Current Developments in Monetary and Financial Law

Current Developments in Monetary and Financial Law

Volume 2

International Monetary Fund

© 2003 International Monetary Fund

Cataloging-in-Publication Data

Current developments in monetary and financial law / Legal Department.—
    Washington, D.C. : International Monetary Fund.
    v. : cm.

Includes bibliographical references.
ISBN 1-55775-796-8 (volume 1)
ISBN 1-58906-176-4 (volume 2)

1. Banking law—Congresses. 2. Monetary policy—Law and
legislation—Congresses. 3. Financial policy—Law and legislation—
Congresses. 4. Financial crises—Congresses. 5. Banks and banking—State
supervision—Congresses. 6. Banks and banking, International—Congresses.
7. Bank and banking, Central—Congresses. 8. Economic and Monetary
Union—Congresses. 9. Payment systems—Congresses. I. International
Monetary Fund. Legal Dept. II. IMF Institute.
K1066.C97 1999

92-16996
CIP

Price: $65.00

Please send orders to:
International Monetary Fund, Publication Services
700 19th Street, N.W., Washington, D.C. 20431, U.S.A.
Telephone: (202) 623-7430; Telefax: (202) 623-7201
E-mail: publications@imf.org
Internet: http://www.imf.org

Contents

Page

Preface .... *xi*

I. THE INTERNATIONAL MONETARY FUND

1 Provision of Information to the IMF
   François Gianviti 3

2 Economics of IMF Arrangements: An Introduction
   Gregory C. Dahl 21

3 The Stand-By Arrangement: Its Legal Nature and Principal Features
   Ross Leckow 33

4 The IMF's Relationship with the World Bank: The Cooperative Framework
   William E. Holder 51

II. OTHER INTERNATIONAL FINANCIAL INSTITUTIONS

5 International Financial Institutions and Their Discontents
   Jerome I. Levinson 71

6 Recent Developments in the European Central Bank
   Antonio Sáinz de Vicuña 79

7 International Finance Corporation: History and Current Operations
Carol Mates 101

8 Competencies of the European Community on International Monetary Fund Matters: An Overview of the Key Legal Issues
Bernhard Steinki 109

III. ARCHITECTURE OF THE INTERNATIONAL MONETARY SYSTEM

9 Prevention of Financial Crises: An Overview of the Public Sector Aspects of the International Financial Architecture
John Hicklin 151

10 Involving the Private Sector in the Avoidance and Resolution of Crisis
Mark Allen 167

11 Role of the IMF in Promoting Fiscal Transparency
Marco Cangiano 181

12 Legal Aspects of the IMF's Code of Good Practices on Transparency in Monetary and Financial Policies
Roy C.N. Baban 203

IV. INTERNATIONAL CAPITAL FLOWS

13 Liberalization of Capital Movements: A Possible Role for the IMF
François Gianviti 217

14 A Dozen Things to Love (or Hate) About Capital Flows
    Vincent Raymond Reinhart 233

15 Tax Aspects of Offshore Financial Centers
    Victor Thuronyi 263

V. CENTRAL BANKING

16 Central Banks and International Financial Volatility
    Luis Jácome Hidalgo 283
Comment
    George Iden 311

17 Responsibility of Central Banks for Stability in Financial Markets
    Garry J. Schinasi 317
Comment
    Cynthia Lichtenstein 337

18 Central Bank Responsibility for Exchange Rate Policy and Implementation
    Karen H. Johnson 341

19 Current Challenges in Foreign Exchange Reserves Management
    Jennifer Johnson-Calari 357

VI. SUPERVISION AND REGULATION OF FINANCIAL INSTITUTIONS

20 Selective Bank and Environmental Developments: Supervisory Trends upon Entering the Twenty-First Century
    Joseph Norton 369

Comment
    Mark A. Cymrot 435

21 Legal Issues Incident to Holding Central Bank Assets Abroad
    Thomas C. Baxter, Jr., and Robert B. Toomey 447

22 Assessing the Case for Unified Financial Sector Supervision
    Richard K. Abrams and Michael W. Taylor 463

23 Supervision of Financial Institutions in the United Kingdom
    William Blair 489

24 Converging Standards for Evaluating Banking Supervision in Individual Countries
    Ricki Tigert Helfer 503

25 Some Aspects of the Discretion of Bank Regulators in Addressing Banking Problems
    Tobias M.C. Asser 521

26 Key Legal Aspects of Bank Restructuring
    Jan Willem van der Vossen 541

27 Five Observations About Banking Failures
    Ross S. Delston 571

28 Impact of Bank Secrecy on the Rule of Law in the World
    John W. Moscow 579

29 Internet Banking: Some Recent Legal Developments
    John Jin Lee 591
Comment
    Brian W. Smith 603

VII. MONETARY AREAS AND EXCHANGE ARRANGEMENTS

30 Dollarization: A Primer
Tomás J.T. Baliño 613

31 Dollarization and Euroization
Michael Gruson 629

32 Strongly Anchored Currency Arrangements
Alain Ize 641

33 Common Currencies, Single Currency, and Other Forms of Currency Arrangements
Jean-Victor Louis 657

34 Legal Tender: A Notion Associated with Payment
Kazuaki Sono 679

VIII. PAYMENT SYSTEMS

35 CPSS Core Principles for Payment Systems
Gregor Heinrich 691

36 Institutional Framework and Implementation of the Core Principles for Systemically Important Payment Systems
Omotunde E.G. Johnson 723

37 TARGET: Trans-European Automated Real-Time Gross Settlement Express Transfer System of the European System of Central Banks
Erwin Nierop 751

IX. DORMANT ACCOUNTS

38 Swiss Law on the Treatment of Dormant Accounts: A Comparison with European and U.S. Law
Michael Bradfield and Pamela Sak 773

39 Summary Review of the Claims Resolution Tribunal for Dormant Accounts in Switzerland
Roberts B. Owen 799

X. GOVERNANCE

40 Managing the Global Economy: The Role of Governance
Rainer Geiger 813

APPENDIX

I Code of Good Practices on Transparency in Monetary and Financial Policies: Declaration of Principles 833

Biographical Sketches 853

Preface

The Legal Department and the Institute of the IMF held their seventh biennial seminar for legal advisers of central banks of member countries on May 9–19, 2000. As in earlier seminars, presentations were made by officials of the IMF and other international organizations, officials of central banks and regulatory agencies, representatives of the private sector, lawyers, and scholars. The papers published in this volume are based on these presentations. The views they express are those of their authors and should not be attributed either to the IMF or to any institution with which the authors are affiliated.

The seminar covered a broad range of topics, which are reflected in this volume, including activities of the IMF, developments in the European Monetary Union, the architecture of the international financial system, the supervision and regulation of financial institutions, the role of central banks, payments systems, international financial and monetary relations, and governance.

The preparation of an international seminar, with participants from about forty central banks and speakers coming from different parts of the world, is a complex affair. Many individuals were involved in the preparation of this seminar and the publication of this volume. I wish to express our particular gratitude to Hermann Krull, who helped organize the seminar; Robert Effros, who participated in the preparation and was the moderator of the seminar; Alice Peñalosa, Stella Ymar, Esther Parsons and Linda Byron, who made the necessary arrangements and ensured the smooth functioning of the seminar; Deidre Gantt, Julia Baca, and Christopher Matson, who prepared the manuscript; and Roy Baban and Glenn Gottselig, of the Legal Department, as well as Archana Kumar, their counterpart in the External Relations Department, who oversaw the preparation and publication of this volume.

FRANÇOIS GIANVITI

The General Counsel

I. The International Monetary Fund

Chapter 1

Provision of Information to the IMF

FRANÇOIS GIANVITI

In the fulfillment of its mandate, the International Monetary Fund (Fund) collects and uses different types of information, which bear on a wide variety of subjects. For instance, the Fund collects quantified economic data on countries' monetary reserves, external trade, balance of payments, exchange rates, budgetary resources and expenditure, etc. The Fund also collects information on national legislation, mainly exchange control regulations, trade regulations, fiscal and banking legislation, and more generally economic and financial legislation. Last but not least, the Fund is interested in the policy intentions of its members, both those that will have a direct effect on the exchange rate of their currencies or on their balance of payments and those that may have an indirect effect through fiscal, monetary and other economic or financial policies. In order for the Fund to have a significant role in the prevention or resolution of international financial crises, whether they affect one or several countries, the provision of accurate and timely information is essential.

(a) Some of the information used by the Fund is readily available through publications or on various websites. Publicly available information, however, is not always sufficient for the Fund. Sometimes data are published after a long period of time, when they are no longer relevant for policy decisions. For instance, a decision to adjust the exchange rate cannot be based on three-month-old reserves and balance of payments data. In other cases, the information needed is not publicly available. It may be that this type of information is of interest to no one but the Fund. More probably, the reason is that the country generating the information does not want to disclose it to anyone but the Fund, essentially because, if disclosed to the public, the information could have a negative effect on the achievement of the country's monetary, economic, and financial objectives (e.g., an intention to make periodic adjustments in the exchange rate). When information is received from a member country on a confidential basis, the Fund may use it but is not at liberty, without the member's consent, to publish the information or to disclose it to a person who is not bound to preserve its confidentiality.

(b) In order to obtain information that is not publicly available, the Fund has to turn to the member that can generate and provide such information. Three approaches may be used.

The first one is to ask the member to provide the information. As long as the information is reasonably related to the achievement of the Fund's purposes, it may be requested by the Fund. In that case, the member is free to decide whether or not to provide the information. Essentially, this type of approach is used for information that is not so much needed by the Fund but rather collected by the Fund for the general benefit of its membership and the preparation of statistical and other studies. It is "additional" to the information needed by the Fund, and will not be discussed here. The relevant provision is Article VIII, Section 5(c):

> The Fund may arrange to obtain further information by agreement with members. It shall act as a centre for the collection and exchange of information on monetary and financial problems, thus facilitating the preparation of studies designed to assist members in developing policies which further the purposes of the Fund.

A second approach is to require the member, as a legal obligation, to provide the information that is found necessary by the Fund for one or more of its activities. The relevant provision is Article VIII, Section 5 where one finds both a list of the minimum information that must be provided to the Fund (e.g., on balance of payments) and a power for the Fund to require additional information if found necessary by the Fund. This additional information may, like the preestablished list, apply to all members or, alternatively, if the Fund so decides, on a case-by-case basis. A breach of that obligation by a member may give rise to sanctions under the Articles.

In the context of surveillance under Article IV, there are similar provisions both on each member's obligation to provide certain information (on exchange arrangements) and on the Fund's power to require information (for surveillance over exchange rate policies).

A third approach has been developed by the Fund in the exercise of its powers to adopt policies on the use of its resources. As a condition for accessing Fund resources, either in the form of purchases from the General Resources Account or in the form of loans from an administered account (e.g., the former Enhanced Structural Adjustment Facility (ESAF), the present Poverty Reduction and Growth Facility (PRGF), and the Heavily Indebted Poor Countries (HIPC) Initiative), the Fund specifies certain targets that need to be reached or actions that need to be taken (or avoided). Information on the fulfillment of these conditions is essential and must be accurate. Otherwise, false information could be provided to the Fund, on the basis of which resources would be made available while the specified objectives had not been achieved. Even if a finding of breach of obligation cannot be made, a "civil" remedy, such as a repayment to the Fund, can be envisaged.

Only the second and third approaches will be examined, that is, firstly, the provision of information as an obligation under the Articles and, secondly, the provision of information as a condition for the use of Fund resources.

The Provision of Information as an Obligation under the Articles

As explained above, several provisions of the Fund's Articles confer upon the Fund the power to require information from its members. The most general provision is Article VIII, Section 5, which applies to all types of information deemed necessary by the Fund. There are also specific provisions on information relating to surveillance, but their scope is limited, their usefulness is questionable, and differences in the wording of these provisions raise questions of interpretation.

In any case, all these provisions deal with the provision of information to the Fund. There is no obligation for members under the Articles to publish information and the Fund has no authority to impose such an obligation.

Moreover, under all these provisions, information is required as a matter of obligation. A failure to comply with that obligation constitutes a breach of obligation under the Articles and sanctions may be imposed by the Fund.

Obligations Under Article VIII, Section 5

The drafters of the Articles had two choices. The first was to list all the information they regarded as necessary for the activities of the Fund. However, they were wise enough to realize that, as time passes, new types of data may be regarded as necessary which were not initially foreseen. The second was to give the Fund the power to determine what information it finds necessary. However, there would have been a risk that no general decision be taken, and in fact this is exactly what has happened. If it were not for the list of information set forth in Article VIII, Section 5, the Fund would not have had to this day a general list of data to be provided to the Fund.

The solution found by the drafters of the Articles was to combine the two approaches: they listed what they regarded as the minimum of information necessary for the discharge of the Fund's duties and, in addition, gave the Fund the power to require more information if it deemed it necessary for its activities.

Therefore, two different techniques for the creation of obligations apply to the provision of information, but the underlying criterion remains the same: the Fund may only require what is necessary for its activities. Also certain common conditions, as will be seen, affect the scope and nature of the obligation, but the procedure for requiring information is fundamentally different.

A Common Criterion: Necessity for the Fund's Activities

The Fund may only require the information it needs to fulfill its mandate. Therefore, in principle, the only difference between the list in Article VIII, Section 5, and the additional information that may be required by the Fund is that, for the first category, the Articles themselves declare the information listed in Article VIII, Section 5(a) "necessary for the effective discharge of the Fund's duties" while, for additional information, it is for the Fund to deem such information "necessary for its activities."

Actually, this requirement is not much of a constraint. Indeed, the Fund must act in good faith and may not require information that, in its judgment, is not necessary, but the Fund is not required to say for what activities the information is needed. One activity could be sufficient justification (in spite of the plural "its activities") and the activities of the Fund are numerous and diverse: mainly surveillance and use of Fund resources, but also quota calculations, currency budget, early repurchase expectations, SDR allocations, etc.

There are some activities of the Fund, however, to which Article VIII, Section 5 does not apply and, which, therefore, could not constitute a legal basis for a requirement of information under that provision. Those activities are the technical and financial services provided under Article V, Section 2(*b*), such as technical assistance and the administration of financial contributions for assistance to developing countries (e.g., the former ESAF, the present PRGF and HIPC). The reason is that the provision of such services does not "impose any obligation on a member without its consent" (Article V, Section 2(*b*), last sentence). Therefore, the Fund cannot unilaterally impose an obligation to provide information on users of its services. Assuming that the member consented, the obligation would not be created under Article VIII, Section 5, or otherwise be an obligation provided for in the Articles. Therefore, it could not give rise, in case of failure to provide information, to the imposition of sanctions under Article XXVI for breach of an obligation under the Articles.

Common Conditions

Whether the information is required by Article VIII, Section 5 or by a decision of the Fund adopted under that provision, several rules apply.

The first one is that members are not required to furnish information "in such detail that the affairs of individuals or corporations are disclosed" (Article VIII, Section 5(*b*)). This protection of privacy may seem antiquated at a time when the world wants to know everything about everybody and the Fund is urged to investigate every allegation of scandal concerning governments or central banks of countries using the Fund's resources. In practice, the limitation on the Fund's powers under Article VIII, Section 5 can be remedied by making the provision of specific information a condition for the continued use of Fund resources.

The second rule is actually a combination of two principles. Each member undertakes "to furnish the desired information in as detailed and accurate a manner as is practicable and, so far as possible, to avoid mere estimates" and the Fund must "take into consideration the varying ability of members to furnish the data requested." The general meaning of the rule is rather clear: members must do their utmost to provide accurate information, but they may not always be able to do so and the Fund must take their capacity into account when assessing their compliance with their obligations under Article VIII, Section 5. For instance, the Fund may recognize that certain types of data are inherently subject to a margin of error in the accounts of all members (e.g., errors and omissions in the balance of payments). The Fund may also recognize that some members' data collection systems are weak in certain respects and cannot, at least in the short term, be improved (e.g., trade statistics). Obviously, if a member refuses to provide information or deliberately provides false information ("misreporting"), the question of capacity does not arise and a finding of breach of obligation will be made. It would be wrong, however, to assume that a breach of obligation may only exist in such cases. Even if the misreporting is not voluntary, a finding of breach of obligation may be made by the Fund if it could have been avoided with reasonable diligence. At that point, the question will be whether the Fund wishes to impose a sanction. Clearly, an involuntary breach is less serious than a voluntary breach and should be subject to lesser sanctions or could even be forgiven, particularly if it was an error of minor importance or if it had no significant effect on the Fund's activities.

The third rule is the principle of nonretroactivity. By becoming a member, a country becomes subject to the obligation to provide the information listed in Article VIII, Section 5. This obligation applies prospectively. Similarly, when the Fund requires additional information, it cannot at the same time or later find a member in breach for failing to provide that information before the decision was adopted.

Differences in Procedure

The list in Article VIII, Section 5 is part of the Articles. It may be interpreted by the Fund, but it cannot be restricted by a decision. For instance, by interpretation, the Executive Board could determine a permissible margin of error or a periodicity for the provision of certain types of information listed in Article VIII, Section 5, or specify the type of information (more attuned to current concepts) that would satisfy certain requirements of Article VIII, Section 5 (e.g., national income), but its powers would be limited and would have to be exercised with a view to clarifying, not amending, it.

In contrast, the power to require additional information is an actual power to impose additional obligations on members without their consent or to expand the scope of an existing obligation. Therefore, such a power should be exercised with great caution. On the exercise of that power, a few remarks may be made:

(i) The power to require additional information is conferred upon the Fund. Given the power structure of the Articles and the general delegation given by the Board of Governors to the Executive Board, the powers granted to "the Fund" by the Articles are exercised by the Executive Board. This means that the Managing Director's authority to conduct the ordinary business of the Fund (Article XII, Section 4(*b*)) does not include the power to require information from members, but the Executive Board could decide what information members are obligated to provide when requested by the Managing Director.

(ii) Instead of letting the Managing Director determine the periodicity of the provision of information, the Executive Board may determine that periodicity in its decisions. Absent a specified periodicity (as is the case for the list in Article VIII, Section 5), the obligation is deemed to be continuous, which means that it must be kept up to date by the member. For instance, between consultations between a member and the Fund, current information needs to be provided to the Fund to allow the Managing Director to decide whether a special consultation should be initiated.

(iii) A decision to require the provision of information applies prospectively, but that does not mean that the Fund could not require information on past events. In practice, the ability of the member to provide that information may be limited and the necessity for the information may be questioned if the inquiry relates to an ancient period, but the principle of nonretroactivity would not preclude the possibility of such a decision.

(iv) The main difference between the list in Article VIII, Section 5 and a decision to require additional information is that the former is general in its application while the latter may either be general or country-specific. In fact, the only decisions adopted until now under Article VIII, Section 5 are country-specific. They are adopted in the context of arrangements or other individual decisions allowing members to use the Fund's general resources, and take the form of performance criteria or other conditions specified by the Executive Board, either for all or for some disbursements to the relevant member. Not only is the information country-specific but it is also arrangement-specific or even purchase-specific. For instance, in order to qualify for a disbursement, a member must meet a certain target and, unless information demonstrating that the target has been met is provided to the Fund, the disbursement will not be made. The provision of accurate information is required for a limited purpose, i.e., for the release of resources to the member, but it is required by the Fund for one of its activities and meets the conditions of Article VIII, Section 5 to be regarded as an obligation under the Articles. Consequently, the misreporting of information relating to a performance criterion or other condition specified in a Fund arrangement will normally give rise to a breach of obligation under the Articles. The member's alleged inability to provide accurate information may be taken into account, but this defense will be less convincing than in the case of a general obligation applicable to all members since the member knew the particular importance for the Fund of this type of information and agreed to have it included in the arrangement.

(v) As the obligation to provide information is linked to the existence of a performance criterion, the deletion of that criterion by a waiver of applicability removes the obligation under Article VIII, Section 5. In contrast, a waiver for nonperformance (or nonobservance) does not affect the existence of this obligation because the criterion survives; the member is merely exempted from meeting that condition.

Article VIII, Section 5 is by far the most comprehensive provision of the Articles on the furnishing of information to the Fund. At the time of the Second Amendment, a few more provisions were inserted in Article IV, which seem to duplicate Article VIII, Section 5.

Obligations Under Article IV

Two provisions of Article IV require the furnishing of information to the Fund and their formulation is like a reminder of the dual structure of Article VIII, Section 5: they combine a requirement to provide certain information with a power to require additional information.

The first provision is similar to the list in Article VIII, Section 5 in that it defines certain information that must be provided to the Fund, for which no further decision of the Fund is required. Article IV, Section 2 provides:

> (*a*) Each member shall notify the Fund, within thirty days after the date of the second amendment of this Agreement, of the exchange arrangements it intends to apply in fulfillment of its obligations under Section 1 of this Article, and shall notify the Fund promptly of any changes in its exchange arrangements.
>
> (*b*) Under an international monetary system of the kind prevailing on January 1, 1976, exchange arrangements may include (i) the maintenance by a member of a value for its currency in terms of the special drawing right or another denominator, other than gold, selected by the member, or (ii) cooperative arrangements by which members maintain the value of their currencies in relation to the value of the currency or currencies of other members, or (iii) other exchange arrangements of a member's choice.
>
> (*c*) To accord with the development of the international monetary system, the Fund by an eighty-five percent majority of the total voting power, may make provision for general exchange arrangements without limiting the right of members to have exchange arrangements of their choice consistent with the purposes of the Fund and the obligations under Section 1 of this Article.

The second provision is Article IV, Section 3(*b*), which requires each member to provide the Fund with the information necessary for such surveillance. The general objective resembles and probably duplicates the power in Article VIII, Section 5 to require additional information when it is deemed by the Fund necessary for its activities. However, a closer comparison shows a number of differences. First, while Article VIII, Section 5 clearly gives the Fund the power to decide what information is necessary, Article IV, Section 3(*b*) leaves the question open. Clearly, the answer must be the same as in Article VIII, Section 5: only the Fund, that is, the Executive Board, can make such a determination as it determines the scope of each member's obligation. However, the Executive Board has not adopted any general or country-specific decision implementing that provision or even found a member to be in breach of that obligation.

Another point worth noting is that the two limitations in Article VIII, Section 5, concerning the privacy of individuals or entities and the members' ability to provide information, do not appear in Article IV, Section 3(*b*).

Consequences of a Breach of Obligation Under the Articles

The most extreme example of sanctions imposed on a member for a breach of its obligations under the Articles was the expulsion of Czechoslovakia in 1954 for refusing to provide information in accordance with Article VIII, Section 5. It was an exceptional case in many respects because it occurred in the context of the cold war and the tension was compounded by what was regarded as a defiant attitude of the country.

Today, it is not so much the refusal to provide information but rather the provision of misleading information which is a cause for concern, particularly misreporting by countries using the Fund's general resources and receiving financial assistance from the Fund without fulfilling the conditions specified by the fund.

When it appears to the Managing Director that a breach of obligation has occurred, he must report the matter to the Executive Board. As there is no statute of limitations in the Articles or in decisions of the Fund, a breach of obligation may be detected years later and reported to the Executive Board.

A breach of obligation may give rise to sanctions in accordance with Article XXVI, Section 2, which provides for an escalation of penalties against continuing offenders. The first sanction is a declaration of ineligibility to use the Fund's general resources but under rule K-2 the Fund may prefer to limit or suspend the use of those resources by the member. As there is no obligation for the Fund to impose penalties, the member's attitude, and particularly its good faith and repentance, are taken into account by the Fund when deciding whether to impose a sanction and the nature of the sanction.

In the context of misreporting, the most difficult question is the distinction between good faith and bad faith. Although good faith is not by itself sufficient for a complete exoneration, it often plays a decisive role when it comes to imposing sanctions. There are difficulties, however, with this distinction. The first is that, in many cases, there is no clear evidence of good or bad faith. In other words, the information is patently false, but the circumstances that led to the misreporting are disputed. The second is that misreporting usually involves a number of officials, at different levels of responsibilities, who may or may not have acted in concert; since a country has no mind of its own, its good or bad faith is only the good or bad faith of its officials, but which officials? Should it be the head of state or government, the minister, central bank governor, or other officials who transmitted the information to the Fund, the statisticians who collected, assessed, and processed the information, or the employees of the Treasury, customs, the central bank, and other agencies who generated the initial data? What if a ministry official misled his minister or the minister misled the head of state? The third difficulty is that, by the time the misreporting is detected, there may be a new minister or a new central bank governor who will claim that his country should not be penalized for the wrongdoings of his predecessor.

Therefore, rather than imposing any of the sanctions contemplated in Article XXVI, Section 2, the Fund often prefers to settle the dispute with the member: one or several early repurchases are made, internal procedures are strengthened to avoid future offenses, and a press release informs the public of the sin committed and the remedies provided.

The Provision of Information as a Condition for the Use of Fund Resources

Unlike membership obligations which are governed by the Articles and may not (with one exception for Article VIII, Section 5) be extended by the Fund, the scope of Fund conditionality is only defined in terms of the Fund's purposes, which are not themselves very constraining. Therefore, without imposing obligations on its members, the Fund may use its resources to induce them to take or refrain from certain actions. This influence is limited in two respects: it does not apply to members that do not use Fund resources and, even for members who use those resources, it applies only as long as the financing has not been fully disbursed (unless there is hope for more). For instance, trade liberalization is not an obligation under the Fund's Articles but it has been part of Fund conditionality for many years.

A similar distinction can be made with respect to the publication of information. The Fund may not impose on a member an obligation to publish information but it may and does recommend the publication of certain information. Consideration may be given at some point to making that publication an element of Fund conditionality. A small step has already been taken in that direction: members using Fund resources are supposed to publish their letters of interest, unless they explain to the Fund why, in their judgment, such a publication would not be desirable.

As explained above, Article VIII, Section 5 is drafted in such broad terms that it can apply to any of the Fund's activities, including the use of the Fund's general resources. However, a finding of breach of obligation is a serious matter because of its impact on the country's reputation as a subject of international law and as a borrower in capital markets, not to mention the possibility of sanctions under the Articles. Therefore, before a finding of breach of obligation can be made, certain conditions must be met: in particular, it must be determined whether the member had the capacity to provide the information. Also there are limits on the type of information that may be required (e.g., privacy). For all these reasons, two special sets of rules for information in the context of Fund-supported programs were adopted, the first one in 1984 for arrangements in the General Resources Account and later, in 1998, a second one for the Enhanced Structural Adjustment Facility (now replaced by the Poverty Reduction and Growth Facility). Though amended on July 27, 2000, the two sets of rules remain very similar. They are usually referred to as guidelines on misreporting, either for the General Resources Account (GRA) or for the Poverty Reduction and Growth Facility.

The GRA Guidelines

The Guidelines do not define the information that needs to be provided to the Fund; this is done in the context of arrangements and other individual decisions governing purchases. The purpose of the Guidelines is to define what constitutes misreporting in the context of such decisions and the remedies for misreporting. Interestingly enough, the Guidelines do not refer to Article VIII, Section 5 because they apply in cases where this provision does not necessarily apply, and the remedies are different.

Scope of Misreporting Under the GRA Guidelines

Initially, the GRA Guidelines applied only to purchases under stand-by or extended arrangements. Since July 2000, they also apply to outright purchases, i.e., purchases made outside an arrangement (purchases under the Supplemental Reserve Facility (SRF) are made under a stand-by or extended arrangement; purchases under the Contingent Credit Lines (CCL) are made under a stand-by arrangement).

In the preparation and implementation of a Fund-supported program, a considerable amount of information is provided by the member to the staff and management of the Fund, but only part of that information reaches the Executive Board and, within that part, only a fraction will be required to determine whether performance criteria or other conditions specified by the Executive Board have been met. For instance, there may be a number of "prior actions" the member intends and is expected to take before the arrangement is approved by the Executive Board, but these prior actions are normally not identified as conditions for purchases under the arrangement. Nor is there a clause in Fund arrangements subjecting the validity or effectiveness of the arrangement to such prior actions. Therefore, it is possible that, after approving an arrangement and authorizing purchases, the Fund discovers that its assumptions concerning the member's program are false and that it has been misled by inaccurate information provided by the member.

This type of problem is not uncommon in the context of business contracts. Lawyers are familiar with the concepts of error, fraud, or misrepresentation and their effects on the validity of contracts. However, Fund arrangements raise particular problems, for different reasons. First of all, they are not contracts but decisions of the Fund. That in itself, however, would not be decisive: unilateral acts may be vitiated by error or fraud. Secondly, they are governed by international law, but again the principles governing the validity of treaties or unilateral acts in international law are derived from those of private law. Thirdly, and more importantly, error and fraud are not always sufficient for a judge to declare the contract void. The party that claims to have been the victim of error or fraud when entering into a contract has the burden of proving that, if it were not for the error or fraud, that contract would not have been made. In the case of a dispute between the Fund and a member country, there is no established judicial or arbitral procedure to rule on the merits of the Fund's claim. The Fund is both the creditor and the judge in its own dispute. As creditor it can claim that its consent was vitiated, even though there may have been only very minor discrepancies, and then, acting as judge in its own cause, rescind the commitment resulting from the arrangement. Not only would such an approach undermine the confidence of members in the Fund's support but it could create a perception that the Fund is acting arbitrarily and capriciously vis-à-vis some members.

These are exactly the risks the GRA Guidelines tried to avoid. To prevent any suspicion of arbitrariness and subjectivity, the Guidelines established a system based on objectively prespecified conditions: only misreporting bearing on performance criteria or other conditions identified in the relevant individual decision of the Fund can be taken into account. Under this system, there is no room for hypothetical speculation concerning what could have been or should have been. Only what has been identified as essential is relevant.

In the case of an arrangement, misreporting may occur at all stages of the arrangement—initial approval as well as subsequent reviews, provided that conditions are specified. It may also occur in the context of waivers: if a waiver for nonperformance is qualified by stating that it is granted on the assumption that the deviation did not exceed 5 percent and it is later found that the deviation exceeded that percentage, then the Guidelines apply to the purchase made pursuant to the waiver. Absent prespecified conditions, however, the Guidelines do not apply.

Nature of Misreporting Under the GRA Guidelines

A finding of misreporting under the Guidelines is based on purely objective criteria. It may be made regardless of the capacity of the member to collect information and of its good faith in communicating it to the Fund. The lack of capacity may be a defense against the imposition of sanctions for violation of Article VIII, Section 5, but it is not relevant in the context of the Guidelines. Nor is the good faith defense relevant, although it is often used by the authorities to protect at least their reputation. The reason for this objective approach to misreporting is that the purpose of the Guidelines is to safeguard the Fund's resources and ensure their proper use. If specified conditions (therefore, by definition, conditions that are important to the success of the program) have not been met, it must be assumed that these resources are at risk and/or that they are not being used in accordance with the purposes for which they were provided.

Procedure and Remedies Under the GRA Guidelines

"Whenever evidence comes to the attention of the staff indicating that a performance criterion or other condition applicable to an outstanding purchase made in the General Resources Account may not have been observed, the Managing Director shall promptly inform the member concerned" (GRA Guidelines, as amended July 27, 2000).

Once an investigation for misreporting has been initiated, the Managing Director must promptly inform the member concerned. If the Managing Director concludes, after consultation with the member, that the performance criterion or other condition has not been observed, which means that the member has made a purchase to which it was not entitled ("noncomplying purchase"), he must submit a report to the Executive Board together with recommendations. If the noncomplying purchase was made no more than four years before the Managing Director informed the member, the Executive Board may either call upon the member to make a repurchase equal to the outstanding amount of the purchase or grant a waiver for the nonobservance of the performance criterion or other condition.

In order to grant a waiver, the Executive Board must "normally" find either that "the deviation from the relevant performance criterion or other condition was minor or temporary" or that "subsequent to the purchase, the member had adopted additional policy measures appropriate to achieve the objectives supported by the relevant decision."

When granting a waiver, the Executive Board may specify certain conditions. Sometimes, the member makes a voluntary repurchase of the outstanding amount of the noncomplying purchase, which prevents any further action under the Guidelines by the Fund.

If a waiver is not granted, the Executive Board will take a decision whereby the member will be "expected" to repurchase the outstanding amount of the noncomplying purchase within a specified period (normally 30 days from the date of the decision). If the repurchase is not made as expected, the member's further access to the Fund's resources, including PRGF loans, is suspended. If the member persists in not making the repurchase, a limitation on the member's access to Fund resources, followed by a declaration of ineligibility, may be decided under Article V, Section 5.

It would have been possible to envisage a repurchase obligation rather than a repurchase expectation but this type of remedy would have required a general decision applicable to all members (because of the principle of uniform treatment for repurchase obligations) and a high majority (85 percent of the total voting power). Moreover, once the repurchase obligation had been created, a postponement would have required that the conditions set forth in Article V, Section 7(*g*) be met.

In addition to the remedies under the Guidelines, a finding of breach of obligation under Article VIII, Section 5 may be made and sanctions may be imposed under Article XXVI if the relevant conditions (explained above) are met. The time limit specified in the Guidelines does not apply to the initiation of a procedure for breach of obligation and the imposition of sanctions under Article XXVI.

The PRGF Guidelines

In 1998, the Executive Board adopted PRGF Guidelines on misreporting very similar to the GRA Guidelines. There are certain differences, however. One is in the consequences of a failure by the member to meet a repurchase expectation: a penalty interest rate is charged on the amount that has not been repaid.

A more important difference, however, is that the provisions of the Articles concerning the obligation to provide information to the Fund (Article V, Section 5) and its sanctions (Article XXVI, Section 2) do not apply because PRGF obligations are not obligations under the Articles.

Conclusion

Sanctions and other remedies may be a deterrent that will induce members to report accurate information to the Fund.

An ounce of prevention, however, is often worth a pound of cure. Therefore, central banks as users of Fund resources will be subject to an ex ante process to provide reasonable assurance to the Fund that the central bank's control, accounting, reporting, and auditing systems in place to manage resources, including Fund disbursements, are adequate to ensure the integrity of operations (Acting Chairman's statement of March 23, 2000). Safeguard assessments will be conducted by Fund staff. If, on the basis of documents provided and discussions with independent auditors, the staff concludes that the central bank's control, reporting, and auditing mechanisms appear adequate to safeguard the Fund's resources, no further steps need be taken. In other cases, a second stage of assessment would include an on-site review by a multidisciplinary team as a prior condition before presentation of an arrangement to the Executive Board for approval or at least before the first review.

Chapter 2

Economics of IMF Arrangements: An Introduction

GREGORY C. DAHL

Fund arrangements with member countries are best understood by reference to the context within which they arise. They are a mechanism by which member countries can seek temporary financing to assist them in addressing a balance of payments problem. Like the majority of us who visit a doctor or dentist only when our illness, pain, or fear of a major crisis is greater than the discomfort of seeing the doctor, most countries seek the assistance of the Fund only when they already have a serious balance of payments problem or a full-blown crisis. There have been a few precautionary arrangements, but they are relatively rare.

The purpose of Fund arrangements, therefore, is to assist members to address balance of payments problems. Fund arrangements provide access to Fund resources in support of a program of economic and financial policies aimed at redressing external imbalances of a member through orderly adjustment to avoid or mitigate a crisis, with the objective of achieving a sustainable balance of payments position.

The programs supported by Fund arrangements always contain some balance of external financing and adjustment, reflecting the fact that the international community is willing to provide financial support only if the member is taking steps to address the issues that gave rise to its balance of payments problem. The external financing is largely from official sources, from the Fund and others. (If the member has access to private financing it would most likely not have a balance of payments problem and would not seek a Fund program.) The available official financing is, unfortunately, quite limited. The financing is therefore temporary and is aimed at financing an adjustment process leading relatively quickly to a sustainable position in which the member no longer depends on such exceptional official financing. However, the program must also provide for adequate financing to ensure the success of the program, i.e., there can be no ex ante financing gap. Thus, the Fund often plays a catalytic role during program negotiations in arranging sufficient financing from all sources to meet the financing need during the adjustment period.

For its part, the member country must take adjustment measures to address the origin of its balance of payments problem, and phased access to Fund resources is based on adequate performance in relation to program objectives, through policy conditionality. The adjustment to be undertaken usually involves restraining demand and structural reforms.

The external financing and adjustment effort included in programs are often seen as substitutes, i.e., more external financing means a less rapid and difficult adjustment effort. If there were no IMF and no financing mechanism provided by the international community for balance of payments problems, it is clear that countries would need to face their balance of payments problems anyway, and their adjustment would be that much more difficult. Even with the existing institutional framework, countries always have the option of going it alone, and obviously they seek Fund support because it reduces the pain of adjustment. However, it is important to note that in practice there is also some complementarity to financing and adjustment: the international community is more willing to assist a member that is making a stronger and more credible effort to address its problems. Thus, a strong program attracts more financing, and the chances of success rise sharply as the adjustment effort is strengthened.

External and Internal Imbalances

But on what grounds does the Fund insist on domestic demand-restraining measures and policy reforms as key elements of the conditionality for Fund arrangements? How is it that, for example, such internal policies as the level of the budget deficit become key points in negotiations for a Fund-supported program? This is where economic relationships come into play.

Economics shows us that external and domestic balances are closely linked. If there are external (balance of payments) problems, economic analysis tells us what are the nature and origin of these problems, and thus how to adjust external and domestic policies to redress the imbalances. The Articles of Agreement reflect a general understanding of the linkage between such policies, although the economic models describing these linkages were developed subsequently. Article I (Purposes) states in part that the Fund is "to facilitate the expansion and balanced growth of international trade and to contribute thereby to high levels of employment and real income and the development of productive resources" and "to give confidence to members by making resources temporarily available to them under adequate safeguards, thus providing them with opportunity to correct maladjustments in their balance of payments without resorting to measures destructive of national or international prosperity." The phrase "adequate safeguards" provides authority or the Fund to impose "conditionality" when it extends credit to help ensure that the balance of payments problems would be addressed and that the Fund would be repaid.[1]

So let us now turn, briefly, to the economics. A basic identity of the national income accounts tells us that

GNDI − A = CAB,

where

GNDI = gross national disposable income,

CAB = the current account of the balance of payments,

and

---

[1] The basing of Fund lending on conditions relating to policy actions designed to redress imbalances is fundamental to the conceptual basis of the Fund, and may be contrasted with recent proposals that the Fund be transformed into a classic lender of last resort, lending against collateral at penalty interest rates but with no policy conditions. Such a transformed Fund would be a much simpler institution, with more automatic lending mechanisms. But it is not at all clear how this could work in practice with sovereign borrowers. What collateral could be used for such operations? Could a country pledge, for example, its land, or its future tax revenues? What happens when governments change and repudiate the policies of their predecessors? What would prevent the excesses of sovereign borrowing that have been the source of many problems in the past?

$$A = C + I$$

or "absorption" equals consumption plus investment. In other words, if the economy absorbs more than it produces (= income), the extra goods and services must come from abroad as reflected in a deficit in the current account of the balance of payments.

But from the balance of payments we know that a current account deficit must be financed, i.e., the current account balance plus the capital and financial account balance must equal the change in reserves. Any deficit in the current account must be covered by a net inflow of capital or a drawdown in reserves. If there is a current account deficit, the question then becomes: is it sustainable, i.e., can the financing flows be maintained without precipitating a crisis of confidence, a cutoff or reversal of the flows, and a brutal adjustment as imports are curtailed? If the deficit is being paid for by a decline in reserves, it is obvious that the answer is no, it is not sustainable, since reserves at some point will be exhausted, precipitating a crisis and requiring adjustment.

If the financing is not sustainable and adjustment is required, what form must it take? With reference to the above conceptual framework, adjustment could involve either an increase in domestic output or a decline in absorption. Unfortunately, in most cases an increase in domestic output is not possible in the short run, so a decline in absorption is inevitable. This is the logic of the emphasis in adjustment programs on demand management to reduce absorption.

So how do we reduce absorption?

The Monetary Approach to the Balance of Payments

IMF economist Jacques Polak developed a model in the 1950s which initiated what came to be called the "monetary approach to the balance of payments," linking domestic and external balances and policies. The main focus of this approach was on domestic credit expansion. Briefly, the argument ran as follows: an expansion in credit, e.g., to the government, gives rise directly to an increase in money. For example, if the central bank gives credit to the government, it does so by creating new deposits or printing new cash, either of which creates new base or "high-powered" money.

However, since economic actors have some level of desired money balances—"demand for money"—an increase in the supply of money, other things being equal, will give rise to more spending as people seek to return to their desired level of money holdings. Some proportion of new spending will be for imports, increasing the current account deficit of the balance of payments. If the authorities are maintaining a fixed or managed exchange rate, they will be obliged to sell reserves to keep the value of the local currency from depreciating as the demand for imports rises, and reserves will fall. The rest of the new spending will be for domestically produced goods, whose supply will probably be constrained, so their prices will rise. Domestic goods will thus become more expensive relative to imported goods, and some demand will shift towards imported goods, further increasing the current account deficit and the resulting decline in reserves. However, as the central bank sells reserves, it buys domestic money, thus contracting the money supply. As this process continues, money will contract until a new equilibrium is reached at which economic actors again hold the amount of money they desire.

Thus, a given increase in credit will eventually be reflected, through the mechanisms just described, in a decline in reserves. The problem is that borrowers such as governments rarely need a one-time credit. Needs are ongoing, and the flow continues. But a continuing flow of new credit implies, from the above relationships, a continuing decline in reserves. At some point reserves will hit bottom, or speculators will see that reserves will inevitably hit bottom, and they will attack the currency. Thus, a crisis is inevitable. The obvious prescription in this case is to limit the expansion of credit. Thus, Fund-supported programs always have some kind of limit on credit in the financial system. Since the origin of the excess credit creation is often the credit demands of the government, programs usually also focus on the budget deficit and its financing. Some have said that "IMF" stands for "it's mostly fiscal."

The key insight of the monetary approach to the balance of payments is that a change in a domestic economic variable (credit) becomes a major determinant of the balance of payments position and of the ability of the country to meet its foreign payments obligations. Domestic and external imbalances are closely linked.

We have assumed above a fixed or managed exchange rate regime. But the result is similar with a floating exchange rate, except that instead of reserves declining as credit expands, the exchange rate depreciates, further worsening domestic inflation and perhaps contributing to an inflationary spiral.

Note that the monetary approach to the balance of payments assumes that the capital account of the balance of payments is mostly autonomous. This is still true of many developing countries with little access to capital markets and a high dependency on official financial flows. But for emerging market countries and more developed countries, the capital account has taken on a vastly greater importance, and a rather different conceptual framework with greater focus on the composition of external borrowing and on financial sector soundness applies. Even for these countries, however, domestic policies are the major determinant of the balance of payments position.

The Rationale for Stabilization Policies

We see, then, that domestic policies can lead to a situation where a balance of payments crisis becomes inevitable. If reserves approach zero, either the country begins to incur arrears in foreign payments and loses its credit-worthiness or it is forced to abandon its exchange rate commitment, often with negative consequences. To restore stability and equilibrium, an adjustment in policies becomes necessary. Since such an adjustment will sooner or later be forced by a crisis anyway, perhaps in chaotic circumstances, an orderly and managed adjustment is clearly better. Thus the need to have an adjustment program.

It must also be noted that, while demand restraint and adjustment are painful, the alternatives are worse. Inflation and payment problems impede investment and negatively affect growth. High inflation can lead to currency substitution and capital flight, worsening inflation and pressure on the exchange rate. If the authorities resort to price, exchange, and trade controls to try to stabilize the situation, economic distortions and impediments to investment are introduced that further damage growth and output performance. Although not long ago quite a few countries tried to cope with the effects of inflationary domestic financing by imposing extensive controls on their economies, it is now widely recognized that such policies lead to dramatically poorer economic performance relative to more liberal, market-friendly economic policies, and they have been largely abandoned.

Stabilization Policies

So what things, in brief, constitute stabilization policies?

First, and perhaps foremost, is fiscal policy. The budget deficit must be contained within a limit that can be financed with non-inflationary domestic borrowing and sustainable external borrowing. This means limiting expenditures and assuring adequate revenues, both of which can be difficult.

Monetary policy is also critical. A major influence on monetary policy in many countries is fiscal policy, i.e., the demands of the government for credit. But the monetary authorities are also responsible for the regulatory and financial environment in which the banks and other financial institutions operate, and they are thus in a position to influence the level of interest rates, credit, and money in the economy. There are many interesting technical issues relating to the way in which monetary policy is formulated and conducted, including the choice of quantitative targets (money, inflation, nominal income, etc.), the choice of instruments to use to achieve the targets, the rules to be applied, and the degree of transparency in the process.

The monetary authorities are usually also responsible for exchange rate policy and for the management of the official reserves. The exchange rate is a critical price in most economies, setting the relative price of tradable goods to nontradable goods. Exchange rate policy is also closely interrelated with monetary policy, because the purchase and sale of reserves has a direct counterpart in the creation or absorption of money, and because the exchange rate is often an important factor in domestic inflation, directly influencing the ultimate objective of monetary policy, which is the stability of the value of the currency.

Many countries also continue to be involved to some extent in price policies, although price regimes have generally become more liberal in recent years. The government, of course, sets the level of public sector wages and salaries, and may also have a role in determining wage rates in the private sector. Wage policy, in turn, can be key in stabilizing an economy. There may also be administered prices in an economy for important consumer items such as energy, basic foodstuffs, transportation and communications, and/or public bodies that regulate monopolies in these and other areas.

It is also important to note that economic policymaking for stabilization requires making decisions in real time based on available information regarding the current state of the economy, which is always incomplete and provisional. These data deficiencies present a major challenge to policymaking, a challenge which increases in times of crisis when economic variables are moving faster and past economic relationships no longer hold. Even in the best of times, basic economic relationships on which policies are based, such as the demand for money, are subject to variation and may be hard to estimate. Economies are also subject to unpredictable and external influences ("exogenous shocks"). For these reasons, Fund-supported programs provide for frequent reviews—a reconsideration of the program by the Executive Board of the Fund in the light of recent performance and developments—allowing for the possibility of a readjustment of the program and conditionality as needed to take account of unforeseen developments. Thus, although economic analysis may be rather imprecise, especially in times of crisis and stabilization, the reviews provide a feedback mechanism that ensures that program objectives can be met.

Structural Policies

Stabilization policies in Fund-supported programs are usually coupled with structural policies designed to increase growth and output in the medium term, i.e., to improve supply rather than to contract demand. Structural policies might include, for example, financial sector reform, bank restructuring, pension and health system reforms, price liberalization, public enterprise reform and privatization, trade reform, public expenditure reforms, tax structure or administration reforms, legal reform, and reforms aimed at improving transparency and governance.

Structural policies usually have many close interlinkages with stabilization policies. For example, a weak and illiquid banking system may force the central bank into extending short-term credits in order to keep the payments system functioning, but with the result of undermining the overall monetary policy and presenting bankers with perverse incentives (credit going to poorly rather than well-performing banks). Similarly, money-losing public enterprises or poorly structured pension and health systems may be an enormous financial burden on the budget and/or the banking system. Reforms may often entail a short-term cost but with the prospect of significant cost savings in the longer term, and these trade-offs need to be taken into account when formulating the short-term program.

Issues in Program Design

There are many interesting issues in the design of Fund-supported programs. Among them are

1. *The proper balance between adjustment and financing.* It must be judged on a case-by-case basis taking many factors into account.

2. The proper mix of *macroeconomic stabilization policies versus structural reform*, and the related issue of *the role of the Fund vis-à-vis other institutions* such as the World Bank. The many interlinkages between structural issues and macroeconomic performance require the Fund to address a range of structural issues, but collaboration with other institutions possessing more expertise in structural matters can reduce the burden on the Fund and the level of Fund conditionality in these areas.

3. *"Ownership" of programs by the authorities.* Program design has traditionally relied heavily on the expertise of Fund staff, but credible programs require the full commitment of the authorities, which may be enhanced by a fuller involvement of the authorities in program formulation. However, more dialog in program formulation necessarily means a longer process, and more latitude given to the authorities in terms of performance and conditionality implies a somewhat more subjective evaluation process and thus more uncertainty

regarding whether or not the Fund may lend its support.

4. *The pace and sequencing of policies and reforms.* In situations where a wide range of stabilization policies and structural reforms is needed, it is usually impossible for the authorities to do everything at once. Priorities must then be set and schedules established, for which there is often little guidance from economic theory.

5. *Nominal versus real programming.* Short-term economic and financial stabilization policy (often called "financial programming") centers on nominal economic variables, with inflation and growth variables set as objectives. In practice, the instruments are generally available to achieve a given nominal output objective, but the split of that nominal growth between inflation and real growth is difficult to predict. If programs are too tight in nominal terms, growth may suffer, and if they are too loose, inflation may be higher than necessary. But, given our present state of economic science, the proper level in the context of real-time decision making depends largely on judgment. Different kinds of policies, such as structural reforms, may also be needed to encourage positive real growth, beyond the beneficial effects of macroeconomic stabilization.

6. *Protection for the poor and vulnerable.* The Fund's approach to stabilization and adjustment focuses primarily on macroeconomic variables, and a major criticism in the past has been that these programs have ignored the fact that the burden of adjustment may fall unfairly on vulnerable social groups, while the relatively well-off may have the means to protect their own interests. Thus, specific consideration of the impact of programs on the poor, and provision of social safety nets, have been introduced into Fund programs.

7. *Simplification of program and conditionality issues.* In addition to enhancing "ownership," simpler programs with fewer and more focused conditionalities may be easier to understand and to explain to the public, increasing their credibility and the likelihood of success. The Fund has been reexamining its policies with a view to simplification.

8. *Capital rather than current account problems.* The increasing frequency of balance of payments crises in emerging market economies arising from the capital account rather than the more traditional domestic and current account imbalances has required a new assessment of the role of the Fund, with much more involvement in financial sector issues and an enhanced role in surveillance of the global monetary system to include more emphasis on financial developments and financial sector soundness.

In all these areas, the Fund continues to evolve in response to the changing global environment and the needs of its members.

Chapter 3

The Stand-By Arrangement: Its Legal Nature and Principal Features

ROSS LECKOW

In the popular press, IMF stand-by arrangements are a subject of enormous attention and, at the same time, considerable misunderstanding. Most "IMF watchers" acknowledge that the stand-by arrangement is the principal legal instrument through which the Fund extends financial assistance to its members. However, few understand how a stand-by arrangement is structured or how it operates. Press reports abound of the Fund extending "stand-by loans" in support of programs of economic reform, or signing "stand-by agreements" with the authorities of member countries.[1] These reports ignore the stand-by arrangement's specific and, in many ways, unique characteristics. They also fail to recognize the manner in which the stand-by arrangement's principal features have evolved over time in order to meet the changing needs of the Fund and its members.

This paper examines the legal nature of a stand-by arrangement, its structure, and principal features.[2] It first reviews a few basic concepts of Fund financing before turning to the stand-by arrangement's legal character and manner of operation. The paper subsequently discusses some recent changes in the operational features of stand-by arrangements, and it ends with a brief conclusion.

---

[1] *See Ecuador Set to Secure IMF Deal*, Financial Times of London (May 4, 2001); *IMF Support Lifts Emerging Markets Debt*, Financial Times of London (May 1, 2001).

[2] This paper will focus on the most common and well-known form of Fund arrangement—the "upper credit tranche" stand-by arrangement through which the Fund provides financial assistance in the upper credit tranches to help members overcome general balance of payments problems. While the Fund has developed other types of arrangements—for example, the extended arrangement under the Extended Fund Facility—these other instruments have drawn on many of the principal features of the upper credit tranche stand-by arrangement.

Basic Principles of IMF Financing

Several important principles of Fund financing are reflected in the structure and operation of a stand-by arrangement. Central to these principles is the purpose of Fund financing in the General Resources Account. As specified in Article I (v) of the Articles of Agreement (the "Articles"), the purpose of Fund financing is "[t]o give confidence to members by making the general resources of the Fund temporarily available to them under adequate safeguards, thus providing them with [the] opportunity to correct maladjustments in their balance of payments without resorting to measures destructive of national or international prosperity."[3] Stated simply, the Fund provides financial assistance to member countries (i.e., members) experiencing balance of payments difficulties in order to allow the authorities of these countries to address these problems without having to impose restrictive measures that may damage that country's economy or those of other countries.[4] Under the Articles, the Fund may only provide financial support to a member to help that member deal with a problem in its balance of payments.[5] The Fund may not provide financing for other purposes—for example, to finance a particular project or the budget deficit of a member government.

Most Fund financing is provided to members through the General Resources Account under which the Fund normally makes available the resources which countries pay to the Fund at the time of membership or when their quotas in the Fund are periodically increased.[6] Financial assistance in the General Resources Account does not take the form of loans but, rather, of purchases and repurchases of currency.[7] Members receiving financial support purchase Special Drawing Rights ("SDRs") or a currency they need (e.g., U.S. dollars) with their own currency and, when the obligation to repay falls due, repurchase their own currency with SDRs or a

---

[3] Articles of Agreement of the International Monetary Fund, art. I (v) [hereinafter Articles of Agreement].

[4] F. Gianviti, "The International Monetary Fund and External Debt," *in* 215 Recueil des Cours 209, 246 (1989).

[5] *See Id.* at 226.

[6] Richard Edwards, *International Monetary Collaboration*, 222 (1985).

[7] Gianviti, *supra* note 4, at 225.

currency acceptable to the Fund.[8] Members receiving financial support pay charges on the balances of their currency that the Fund holds as a result of such assistance.[9]

When a member requests a purchase, the Articles require the Fund to satisfy itself that the request is consistent with the provisions of the Articles and, inter alia, the Fund's policies on the use of its financial resources.[10] The Fund must also determine that the member requesting a purchase (other than a reserve tranche purchase) actually has a balance of payments need. A member requesting such a purchase must represent that the money is needed in order to address a balance of payments problem.[11] For its part, the Fund may question whether such a need exists and, ultimately, may deny the member's request.[12]

The Articles require that Fund financing help a member requesting assistance to address its balance of payments problems in a manner that is consistent with the Articles. Financial support must be provided under conditions that ensure that the money the country receives will ultimately be paid back.[13] In order to meet these conditions, the Fund normally extends financial assistance to a member only if the member is prepared to take the steps necessary to address its balance of payments difficulties.[14] This is accomplished through the member implementing a program of economic reform

---

[8] Articles of Agreement, *supra* note 3, art. V, secs. 3 (b) and 7; Edwards, *supra* note 6, at 223.

[9] Articles of Agreement, *supra* note 3, art. V, sec. 8. *See also* Gianviti, *supra* note 4, at 227; Edwards, *supra* note 6, at 229.

[10] Articles of Agreement, *supra* note 3, art. V, sec. 3 (c). *See also* Gianviti, *supra* note 4, at 226.

[11] Articles of Agreement, *supra* note 3, art. V, sec. 3 (b)(ii).

[12] *See* Gianviti, *supra* note 4, at 226.

[13] More specifically, the Articles provide that the Fund "shall adopt policies on the use of its general resources, including policies on stand-by or similar arrangements, and may adopt special policies for special balance of payments problems, that will assist members to solve their balance of payments problems in a manner consistent with the provisions of this Agreement and that will establish adequate safeguards for the temporary use of the general resources of the Fund." Articles of Agreement, *supra* note 3, art. V, sec. 3 (a).

[14] *See* Edwards, *supra* note 6, at 249.

that deals with the problems that gave rise to the balance of payments crisis. In this manner, the country will resolve its balance of payments difficulties and, at the same time, improve its external position to the point where it will be able to repay the Fund.

How does the Fund support a member's program of economic reform? The Fund's "founding fathers" envisioned a world in which the balance of payments crises with which the Fund would be confronted would be relatively short-term in nature.[15] In the Fund's early years, many assumed that a member could resolve its balance of payments difficulties relatively quickly, and that its reform efforts could be adequately supported by a single purchase or a few purchases from the Fund. Over time, it was recognized that, in many cases, a member's reform efforts could not be adequately supported through a few stand-alone purchases from the Fund, and that members could more effectively resolve their balance of payments difficulties within the context of a more permanent framework for Fund financial assistance. There emerged the belief that a member could more efficiently implement a program of economic reform if it had the assurance that the Fund would provide financing over the program's life without scrutinizing each request for a purchase within that period. It was against this background that the concept of the Fund arrangement was born.[16]

---

[15] For example, the Fund decided in 1946 that the "authority to use the resources of the Fund is limited to use in accordance with its purposes to give temporary assistance in financing balance of payments deficits on current account for monetary stabilization operations" (Pursuant to Decision No. 71-2, adopted September 26, 1946), *reprinted in Selected Decisions and Selected Documents of the International Monetary Fund*, Twenty-Fifth Issue 128 (December 31, 2000) [hereinafter S*elected Decisions*].

[16] Joseph Gold, *Financial Assistance of the International Monetary Fund: Law and Practice*, 12 (1985). See also H. James, *International Monetary Cooperation Since Bretton Woods*, 81 (1996).

The Stand-By Arrangement and Its Principal Features

The stand-by arrangement is, in many ways, a creature of necessity. The first arrangement was approved for Belgium in 1952[17] and the structure and principal features of the arrangements that followed have evolved continuously in order to adjust to the changing needs of the international community.

The Conceptual Basis of a Stand-By Arrangement

The stand-by arrangement is defined in Article XXX (b) of the Articles as "a decision of the Fund by which a member is assured that it will be able to make purchases from the General Resources Account in accordance with the terms of the decision during a specified period and up to a specified amount." This definition sets out several important features which require closer examination.

A stand-by arrangement is a decision of the Fund.[18] More specifically, it is a unilateral decision of the Fund's Executive Board setting out the terms and conditions under which a member will be able to make purchases during a designated period and up to a specified amount. As a unilateral decision of the Executive Board, a stand-by arrangement is not a contract between the Fund and the member.[19] While it is not clear whether the Fund would be legally precluded from providing its resources to members through the conclusion of loan agreements,[20] the noncontractual approach offers a

---

[17] J. Keith Horsefield, *The International Monetary Fund, 1945–1965 I*, 329 (1969).

[18] *See* Gianviti, *supra* note 4, at 254; Edwards, *supra* note 6, at 267.

[19] Joseph Gold, *The Stand-By Arrangements of the International Monetary Fund*, 50 (1970). The Fund has adopted *Guidelines on Conditionality* which provide that "[s]tand-by arrangements are not international agreements and therefore language having a contractual connotation will be avoided in stand-by arrangements and letters of intent." *See Guidelines on Conditionality* (Decision No. 6056-(79/38), adopted March 2, 1979), *reprinted in Selected Decisions*, *supra* note 15, at 149. It follows that a stand-by arrangement cannot be regarded as an international agreement as the Fund, in light of the language quoted above, cannot be regarded as having the intention to contract necessary to support the formation of an agreement.

[20] Sir Joseph Gold has identified three questions that would need to be addressed before the Fund could make use of contractual instruments in

number of practical advantages. In particular, reliance upon a contractual commitment would discourage members from taking the tough measures that may be required to resolve a balance of payments problem. Having embarked upon a program of economic reform, a member may, for whatever reason, find itself unable to successfully implement the program. In these circumstances, the member would not want to be found to be in breach of its contractual obligations to the Fund, thereby exposing itself to the stigma associated with breach of contract, and to the possibility of triggering cross default provisions contained in loan agreements with other creditors.[21]

A stand-by arrangement, although not a contract, is a legal instrument which gives the member certain legal rights. The principal legal right accorded to the member is the "assurance" that it will be able to make purchases under the arrangement.[22] The member, subject to the conditions of the arrangement, may request purchases without the Fund scrutinizing each request to determine whether it is consistent with the Fund's Articles and policies or whether a balance of payments need actually exists. As long as the member meets the conditions stipulated under the arrangement, it will be able to request purchases without further challenge by the Fund.

---

providing its resources to members in the General Resources Account: (i) whether the definition of a stand-by arrangement in Article XXX (d) as a "decision of the Fund" precludes the Fund from providing financing in the General Resources Account through contractual instruments; (ii) whether agreements that (as is often the case under a stand-by arrangement) left some of the conditions for purchases to be specified at a later date would be regarded as an "agreement to agree" and, therefore, not a contract; and (iii) whether certain provisions of an arrangement that give the Fund the discretion to suspend the member's right to make purchases are so broad in nature as to give rise to an "illusory agreement" which is not a contract. *See* Joseph Gold, *The Legal Character of the Fund's Stand-By Arrangements and Why It Matters*, IMF Pamphlet Series No. 35, 45 (1980).

[21] *Id.* at 38, 41. One consequence that flows from the avoidance of a contractual approach is that a member may request a stand-by arrangement without having to satisfy its domestic legal requirements for the conclusion of an international agreement. Moreover, as a stand-by arrangement is not an international agreement, it cannot be registered under Article 102 of the Charter of the United Nations.

[22] *See* Gianviti, *supra* note 4, at 255; Edwards, *supra* note 6, at 267.

At the same time, this assurance is subject to a number of limitations and conditions. First, the stand-by arrangement only commits financial support to a member for a designated period and up to a specified amount.[23] The arrangement will normally be put in place for the same length of time that the member's program is to cover—generally, one year but for as long as three years.[24] The amounts to be committed are determined on the basis of the member's quota and access policies which the Fund has adopted.

The arrangement provides that purchases may only be made if the member meets the conditions that are specified in the arrangement.[25] These conditions normally require the member to meet key macroeconomic targets or to implement specific structural measures that are drawn directly from the member's program, and are incorporated into the terms of the arrangement. The rationale for this approach is that the member should only be permitted to purchase if it is successfully implementing the program that the arrangement is supporting. These various conditions are known as the "conditionality" of the arrangement.

While these targets and measures are established as conditions for purchase, the member is under no legal obligation to meet them.[26] The only legal consequence which arises from the failure of a member to meet a condition for purchase is that the member will be deprived of the right to purchase under the arrangement.[27] The member will not be in breach of an obligation. Rather, the member is free to "walk away" from its program and the arrangement at any time.[28]

---

[23] *See* Gold, *supra* note 19, at 84–95; Gianviti, *supra* note 4, at 254.

[24] The *Guidelines on Conditionality* provide that "[t]he normal period for a stand-by arrangement will be one year. If, however, a longer period is requested by a member and considered necessary by the Fund to enable the member to implement its adjustment program successfully, the stand-by arrangement may extend beyond the period of one year. This period in appropriate cases may extend up to but not beyond three years." *Guidelines on Conditionality, supra* note 19, at 149.

[25] *See* Gianviti, *supra* note 4, at 255; Edwards, *supra* note 6, at 267.

[26] Edwards, *supra* note 6, at 267.

[27] Gold, *supra* note 19, at 141; Gianviti, *supra* note 4, at 256.

[28] Joseph Gold, *Interpretation: The IMF and International Law*, 363 (1996).

The Fund will only approve an arrangement for a member at the member's request. The member's program (including the measures that are established as conditions for purchase under the arrangement) is, in practice, formulated by the member in consultation with the Fund.[29] In approving an arrangement for a member, the Fund must be satisfied that the member's program will be successfully implemented and will contribute to the resolution of the member's balance of payments problems. The Fund normally obtains the necessary assurances for this purpose by working with the member on the formulation of the program and reaching understandings on its features. As a matter of practice, the member's program will be described in a statement of economic policies from the authorities of the member country—often called a letter of intent or memorandum of economic policies—in which the authorities, in support of their program, request a stand-by arrangement from the Fund. The Fund will then approve the stand-by arrangement, including the specific terms and conditions for purchases under the arrangement.

Principal Features of an IMF Arrangement

Stand-by arrangements invariably embody several principal features—in particular (i) the phasing of purchases, (ii) performance criteria, and (iii) program reviews by the Executive Board.[30]

Phasing of Purchases

The first important feature of a stand-by arrangement is the concept of phasing. Rather than making all the committed resources available to the member immediately, the arrangement provides or "phases" specified amounts at designated intervals over the arrangement's life.[31]

The phasing of purchases is designed to ensure that financial assistance will be provided to the member gradually over the life of its program as it implements the measures contemplated in the

---

[29] Edwards, *supra* note 6, at 249; Gianviti, *supra* note 4, at 253.
[30] Stand-by arrangements in the first credit tranche (as opposed to upper credit tranche stand-by arrangements) do not provide for the phasing of purchases, and do not subject purchases to the observance of performance criteria or the completion of reviews. *See* Gianviti, *supra* note 4, at 256.
[31] Gold, *supra* note 19, at 120.

program. As each purchase is made available, the member may request the purchase if it meets the conditions established under the arrangement. To the extent that a member does not purchase an amount when it is made available, the member may do so later as long as it meets the specified conditions.

Performance Criteria

Probably the most common and well-known conditions established under a stand-by arrangement are the performance criteria. A performance criterion is a target or measure drawn from a member's program whose observance or implementation is made a condition for purchase under an arrangement approved for the member.[32] Performance criteria serve as signposts which help the Fund determine whether a program is being successfully implemented. A member requesting a purchase under an arrangement must demonstrate that it has met all applicable performance criteria established under the arrangement.

Broadly speaking, performance criteria fall into two categories.[33] The first and most common type are quantitative performance criteria which specify quantitative macroeconomic targets that must be met before the member will be permitted to make purchases.[34] These targets normally cover the most important macroeconomic features of a member's program such as the level of net international reserves, the net domestic assets of the banking system, the size of the budget

---

[32] *See Id.* at 140. The Fund first made use of performance criteria in stand-by arrangements for Latin American countries in the late 1950s. *See* E.G. Spitzer, *Stand-By Arrangements: Purposes and Form* in Horsefield, *supra* note 17, at II, 484.

[33] The *Guidelines on Conditionality* provide that "[t]he number and content of performance criteria may vary because of problems and institutional arrangements of members. Performance criteria will be limited to those that are necessary to evaluate implementation of the program with a view to ensuring the achievement of its objectives. Performance criteria will normally be confined to (i) macroeconomic variables, and (ii) those necessary to implement specific provisions of the Articles or policies adopted under them. Performance criteria may relate to other variables only in exceptional cases when they are essential for the effectiveness of the member's program because of their macroeconomic impact" *(supra* note 19, at 150).

[34] Gold, *supra* note 19, at 148; Gianviti, *supra* note 4, at 255.

deficit, and the amount of nonconcessional external borrowing by the government. The second type are structural performance criteria which require the member, as a condition for purchase, to implement structural measures that are important for the success of the program. Some of these conditions require the member to take positive action—for example, to enact a piece of legislation such as a bankruptcy law. In other cases, the performance criterion will require the member to refrain from taking particular action—for example, from imposing exchange restrictions.[35]

Traditionally, reliance upon structural performance criteria was relatively rare and was generally limited to a narrow range of measures. The past decade has witnessed much greater use of structural conditionality as the international community has recognized the need for countries to address underlying structural problems in order to achieve macroeconomic stability. Structural conditionality has been particularly important in members' programs supported under the Enhanced Structural Adjustment Facility and, more recently, the Poverty Reduction and Growth Facility, and also in the programs of the formerly socialist countries.[36]

While the Fund may draw on a wide range of measures from the member's program in establishing quantitative or structural performance criteria, there are limits. In particular, a performance criterion cannot require a member to take action that would be inconsistent with the purposes of the Fund or with other provisions of the Articles. For example, the Fund cannot set performance criteria whose implementation would require the removal of restrictions on

---

[35] The text of the Fund's standard form stand by arrangement includes performance criteria respecting the imposition or intensification of exchange restrictions, the introduction or modification of multiple currency practices, the conclusion of bilateral payments agreements that are inconsistent with Article VIII of the Fund's Articles, and the imposition and intensification of import restrictions for balance of payments purposes. *See Stand-By and Extended Arrangements—Standard Forms* (Decision No. 10464-(93/130), adopted September 13, 1993), *reprinted in Selected Decisions, supra* note 15, at 173.

[36] Conditionality in Fund-Supported Programs—Overview (IMF Staff Report, February 20, 2001), par. 6 *available at* http://www.imf.org/external/np/pdr/cond/2001/eng/overview/index.htm.

capital movements.[37] The liberalization of capital movements is not a purpose of the Fund and Article VI, Section 3 expressly recognizes the right of members to restrict the capital account.[38] The establishment of a performance criterion requiring the elimination of such measures would be inconsistent with the Fund's purposes and would effectively deny the member the exercise of a right expressly recognized under the Articles.

The Fund has put in place policies that prohibit the establishment of other types of measures as performance criteria. The Fund's *Guidelines on Conditionality* require the Fund, in helping members design programs of economic reform, to "pay due regard to the domestic social and political objectives" of members.[39] The Fund could not establish a performance criterion related to the human rights record of a member. Moreover, Fund policy prohibits the establishment of performance criteria requiring a reduction in a country's military spending.[40]

At the same time, it would appear that the acceptable boundary of conditionality has been gradually expanding. Over the past decade, many international financial organizations have recognized the importance of improving good governance in member countries in order to facilitate meaningful macroeconomic reform. Fund staff guidelines have been developed which contemplate the establishment

---

[37] See William E. Holder, Fund Jurisdiction over Capital Movements—Comments, Panel on "Preventing Asian Type Crises: Who If Anyone Should Have Jurisdiction over Capital Movement?," 5 ILSA Journal of International and Comparative Law 407, 411 (1999).

[38] Article VI, Section 3 provides that "[m]embers may exercise such controls as are necessary to regulate international capital movements, but no member may exercise these controls in a manner which will restrict payments for current transactions or which will unduly delay transfers of funds in settlement of commitments, except as provided in Article VII, Section 3 (b) and in Article XIV, Section 2."

[39] *Guidelines on Conditionality*, supra note 19, at 149.

[40] See *Concluding Remarks by the Acting Chairman, Military Expenditure and the Role of the Fund* (EBM/91/138, October 2, 1991), reprinted in *Selected Decisions*, supra note 15, at 448. In the *Concluding Remarks*, it is noted that "Directors agreed that data on military expenditures should not serve as a basis for establishing performance criteria or similar conditions associated with Fund-supported programs."

of performance criteria to improve good economic governance.[41] The programs of economic reform of some members have begun to reflect greater concern with these issues. For example, the Kenyan program supported by an ESAF arrangement from the Fund provided for the establishment of an anti-corruption authority designed to combat corruption in the Kenyan government.[42]

Members often fail to meet performance criteria, either because they did not properly implement the measures provided for in their programs or because of exogenous developments which were beyond their control. Where a member fails to meet a performance criterion, it will not be able to request purchases under the arrangement.[43] In these circumstances, the Fund may grant a waiver for the nonobservance of the performance criterion and permit a purchase to be made.[44] As the purpose of performance criteria is to ensure that the Fund will only provide financing to a member when it is successfully implementing its program, a waiver will only be granted if the Fund is satisfied that, notwithstanding the nonobservance, the program is on track. The Fund will normally grant a waiver only if the extent of the nonobservance is so minor as to be self–correcting, or the member adopts corrective measures to bring the program back on track.[45]

---

[41] *See IMF Adopts Guidelines Regarding Governance Issues* (IMF News Brief 97/15, August 4, 1997) *available at* http://www.imf.org/external/np/sec/nb/1997/nb9715.htm. The Guidance Note provides that "[t]he use of conditionality related to governance issues emanates from the IMF's concern with macroeconomic policy design and implementation as the main means to safeguard the use of IMF resources. Thus, conditionality, in the form of prior actions, performance criteria, benchmarks, and conditions for completion of a review, should be attached to policy measures including those relating to economic aspects of governance that are required to meet the objectives of the program. This would include policy measures which may have important implications for improving governance, but are covered by the IMF's conditionality primarily because of their direct macroeconomic impact."

[42] *See Moi Weighs Tough Corruption Probe*, Financial Times of London (July 28, 1997); *see also IMF Rules out Early Loan Agreement With Nairobi*, Financial Times of London (February 19, 1998).

[43] Gold, *supra* note 19, at 144; Gianviti, *supra* note 4, at 255.

[44] Gianviti, *supra* note 4, at 256.

[45] Edwards, *supra* note 6, at 268.

Reviews by the Executive Board

A second important type of condition established under a stand-by arrangement is the review by the Executive Board of the implementation of the member's program. Stand-by arrangements typically provide that, after a specified point in time during the arrangement, the member's right to make further purchases will be interrupted until the Fund's Executive Board completes a review of the implementation of the program by the member.[46] In the review, the Executive Board seeks to determine whether the program is being successfully implemented and is "on track," and will only complete the review if it is satisfied that this is the case. The Board will look not only at the member's observance of performance criteria but at other features of the program as well.[47] A member's memorandum of economic policies often identifies specific elements to be examined in the course of a review but the Board is not limited to a consideration of these issues. The Board has discretion in identifying the range of factors it takes into account. For example, the Board may take into account the effect of an exogenous event that was not contemplated at the time the program was formulated but which may jeopardize the successful implementation of the program.

A program review allows the Fund not only to consider past performance but to make adjustments to the conditionality of an

---

[46] As late as the early 1970s, reliance upon review clauses in stand-by arrangements was relatively rare. As Sir Joseph Gold wrote in 1970, "[t]he Fund has made rare use of this kind of review clause. It has been adopted in some cases in which the outlook for the member was unusually difficult to predict and in which, therefore, this uncertainty made it difficult to reach a judgment on the stabilization measures that the member was undertaking." *See* Gold, *supra* note 19, at 138. By the time of the adoption of the *Guidelines on Conditionality,* Executive Board reviews had become a more common feature of a stand-by arrangement.

[47] Stand-by arrangements, in some cases, provide for the completion of more focused reviews which are limited in scope to the examination of one particular question—for example, the financing of the program. Financing assurances reviews are normally provided for when an arrangement is approved for a member before the member has reached agreement with private creditors on the rescheduling of its external obligations. *See The Acting Chairman's Summing Up on Fund Policy on Arrears to Private Creditors—Further Considerations* (EBM/99/64, June 14, 1999) *reprinted in Selected Decisions, supra* note 15, at 199.

arrangement in light of changing circumstances—for example, by establishing new or modifying existing performance criteria.[48] Reliance upon Board reviews is particularly useful in arrangements that support programs whose implementation is subject to uncertainty and change.[49] Fund arrangements in recent years have placed greater reliance upon program reviews by the Executive Board. This was particularly the case with arrangements for some countries of the former Soviet Union where the Fund, in the early and mid-1990s, often found itself committing assistance in uncertain macroeconomic situations.[50]

Recent Developments with Respect to Stand-By Arrangements

Stand-by arrangements have evolved in order to meet the changing needs of the Fund and its members. This has always been the case in the past and will invariably continue to be so in future. Two recent developments in this area concern (a) the role of prior actions; and (b) the use of stand-by arrangements to make available resources under the Fund's special policies.

Prior Actions

Prior actions are an important feature of a member's program of economic reform. These are generally structural measures which the member implements before requesting a new Fund arrangement, the completion of a review, or the waiver for the nonobservance of a performance criterion. These measures are taken "up front" in order

---

[48] Gianviti, *supra* note 4, at 256.

[49] The *Guidelines on Conditionality* provide that "[i]n programs extending beyond one year, or in circumstances where a member is unable to establish in advance one or more performance criteria for all or part of the program period, provision will be made for a review in order to reach the necessary understandings with the member for the remaining period." *See Guidelines on Conditionality, supra* note 19, at 151. In recent years, Executive Board reviews have become more frequent.

[50] For example, the 12-month stand-by arrangement in an amount equivalent to 4.3 billion Special Drawing Rights approved for the Russian Federation on April 11, 1995 provided for monthly Board reviews of performance. *See IMF Approves Stand-By Credit for Russia* (IMF Press Release No. 95/21, April 11, 1995), *available at* http://www.imf.org/external/np/sec/pr/1995/pr9521.htm.

to demonstrate the member's commitment to the success of its program. The Fund often expects such measures to be put in place by members whose programs have historically been characterized by poor track records of implementation.

While the Executive Board will be informed whether these measures have been taken, their implementation has, until recently, seldom been made a condition under the arrangement. Rather, the Board, having been advised that the measures are in place, has simply adopted the relevant decision—that is, approving an arrangement, completing a review, or granting a waiver for nonobservance—without making implementation an express condition under the decision. This has been the case even if the measures may, as a practical matter, have been particularly influential factors in the decision-making process of some Directors.

The consequence of this approach was that the implementation of the relevant prior actions did not form part of the conditions established under a member's stand-by arrangement. In these circumstances, the Fund had no legal recourse against a member that provided the Fund with incorrect information on the implementation of its prior actions. The Fund's Articles and policies set out certain remedies to address cases in which members have "misreported" information respecting the observance of conditions established under an arrangement.[51] Generally speaking, these remedies do not apply to

---

[51] The Fund has put in place guidelines on misreporting under Fund arrangements which, subject to certain conditions, provide that, where a member makes a purchase on the basis of erroneous information that leads the Fund to mistakenly believe that all conditions applicable to the purchase under the arrangement were met, the member will be "expected" to make a prompt repurchase of the amount unless the Fund grants a waiver. *See Misreporting and Noncomplying Purchases under Fund Arrangements—Guidelines on Corrective Action* (Decision No. 7842-(84/165), adopted November 16, 1984, as amended) *reprinted in Selected Decisions, supra* note 15, at 160. In addition, Article VIII, Section 5 of the Articles requires members, subject to certain conditions, to report accurate information to the Fund. A member that fails to comply with the requirements of this provision will be in breach of an obligation under the Articles and may be subjected to the sanctions specified in Article XXVI, Section 2—that is, a declaration of ineligibility to use the general resources of the Fund, the suspension of

the misreporting of information that does not relate to such a condition.

A number of recent cases in which members have misreported information respecting the implementation of their programs of economic reform have compelled the Fund to reassess this approach. In July 2000, the Executive Board established a policy of incorporating conditions into decisions on stand-by arrangements which require the member to have implemented specified prior actions in the manner reported to the Executive Board.[52] This new approach will allow the Fund to apply its legal framework for misreporting to cases involving prior actions.

Stand-By Arrangements and Special Policies

The Articles require the Fund to establish "policies" on the use of its general resources which specify the types of balance of payments problems the Fund will finance and the applicable conditions. The Fund has put in place the "credit tranche policies" for general balance of payments problems and "special policies" for special types of balance of payments problems.[53]

Historically, the stand-by arrangement has been the instrument through which the Fund makes available financing under the credit tranche policies to address a general balance of payments problem.[54] Other means have been used to provide resources under the special policies of the Fund to deal with special types of balance of payments difficulties. In recent years, this approach has changed. The Fund has begun to use stand-by arrangements to make available resources under its special policies in combination with resources under the credit tranche policies. Two recent examples of this approach are the Supplemental Reserve Facility and the Fund's policy on Contingent Credit Lines. These two special policies are designed to address cases

---

voting and certain other related rights, and, ultimately, compulsory withdrawal.

[52] *See Establishment of General Policy to Condition Decisions in the General Resources Account on Accuracy of Information Regarding Implementation of Prior Actions* (Decision No. 12250-(00/77), adopted July 27, 2000) *reprinted in Selected Decisions, supra* note 15, at 162.

[53] Gianviti, *supra* note 4, at 250.

[54] *Id.* at 251.

in which members require massive amounts of financial support in order to address balance of payments problems arising from different types of sudden and large losses in market confidence in the member's economy.[55] In both cases, resources are provided under a stand-by arrangement in conjunction with resources under the credit tranches. Given the large amounts of financial assistance which the Fund commits, both policies require members to meet very strict levels of conditionality.[56] The stand-by arrangement provides the appropriate mechanism to ensure that resources are only made available if the conditionality contemplated by the Fund is being met.

Conclusion

Since its creation almost 50 years ago, the stand-by arrangement has been a potent weapon in the Fund's arsenal that has helped members resolve their balance of payments difficulties and restore exchange stability. Central to the success of the stand-by arrangement has been its reliance upon the member's own efforts to address a balance of payments problem and its focus on the member's program of economic reform. It is this emphasis on the member's policies that has allowed the stand-by arrangement to serve as a catalyst for the financial support of the entire international community. The commitment of resources under a stand-by arrangement represents the Fund's endorsement of the member's program of economic reform— a "seal of approval" that encourages other creditors, both public and private, to lend their support. In this manner, the stand-by arrangement serves as an instrument of cooperation not only between the Fund and individual members but for the international community as a whole.

---

[55] *See Supplemental Reserve Facility and Contingent Credit Lines* (Decision No. 11627-(97/123) SRF, adopted December 17, 1997, as amended), *reprinted in Selected Decisions*, *supra* note 15, at 223.

[56] *See IMF Tightens Defenses Against Financial Contagion by Establishing Contingent Credit Lines* (IMF Press Release 99/14, April 25, 1999) *available at* http://www.imf.org/external/np/sec/pr/1999/pr9914.htm.

Chapter 4

The IMF's Relationship with the World Bank: The Cooperative Framework

WILLIAM E. HOLDER

The International Monetary Fund (Fund) and the International Bank for Reconstruction and Development (World Bank) have worked closely together for more than fifty years. Both emerged from the Bretton Woods Conference in 1944 and were designed as part of the new post-war economic order, together with the intended International Trade Organization.

Both the Fund and the Bank operate within their given mandates, as prescribed by their respective Articles of Agreement. At the same time, both institutions have adapted their functions to react to changing world conditions and the demands of their membership.

In so doing, the overlap of activities has increased; in particular, it is generally accepted that macroeconomic and structural policies interact substantially and cannot be evaluated separately. In addition, the general goal of assisting the stability, growth, and poverty alleviation of their members has served to add to the conception of commonality.

Since the time of the Bretton Woods Conference, the common membership has expected the Fund and the Bank to cooperate in a mutually supporting fashion. Indeed, the justification for maintaining two separate organizations probably depends upon that cooperative element:

> Their functions remain separate in that the IMF is primarily a monetary and not a development institution; but effective institutionalized cooperation between the two is needed if there is

not to be a widespread rejection of the Bretton Woods twins on the part of their members, clients, and owners.[1]

Then what is the accepted framework for this cooperation? The two constitutive treaties in fact contain little on the subject, and certainly make no attempt to delineate mutually exclusive economic jurisdiction. One possibility would be for the two institutions to negotiate a treaty instrument to clarify substantive areas and procedural techniques: that approach has lacked attraction. Instead, as described below, the institutions have adhered to an informal statement of roles and modalities, in the form of memoranda entered into by the Managing Director of the Fund and the President of the Bank, and the ongoing implementation of the principle of cooperation by active interchange and an attendant culture.

Structure and Relationship

The Articles and Competence

The purposes and functions ascribed to the Fund and the Bank require timely study for their comprehension. It is fair to say that they are substantially different in basic orientation: the Fund's focus is on the balance of payments, exchange rate stability, and the international monetary system; the Bank's focus is on investment for development and on particular projects.[2]

In summary, the purposes of the Fund are:

- promotion of international monetary cooperation;

- facilitation of the growth of international trade;

- promotion of exchange rate stability;

- assistance in the establishment of a multilateral system of payments; and

---

[1] Harold James, *International Monetary Cooperation Since Bretton Woods*, Oxford University Press (1996), p. 617.

[2] *See* Article III, Section 4(vii), in addition to Article I, IBRD Articles of Agreement.

- provision of temporary balance of payments assistance to members.[3]

These purposes were supplemented by the First and Second Amendments (although without amendment of the purposes specified in Article I). Under the First Amendment, the Fund could respond to the need for international liquidity by the creation of Special Drawing Rights. Under the Second Amendment, the Fund was to oversee the international monetary system in the interests of financial and economic stability and to oversee members' obligations with respect to their exchange rate policies.

For the Bank, the purposes are:

- facilitation of investment of capital for the reconstruction of economies destroyed in the war, and the development of productive facilities and resources in less developed countries;

- promotion of private investment, and to supplement private investment by injecting its own capital or by guarantees; and

- promotion of international trade and balance of payments equilibrium by encouraging international investment.[4]

Unlike the Fund, the Bank has added purposes by creating new entities within "the Bank Group," namely, the International Development Association (IDA), the International Finance Corporation (IFC), the International Center for the Settlement of Investment Disputes (ICSID), and the Multilateral Investment Guarantee Association (MIGA).

Structural Ties

Both the Fund and the Bank operate as separate juridical entities, pursuant to their Articles and in accordance with international law. While their common ancestry led to some similarities of structure,

---

[3] Article I, IMF Articles of Agreement.
[4] Article I, IBRD Articles of Agreement.

both enjoy their own resources and decision making and there is no attempt to link their functions organically—as there was, for example, between the Fund and the GATT (and now the WTO). Clearly, neither institution is subjugated to the other.

In one respect, the Bank is tied to the Fund, in that the Bank's Articles require membership in the Fund as a precondition to membership in the Bank.[5] In the event, however, that a country ceases to be a member of the Fund, a special procedure may allow it to remain a member of the Bank; cessation of membership in the Bank after the expiration of three months can be prevented by a majority of three-fourths of the total voting power agreeing to the maintenance of membership.[6] At the time of writing this paper, membership in the Fund and the Bank is completely common.

The Fund's Articles indicate another possible linkage, by envisaging relations with other organizations: "The Fund shall cooperate within the terms of this Agreement with any general international organization and with public international organizations having specialized responsibilities in related fields."[7] Pursuant to this provision, the Fund has entered two international agreements, one with the United Nations,[8] which brings it into association with the United Nations as a specialized agency, and one with the World Trade Organization.[9] This provision, however, has not been relied on in order to further relations with the World Bank by entering a formal international agreement.

For the performance of particular functions, however, the Fund and the Bank have engaged in joint activities, including joint committees. In 1974, for example, the two Boards of Governors, by parallel resolutions, established the Joint Ministerial Committee of the Boards of Governors of the Bank and the Fund on the Transfer of Real Resources to Developing Countries (the Development

---

[5] Article II, Section 1.
[6] Article VI, Section 3.
[7] Article X. The Bank has the same provision (Article V, Section 8 (a)).
[8] Agreement Between the United Nations and the International Monetary Fund, *Selected Decisions, Twenty-Fifth Issue*, pp. 651–57.
[9] Agreement Between the International Monetary Fund and the World Trade Organization, *Selected Decisions, Twenty-Fifth Issue*, pp. 705–10.

Committee).[10] The Committee is serviced by joint contributions of the staffs, and the managements and Boards collaborate closely with respect to it. The International Monetary and Financial Committee (formerly Interim Committee), in contrast, is constituted as an advisory committee within the Fund only, and is not established with the Bank.[11]

Other organic linkages exist. In a few instances, an appointed Executive Director is selected to serve on the Executive Board of the Fund and on the Board of the Bank at the same time. Occasionally, also, the two Executive Boards have furthered a common topic by deliberating jointly. Finally, the Fund and the Bank, since the beginning, have held their Annual Meetings jointly, supported by a joint secretariat and bringing efficiency to the enterprise.

In the same way, some administrative services are combined, according to agreed terms, for example, a joint library and a combined health service. Similarly, some training exercises for member countries call for inter-institutional support.

Both the Fund and the Bank are parties, also, to the agreement establishing the Joint Vienna Institute, a training center in Vienna, Austria, which itself operates as a separate international legal entity.[12]

Framework for Cooperation

Early Years

From the first years of the Fund and the Bank, the need for close collaboration, especially concerning financial assistance to members, was treated as of the highest importance; the Joint Standing Committee of the Bank and the Fund acted to ensure this goal. In 1946, the first year of operation of the Bretton Woods institutions, the Joint Committee produced a Report on Provisional Procedures for Liaison Between the Fund and the Bank on Financial Assistance to Members, which was adopted by the respective Executive Boards.

---

[10] *Selected Decisions, Twenty-Fifth Issue*, pp. 606–11.
[11] *Selected Decisions, Twenty-Fifth Issue*, pp. 602–605.
[12] Agreement for the Establishment of the Joint Vienna Institute, *Selected Decisions, Twenty-Fifth Issue*, pp. 689–99. The other participants in the JVI are the BIS, the EBRD, the OECD, and the WTO.

Specifically, the institutions agreed that their actions were complementary in many respects, and that there should be close collaboration on financial assistance to members, with due regard to the responsibilities of each institution. On this basis, the Fund and the Bank were to be kept informed of matters of interest to them, and to be free to express an opinion. Specifically, the Fund was to communicate regularly to the Bank on the financial standing of members, the intention to declare a member ineligible, decisions concerning par values, and significant proposed and actual actions relating to exchange restrictions. The Bank, in turn, was to communicate prospective loan policies and programs, details of prospective and actual loan applications, decisions of the Loan Committee, and related loan reports of special interest to the Fund.

As the two institutions proceeded to develop their institutional practices, the two staffs developed a good deal of mutual support and interaction. At the same time, tensions and differences also occurred, leading to assertions of transgression. Upon occasion, for instance, allegations of intrusion into primary fields of competence surfaced. For example, on one occasion in 1949, the Fund protested that the Bank, instead of acting on a loan application of a member, was offering its advice to the country on monetary and exchange matters. The objection was made not because the advice was wrong, but as a matter of jurisdictional competence. In the view of the Fund, each institution should adhere to the "appropriate specialization"; thus, the Bank would be directly and primarily concerned with investment, production, and commodity problems, all of which related to long-run real economic positions of its members. The Fund would be directly and primarily concerned with exchanges, reserves, and monetary policy, all bearing on the immediate balance of payments of its members. According to this view, specific advice on monetary policy would be communicated by and through the Fund.

Perhaps indicative of the atmosphere, a joint committee appointed to look into the budget aspects of closer cooperation in 1952 was unable to make progress on joint operations for the collection and compilation of basic economic data needed by both institutions and the use of technical expertise in staffing missions and carrying out research projects.[13]

Formalizing Collaboration

Since 1966, the Fund and the Bank have dealt with the challenge of enhanced collaboration by a special technique. The Managing Director of the Fund and the President of the World Bank negotiate a document to which they can subscribe in their own names, which is then submitted (initially in parallel documents but later as joint memoranda) to the respective Executive Boards for approval. Such a document is not seen as creating an international agreement between the institutions, or even an "arrangement" to cooperate with another international organization.[14] As indicated above, it was open to the Fund to enter a more formal international agreement, but to do so would have run counter to the view that the flexibility of the more informal device should be retained.

1966 Outline of Procedures

The 1966 memoranda were made up of two parts. In January 1966, the two heads forwarded a document dealing with the procedures of collaboration, entitled "Further Steps for Fund/Bank Collaboration," to their respective executive boards, each of which approved it. The memoranda noted the existing close contact of the two staffs, and called for greater collaboration by means of exchange of information, including that relating to prospective missions and views on countries. Specifically, inconsistent evaluations were to be avoided, and each institution was to serve as the source of information for the other for basic information within the primary concern of the other.

To encourage the desired level of cooperation, parallel missions, and the attachment of staff members for missions of the other institution, were to be considered as an appropriate means of cooperation.

---

[13] Keith Horsefield, *The International Monetary Fund, 1945–1965*, Vol. 1, pp. 340–41.

[14] In 1966, such an arrangement would have required Boards of Governors approval. While the Fund's Second Amendment removed the requirement, for the Bank it is still in place (Article V, Section 2(b)(v)).

1966 Memorandum on Competence

In December 1966, further parallel memoranda elaborated on the issue of institutional competence. The stated objectives of the memoranda were to ensure that organizational views on economic policy matters were consistent, and that members should not be faced with contradictory or conflicting advice. At the same time, the memoranda admit the reality of substantial common interests and a shared concern with the economic and financial structure and progress of the institutions' members. Thus, there is no attempt to draw strict jurisdictional boundaries.

The memoranda build on the concept of areas of "primary responsibility," which, as noted earlier, had permeated thinking since the beginning, and elaborated on the consequence for each institution, as follows.

> 4. As between the two institutions, the Bank is recognized as having primary responsibility for the composition and appropriateness of development programs and project evaluation, including development priorities. On those matters, the Fund, and particularly the field missions of the Fund, should inform themselves of the established views and positions of the Bank and adopt those views as a working basis for their own work. This does not preclude discussions between the Bank and the Fund as to those matters, but it does mean that the Fund (and Fund missions) will not engage in a critical review of those matters with member countries unless it is done with the prior consent of the Bank.

> 5. As between the two institutions, the Fund is recognized as having primary responsibility for exchange rates and restrictive systems, for adjustment of temporary balance of payments disequilibria and for evaluating and assisting members to work out stabilization programs as a sound basis for economic advance. On these matters, the Bank, and particularly the field missions of the Bank, should inform themselves of the established views and positions of the Fund and adopt those views as a working basis for their own work. This does not preclude discussion between the Bank and the Fund as to those matters but it does mean that the Bank (and Bank missions) will not engage in a critical review of those matters with member countries unless it is done with the prior consent of the Fund.

This identification of primary responsibilities is balanced, however, by the recognition of areas of shared responsibilities, with consequential instructions to the staff:

> 6. In between these two clear-cut areas of responsibility of the Bank and the Fund, respectively, there is the broad range of matters which are of interest to both institutions. This range includes such matters as the structure and functioning of financial institutions, the adequacy of money and capital markets, the actual and potential capacity of a member country to generate domestic savings, the financial implications of economic development programs both for the internal financial position of a country and for its external situation, foreign debt problems, and so on. In connection with all such matters, efforts should be made to avoid conflicting views and judgements, through continuing close working relations between the respective area departments and other means. In particular, field missions of each institution should acquaint themselves with the views and judgements, through continuing close working relations between the respective area departments and other means. In particular, field missions of each institution should acquaint themselves with the views and judgements of other institution prior to departure. Returning missions should also arrange for frank discussions between staff members of the two institutions, especially where there may be reason to believe that differing views have emerged or may emerge.

Finally, the memoranda recognized that within this area of common interest full uniformity of views could not be expected; nonetheless, close working relations should encourage efforts to avoid conflicting views and judgments.

The memoranda were distributed to the two Boards but not discussed, with the understanding that they would be circulated to staff for guidance in coordinating operations.

The 1970 Memorandum

In February 1970, a further note elaborated on procedures, for the first time entitled as a joint memorandum of the Managing Director and the President.

In various respects, the memorandum confirmed and consolidated existing practices and the 1966 understandings. In particular, the memorandum prescribed staff exchanges preceding Fund consultation and use of resources missions, and Bank economic missions, oral debriefing upon return, circulation of draft documents for comment before distribution, and exchange of final documents. Meanwhile, parallel missions were to be encouraged, with a view to lightening the burden on governments, and input from resident missions welcomed. In the same way, while technical assistance was seen as reflecting the special responsibilities of each institution, so that issues of coordination were seen as minimal, nonetheless the need for appropriate exchanges and mechanisms was recognized.

The 1989 Concordat

A further concentrated review of the arrangements was undertaken in 1989, again under the nature of a Joint Memorandum of the two heads (which has attracted the description of "the 1989 Concordat").

The 1989 Concordat confirmed the soundness of the 1966 Guidelines, while seeking to reinforce them, and recognized the increasing overlap of activities, especially given the intermingling of macroeconomic and structural policies.

The 1989 Concordat reaffirmed the concept of primary responsibilities, especially in functional terms, and offered an updated formulation:

> The Fund has among its purposes the promotion of economic conditions conducive to growth, price stability, and balance of payments sustainability and is required to exercise surveillance on a continual basis over the performance of its members as defined by Article IV. The Fund is empowered to provide temporary balance of payments financing to members to enable them to correct maladjustments in their balance of payments without resorting to measures destructive of national or international prosperity. Thus, the Fund has focused on the aggregate aspects of macroeconomic policies and their related instruments—including public sector spending and revenues, aggregate wage and price policies, money and credit, interest rates and the exchange rate. The Fund has to discharge responsibilities with respect to surveillance, exchange rate matters, balance of payments, growth-oriented stabilization policies and their related instruments. These are the areas in which

the Fund has a mandate, primary responsibility, and a record of expertise and experience.

The Bank has the objective of promoting economic growth and conditions conducive to efficient resource allocation, which it pursues through investment lending, sectoral and structural adjustment loans. Thus, the Bank has focused on development strategies; sector and project investments; structural adjustment programs; policies which deal with the efficient allocation of resources in both public and private sectors; priorities in government expenditures; reforms of administrative systems, production, trade and financial sectors; the restructuring of state enterprises and sector policies. Moreover, as a market-based institution, the Bank also concerns itself with issues relating to the creditworthiness of its members. In these areas, except for the aggregate aspects of the economic policies mentioned in the previous paragraph, the Bank has a mandate, primary responsibility, and a record of expertise and experience.

Accordingly, while the Fund and the Bank could be expected to pursue their interests incidental to their purposes and functions, each institution should rely as much as possible on analyses and monitoring of the other institution when matters fell within the primary responsibility of the other institution. In addition, when faced with divergent views, the escalating involvement of senior staff, management, and Executive Boards was called for.

On the procedural side, the Concordat then spelled out the modalities for enhanced collaboration: intensification of staff and management contacts; the search for common positions on conditionality and major advice to countries; greater exchange of information; and the attachment of staff to missions of the other institution.

In order to achieve improved collaboration on adjustment programs, on the side of the Bank, reference would be made to the country's relations with the Fund, the status of negotiations with the Fund, and the existence of an arrangement and the completion of relevant reviews. In the absence of an arrangement, and when economic circumstances may have changed significantly, Fund staff's view on the macroeconomic situation would be solicited. Conversely, before Fund approval of financial assistance involving an adjustment program, the Fund would seek the Bank's views.

To promote cooperation relating to the debt strategy, in which both the Fund and the Bank interact with commercial and official financing communities, the parties agreed to establish a task force to promote cooperation, analysis, and the exchange of information.

A further area of common interest concerned overdue obligations to the institutions: how should overdue obligations to the other institution affect the approval of financial assistance? In short, each would take the matter into account, to such an extent as inhibiting a recommendation of financial assistance to the respective Board, in the event that the existence of such arrears prevented the assurance of adequate financial safeguards in the lending operation.

Finally, the memorandum asserted that cross-conditionality was to be avoided; though the relevant assessments of the other institution would remain an important element, the ultimate financing decision had to rest with the relevant Executive Board taking the decision.

Collaboration in Practice

The 1989 Concordat continues as the guiding framework for Fund/Bank collaboration. Within that framework, collaboration has intensified, in light of the emerging conditions of the international economic and financial system and the initiatives of the two institutions. In particular contexts, the Executive Boards have returned to the matter in order to ensure efficiency and consistency, for example, concerning assistance to the former Soviet Union, public expenditure issues, and financial sector and financial system issues. In some current developments, in particular, the mutual accommodation of institutional actions seems to be taking on the form of joint ventures.

IMF Surveillance

Under the Articles, the Fund exercises regulatory powers, including Article IV surveillance. Fund surveillance involves an intensive dialogue with each member, a review of its economic and financial system and developments, and a periodic assessment by the Executive Board. This examination is based on the member's fiscal, exchange rate, trade, and monetary policies, and extends to other areas than the macroeconomic performance of a country: financial sector, labor market, military expenditure, economic aspects of governance, and the social sector. Following the Mexican financial crisis in 1995, and the Asian crisis beginning in 1997, the Fund has worked vigorously to broaden and deepen its surveillance function.

While the Bank has no stipulated surveillance function, the Bank's shift to sectoral and structural adjustment lending, and the carryover of macroeconomic elements to the development process, have enlarged the degree of overlap with the Fund's practices.

Accordingly, pursuant to the Concordat, the Fund, in carrying out its surveillance function, draws on the Bank's work; for areas where the Bank has primary responsibility, the staff seeks to integrate the Bank's view and analysis.

The synthesis might not always be easy. First, the Fund has a statutory duty to conduct surveillance; this responsibility cannot be delegated. Second, the Fund entertains surveillance for all of its members. Meanwhile, the Bank's involvement, especially in the industrial countries, is limited.

As an adjunct to its surveillance under Article IV, and in the context of steps toward a new international architecture, some of the Fund's initiatives have been taken in close connection with the World Bank.

First, within the last three years, and especially in the light of the Asian crisis, the Bank and the Fund have sought to strengthen their work on financial vulnerability of countries, and in this respect have acted in a joint fashion.

For this purpose, the institutions created a Bank-Fund Financial Sector Liaison Committee (made up of senior staff), and a joint work program was put in place. In May 1999, a pilot project was begun under the Financial Sector Assessment Program (FSAP), utilizing joint Fund/Bank missions charged with preparing comprehensive assessments of members' financial systems, and delivering them to national authorities.

Given the sensitivity of the FSAP reports, these reports are not to be distributed to the Executive Boards; however, each institution will utilize the reports for ongoing work. In the Fund, the FSAP reports are seen as feeding information into and contributing to the Article IV surveillance process, in that the staff prepares a document, the Financial System Stability Assessment (FSSA), for discussion by the Executive Board. For an interim period, the policy has been adopted that the Fund will not agree to the publication of the FSSA for particular countries, subject to later review and in light of the experience gained under the pilot project.[15] On the Bank side, the FSAP will likewise provide information for the Bank's ongoing work on the financial sector, including lending and other aspects, and a summary Financial Sector Assessment (FSA) will be given to the Bank's Executive Directors for information.

Secondly, the Fund is working to identify and assess observance of standards and codes relating to the financial sector. It has been accepted that, while the Fund has a central coordinating role, it will draw on the work of other standard-setting bodies in the process. Nominally, the Fund's focus will be on areas of direct operational concern to it, identified as data dissemination, monetary and financial policy transparency, fiscal transparency, and banking supervision. For other standards, the Fund co-opts the expertise of other expert bodies, including the World Bank. On this basis, the Fund has experimentally produced models of Reports on the Observance of Standards and Codes (ROSCs), which are permitted to be published by the national authorities. In support, the World Bank has begun to organize its involvement in this standards exercise, by identifying areas where it intends to make its own assessments of standards, including accounting, auditing, and corporate governance (with the OECD). Accordingly, the Bank has already contributed some assessments to the completed ROSCs.

The FSAP exercise has already spawned a related product, the Basel Core Principles Assessment (CPA), which aims to judge the adequacy of the rules of banking supervision as well as the supervisors' ability to monitor and limit major risks being faced by banks. Of the CPAs carried out so far, most have been carried out by the Fund, a few by the Bank, and the rest jointly.

---

[15] In December 2000, the Fund's Executive Board authorized the publication of FSSAs subject to the consent of the member. *See Selected Decisions, Twenty-Fifth Issue,* p. 126.

Financial Assistance

The provision of the Fund's financial assistance to members generally rests on an adjustment program developed by the member in close consultation with Fund staff. Demonstrably, over the years structural elements have proliferated, for example, under the Extended Fund Facility and the Structural Adjustment Facility and its successors. In this situation, the arrangement is that, for macroeconomic and structural measures that fall within the other institution's area of primary responsibility, there is to be a conscious sharing of the elements of policy design, implementation, monitoring, and evaluation; this sharing of responsibility is to be clarified with the country authorities.

In numerous cases, the Fund and the Bank provide financial assistance at the same time, in which case the interaction between the Bank and the Fund intensifies. In particular, for a Fund-supported program, the requirement is that the program be fully financed, and this may rely on coincidental Bank lending. Moreover, the Fund, in approving an arrangement, seeks the assurance from the Bank that the supporting structural policies are in place.

The question therefore arises whether the country might at times be forced to deal with both the Fund and the Bank in order to gain assistance from either. In addition, even from the point of view of each institution, there might be a concern for the loss of effective independence, and the imposition of "cross-conditionality." Each institution has denied that the reliance on the other in certain respects amounts to cross-conditionality, in the sense that one institution does not treat the views of the other as binding, and thus a decision by one institution on financing is not subject to veto by the other.

Even so, the complexities and the pressures upon the institutions are likely to vary with the precise situation. The view can be taken, for example, that financing in crisis situations has put these traditional mechanisms under strain, as was demonstrated by the response to the recent Asian economic and financial crisis. In such situations of severe financial crisis involving a collapsing exchange rate, capital flight, and pervasive domestic and external debt, speedy financial assistance is crucial; there is an immediate need for a short-term stabilization program and prompt liquidity support. Notably, even the expectation of forthcoming Fund support may help to turn the tide. Overall, it seems to be recognized that the Fund's organization, policies, and procedures allow it to act within a matter of weeks, and even to contribute valuable signals within days. Meanwhile, the Bank's structural reform programs have a relatively lengthy time horizon, with financing tied to the long-term objectives of capacity building and implementation.

In this situation, the Fund has been prepared to take the initiative and has assumed responsibility for the negotiation of the member's stabilization program. During the process, the Bank is consulted, and invited to contribute, especially on structural issues, backed up by cross-participation in the respective missions. In extreme situations, however, where the Bank's data and analysis of a country is lacking, it follows that Fund management and staff may need to proceed with recommending high-priority structural adjustment reforms without the normal in-depth work of the Bank.

In the area of financial assistance to low-income countries, indications are that Bank-Fund collaboration will fuse as a common effort. The Fund's concessional financial assistance to its poorest members and its alleviation of the debt burden of deeply-indebted members, under the Poverty Reduction and Growth Facility (PRGF) and the Debt Initiative for the Heavily Indebted Poor Countries (HIPC), assume parallel action of and close association with the Bank, accentuated by the adoption of an explicit focus on poverty reduction, as a basis of both the PRGF and the HIPC.

Under this strategy, the two institutions have come to work in tandem. In particular, the joint assistance, as well as that of other contributors, is premised on a common document that is to be produced by the member, the Poverty Reduction Strategy Paper (PRSP), which is then to be endorsed by the Boards of both the Fund and the Bank. The PRSP will thereby serve as the central mechanism for developing and coordinating concessional lending to low-income countries, including the commitment of resources under the HIPC.

Program design will thus seek to integrate even more explicably macroeconomic policies and poverty reduction. In this enterprise, the Fund and the Bank are expected to contribute within their traditional areas of expertise. Accordingly, Fund staff will advise on macroeconomic policies, together with certain related structural areas, including exchange rate and tax policy, and fiscal management. Bank staff will take the lead in the design of poverty reduction strategies and their monitoring, structural and sectoral issues, social issues, and the costing of particular poverty reduction expenditures. Common areas would include the establishment of an environment conducive to private sector growth, trade policy, financial sector development, and governance and transparency.

Recent institutional actions emphasize the jointness of the enterprise. First, the Fund and the Bank issued a joint paper entitled "Poverty Reduction Strategy Papers: Operational Issues," which is designed to guide implementation of the process. Second, in April 2000 they acted to establish a Joint IMF/World Bank Implementation Committee (JIC) to work on the HIPC initiative and the PRSP program.[16]

Comment

The relationship between the Fund and the Bank has been subject to a vigorous evolution. The principles underlying that relationship have been remarkably consistent from the 1946 approach to the 1989 Concordat, and during the last decade. In general, that approach includes: (i) full consultation and frank exchange of views, including the formulation of program design and policy advice, with procedures for the settlement of differences; (ii) open communication to members of the respective primary responsibilities for policy advice and reform; and (iii) adherence by each institution to its responsibilities under its Articles, including the need for it to act independently in making its financing decisions.

At the same time, the 1989 Concordat, like the earlier framework documents, is seen as a living document. It has been revisited in the context of particular developments, and polished and adjusted in order to reach an accommodation that is both compatible to the institutions and that will give assurance that the interests of the membership are being served.

---

[16] IMF Press Release No. 00/30, April 16, 2000.

In addition, there has been a steady elaboration of operational mechanisms. For example, hierarchical counterparties for management and staff have been identified, and steps taken to pinpoint responsible decision makers within each institution, so that direct dialogue can be enhanced and differences settled more readily. Similarly, the long-established practices for the exchange of Board documents have been fortified. Further, under a new electronic information system, access to information will be easier and the information more current. Finally, common guidelines on confidentiality of information, especially when external experts are engaged, will further strengthen assurances in that regard.

The interaction between public international organizations has become a matter of great interest and significance, especially because organizations tend to interpret their competence broadly, and to take initiatives within that competence, in order to achieve their objectives and thus to satisfy the demands and expectations of their membership.

For various reasons, the experience of the relationship between the Fund and the Bank is illustrative. Clearly, the common membership has supported the growth of functions and instruments of both institutions, leading to greater overlap of activities. Yet calls for greater cooperation and a better division of labor between the institutions are legion.

Even so, as outlined above, the relationship between two independent entities, separate legal persons under international law, continues to be founded on informal and flexible arrangements and, in particular, the 1989 Concordat. While avoidance of more formal arrangements may seem surprising, the evolution of the situation can fairly be viewed, in the light of experience, as relatively successful.

Moreover, within certain areas of activity, there is a move from mutual support to jointness, in particular relating to the FSAP and the PRGF/HIPC. If these ventures are successful, the pressures for more joint enterprises are likely to increase. In that event, questions might be raised about the need for more formal integration of the two organizations, either by elaborating on the 1989 Concordat or by more formal agreement.

II. Other International Financial Institutions

Chapter 5

International Financial Institutions and Their Discontents

JEROME I. LEVINSON

Two events have highlighted the discontent with the IMF and the World Bank: first, the issuance of a report by the majority of an International Advisory Commission on International Financial Institutions, and accompanying dissenting statements; and second, high-profile protest demonstrations in Washington at the April 2000 meetings of both institutions. Coming from opposite ends of the American political spectrum, the two events converge in evidencing a widespread discontent with the operations and priorities of both institutions.

Both the Commission and the protests, in my opinion, arise out of the evolution of the international trade, investment, and finance system of the past two decades. That evolution has transformed domestic U.S. politics with respect to the international economy. The culminating event was the East Asian financial crisis that unfolded in November 1997 and the request of the U.S. administration for additional funding for the IMF to cope with the developing crisis.

That crisis served as a catalyst for two strains of criticism of the IMF: the center-left of the Democratic Party in the Congress, particularly in the House, demanded, as the price of their support, that the legislation include provisions that instructed the U.S. Executive Director in the IMF to use the "voice and vote" of the United States to (i) advance core worker rights as a part of IMF programs, and (ii) to ensure that IMF programs that included labor market flexibility measures as a condition of financing were compatible with core worker rights. That demand reflected a widespread feeling among Democrats, and their labor allies, that IMF programs are biased in favor of capital and corporate interests. If the IMF legislation was to obtain congressional passage, the U.S. administration, Wall Street, and the congressional leadership had to accept a provision in the legislation along the above lines.

For the first time, the legislation appropriating IMF funding included such a worker rights provision, but this approach neither questioned the existence of the IMF or its relevance, nor did it impose conditions directly upon the IMF; rather, it respected the multilateral character of the institution by imposing the policy conditions upon the U.S. Executive Director (USED) in the IMF, and the U.S. Treasury Department, the principal agency responsible for U.S. policy relating to the international financial institutions. Understood in these terms, it represented a relatively conservative approach to policy reform in the IMF. It was a reformist rather than an abolitionist strategy.

At the same time, the Asian financial crisis catalyzed sentiment in conservative U.S. academic and congressional circles that the IMF no longer served a useful purpose; on the contrary, it contributed to successive crises by increasing "moral hazard." The East Asia crisis, in this view, arose directly out of the 1994/95 bailout of Mexico: the resolution of the East Asia crisis should have been left to the private capital markets to sort out. This view received its most dramatic expression in a *Wall Street Journal* article by George Shultz, William Simon, and Walter Wriston. Shultz had been Secretary of State and Simon had been Secretary of the Treasury in former Republican administrations; Wriston had been a former chief executive officer of Citicorp. The article called into question the rationale for the very existence of an IMF, and because of the personal prestige of the authors, it caused something of a sensation.

The legislation approving additional funding for the IMF provided for a Congressional Advisory Commission on International Financial Institutions (IFIs), which was to examine U.S. policy with respect to these institutions, including the question of whether they ought to continue to exist. For purposes of the Commission, the World Trade Organization (WTO) was included in the definition of IFIs, indicating, in my view, that the Congress wanted the question of international finance examined within a broader context: that is, trade, investment, and finance would be considered as an integrated whole.

The Advisory Commission consisted of eleven members: six appointed by the Republican majority leaders in the Senate and the

House and five appointed by the Democratic minority leaders in both chambers. The Chairman (Professor Allan Meltzer of Carnegie-Mellon University) was drawn from among the majority members. I was one of the Democratic appointees. The various reports, a majority report (eight members), a joint dissent (three members), and my own separate, and somewhat lengthy dissent, reflected the deep divisions within the Commission and, in my opinion, within American society, concerning not only the institutions which are the subject of the Commission inquiry but also the more general process in the international economy that we in shorthand refer to as "globalization." One member signed both the majority report and the joint dissent.

The majority, consisting of the six Republican members and two Democratic appointees, Professor Jeffrey Sachs of Harvard University and Richard Huber, formerly chief executive officer of the Aetna Corporation, recommended a highly constricted role for the IMF: only member countries of the IMF that are prequalified are eligible for IMF financing; that financing is at a penalty rate of interest for a maximum period of 120 days, with a one-time-only rollover for an additional 120 days. Initially, the majority had a collateral requirement, an IMF preferential claim on tax revenues, specifically customs revenues, but in the final report this requirement was dropped.

The prequalification requirements relate to financial ratios for financial sector institutions; in the final meeting of the Commission, one dissenting member, Fred Bergsten, severely criticized the absence of macroeconomic criteria. In response to this criticism, unspecified fiscal criteria were added. Program conditions attached to IMF financing are specifically barred. During a five-year transition period, nonqualifying countries would be enabled to borrow, but only at a super-penalty rate of interest.

Initially, the majority members of the Commission voted to have the IMF discontinue Article IV consultations, but at the same time, they proposed the IMF be a disseminator of best practices. The illogic of discontinuing Article IV consultations, the means by which the IMF informs itself of best practices, but expecting the Fund to disseminate such practices among the member countries, finally dissuaded the Majority from recommending discontinuing Article IV consultations. Longer-term lending facilities (including a poverty reduction initiative) are proposed to be terminated.

The IMF, then, according to the Majority, has a restricted financing role as lender of last resort in a systemic crisis, or, when a country, through no fault of its own, finds itself in temporary dire financial straits, deprived of market access. It is a nineteenth-century Bagehot conception of a central bank but without the money creation function; that conception assumed a single political entity in a country with basically solvent financial institutions operating within a market economy with relatively well-developed financial markets. Any interruption of market access could be assumed to be an aberration and temporary in nature.

Countries which have problems which are structural in character are assigned by the Majority to the World Bank (and regional development banks). However, under the Majority proposal, the World Bank would be divested of financing responsibility in any of the countries of Latin America or Asia. It becomes a super-development bank for Africa, at least until the African Development Bank has matured sufficiently to assume exclusive responsibility for financing development in the region. To the extent there is a development financing function at all for the other regions, that function is to be carried out by the regional development banks. But the criteria for eligibility for financing from these institutions are set at such a high bar that, for example, in Latin America, eleven countries are excluded from eligibility for development financing, including the ones with the largest populations.

It is a proposal that, in effect, says that for the more developed countries in Latin America and Asia, development financing is now irrelevant; they should rely, for development finance, exclusively upon the private financial markets. Moreover, the specifics of the majority proposal that allow for continued development financing for a limited number of countries by the regional development banks are so impractical and implausible that it is difficult to know whether they are simply naive or a cynical attempt to indirectly kill off all public development financing.

The World Bank ultimately becomes a source of "public goods," addressing such issues as tropical disease, for example, malaria and

AIDS, which are at present not being adequately addressed. It also becomes a coordinator of other aid givers. In my view, the World Bank, politically, does not survive as a super-development bank for Africa or as a super-international public health agency, nor, politically, do the regional development banks survive with their most important members deprived of eligibility for finance from these institutions.

The joint dissent outlined a different conception: the IMF should continue to be a source of financing for countries that, for one reason or another, find themselves in balance of payments difficulties. The original conception of the Fund remains valid: it is desirable that countries in financial difficulty not resort to destructive policies that have the potential to set off a competitive cycle of policy choices that lead to harmful systemic problems. Such IMF financing should be accompanied by an agreement on program conditions that address the underlying causes that led to the balance of payments problem. That is a major difference with the Majority proposal: a continued role for programmatic content to accompany IMF financing.

The joint dissent, however, shared the view with the Majority that the IMF should not be a frontline permanent poverty-fighting agency. It must assess the social impact of a specific program, but structural reform not proximately linked to the balance of payments problem should be left to the World Bank and regional development banks. This conception, then, urged a continued development financing role for the development banks, even for the more advanced developing countries. Development financing provided an assured source of long-term finance for high-value projects and programs, primarily related to human capital development but also for a limited number of high-value physical infrastructure projects. That financing is not subject to the vagaries of the private financial markets. It also has a policy content that is not characteristic of private financing. In general terms, it is this conception that has been articulated by the Secretary of the Treasury, the Council on Foreign Relations and Institute for International Economics Task Force on International Finance, and a similar task force of the Overseas Development Council.

Neither the Majority report nor the joint dissent, however, recognized the other source of discontent with the Bretton Woods institutions: the perception that they are critical elements in the development of a profoundly inequitable two-track international trade, investment, and finance system, a rule-based system for the protection of corporate property rights but no protection for core worker rights and the environment. It is that perception, in my view, that fueled the demonstrations in Seattle and Washington. It is what was fundamentally at issue in the intense debate in this country over granting permanent normal trade status to China. It is the issue that I addressed at some length in my separate dissenting statement.

The issue arises most acutely in connection with the IMF/World Bank emphasis upon labor market flexibility measures, which is short-hand for measures that make it easier for companies to fire workers without significant severance payments and weaken the capacity of trade unions to negotiate on behalf of their members, all for the purpose of driving down urban union wages and benefits so as to make a country's goods more internationally competitive.

Joseph Stiglitz, formerly Chief Economist of the World Bank, has noted, with respect to labor matters, that this emphasis reflects an excessively economic view, through the even more narrow prism of neo-classical economics. This labor market intervention by the Bretton Woods institutions is contrasted with their indifference to the abuse of core worker rights, particularly freedom of association and collective bargaining, where countries use the coercive power of the state to effectively deny workers these rights, even where the country's own constitution and labor laws, at least nominally, guarantee such rights.

Indeed, the World Bank is of the view that it cannot support freedom of association and collective bargaining because economic studies, according to the Bank, are inconclusive as to whether freedom of association and collective bargaining make a positive contribution to economic development. Hence, through some truly bizarre reasoning, the World Bank legal staff concludes that freedom of association and collective bargaining are "political" in nature. Under its charter, the Bank is consequently prohibited from intervening to support such rights in the conditions that attach to its financing. In contrast, according to the World Bank, labor market flexibility measures clearly contribute to economic development and therefore are not political; they have increasingly become an integral part of the conditionality requirements of both World Bank programs.

Both institutions are, then, perceived as doing the dirty work for big capital, both domestic and foreign, to the disadvantage of workers, in both developed and developing countries. Mr. Stanley Fischer, First Deputy Managing Director of the IMF, denies that IMF intervention is so one-sided, but that is the way it is perceived by trade unions, particularly in Latin America and Asia, and critics in the Congress. We run the risk of creating, in both the industrialized world and the borrowing member countries of the Bretton Woods institutions, an increasingly alienated and embittered working class, with incalculable social and political consequences. The apparent indifference of the Bretton Woods institutions to this tendency fuels the view that they are dominated by a one-dimensional, excessively technocratic economic theology which is socially and politically tone-deaf.

The neo-classical economic model, promoted by the World Bank and IMF, is not confined to the labor market but represents a more general approach to development: public sector intervention is suspect or worse; privatization, in any and all circumstances, is preferred. Growing income inequality within countries is of lesser consequence than economic efficiency considerations. It is ironic that this neo-classical economic view now predominates in the Bretton Woods institutions. Lord Keynes and Harry Dexter White, the two men most responsible for the design of the Bretton Woods system, fought all of their professional lives against that same neo-classical model. The institutions they designed to insulate the world economy against the limitations of that economic philosophy have now become the means by which that philosophy is imposed upon the borrowing member countries of the two institutions.

I would go further and argue that, taken in conjunction, the policy priorities of the Bretton Woods institutions undermine the institutional basis for development within the framework of democratic political institutions. That is because they have focused so strongly upon creating the conditions in their borrowing member countries for attracting capital, particularly FDI, that they have fostered a growing concentration of ownership of income-earning assets and income inequality. Who, after all, can buy the former state-owned assets? The answer is domestic monopolies and oligopolies and the multinational corporations. The role of the state-owned industries as a counterweight to these private agglomerations of capital is destroyed by the privatization programs.

The most important possible source of countervailing power within civil society—a vigorous trade union movement independent of government control—is deliberately weakened through labor market flexibility measures. The combination of the two policies—privatization of state-owned industries, under any and all circumstances, and labor market flexibility—undermines the basis for development with a balance of institutions that can assure a more equitable distribution of the fruits of economic growth.

So long as this is the case, there is no possibility, in my view, of assembling a broad-based consensus within this country for support of the these institutions. On the contrary, I anticipate that public, although not elite, support will continue to weaken. There is, then, a dilemma: there is a compelling case for development finance to complement the private financial markets, even with respect to the more advanced developing countries, but the Bretton Woods institutions, in promoting their neo-classical economic philosophy, have overreached. They are engaged in a project of remaking the economies of their borrowing member countries along lines that would never be accepted, politically, in their major non-borrowing member countries. In so doing, they are promoting an increasingly inequitable international economic system. They undermine support in American society for what should be a noble enterprise: raising the standard of living of many people who do not at present share in the global economy.

Chapter 6

Recent Developments in the European Central Bank

ANTONIO SÁINZ DE VICUÑA

This article provides information on the main developments that occurred at the European Central Bank (ECB) since its establishment in June 1998. It supplements the general description of the legal preparations made by the European Monetary Institute (EMI) for the European Monetary Union and for the establishment of the ECB published earlier.[1]

Institutional Issues

The ECB: Internal Organization

The management of the ECB is organized by way of nine Directorates General,[2] nine Directorates, and 50 Divisions. Five[3] of the Directorates and two[4] of the Divisions report directly to Executive Board members. Following the model of several central banks, the Executive Board, irrespective of its collegial responsibility, has allocated internal executive managerial competences among its members as follows:

---

[1] Antonio Sáinz de Vicuña, "Institutional Aspects of the European Central Bank," in *Current Developments in Monetary and Financial Law*, Volume I (IMF, 1999), pp. 291–97.

[2] Legal Service, Administration and Personnel, Economics, Research, International and European Relations, Payment Systems, Statistics, Information Systems and Operations. The ECB Representative in Washington, D.C., and the Coordinator of Counsel to the Board have also the category of Director General.

[3] Directorates are hierarchically below Directorates General. The following five Directorates report directly to Executive Board members: Secretariat and Language Services, External Relations, Internal Audit, Banknotes, and Controlling and Organization.

[4] Divisions are hierarchically below Directorates. The following two report directly to Executive Board members: Prudential Supervision and Middle Office.

President (W. Duisenberg): Secretariat (D), External Relations (D), and Internal Audit (D); Vice President (C. Noyer): Legal Service (DG), Administration and Personnel (DG), and Middle Office (d); O. Issing: Economics (DG) ("applied economics"), Research (DG) ("conceptual economics"); T. Padoa-Schioppa: International and European Relations (DG), Payment Systems (DG), and Prudential Supervision (d); E. Domingo Solans: Banknotes (D), Statistics (DG), and Information Systems (DG); S. Hamalainen: Operations (DG) (monetary policy, foreign reserves management) and Controlling and Organization (D) (ECB budget and internal organization).

ECB Staff

Since its establishment in June 1998, the ECB has been a growing organization. By the end of 1998, it had 534 staff members. One year later, in December 1999, it had 732 staff members. The figure foreseen by the end of 2000 is about 1,000 staff members, which still cannot compare with the some 50,000 people who staff the national central banks (NCBs) of the Eurosystem.

Recruitment is roughly 50 percent from NCBs and 50 percent from the market. The average age for staff members is about 35 years, with an even distribution of European Union (EU) nationalities, although there is no rule regarding nationality quotas.

Staff members are recruited under a contract of employment and do not have a civil service statutory nature. Such employment contracts are not subject to German law, but rather are European Union based (based on principles common to the member states and on EU employment law).

Salaries are subject not to German tax but to a community tax that applies to all dependents of European institutions and bodies.

The conditions of employment foresee staff representation by way of a Staff Committee with a consultative function (i.e., not bargaining capacity). In addition, staff may be represented by trade unions, one of which is relatively active in the ECB.

ECB Finances: Own Funds

The ECB has as main sources of income the operations made with its own funds, namely, capital and reserves.

The Statute established an initial authorized capital of EUR 5,000 million. The paid-in capital amounts to EUR 3,999 million, and, in the year 2000, the Council adopted a regulation allowing the Governing Council to call additional capital up to an additional EUR 5,000 million so as to reach a maximum authorized figure of EUR 10,000 million. The ECB received its capital from its shareholders on January 1999 under two different classes of shares:

- Type "A" shares, 100 percent paid, with full voting and economic rights:

Bundesbank:	24.49%
B de France:	16.83%
B d'Italia:	14.89%
B de España:	8.89%
De Nederlandsche Bank:	4.27%
BN Belgique:	2.86%
Austrian NB:	2.35%
B de Portugal:	1.92%
Finnish CB:	1.39%
CB Ireland:	0.84%
BC Luxembourg:	0.14%
TOTAL:	78.93%
	(EUR 3.947 million)

- Type "B" shares, only partially disbursed (5 percent), with no voting rights and with neither rights on ECB profits nor liability for losses:

B of England:	14.68%
Sveriges RB:	2.65%
B of Greece:	2.05%
Danmarks NB:	1.67%
TOTAL:	21.05%
	(EUR 52.6 million)

During 2000, the European Council agreed to the adoption of the euro by the Hellenic Republic and thus accepted the Bank of Greece within the Eurosytem with effect from January 2001. The Bank of Greece will have to fully subscribe its share in the capital of the ECB by that date.

The ECB is also the recipient of foreign reserve assets from its shareholders. This will be explained below.

The Eurosystem: Its Decision-Making Bodies

The Treaty speaks only of the European System of Central Banks or ESCB, which includes all 15 NCBs of the European Union plus the ECB. However, the Treaty gives different rights to those members of the ESCB who have adopted the euro as compared with the so-called Member States with a derogation (or with an "opt-out," the United Kingdom and Denmark). The group of NCBs of the member states that have adopted the euro, together with the ECB, operate under a centralized decision-making mechanism as a group, and this warrants a term that identifies this group as different from the ESCB. The Governing Council of the ECB decided in 1998 that the group should be called "Eurosystem."

The Eurosystem is governed by the Governing Council, its supreme decision-making body. It is composed of the 11 Governors of the NCBs of the euro zone[5] plus the six Executive Board members. They participate in a personal capacity and not as representatives of any specific country or NCB, are seated in alphabetical order, and decide by the rule of "one man, one vote" and simple majority rule. However, there are a series of listed decisions related to shareholders' rights, where the Governing Council takes the shape of a shareholders' meeting: it is the NCBs who vote on a weighted manner, and the members of the Executive Board receive a zero voting weight.

---

[5] Plus the Governor of the Bank of Greece as observer during the second half of 2000 and as full member from January 1, 2001.

The Governing Council is subject to the ECB Rules of Procedure approved in 1998. It meets twice a month, on every second Thursday, and the Rules allow for possible teleconference meetings.

The second decision-making body of the Eurosystem is the ECB's Executive Board with three main areas of competence:

- Preparation of Governing Council meetings and decisions. It organizes the preparatory work of the ECB, supervises all papers before submission to the Governing Council, prepares the agenda for Governing Council meetings, and makes the proposals for decisions.

- Implementation of Governing Council decisions. The Executive Board is vested with an executory task: to implement Governing Council decisions. It is also recipient of delegated powers from the Governing Council, the most important of which is worth mentioning: the carrying out of the weekly liquidity tender and the adoption of the weekly decision on liquidity allotment.

- Executive management of the ECB. As mentioned above, the Executive Board is the superior managerial body of the ECB, and to that end every ECB department has been allocated to one of the Executive Board members. Irrespective of this allocation, responsibility is collective.

The Board is subject to its own Rules of Procedure. It meets every Tuesday.

The third decision-making body of the ECB is the General Council, composed of the governors of all the NCBs of the European Union and the President and Vice-President of the ECB.

It has four main areas of competence:

- Coordination of policies between Eurosystem and "out" NCBs;

- Preparation for integration into the Eurosystem of "out" NCBs;

- ECB shareholder issues affecting "out" NCBs (i.e., matters related to the "B" series of ECB shares); and

- Advisory functions to Governing Council.

The Statute imposes on the Governing Council the duty to inform the General Council of all its decisions. It has its own Rules of Procedure; it meets four times a year.

The ESCB Committees

Integration of the NCBs of the euro area is not only by participation of the relevant governors in the decision-making bodies of the ECB but also on a technical level by participation in the bodies that prepare the papers that will serve as a basis for decisions: namely, the ESCB Committees, organized by the Governing Council in 1998. They are the following: Accounting and Monetary Income Committee (AMICO); Banking Supervision Committee (BSC); Banknote Committee (BANCO); Budget Committee (BUCOM); External Communications Committee (ECCO); Information Technology Committee (ITC); Internal Auditors Committee (IAC); International Relations Committee (IRC); Legal Committee (LEGCO); Market Operations Committee (MOC); Monetary Policy Committee (MPC); Payment and Settlement Systems Committee (PSSC); and Statistics Committee (STC).

ESCB Committees do not have decision-making capacity, but are essential for decision making by the Governing Council. With the exception of the Budget Committee, all ESCB Committees report to the Governing Council via the Executive Board, which has the statutory duty to prepare Governing Council meetings.

The ESCB Committees have the capacity to create subgroups when needed: in the year 2000, the number of subgroups reached 50.

The Legal Framework

The legal framework under which the Eurosystem operates may be classified as follows:

- European Community legal acts, which may be subclassified in the following two categories:

— Complementary legislation, meaning the legal acts that the Statute of the ESCB had foreseen to complete the legal framework of the Eurosystem, in a list which is *numerus clausus*:

- Specification of the cases where Member States are obliged to submit draft legislative provisions to the ECB for opinion.

- Fixing of the capital key which serves to allocate own funds and profits of the ECB between its shareholders, which is revised every five years.

- Establishment of the limits whereby the Governing Council is authorized to call additional capital from its shareholders.

- Establishment of the limits whereby the Governing Council is authorized to ask for additional transfers of foreign reserve assets to the ECB from its shareholders.

- Specification of persons who may be subject to statistical obligations imposed by the ECB, and legislative power given to the ECB to that effect.

- Specification of persons who may be subject to minimum reserves imposed by the ECB, basic parameters thereto and legislative power given to the ECB to that effect.

- Authorization for other monetary instruments imposing obligations on third parties (so far unused).

- Regime under which the ECB may impose sanctions for breaches of obligations vis-à-vis the ECB, and legislative power given to the ECB to that effect.

External regime of the euro: the Council of Ministers has the authority to establish the external regime of the euro, and it has done so, so far, with respect to San Marino, Vatican, Cape Verde, Monaco, the franc zone, and St. Pierre Miquelon, and Mayotte. The ECB takes an active role in assisting the Council thereto, and is officially consulted before decisions are taken.

- ECB legal acts, foreseen in the Statute, which may be classified in five categories:

    - Binding on everyone (having "general application"): ECB Regulations, which are like "laws," directly applicable on participating Member States upon publication in the Official Journal of the European Communities. So far the ECB has legislated in only three areas: statistics, ECB sanctions, and minimum reserves. Other areas which may be subject to ECB legislation are monetary policy and payment and clearing systems, although the ECB has preferred a contractual approach in those areas.[6]

    - Binding on all ESCB members ("out" NCBs included): ESCB Agreements. The only legal mechanism to bind the NCBs of the Member States that have not adopted the euro is by way of contract. The Statute preserves for them in its integrity their existing national powers.

    - Binding only on Eurosystem NCBs: Guidelines and Instructions. The "guidelines" are, in spite of their name, legally binding acts that NCBs of participating Member States are obliged to comply with and which the European Court of Justice is empowered to enforce. Guidelines are drafted as other legislation with a preamble and articles, and although not necessarily public, the ECB may decide to publish them in the *Official Journal of the Communities* for general notice. Guidelines may only be adopted by the Governing Council (although it may delegate that power to the Executive Board). "Instructions" are the legal acts of the Executive Board, binding on participating NCBs, and are only of executory nature.

---

[6] Except, as mentioned, for minimum reserves, organized by regulations.

- Binding internally within the ECB: Decisions and Administrative Circulars. Decisions are acts adopted either by the Governing Council or by the Executive Board in its domain of competence, in matters internal to the ECB and without external effect. Decisions are also used to document "shareholder" resolutions of the Governing Council, i.e., decisions having effect on the ECB shareholders such as those on allocation of monetary income, on remuneration of intra-ESCB balances, or on risk allocation. Administrative Circulars are the legal acts adopted by the Executive Board in the domain of internal organization of the ECB.

- Soft law (nonbinding acts): The Statute foresees two kinds, the Recommendations and the Opinions. While "Recommendations" are issued *motu propio* and address policy issues, "Opinions" are normally issued upon previous consultation by the Community or a Member State on a draft legislative provision (although they may be theoretically issued as well upon its own initiative by the ECB).

The general regime for ECB legal acts is to be found not only in the Treaty and ESCB Statute but also in the ECB Rules of Procedure. Since its establishment in June 1998, the ECB has enacted more than 90 binding acts altogether and more than 170 nonbinding acts (including EMI opinions). Public ECB legal acts are reproduced in the yearly edition of the "ECB Compendium," available free of cost and accessible through the ECB's website.

Basic Tasks

Monetary Policy

The ECB has organized the single monetary policy along three kinds of instruments:

Minimum reserves. These are cash amounts that credit institutions need to keep deposited with the Eurosystem. Some 7,900 credit institutions established in the euro area are subject to minimum reserves.

The basic regime is to be found in a European Community Regulation and in an ECB Regulation, and may be summarized as follows:

- The amount to be deposited is 2 percent of banks' qualifying liabilities.

- Such amount is to be calculated as an average for the maintenance period, which is one month. This permits the minimum reserves to operate as a liquidity buffer for credit institutions, with a stabilizing effect on interest rates.

- The reserves are to be deposited with NCBs and not with the ECB.

- Deposits are remunerated at the benchmark ECB repo rate.

- Breaches to minimum reserves are subject to ECB Sanctions, the regime of which is set in a European Community Regulation and an ECB Regulation, giving the Executive Board the ordinary sanctioning authority, with a right of appeal to the Governing Council; NCBs detect the breaches.

Open market operations. The Eurosystem provides liquidity (or withdraws liquidity if needed) by way of tenders of liquidity granted against taking, by way of pledge or by temporary transfer of title (repo) eligible collateral.

Approximately 2,500 credit institutions are entitled to participate in open market operations, although only some 200 are eligible for fine-tuning operations. The maximum number of bidders for liquidity in 1999 was 1,068 credit institutions, while the minimum number in 1999 was 302 credit institutions.

The ECB has kept a fixed rate tender procedure for one and a half years, whereby credit institutions were asked for liquidity needs and the Executive Board would make a weekly decision on liquidity allocation on a lineal manner, as a percentage of total liquidity demand. The rates applied during this period have been:

- 3 percent from January to April 1999;

- 2.5 percent from April to November 1999;
- 3 percent from November 1999 to February 2000;
- 3.25 percent from February to March 2000;
- 3.50 percent from March to April 2000; and
- 3.75 percent from April to June 2000.

Fixed rate tenders create a tendency to overbidding. Although the average in 1999 was a 10.8 percent allotment, in spring 2000 it approximated 1 percent allotment. Because of this tendency, in June 2000 the ECB switched to the system of variable rate tenders, whereby the ECB would post a minimum rate for tenders but admit higher rates from bidders, and allocate the amount of liquidity to be injected into the banking system to the higher bidders as per the rates offered. The minimum rate was initially set at 4.25 percent, and raised to 4.50 percent in August 2000.

Tenders are announced on Mondays, allotted on Tuesdays, and settled on Wednesdays. Eurosystem financing needs to be repaid in 15 days. Three-month financing operations have been also used, by way of monthly variable rate tenders. Fine-tuning operations are also possible, but there has been only one for Y2K reasons at the end of 1999.

Standing facilities. These consist of a unilateral undertaking by the Eurosystem to admit overnight deposits below market rates for the excess liquidity of credit institutions, and to lend overnight amounts above market rates against eligible collateral in cases of liquidity needs. The standing facilities have a "corridor" function for market interest rates, whereby the lending facility sets the upper limit and the deposit facility sets the bottom limit. Interest rates of the standing facilities have moved together with the benchmark refinancing rate, except for a short "narrow band" in January 1999.

Loans and deposits under the standing facilities are held at NCBs, not at the ECB. The opening times for standing facilities are synchronized with the operating hours of the TARGET payment system, so that unfounded payment orders have an automatic access to the lending facilities at the end of the day, and unprocessed orders are converted into overnight deposits at the end of the day.

Cross-Border Use of Collateral

In order to avoid any market compartmentalization, the ECB has organized the possibility for Eurosystem counterparties to mobilize their available collateral irrespective of its location in Europe. Two mechanisms have been accepted in this respect:

- The Correspondent Central Bank Model (CCBM). This is a multilateral arrangement by which every NCB accepts to act as correspondent NCB (CCB) to hold collateral for the lending NCBs. The use of CCBM has increased since it started in January 1999. Fees are charged and were increased in October 1999. So far the main CCB has been Banca d'Italia, while the main lender NCBs under CCBM are the Bundesbank and De Nederlandsche Bank. The main practical problem of the CCBM is that it does not permit delivery-versus-payment (DVP), with the consequence of higher immobilization of assets.

- The links between Securities Settlement Systems (SSSs). The European Central Securities Depository Association (ECSDA) has organized a network of bilateral links, technical and contractual, between SSSs, following which book-entry (dematerialized or immobilized) securities "travel" from the register of one SSS to the register of the other. This facility, together with the implementation of the Settlement Finality Directive (establishing the *situs* of the securities in the place where such security is registered), and the redenomination into the euro of a big portion, if not all, of the securities placed in the euro area, has created a new scenario for the cross-border use of securities for collateral purposes. The links will permit DVP at the latest by 2002. A total of 62 bilateral links have been approved by the ECB for use by the Eurosystem, and some more are in the pipeline.

In addition to the links between SSSs, the following major SSSs are merging:

- The French SICOVAM will merge with the Belgian Euroclear as of January 1, 2001.

- The German Deutsche Borse Clearing has merged with Luxembourg's Cedel, to form Clearstream.

Since all merging SSSs had bilateral links with many other SSSs, cross-border use of collateral in Europe may be done in real time.

Foreign Reserves Management

As the Statute foresees, at the start of monetary union in January 1999, the participating NCBs transferred to the ECB an amount of EUR 39,468 million in foreign currency assets, split in accordance with the ECB capital key, and receiving as compensation a nonredeemable claim for the equivalent amount in euro. A Council Regulation adopted in 2000 allows for further transfers to replenish the foreign reserve assets up to an amount of EUR 50,000 million.

The initial composition of the foreign reserve assets transferred to the ECB was as follows:

- Gold: approximately 15 percent;
- US$ securities: approximately 80 percent; and
- Yen securities: approximately 5 percent.

Foreign reserve assets are kept through selected intermediaries in New York, London, Tokyo, Singapore, and also within the euro area.

Although foreign reserve assets are the property of the ECB in whose balance sheet they are accounted for, their management is organized in a decentralized manner, through the dealing rooms of the NCBs and under a "disclosed agency" basis.

Such management is subject to two kinds of parameters: the Strategic benchmark, decided by the Governing Council; and the Tactical benchmark, decided from time to time by the Executive Board within the strategic benchmarks.

These benchmarks are defined by specifying the following elements:

- currency distribution,
- ranges for interest rates and interest fluctuations,

- eligible assets,
- permissible operations, and
- limits for credit risk exposures.

Payment Systems

The ESCB has put in place a real-time gross settlement system organized by way of a basic ECB Guideline and agreements with the nonparticipating NCBs, under the name of TARGET. This system started operations on January 4, 1999, and from its start it has channelled funds for amounts beyond the initial estimations. There is a progressive shift from payments effected through correspondent banking into TARGET, and a steady decrease in the average amount transferred through TARGET.

One major computer breakdown in one NCB terminal occurred in February 1999, and the consequent claims were settled swiftly through a common Eurosystem procedure organized by the Governing Council.

At the end of 1999, the Settlement Finality Directive had been implemented by most EU Member States, with the following main legal effects:

- irrevocability of payment orders and of securities transfer orders;

- nonretroactivity of insolvencies for payment orders (finality);

- insulation of collateral from insolvency proceedings ("ring fence"); and

- clear conflict-of-law rules for book-entry securities (the so-called PRIMA—primary intermediary account—criterion).

It is perhaps important to mention that the NCBs carry out oversight functions vis-à-vis domestic large-value payment systems, while the ECB carries out oversight of cross-border large-value payment systems. There are currently two cross-border large-value payment systems:

- One, operative since January 1999 under the name Euro 1, a netting system organized by the Euro Banking Association, settled at the ECB; and,

- The second, operational only as from 2001: Continuous Linked Settlement (CLS), organized in New York and London, for payment-vs-payment (PvP) in different currencies. Since the euro will be one of the major settlement currencies, the ECB has been involved in the preparatory work and will oversee its operation from the European side.

Euro Banknotes

The huge project of launching a full set of new and common monetary signs within 12 countries may be summarized in the following manner:

Production

- Decentralization. The ECB has no printing works, and thus it had to rely on the NCBs' printing works. It was decided to retain the existing structural framework: each NCB produces all the banknotes it will need within its respective jurisdiction. The alternative option of charging each of the printing works with the production of only one denomination ("pooling option") was rejected and left for future times.

- Centralization where convenient. The ECB was entrusted with obtaining the necessary patents and licenses and the basic supplies (paper, ink, etc.) for the whole Eurosystem by appropriate public tender procedures. In addition, in order to ensure total homogeneity of all banknotes, the ECB was entrusted with the centralized quality control.

Protection

- Against counterfeiting. The ECB decided to create the Eurosystem's central analysis center and database for counterfeits, and promote the preparation of a Community legal act that will organize the cooperation of law enforcement agencies by vesting the necessary means in Europol, and supporting the coordination between Europe and third countries through Interpol. Such a legal act, a Council Regulation, is forthcoming. In 1999, Europol was given the necessary legal competences to coordinate law enforcement agencies of Member States for the fight against counterfeiting. In addition, a Framework Decision was adopted by the Council of Justice Ministers to harmonize the penal treatment of euro banknote counterfeiting.

- Against illicit reproduction. To avoid reproductions that the public may confuse with a real banknote, all Member States have to recognize the copyright on the design of the euro banknotes in the ECB. All NCBs are entrusted with taking all necessary action to enforce ECB's copyright in their respective jurisdictions. Conditions under which reproduction of banknotes is generally authorized were laid down in an ECB public legal act.

Promotion

The ECB has put in motion a macro campaign in all relevant European media to inform the public about the new banknotes, in coordination with the NCBs.

Changeover

The Council of Ministers (ECOFIN), evaluating the inconveniences of the dual-currency period, decided that the cash changeover should be activated so as to achieve the bulk changeover within the first 15 days of 2002, and the main part of the rest within the first two months of 2002. National laws would be enacted to achieve the above goal. The Eurosystem decided, accordingly, to organize a system permitting the front-loading of banknotes in the last quarter of 2001, and facilitating the tasks of credit institutions in this respect. In addition, Eurosystem NCBs are to exchange at par value national banknotes against euro banknotes without cost to the public during that transitional period.

Other Tasks

International Representation of the ESCB

International Organizations

The decision-making bodies of the IMF agreed to grant the ECB an observer status in its Interim Committee and Executive Board. Following that decision, the ECB decided to have a permanent representative office in Washington, D.C., with the function to liaise with U.S. monetary authorities and to provide support to the ECB's observer in the IMF.

At the OECD, the ECB agreed with the Commission that the ECB represents the Community in monetary matters dealt with at the OECD.

With regard to the BIS, its shareholders agreed to raise its capital and offer it to the ECB, which became a shareholder. The ECB has regular membership in most BIS committees.

International Groupings

The ECB is represented in G-7, G-10, and G-20 meetings.

European Bodies

The ECB is represented in the Economic and Financial Committee (EFC), which meets once a month; the EuroGroup (formerly "Euro 11"), which meets once a month and prepares ECOFIN meetings; and the ECOFIN Council, which meets once a month.

Bilateral Relations

With the United States, reference was made above to the ECB's Permanent Representative Office in Washington, D.C., to liaise with the Federal Reserve System and with the Department of the Treasury.

With Central and Eastern European countries candidates for accession to the EU, the ECB has established regular relations with the NCBs of Poland, Estonia, the Czech Republic, Hungary, Slovenia,

Cyprus, Latvia, Lithuania, Slovakia, Bulgaria, Romania, and Malta. Three different periods may be seen for those countries:

- Prior to accession to the EU, they have to comply with the so-called Copenhagen criteria, with which the ECB is concerned only by the shape of the financial markets, implementation of the financial EU "acquis," and on achieving NCB's independence.

- Upon accession, they have to follow the "convergence criteria" inclusive of participation in ERM 2. During that period, NCBs become members of ESCB as "out" Member States, acceding the General Council.

- Upon satisfaction of the "convergence criteria," integration into Eurosystem.

- With NCBs of third countries important to the ECB: Japan, Switzerland, Norway, Turkey.

It is worth mentioning the phenomenon of "euroization," namely, the unilateral introduction of the euro as official currency by Kosovo, Montenegro, East Timor, and Andorra. The ECB takes the view that international comity requires prior consent of the authorities issuing the currency. The limited dimension of the territories involved, and the practical absence of money creation because of its limitation to banknotes and coins, reduce the importance of such phenomena.

Supervision of Euro Financial Markets

The Treaty has not given the ECB any function regarding "microprudential supervision" (i.e., bank inspections). The ECB's only concern is with what has been termed as "macroprudential supervision." In this context, the main developments in the euro financial markets monitored by the ECB have been the following:

- The integration of the euro money markets, the success of which is shown by the general usage of the new euro-wide reference interest rates, the Euribor and the Eonia, and corresponding disappearance of the national reference rates (FIBOR, PIBOR, MIBOR, etc.). Such integration was essential for the singularity of monetary policy, and it has been achieved thanks to an intensive use of TARGET. However, while the uncollateralized money market is totally integrated, there are deficiencies in the integration of the cross-border collateralized or repo market, one of the reasons being lack of legal and regulatory harmonization in the securities "leg" of that market.

- The process to integrate equity markets, following the huge redenomination into the euro of the stock of all major euro-area listed corporations, and the switch into euro of market price quotations in all euro-area stock exchanges. Market integration and consolidation are further shown by the initial 1999 project to integrate eight major European stock exchanges, subsequently superseded by the Euronext project (ongoing merger between the stock exchanges of Paris, Brussels, and Amsterdam), on the one hand, and by the iX project (merger between the London Stock Exchange and the Deutsche Börse of Frankfurt, perhaps with Sweden's OM as third entity), on the other hand. This is still not the final picture: the stock exchanges of Milan and Madrid have signed memoranda of understanding with the parties to the iX project, conversations are taking place between Euronext and iX, and the U.S. NASDAQ has opened shop in the United Kingdom with plans to associate itself with some European projects.

- Integration of the public debt market, where the whole public debt of the 11 participating Member States was redenominated into euro on January 1999. The process toward integration is shown by the creation and development of a common trading platform called Euro-MTS, a screen-based electronic system based in Milan organized jointly by the primary dealers of the seven major euro-area public debt issuers (Belgium, Spain, Germany, France, Italy, the Netherlands, and Austria), and by the works of the so-called Brouhn's Group trying to establish synchronization mechanisms between issuers, leading perhaps to the creation of a single public debt issuing agency.

- In the bond market, the International Securities Market Association (ISMA) has launched a trading system called COREDEAL with central electronic price-making replacing the still predominant direct OTC trades. In addition, three initiatives are under way to have euro-wide central counterparties (single counterpart for market participants instead of them having to find ad hoc OTC counterparts): (i) The London Clearing House launched Repoclear on August 1999 as central counterpart for euro-denominated repos; (ii) Clearnet (Paris-based central counterpart) is to become a French-Belgian-Dutch central counterpart; (iii) the German-Luxembourg merged security settlement system named Clearstream (see below) is launching the European Clearing House based on the Swiss-German Frankfurt-based Eurex derivatives market.

In 1999, the ECOFIN endorsed a legislative program of the European Commission to update and develop the Community Directives on the financial markets (Financial Services Action Plan). The ECB is represented in the top group organizing such legislative developments (Financial Services Policy Group) and in the several groups dealing with the individual topics. More recently, the ECOFIN created a Committee of Seven Wise Men with the mandate to investigate and report about the integration of the euro securities markets in Europe; such Committee, due to report in spring next year, may be the origin of important legislative and institutional initiatives concerning the European capital markets.

Microprudential supervision schemes are still the same as before monetary union; their legal framework mainly predates the Treaty of Maastricht, which left all options open.

There is an ongoing debate about the proper way to organize microprudential supervision after monetary union. Consolidation and integration of the credit market renders the existing scheme inadequate.

The NCBs of Austria, Italy, and Ireland have received microprudential supervision competences after monetary union. The Bundesbank has requested such functions.

The Banking Supervision Committee (BSC) of the ECB is already an embryo of a forum for increased cooperation between European supervisors.

The ECB achieved a working solution to organize the emergency liquidity assistance (ELA) by Eurosystem members, characterized as follows:

- The basic competence for ELA operations lies with the NCBs.

- Transparency obligations are established for ELA operations within the Eurosystem.

- Collateral for ELA operations is required.

- The liquidity impact is to be managed by the Eurosystem.

- Institutional preference is for "market" solutions.

Statistics

A single monetary policy requires harmonized monetary aggregates: M1, M2, and M3. They form the so-called first pillar of the Eurosystem's monetary policy strategy. The ECB has an exclusive competence to organize the definition and elaboration of such monetary measures. In addition, a harmonized balance of payment statistics is produced by ECB.

For "second pillar" (inflation indicators), and other statistics of interest for the Eurosystem, the ECB shares its competence with Eurostat, in whose committees and groups the ECB is duly represented.

The above summary is organized by several legal acts: 1 EC Regulation, 1 ECB Regulation, 1 ECB Guideline, 2 ECB Recommendations.

ECB sanctions are possible, but so far no sanctions have been imposed.

Advisory Function

Since its establishment, the ECB has been consulted nearly 100 hundred times. Consultations on draft Community legal acts and draft national legislation seldom fall below two per month. The year 1998 was a very busy year in this regard, 1999 and 2000 were less so.

In addition, the ECB provides informal advice to accession countries (on statistics, payment systems, legislation, etc.).

The ECB has produced its first Convergence Report on a candidate country: Greece. The EMI examined and advised on the convergence of Member States in 1998.

Chapter 7

International Finance Corporation: History and Current Operations

CAROL MATES

I am going to speak a bit about the history of the International Finance Corporation (IFC) and IFC's current operations. To give you an idea of day-to-day work that lawyers do in the Legal Department of IFC, I'll discuss some projects that I've worked on recently that I think are particularly interesting.

IFC is the organization in the World Bank Group that was established to promote development exclusively through the private sector. IFC was formed in 1956, about 10 years after the World Bank started operations. From the legal point, it is interesting to note that IFC's charter, its Articles of Agreement, prohibit it from accepting a host government guarantee for any of its loans or financial assistance, which complements the World Bank's charter requirements that the World Bank *must* take a government guarantee to support any financial assistance that it renders. A member government must first join the IMF in order to be eligible to join the World Bank; and to be a member of IFC, a country must be a member of the World Bank. At the time of writing, IFC had 174 member governments.

When I joined IFC's Legal Department in 1981, I thought that all of the most exciting developments had occurred and that all of the countries in the world that could be members of IFC were already members, because, at that time, membership was effectively limited to the non-communist world. There were really only a few small island nations left, perhaps, that might someday become member countries, and part of the fun of being an IFC lawyer was to do the first IFC project in the country. Why? Because that meant a trip to the country, a week's discussion with local counsel on what the laws of the country were as they related to private sector investments, discussions with authorities in the country as to the role of the legal status of IFC's immunities in the country, discussions with Ministry of Finance and central bank officials as to any applicable exchange control requirements, etc. Well, I didn't realize how wrong I was because, in the early 1990s, after the Soviet Union fell apart, we had many more countries that started joining the IMF, the World Bank, and then IFC, and there were a lot of new countries for us to do investments in, a lot of new countries for us to figure out the laws of, including the investments laws and regulations, and many opportunities to have discussions with some of our colleagues.

One other interesting feature about IFC's charter is that IFC is prohibited from exercising management control of an enterprise. Exactly what is meant by "management control" is not specified in IFC's charter, and this has sometimes been the subject of discussions at Executive Board meetings or internal meetings. The restriction is generally understood to mean that IFC should not be the sponsor or the main force behind any particular project. In practice, what this has traditionally meant is that IFC is generally approached by a private sector sponsor, which has an idea to develop a particular project in a developing member country. IFC will appraise the project to assure that its criteria as to development impact, financial viability, etc., are met. If the project meets IFC's technical and financial criteria, IFC can assist with loan financing, equity or quasi-equity financing, and also usually with some technical assistance depending on how sophisticated the sponsors are and how developed the country is.

Recently, IFC has been exploring whether it should get much more involved in the development stage of projects, in order to see if it can help prepare many of our less developed "frontier" country members to be more receptive to particular private sector investments which will help fight poverty and advance other host government and World Bank Group goals. So, in two unusual projects, IFC actually went out to help develop a project before there was any private sector sponsor, in order to attract potential private sector sponsors. It is also very important to note that IFC's private sector sponsors by no means have to be foreign investors. IFC may provide financing to local investors or foreign investors in a developing member country; the key criteria are that the project being financed is privately controlled and managed.

In recent years, IFC has faced a number of interesting legal issues on what the interpretation of a "private" company is and what levels of state participation in a private company may be permissible to qualify for IFC financing. Beginning in the very late 1980s, when the world was moving more toward a model of privatization and market-based economics, IFC financed projects in a number of countries that were in the process of privatization. There were a few financing transactions in telecom projects *prior* to privatization—for example, one such pre-privatization investment was in the former Yugoslavia Republic of Macedonia (FYRM) where IFC made a loan to a 100 percent government-owned telecom company in order to show support for the company and its proposed privatization. IFC generally insists that a company be privately managed, in other words, managed generally on a for-profit basis, by a board of directors who are looking at it as a private sector enterprise as opposed to really a quasi-governmental arm. Therefore, in some cases IFC has agreed to finance a project despite the fact that, hopefully temporarily, there may be more than 50 percent government ownership, so long as there is an intention of the government to divest.

In addition to providing its own funds, IFC also has a mobilization role, a catalytic role, in bringing new capital into a country. This is accomplished through IFC's loan syndication program, which by now is well known in the market as the IFC "B" Loan program. From the legal point of view, the entire loan is an IFC loan and IFC is the lender of record. The "A" Loan portion is funded for IFC's own account, while the "B" Loan portion is funded by commercial banks, which affords the commercial banks the opportunity to invest in a country that perhaps their credit committees might be a bit nervous about *except* for the fact that, under the "B" Loan "umbrella," the "B" Loan benefits from the implicit political risk cover of IFC. It is also worth noting here that the IFC political risk cover or umbrella is not a de jure cover, i.e., not a legal cover; it is really more of a de facto political cover because of the relationship between IFC and its member countries. In fact, the IFC's "preferred creditor" status, by which, generally speaking, if there is a foreign currency shortage in a country, our member countries have generally allocated the available foreign exchange to repayment of obligations due to the multilateral institutions, including IFC, is also not a legally mandated privilege. IFC also serves as an equity catalyst because its presence in a transaction often mobilizes private sector investors to enter into projects that IFC is financing. IFC also provides hedging products services to clients, so that IFC may be an intermediary and deal with a commercial bank counterparty on one end and the client private sector company in the developing country on the other. IFC offers advisory services through a number of facilities and advises governments in privatization of state-owned assets and also advises governments on how to make a better investment climate in the country, through entities such as FIAS and also directly.

An area of increasing importance today is IFC's collaboration with the World Bank. Mr. Wolfensohn became IFC's President about six years ago. He is the President of the World Bank Group, the President of the Bank, IFC, MIGA and, of course, IDA. There has been a big emphasis over the last six years on collaboration. The overall mission statement of IFC is poverty reduction through the private sector in order to improve people's lives, and the belief that economic growth can help to mitigate poverty in our developing member countries, and we now work much more closely with the World Bank than in previous years. This includes, on the legal side, increasing collaboration between the two legal departments.

The Global Products Groups previously alluded to are very recent innovations. What that means is that in areas such as telecommunications, the group working on it at the World Bank would be merged with the group working on it at IFC, into one department. So you will have the IFC team members working on doing the transactions together with many of the Bank people working on giving policy advice to the governments. Where does this leave the lawyers who previously would have advised the World Bank policy people, who might have been economists, or the IFC lawyers advising the IFC Investment Officers doing the transactions, who are probably MBA types? Well, we don't know yet, but perhaps next year we'll be able to tell you. It's a challenge for the lawyers of both IFC and the World Bank to see how, on an operational basis, this may change or broaden our work.

Some new areas at IFC, in addition to Global Product Groups, are increasingly more attention to integrating environmental and social matters into our mainstream project processing. We are also having a push into what we call "frontier markets." The frontier markets are markets where there has not to date been significant private sector investment, which would include certain parts of the world such as sub-Saharan Africa, the new Central Asian republics, and Central America. This poses many challenges for the lawyers in particular, because we are working with untested legal systems, and because we do project finance, which relies greatly on clear legal regimes and which is limited or nonrecourse to any sponsor, guarantor, and certainly nonrecourse to the host government.

IFC is dependent on getting repaid for its loans and getting a return on its equity from the contractual structure of a project, or if that fails, its ability to go into court, generally a local court, to enforce its security interests, generally being a mortgage and a pledge on equipment. Of course, in many countries where there is a weak legal system, many countries which have had nonmarket economies for many years or their entire existence, the laws are just either being put on the books or a bit rusty and in many cases they don't really work. So, our work in the frontier markets requires a lot of legal work. Often its not cost effective in the sense that the amounts invested in the project would probably never justify the amount of legal work, legal due diligence that must go into the project if one were going to do it purely on a commercial type of profit return. And that's, of course, where we as a legal department in a development institution come in because we see it as our role to understand the legal system in the country and, increasingly through our colleagues in the World Bank Legal Department, to give feedback to the governments in these countries as to what we think works to attract foreign investment and what we think doesn't work to attract foreign investment.

Some of you, in terms of your role as Bank supervisory regulators, may have seen the interplay between the extent to which security interests in your country can be good and which can shore up the banking sector. In a number of countries that I have seen, banks really might be insolvent because they can't foreclose on any security collateral for loans and the loans are not good so the loans end up being carried on the books for years and years hoping that somehow they will get paid back. And often, when countries implement laws providing for registry systems for good security interests on land or equipment, this can be used to help banks collateralize loans, make more effective loans, and thereby shore up the banking system.

One other thing that IFC is doing in recent times is putting more staff in the field—decentralizing. We are also putting lawyers in the field so some of you who perhaps did not have much to do with IFC in the past might find that you are being asked a question by people in your government about IFC—such as "what does IFC do," why is IFC asking for this change in law or this clarification of interpretation—and this may be because of IFC's increased positioning of staff in the field.

Just to give you an idea, in summary, of some kinds of items that IFC lawyers work on, I will tell you what I've been working on. Recently, I've been working on power projects. These are independent power projects, called IPPs, and they are very complicated from the legal standpoint. Generally, investment in an IPP occurs in conjunction with, or just after, a country has liberalized the energy sector and split up the energy sector into energy generation, distribution, and transmission. Very often, these three sectors will be privatized, thereby reducing a huge drain on the balance sheet of the country. To improve generating capacity in the country, as you know, many countries have invited foreign power generators into the country. I've recently signed, just last week, documentation providing for an IFC loan to a power project in Kenya, which is the first power project IFC has done in sub-Saharan Africa, and which did not have a government guarantee of the obligations of the utility off-taker. We are very, very, heartened by that development and hope that this will be something that will really enable government resources and balance sheets to be freed up if we are able to replicate this in other countries.

I've also been involved in telecom and transport infrastructure financings, both post-privatization, expansion, and modernization projects and, as I mentioned previously, a pre-privatization telecom deal in FYRM.

That's power, telecom, and transport. I recently participated in the financing of an elevated mass transit system in Bangkok which we are very proud of because we disbursed at the height of the Thai baht crisis, and we watched the exchange rate go from 25 to 54 and settle down somewhere around 35. IFC, as a reliable development partner, was instrumental in helping other lenders—a German bank, Kreditanstalt für Wiederaufbau (KfW), and Thai banks. We were prepared to ride out the storm. We knew that this crisis would ultimately be reversed.

Last, I mentioned that I also work in venture capital funds. This is an instrument that we use as a type of financial intermediary, basically to bring financing to small- and medium-scale enterprises that IFC might not be able to directly finance because they would be too expensive. One that I just closed recently is called the Renewable Energy and Energy Efficiency Fund, and it's going to be financing different forms of power generation distribution and will also get into exciting things such as solar energy, wind farms, and biomass, and we hope will make a profit doing it. I hope that I have given you a better understanding of the IFC and its work.

Chapter 8

Competencies of the European Community on International Monetary Fund Matters: An Overview of the Key Legal Issues

BERNHARD STEINKI

If one were asked to write a memorandum on the respective powers of the European Central Bank (ECB), the Commission, the Council of Ministers, and the European Parliament in the exercise of the IMF membership of the EU/euro area countries,[1] it would be no surprise if the memorandum contained a long list of questions and

---

[1] Outside legal documents and legal writing, often no distinction is made between the European Union and the three separate Communities (i.e., the *European Community (EC)*, the *European Community for Coal and Steel (ECCS)*, and the *European Atomic Energy Community (Euratom)*). However, legally speaking these are separate entities, the European Union and each Community regulating different areas and forms of European cooperation. The main text for economic integration is the Treaty Establishing the European Community (the EC Treaty) which contains, inter alia, the provisions on the common market, the customs union, the common agricultural and trade policy, and also the framework for economic and monetary union. The *Treaty on European Union* (adopted in Maastricht in 1992), as amended by the Amsterdam Treaty (effective May 1, 1999), contains provisions on a Common Foreign and Security Policy (CFSP) and on Police and Judicial Cooperation in Criminal Matters. The term European Union is used as an umbrella term to cover the European Communities (so-called "first pillar" of the European Union), the Common Foreign and Security Policy ("second pillar"), and the Provisions on Police and Judicial Cooperation in Criminal Matters ("third pillar"). Whereas the European communities each have legal personality, the European Union does not. Legal acts of the European Union always indicate on which basis the European Union acts (EC, Euroatom, CFSP, etc.). Since in the area of economic and monetary union, the EC Treaty is the legal basis, the terms EC law/Community law, European Community, and Community institutions will be used in this paper, and not the broader terms EU law, European Union, and European Union institutions. When referring to the EU/EC members, the term EU Member States, or simply Member States, will be used.

unresolved issues but few definitive answers. The main reason for this likely outcome is that the Treaty Establishing the European Community (the "EC Treaty")—the legal foundation for European economic and monetary union ("EMU")—does not comprehensively regulate the external aspects of EMU. It contains only a few provisions on the international implications of EMU, and the application of these Treaty provisions, for example, with regard to the IMF, raises numerous questions of interpretation.

There are clear signs that something has changed in the way the EU Member States exercise their membership in the IMF since January 1, 1999. The Community requested and obtained an observer status for the ECB with the Executive Board of the IMF.[2] The IMF now conducts surveillance over the monetary and exchange rate policies of the members of the euro area (euro area Article IV consultation).[3] For this purpose, an agreement was reached in February 2000 between the Economic and Financial Committee (EFC)[4] of the European Community and the ECB on how to determine the position of the euro area/the Community for the euro area Article IV consultation. Moreover, Executive Directors appointed and elected by the EU Member States have set up consultation and coordination procedures at the IMF with the participation of the ECB representative and a Commission representative. It also has to be noted that Mr. Köhler, a national of Germany, was officially nominated at an Executive Board meeting to succeed Mr. Camdessus as Managing Director of the IMF by a national of Portugal from an Executive Director's office on behalf of the EU Member States.[5] Portugal held the Presidency of the European Union at the time.

EMU seems to have triggered a process that will lead to more common European positions on IMF issues, a greater involvement of the European institutions on IMF matters, and ultimately a stronger

---

[2] Executive Board Decision No. 11875-(99/1), adopted December 21, 1998; *Selected Decisions and Selected Documents of the International Monetary Fund* (*Selected Decisions*), Twenty-Fifth Issue, p. 478.

[3] Executive Board Decision 11846-(98/125), adopted December 9, 1998, *Selected Decisions*, Twenty-Fifth Issue, p. 28.

[4] See Article 114 EC Treaty.

[5] See IMF Press Release No. 00/18, March 14, 2000, http://www.imf.org/external/np/sec/pr/2000/pr0018.htm.

representation of the Community in the IMF. These developments warrant a closer look at how Community law addresses the IMF membership of the EU Member States, and how the legal framework has been implemented so far.

This paper is structured as follows: the next section deals with the relevance of Community law for the IMF membership of the EU/euro area countries; the third section gives an overview of the key provisions of the EC Treaty on the external relations of EMU; the fourth section summarizes the conclusions of the meetings of the European Heads of State and Government of Luxembourg (1997) and Vienna (1998) on the external relations of EMU; the fiftth section discusses some of the issues that need to be addressed in determining the substantive competencies of the Community on IMF matters; the sixth section analyzes the roles of the respective Community institutions on IMF matters; and the last section looks at how Community competencies can be exercised under the IMF's Articles of Agreement.

Relevance of Community Law for the IMF Membership of the EU Member States

The EC Treaty cannot unilaterally change the rights and obligations of the EU Member States under the IMF Articles of Agreement. Since all EU Member States had ratified the IMF Articles of Agreement before they ratified the Maastricht Treaty, they are bound under public international law to continue to fulfill all obligations under the Articles of Agreement and are entitled to enjoy all rights thereunder.[6] However, Community law could affect the way the EU Member States exercise their IMF membership.

The exercise of the IMF membership of a country is typically set out in national law. For example, the German law on the IMF regulates the appointment of the German Executive and Alternate Executive Director, the fulfillment of the financial obligations of Germany towards the IMF, the cooperation between the Ministry of Finance and the Deutsche Bundesbank on IMF matters, and the power

---

[6] *See* Hector Elizalde, "The Economic and Monetary Union and the International Monetary Fund," in *Current Developments in Monetary and Financial Law*, Vol. 1, 1999, p. 303.

of the Minister of Finance to instruct the German Executive Director on his/her positions and voting in the Executive Board.[7] The U.S. Congress has also adopted a number of laws on the exercise of the U.S. IMF membership. These laws require congressional approval for certain acts in the exercise of the U.S. IMF membership, or set legislative mandates on how the Treasury Secretary shall instruct the U.S. Executive Director in the exercise of his/her office.[8] It is with regard to the exercise of the IMF membership that Community law—similar to national laws—can be relevant.

Under Community law, where the Community has exclusive competence, it is able to exercise it independently within the framework of other international organizations. Moreover, on matters of exclusive Community competence, the Member States are no longer competent to act within other international organizations.[9] The Member States have to facilitate the achievement of the Community's tasks and at the same time abstain from any measure that could jeopardize the attainment of the objectives of the Treaty. The European Court of Justice has decided that, if the rules of an international organization do not allow the Community to accede as a member, Article 10 EC Treaty binds the Member States and the institutions of the Community to use every means at their disposal to ensure the participation of the Community in international conventions if the Community must do so to in the exercise of its exclusive competence. Article 10 EC Treaty further obliges the Member States to take all appropriate measures to ensure fulfillment of the obligations arising out of the Treaty or resulting from action taken by the institutions of the Community.[10]

With regard to the IMF, a determination is necessary regarding which Community competencies are implicated by the IMF

---

[7] Bundesgesetzblatt 1978 II p. 13, amended by Bundesgesetzblatt 1991 II p. 815 and Bundesgesetzblatt 2000 II p. 799.

[8] *See* recently published report by the U.S. General Accounting Office on *International Monetary Fund—Efforts to Advance U.S. Policies at the Fund*, dated January 23, 2001 (GAO-01-214), which lists 60 provisions of federal law that set forth U.S. policy toward the Fund (report available via www.gao.gov).

[9] Rachel Frid, *The Relations between the EC and International Organizations* (1995), p. 214.

[10] *Id.*, p. 216, with further references.

membership of the EU/euro area countries, and how these competencies can be exercised under the current Articles of Agreement. Looking at the purposes, the activities, the organizational structure, and decision making of the IMF, as well as the specific rights and obligations of IMF members, the following concrete examples illustrate the question on the competencies of the Community on IMF matters:

- On decisions touching the fundamentals of the IMF membership, e.g., amendments of the Articles, quota increases, or Special Drawing Rights (SDRs) allocations, what is the involvement of the Community institutions in the decisions taken by the Member States on these issues?

- Which of the wide range of issues that are decided by the Executive Board on a daily basis (e.g., surveillance, access to Fund resources, Heavily Indebted Poor Country (HIPC) Initiative issues, or issues concerning the global financial architecture) implicate Community competencies?

- Are Community institutions included in the consultation procedures between Executive Directors and the EU Member States appointing or electing them, and what is their exact role in this regard? Could a legal act adopted at Community level—similar to national laws concerning the IMF—provide for the powers of Community institutions to instruct European Executive Directors on IMF matters?

- Does Community law require those EU Member States that elect Executive Directors to form euro area/EU-only constituencies?

- Is there a role for the Community in the appointment and election of Executive Directors/Alternate Executive Directors by the euro area countries/EU Member States? Is there a procedure to ensure that policy positions adopted by the Community institutions are respected by the "European" Executive Directors in their participation (statements and voting) in the Executive Board?

- What form of representation of the Community in the IMF would be consistent with the distribution of competencies under the EC Treaty? Does Community law require the membership of both the Community and the Member States, or should the Community be the sole IMF member, replacing the Member States?

The Key Provisions of the EC Treaty on the External Representation of EMU

The EC Treaty has no specific regime for the Community's relations with the IMF. Only one provision in a protocol attached to the EC Treaty, namely, the Statute of the European System of Central Banks and the European Central Bank ("ESCB Statute"), expressly mentions the IMF.[11] However, the EC Treaty contains a number of provisions on the external relations of EMU in general. These provisions, supplemented by the case law of the European Court of Justice, will have to be relied on in determining the Community law framework for the exercise of the IMF membership of the EU Member States.

The central provision for the external relations of EMU is Article 111 EC Treaty.[12] Paragraphs (1) and (2) of this provision deal with exchange rate policy, paragraph (3) with the negotiating of international agreements concerning monetary and exchange-regime matters, paragraph (4) with the adoption of positions of the Community at the international level as regards issues of particular relevance to economic and monetary union and the international representation of the Community as regards EMU, and paragraph (5) with the power of the Member States to negotiate and conclude agreements outside the competencies of the Community. Article 111 EC Treaty only applies to those Member States that participate in monetary union (see Article 122 (4) EC Treaty). Of the 15 EU Member States, the United Kingdom, Sweden, and Denmark currently do not participate in EMU. These members neither vote in, nor are they bound by, decisions adopted on the basis of Article 111 EC Treaty. The following overview of Article 111 paragraphs (3), (4), and (5) EC Treaty illustrates that the application of each of these provisions with regard to the IMF requires a determination as to what

---

[11] Article 30.5 of the Statute of the European System of Central Banks and the European Central Bank provides: "The ECB may hold and manage IMF reserve positions and SDRs and provide for the pooling of such assets."

[12] The numbering of Articles of the EC Treaty cited in this contribution corresponds to the revised numbering of the EC Treaty after the entering into force of the Treaty of Amsterdam, amending the EC Treaty, on May 1, 1999.

IMF matters are affected by the Community's competence for monetary and exchange rate matters (or other Community competencies). The EC Treaty leaves it to future decisions of the Community institutions to make that determination.

Article 111 (4) EC Treaty: Position of the Community at the International Level—International Representation

Article 111 (4) reads as follows:

> The Council shall, on a proposal from the Commission and after consulting the ECB, acting by a qualified majority decide on the position of the Community at international level as regards issues of particular relevance to economic and monetary union, and acting unanimously, decide its representation in compliance with the allocation of powers laid down in Articles 99 and 105.[13]

Both parts of Article 111 (4) EC Treaty are directly relevant for the Community's relations with the IMF. Article 111 (4), second alternative EC Treaty is the legal basis for a decision by the Council[14] on the representation of the Community in the IMF. The reference to Article 99 and 105 clarifies that the Council, in its decision on the

---

[13] The Heads of State and Government of the EU agreed to amend this provision at the European Council meeting which took place in Nice during December 7–9, 2000 by Article 2.6 of the Treaty of Nice (OJC80/1 of March 10, 2001) as follows: "Subject to paragraph 1, the Council, acting by a *qualified majority* on a proposal from the Commission and after consulting the ECB, shall decide on the position of the Community at international level as regards issues of particular relevance to economic and monetary union and on its representation in compliance with the allocation of powers laid down in Articles 99 and 105" (emphasis added). Thus the Council would no longer be required to decide unanimously the representation of the Community as regards EMU. However, the amendments of the EC Treaty agreed on in Nice still have to be ratified by all 15 EU Member States to become effective.

[14] The Council consists of a representative of each Member State at ministerial level, authorized to commit the government of that Member State, Article 203 EC Treaty. On EMU issues, the Council typically meets in the composition of economic and finance ministers. The Council takes decisions by majority of its members except provided otherwise. Where the Council is required to act by "qualified majority," the weighed voting set out in Article 205 EC Treaty applies (see note 43 below).

representation of the Community, has to respect the powers allocated to the ESCB (reference to Article 105, which sets out the objectives and tasks of the ESCB) and the competencies of the Member States for economic policy (reference to Article 99, which sets out a surveillance mechanism for those areas of economic policy that largely remain in the competence of the Member States). Article 111(4), first alternative EC Treaty is the legal basis for positions of the Community on IMF matters of particular relevance to EMU.

The application of Article 111(4) EC Treaty with respect to the IMF requires a determination of (i) what IMF matters can be considered *"issues of particular relevance to economic and monetary union,"* and (ii) what representation of the Community in the IMF is *"in compliance with the allocation of powers laid down in Articles 99 and 105."*

Negotiation by the Community of International Agreements Concerning Monetary and Exchange-Regime Matters (Article 111(3) EC Treaty)

Article 111(3) EC Treaty provides the following with respect to international agreements:

> (3) By way of derogation from Article 300, where agreements concerning monetary or foreign exchange regime matters need to be negotiated by the Community with one or more States or international organizations, the Council, acting by a qualified majority, on a recommendation from the Commission and after consulting the ECB, shall decide the arrangements for the negotiation and for the conclusion of such agreements. These arrangements shall ensure that the Community expresses a single position. The Commission shall be fully associated with the negotiations.

Article 111(3) EC Treaty sets aside the general regime for treaty negotiations contained in Article 300 EC Treaty and is limited to two areas of exclusive competence of the Community: monetary and foreign exchange–regime matters. Article 111(3) EC Treaty could be relied on for future amendments of the IMF Articles of Agreement. However, the EC Treaty does not contain a definition of "agreement concerning monetary and exchange-regime matters." In the case of an amendment of the IMF Articles of Agreement, a determination will become necessary as to whether the amendment is to be qualified as an "agreement concerning monetary and exchange-regime matters," or whether the specific subject matter of an amendment falls outside that category.

Two examples illustrate this point: The Third Amendment of the Articles, which became effective in 1992, introduced changes to Article XXVI of the Articles by providing for the possibility of suspending voting and related rights of members that do not fulfill their rights under the Articles. The Fourth Amendment, which is not yet effective, consists of a special one-time allocation of Special Drawing Rights (SDR). If adopted today, would both amendments fall under Article 111(3) EC Treaty?

International Treaties by the Member States (Article 111(5) EC Treaty)

Article 111(5) EC Treaty reads as follows:

5. Without prejudice to Community competence and Community agreements as regards economic and monetary union, Member States may negotiate in international bodies and conclude international agreements.

The application of Article 111(5) EC Treaty requires a determination of what constitutes *"community competence and Community agreements as regards economic and monetary union."* The powers of the Member States to negotiate on IMF matters and to conclude amendments to the IMF Articles of Agreement in the future are limited by the Community's competencies as regards economic and monetary union.

As can be seen from this brief overview of Article 111 paragraphs (3), (4), and (5) EC Treaty, the EC Treaty addresses the international dimension of EMU only in very general terms, but leaves it largely to future decisions of the Council to determine its precise implications.

In the run-up to January 1, 1999, the Community institutions and the Member States had to come up with a first interpretation of Article 111 EC Treaty.

The European Council Meetings of Luxembourg (December 1997) and Vienna (December 1998)

As part of the preparations for the start of EMU on January 1, 1999, an attempt was made by the Member States and the Community to adopt a formal Council decision on the basis of Article 111(4) EC Treaty on the external representation of EMU, including its representation in the IMF. Twice, at its summits in Luxembourg in December 1997 and in Vienna in 1998, the Heads of State and Government of the European Union, meeting as the European Council,[15] dealt with the issue of external representation of EMU and gave directions for the future work of the Community institutions, which are contained in the Presidency Conclusions of these meetings.[16]

Luxembourg Council Conclusions

Paragraph 46 of the Luxembourg conclusions reads as follows:

> 46. The Council and the European Central Bank will fulfill their tasks in representing the Community at international level in an efficient manner and in compliance with the distribution of powers laid down in the Treaty. The Commission will be associated with external representation insofar as necessary to enable it to fulfill the role assigned to it by the Treaty.

---

[15] Article 4 of the EU Treaty provides for the following with regard to the European Council: "The European Council shall provide the Union with the necessary impetus for its development and shall define the general political guidelines thereof. The European Council shall bring together the Heads of State or Government of the Member States and the President of the Commission. They shall be assisted by the Ministers for Foreign Affairs of the Member States and by a Member of the Commission. The European Council shall meet at least twice a year, under the chairmanship of the Head of State or Government of the Member State that holds the Presidency of the Council. The European Union shall submit to the European Parliament a report after each of its meetings and a yearly written report on progress achieved by the Union."

[16] Luxembourg European Council Conclusions, see Bulletin EU 12/97, http://europa.eu.int/council/off/conclu/dec97.htm. Vienna European Council Conclusions, see Bulletin EU 12/98, http://europa.eu.int/council/off/conclu/dec98.htm.

The Council also adopted a Resolution on Economic Policy Coordination in Stage 3 of EMU and on Treaty Articles 109 and 109(b).[17] In Part II of this resolution under Implementing the Treaty Provisions on the Exchange-Rate Policy, External Position and Representation of the Community (Article 109), the European Council made the following statements:

> 9. The Council should decide on the position of the Community at international level as regards issues of particular relevance to economic and monetary union, in accordance with Article 109(4). *These positions will be relevant both to bilateral relations between the EU and individual third countries and to proceedings in international organizations or informal international groupings.* The scope of this provision is necessarily limited as only euro-area member states vote under Article 109 (emphasis added).
>
> 10. The Council and the European Central Bank will carry out their tasks in representing the Community at international level in an efficient manner and *in compliance with the allocation of powers laid down in the Treaty.* On *elements of economic policy other than monetary and exchange-rate policy,* the Member States should continue to present their policies outside the Community framework, while taking full account of the Community interest. The Commission will be involved in external representation *to the extent required to enable it to perform the role assigned to it by the Treaty.* Representation in international organizations should take account of those organizations rules. *With particular regard to the Community's relations with the International Monetary Fund, they should be predicated upon the provision in the Fund's Articles of Agreement that only countries can be members of that institution. The Member States, in their capacities as members of the IMF should help to establish pragmatic arrangements which would facilitate the conduct of IMF surveillance and the presentation of Community positions, including the views of the ESCB, in IMF fora* (emphasis added).

Analysis of the Luxembourg Conclusions

The European Council Resolution determines two important issues: First, that the representation of the Community will largely lie in the hands of the Council and the ECB, and that the Commission

---

[17] The Treaty of Amsterdam changed Article 109 and 109(b) to Article 111 and 113 EC Treaty, respectively.

will only *"be involved in the external representation to the extent required to enable it to perform the role assigned to it by the Treaty."* This conclusion assigns the Commission a much weaker role in the external representation of EMU than for other areas of Community competencies.[18] Second, that the Community will not seek an amendment of the IMF Articles of Agreement but rather, in light of the current Articles of Agreement, will seek *"to establish pragmatic arrangements which would facilitate the conduct of IMF surveillance and the presentation of Community positions, including the views of the ESCB, in IMF fora."*

By providing that the Council and the European Central Bank represent the Community *"in compliance with the allocation of powers laid down in the Treaty,"* and that the Member States continue to present their policies *"on elements of economic policy other than monetary and exchange-rate policy"* outside the Community framework, the European Council conclusions simply paraphrase Article 111(4), second alternative, which—as mentioned above—requires that the representation of the Community as regards EMU be in compliance with the allocation of powers as laid down in Articles 99 and 105. However, the European Council conclusions give little indication as to the substance of the distribution of powers on IMF matters between the Member States and the Community and among the Community institutions. The Resolution simply states that pragmatic arrangements shall "facilitate the conduct of IMF surveillance" and "the presentation of Community positions, including the views of the ESCB, in IMF fora."

Moreover, while the Council Resolution provides with regard to common positions that "[t]hese positions will be relevant both to bilateral relations between the EU and individual third countries and to proceedings in international organizations or informal international groupings," it does not address how positions adopted by the Council on IMF matters could be implemented within the IMF's organizational structure.

---

[18] *See*, for example, Article 302 EC Treaty, which reads as follows: "It shall be for the Commission to ensure the maintenance of all relations with the organs of the United Nations and of its specialized agencies. The Commission shall also maintain such relations as are appropriate with all international organizations."

The Vienna European Council Conclusions (December 1998)

Under the heading "Europe as a Global Player" the Council concluded:

14. ... The European Council endorses the report of the Council on external representation of the Community, which foresees that the president of the ECOFIN Council, or if the president is from a noneuro area Member State, the President of the Euro 11, assisted by the Commission, shall participate in meetings of the G7 (Finance) (see annex II). *The ECB, as the Community body competent for monetary policy, should be granted an observer status at the IMF board. The views of the European Community/EMU on other issues of particular relevance to the EMU would be presented at the IMF board by the relevant member of the Executive Director's office of the Member States holding the euro presidency, assisted by a representative of the Commission.* The European Council invites the Council to act on the basis of a Commission proposal incorporating this agreement (emphasis added).

Annex II to the Presidency Conclusions contains a report by the Council (Economic and Finance Ministers) to the European Council (Heads of State or Government) on the stage of preparation for stage 3 of EMU, which deals with the external representation of the Community in greater detail.

The main passages in the report with relevance for the IMF read as follows:

3. The external representation in Stage 3 of EMU will imply changes in the current organization of fora. Therefore, third countries and institutions will need to be persuaded to accept the solutions proposed by the European Union. The Council considers that a pragmatic approach might be the most successful which could minimize the adaptation of current rules and practices provided, of course, that such an approach resulted in an outcome, which recognized properly the role of the euro.

4. It follows from the Treaty that a distinction has to be made between the representations:

- Of the Community at international level as regards issues of particular relevance to economic and monetary union (Article 109(4)), and

- On matters which do not belong to the Community competence, but on which it may be appropriate for Member States to express common understandings.

5. As regards the first indent of paragraph 4—the representation of the Community at international level as regards issues of particular relevance to EMU—the Council believes that, while trying to reach early solutions pragmatically with international partners, these solutions should further develop over time adhering to the following principles:

- The Community must speak with one voice;

- The Community shall be represented at the Council/ministerial level and at the central banking level;

- The Commission "will be involved in the Community external representation to the extent required to enable it to perform the role assigned to it by the Treaty."

- As regards the second indent matters, which do not belong to Community competence, the Council considered it useful to develop pragmatic solutions for the external representation.

6. In developing those pragmatic solutions, the Council concentrated its work on three important areas:

- Representation at the G-7 Finance Ministers' and Governors' Group

- Representation at the International Monetary Fund

- Composition of ECOFIN delegations to third countries

Concerning the IMF, the report provided:

13. The Council considers that pragmatic solutions for presenting issues of particular relevance to EMU may have to be sought which do not require a change in the Articles of Agreement of the IMF:

A first necessary step has already been taken; the IMF Executive Board has agreed to grant the ECB an observer position at the Board;

Secondly, the views of the European community/EMU would be presented at the IMF Board by the relevant member of the Executive Director's office of the Member State holding the Euro 11 Presidency, assisted by a representative from the Commission.

The draft Commission proposal for a Council decision was not published together with the Luxembourg Presidency conclusions. The draft decision provides in Article 4 that representatives of both the ECB and the Commission should be allowed to attend meetings of the Executive Board on issues of relevance to EMU. The explanatory memorandum envisaged an observer office of the Community at the IMF, consisting of Commission and ECB representatives.

Analysis of the Vienna Conclusions

The Vienna conclusions provide further guidance on the application of Article 111(4) EC Treaty. It appears that the European Council is of the view that the IMF covers matters that partly fall in the competence of the Community (paragraph 4, first bullet of the Council report), and that partly remain in the competence of the Member States (paragraph 4, second bullet of the Council report). The Council seeks "pragmatic solutions" for both areas.

However, as in Luxembourg the year before, the European Council refrained from addressing in more detail which IMF matters remain in the competence of the Member States and which—as a result of EMU—fall in the competence of the Community. More specifically, while the European Council expressed the wish that *"[t]he ECB, as the Community body competent for monetary policy, should be granted an observer status at the IMF board,"* it did not indicate which IMF matters discussed and decided by the Executive Board fall under the competence of the ECB. The Vienna European Council conclusions were (again) limited to the formal aspects of the representation of the Community in the IMF without addressing the substantive distribution of competencies between the Community and the Member States.

The Luxembourg and Vienna conclusions have largely been followed with regard to the IMF, despite the absence of a formal Council decision on the issue. The notable exception concerns the request for the presence of a Commission representative at Executive Board meetings, which was not granted by the Executive Board. The ECB representative is now invited to meetings of the Executive Board in accordance with the Executive Board decision on the ECB observer, and a member of the Executive Director's office holding the Presidency of the European Union can present the position of the European Community/euro area at Board meetings on the surveillance of the euro area. Moreover, there are extensive consultations on IMF matters among the euro area/EU Member States, in particular in the Economic and Financial Committee of the Community, the International Relations Committee of the European Central Bank and among European Executive Directors with the participation of the ECB representative and a Commission representative from the EU delegation in Washington, D.C.

Despite these developments, it remains largely unclear what specific competencies the Community has on IMF matters and what role the Community institutions play in the exercise of the IMF membership of the euro area/EU countries. One of the reasons for this uncertainty might be that it is not obvious how the new Community competencies translate into specific powers on IMF matters, and how a representation of the Community in the IMF should look like that is in compliance with the EC Treaty.

Experience with other international organizations (e.g., World Trade Organization, International Labor Organization, or the Food and Agriculture Organization) shows that a complex analysis of all aspects of an international organization is required to determine the implications of Community competencies for the relations of the Member States and the Community with that organization, and that the result is often a rather complex arrangement of representation. The following section gives an overview of the purposes of the IMF, its financial operations and other activities, and the rights and obligations of individual members that potentially implicate Community competencies.

Determination of the Competencies of the Community on IMF Matters

The two competencies of the Community that are most relevant for its relations with the IMF are its competencies for monetary and exchange rate policy. However, other competencies in the areas of trade, the common market (in particular for financial services), international payments, and capital movements might also be relevant.

Purposes of the IMF

The purposes of the IMF are set out in Article I of the Articles of Agreement. They can be summarized as follows: (i) to promote international monetary cooperation, (ii) to facilitate the expansion and balanced growth of international trade, (iii) to maintain orderly exchange arrangements among members, (iv) to assist in the establishment of a multilateral system of payments in respect of current transactions between members and in the elimination of foreign exchange restrictions, and (v) to provide financial assistance to members to allow them to correct maladjustments in their balance of payments.

Of the general purposes of the IMF, the promotion of international monetary cooperation (Article I (i)), the maintenance of orderly exchange arrangements (Article I (iii)), and the elimination of exchange restrictions (Article I (iv)) are closely related to the Community's competence for monetary and exchange rate policy and to Community competencies under Article 56 of the EC Treaty.[19]

Given the Community's competence for the internal market and its exclusive competence on trade matters, the IMF's purpose of facilitating the expansion and balanced growth of international trade (Article I (ii)) is also closely related to Community competencies.

---

[19]Article 56 reads as follows: "(1) Within the framework of the provisions set out in this Chapter, all restrictions on the movement of capital between Member States and between Member States and third countries shall be prohibited. (2) Within the framework of the provisions set out in this Chapter, all restrictions on payments between Member States and between Member States and third countries shall be prohibited." *See also* Articles 57 to 60 EC Treaty.

The IMF purpose of balance of payments assistance is more difficult to relate to a Community competence. Among the euro area countries, a system of balance of payments assistance no longer exists. Only in very exceptional circumstances can the Council decide on financial assistance of the Community to a Member State.[20] The European Central Bank and the national central banks are prohibited from extending credit to Community bodies or the Member States.[21] Articles 119 and 120 EC Treaty provide for a balance of payments assistance regime for those EU Member States that are not part of the euro area.[22]

One could argue that the Community competence for monetary and exchange rate policy implies the power to provide balance of payments assistance to third countries as part of the external cooperation in the area of monetary and exchange rate policy, and to obtain balance of payments assistance in case of a balance of payments need. Under this analysis, the Community would have in principle the power to provide financing to, and receive financing from, an international institution like the IMF. However, direct access by the Community to IMF resources would require an amendment of the Articles of Agreement.

Operations and Activities of the IMF

The operations and activities of the IMF could implicate competencies of the Community. The Articles of Agreement contain provisions on surveillance, financial operations, and other specific activities of the IMF.[23] These activities can be grouped together under the following categories:

---

[20] *See* Articles 100 and 103 EC Treaty.
[21] *See* Article 101 EC Treaty.
[22] *See* Article 122(6) EC Treaty, which provides that "Articles 119 and 120 shall continue to apply to a Member State with a derogation."
[23] The IMF's annual report, published for the IMF's annual meetings around September each year, and the IMF's website (www.imf.org) provide a useful overview of how the Articles of Agreement are implemented in the day-to-day business of the IMF.

Surveillance

According to Article IV, Section 3 of the Articles, the IMF is charged to oversee the international monetary system in order to ensure its effective operation, and the IMF shall oversee the compliance of each member with members' obligations regarding exchange arrangements under Article IV, Section 1 of the Articles. Article IV, Section 1 reads as follows:

> Recognizing that the essential purpose of the international monetary system is to provide a framework that facilitates the exchange of goods, services, and capital among countries, and that sustains sound economic growth, and that a principal objective is the continuing development of the orderly underlying conditions that are necessary for financial and economic stability, each member undertakes to collaborate with the Fund and other members to assure orderly exchange arrangements and to promote a stable system of exchange rates. In particular, each member shall:
>
> (i) endeavor to direct its economic and financial policies toward the objective of fostering orderly economic growth with reasonable price stability, with due regard to its circumstances;
>
> (ii) seek to promote stability by fostering orderly underlying economic and financial conditions and a monetary system that does not tend to produce erratic disruptions;
>
> (iii) avoid manipulating exchange rates or the international monetary system in order to prevent effective balance of payments adjustment or to gain an unfair competitive advantage over other members; and
>
> (iv) follow exchange policies compatible with the undertakings under this Section.

With regard to the specific obligations that are subject to surveillance by the IMF, the obligation to avoid manipulating exchange rates to prevent balance of payments adjustment or to gain unfair competitive advantages (Article IV, Section 1(iii)), and the obligation under Article IV, Section 1(iv) to follow exchange rate policies compatible with Article IV, Section 1, largely relate to competencies that are now at the Community level.

The obligations under Article IV, Sections 1 (i) and (ii) relate to competencies both at the Member State and the Community level. The economic and financial policies necessary to foster orderly economic growth are still largely determined by the Member States, even if they are subject to Community surveillance procedures.[24] The Community, on the other hand, is responsible for monetary policy, which is critical for "reasonable price stability." The obligation to foster orderly underlying economic and financial conditions relates to competencies of both the Member States (e.g., fiscal, social, and structural policies) and the Community (internal market, trade, and monetary and exchange rate policies), while the obligation to seek a monetary system that does not tend to produce erratic disruptions relates to the Community's competence for monetary and exchange rate policy.

Financial Operations and Support for Member Countries

As mentioned above, the IMF can provide balance of payments assistance to its members. The IMF has three main channels through which it can make financial resources available to its members: The General Resources Account (GRA), the Poverty Reduction and Growth Facility Trust (PRGF Trust), and the Special Drawing Rights Department (SDR Department).

The general resources of the IMF consist mainly of the quota payments of the members, but can be supplemented by borrowing from special borrowing arrangements, notably the New Arrangements to Borrow (NAB) and the General Arrangements to Borrow (GAB).[25] The resources from the GRA are made available through a number of

---

[24] Article 99 EC Treaty, and secondary legislation adopted on the basis of Article 99 EC Treaty, so-called "Stability and Growth Pact," Council Regulations (EC) 1466/97 and 1467/97 of July 7, 1997.

[25] GAB (1962) and NAB (1998) together amount to SDR 34 billion (about US$43.1 billion at end-March 2001 exchange rates). Participants of the NAB are Australia, Austria, Belgium, Canada, Denmark, Deutsche Bundesbank, Finland, France, Hong Kong Monetary Authority, Italy, Japan, Korea, Kuwait, Luxembourg, Malaysia, Netherlands, Norway, Saudi Arabia, Singapore, Spain, Sveriges Riksbank, Swiss National Bank, Thailand, United Kingdom, and United States. The GAB contains a sub-set of the NAB members. For details on the NAB and GAB *see Selected Decisions*, Twenty-Fifth Issue, p. 366 (GAB) and p. 397 (NAB).

facilities, depending on the nature and size of the balance of payments problem.[26] Balance of payments assistance to low-income countries may also be provided through a special trust (the Poverty Reduction and Growth Facility (PRGF) Trust) at concessional terms.[27] Through the Special Drawing Rights (SDRs) Department members with a strong balance of payments and reserve positions provide unconditional liquidity to countries with balance of payments needs and a weak reserve position.[28]

The central question from the Community perspective concerning the IMF's balance of payments assistance function is whether financial contributions by the EU/euro area members to the IMF to finance balance of payments assistance to third countries, or the right of the EU Member States under the Articles of Agreement to obtain balance of payments assistance in case of balance of payments need, affect any Community competencies.

As mentioned above, one could argue that the Community's competence for monetary and exchange rate policy includes the power to participate in a cooperative organization with a mandate to provide balance of payments assistance. Under this analysis, balance of payments assistance would be regarded as a form of exchange rate policy in a wider sense. The question is whether a Community competence in this regard would be exclusive in the sense that the Member States would be prevented from providing bilateral balance of payments assistance to third countries or from participating in a multilateral organization with a balance of payments assistance mandate. There is nothing in the EC Treaty that would suggest that the power to provide international balance of payments assistance is exclusively tied to the competence for monetary and exchange rate

---

[26] *See* IMF *Annual Report 2000*, p. 68.
[27] *See Selected Decisions*, Twenty-Fifth Issue, p. 44. As of April 30, 2000, 29 members had loan arrangements under the PRGF with agreed amounts of SDR 3.516 billion and undrawn balances of SDR 2.018 billion. Total loans outstanding under current and previous arrangements amounted to SDR 5.77 billion to 56 members; see p. 211 and 214 of *Annual Report 2000*.
[28] The overall allocation of SDR currently amounts to SDR 21.43 billion, which would be doubled under the Fourth Amendment to SDR 42.86 billion. For the existing allocation and the proposed allocations under the Fourth Amendment, *see Annual Report 2000*, Appendix II, Table 12.

policy. Financial assistance for balance of payments purposes can be provided as part of the general international financial cooperation of a country, which in the case of the EU largely remains in the competence of the Member States.

Concerning access of euro area Member States to IMF resources, some argue that access by a euro area country to IMF resources would breach the prohibition contained in Article 101 EC Treaty that the ECB and the national central banks are prohibited from extending credit to a Member State or Community bodies. This argument is based on the assumption that at least one euro area Member State would continue to contribute to the operational budget of the IMF through its national central bank (NCB), in which case the balance of payments assistance for a euro area country by the IMF could be indirectly cofinanced by the NCB of another euro area member.

It has to be noted in this regard that Council Regulation No. 3603/93 of December 13, 1993 specifies definitions for the application of the prohibitions referred to in Articles 104 and 104a (now 101 and 102) EC Treaty. This regulation contains a number of exceptions to the prohibition of monetary financing. In particular, Article 7 stipulates that the financing by the ECB or by the NCBs of obligations falling upon the public sector vis-à-vis the IMF shall not be regarded as credit facility within the meaning of Article 101 of the EC Treaty. Unless this interpretation is changed, Article 101 EC Treaty does not seem to provide an argument against access to IMF resources by individual EU Member States.

Access to IMF resources is currently not a major issue for the euro area countries. However, the participation in the IMF decision-making bodies on financial assistance to third countries are important elements of the foreign (financial) policy of the EU Member States. Coordination on these matters not only takes place at the Community level but also at country groupings like the G-7 or the G-10. It appears from the foregoing that the Community and the Member States share competencies for international balance of payments assistance.

The Heavily Indebted Poor Countries (HIPC) Initiative

In 1996, the IMF and the World Bank launched the HIPC Initiative[29] to provide debt relief for members with unsustainable external debt levels. Together with other multilateral international financial institutions (e.g., the African Development Bank, the Inter American Development Bank), official bilateral creditors (Paris Club), and commercial creditors, a framework was created to reduce the external debt levels of the poorest countries to sustainable levels.[30] Both the Community and the Member States have competencies in the area of international development cooperation (see Article 177 EC Treaty).

Global Financial Architecture—Financial Sector Issues

The financial crises of the 1990s exposed weaknesses in the international monetary and financial system. In response, the IMF is now involved in the reform efforts regarding the global financial architecture.[31] Some of the financial architecture issues discussed and decided by the Executive Board implicate Community competencies, for example the Code on Good Practices on Transparency in *Monetary* and Financial Policies, while others relate to policy areas for which the Member States remain responsible.

Obligations of Members

Membership in the IMF entails a number of specific obligations, in particular, concerning exchange arrangements, restrictions on payments and transfers for current international transactions, provision of economic information, and financing of the IMF. The fulfillment of these obligations implicates Community competencies.

---

[29] In 1999, the debt relief under the HIPC Initiative was augmented and the procedure streamlined. The HIPC Initiative is, therefore, often referred to as the *Enhanced* HIPC Initiative.

[30] IMF assistance under the HIPC Initiative is provided through a Trust for Special PRGF Operations for the Heavily Indebted Poor Countries and Interim PRGF Subsidy Operations, *see Selected Decisions*, Twenty-Fifth Issue, p. 80.

[31] *See* overview on page 37 of IMF *Annual Report 2000*, and Progress in Strengthening the International Financial Architecture—A Factsheet, dated July 31, 2000, at IMF web pages: http://www.imf.org/external /np/exr/facts/arcguide.htm.

Exchange Arrangements

Article IV of the Articles contains obligations concerning exchange arrangements. The general obligation is "to collaborate with the Fund and the other members to ensure orderly exchange arrangements and to promote a stable system of exchange rates" (Article IV, Section 1).[32] On exchange-regime matters all competencies are transferred from the Member States to the Community level. According to Article 111(1) EC Treaty, the Council can conclude formal arrangements for the euro in relation to non-Community currencies, and adopt, adjust, or abandon the central rates of the euro within the exchange rate system. In the absence of an exchange rate system referred to in Article 111(1) EC Treaty, the Council can formulate general orientations for exchange rate policy in relation to these currencies. In the absence of such guidelines, the ECB appears to be responsible for exchange rate policy. Article 105(2), second indent EC Treaty assigns the ESCB the task to "conduct foreign exchange operations consistent with the provisions of Article 111."

---

[32] The full text of Section 1 reads as follows:

"Recognizing that the essential purpose of the international monetary system is to provide a framework that facilitates the exchange of goods, services, and capital among countries, and that sustains sound economic growth, and that a principal objective is the continuing development of the orderly underlying conditions that are necessary for financial and economic stability, each member undertakes to collaborate with the Fund and other members to assure orderly exchange arrangements and to promote a stable system of exchange rates. In particular each member shall:

(i) endeavor to direct its economic and financial policies toward the objective of fostering orderly economic growth with reasonable price stability, with due regard to its circumstances;

(ii) seek to promote stability by fostering orderly underlying economic and financial conditions and a monetary system that does not tend to produce erratic disruptions;

(iii) avoid manipulating exchange rates or the international monetary system in order to prevent effective balance of payment adjustment or to gain an unfair competitive advantage over other members; and

(iv) follow exchange policies compatible with the undertaking under this section."

Given the loss of competencies for exchange rate matters at the Member State level, it is the Community that is today in a position to collaborate with the IMF and the other members to ensure orderly exchange arrangements and to promote a stable system of exchange rates. Although the Community is not a party to the IMF Articles of Agreement, in light of the European Court of Justice's jurisprudence on the binding effects of the GATT (1947) agreement for the Community, the Community has to be considered bound by the obligations under the IMF Articles of Agreement with regard to exchange arrangements.[33]

Avoidance of Restrictions on Current Payments Arrangements

According to Article VIII, Section 2(a) of the Articles, no member shall without the approval of the Fund impose restrictions on the making of payments and transfers for current international transactions. Both the Community and the Member States are in a position to take measures that could constitute restrictions falling under Article VIII, Section 2(a) of the Articles. The same is true for discriminatory currency practices under Article VIII, Section 3 of the Articles. The EC Treaty (Articles 56 to 60) has a chapter on the free movement of capital and payments which sets out Community law obligations in this regard and provides for Community powers to impose in exceptional circumstances restrictions on capital movements and payments. As a result, Article VIII, Sections 2 and 3 of the Articles relate to competencies both of the Community and the Member States.

Economic Information

Under Article VIII, Section 5 of the Articles, the IMF can require members to furnish it with the information necessary for its activities. Information required under Article VIII relates to areas of Community and Member State competencies. For example, the ESCB is responsible "to hold and manage the official reserves of the Member States" (Article 105(2), third indent EC Treaty), while the Member States are still responsible for producing national balance of payments statistics and national income statistics.

---

[33] *See* commentary to Article 234 (now 307) of the EC Treaty in Groeben, Thiesing, Ehlermann, Kommentar zum EU-EG-Vertrag, Zweite Auflage (1997), p. 584.

Financial Obligations

The most important financial obligation under the Articles is the obligation to make quota subscription payments. Part of the subscription payment is made in reserve currency, the remainder in the currency of the member.[34] Participation in the SDR Department may involve the obligation to provide foreign currency against the SDRs of another member, either in voluntary agreements or in transactions by designation.[35] Under the New Arrangements to Borrow (NAB) and the General Arrangements to Borrow (NAB) participants may be obliged—upon activation of these borrowing arrangements—to provide additional resources to the IMF.[36] Members that have committed resources to the PRGF Trust or the HIPC Initiative have to fulfill their financial obligations with regard to these two activities of the IMF.[37]

As discussed above, the financing of the balance of payments assistance activity of the IMF by the Member States does not appear to implicate exclusive competencies of the Community. The Member States remain competent to incur and fulfill the type of financial obligations resulting from the IMF Articles of Agreement. However, the Community would also be competent to assume such financial obligations.

Rights under the Articles of Agreement

The Right to Access IMF Resources (Article V, Section 3 of the Articles)

Under the conditions set forth in Article V, Section 3 of the Articles, as further specified by Executive Board decisions implementing Article V, Section 3, IMF members are entitled to receive balance of payments assistance from the IMF. This right of the EU/euro area Member States does not appear to be affected by the EC Treaty. As long as the member complies with the fiscal targets set

---

[34] Article III, Section 3 of the Articles.
[35] Article XIX, Sections (2) and (5) of the Articles.
[36] The NAB were activated for the first time in December 1998.
[37] Concerning the financing of the PRGF Trust and the HIPC Initiative see IMF *Annual Report 2000*, p. 126.

out in the 1997 Stability and Growth Pact,[38] Community law does not restrict the right to obtain external financing in case of balance of payments need (including financing from the IMF). However, if, to achieve IMF program targets, the Member State had to take measures in areas of exclusive Community competence (for example, monetary policy or exchange rate policy), it could be the case that without the cooperation of the Community institutions, the Member State would no longer be in a position to agree on a program with the IMF.

On the other hand, if the Community institutions decided that the Community/euro area as a whole had a balance of payments problem, the question is whether the Community could adopt a decision requesting the Member States to seek financial assistance from the IMF and requiring that the use of such assistance be determined at the Community level. One could argue that such a decision could be based on the Community's competencies for monetary and exchange rate policy. In such an unlikely scenario, the ECB would be in a position to act as fiscal agent for the Member States in their relations with the IMF (see Article 30.5 of the Statute of the European System of Central Banks and the European Central Bank).

Right to Appoint or Elect Executive Directors

The right to appoint Governors to the Board of Governors, and the right to appoint or elect Executive Directors to the Executive Board are two important rights of IMF members under the Articles of Agreement.[39] Given the central role of Executive Directors in the decision making of the IMF, the question is whether competencies of the Community on IMF matters give it the right to participate in the selection process of Executive Directors. Traditionally, those Member States that appoint Executive Directors have always appointed their own nationals. Member States that elect Executive Directors have chosen nationals from the countries that form a constituency. While there seems to be no legal obligation on the part of the Member States to coordinate the appointment and election of Executive Directors, one could argue that the power of the Council under Article 111(4) EC Treaty to decide the representation of the

---

[38] *See* footnote 24.
[39] Article XII, Section 2 (Board of Governors) and Section 3 (Executive Board).

Community in the IMF could include rules on the appointment and election of Executive Directors. It would require a unanimous decision by the Council.

The Respective Roles of the Community Institutions in the Community's Relations with the IMF

Another area that raises a number of questions concerns the respective roles of the Community institutions, in particular the Council, the ECB, and the Commission concerning those IMF matters that fall within the competence of the Community. For example, for the annual surveillance of the monetary and exchange rate policy of the euro area, which Community body is competent to determine the position of the euro area/the Community?

Vienna Conclusions and Article 105 EC Treaty

As mentioned above, the European Council meeting in Luxembourg (1997) had concluded that "[t]he Council and the European Central Bank will fulfill their tasks in representing the Community at international level in an efficient manner *and in compliance with the distribution of powers as laid down in the Treaty. The Commission will be associated with external representation insofar as necessary to enable it to fulfill the role assigned to it by the Treaty*" (emphasis added).[40]

The Vienna European Council Conclusions contain the following statement with regard to the respective distribution of roles between the ECB observer and the Council representative (emphasis added):

> The ECB, as the Community body *competent for monetary policy*, should be granted an observer status at the IMF board. The views of the European Community/EMU on *other issues of particular relevance to the EMU* would be presented at the IMF board by *the relevant member of the Executive Director's office of the Member States holding the euro presidency*, assisted by a representative of the Commission.

---

[40] Paragraph 46 of the Luxembourg European Council meeting Conclusions.

It is no surprise that the European Council, which refrained from giving any indication as to the substance of the distribution of competencies between the Member States and the Community, also refrained from addressing in detail the respective roles of the Community institutions as regards the exercise of Community competencies. For example, while the Vienna conclusions provide that the ECB should be granted an observer status at the IMF Executive Board, it is left open on which IMF matters the competence of the ECB becomes relevant. It is also left open which IMF matters would be taken up by the Council in the form of common positions on issues of particular relevance to EMU, or what participation of the Commission is "necessary to enable it to fulfill the role assigned by the Treaty."

Concerning the ECB, the Statute of the European System of Central Banks and the European Central Bank (the ESCB Statute) as part of the EC Treaty contains a number of provisions on the international cooperation of the European System of Central Banks.

International Cooperation of the ECB/ESCB

Article 6 ESCB Statute reads as follows:

6.1 In the field of international cooperation involving the tasks entrusted to the ESCB, the ECB shall decide how the ESCB shall be represented.

6.2 The ECB, and subject to its approval, the national central banks may participate in international monetary institutions.

6.3 Article 6.1 and 6.2 ESCB Statute shall be without prejudice to Article 111(4) of the EC Treaty.

The application of Article 6.1 requires an interpretation of what is covered by "international cooperation involving the tasks of the ESCB." The tasks of the ESCB are set out in Article 105 EC Treaty.

Tasks of the ESCB—Article 105 EC Treaty

Article 105 EC Treaty attributes the following tasks to the ESCB:

2. The basic tasks to be carried out through the ESCB shall be:

- to define and implement the monetary policy of the Community;

- to conduct foreign exchange operations consistent with the provisions of Article 111;

- to hold and manage the official reserves of the Member States;

- to promote the smooth operation of payment systems.

5. The ESCB shall contribute to the smooth conduct of policies pursued by the competent authorities relating to the prudential supervision of credit institutions and the stability of the financial system.

6. The Council may, acting unanimously on a proposal from the Commission and after consulting the ECB and after receiving the assent from the European Parliament, confer upon the ECB specific tasks concerning the policies relating to the prudential supervision of credit institutions and other financial institutions with the exception of insurance undertakings.

The most relevant tasks of the ESCB with regard to the IMF are (i) monetary policy (Article 105(2), first indent EC Treaty), (ii) the conduct of foreign exchange operations (Article 105(2), second indent EC Treaty), and (iii) the holding and managing of the official reserves of the Member States (Article 105(2), third indent EC Treaty).

While the presentation of the ESCB's monetary policy within the IMF through the ECB observer is clearly covered by its task "to define and implement the monetary policy of the Community," it is unclear how the other tasks of the ESCB/ECB translate into specific competencies on IMF matters. On exchange rate matters, the Council has competencies in accordance with Article 111(1) and (2) EC Treaty. One would assume that the February 2000 understanding between the ECB and the Economic and Financial Committee regulates in detail how the ECB and the Council cover exchange rate policy issues. However, this understanding has not been published. In addition, while it is clear that Community institutions are now responsible for formulating and presenting the monetary and exchange rate policy of the Community, it is unclear whether with regard to the monetary and exchange rate policy of non-EU IMF members the Community institutions have a role in determining common positions. For example, does Community law require a common position on the monetary and exchange rate policy of the United Sates or Japan for the Article IV consultation of these countries, or are common positions limited to the monetary and exchange rate policy of the euro area? It is not obvious whether the common monetary and exchange rate policy of the euro area has to include a common position on the monetary and exchange rate policy of third countries. However, if such common positions were adopted at the Community level, they would be binding on the Member States.

Holding of IMF Reserve Positions and SDR and Pooling of Such Assets

With regard to the holding of IMF reserve positions, Articles 30.5 and 30.6 ESCB Statute provide for the following:

> 30.5 The ECB may hold and manage IMF reserve positions and SDR and provide for the pooling of such assets.

> 30.6 The Governing Council shall take all other measures necessary for the application of this Article.

Under the Articles of Agreement, only the Member States can legally hold reserve positions and be allocated SDR in the SDR Department.[41] However, the Articles do not prevent the EU/euro area members from entrusting the ECB with the operational aspects of their quota payments and their participation in the SDR Department as long as the Member States, as the IMF members, continue to comply with their obligations under the Articles. The quota payments and SDR allocations/holdings would legally remain financial positions of the Member States despite the operational involvement of the ECB as their fiscal agent.

---

[41] However, the Articles do provide for the status of a prescribed holder of SDRs for nonmembers. A prescribed holder may exchange SDR against freely usable currencies in transactions by agreement with IMF member countries and other prescribed holders (Article XVII, Section 3 of the Articles). The ECB was approved as a prescribed holder of SDRs on November 15, 2000; *see Selected Decisions*, Twenty-Fifth Issue, p. 524.

The central question concerning Article 30.5 and 30.6 ESCB Statute is which body decides whether the ECB is involved in managing the reserve position and SDRs. Could the Governing Council of the ECB take such a decision on the basis of 30.6 ESCB Statute on its own, or would such a decision be taken at the political level by the Council?

In this regard, Article 6.3 ESCB Statute on the international cooperation of the ESCB could be relevant. Article 6.3 of the ESCB Statute provides that "Article 6.1 and 6.2 ESCB Statute shall be without prejudice to Article 111 (4) of this Treaty." Article 111 (4) of the EC Treaty stipulates that the decision by the Council on the representation of EMU has to be "in compliance with the powers laid down in Articles 99 and 105." Seen together, these provisions can be understood to mean that the Council decides on the external representation of the Community, thereby taking into account the powers allocated to the ESCB under Article 105 EC Treaty. The ECB on the other hand, when deciding on the international cooperation involving the tasks entrusted to the ESCB, is bound to respect the Council decision(s) on the external representation of EMU. With regard to the decision on the management, holding and pooling of reserve positions and SDRs, it would appear that such a decision could not be taken by the ECB without the approval of the Council.

Concerning the role of the ECB on IMF matters, a distinction might be necessary between those matters that have to be covered by the ECB and are protected by its independence (e.g., the representation of the monetary policy of the ESCB) and other matters where the ECB would act more as an agent of the Community within parameters set by the Council. It remains to be seen what role the ECB will have on "other IMF" matters that do not directly affect the definition, implementation, and representation of the ESCB's monetary policy.

The Role of the Commission

The Luxembourg European Council had concluded with regard to the Commission that "[t]he Commission will be associated with external representation insofar as necessary to enable it to fulfill the role assigned to it by the Treaty. The report by the Council to the

Vienna European Council had concluded with regard to the IMF that "the views of the European Community/EMU would be presented at the IMF Board by the relevant member of the Executive Director's office of the Member States holding the Euro 11 Presidency, *assisted by a representative from the Commission"* (emphasis added).

This raises the question of the role of the Commission on IMF matters, both with regard to its competencies on substantive issues and its role in the formal representation of the Community in the IMF. The Commission has a central role in the implementation of Article 111(4) EC Treaty. Under both alternatives of Article 111(4) EC Treaty, the Commission has the exclusive right of initiative, i.e., only the Commission can make a proposal for a common position on an issue of particular relevance to EMU and for a Council decision on the representation of the Community in the Fund. A decision on the position of the Community as regards issues of particular relevance to economic and monetary union is taken by "a qualified majority." This means that the regime of weighted voting set out in Article 205 EC Treaty applies to these decisions.[42] In accordance with Article 250 EC Treaty, the Commission proposal can only be amended by the Council through a unanimous decision; the Council is not in a position to amend the Commission proposal by a qualified majority.[43]

---

[42] At present France, Germany, Italy, and the United Kingdom each have 10 votes. Spain has 8, while Portugal, the Netherlands, Greece, and Belgium each have 5. Austria and Sweden each have 4, Denmark, Ireland, Finland each have 3, and Luxembourg has 2 votes. Sixty-two votes in favor are needed where the EC Treaty requires a decision on a proposal from the Commission. However, under the draft Treaty of Nice, the present Article 205(2) of the EC Treaty will be replaced on January 1, 2005 by the following regime of weighted voting: France, Germany, Italy, and the United Kingdom will each have 29 votes. The other votes are distributed as follows: Spain, 27; the Netherlands, 13; Belgium, Greece, and Portugal, 12; Austria and Sweden, 10; Denmark, Ireland, and Finland, 7; and Luxembourg, 4. Acts of the Council shall then require for their adoption at least 169 votes in favor cast by a majority of the members. According to Article 122(5) EC Treaty, the EU Member States who do not participate in monetary union do not vote on decisions under Article 111 EC Treaty. The majorities will therefore be different, depending on the membership of monetary union.

[43] Article 250 EC Treaty provides in this regard: (1) Where, in pursuance of this Treaty, the Council acts on a proposal from the Commission, unanimity shall be required for an act constituting an

This procedural rule gives the Commission considerable influence since its proposals can either only be modified unanimously or be rejected entirely.

Decisions on the representation of the Community as regards EMU have to be taken unanimously by the Council under the current version of the EC Treaty. After the entering into force of the amendments agreed in the Nice Treaty, the Council will take these decisions with a qualified majority.

The Commission also has significant competencies on matters that affect the Communities relations with the IMF. For example, the Commission has a lead role in the accession process of the EU accession countries, many of which have or had IMF-supported programs. On trade issues and with regard to the Common Market, the Commission has extensive powers. IMF staff maintain regular consultations with Commission officials.

The explanatory memorandum to the previously mentioned Commission proposal for a Council decision on the external representation of EMU made reference to a Community "Observer Office" at the Fund that would be made up of the Commission and the ECB. It remains to be seen whether the direct institutional links between the Fund and the Community will be limited to the ECB observer, or whether in the future the Community will establish broader relations with the Fund and would be represented not only by the ECB and the Council but also by the Commission.

Exercise of Community Competencies under the Current Articles of Agreement

This following section gives an overview of how competencies of the Community institutions on IMF matters could be exercised under the current Articles of Agreement.

---

amendment to that proposal, subject to Article 251(4) and (5). (2) As long as the Council has not acted, the Commission may alter its proposal at any time during the procedures leading to the adoption of a Community act.

The IMF Decision-Making Bodies

The IMF is a country-based international organization, membership is limited to countries, and an international organization cannot become a member of the IMF under the current Articles of Agreement.[44] It is a financial institution with a rather unique financial structure. Each IMF member is assigned a quota expressed in Special Drawings Rights, the IMF's unit of account.[45] Quotas are based on a number of economic criteria and are subject to review every five years.[46] Each member has to make subscription payments for its quota, partly in reserve currency, partly in domestic currency.[47] The voting power of members in the IMF's decision-making bodies is determined by the quota assigned to each member.[48]

The IMF has two decision-making bodies, the Board of Governors and the Executive Board. The Board of Governors consists of one Governor and one Alternate appointed by each member. The Board of Governors is the highest decision-making body of the IMF. All powers not directly conferred to the Executive Board or the Managing Director are vested with the Board of Governors. The main decision-making body, however, is the Executive Board to which the Board of Governors has delegated the exercise of all powers of the Board of Governors, except the powers

---

[44] Article II of the Articles of Agreement.

[45] The valuation of the SDR is determined by the Executive Board (Article XV, Section 2). Since January 1, 2001, the SDR value has been determined by a basket of currencies, which are weighted according to a currency-based method (in contrast to the member-based approach applied before). The basket currently consists of the U.S. dollar (US$0.5770), the Japanese yen (yen 21), the euro (0.4260), and the pound sterling (0.0984); see *Selected Decisions*, Twenty-Fifth Issue, p. 519.

[46] See Article III of the Articles of Agreement. As of February 28, 2001, the United States has the largest quota with SDR 37,149.3 million (17.49 percent of total quota), followed by Japan with SDR 13,312.8 million (6.27 of total quota), Germany with SDR 13,008.2 million (6.12 percent of total quota), France with SDR 10,738.5 million (5.06 percent of total quota), and the United Kingdom with SDR 10,738.5 million (5.06 percent of total quota).

[47] Article III, Section 3(a) of the Articles.

[48] Article XII, Section 2(e) of the Articles (Board of Governors) and Article XII, Section 3(i) and (iii) of the Articles (Executive Board).

conferred directly on the Board of Governors by the Articles.[49] The Executive Board currently has 24 Executive Directors, and is chaired by the Managing Director of the IMF.[50] The basic rule is that the five members with the largest quota each appoint an Executive Director while the other members form constituencies to elect Executive Directors.[51] Elections of Executive Directors take place at intervals of two years.[52] Voting in the decision-making bodies of the IMF is by weighted voting. Each IMF member is assigned 250 votes plus one additional vote for each part of its quota equivalent to 100,000 SDR.[53] In the Board of Governors, each Governor casts the votes allotted to the member appointing him.[54] In the Executive Board, an Executive Director casts the votes allotted to the member appointing him, or the votes that counted toward his election.[55] Executive Directors elected by several members cannot split their vote.[56]

Participation of the IMF Members in the Decision Making of the Fund

The IMF members participate in the decision making of the IMF through the Executive Directors appointed or elected by them. In this respect, the representation of members in the Executive Board is different from most other international organizations where countries are represented in the decision-making bodies through national delegations often headed by an ambassador. The five members that appoint Executive Directors have the most direct influence over "their" Executive Directors. The same is currently true for the Executive Directors elected by Russia, China, and Saudi Arabia, which each form constituencies of their own. Executive Directors that are elected by a group of countries are integrated in consultation procedures with the authorities of all countries electing them.

---

[49] *See* Article XII, Section 2(b), Article XII, Section 3(a) of the Articles and Section 15 of the IMF By-Laws.
[50] For up-to-date composition of the Executive Board see http://www.imf.org/external/np/sec/memdir/eds.htm.
[51] Article XII, Section 3(b) of the Articles (currently the United States, Japan, Germany, France, and the United Kingdom).
[52] Article XII, Section 3(d) of the Articles.
[53] Article XII, Section 5(a) of the Articles.
[54] Article XII, Section 2(e) of the Articles.
[55] Article XII, Section 3(i) (i) and (ii) of the Articles.
[56] Article XII, Section 3(i) (iv) of the Articles.

There are basically no rules on which countries can form a constituency to elect "their" Executive Director. In particular, there are no rules that would provide for regional constituencies. EU countries, for example, do not form EU-only constituencies, but are part of rather diverse constituencies. Ireland and Spain are in constituencies with only non-European countries. As of August 15, 2001, nationals from Belgium, Finland, Italy, and the Netherlands are elected Executive Directors, and nationals from Austria, Greece, Ireland, Spain, and Sweden are Alternate Executive Directors.[57]

In this institutional framework, there are two avenues through which Community competencies on IMF matters could be exercised.

First, with regard to decisions on IMF matters that are taken directly by the authorities of the euro area countries (for example, acceptance of amendments to the Articles of Agreement, consent to quota increases, appointment of Executive Directors, or formation of constituencies to elect Executive Directors) binding decisions by the Community institutions could produce direct legal effects on the Member States under general principles of Community law.

Second, on the large majority of IMF matters that are discussed and decided by the Executive Board, the exercise of Community competencies is limited to its influence over Executive Directors in a similar fashion as national authorities can influence Executive Directors.

National authorities have two main tools to influence Executive Directors: consultation and instruction. While the normal procedure will be consultation, national laws do provide for formal instructions. This raises the question whether (i) the Community institutions, as a matter of Community law, have to be included in the consultation procedures between Executive Directors and "their authorities," and (ii) whether the Community could issue instructions, whether on a case-by-case basis or in general form, similar to national legislation, on the positions and voting of EU Executive Directors.

---

[57] *See* http://www.imf.org/external/np/sec/memdir/eds.htm.

It appears that the common positions adopted following the procedures set out in the February 2000 understanding in the EFC are followed by the Executive Directors in the Article IV consultation of the euro area. If these positions were adopted on the basis of Article 111(4) EC Treaty, they would be binding for the Member States, and the Member States in their consultation with Executive Directors would have to ensure that the Executive Directors represent the position determined at the Community level. Further, if one accepts that the Community's competence for monetary and exchange rate policy includes the power to provide and receive balance of payments assistance in the context of a multilateral organization like the IMF, one could take the view that the Community could adopt common positions on these matters with binding effects for the Member States (for example, a common position on decisions concerning the Stand-By Arrangement for Turkey). A similar line of reasoning could conclude that the Community could adopt common positions on the monetary and exchange rate policy of third countries, which again would be binding on its Member States. Such common positions could be adopted on the basis of Article 111(4) EC Treaty. However, while it seems possible that the Community could adopt common positions on issues of access to IMF resources and surveillance of third countries, it does not appear that the Community is under a legal obligation to do so.

Conclusion

The EC Treaty could have provided for a clearer framework for the external relations of EMU. However, it is not unusual that the external relations of the Community are scarcely regulated and give rise to numerous questions of interpretation because most Treaty provisions in this area contain compromise language agreed to at the last minute of Treaty negotiations.

The IMF membership of the euro area countries clearly implicates Community competencies, in particular for monetary and exchange rate policy. However, it is less obvious how these competencies translate into specific powers on IMF matters. Article 111(4) EC Treaty appears to give the Council a certain discretion whether to leave the responsibility for IMF matters with the Member States, or to adopt binding common positions and formal decisions on the representation of the Community in the IMF, which would lead to more decision making on IMF matters at the Community level. The majority requirements for decisions under Article 111(4) EC Treaty require broad consensus at the Community level on how to proceed. It remains to be seen whether the Community has the political will to agree on common policies on IMF matters. Absent such decisions, the Member States appear to continue to exercise their IMF membership largely as a matter of national competence, subject to nonbinding consultation and coordination at the Community level (with the notable exception of the presentation of the monetary and exchange rate policy of the euro area at the Executive Board).

III. Architecture of the International Monetary System

Chapter 9

Prevention of Financial Crises: A Overview of the Public Sector Asp... the International Financial Architecture

JOHN HICKLIN

The use of the word "architecture" to describe the work undertaken to improve the functioning of the international financial system in the wake of the financial crises of the 1990s is firmly established, despite some awkwardness of the terminology. It is awkward not only because it is a term adopted from another profession, but because it suggests sweeping changes, a new design, and even, perhaps, a starting from scratch. However, most of the wide-ranging topics grouped under this rubric of architecture are more accurately described as revisions, adaptations, or other incremental changes to the policies or practices of the various participants in the international financial system. This paper reviews the collection of tasks under the overall heading of architecture, with a focus on the public sector aspects; that is, the changes in policies and practices that both national and international official bodies, ranging from individual member country governments to the IMF itself, are adopting. The initiatives constitute a lengthy and challenging mandate for the international community, their incremental nature notwithstanding, but it is useful to recognize that the present cooperative efforts to reform the international financial system are more evolutionary than revolutionary.

The Main Areas of the Reform of the International Financial Architecture

One way to approach the broad and complex set of issues subsumed under the architecture is to break it into five main initiatives of crisis prevention and two of crisis resolution, along with one additional item, which is the overall organization of the international financial community, e.g., the role of the Fund and of other institutions and fora, such as the Financial Stability Forum, the G-20, the G-24, and others. This approach draws on a key IMF report on the international financial architecture, the semiannual statement and report of the IMF Managing Director to the IMF's ministerial body (the International Monetary and Financial Committee, or IMFC) on the reform of the IMF and of the international financial system.[1]

The five topics of crisis prevention are:

1. Transparency and Accountability;

2. Developing and Assessing Standards, Principles, and Guidelines;

3. Strengthening Financial Systems;

4. External Vulnerability;

5. Capital Account Liberalization, Capital Controls, and Exchange Rate Regimes.

These crisis prevention topics tend to be associated more with the involvement of the public sector, rather than private sector, but as will be discussed below, there are limits to this distinction.

The two main areas associated with crisis resolution and management are:

6. Involving the Private Sector in Forestalling and Resolving Crises; and

7. The Reform of the IMF's Financial Facilities.

It should be noted that the reform of Fund facilities also deals with crisis prevention.

---

[1] The most recent of these reports at the time of the Seminar was "The Statement and Report of the Acting Managing Director to the International Monetary and Financial Committee on Progress in Reforming the IMF and Strengthening the Architecture of the International Financial System," April 12, 2000. An update of the report was released at the time of the World Bank–IMF Annual Meetings and is dated September 19, 2000. This Seminar paper lays out the status of the reform initiatives up to May 2000, but the September 2000 and subsequent papers, along with other materials on the IMF external website (www.imf.org), provide information on the main areas in which there has been further progress since then.

The additional topic noted above, which is not mentioned explicitly in the IMF architecture report, but which is certainly part of the agenda, is:

8. The Organization of the International Financial Community.

An Overview of the Reform Efforts

To gain a good overview of the reform efforts, it is useful to ask what binds together these quite diffuse topics. One factor is that many of the individual ideas were specifically initiated in response to the particular features of what some observers have called "a new breed of crisis": the series of financial crises that began with Mexico in the mid-1990s and then resumed in the late 1990s with the developments in Asia, Russia, Brazil, and elsewhere. Certainly, these events still involved elements of the macroeconomic imbalances that had characterized "old-fashioned" crises, such as large fiscal or current account deficits. But the key feature of the new crises has been the role of large, short-term, cross-border private capital flows, or more broadly, the new reality of globalized international capital markets, made possible, in part, by rapid technological changes.

These international capital flows—both inflows and outflows—are influenced by perceptions of the asset-liability structure of an economy. But the flows themselves have the power to produce dramatic stock imbalances in the asset-liability position of the banking sector, or in the financial, corporate, and public finance sectors more generally. The centrality of cross–border capital flows in the new crises accounts for many of the other defining features of recent financial turmoils, such as the speed with which they develop. The days are gone when discussions between the IMF and national authorities could take place at a predictable, if not a leisurely, pace, which might extend over the course of several months and leave the authorities the breathing space to decide whether they wanted to take reforms this month, next month, or wait a little while longer until the political momentum for enacting changes was in place. Now, large, short-term, cross-border private capital flows can generate crises, which require policy responses where speed, timing, and magnitude are critical factors.

Another defining feature of the recent financial crises that derives from the central role of international flows of private capital is that many different players are involved in each of the eight main areas of the architecture listed above. It is no longer just a question of the IMF advising that something should or should not be done by member countries, nor of national authorities deciding on their own, without thought of the private sector's response, to effect changes in their domestic policy and regulatory environment. Now, the private sector is crucially involved in many of these changes. Thus, while Topic 6—involving the private sector in preventing or forestalling and resolving crises—is the most high-profile area involving the nonofficial sector, the private sector also has roles to play under the five "crisis prevention" topics.

For example, in the area of transparency and accountability, the objective is not just to make public bodies more transparent and accountable, but also the private sector. Objectives for the private sector include better accounting rules and more-transparent company statements, with the goal of helping markets to make better-informed choices. A second example relates to the realization that the financial markets now share the driving seat with country authorities in terms of the direction of economic policy. The private sector pushes and pulls the levers of economic decision making by its reactions to government policies and the announcement of economic information, reactions that it signals in the form of investment and other financial behavior. Following the Mexico crisis, the Fund established the Special Data Dissemination Standard (SDDS), which would allow the markets a better assessment of country data provision by providing guidelines for good data dissemination practices. The Fund's role in the process was getting the system in place, and the country authorities' role was to use the system to achieve better data dissemination. However, the ultimate objective is that the private sector would, in reaction to what the SDDS could help reveal about country data practices, be sending feedback directly to the countries themselves. These are examples of how the private sector is intimately involved even in the reforms to the architecture that are mostly considered "public sector."

It is important to note that while it was in Mexico, Asia, Russia, and elsewhere that the "new breed of crisis" first appeared, this does not mean that the architecture agenda only relates to those countries or regions. The lessons learned and the potential for changes in policy and regulatory frameworks have very broad and far-reaching implications for all economies—industrial, emerging market, low-income, and transition.

Another thing that binds the topics under the reform of the international financial architecture is that many of them come under the broad context of strengthening IMF surveillance, the Fund's overseeing of the economic health of its member countries by continually assessing their circumstances and policies. Relatedly, many of these same reform initiatives (which the reader is reminded are mostly incremental changes to policies and practices already in place) are covered by the IMF's basic mandate as set out in the Articles of Agreement. While the reform initiatives are new and important, they fit in well with the Fund's responsibilities as drafted by its founders over 50 years ago. Thus, apart from the occasional radical proposal from among the many officials, academics, and commentators who have contributed to the debate on the reform of the international monetary and financial system in the wake of the recent crises, such as the proposal that the international financial institutions should be abolished altogether, most of the initiatives are relevant to the IMF's quintessential mandate to promote international monetary cooperation, exchange stability, and orderly exchange arrangements, and to foster economic growth and high levels of employment.

Transparency and Accountability

A few years ago, the IMF provided little information to the markets or the general public on its views on member country policies or on its financial arrangements. There has been a sea change in the transparency of the IMF. As a visit to the IMF's external website (www.imf.org) will suggest, it would now be much quicker and easier to list the few documents that the IMF does not make public, than to name the many operational, policy, and statistical reports that are posted there.

Perhaps the most dramatic change in transparency has been the release of the Fund's views on country policies. In its work on country surveillance, the Fund now releases, if the member country agrees, a Public Information Notice (PIN), which is a summary of the Executive Board's views on a member country's policies as discussed in the annual Article IV consultation. Under financial arrangements with a member country, the Fund now releases, again with the member's permission, letters of intent, memoranda of economic and financial policies, and other program documents. Despite the inevitable tension between the role of the Fund as a confidential advisor and, simultaneously, as a source for information and views on country policies to markets and to the public, the Fund membership has embraced transparency. About 80 percent of countries release PINs and about the same percentage release documents on their financial arrangements with the Fund. Moreover, a pilot project for the release of the Article IV staff reports, which are the full analyses by the IMF staff on an economy's strengths and vulnerabilities that go to the Board and form the basis of the Board's surveillance discussions, has been under way for almost a year. While the Fund staff anticipated that countries' reservations about this additional transparency measure might limit participation in the pilot, 60 countries, or a third of the membership, have volunteered to be in the pilot.[2]

The objectives of these transparency initiatives have been not only to make the Fund more accountable but also to better inform markets and other constituencies and civil society within countries on the complexities of economic debate and the nature of the policies being adopted.

Developing and Assessing Standards, Principles, and Guidelines

A second area of architectural reform, which is related to transparency, is the body of work that has been going on in the Fund and in other international institutions and fora to help develop and disseminate internationally accepted standards and codes deemed important to sound economic and financial systems, and also to help countries implement these standards and codes. Through these

---

[2] Following the IMF Executive Board's review of the pilot project, the voluntary release of staff reports for Article IV consultations and use of Fund resources was made a regular policy (*see* www.imf.org).

initiatives, national authorities can be more transparent about the way that their governments go about business.

The Fund has developed standards and codes on data dissemination, fiscal transparency, and monetary and financial policy transparency, which have been well received by the membership and increasingly recognized by the private sector. As suggested above, the Special Data Dissemination Standard (SDDS) was developed by the Fund to enhance the availability of timely and comprehensive statistics and therefore contribute to the pursuit of sound macroeconomic policies by countries, as well as the improved functioning of financial markets. Specifically, the SDDS is aimed at countries that access, or are preparing to access, the international capital markets.[3] The SDDS, which was initiated in 1996 in response to the Mexican financial crisis, has continued to evolve, and has been recently reinforced significantly in the area of reserves and external debt, key data weaknesses in the crises of the late 1990s. Forty-seven countries subscribe to the SDDS, which has resulted in quite sharp improvements in their national statistical systems, along with a better appreciation of the complexity of the issues involved in making reliable data more available to the public.

The second standard that was developed at the Fund was the Code of Good Practices on Fiscal Transparency (1998), and the third, the Code of Good Practices on Transparency in Monetary and Financial Policies (1999). One of the key lessons of the Asian crisis was that many of the crucial policy mistakes were not evident, even to other policymakers within the government, let alone to private investors, other market participants, or citizens. The fiscal Code and the monetary and financial policy Code are voluntary guides to help countries make their policies and policymaking more transparent. These Codes are being reflected in the surveillance advice given to national authorities and the technical assistance provided by the Fund.

A fourth standard that the Fund uses in its operations is the Basel Committee's Core Principles on Effective Banking Supervision (BCP). As the name suggests, the Basel Committee was instrumental

---

[3] The Fund's General Data Dissemination System (GDDS) was established in 1997 for other member countries not yet at the point of accessing the international capital market.

in establishing this code, but the Fund, the World Bank, and other bodies contributed extensively. The BCP, along with a methodology for assessing compliance with the principles, is being used by the Fund and the Bank as a key element of their joint work to help strengthen national financial systems.

While these four standards are the most central to the IMF's operations, there is a range of others: standards on securities regulation (by the International Organization of Securities Commissions (IOSCO)); insurance (by the International Association of Insurance Supervisors (IAIS)); payment and settlement systems (by the Committee on Payment and Settlement Systems (CPSS)); accounting and auditing (the International Accounting Standards Committee (IASC) and the International Federation of Accountants (IFAC)); corporate governance (Organization for Economic Cooperation and Development (OECD)); and bankruptcy provisions. These and other standards can be useful to the sound conduct of economic and financial policies.

Once standards are developed and disseminated, implementation becomes key. Assessment by independent and expert assessors can be an incentive for the effective implementation of standards. There is now the basic understanding among the international community that the Article IV surveillance process at the Fund is likely to provide the appropriate framework within which discussions on countries' adherence to standards can take place. The exact modalities of doing those assessments are still experimental. The IMF and the Bank have been producing Reports on the Observance of Standards and Codes, or ROSCs, which are summary assessments of countries' adherence to individual codes and standards. Many countries have now volunteered to be in the ROSC pilot. The Fund has been producing ROSCs on its data and fiscal transparency standards; the Fund and the Bank have been working together on assessing financial sector standards under the joint Financial Sector Assessment Program (FSAP), which is described below; and the Bank is looking at the assessment of some of the more newly developed standards on corporate governance, accounting and auditing, and bankruptcy provisions. The range of standards encompasses areas where the Fund does not have a core expertise, and where the institution will need to draw on the expertise of the other institutions that have been critically involved in the development of standards.

While the *raison d'être* for developing and implementing standards of good practices is simple, there are many complexities to the assessment process. An important one is the extent to which third-party assessment is critical to the credibility of the assessment. Another concerns the publication of these assessments; the publication of the experimental ROSCs is voluntary. But many would argue that without publication and dissemination of the results of the assessments, so that policymakers and markets can see where a country stands in relation to an accepted international benchmark, their value is considerably reduced. Others argue that, in the first instance, it is the authorities that need to see the assessments and not the markets or others, since the fundamental aim is for the country to muster the resources, time, and any needed international assistance to strengthen implementation, without being pressured by the markets. These issues are still under debate by the international community.[4]

Strengthening Financial Systems

Many member countries (not just those associated with the financial crises of the mid- to late-1990s) have experienced banking crises in the last 20 years, and it is well recognized that financial sector weaknesses lay at the heart of the Asian crisis. In the last two years, the international community has called for the IMF and the World Bank to pool their resources and strengthen their efforts to assess the state of financial sectors as a key tool of crisis prevention. A key manifestation of the enhanced financial sector surveillance is the Financial Sector Assessment Program (FSAP). The joint Fund-Bank FSAP provides an in-depth analysis and evaluation of the strengths, risks, and vulnerabilities of a country's financial sector, using tools such as macroprudential indicators and stress testing. Participation in the program is voluntary. To date, there have been 12 pilot FSAPs, and 24 more countries are now participating. The response here has been clear and strong. FSAPs have proved very valuable in highlighting vulnerabilities and developmental needs;

---

[4] The IMF Board discussion in early 2001 helped to clarify these issues (*see* www.imf.org).

enhancing Fund surveillance; providing input to IMF-supported programs; and helping to prioritize technical assistance requirements. FSAPs provide a comprehensive assessment of the state of the financial system, bringing in experts from around the world on banking, securities regulation, insurance, and payment systems.

External Vulnerability

The new reality of large, short-term, cross-border private capital flows increases the need for the early detection and management of vulnerability to external shocks, and this is a fourth component of the architectural reform. The IMF has been considering new ways of identifying and managing vulnerability linked to external debt and reserves. A new template for reporting data on international reserves and foreign currency liquidity has been agreed on; the prescriptions for reporting data on external debt to the Fund have been strengthened; the Fund is working with the Bank on a set of draft guidelines on public debt management; and the Fund is also developing a framework for sound practices in the management of foreign exchange reserves. The IMF has been drawing on the body of literature on early warning systems and vulnerability indicators, as well as conducting internal research and analysis. Identifying and managing vulnerability constitutes another area of the financial architecture that spans the public and private sectors.

Capital Account Liberalization, Capital Controls, and Exchange Rate Regimes

This topic encompasses some relatively controversial policy issues, including the pace and sequencing of capital account liberalization; the role of capital controls; and issues related to exchange rate regimes, which are central to the Fund's mandate. What role does the sequencing of capital account liberalization play in making a country vulnerable to crises? How does the choice of exchange rate regime, such as the alternatives of a pegged or floating system, make a country more or less vulnerable to a financial crisis? There are many different views on this broad spectrum of issues, and this is an area where the international community has not reached a resolution, in the same way that there is a consensus on the value of transparency measures or the importance of internationally accepted standards. One lesson that seems clear, though, is that in these areas of capital account and exchange rate policies, simple answers or hopes for a single "silver bullet" that will protect an economy over time from all potential shocks are bound to be misleading.

Two examples may illustrate this point. First, it is widely held that the maintenance of pegged exchange rate regimes contributed to the problems of several of the crisis countries in the late 1990s. However, the alternative of a rigidly fixed regime (a currency board, or adapting another currency) requires fundamental policy and institutional changes that may not be desirable or feasible. Another alternative of a "fully floating" regime is extremely rare, since in practice most central banks intervene in one way or another because they wish to smooth out fluctuations in demand or supply of foreign exchange and/or target particular levels of international reserve holdings. If the resulting policy prescription is, in fact, for "greater flexibility than a pegged rate," considerable judgment is required about the degree of flexibility and the means by which the credibility of the policy can be established. Another example of less than clear-cut policy prescription is the desirability of controls on particular forms of capital flows. After all, if some flows can have undesirable consequences, why not stop them? In practice, there is good advice to be given on preventing particular policies (legal, regulatory, or supervisory) that encourage the "wrong" type of flows, but outright bans on particular flows can often run into practical problems of ineffectiveness, given the ability in modern systems to circumvent specific regulations.

Involving the Private Sector in Forestalling and Resolving Crises

This topic, in many ways the most complex and in some ways the most controversial of all of the components of the architectural reform, is the subject of another paper in this volume, and will not be addressed further herein.[5]

---

[5] See the next chapter.

The Reform of the IMF's Financial Facilities

This seventh topic concerns adapting the range of facilities available to the Fund to assist its members, in order to enhance both crisis prevention and crisis resolution, and to help ensure a more efficient use of the Fund's financial resources. Part of the work in this area has been a housecleaning exercise to eliminate some little-used existing facilities and simplify others. Another part is much more fundamental, addressing the overall level of access of a member to Fund financial support; the rates of interest and other terms on the use of Fund resources; the very rationale of Fund financing, i.e., whether it is for the resolution of shorter-term policy problems or longer-term structural issues; and the extent to which Fund financial support may increase or decrease moral hazard.

Some have argued that countries with a history of involvement with the Fund through the actual use of Fund financial resources were better prepared for the turmoil of the late 1990s by having undertaken policy reforms within the context of a Fund-supported program before the crises hit. For example, countries that had had Fund precautionary arrangements[6] were often in a stronger position when financial volatility increased with the Asian crisis because they had built a consensus to undertake policy commitments and reforms, making them stronger and more resilient to shocks. This beneficial element of proactivity associated with precautionary arrangements got extended last year to a new IMF financial facility, the Contingent Credit Lines (CCL).

The CCL is the second facility created in response to the "new breed of financial crisis," as manifested by the crises of the late 1990s. The Supplementary Reserve Facility (SRF), created in December 1997 at the height of the Asian crisis, provides financial assistance to a country experiencing exceptional balance of payments difficulties due to a large short-term financing need resulting from a sudden and disruptive loss of market confidence reflected in pressure

---

[6] A precautionary arrangement is a stand-by or an extended arrangement under which the member agrees to meet specific conditions for use of IMF resources and make policy reforms even though it has indicated to the Executive Board its intention not to make drawings.

on the capital account and the member's reserves. With the SRF in place as a bold new Fund facility to address crisis management, the Fund began to work on a new facility focused on crisis prevention. The CCL is a precautionary line of defense readily available to member countries with strong economic policies. It is designed to prevent future balance of payments problems that might arise from international financial contagion. The essence of the CCL is that a country that undertakes certain preconditions and has its house in good economic order can be eligible for a rapid review of its position and Fund financial support, should it be affected by unfavorable changes in the international financial environment. The preconditions include that the policy framework of the country is satisfactory; that there has been progress in adherence to some of the various international standards described above, including subscription to the SDDS; and that there are sensible debt and risk management policies in place. The CCL has not actually been used yet, and one of the items under discussion in the review of Fund financial facilities concerns improving the usability and effectiveness of this facility.

The Organization of the International Financial Community

The reform of the international financial system includes the institutional organization of the international financial community. The Fund's relationship with the World Bank has been extended and strengthened, particularly in the financial sector area. Ties with other established official international bodies have been deepened, and links have been established with newer and more informal fora, such as the Financial Stability Forum (FSF). The FSF was established by the G-7 countries, but now has wider representation. Its purpose is to help promote international financial stability through enhanced information exchange and international cooperation in financial market supervision. In this regard, the FSF has played a role in bringing together not just central bankers and finance ministry officials but also representatives of the national supervisory agencies; the latter had often not been at the same table in the discussions of these various reforms, and yet they are obviously key players in many of these architectural initiatives. The proliferation of groups and fora is not without tension, for example, in terms of the selective membership in some cases. While Fund management and staff have worked with various fora, Fund decisions are ultimately taken by the

IMF's Executive Board and its ministerial group, the IMFC, through which the views of all of the countries of the Fund's near-universal membership are reflected.

Concluding Remarks

With this extensive, albeit summary, list of reform initiatives laid out, a natural question is whether these ideas have truly affected the operation of the international financial system to date, or are likely to do so. Are these reforms, even though intended to be evolutionary rather than revolutionary, fundamental, or are they tinkering at the margin?

Other periods of rapid change provide historical parallels. An example is the kind of intellectual change that took place at the time of the Industrial Revolution. Over a short space of time, technology in the goods markets produced developments that would have not been feasible a relatively few years earlier. One outcome of this was a rapid move towards establishing standards and codes. Standards for the production of various metals and for the measurement of temperature, time, and other parameters began to develop in Western Europe in the late eighteenth century, because the changes wrought by the Industrial Revolution made them important. Another outcome was the sharing of intellectual property between scientists (botanists, chemists, physicists, and others) with other disciplines, such as lawyers, businessmen, and financiers, and the search for a public framework that could secure the benefits of technological advancement. Today, one result of dramatic technological change is the globalization of the financial markets, and some parallels apply. International standards and codes of good practices are increasingly recognized as a global public good that helps ensure that economies function properly at the national level, which is a key prerequisite for a well-functioning international system. The "interconnectedness" of the international financial markets means that policymakers need to talk to statisticians, financial supervisors, lawyers, and accountants, all of whom bring different perspectives to the complexities of a global economy, and to creating a public framework that secures the benefits of capital flows, while reducing the risks of crises.

Much more needs to be done to make sure that the global financial system provides a solid foundation for economic and human development. But it is fair to say that the way the world makes economic policy and does financial business is changing because of the reforms of the international financial system that are under way. There are numerous examples of governments becoming more transparent and prudent in their policy framework, and of the private sector responding to such initiatives by differentiating more finely between country cases. A key test of the collection of reforms will not be that all crises are prevented, but that the probability of crises will be lower, especially those triggered by misunderstandings concerning a country's circumstances.

Chapter 10

Involving the Private Sector in the Avoidance and Resolution of Crisis

MARK ALLEN

The Mexican crisis of 1994 was memorably described by the Managing Director of the Fund, Mr. Camdessus, as the first financial crisis of the twenty-first century. Since then there have been crises in Thailand, Korea, Indonesia, Russia, the Czech Republic, Brazil, and Ecuador—all occurring before the twenty-first century had officially started. At the present rate, it is going to be quite a perilous century.

The main features of these crises have been the sudden loss of confidence by investors in a given country, the precipitate withdrawal of funds, and contagion, or fears of contagion, to other emerging market economies. In terms of the destruction of prosperity that these crises can wreak, they are very dangerous indeed.

In addition to the sheer virulence of these crises, the international community has several concerns about how to handle them. Restoring confidence and helping countries avoid the worst contractionary effects of the crisis require the injection of large amounts of public sector money. This has to be provided in a context of little domestic political support within industrial countries for bailing out the private sector. There is also concern that the use of large amounts of official resources leads to a mispricing of risk, creates moral hazard, and lays the seeds of even larger crises to come.

Since the crisis is triggered by the exit of private sector capital, and since the provision of official money goes, among other things, to ensure that the private sector gets paid, it is understandable that there are calls to find ways of ensuring that the private sector remains exposed to countries in crisis. But this is easier said than done. Nevertheless, as the official sector gradually develops a more coherent approach, the roles of the official and private sectors are beginning to be more clearly defined.

The program of the official sector, with the Fund playing a central role, has four aspects:

- action to prevent crises or reduce their incidence;
- ex ante measures to make it easier to handle crises;
- techniques for handling crises once they strike; and
- techniques for resolving crises.

On the first area, measures that are being taken by the international community to reduce the incidence of crises or their virulence, John Hicklin has already spoken.[1] As far as the relation of the work in this area with the private sector is concerned, the principal idea is that more and better information will allow commercial lenders to take better decisions (and that countries will not allow themselves to become vulnerable). The hope is that markets will not allow unsustainable positions to arise, and that any loss of confidence will come at an earlier stage, forcing earlier correction of policies. Better a smaller crisis earlier than a bigger crisis later. Information should flow as data and Fund surveillance activities become more transparent, and as countries adhere to relevant standards and codes.

But while this work may reduce the frequency of crises or their size, it will not eliminate them altogether. Markets, and particularly asset markets, are prone to sudden adjustments of value. Data may be there for all to see, but may not be internalized or fully understood by the market. When financial markets reappraise the creditworthiness of a counterparty, loss of confidence is likely to be reflected in a sudden withdrawal of funds and in a downward revision of the creditworthiness of those holding claims on the same counterparty. Even the provision of extensive, accurate, and timely data does not prevent the sudden loss of confidence in a country. So the next strand of work has been to see if action can be taken that would help prevent the withdrawal of funds from a country by the private sector in the event of such a shock.

---

[1] See the preceding chapter.

To what extent can ex ante measures be taken to ensure that the private sector will remain engaged should a crisis hit? Are there certain forms of international finance that should be encouraged and others discouraged to make it easier to cope with a drying up of international liquidity or to prevent it? The Fund and the official community more generally have been exploring a number of approaches in this regard.

One approach has been to establish insurance mechanisms for countries to give markets assurances that the country involved will have the resources to defend its currency and pay its debts on time. The simplest way to do this is of course to build up foreign exchange reserves, and emerging market countries have been very active in reducing their vulnerability in this way. The rule of thumb for an adequate reserve level for such countries has changed from the traditional three months of imports of goods and services to a broader measure allowing reserves to cover in addition all the country's short-term external obligations.

Accumulating additional reserves is expensive, however, and so countries have been considering other insurance mechanisms to give the private sector confidence in the event of a crisis. One possibility is to arrange a line of credit with private sector institutions that can be drawn in an emergency. Mexico and Argentina have tried such an approach, but with mixed results. One difficulty is pricing such lines: while it may be possible to contract them at a time when the country's borrowing costs are low, when the time comes to draw on such a line, pricing may be much tighter. Either the use of such a line of credit becomes very expensive to the country, and possibly more than it can afford even in a crisis, or the private sector may be concerned that it will take losses in the event of the line's being drawn. To avoid the latter outcome, private sector institutions will hedge their potential exposure, to avoid having to increase exposure to a country at an undesirable time. In practice, this seems to have happened in the case of Mexico, which drew on its line of credit, which had been priced to the country's advantage, but found that international creditors promptly cut their exposure to Mexican corporates, raising the cost of credit to a large part of the Mexican economy and offsetting the benefit of the use of the contingent line.

Other mechanisms of this sort suffer from similar drawbacks in practice. Thus, for example, little action was taken on a proposal to incorporate rollover clauses in bond contracts, which would have allowed the sovereign debtor to roll over amortization for a year at its discretion should it face a financing crisis. The fear was that such insurance would either be very expensive or creditors would take hedging action to offset their increase in exposure and that would render the insurance useless.

Another approach to having the private sector provide insurance has been to provide some official guarantee for the facility, say through the World Bank. While this approach could ensure the provision of quite large amounts of financing, there are doubts about whether it actually engages the private sector in a fundamental sense. Markets are adept at splitting such guarantee operations into their component parts, and thus a guaranteed or partially guaranteed line of credit would be split into that part of the claim that represents sovereign risk (i.e., the claim on the country involved) and that part that is a claim on the official guarantor. That part of the operation that involves pure sovereign risk is likely to be treated in the same way as the simple credit line described above, with all the attendant problems. That part of the insurance that consists of the official guarantee is likely to be treated by the market as a claim on the official guarantor. Since markets tend to discount slightly the value of more complicated instruments, the official sector can almost certainly provide resources to the emerging market country more cheaply if it lends directly.

This reasoning is one factor behind the decision of the Fund to establish a Contingent Credit Line facility (CCL). Here, the Fund provides insurance to those of its members that request it and which meet certain criteria in terms of the strength of their economic policies. This assistance can be quite substantial (normally 300 to 500 percent of quota) and can be used if the member is hit by contagion from a crisis that occurs elsewhere.[2]

---

[2] Since this presentation was written, in November 2000, the CCL facility was simplified and made more automatic in its use, thus making it a closer substitute for owned international reserves. Nevertheless, as of June 2001, no member has applied for access to this facility.

Another approach to involving the private sector ex ante in actions that might reduce the risk of crises has been to promote a better flow of information between sovereign debtors and their private sector creditors. Sovereigns are encouraged to establish investor relations programs that will allow those holding claims on the country to be fully informed about policy actions that might affect the value of their claims and will establish a mechanism whereby questions about policies and clarification of official statements and data can be issued promptly. Such investor relations programs, modeled on the similar operations of corporate borrowers, are expected to build market confidence in countries, as well as provide channels by which market participants can let their concerns be passed through to the sovereign's policymakers. This should provide a means of preventing the buildup of vulnerabilities, as well as establishing a framework that might allow a sovereign to reach agreement with creditors on how a crisis might be handled.

In the debt crises of the 1980s, it proved possible to restructure debt after a period of standstill, in part because the main creditors were international commercial banks sharing common interests and with the flexibility to agree jointly on how the claims might be restructured. Since the start of the 1990s and following the conversion of a large part of bank loans into Brady bonds, the bulk of new sovereign debt has been in securitized form. These instruments are usually held widely and anonymously, and the holders have more divergent interests than did the commercial bank creditors of the 1990s. Furthermore, the legal instruments underlying these claims frequently provide for no amendment of their terms and for the sovereign to waive immunity and submit disputes with its creditor to foreign courts. Default on one bond normally triggers default on others, almost ensuring that concern over the servicing of one instrument would precipitate a crisis for the holders of other instruments. The rigidity of normal bond documentation was thought to be a major obstacle to the restructuring of claims, even when such a restructuring might be in the interests of the creditors as a group, by strengthening the longer-run payments capacity of the debtor.

To facilitate the restructuring of bonds but with appropriate safeguards for the creditors, countries are encouraged to incorporate collective action clauses in their bonds, allowing a qualified majority of bondholders to agree to an amendment of the conditions of the bond. Such collective action by creditors is generally permitted under English law and normally forms part of international bonds issued in London. However, this is not normal practice for bonds issued in New York, although New York law does not prevent their use. One problem with making the use of such clauses more general is a fear by sovereigns that it will increase their borrowing costs. Indeed, at a time when the sovereign is trying to persuade the markets to buy its bonds, introduction of an unusual clause that focuses on the possibility that the debtor might be unable to implement the terms of the agreement is often considered problematic.[3] To overcome this problem, some industrial sovereigns, namely, Canada and the United Kingdom, have introduced such clauses in their own international bonds. Little progress, however, has been made in encouraging the use of such clauses, partly for the reasons just stated, and partly because ways have been found of achieving the same effect through the use of "exit consents" (notably in the case of Ecuador) when a majority of creditors wishes to amend the terms of a bond despite the opposition of a minority.

One final area of international action to reduce the risk of crisis which has been explored is the functioning of international capital markets themselves. Concerns were expressed that the regulatory system under which private market participants operated gave excessive encouragement to short-term credit over longer-term exposure, and thus collectively created more unstable systems. In particular, the risk weighting of banks' short-term exposure under the Basel Capital Adequacy standards appeared to be based on the assumption that such lending was much less risky than longer-term lending, a proposition which the continuing volatility of international capital markets made doubtful. Insofar as short-term lending is more risky than considered hitherto, the revision of the Basel Capital Adequacy standards should correct the problem, and the relative price of short-term and longer-term borrowing should adjust. Another systemic factor thought to be behind financial crises, particularly those in Asia and Russia, was the highly leveraged activities of hedge

---

[3] The argument could be made that a well-designed collective action clause would increase rather than decrease the expected return to creditors, if it ensures that creditors continue to get paid in full in good states of the world, while reducing the likelihood that a creditor panic will lead to a destruction of payments capacity in bad states.

funds. Following the LTCM affair, supervisors have required banks and certain other counterparts to be more careful in their lending to such institutions, and there has since been a considerable decline in leverage.

Some of the actions described above should be useful in reducing the incidence of crises, reducing their size, and making them somewhat easier to manage. But they will not eliminate crises, nor do they guarantee that those crises that occur will not be severe and dramatic. Therefore the international community has also been looking to strengthen its ability to handle crises. As described above, when a country with large exposure to international capital markets loses market confidence, the resulting outflow of capital as both non-resident creditors and residents look for safe havens can be overwhelming and destructive. Two choices present themselves in such a situation: to take action to prevent or reverse the loss of market confidence as soon as possible, or to let the crisis play out and seek to rebuild relations with creditors over a longer period.

If the choice is to restore market confidence as quickly as possible, the most important action is that taken by the country itself. If it can show that its policies are worthy of support and are tackling the reasons behind the markets' doubts, then confidence may come back. But things are not always so simple. If the government has taken actions that have led to the loss of confidence, it may have a hard time convincing the markets to believe in the reversal. The lack of confidence may be related to the markets' disbelief in the government's political will to implement changes, particularly if the policy corrections are socially and politically difficult. The markets may also want to see international endorsement of policies and the public contracting implicit in an arrangement with the Fund.

The second and complementary way of restoring confidence is to show that there is enough money available to finance any withdrawal of funds by creditors, so there is no pressing reason for creditors to leave. Thus international support packages to supplement the country's international reserves can play an important role. This is akin to the lender of last resort function in traditional central banking, which has become a fashionable way to describe the Fund's role in this area.

There continue to be cases where the combination of strong policy action and the provision of international liquidity are successful in averting crises and restoring confidence. One such example was the Czech Republic in 1997, and another Argentina in 1998, at the time of the Russian and Brazilian crises. The program with Turkey in early 2000 also had this effect initially. But not all cases have been successful. In Korea, Indonesia, Thailand, and Brazil, the initial combination of adjustment and official support was not adequate to restore confidence.[4] That only came with a second round of policy changes, combined with other actions to dissuade creditors from leaving. In the case of Russia, the crisis was not averted.

In cases where the country in difficulty introduces a strong and convincing adjustment program, the financing by the Fund (and other international support) is intended to be purely catalytic. The official financing combined with the adjustment are expected to be sufficient to reverse the markets' loss of confidence and lead to a rapid return of capital market financing for the country. This sort of purely catalytic Fund support has a long and successful history in the Fund's operations. However, given the size of the potential outflows, the amounts of money that the official sector may need to put at risk to ensure this catalytic function are often very much greater than in the past. This approach runs the risk of leaving the public sector exposed in a failed adjustment effort, having provided the resources to allow a good part of the private sector to be repaid.

If the risk to the public sector of being left exposed to the country following the exit of the private sector is considered too high, further action must be taken to ensure that the private sector stays involved during a crisis and doesn't reduce its exposure, precipitating further panic. This involves various techniques to discourage or prevent the private sector from reducing its exposure. They range from light-touch approaches to ensure that creditors do not misinterpret each others' actions, through agreements with groups of creditors to maintain exposure, to more drastic action where the sovereign limits payments to creditors.

---

[4] Since this presentation was prepared, growing market doubts about Argentina and Turkey have required that these countries adopt tighter adjustment policies and that specific action be taken to ensure the continued engagement of private creditors.

When confidence in a country is shaky, one reason that a creditor may rush for the exit and seek to withdraw funds is a fear that other creditors are already doing the same thing, and there will soon be little money left. If each creditor knew that others were maintaining their exposure, there would be much less reason to seek to move out quickly. In such circumstances, there may be a role for a mechanism to inform creditors of the actions of others, and such a technique was applied in Brazil. In this case, a monitoring system was put in place to measure each bank creditor's exposure and changes in it, allowing banks to question each other when they saw changes. This device proved successful in Brazil (although it was not applied until a number of smaller banks had withdrawn their funds), and the Fund has encouraged other countries to put similar monitoring systems in place for use in a crisis.

But this approach may not be successful and it may be necessary to seek more formal agreement of creditors to maintain exposure, as was done with commercial bank creditors in the 1980s debt crises. Between December 1997 and January 1998, an agreement was sought with Korea's commercial bank creditors that they would maintain exposure. This was backed by a monitoring system based on data supplied by Korean bank counterparts, combined with moral suasion on the part of creditor bank supervisors to ensure that the agreement was implemented. In the event, confidence returned rapidly, and banks agreed to exchange their short-term exposure into longer-term instruments that Korea could service with less difficulty. Similarly, moral suasion was used to persuade Japanese banks to maintain their exposure in Thailand in 1997.[5]

But these techniques involving a mixture of creditor agreement and moral suasion from creditors' supervisors will not work everywhere. Crises do not only, or even mainly, involve bank claims. The sources of pressure may be the bond market, with a failure to roll over short term or other maturing exposure, or the pressure may

---

[5] A voluntary agreement was also reached with the main creditors of Turkey's banks in late 2000 to maintain their exposure, in return for a guarantee by the Turkish government. However, banks only expressed a willingness to maintain their own proprietary exposure, and argued that much of the exposure booked through them to Turkey was actually exposure of their clients over which they had no control and for which they could assume no responsibility.

reflect residents fleeing domestic assets. For example, the *tesobonos*, U.S. dollar-denominated bonds held largely by nonresidents, were the main source of pressure in Mexico in 1994. In Russia in 1998, the unloading of short-term government bonds, *GKO*s, were the main source of pressure. In these cases, light-touch coordination or moral suasion from supervisors is unlikely to be effective. Creditors are too numerous, their interests too divergent to be coordinated, and supervisory authorities have neither the willingness nor the ability to intervene.

In some circumstances there may be scope for an agreement with bondholders to restructure claims, by exchanging them for others whose payments profile the country is more able to meet. However, the cost of persuading creditors to cooperate may be high, particularly since the secondary market yields on the country's debt are likely to be very high, given the imminence of the crisis. Indeed, the cost of persuading sufficient bondholders or other creditors to extend maturities may exceed the country's payments capacity, and thus the operation may not result in the sought increase in confidence.

In these cases, the only way to prevent a sharp outflow of capital may be through the imposition of exchange restrictions and the government's defaulting on its obligations. These, of course are drastic remedies, and can only be considered when the other options facing a country in a crisis are equally unpalatable. They risk damaging the country's prospects for returning to the capital markets (in other words, imposing a long-run premium on its cost of capital), and they lay it open to litigation. Nevertheless, there will be cases where this is the only practical approach.

When the main source of pressure on the country is the need to repay certain instruments held largely by foreign creditors, it may be possible to limit the default to those instruments, with little collateral damage. Things are more complicated, though, where the same instruments are held by both residents and nonresidents, particularly where the latter includes domestic financial institutions. A default on instruments held by local banks can severely damage bank balance sheets, as indeed can any action that results in a reduction in the market value of their assets. In such circumstances, government backing may be needed if there is not to be a run on banks, and even with such backing, there may be such a loss of confidence in the currency as to cause a run on the foreign exchange reserves. In these cases, there would almost certainly have to be widespread imposition of exchange controls, which could prove immensely damaging to the domestic economy and its longer-term prospects.

In principle, actions to lock creditors while adjustment measures can take hold could be in the interests of the creditors as a group. They should allow the country to recover more quickly, thus increasing the aggregate returns to investors. But this will only be the case if the country uses the respite to adjust. The question has been raised concerning the role the Fund should play in a country's decision to use exchange controls. It has been suggested that the Fund should be in a position to certify that a country needs to invoke exchange restrictions, offering creditors at the same time the assurance that adjustment is well in hand. It has been suggested that Article VIII, Section 2(b) of the Fund's Articles of Agreement might be amended to this effect, allowing the Fund to sanction a standstill on debt payments and associated exchange controls, thus reducing the ability of creditors to litigate, and perhaps the damage to the country's long-run reputation. However, international agreement on this matter remains far away.

To summarize the level of agreement in the international community on managing private sector involvement in financial crises: in some cases, it remains appropriate to rely on the Fund's catalytic approach and not require specific action to keep the private sector engaged. This will be the case where the financing gap is sufficiently small to be financeable with Fund resources. Similarly, there is agreement that in cases where there is a large financing gap and the country does not have good prospects of market access, or where its debt burden is unsustainable, provision of Fund resources should be conditioned on the private sector bearing part of the burden. This covers cases where a country, which has not created the conditions for using market financing efficiently, has gone in too deeply. In many such cases, restoring medium-term viability will require reorganizing and possibly reducing the debt burden. In some of these cases, the concomitant involvement of the Paris Club will also mean that debts need to be rescheduled.

For countries with substantial capital market involvement and which are expected to continue to tap the markets as their main source of financing, there is agreement that private sector involvement will have to be handled on a case-by-case basis. But this doesn't mean that controversies have been laid to rest.

The willingness to use large financing packages without requiring a commitment from the private sector on its continued involvement risks using large amounts of official money with uncertain chances of success. It risks creating a class of countries that are considered "too big to fail," and making the private sector less concerned about the underlying creditworthiness of their investments. But use of such large financing packages in individual cases can minimize market disturbance and contagion.

Some argue that private sector involvement should be required as soon as the amount of official financing exceeds some level. But there are problems with implementing this approach. The first is that it is not clear that private sector involvement can be secured at the outset in these cases through voluntary agreements. Even the approach to creditors for an extension of maturities may precipitate a rush for the exits, leaving the country with no option other than comprehensive default on sovereign obligations and the re-erection of a wall of exchange controls. In any case, it may be hard to say at the start of the adjustment process exactly how confidence will be restored, in other words, how large the temporary financing gap will be and precisely in which form capital will come back into the country. Finally, clear rules that signal when exchange controls and default will be implemented are likely to tempt the market into speculating against the application of those rules. Thus a system of rules of this nature could be highly destabilizing to the markets.

The private sector wants both clear rules and less willingness of the public sector to seek its concerted involvement. The second point on concerted involvement is, of course, special pleading. But the call for clear rules raises some difficult issues. As already mentioned, clear rules will tempt the markets into creating instruments that allow them to circumvent those rules. The market may turn out to be very creative in this connection.

So the debate on precisely how to handle a crisis continues.

Finally, in the matter of restructuring debt, there has been some progress. It was feared by many observers that it would prove very difficult to restructure bond debt, because of problems of getting sufficient creditors to agree and the dangers of litigation. In practice, these problems seem to be fewer than first thought. The experience of successful bond exchanges in Pakistan and Ukraine, and possibly some of Russia's experience in negotiating with its creditors, shows that restructuring bonds is quite feasible, although it may not be compatible with a rapid restoration of market access. However, we are not yet at the end of interesting cases where litigation may prove a problem.

Postscript

Since this presentation was prepared in May 2000, work at the Fund in the area of private sector involvement in crisis prevention and resolution has developed further. The official community agreed in Prague on a framework for crisis resolution that has clarified the options available to the official community when facing a crisis.[6] Within the Fund, there has been further discussion of the use of payments standstills by debtors and the mechanisms by which bond debt can be renegotiated.[7] Discussions continue on the relative treatment of public and private sector claims in the Paris Club when a country's debt needs to be restructured.[8]

In terms of practical experience, Ecuador has also managed to restructure its debt, although the private sector has reservations about some of the techniques employed. Finally, developments in Argentina and Turkey have shown other facets of the problems involved in managing crises that will be important in future cases.

---

[6] *See* communique of the International Monetary and Financial Committee of the Board of Governors of the IMFC, September 24, 2000 (www.imf.org/external/np/cm/2000/092400.htm). *See also* Statement of the Managing Director to the International Monetary and Financial Committee on Progress in Strengthening the Architecture of the International Financial System and Reform of the IMF, September 19, 2000 (www.imf.org/external/np/omd/2000/02/state.html).

[7] *See* Summing Up by the Acting Chairman on Involving the Private Sector in the Resolution of Financial Crises Restructuring International Sovereign Bonds, January 24, 2001 (www.imf.org/external/pubs/ft/ series/ 03/index.htm).

[8] *See* Involving the Private Sector in the Resolution of Financial Crises: The Treatment of the Claims of Private Sector and Paris Club Creditors—Preliminary Considerations, June 27, 2001(www.imf.org/External/NP/psi/2001/eng/062701.pdf).

Chapter

11 Role of the IMF in Promoting Fiscal Transparency

MARCO CANGIANO

In recent years the IMF has been at the vanguard in promoting fiscal transparency. To this end, the IMF has, among other activities, developed a standard against which the transparency of fiscal management systems can be assessed. This standard is represented by the *Code of Good Practices on Fiscal Transparency—Declaration on Principles* (henceforth the Code). The Code, adopted by the IMF Interim Committee[1] in April 1998, is one element in a wider effort to promote international standards and codes as a means of improving economic and financial management. In particular, the adoption of standards is the beginning of a difficult process of assessing and reducing vulnerabilities in the context of a new financial architecture.

The main purpose of this paper is to describe the rationale, objectives, structure, and requirements of the Code and to discuss some implementation issues. In the process, the paper also shows how recent efforts to promote fiscal transparency have to be seen in the context of a broader attempt by the IMF to encourage the observance of standards relevant to economic policymaking, to foster good governance, and to strengthen the architecture of the international financial system.

A Brief Historical Digression

Transparency as a key element of good governance is certainly not a new concept. Although *in nuce,* this concept was already present in the writings of political philosophers in ancient Greece, such as Plato and Aristotle.[2] This tradition carried on to Roman times in the

---

Note: This paper draws from earlier presentations and papers on this topic prepared by Richard Hemming, whom the author wishes to thank.

[1] Now the International Monetary and Financial Committee.
[2] *See*, for instance, Plato's *The Republic* and Aristotle's *Politics*.

writings of Cicero, in particular his *Res Publica*, in which the word "honorability" came to sum up the virtues required of policymakers. Jumping to the Middle Ages, the contraposition between good and evil government found a synthesis in a fresco by Ambrogio Lorenzetti in the Public Palace in Siena.[3] On one side of the fresco, the *buon governo*, the consequences of good government are represented as harmony, justice, and a plentiful supply of agricultural products; on the other side, the *mal governo*, poor government, brings about tyranny, injustice, and famine.

The desire to enhance transparency in public affairs became pressing in the period preceding the French Revolution. During the eighteenth century, the French royal treasury lived in a state of almost perpetual fiscal crisis, mainly due to the need to finance extravagantly expensive wars. By the late 1780s, the national debt had grown to enormous proportions and was largely held by a huge class of *rentiers*, which was well prepared to fight in defense of their interests. This state of business is brilliantly summarized by the following excerpt from Hippolyte Taine's *Les origines de la France contemporaine*:[4]

> ...from then on, public affairs were no longer solely the King's affairs. His creditors became concerned about his expenditure; for it was their money that he was wasting; if he mismanaged things, they would be ruined. They desired to know his budget in detail, to check his books; a lender always has the right to inspect his surety. Here, then, we see the bourgeois raising their heads and beginning to look more closely at that great machine whose workings, now open to the gaze of even the lowest, had up until then been a state secret...

In recent times, transparency and accountability have found new impetus in the reforms carried out in New Zealand from the mid-1980s to the mid-1990s.[5] These reforms culminated with the passage of the Fiscal Responsibility Act (FRA) in June 1994. With this legislation, New Zealand has taken an innovative institutional

---

[3] I am indebted to George Kopits (1998) for drawing my attention to this masterpiece of Italian art.

[4] Hippolyte Taine, *Les origines de la France contemporaine*, Hachette (1876–1885).

[5] A concise account of New Zealand's reforms can be found in Cangiano (1996).

approach to fiscal policy, balancing principles of responsible fiscal management with a degree of policy flexibility. As the culmination of earlier reforms, it emphasizes transparency and accountability, and imparts a strong medium- and long-term orientation to fiscal policy. Rather than prescribing quantified fiscal targets, the FRA imposes fiscal discipline by setting principles for responsible fiscal management as legislative benchmarks.[6] The FRA permits the government to depart temporarily from these fiscal principles, provided it explains its reasons and indicates how, and within what time frame, it plans to return to them. Future governments remain free to select different fiscal objectives, as long as they are consistent with the FRA's principles. A crucial premise of the FRA is that increased transparency will promote prudent fiscal policy and better fiscal outcomes. Toward this end, the Act made the adoption of generally accepted accounting practices (GAAP) mandatory for the whole government and introduces a number of specific disclosure requirements on fiscal policy intentions and objectives as an essential precondition for government accountability and transparency, and ultimately, to raise its credibility.

The IMF Code

Fiscal Transparency as a Key Aspect of Governance

The 1996 Interim Committee Declaration focused on the importance of sound economic policies to achieving sustainable growth across the IMF membership. In this connection, it emphasized key aspects of good governance in the IMF area of competence—the promotion of macroeconomic stability, balance of payments viability, and orderly economic growth. While recognizing that the responsibility for governance issues lies first and foremost with country authorities, the declaration went on to highlight efficiency

---

[6] These principles are: (i) reducing total Crown debt to prudent levels by ensuring fiscal operating surpluses every year until this is accomplished; (ii) once they are achieved, maintaining these levels, by ensuring that, on average, over a reasonable period of time, the total operating expenses of the Crown do not exceed its total operating revenues; (iii) achieving and maintaining sufficient levels of Crown net worth that provide a buffer against factors that may impact adversely on the Crown's net worth in the future; (iv) managing prudently the fiscal risks facing the Crown; and (v) pursuing policies that are consistent with a reasonable degree of predictability about the level and stability of tax rates for future years.

and accountability of the public sector as one particular aspect of good governance. It then mentioned fiscal transparency and referred to quite specific sources of nontransparency, such as off-budget transactions and quasi-fiscal operations, as a way to address governance issues.[7]

The recent Asian crisis is perhaps the first clear example where lack of fiscal transparency was at the root of broader governance concerns. The crisis pointed to the need to increase the efficiency of global financial markets by providing the participants more and better information. At the same time, this crisis offered strong evidence that conventional budgets do not provide a true account of a country's financial condition and of the fiscal risks it faces from sudden shifts in capital flows and stocks. At the eve of the crisis, most of the Asian "tigers" reported favorable budget conditions and international organizations judged their finances to be soundly managed. Once the crisis unfolded, however, fiscal conditions deteriorated rapidly, as economic activity contracted and budget deficits escalated. The failure to look beyond the official government accounts meant that underlying sources of fiscal vulnerability were ignored. In particular, a lack of transparency masked pervasive off-budget involvement in various sectors of the economy for which the government was not held accountable. Further, the expectation was created that the government stood behind these sectors and would bail them out in a crisis. As a matter of fact, the share of public debt into GDP increased sharply during the crisis in most of the crisis countries when the government did in fact bail out some institutions.

---

[7] The IMF has a mandate to work on governance issues. This is reflected in "The Role of the IMF in Governance Issues—Guidance Note" (http://www.imf.org/external/np/sec/nb/1997/nb9715.htm#I2), which was issued in August 1997. The guidelines place boundaries on IMF involvement. Specifically, it is emphasized that: national authorities are primarily responsible for governance issues; IMF staff should focus only on economic aspects of governance; they should not make judgments of a political nature; they should not be influenced by the interests of other countries; and poor governance should be of concern to the IMF only where it affects the authorities' ability to design and implement appropriate macroeconomic policies. As it turns out, the second and fifth of these guidelines give the IMF considerable scope to address governance issues as part of its surveillance of macroeconomic policies, in the design of IMF-supported programs, and in connection with providing technical assistance.

Following the 1996 declaration, IMF staff developed the Code as a major contribution to promoting better governance. This was rapidly followed by standards and codes in other areas. As a whole, the set of standards and codes have the same effect, in that they place obligations on policymakers and those that implement policies which limit the scope for practices that characterize a breakdown in governance, including corruption.

A Definition of Fiscal Transparency

Fiscal transparency is defined as easy access by the public to the structure and functions of government, to its fiscal policy intentions, to public sector accounts, and to fiscal projections (Kopits and Craig, 1998). A number of countries have in recent years introduced fiscal management practices that reflect a high level of fiscal transparency. Australia and New Zealand have been leaders in this regard. However, given the diversity of economic and institutional characteristics across countries, the best practices adopted in a few advanced economies cannot provide a basis for a universal standard of fiscal transparency, especially when cultural characteristics and levels of economic development are very different. The Code is, therefore, based upon good practices of fiscal management that are judged appropriate to the IMF membership as a whole. It is, of course, hoped that countries will attempt to exceed these minimum standards.

The Rationale Behind the Code

Along with the broader governance concerns, there are three main factors behind the Code: the increasing role played by markets; accountability relations between policymakers and the public; and the new emphasis put on the management of fiscal policy and fiscal risks.

As markets are largely driven by expectations, the risk of having markets misread policy intentions has forced countries to broaden the range of information made available to markets. If secrecy in policy formulation used to be the norm, now markets put a premium on openness and transparency.

Whereas fiscal transparency is about the availability of information, accountability is about the relationship between policymakers and the public. But, as it has become increasingly evident in the Australian and New Zealand experiences, transparency and accountability are the two sides of the same coin. And together they constitute the backbone of good fiscal management.

Perhaps the single most important feature of the Code is that it broadens the concept of fiscal management beyond that of managing the public finances as defined by conventional budget and public accounts documents. While the need for comprehensive, timely, and reliable budget estimates and public accounts is strongly emphasized in the Code, it is clearly recognized that, by themselves, these are not enough. The dimensions of fiscal transparency—and, implicitly, fiscal management—are extended to include any activity of a fiscal nature. Transparent fiscal management practices, according to the Code, must disclose all forms of off-budget fiscal activity, and fiscal policy statements are required to look beyond a single year. Fiscal transparency is therefore a prerequisite for good fiscal management to the extent that transparency penalizes inefficient policies that may lead to large deficit and an unsustainable debt position.

The Objective of the Code

The Code can be seen as a benchmark against which countries may assess fiscal transparency and, more generally, fiscal management. The principal aim of the Code is therefore to promote fiscal transparency and thereby make governments more accountable for the design, implementation, and outcome of fiscal policy. This is expected to exert discipline on policymakers and to provide needed information to the private sector in general and the financial market in particular. In turn, this would lead to better and more credible policies, to a less uncertain policy environment, and to an earlier and smoother fiscal policy response to emerging economic problems. Ultimately, fiscal transparency should be associated with, and may directly result in, improved economic performance. There are, of course, circumstances where, for particular periods, full transparency may not be appropriate or may be precluded by the costs involved. But the usual presumption should be in favor of improved fiscal transparency.[8]

---

[8] In the late 1800s, some economists such as Puviani defended the use of fiscal illusions. More recently economists of the public choice school have argued that
(continued)

Structure of the Code

The Code is based upon a hierarchy of principles and practices. The organizational framework for the Code is provided by four general principles that are the key elements of fiscal transparency (Box 1). Specific principles expand upon these four general principles.

The first general principle—**Clarity of Roles and Responsibilities**—is the foundation of the other three principles, since the clear identification of a boundary between the public and private sectors and, separately, of policy and management roles within government, together with a clear legal and administrative framework for fiscal management are prerequisites for the transparent design and implementation of fiscal policy. When the frontier between the public and private sectors or between policy and management is not well defined, problems inevitably arise, as the experience of many countries, especially those in transition, indicates.

The second general principle—**Public Availability of Information**—covers the need for the timely and adequate provision of high quality fiscal information, accompanied by a public commitment to make this information widely available to the public. In many countries, the information available is limited while in other cases individuals who are not part of the government have difficulty in getting access to relevant information even when this information is of relevance to them. There is often a tendency in government to control the available information making it difficult for private individuals to obtain access.

---

governments have a bias against transparency. It has also been argued that transparency may foster voters' confidence and ultimately a larger government.

> **Box 1. Code of Good Practices on Fiscal Transparency—Declaration of Principles**
>
> **Clarity of Roles and Responsibilities**
>
> - The government sector should be clearly distinguished from the rest of the economy, and policy and management roles within government should be well defined.
> - There should be a clear legal and administrative framework for fiscal management.
>
> **Public Availability of Information**
>
> - The public should be provided with full information on the past, current, and projected fiscal activity of the government.
> - A public commitment should be made to the timely publication of fiscal information.
>
> **Open Budget Preparation, Execution, and Reporting**
>
> - Budget documentation should specify fiscal policy objectives, the macroeconomic framework, the policy basis for the budget, and identifiable major fiscal risks.
> - Budget data should be classified and presented in a way that facilitates policy analysis and promotes accountability.
> - Procedures for the execution and monitoring of approved expenditures should be clearly specified.
> - Fiscal reporting should be timely, comprehensive, and reliable, and should identify deviations from the budget.
>
> **Independent Assurances of Integrity**
>
> The integrity of fiscal information should be subject to public and independent scrutiny.

The third general principle—**Open Budget Preparation, Execution, and Reporting**—deals with the budgetary process, and thus goes to the core of fiscal transparency. In many countries, the budgetary process is an arcane and almost mysterious one, which is often poorly understood. In some countries, only a handful of individuals fully understand this process. Furthermore, at times, the effective budgetary process is very different from the formal one described by the laws or the regulations of the countries.

Finally, the fourth general principle—**Independent Assurances of Integrity**—requires that fiscal information, and assumptions underlying it, are open to external scrutiny or, additionally or alternatively, that a competent and independent agency takes the legal responsibility of verifying the quality and the accuracy of the available information.[9] Statistical misreporting in the financial or fiscal areas is recognized as a major problem for quite a few countries. Beyond the normal requirement that government accounts should be externally audited, the integrity of fiscal information should be further ensured by subjecting macroeconomic forecasts underlying budgets to scrutiny by independent experts and by ensuring that the national statistical office has institutional independence.

The Manual on Fiscal Transparency

The Code is a relatively short document that identifies various good practices of fiscal management. Elaboration of these practices is provided in a much longer document titled the *Manual on Fiscal Transparency* (the Manual). The Manual sets out the detailed requirements that make up the overall standard of fiscal transparency proposed in the Code. This is a standard that most countries should seek to meet. However, because fiscal management systems vary considerably across countries, and in particular because systems and administrative procedures are much less developed in some countries than in others, flexibility is required in applying the Code. To this end, the Manual proposes a minimum standard of fiscal transparency, the requirements of which are to be given highest priority by those countries that are some way from meeting the overall standard of the Code. The minimum standard emphasizes the provision of comprehensive, reliable, and timely budget and accounting reports. This is viewed as a fundamental requirement for assessing a country's fiscal policies, and all countries aspiring to participate fully in international financial relations, and seeking to benefit from the recognition of their good fiscal management practices, should aim to meet the minimum standard. In a world becoming progressively more globalized and in which decisions by foreign investors may have a

---

[9] Once again, a similar concept can be found in Aristotle's *Politics*, book 6, fragment 8: "But since many, not to say all, of state offices handle the public money, there must of necessity be another office which examines and audits them, and has no other functions."

great impact on a country's economy this requirement acquires particular significance.

Requirements of the Code

The Manual provides a detailed explanation of the various requirements of the Code. However, highlighting a few of these requirements will give an indication of the extent to which the scope of the Code goes beyond the more familiar good practices of budgeting and expenditure management.

Coverage

The Code is directed at the general government (i.e., the central government and lower levels of government), but its coverage extends beyond narrowly defined budgetary activities. It also covers: extrabudgetary activities; quasi-fiscal activities undertaken by the central bank, public financial institutions, and nonfinancial public enterprises; and regulation of the private sector.[10] All of these have proved to be important means through which governments extend their influence over the rest of the economy without being constrained by formal budget approval, execution, monitoring, and reporting procedures.[11]

Taxation

Not only should taxation have a legal basis, but there should also be clear and accessible criteria governing the administrative application of tax laws. The tax laws themselves should be widely available and should be clearly written to prevent or reduce alternative interpretations. Taxpayer rights and obligations should be

---

[10] The application of the principles of the Code to lower levels of government as separate entities—as distinct from the current emphasis on their inclusion as part of general government—and the extension of the Code to nonfinancial public enterprises are to be considered. In fact, in a few decentralized countries such as Brazil and Argentina, subnational governments have shown interest in applying the principles of the Code.

[11] See, for instance, Tanzi (1998). Many of these activities as well as the use of tax expenditures, give rise to inefficiencies and as such are often inherently undesirable. However, the Code stops short of recommending against their use. But it is expected that being transparent about such activities will reduce the incentive to policymakers to make use of them.

clearly stated, and all decisions made by the tax administration should be open to independent review. Discretionary decisions on the part of tax administrators should be kept at a minimum and political figures should not interfere with the day-to-day administration of taxes, as discussed in Tanzi (2000).

Ethical Behavior

The behavior of public servants should be governed by standards which require that they act in the public interest, avoid conflicts of interest, satisfy any disclosure requirements, respect the confidentiality of information, etc. Corruption in any form should not be tolerated and corrupt acts should be punished. The opportunities that promote corruption should be minimized.

Commitment to Publication

The government should make an explicit commitment to the timely disclosure or publication of information on all the fiscal and quasi-fiscal activities covered by the Code. The commitment should be either in the form of a legal obligation or should involve explicitly adopting a relevant system or standard such as the IMF's General Data Dissemination System or Special Data Dissemination Standard (see below). Among other things, these require that advance release date calendars for fiscal reporting should be announced, to provide clear indication of a commitment to publication.

Fiscal Policy Objectives

A key requirement of the Code is that the budget documentation should place the annual budget in a broader fiscal policy framework. This would involve clearly and explicitly specifying fiscal policy objectives and relating these to broader macroeconomic objectives. The budget documentation should thus specify the objectives or the outcomes to be achieved by major government programs (e.g., the improvement in health indicators expected as a result of health spending changes or in test scores as a result of changes in educational spending, etc.), and should report on performance relative to these objectives. Any fiscal rules that have been adopted should be explicitly stated, and fiscal outcomes should be assessed against these rules. An assessment of the sustainability of fiscal policy should also be provided, with detailed projections being undertaken for programs with significant longer-term financial consequences (e.g., social security).[12] The assumptions underlying these projections should be made explicit.

Fiscal Risks

The major risks to the budget should be identified and, where possible, quantified. Such risks include economic developments at variance from the forecasting assumptions underlying the budget as, for example, changes in interest rates or in economic activity, contingent liabilities (e.g., guarantees that may be called), the uncertain costs of specific expenditure commitments, and new commitments that may have to be made. In many countries, particularly those likely to be most vulnerable, much fiscal activity is conducted through various off-budget measures, such as guarantees, extrabudgetary funds, quasi-fiscal activities, or tax expenditures. Such measures imply that official statements about the government's fiscal position are often misleading.[13] Not only is accountability of the government sector and sectors in receipt of off-budget support diminished in the process, but also expectations are created that government stands behind the supported sectors and will bail them out in the event of a crisis. The concept of fiscal vulnerability as a situation where the government is exposed to the possibility of failure to achieve its broad fiscal policy objectives is relatively new. Along with analytical work on contingent liabilities and risk analysis now underway with assistance from the World Bank, this work will be an important element of the government's assessment of fiscal risks, and the results, together with other relevant material can be consolidated in a comprehensive statement of fiscal risks as illustrated in Box 2 below.[14]

---

[12] For a discussion of fiscal sustainability, *see* Chalk and Hemming (2000).

[13] These measures may, however, be taken into account by the markets in a general sense. A lack of perceived transparency in fiscal management (evidenced by general reference to quasi-fiscal or other off-budget support of other sectors), which may give rise to borrowing or investment premiums in a stable environment, may become pivotal in encouraging capital flight under volatile conditions.

[14] The very concept of fiscal vulnerability assessment has been developed by Hemming and Petrie (1999). For ongoing research on contingent liability, see Polackova (1999) and Petrie (2000). Allan (2000) highlights the role of the Code in linking transparency and vulnerability assessments.

Implementation Issues

The adoption of the Code by the IMF Interim Committee places no obligation on countries to put in place all the good practices it proposes. Instead, implementation is to be voluntary, and steps have been taken with this in mind. In addition to preparing the Manual, the IMF has also developed a questionnaire that is structured like the Code and the Manual. This questionnaire can be used by a country to assess how its fiscal management system compares with the requirements of the Code. A summary self-evaluation report can then be used to highlight the strengths and weaknesses of the country's fiscal management system, and to provide a basis for formulating plans to improve fiscal transparency. The Code, the Manual, the questionnaire, and the self-evaluation report are available on the IMF's external website.[15] The IMF also plans, and indeed it has already begun, to work directly with countries seeking to improve fiscal transparency by meeting the requirements of the Code.[16] In particular, it can provide technical assistance to countries that want to assess the transparency of their fiscal management systems, that need help designing plans for improving fiscal transparency and/or require support with implementing those plans.

A number of countries have completed, or are in the process of completing, the fiscal transparency questionnaire, and a few advanced economies have made the completed questionnaire report available on national websites (e.g., New Zealand, the United Kingdom,[17] and the United States). Australia has also published a comprehensive assessment of its compliance with a wide range of standards on its treasury website. The initial expectation was that, either independently or in conjunction with IMF staff, an increasing number of countries would complete and publish the questionnaire. Subsequent monitoring would then be relatively informal, with IMF staff discussing fiscal transparency issues with country authorities on

---

[15] The questionnaire and self-evaluation report can be downloaded from http://www.imf.org/external/np/fad/trans/index.htm.

[16] This refers to the requirements of the minimum standard or the overall standard of the Code, whichever is appropriate. The implementation of the minimum standard is also voluntary.

[17] The United Kingdom has published only the self-evaluation report, but it is quite detailed.

a case-by-case basis, usually in the context of the Article IV surveillance process. As it turns out, and as described below, reporting on and monitoring the observance of standards in general has become more formal.

Standards and Financial Architecture

Standards

The fiscal transparency Code is one of four standards in areas of core interest to the IMF. The others cover data dissemination, monetary and financial policy transparency, and banking supervision.

Data Dissemination

The General Data Dissemination System (GDDS) became operational in May 2000. Its aim is to foster improvements in the quality of economic, financial, and socioeconomic data. There are currently nine participating countries for which information on their statistical systems and plans for improvement is published on the IMF's Data Standards Bulletin Board (DSBB). For countries seeking access to international capital markets, there is a more demanding Special Data Dissemination Standard (SDDS). This has been in place since March 1996. The 47 current subscribers to the SDDS provide information about their data dissemination practices, which is published on the DSBB, and have undertaken to make their data available on a country website linked to the DSBB. The SDDS has recently been strengthened, particularly to increase the comprehensiveness of information that is reported on international reserves and external debt. Further information about the GDDS and SDDS is available on the *Standards and Codes* website (http://dsbb.imf.org/).

Box 2. Toward a Statement of Fiscal Risk

Material on the following topics could be incorporated in a statement of fiscal risk:

Effectiveness of Budget Control and Discipline

Assurance should be provided that budget estimates of revenue are reliable and that control mechanisms for expenditure are adequate. A table should be presented with the budget estimates showing variation between original budget estimates and final outcomes with an explanation of the source of variation (e.g., changes in economic parameters, supplementary budget provisions for policy change, contingencies, or revenue shortfall). Such a table provides important information to the public, but it also helps the Ministry of Finance identify weaknesses in fiscal management.

Government Guarantees

Government guarantees should be fully disclosed in the budget and as a memorandum item in the government accounts. Plans are to set realistic limits for issuance of all kinds of guarantees in the annual budget law. In the budget document, tables should be presented providing a listing by: category of all outstanding guarantees; item of all new guarantees issued or to be issued over the forthcoming year; and item of all guarantees that have been called. Some broad indication should be given of the risk of further calls during the year and how the budget addresses such risks (e.g., by an allowance in an appropriated contingency reserve).

Other Contingent Liabilities

Other contingent liabilities may arise from legal proceedings against government and privatization may give rise to contingent liabilities by way of indemnities to the purchaser of assets. The Ministry of Finance or the Treasury should maintain records of all such forms of legal liability and declare these in a statement of fiscal risks. Some liabilities arise because government is assumed to have an implicit obligation (for instance in the case of bank failure). These would not be included in a formal assessment of risk—because of the potential moral hazard such an assessment would entail. However, an indication should be given of action taken to mitigate such implicit risks.

Variation of Economic Assumptions

Changes in the economic environment are another element of risk that may affect both the annual budget (and medium-term budget estimates, if developed as part of the budget presentation). It is suggested that, alongside the development of the formal macroeconomic framework, simulations of the effects of changes in key economic parameters (e.g., GDP, inflation, wage rate changes, and interest rate changes) should be calculated. A table showing the impact of changes in economic parameters for at least the budget year should be included in the statement of risk.

Risk Mitigation Measures

The risk statement in the budget document should include a description of all measures that the government is taking to mitigate risks. Such measures could include a contingency fund provision, introduction of medium-term planning procedures, or specific policies to strengthen particular sectors of the economy and reduce the risk of implicit contingent liabilities.

Monetary and Financial Policies

A Code of Good Practices on Transparency in Monetary and Financial Policies, developed in conjunction with the World Bank, national central banks, and other agencies, was endorsed by the IMF Interim Committee in September 1999. In terms of objectives, structure, and requirements, there is a parallel with the fiscal transparency Code. Thus, the emphasis is on the provision of information on monetary and financial policies that is comprehensive, understandable, timely, and readily accessible to the public. This Code is also available on the *Standards and Codes* website. Assessments of compliance with the monetary and financial policies transparency Code are made in connection with a joint IMF/World Bank Financial Sector Assessment Program (FSAP) launched on a pilot basis in May 1999. The FSAP looks in-depth at financial sector risks and vulnerabilities.

Banking Supervision

The *Basel Core Principles for Effective Banking Supervision* include requirements for clarity of the objectives of banking supervision, information sharing between supervisory agencies at home and abroad, and obligatory publication of financial statements by banks. The principles also emphasize assurance of quality of information by requiring consolidation of accounts in prudential reporting, appropriate internal controls and risk management systems, and independent verification of reported information. They therefore have a significant transparency element. However, the principles go beyond transparency, covering all the basic elements of an effective supervisory system.

The principles are available on the Bank for International Settlements (BIS) website (http://www.bis.org/publ/bcbs30a.htm).

Noncore Standards

There are also a number of other standards relevant to the work of the IMF that are the responsibility of other organizations. These include standards relating to corporate governance, accounting practices of the private and public sectors, and securities market and insurance supervision. A compendium of international standards is maintained by the Financial Stability Forum (FSF), which was established in early 1999 to promote an exchange of information and cooperation between agencies and institutions involved in financial market supervision and surveillance. The compendium is available on the FSF website (http://www.fin.gc.ca/newse99/99-110_1e.html).

Compliance with Standards

In response to an initial call by the group of countries referred to as the G-22, which was subsequently bolstered by other groups (G-7, G-20), the IMF has embarked upon the preparation of experimental *Reports on the Observance of Standards and Codes* (ROSCs)[18] ROSCs are a collection of modules, each module including a description of practice (prepared by the country, the IMF staff, or usually both) in the area covered by a core standard and an IMF staff commentary on compliance with that standard.

Thus far, 12 ROSC fiscal transparency modules have been published on the Fund's Standards and Codes external website, including Australia's self-assessment (which is formally treated as a ROSC).[19] Twelve modules are under way, ten of which are close to completion.

Work on further 20 modules should commence and be largely completed during FY 2001 (Table 1). Of the modules so far completed or under way, 7 have required specific technical assistance missions, 4 have been prepared with assistance from the fiscal economist assigned to the relevant area department mission, and the others have been prepared only with assistance from headquarters.

Concluding Remarks

This paper has presented in some detail the effort made by the IMF to address governance concerns. The focus has been on fiscal transparency as one of the key elements of governance. The increasing role played by markets has added to governments'

---

[18] *See* Canadian Department of Finance (1998). The G-20, which in some respects is the successor group to the G-22, formally requested all group members to undertake assessments against IMF standards and codes.

[19] Published in the IMF's Standards and Codes website: http://www.imf.org/external/np/rosc/index.htm.

information requirements. Fiscal transparency is foremost concerned with availability of information. But from this perspective, fiscal transparency is also the main tool to enhance accountability relations between policymakers and the public. Enhanced transparency and accountability also broaden the very concept of fiscal management beyond that of managing the public finances as defined by conventional budget and public accounts documents to include any activity of a fiscal nature. In this regard, it helps governments focus on the objectives of fiscal policy and lengthen the time horizon beyond the budget fiscal year.

An increasing number of countries have shown interest in carrying out a fiscal transparency assessment either in the form of self-evaluation or with the assistance of IMF staff. Since its launch in March 1998, 26 countries have participated in the exercise and an additional 20 are likely to complete the exercise by 2001. As to changes to bring national practices in line with minimum standards, it is perhaps too early to judge. Over the short run, the policymakers of some countries may not show much enthusiasm for the proposed changes as they may fear that greater disclosure might precipitate some undesirable reaction on the part of the market or might reduce their degree of freedom in policy actions. However, over the long run it will be increasingly more difficult for poor policies to hide behind the veil of nontransparency or for policymakers to exploit fiscal illusions.

Table 1. Fiscal Transparency Module Progress Report as of September 2000 [1]

Country	Published	Approved for Final Publication	Waiting for Final Approval	Internally Reviewed	Ongoing	Planned [2]
Argentina	X					
Australia	X					
Bulgaria	X					
Cameroon	X					
China-Hong Kong SAR	X					
Czech Republic	X					
Greece	X					
Tunisia	X					
Turkey	X					
Uganda	X					
Ukraine	X					
United Kingdom	X					
Azerbaijan		X				
India		X				
Korea		X				
Papua New Guinea		X				
France			X			
Lebanon			X			
Pakistan			X			
Poland			X			
Russian Federation			X			
Sweden			X			
Uruguay			X			
Hungary					X	
Mozambique					X	
Nicaragua						X

[1] The first set of ROSCs on Argentina, Australia, and the United States was published in April 1999. A second set was published for Bulgaria, the Czech Republic, Hong Kong SAR, Tunisia, and Uganda in Septemeber 1999. ROSC fiscal transparency modules for Ukraine and Cameroon wer also published in September 1999, and one for Greece was published in October 1999.

[2] Agreed with the national authorities, not yet under way.

References

Allan, William, 2000, Linking Transparency and Vulnerability Assessments—The Role of the IMF Fiscal Transparency Code, IMF Fiscal Affairs Department mimeograph.

Canada Department of Finance, 1999, "G-20 Commits to Efforts to Reduce Vulnerabilities to Global Financial Crises," *Finance Canada News Release* 99–110, December 16 (http://www.fin.gc.ca/newse99/99-110_1e.html).

Cangiano, Marco, 1996, Accountability and Transparency in the Public Sector: The New Zealand Experience, IMF Working Paper 96/122 (Washington: International Monetary Fund).

Chalk, Nigel, and Richard Hemming, 2000, Assessing Fiscal Sustainability in Theory and Practice, IMF Working Paper 00/81 (Washington: International Monetary Fund).

G-22, 1998, Report of the Working Group on Transparency and Accountability, October.

Kopits, George, 1998, *Calidad de Gobierno. Trasparencia y Responsbilidad* (Buenos Aires: Fundación Macri).

──, and Jon Craig, 1998, "Transparency in Government Operations," Occasional Paper No. 158 (Washington: International Monetary Fund).

IMF Interim Committee Declaration, 1996, "Partnership for Sustainable Global Growth" (Washington: International Monetary Fund).

IMF Survey, October 14, p. 327. (Washington: International Monetary Fund).

Hemming, Richard, "The IMF Code of Good Practices on Fiscal Transparency," *Commonwealth Ministers Reference Book 1999/2000* (London: Kensington Publications Limited).

———, and Murray Petrie, 2000 "A Framework for Assessing Fiscal Vulnerability," IMF Working Paper 00/52 (Washington: International Monetary Fund).

Petrie, Murray, 2000, "Financial Accountability to Capture Risk: A Framework with Application," IMF Fiscal Affairs Department mimeograph.

Polackova, Hana, 1999, "Contingent Government Liabilities: A Hidden Fiscal Risk," *Finance and Development*, International Monetary Fund, March, pp. 46–49.

Tanzi, Vito, 1998, "The Role of the State and the Efficiency of Fiscal Instruments," in *Public Finance in a Changing World*, ed. by Peter Sorensen (McMillan: London).

———, 2000, "The Role of the State and the Quality of the Public Sector," IMF Working Paper 00/36 (Washington: International Monetary Fund).

Chapter 12

Legal Aspects of the IMF's Code of Good Practices on Transparency in Monetary and Financial Policies

ROY C.N. BABAN

In the wake of the recent Asian crisis, the IMF launched a number of initiatives aimed at avoiding future crises. Among these initiatives, which were termed pillars of a "new architecture of the international financial system," was the promotion of the observance by Fund members of certain standards and codes prepared by international entities and professional associations and the development of new codes.[1]

Reflecting the Fund's comparative expertise in macroeconomic management, the Fund developed the Code of Good Practices on Fiscal Transparency[2] in 1998 and the Code of Good Practices on Transparency in Monetary and Financial Policies: Declaration of Principles[3] in 1999 as guides for members' efforts to increase transparency in these areas.

This paper focuses on the provisions of the Code of Good Practices on Transparency in Monetary and Financial Policies (hereafter "the Code") that prescribe the use of law and legal processes to achieve transparency in certain matters. Observance of

---

[1] The other pillars include: increasing transparency in economic data and decision making; strengthening the financial sector; involving the private sector in crisis prevention; modifying Fund facilities; and addressing other systemic issues, principally the adoption of appropriate exchange rate regimes. *See* "Report of the Managing Director to the International Monetary and Financial Committee on Progress in Strengthening the Architecture of the International Financial System and Reform of the IMF," September 19, 2000, http://www.imf.org/external/np/omd/2000/02/report.htm. *See also* François Gianviti, "The Reform of the International Monetary System (Conditionality and Surveillance)," *The International Lawyer*, Spring 2000, Vol. 34, No. 1, pp. 107–116.

[2] *See* the preceding chapter.

[3] For an introduction to the Code and its text, *see* www.imf.org/external/np/mae/mft/code/index.htm. The text is also reproduced in this volume as Appendix I.

these provisions would lead to other consequences, in particular, the promotion of institutional independence, accountability, and public consultation that may not otherwise ensue if transparency were to be achieved only by publication.

Definition of Transparency and Structure of the Code

In the introduction to the Code, transparency is defined as "an environment in which the objectives of policy, its legal, institutional, and economic framework, policy decisions and their rationale, data and information related to monetary and financial policies, and the terms of agencies' accountability, are provided to the public on an understandable, accessible and timely basis."[4] Such an environment is deemed to increase the effectiveness of monetary and financial policies, promote the efficiency of markets, and promote good governance in central banks and financial agencies, particularly those granted high levels of autonomy.[5]

The Code is divided into two parts. The first refers to "central banks" (defined as central banks or other authorities in charge of monetary policy) and the second refers to "financial agencies" (defined as "governmental units having exclusive or primary responsibility for the regulation, supervision, and oversight of the financial and payment systems").[6] In turn, each part is divided into four sections: (i) clarity of roles, responsibilities, and objectives; (ii) open process for formulating and reporting decisions; (iii) public availability of information on monetary/financial polices; and (iv) accountability and assurances of integrity.

Legal Status of the Code in the IMF

The Fund's development of the Code did not give rise to new obligations under the Fund's Articles of Agreement.[7] In other

---

[4] *Id.*, p. 2.
[5] Id.
[6] *Id.*, p. 11–12.
[7] For an examination of the status of standards and codes under international law, *see* Mario Giovanoli, A New Architecture for the Global Financial Market: Legal Aspects of International Financial Standard Setting, *International Monetary Law: Issues for the New Millennium*, Oxford University Press, 2000, pp. 3–59. The
(continued)

words, observance of the Code by members is voluntary. However, the Fund encourages observance of the Code through: (i) an examination of the extent of observance by members as part of Fund surveillance; (ii) closer examination of observance through voluntary pilot programs; (iii) the specification of observance of elements of the Code as part of conditionality for Fund credit; and (iv) the provision of technical assistance. These avenues for increasing observance are discussed further below.

Surveillance

Under Article IV of the Fund's Articles, the Fund is charged with overseeing the international monetary system. To fulfill this function, it conducts "firm surveillance over exchange rate policies of members" under Article IV, Section 3(b), and members are obliged to cooperate in this task. Since exchange rate policies could not be examined meaningfully in a vacuum, the Fund conducts its appraisal of a member's exchange rate policies "within the framework of a comprehensive analysis of the general economic situation and economic policy strategy of a member."[8] The phrase "comprehensive analysis" implies that Fund surveillance has a wide scope. In conducting Article IV consultation discussions with a member, Fund staff may deem information about the extent of a member's observance of the Code as particularly relevant for surveillance and bring it to the attention of the Executive Board of the Fund. At the Executive Board, peer pressure may be exercised upon the member to make progress with respect to such observance.

Pilot Programs

Information about a member's observance of the Code and other standards and codes may also feed into the Fund surveillance process through two voluntary pilot programs. In 1999, the staffs of the Fund and World Bank began preparing *Reports on the Observance of Standards and Codes* (ROSCs). These reports examine the extent to which participating members observe certain internationally

---

author argues that international standards are soft law that should be given appropriate legal status (i.e., enforceability) under international law.

[8] "Surveillance Over Exchange Rate Policies," *Selected Decisions*, Twenty-Fifth Issue, p. 13.

recognized standards and codes.[9] ROSCs are key components of the Financial Sector Assessment Program (FSAP), which the Fund and World Bank jointly launched later in the same year.[10] Under this program, participants undergo examinations of the strengths, risks, and vulnerabilities of their respective financial sectors. Reports arising from these examinations, namely, Financial Sector Stability Assessments (FSSAs) by Fund staff and Financial Sector Assessments (FSAs) by World Bank staff, may be published with the consent of the member involved.[11]

In this context, the Fund and World Bank have identified the relevant standards and codes to include: (i) the Special Data Dissemination Standard,[12] Code of Good Practices on Fiscal Transparency,[13] and Code of Good Practices on Transparency in Monetary and Financial Policies (International Monetary Fund); (ii) the Core Principles for Effective Banking Supervision (Basel Committee on Banking Supervision);[14] (iii) the International Accounting Standards (International Accounting Standards Committee, IASC);[15] (iv) the International Standards on Auditing (International Federation of Accountants, IFA);[16] (v) the Objectives and Principles of Securities Regulation (International Organization of Securities Commissions, IOSCO);[17] (vi) the Insurance Supervisory Principles (International Association of Insurance Supervisors, IAIS);[18] and (vii) the Core Principles for Systemically Important Payments Systems (Committee on Payments and Settlements System).[19] In addition, ROSCs may cover corporate governance, using the OECD Corporate Governance Principles[20] as a baseline, and

---

[9] *See* Reports on the Observance of Standards and Codes (ROSCs), www.imf.org/external/np/rosc/rosc.asp.
[10] *See* Financial Sector Assessment Program (FSAP), www.imf.org/external/np/fsap/fsap.asp and http://website92.worldbank.org/html/fsap_home.html.
[11] For FSSAs, *see* www.imf.org/external/np/fsap/fsap.asp#cp.
[12] *See Selected Decisions*, Twenty-Fifth Issue, pp. 451–69.
[13] *See* www.imf.org/external/np/fad/trans/index.htm.
[14] *See* www.bis.org/publ/bcbsc102.pdf.
[15] *See* www.iasc.org/uk/cmt/0001.asp.
[16] *See* www.ifac.org.
[17] *See* www.newrisk.ifci.ch/144440.htm.
[18] *See* http://www.iaisweb.org/framesets/pas.html.
[19] *See* http://www.bis.org/publ/cpss43.htm.
[20] *See* http://www1.oecd.org/daf/governance/principles.pdf, p. 10.

insolvency and creditor rights. The Fund has focused primarily on categories (i) and (ii) above.

In the preparation of ROSCs, the Fund and World Bank have adopted a modular approach because of the number of potential participants, the number of standards and codes, differing priorities, and the resource intensity of preparing these reports. Consequently, the coverage and timing of ROSC modules may differ from one participating member to another. ROSCs are published.[21]

Conditionality

In formulating conditionality for Fund credit to a member, the Fund may decide to include the member's subscription to the relevant standards or codes or observance of an element thereof as a condition of eligibility, a prior action,[22] or a structural performance criterion.[23] Such inclusion does not change their legal status in the Fund. Observance of elements of standards and codes remains voluntary, even if the Fund decides to include such observance as a condition for use of Fund credit, because such use is optional to a member.[24] The macroeconomic nature or macroeconomic impact of observance of the relevant standards and codes and, thus, the consistency of their observance with the Fund's Guidelines on Conditionality, has not been controversial.[25]

---

[21] *See* ROSC modules by country in www.imf.org/external/np/rosc/rosc.asp.

[22] Prior actions are measures that a member must implement prior to the Fund's consideration of its application for Fund credit. For some circumstances under which the Fund may require prior actions, *see Selected Decisions*, Twenty-Fifth Issue, pp. 74, 162–3, 195, and 252–53.

[23] Nonobservance of a structural or quantitative performance criterion interrupts a member's ability to draw on credit under a Fund arrangement (*see* "Relationship Between Performance Criteria and Phasing of Purchases Under Fund Arrangements—Operational Guidelines," *id*., pp. 151–54). In contrast, nonobservance of indicative targets or structural benchmarks do not interrupt a member's ability to draw.

[24] For the legal aspects of arrangements for use of Fund resources, *see* Chapter ... above.

[25] The Guidelines on Conditionality state: "Performance criteria will normally be confined to (i) macroeconomic variables, and (ii) those necessary to implement specific provisions of the Articles or policies adopted under them. Performance criteria may relate to other variables only in exceptional cases when they are essential
(continued)

So far, the Fund has established a direct link between standards and access to Fund credit only in respect of Contingent Credit Lines (CCLs). As a condition of eligibility, contingent financing will be committed only to members that have subscribed to the Special Data Dissemination Standard.[26] In contrast, the Fund will be only "taking into account the extent of the member's adherence to relevant internationally-accepted standards," including the Basel Core Principles for Banking Supervision and the two Fund codes on transparency.[27]

In the absence of such direct link for other Fund facilities, the Fund exercises judgment, within the broad principle of uniformity of treatment, on whether or not to include observance of elements of relevant standards and codes as prior actions or structural performance criteria, in light of its appropriateness as part of a package of conditionality.

Technical Assistance

At a member's request, the Fund may decide to provide technical assistance, as authorized by Article V, Section 2(b). In the present context, the Fund has provided technical assistance to members wishing to increase the extent of their observance mainly of those standards and codes within the Fund's direct operational focus, namely, data dissemination, fiscal transparency, monetary and financial transparency, and banking supervision.

Transparency Through Law

In recent years, the need to update the central bank laws of republics of the former Soviet Union and allied states that had become members of the Fund and the negotiations leading to the establishment of the European Central Bank have given fresh impetus to the identification of the principles that underlie "good practices" in central bank law. At the broadest level, even taking account of differences in central banking cultures and legal systems, the

---

for the effectiveness of the member's program because of their macroeconomic impact" (*id.*, p. 150).
[26] *Id.*, p. 237.
[27] *Id.*

examination of good practices has pointed to the values of transparency, independence, accountability, and public consultation. While the Code is meant to promote transparency, its choice of matters that are to be made transparent through law also reflects these other values.

In most legal systems, laws are a matter of public record. Indeed, they generally do not become effective until published in an official gazette or similar publication. Thus, laws may be chosen as vehicles for transparency. In so doing, other considerations come into play. First, as laws generally reflect the culmination of a process by which the executive and legislative branches of government reach an agreement, they are not easily amended or reversed. Thus, laws tend to incorporate elements that are envisaged to be stable over the long term. Second, the degree of precision in laws that is necessary for enforcement contributes to transparency. Finally, laws generally specify consequences for noncompliance, thereby bolstering accountability.

Section 1.1 of the Code provides that the following should be included in law: (i) the ultimate objective(s) of monetary policy; (ii) the responsibilities of the central bank; (iii) authority of the central bank to utilize monetary policy instruments; (iv) broad modalities of accountability of the central bank for the conduct of monetary policy and other responsibilities; (v) authority of the government, if any, to override the central bank, the conditions under which this authority may be invoked, and the manner in which it is publicly disclosed; (vi) procedures for appointment, terms of office, and any general criteria for removal of the heads and members of the central bank's governing body.[28] In contrast, the Code is less prescriptive about transparency through law for financial agencies. Section 5.1 provides only that the broad objective(s) and institutional framework of financial agencies should be "clearly defined, preferably in relevant legislation or regulation." This difference in approach was brought about by the greater variation among institutional arrangements for

---

[28] Reflecting the wide variety of practices on how exchange rates for currencies of Fund members are determined, the Code does not provide that institutional responsibility for foreign exchange policy be specified in law; rather, Section 1.1.4 provides that it should be just publicly disclosed.

financial agencies across the membership than those for central banks.

The commentary to the Code, which is contained in a Supporting Document,[29] notes the diversity of objectives among central banks. Objectives include, for example, a single qualitative objective (e.g., price stability), multiple qualitative objectives (e.g., price stability with sound development), or a single qualitative objective combined with a quantitative objective (e.g., price stability plus a numerical inflation target).[30] Clearly, the more specific the objective, the easier a central bank may be held accountable for performance. However, the Supporting Document recognizes that specificity in law may reduce a central bank's flexibility to deal with changing circumstances.[31] This is so because the time horizon for a desired shift in course is typically shorter than the period it would take to amend legislation. Thus, the Code's provision that a central bank's ultimate objective(s) be included in law should not necessarily be read to mean that the objective(s) be specified in law in such detail as to preclude flexibility.[32] Where such flexibility is obtained through the adoption of multiple objectives, the Supporting Document urges central banks to disclose their respective priorities so that the public would be aware of potential trade-offs.[33]

Some of the Code's provisions may serve to protect a central bank from governmental interference in its operations and management. Specifying a central bank's responsibilities and authority to utilize monetary instruments in law, as most central bank laws do, would demarcate its jurisdiction but may not be sufficient to shield it from such interference. Hence, the Code provides for transparency under law of the conditions, if any, under which the

---

[29] IMF, "Supporting Document to the Code of Good Practices on Transparency in Monetary and Financial Policies," July 24, 2000 (hereafter "Supporting Document," www.imf.org/external/np/mae/mft/sup/index.htm).

[30] *Id.*, Part 2, pp. 2–4.

[31] *Id.*, Part 2, p. 4.

[32] In New Zealand, for instance, while the Reserve Bank Act states the Bank's objective to be "achieving and maintaining stability in the general level of prices," a quantitative target range is included in a publicly disclosed and periodically renewed Policy Targets Agreement between the Governor of the Reserve Bank and the Treasurer (*id.*, Part 2, p. 3).

[33] *Id.*, Part 2, p. 4.

government may override central bank decisions (Section 1.1.6) and under which heads and members of the central bank's governing body may be removed (Section 1.1.7).

Making transparent any legal process whereby a government may override central bank decisions would tend to reduce the probability that a government would do so. If there were such a directive, the government rather than the central bank would then be directly accountable for the action involved. The Supporting Document's survey of countries with laws that have provisions for government directives to the central bank indicates that none have been issued.[34] In lieu of a directive, a government may seek to obtain a change in central bank decisions by replacing central bank officials. Transparency in the conditions and reasons for such an act would tend to limit resort to this alternative.

The term "modalities of accountability" refers to "the means, methods, and procedures used by a central bank to account for its actions and report on its activities."[35] These would include annual reports, written reports to the legislature, reports in official bulletins, and public appearances by officials before the legislature.[36] The Code's provision that these modalities be specified in law is intended to achieve regular and consistent reporting.[37] Where regular reporting has been established as a matter of custom, law would codify practice. Where there is no custom of regular reporting, the Code's provision is intended to spur the initiation of such reporting.

Transparency Through Public Consultations

In many legal systems, proposed changes in laws are subject to public consultations, such that entities directly impacted by such laws, as well as other interested parties, are given notice and an opportunity to be heard. With open consultations, even parties that are not able to participate in formal processes (e.g., hearings before a legislature) may provide informed commentary, for example, through media editorials. Also, as part of the process of accountability in many

---

[34] *Id.*, Part 2, p. 9.
[35] *Id.*, Part 1, p. 30–31.
[36] *Id.*, Part 2, p. 8.
[37] *Id.*, Part 2, p. 7.

countries, central bank officials are required by law to explain their recent actions and analyses in periodic hearings before governmental authorities, typically legislative committees. As a process for transparency, hearings differ from written reports in two important respects. Hearings are generally unscripted events and testimony is provided in person. In providing opportunities for spontaneous exchanges of views and for the observation of participants' demeanor, hearings may convey information to the public that would not necessarily be available with written reports.

The Code endorses transparency through public consultations. Sections 2.5 and 6.4 provide that there should be a presumption of public consultations in respect of substantive technical changes to the structure of monetary and financial regulations, respectively. The Supporting Document indicates that such consultations may take the form of public hearings, an open period for submission of written comments, posting on a website, or meetings with parties most directly affected.[38] Sections 4.1 and 8.1 also provide that officials of central banks and financial agencies, respectively, should be available to appear before a designated public authority to report on the conduct of monetary or financial policy, explain policy objectives and performance in achieving them, and exchange views on the state of the economy and financial system. Noting that some countries require quarterly appearances by central bank officials during a year, the Supporting Document suggests a frequency of at least once a year, to be augmented by more appearances should there be major new developments affecting monetary policy.[39]

Legal Protections for Official Acts

Legal protections for central banks and financial agency officials in the conduct of their official duties provide assurance that they would not be held personally liable for acts or omissions within the scope of such duties. The forms of such protections vary. Protection may be immunity from suit, or a guarantee of indemnity for legal defense and judgment costs.[40] It may not cover situations involving

---

[38] *Id.*, Part 2, p. 34, Part 3, pp. 22–23.
[39] *Id.*, Part 2, p. 55.
[40] *Id.*, Part 2, p. 65, Part 3, pp. 52–54.

bad faith, misconduct, or willful default.[41] It may be expressed in a generic law that applies to officials generally or in a statute specific to an institution.[42]

Sections 4.4.1 and 8.4.1 of the Code provide for the public disclosure of information on legal protections for officials and staff of central banks and financial agencies, respectively, in the conduct of official duties. Two comments may be made. First, while the texts of these sections refer only to disclosure, the Supporting Document supports the adoption of such protections on the ground that the constant threat of legal action could undermine policymaking in controversial areas, thereby reducing the effectiveness of central banks and financial agencies.[43] This position is in accord with Principle 1 of the Core Principles for Effective Banking Supervision, which states in part: "A suitable legal framework for banking supervision is also necessary, including . . . legal protection for supervisors."[44] Second, protections that are specified in law would, by definition, already be in the public domain. The Supporting Document's rationale for further information is that unwarranted lawsuits are burdensome and could be deterred with the publication of information on the scope and procedures of such protections.[45]

Conclusion

After the outbreak of the Asian crisis, the Fund launched a number of initiatives aimed at establishing a "new architecture of the international financial system" that would be less vulnerable to crises. A pillar of this initiative is the promotion of the observance of certain standards and codes, including the Code of Good Practices on Transparency in Monetary and Financial Policies developed by the Fund. While such observance is voluntary on the part of the Fund's members, the Fund encourages observance through surveillance, pilot programs that focus more closely on observance, conditionality in the

---

[41] *Id.*
[42] *Id.*, Part 3, p. 53.
[43] *Id.*, Part 2, p. 65; *id*, Part 3, p. 52.
[44] *See* www.bis.org/publ/bcbsc102.pdf, p. 13. An explanatory note states that among the components that Principle 1 requires being in place is "protection (normally in law) from personal and institutional liability for supervisory actions taken in good faith in the course of performing supervisory duties" (*id.*).
[45] Supporting Document, Part 2, p. 65.

use of Fund credit, and technical assistance. In the choice of law as a medium for transparency and in the choice of particular elements of the institutional framework for monetary and financial management that are to be made transparent through law, the Code also promotes the values of stability, independence, accountability, and public consultation.

IV. International Capital Flows

Chapter **13**

Liberalization of Capital Movements: A Possible Role for the IMF

FRANÇOIS GIANVITI

At the time of the Bretton Woods Conference, in 1944, during which the Articles of Agreement of the IMF were adopted, a distinction was made between payments for current international transactions, which all Fund members undertook to liberalize over time, and international capital movements, over which they retained the right to impose controls. These two principles were embodied in Article VIII, Section 2(a) (current payments) and Article VI, Section 3 (capital movements). The reason for the distinction may be found in the purposes of the Fund.

Article I, which lists the Fund's purposes, states that one of the Fund's purposes is "[T]o facilitate the expansion and balanced growth of international trade." This does not mean that the Fund was established to liberalize trade; it was only established "to facilitate" international trade through a monetary system conducive to an expansion of international trade. The liberalization of payments for trade in goods and services was seen as an essential element of this monetary system. These payments constitute "payments for current transactions" (Article XXX). Consequently, another purpose of the Fund, also stated in Article I, is "[T]o assist in the establishment of a multilateral system of payments in respect of current transactions between members and in the elimination of foreign exchange restrictions which hamper the growth of world trade."

In contrast, Article I does not mention the liberalization of international capital movements as a purpose of the Fund. At the time of the Bretton Woods Conference, it was expected that controls on capital movements would remain necessary for the foreseeable future and the liberalization of capital movements was not regarded as being as important for international financial relations as the liberalization of current payments. The considerable expansion of capital markets and international capital movements that began in the late 1960s and early 1970s and has continued ever since was not foreseen in 1944.

One major consequence of the decision not to make the liberalization of capital movements a purpose of the Fund can be found in the provisions governing the Fund's financial assistance to its members. While a member may have access to the Fund's general resources to meet a current account deficit, there is a limitation on this access with respect to deficits attributable to capital outflows. Under Article VI, Section 1, a member may not use the Fund's general resources to meet a large or sustained outflow of capital (subject to a few exceptions) and the Fund may request a member to impose controls to prevent such use of its resources. Failure by the member to exercise appropriate controls on capital outflows could result in a declaration of ineligibility to use the Fund's general resources. In fact, the Fund has never found it necessary to request the imposition of such controls, even in recent cases of countries facing major capital outflows.

Under the Fund's Articles, the sovereignty of members applies to both inflows and outflows. For instance, in order to preserve national ownership over local assets (such as land or factories), a member may restrict foreign investments in its territory. Or, a member may be more concerned about short-term capital inflows which, if they are not sterilized, will have an inflationary effect on the local economy and, even if sterilized, may raise the exchange rate to a level that prices local exports out of world markets, not to mention the risk of sudden reflows for speculative reasons. Outflows raise different problems. They may be due to concerns about the country's political stability or the future of the local currency in relation to other currencies, or simply to the attraction of more profitable business opportunities abroad. Depending on the circumstances, the authorities may want to restrict outflows in order to protect the value of the local currency, or to provide local investors with low cost resources (which will create or maintain jobs) by preventing local savings from being invested abroad, or because they want to raise more taxes and fear a loss of their tax base to more frugal jurisdictions.

When imposing restrictions, a country may separately restrict the investment transaction and the payment or transfer related to the transaction. For instance, a member could allow a foreign investor to sell its local investment but prohibit the repatriation of capital. Many countries that have liberalized capital inflows impose limits on foreign direct investments in strategically important sectors of their economies.

The sovereignty of members over capital movements is limited, however, by a broad definition of what constitutes a current payment within the meaning of the Fund's Articles. For instance, the payment of interest on loans or of net income from other investments is regarded as current. Similarly, "payments of moderate amount for amortization of loans or for depreciation of direct investments" are regarded as current. They may not be restricted without the approval of the Fund.

Subject to this, rather minor, qualification, the distinction between current payments and capital movements remains one of the main features of the Fund's Articles, and yet, since 1944, the world's financial relations have undergone considerable changes. Current payments today represent only a small fraction of international transfers. Many countries have entered into international agreements to liberalize capital movements either on a bilateral or multilateral basis. The European Community Treaty, NAFTA, the OECD Capital Liberalization Code, and the General Agreement of Trade in Services are all examples of the trend toward the liberalization of capital inflows and outflows.

In 1976, at the time the Second Amendment of the Fund's Articles was being adopted, a provision was included in Article IV, which recognized the importance of capital movements. The preamble of Article IV, Section 1 states: "Recognizing that the essential purpose of the international monetary system is to provide a framework that facilitates the exchange of goods, services, and capital among countries." One could have expected that the recognition of the importance of capital movements would lead to an amendment of the Fund's purposes and Article VI to achieve a gradual liberalization of capital movements, but neither Article I nor Article VI were amended to that effect.

More recently, in September 1997, a report of the Executive Board recommended an amendment of the Fund's Articles "to make the liberalization of capital movements one of the purposes of the Fund and to extend the Fund's jurisdiction to capital movements." The Interim Committee at its Hong Kong meeting in 1997 endorsed the idea of an amendment of the Fund's Articles to promote "an orderly liberalization of capital movements." In a statement on the Liberalization of Capital Movements Under an Amendment of the Articles, the Committee invited "the Executive Board to complete its work on a proposed amendment of the Fund's Articles that would make the liberalization of capital movements one of the purposes of the Fund, and extend, as needed, the Fund's jurisdiction through the establishment of carefully defined and consistently applied obligations regarding the liberalization of such movements. Safeguards and transitional arrangements are necessary for the success of this major endeavor. Flexible approval policies will have to be adopted. In both the preparation of an amendment to its Articles and in its implementation, the members' obligations under other international agreements will be respected. In pursuing this work, the Committee expects the IMF and other institutions to cooperate closely."

Pursuant to the mandate given by the Executive Board and endorsed by the Interim Committee, the Fund's staff prepared a number of reports examining the policy and legal aspects of a liberalization of capital movements. These reports drew on the experience of unilateral, bilateral and multilateral (EC and OECD) liberalization programs. Particular attention was given to the scope of liberalization, the design of transitional arrangements, and the possibility of reimposing restrictions in cases of major crises.

At the 1998 seminar for central banks' legal advisers, Mr. Hagan and myself discussed the main issues that would have to be addressed in an amendment of the Fund's Articles (cf. *Current Developments in Monetary and Financial Law*, Volume I, IMF, 1999, pp. 7 and 68). Since then, work within the Fund has continued but the context has changed. In the various financial crises of the last few years, heavily indebted countries were faced with major and sudden reflows of foreign capital for which they were unprepared. The international official community was willing to help but concerns were expressed about the moral hazard of bailing out, with official money, countries that had overborrowed and private creditors who had made highly profitable but risky investments.

Therefore, it was no longer clear that the liberalization of capital movements was an objective that should be pursued by the Fund. If it was to be an objective for a particular country, it should be left to the country to decide whether and how to pursue it.

Moreover, rather than trying to convince countries to liberalize capital movements it was perhaps more important to advise them on how to proceed, for instance, by regulating short-term inflows, strengthening their financial systems, etc.

Finally, if a country decided to liberalize capital movements, it should not expect unlimited financing from the Fund and official lenders. The private lenders (banks and bondholders) should participate in the rescue operation, for instance, through debt reduction or debt rescheduling. Private sector involvement could be facilitated if revolving lines of credit were in place and if majority restructuring provisions were included in sovereign and private bond instruments.

At this stage it is not clear whether the Articles of Agreement will be amended to provide for a liberalization of capital movements through an extension of the Fund's jurisdiction. Instead of extending the Fund's jurisdiction, it has been suggested to make the liberalization of capital movements a component of Fund conditionality, similar to trade liberalization. This approach raises several difficulties. The first one is that it would require an amendment of Articles I (purposes) and VI, Section 3 (sovereignty over capital movements) of the Articles. Moreover, a major difference between jurisdiction and conditionality is that jurisdiction applies to all members at all times (except for transitional periods), while conditionality is selective and reversible as it applies only to users of Fund resources and for the duration of the program. Imposed through conditionality, liberalization may be seen as a cost of using Fund resources (i.e., a sacrifice imposed on debtor countries to the benefit of creditor countries) rather than a common goal shared by all Fund members. Another difficulty is that, unlike trade liberalization, which may result in a current account deficit for which Fund resources are available, a large or sustained capital outflow cannot be financed with Fund resources (Article VI, Section 1).

A compromise solution could be found, but it would probably have to combine three elements:

- a voluntary and gradual liberalization, not imposed by the Fund, but decided by each member;

- a willingness of the Fund to provide additional financing for capital outflows; and

- a protection of public and private debtors against actions of foreign creditors, similar to a stay on creditors' actions in the context of insolvency proceedings.

A Voluntary and Gradual Liberalization, Not Imposed by the IMF

"Voluntary" and "not imposed" sound like a tautology, but they are not.

(a) Given the diversity in the levels of economic development and in the financial systems of its members, the Fund would not impose a "one size fits all" approach to capital liberalization. Through surveillance and technical assistance, it could help each member achieve its own objectives in light of its own circumstances. For instance, a member could decide to liberalize certain capital transactions while others would remain subject to restrictions.

What would be the differences with the present system? There would be two differences, both of which would be intended to give confidence to investors.

The first one would be that, once a transaction had been liberalized and as long as it was liberalized, payments and transfers related to that transaction could not be restricted without Fund approval. For instance, assuming that a member authorizes its residents to invest abroad, all payments and transfers related to those investments must be permitted. If, subsequently, investments abroad by residents are prohibited, payments and transfers related to prior investments must still be permitted, unless the Fund approves the restriction. The disruptive practice of prohibiting payments and transfers related to permitted transactions would then disappear. However, if the imposition of restrictions became necessary, in the judgment of the Fund, for balance of payments or security reasons, the member would be authorized to restrict payments and transfers for capital transactions.

The second difference would be that a member could, when or after liberalizing a transaction, notify the Fund that it undertakes not to reimpose restrictions on this transaction. Then the liberalization would become irreversible. No restriction could be imposed by the member on that transaction, except again with Fund approval. In its notification, the member could limit the scope of its undertaking. For instance, it could reserve the right to reimpose certain restrictions or, in the case of a federal system, reserve the right of local authorities to impose restrictions that are within their powers.

One of the reasons why a member may be reluctant to make a commitment of irreversibility is the concern that the Fund may be unwilling to approve the imposition of a restriction in cases where the member finds it necessary. This could be remedied through a system of representation which could only be challenged by the Fund under certain conditions. For instance, if the member stated that the restriction was needed to protect an essential national interest, the restriction would automatically be deemed to be approved unless the Fund, by a special majority of the Executive Board, found the representation unwarranted.

Another area of concern for some members is their freedom to restrict inward direct investments. These investments are often politically sensitive as they affect military, strategic, or cultural sectors in which foreign investments may be seen as a threat to national sovereignty. It would be possible to decide that liberalization of inward direct investment is always reversible. The problem is the definition of what constitutes inward direct investment. If the definition is left to each country, every liberalization becomes reversible. A reasonable solution would be provisionally to leave it to each country to decide whether a particular transaction constitutes inward direct investment, but the Fund would have the power to decide, by a special majority whether a particular type of transaction constitutes inward direct investment; this decision would apply uniformly to all members. In order to impose a restriction on such transactions, a member could then only invoke the preservation of an essential national interest as explained above.

Finally, a member could be reluctant to enter into a commitment to liberalize foreign investments within its territory without a quid pro quo liberalization by other countries. This could be achieved through concerted liberalization, e.g., a group of countries could decide to liberalize the same transactions at the same time vis-à-vis all other Fund members.

A more radical solution would be for each country to enter into a commitment vis-à-vis a specified country or group of countries and to liberalize only on the basis of a reciprocal commitment by those other countries. This would be a system of bilateral or regional commitments, similar to the EC or NAFTA systems. A multilateral organization like the Fund would normally have a preference for multilateral liberalization, as is the case for current payments. Liberalizing vis-à-vis some but not others is regarded as a discriminatory practice, prohibited by Article VIII, Section 3 for current payments. The same approach could apply to capital movements.

(b) A voluntary liberalization is by definition not imposed by the Fund. As there is no obligation to liberalize, how could it be imposed by the Fund? Experience shows, however, that the Fund may impose liberalization even in the absence of obligation. The best example is trade liberalization. There is no obligation under the Fund's Articles to liberalize trade, which is within the jurisdiction of the GATT and GATS administered by the World Trade Organization. However, trade liberalization is often a component of Fund programs.

Therefore, during the discussions that took place within the Fund on a possible amendment for the liberalization of capital movements, some were of the view that conditionality should be used to achieve that objective. This would require an amendment of the Fund's purposes and a deletion of Article VI, Section 3. Once capital liberalization had become one of the Fund's purposes and the right to control capital movements had disappeared, Fund conditionality could be used to liberalize capital movements.

This view did not receive much support. It was felt that, if liberalization was to be achieved, it should be on the basis of either an obligation for all members to liberalize or a purely voluntary decision, without Fund pressure, by each member.

Even if Fund conditionality is not used for the liberalization of capital movements, a member may wish to include at least some form of liberalization in its Fund-supported program, mainly to attract foreign investments and reassure local and foreign investors.

Additional Financing from the IMF

If conditionality is a stick, additional financing is a carrot: it provides an incentive for avoiding restrictions. One of the most interesting features of the recent financial crisis was the unwillingness of countries faced with massive capital outflows to impose restrictions. The reason was rather simple: such restrictions would have hampered their future access to capital markets. An even more interesting feature was that the Fund did not request, as it was authorized by the Articles, the imposition of capital controls. Those countries were given access to Fund resources for unprecedented amounts to face those outflows.

This raises a question of consistency with Article VI, Section 1, which precludes the use of Fund resources for large or sustained capital outflows. Partly, the answer is that some of the outflows were current payments according to the definition in Article XXX. Partly, it is that the reconstitution of a country's reserves and the provision of additional financing to restore confidence are not incompatible with Article VI, Section 1. Finally, in the absence of a definition of what constitutes a large or sustained capital outflow, a precise limit on the level of financing cannot be set.

In recognition of the destabilizing effect of capital outflows and in order to assist its members, the Fund has adopted two new policies.

In December 1997, the Supplemental Reserve Facility (SRF) was created to help members "experiencing exceptional balance of payments difficulties due to a large short-term financing need resulting from a sudden and disruptive loss of market confidence reflected in pressure on the capital account and the member's reserves, if there is a reasonable expectation that the implementation of strong adjustment policies and adequate financing will result, within a short period of time, in an early correction of such difficulties."

Financing under the SRF is additional to what the member may receive under the Fund's credit tranche policies or the extended Fund facility. It is provided for a short period of time (each purchase must be reversed within 2 to 2 years, with an expectation of early repurchase within 1 to 1 years) and at a cost substantially higher than the normal cost of Fund resources (surcharge of 300 basis points, increasing by 50 basis points every six months after one year).

In April 1999, a second decision created the Contingent Credit Lines (CCL) as a preventive financial support against risks of contagion. Under the CCL, resources additional to the credit tranches may be committed before contagion strikes, but they are disbursed only when the risk materializes. In order for a member to qualify for a disbursement, the following conditions must be met: "...as a result of circumstances that are largely beyond the control of the member and that stem primarily from adverse developments in international capital markets consequent upon developments in other countries, the member is experiencing exceptional payments difficulties due to a large short-term financing need resulting from a sudden and disruptive loss of market confidence reflected in pressure on the capital account and the member's reserves, if there is a reasonable expectation that adequate financing and the implementation of any necessary adjustment policies will result, within a short period of time, in an early correction of such difficulties."

Except for the reference to contagion coming from other countries, the activation of the CCL resembles the conditions of the SRF; the cost and duration of the financing are very similar, except that the initial surcharge has been reduced to 150 basis points, in order to make the facility more attractive. The main difference is that the SRF is only available when the crisis strikes, while the CCL allows for a prior commitment of resources subject to certain conditions. In practice, however, the CCL has had no takers. One possible reason is that the conditions for a commitment of resources under the CCL are too stringent; the member needs to meet a broad range of conditions to satisfy the Fund that its policies are adequate and will not, by themselves, create a balance of payments problem. Another reason is that the activation of the CCL is not automatic: the Fund must be satisfied that the member will make the necessary policy adjustments; it may phase the purchases; and impose additional conditions for the disbursements. A third reason is the cost: a commitment fee for a large amount, which may not eventually be released, plus a surcharge (now reduced).

Although it is not often mentioned, there may be a fourth and deeper reason, which is the concern that foreign lenders may see a country's request for a CCL as a sign that the country expects a major financial crisis. If no rain is expected, why carry an umbrella?

In any case, suggestions have been made that easier access to the CCL, perhaps with guaranteed activation in case of contagion, would strengthen confidence and give countries easier access to capital markets. By way of consequence, countries would also feel more confident when liberalizing capital movements if they had the assurance that, in times of crisis, the Fund will stand ready to provide large amounts of financial assistance, even if it is for a short period and with a surcharge.

Realistically, however, the Fund's resources would not be sufficient to meet all the demands for financial assistance in cases of major financial crises. Moreover, the Fund's resources need to be safeguarded and, to that extent, a participation of official lenders and the private sector in the resolution of major crises is necessary.

Another argument against large "bail-out" financing is that it creates a "moral hazard." This argument comes from a perceived analogy between the role of the Fund and the role of central banks. As lenders of last resort, central banks are expected to intervene to stem systematic crises in the banking system but without creating an incentive for risky investments with or by commercial banks. Although the Fund is not a lender of last resort in any realistic sense and its interventions are not limited to systemic crises, the "moral hazard" argument is often used to denounce what is seen as excessive generosity with public money to the benefit of both the mismanaged countries and their greedy creditors. Although the debtor country and its creditors are often lumped together in the "moral hazard" argument, the issue is not the same in both cases.

If the objective is to punish debtor countries for pursuing bad policies, then most countries should be deprived of their access to Fund resources, either for their current account deficit or their capital account deficit. However, the Fund was not established to punish but to assist. A hospital does not refuse to treat the victim of an accident on the ground that he was responsible for the accident. The Fund's assistance is provided for the common good. If the debtor country does not receive financial assistance, it may impose trade and exchange restrictions, which will be detrimental to other members. Moreover, the moral hazard, when applied to a country, would mean that the population should suffer because of the actions of its government. In fact, Fund conditionality will often have that effect because higher interest rates and tighter fiscal policies will affect the standard of living, but this is an unintended result—partly remedied through safety nets—not an objective of Fund conditionality.

The "moral hazard" argument is also used with respect to private creditors, and it is true that the same creditors who charge high interest rates as a risk premium do not want to bear the consequences of their imprudent lending and will insist on full repayment. (It is not clear why official bilateral credits—e.g., for arms sales—are not mentioned as creating a moral hazard.) The problem here is that the only way to avoid the moral hazard of a bailout with public money is to deny the debtor country's request for assistance, at least in part. The result is a default on the country's debt, which will probably make it difficult later for that country to have access to capital markets. Since the Fund's resources are limited, this result may not be avoided, but the reason should not be that the Fund is forcing a country to default in order to punish the creditors, which could be regarded as tortious interference in the country's relations with its creditors.

The rationale for the Fund's decision to limit its assistance can only be the safeguard of its resources, in accordance with the relevant provisions of its Articles: Article I, which defines its purposes; Article V, Section 3(a), which governs access to the Fund's general resources; and Article VI, Section 1, which limits access to the Fund's general resources for capital outflows. Given the particular limitations in Article VI, Section 1, on the provision of financial assistance for capital outflows, these limitations would need to be reviewed in the context of an amendment of the Articles that would promote the liberalization of capital movements.

A Stay on Creditors' Actions

When a country faces a major capital outflow, the foreign exchange held by the banking sector and the monetary reserves of the central bank become insufficient to meet outward payments and transfers. Exchange restrictions may need to be imposed. In addition, the currency has usually depreciated to a point where many local debtors can no longer afford to buy enough foreign exchange to service their external debt. This includes government debt. Inability to pay means default and, at least for private debtors, possible bankruptcy.

Sometimes, the government or public or private entities may find foreign sources of financing: loans, exports, concession contracts. However, foreign creditors may attach these assets, with the result that even essential imports cannot be financed. Some assets may be protected by the debtor country's sovereign immunity, but sometimes the immunity has been waived as a condition for a loan and the creditors will enforce their claim on any assets they can find.

Various suggestions have been made to remedy this situation. The idea of an international bankruptcy court for sovereign debtors has been put forward, but it would be extremely difficult to implement.

A simpler proposal would be to provide for a stay on all creditors' actions against two categories of debtors: those who are prevented from discharging a debt as a result of exchange controls, and sovereign debtors defaulting on an international debt.

There is, in the Fund's Articles, a provision which could be regarded as a partial illustration of this approach. Article VIII, Section 2(b) does offer some protection against creditors when the debtor is unable to fulfill his obligation because of exchange controls imposed consistently with the Fund's Articles. However, this provision does not apply to sovereign debtors' defaults. Moreover, even in the case of exchange controls, it applies only to "exchange contracts" and this expression has been interpreted differently in different countries. The courts of some countries (e.g., France) have adopted a broad interpretation, which would include loan agreements and other contracts creating financial obligations. In other countries (e.g., the U.S. and the U.K.), the courts have adopted a narrow reading and limited the provision to contracts for the exchange of currencies. In another country (Germany), the broader interpretation has been adopted but it has been limited to contracts for current transactions, on the ground that the title of Article VIII, Section 2 deals with restrictions on current payments and that restrictions on capital movements may be imposed without the approval of the Fund.

An amendment of Article VIII, Section 2(b) could provide the basis for an effective stay on creditors' actions. However, some issues would need to be addressed. For instance, approval by the Fund may have to be required, while the present Article VIII, Section 2(b) applies under the sole condition that the restriction be consistent with the Articles. In the case of sovereign default, a condition of uniform treatment of creditors (e.g., between foreign and local creditors and among classes of similar creditors) could be imposed to avoid discrimination. Also, a system of payments in local currency into a blocked account might be envisaged to make sure that, once the stay is lifted, sufficient resources will be available to the creditors. The difficulty in the last instance, however, will be to ensure that the foreign exchange value of the deposits is maintained while the local currency is depreciating.

The unwillingness of a number of major countries, which are also financial centers, to cooperate in a common effort against violations of exchange controls may be contrasted with their calls for international cooperation against money laundering. Oddly enough, the most ardent supporters of a broad definition of money laundering, who also oppose a broad application of Article VIII, Section 2(b), do not seem to realize that the former would indirectly lead to the latter. If the violation of exchange controls constitutes a "predicate offense," then the holding or receipt of illegally obtained or transferred funds would constitute money laundering. The difference with Article VIII, Section 2(b), which provides only for the unenforceability of contracts, is that the perpetrators would be subject to criminal sanctions, with a possible confiscation of the funds.

Conclusion

Globalization has its supporters and its detractors. Its benefits have been so great, however, that it is likely to continue. The question, therefore, is not whether it will take place but how. Capital markets have become so large and provide so much needed financing that they are now a central element of the international financial system. The transformation of the Interim Committee into the International Monetary and Financial Committee (IMFC) was a recognition of the role of the international financial system in the world's economy. As the guardian under the Articles of the international monetary system, which now officially includes the international financial system, the Fund will have to deal with the role of capital markets and the expansion of capital movements. The liberalization of capital movements is taking place and the Fund will have to play its part in this evolution.

Chapter 14

A Dozen Things to Love (or Hate) About Capital Flows

VINCENT RAYMOND REINHART

Free and open international trade in goods and services generally receives widespread support among economists. It might seem paradoxical that there is less confidence in the profession that free and open international trade in financial capital yields benefits everywhere and at all times that exceed the costs. This paper argues that the difference of opinion producing this disparate policy advice is really quite narrow. Most economists would accept a handful of basic propositions about capital flows—reflecting both good and bad and explaining properties of basic economic theory and stylized empirical regularities. Analysts differ, however, in the weight they attach to each.

Introduction

Despite the sense of disarray and dissension sometimes conveyed to those outside the profession, economists by and large tend to agree on many fundamental propositions. Chief among them is the belief that substantial benefits accrue from free and open international trade in goods and services.[1] Indeed, the progress in opening trade in the latter half of the last century, although uneven, could be viewed as the singular triumph of an idea over short-term political expediency. It might seem paradoxical, then, that there is less confidence in the profession that free and open international trade in financial capital yields benefits everywhere and at all times that exceed the costs.

Note: The author has benefited from helpful commentaries made by Carmen Reinhart and Michael Gilbert.

[1] This is a point that recurs in Paul Krugman's popular writings, as in Krugman (1996), that is shown more formally in a survey of economists by Alston, Kearl, and Vaughan (1992). In that survey, more than 90 percent of the respondents held that tariffs and quotas reduce welfare.

Over the years, many economists, including James Tobin (1978), Rudiger Dornbusch (1986), and Jagdish Bhagwati (1998), have suggested slowing the trade in assets across borders.[2] In addition, institutions previously associated with advocacy of untrammeled capital flows—including the IMF—have begun to question just how far to push the opening up of trade in financial assets. Representative of that strain of thought was the product of a recent working group of the Financial Stability Forum, whose membership spans finance ministries, central banks, and securities regulators. In a March 2000 report on short-term capital flows, the working group reported:

> The use of controls on capital inflows may be justified for a transitional period in the face of very strong inflows or as countries strengthen the institutional and regulatory environment in their domestic financial systems, especially if the process of liberalization had not been carried out in a well-sequenced manner. In other words, some measures to discourage capital inflows may be used to reinforce or complement prudential requirements on financial institutions and other resident borrowers.[3]

Such support for limiting the international mobility of capital is by no means universal, with advocates of the free flow of capital including Martin Feldstein (1999) and Michael Dooley (1996), among others.

What this paper argues is that the difference of opinion producing this disparate policy advice is really quite narrow. Most economists would accept a handful of basic propositions about capital flows—reflecting both good and bad and explaining properties of basic economic theory and stylized empirical regularities. Analysts differ, however, in the weight they attach to each. While it is convenient to lay many of these propositions out in terms of simple tools of the economics trade, that technique should not be viewed as an obstacle to understanding. In reality, they are quite intuitive.

These 12 propositions logically fall into three groups, which correspond to the next three sections of this paper. In the next section, I will consider some implications of a fundamental tenet of

---

[2] For Dornbusch's recent views on capital controls, see Dornbusch (2001).
[3] Report of the Working Group on Capital Flows, Financial Stability Forum (2000), paragraph 115, p. 35.

economics: that people enter into trade because they expect to become better off as a result. International capital flows are but one example, essentially involving the exchange of goods across time. That simple proposition has two important implications. For one, the decisions of economic agents will be sensitive to market prices, giving policymakers a means to influence those outcomes through taxes or transfers in a way that is superior to quantitative controls. For another, a choice between current and future consumption ultimately has to be anchored by its income prospects. Simply, fundamentals matter.

The next set of propositions (in Section 3) are empirical in nature and are based on repeated observations that asset prices can sometimes show a remarkable amount of comovement across markets, that it can be difficult to relate those price movements to fundamentals, and that flows can be quite changeable. Moreover, these properties appear with more force in emerging market economies. Simply put, episodes of contagion, in which financial prices move sharply across financial centers in ways at odds with underlying economic developments and capital floods in or dries up, seem more prevalent in markets that are not as far up the ladder of economic progress.

The fourth section addresses some policy implications of simple economic models. Chief among them is the realization that policies are interrelated, known in the literature as the "impossible trinity" or less felicitously as the "trilemma."[4] National authorities can choose only two items from a menu of three: fixed exchange rates, independent monetary policy, and freely mobile capital. Thus, policymakers may, on occasion, be inclined to impose capital controls by an unwillingness to sacrifice the other two devotions of the impossible trinity. The remaining propositions about policy reflect other limitations on what authorities can do: it is easier to slow the entry of capital in good times than delay the exit of capital in bad times; constraining the volatility of one asset price may make other asset prices more volatile, and controls tend increasingly to be evaded over time.

---

[4] For a discussion of the impossible trinity, see Jeffrey Frankel (1999).

By understanding these 12 propositions, it should be easier to put into perspective the sometimes conflicting advice on policymaking, which is dealt with in more detail in the last section.

The Fundamentals of Capital Flows

Underlying the trade theory that explains the flow of goods and services internationally is the notion of equal exchange. Residents of one country bring goods to the world market, say the wine of Portugal in David Ricardo's famous example, and in return receive goods of equal value to them from residents of another country, say English cloth to complete the Ricardian example.[5] That both parties enter voluntarily into the transaction leads to a natural conclusion: the trade must have made each participant no worse off and must have made at least one better off. Had that not been true, the wine would have been drunk in Portugal and the cloth cut to cover the residents of England.

This property can be no less true for the free trade in assets. The difference, though, is that a financial asset adds an intertemporal dimension to the problem, in that its issuance represents a current receipt of revenue that obligates repayment at a later date or dates. A country borrowing on world markets today can engineer consumption outstripping current income as long as it can credibly establish its willingness to spend less than its income in order to repay the debt at a future date.

This point is established more formally in consumer choice theory and expressed clearly in Obstfeld and Rogoff (1997). The simplest example traces back to Irving Fisher's work (Fisher, 1930), which can be applied to two countries instead of two households. Consider a country with income of y_1 and y_2 in terms of a single good in periods 1 and 2. Consumption in both periods, at c_1 and c_2, respectively, is valued, but future benefits are discounted at a constant rate, ∃. Expressing that benefit in terms of an invariant utility function allows us to write what consumers ultimately care about as:

$$u(c_1) + \frac{1}{1+\beta} u(c_2).$$

---

[5] See chapter 7 of Ricardo's *The Principles of Political Economy and Taxation*, which was written in 1817 (Ricardo, 1973).

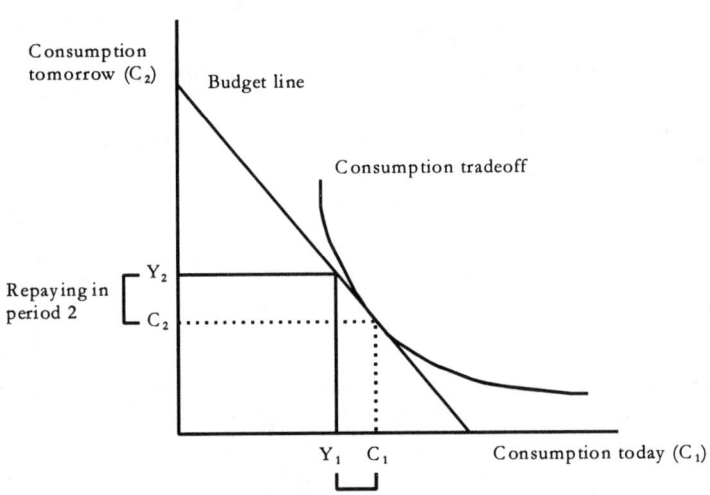

Figure 1: The benefit of intertemporal trade

As is obvious, different combinations of consumption today and tomorrow can attain the same level of utility, producing a family of indifference curve, one of which is depicted as "consumption tradeoff" in Fig. 1.

At the same time, a country must live within its means when viewed over the two periods. That is, any consumption in excess of its income in the first period must be repaid with interest, at the rate r, in the second period. This tells us:

$$(1 + r)(c_1 - y_1) = (y_2 - c_2),$$

which gives the linear "budget line" that slopes down in the figure.

The combination of consumption today and tomorrow where the consumption tradeoff is just tangent to the budget line offers the country the highest attainable level of welfare. In the particular example of the figure, this country would borrow on world financial markets in period 1 to consume more than its income and repay in the second period by consuming less than its income.[6] That outcome, in general, depends on the shape of the utility function, the time profile of income, and the real interest rate. The important point is a comparative one: without trade, the country would be limited to consuming exactly its income in each period, which would not make it as well off as under free trade. Intertemporal trade makes possible the option of consuming any point along the budget line. Unless circumstances satisfy the special case where the tangency of the indifference curve and the budget line occurs at the initial endowment [y_1, y_2], the country will choose a consumption path that involves some borrowing or lending. And that trade makes it better off.[7] The country on the other side of the transaction performs a similar calculation, implying

> *Proposition 1:* The voluntary trade in capital internationally is done only when both parties in a transaction believe it does not make them worse off and at least one better off.

This is not to say that those participants could be wrong in their beliefs or may not be including in their calculations costs to other members of society. It more narrowly says that the fact that trade is voluntary creates a presumption that participants are not knowingly harming themselves.

While most economists would accept this proposition, their judgments about the magnitudes of the benefits accruing from free intertemporal trade differ. To see why, note that the consumption decision could be thought to have two dimensions. Households might choose to consume more or less than their incomes in the first period because their endowments are uneven across the two periods (call this *income smoothing*) or because the rate at which they internally discount the future differs from the market interest rate (call this *interest-rate arbitrage*). For the simplest form of utility, where

---

[6] This, in effect, is a two-period simplification of the intertemporal approach to the current account associated with Buiter (1981) and Obstfeld (1982).

[7] Even in the special case where the tangency of the indifference curve to the budget line occurs at the endowment pair, the possibility of trade makes the country no worse off; rather, it fails to make it better off.

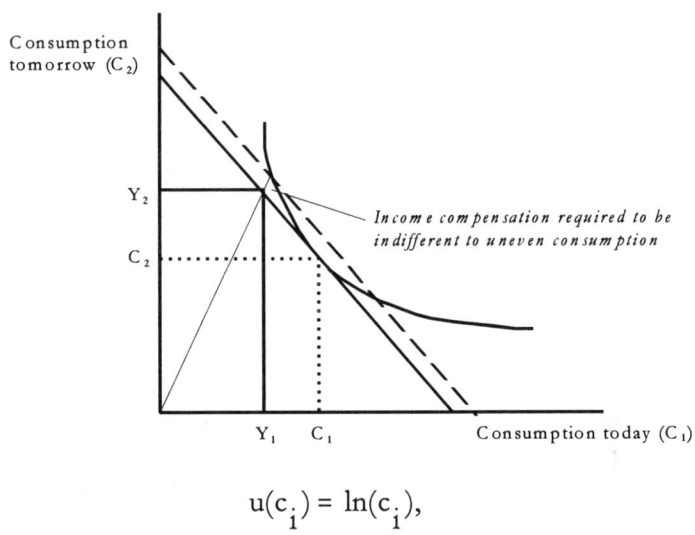

Figure 2: Benefit of smoothing income

[Figure: Graph with axes "Consumption tomorrow (C_2)" vertical and "Consumption today (C_1)" horizontal, showing points Y_2, C_2 on vertical axis and Y_1, C_1 on horizontal axis, with indifference curves and budget lines. Annotation: "Income compensation required to be indifferent to uneven consumption"]

$$u(c_i) = \ln(c_i),$$

the interior condition for optimal consumption takes the form:

$$\frac{1+r}{1+\beta} = \frac{c_2}{c_1}.$$

This simple case can be used to measure separately the benefits of income smoothing and interest rate arbitrage.

To begin this calculation, note that if the world interest rate equaled the rate of time preference ($r = \beth$), a country would want to consume the same amount in each period ($c_1 = c_2$). International trade in assets would permit a country to borrow or lend to smooth uneven endowments to engineer that optimal consumption path, as in Fig. 2. Note that the point where households consume their endowments in each period lies below the indifference curve available when there is free trade in capital—that is the welfare loss associated with halting the mobility of capital. The distance from that point (y_1, y_2) to the preferred indifference curve therefore represents the income compensation required to make the country just willing to accept an uneven consumption pattern. Thus, it is a way of measuring in terms of income the value put on open capital flows. Fig. 3 places numbers to this example. The horizontal axis measures the potential differences between income in the first and second periods as a share of second-period income, as in

$$\frac{y_2 - y_1}{y_1},$$

in percent terms.[8]

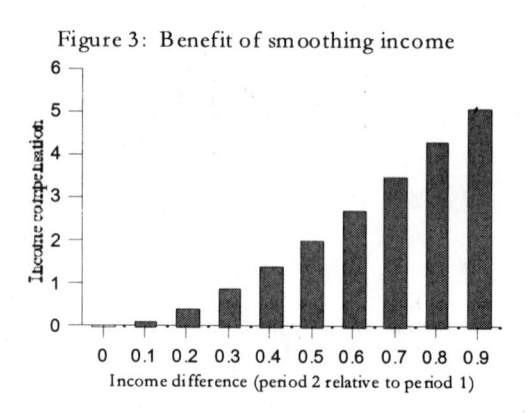

Figure 3: Benefit of smoothing income

[bar chart: Income compensation (vertical axis, 0 to 6) vs. Income difference (period 2 relative to period 1), 0 to 0.9]

The vertical axis plots the overall percent increase in income in both periods necessary to make the country indifferent between consuming exactly those uneven endowments without international trade and smoothing consumption with international trade.[9] It is not until income is substantially uneven over time—more than a one-quarter difference between the two periods—that the required income compensation necessary to offset the welfare loss from restricting capital mobility exceeds 1 percent. But in situations where income is very uneven over time, the compensation can be large—as much as 5 percent.

---

[8] When this measure is zero, income is equal in both periods; as it approaches minus one, all income is earned in the first period; as it gets arbitrarily large, all income is earned in the second period.

[9] This example considers the case where income is deferred ($y_2 > y_1$), but the problem is symmetric in the case where income is front-loaded ($y_1 > y_2$).

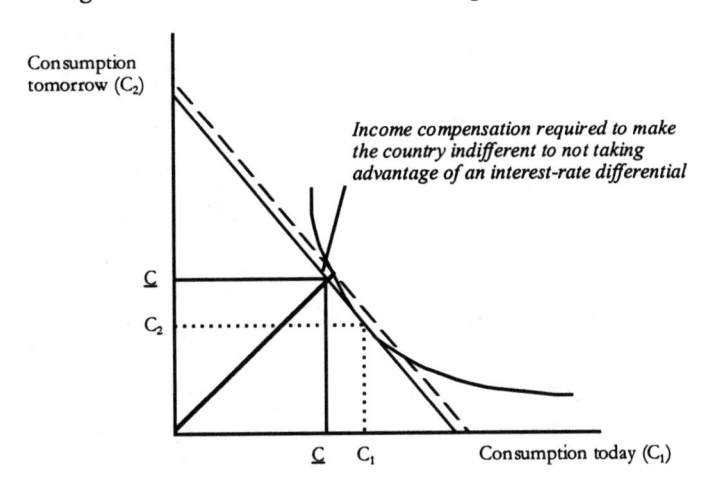

Figure 4: Benefit of interest-rate arbitrage

Income compensation required to make the country indifferent to not taking advantage of an interest-rate differential

The contribution to welfare of interest-rate arbitrage can be calculated analogously. To repeat, by the interior condition for consumption, spending today and tomorrow differ only when the real interest rate, r, differs from the rate of time preference, ∃. In Fig. 4, we ask how much extra income is needed to make a country consume exactly equal amounts in periods 1 and 2 (in the amount c̲) even though the world real interest rate is below the rate of time preference. The income compensation required to keep the country on the same indifference curve associated with the uneven consumption choice (that is produced with trade) but with equal consumption in both periods (if trade is not allowed) can be thought of as measuring the benefit of interest rate arbitrage—or borrowing or lending today to take advantage of the world real rate not equaling the rate of time preference.

Figure 5: Benefit of interest rate arbritrage

[Bar chart: Income compensation (percent) on y-axis (0 to 0.7); Rate of time preference on x-axis (0 to 0.24)]

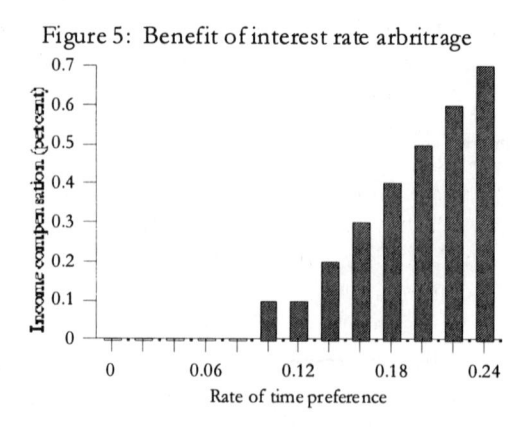

Fig. 5 performs these calculations for the case where the world real interest rate equals 4 percent and the rate of time preference varies from just above zero to as high as 24 percent.[10] As is evident, the income-equivalent benefits of interest rate arbitrage remain modest unless there is a substantial gap between how residents of the country discount the future relative to those in the rest of the world. This leads to a comparative statement most economists would accept:

Proposition 2: In terms of consumption, the benefit from smoothing income is large compared to the benefit of arbitraging interest rate differentials.

Of course, the relative magnitude of the difference between the two aspects of a country's dynamic choice importantly depends on the specification of welfare, including the assumption of a constant intertemporal elasticity of substitution. Indeed, focusing on the demand-side aspects of the effects of interest rates (by working with

---

[10] In general, the effect on current consumption of a change in the world real interest rates is ambiguous. On the one hand, a higher interest rate encourages deferring current consumption. On the other hand, a higher interest rate raises the income from saving, which encourages greater consumption in both periods. With the functional form assumed here, the first effect (the substitution effect) just cancels the second (the income effect). Thus, current consumption is a fixed share of present-discounted income. The question posed in the text is about how an interest rate differential influences relative consumption and welfare. Also note, the example varies the discount factor, not the world interest rate, implying that only the substitution effect is operative.

an endowment economy) may understate the welfare consequences of allowing trade. Production effects as firms equate the marginal product of capital to the real interest rate can be important, an issue discussed in Rogoff (1999).

More generally, an analyst's assessment of whether income smoothing or interest rate arbitrage predominates in international capital markets importantly influences the resulting evaluation of the benefits of those markets. Quite obviously, support for capital mobility will be greatest among those who see world financial markets as fostering borrowing and lending to smooth uneven income prospects—either to build a nest egg for rainy days or a backstop when the rain falls. In contrast, those who read more of financial market activity as responding to differences in interest rates internationally tend to see less benefit in that activity.

But the interior condition explaining consumption behavior also has implications for constructing policies toward international capital flows. To put the issue simply, national authorities have to understand that their citizens desire to smooth consumption. Sometimes that desire implies a willingness to borrow now on world capital markets—in particular, when future income looks rosier or the world real interest rate looks low compared to that at home. If that borrowing is viewed unfavorably by officials, they have two means to constrain their citizens' efforts to trade future income for current consumption. Policymakers can impose a quota (or in some other manner restrict the flow of assets) or place tariffs on goods or a tax on capital flows. For instance, if, as in Fig. 6, the country expected income to rise in the future (seen as the uneven endowments), it would borrow on world markets, allowing it to spend more than current income with funding from abroad (seen by the dashed budget line just tangent to the dashed indifference curve). To stem that inflow of capital, the government could put an explicit limit on capital, represented as the vertical line in the figure drawn to represent an outright ban on new borrowing (thus mandating a consumption choice that lies along the indifference curve drawn with a solid line).

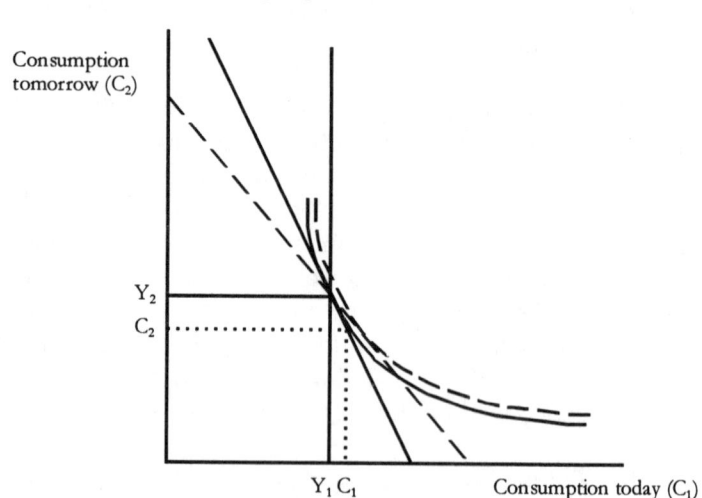

Figure 6: Restricting capital flows

Borrowing from abroad in period 1

In effect, the government imposes (y₂/y₁) as the consumption path. The problem is that, despite the quota, citizens of the country still want to obey the consumption-smoothing condition. The difference between what the public wants, consumption in the ratio (1+ r)/(1+∃), and what they are allowed, consumption in the ratio (y₂/y₁), defines an intervention wedge, T,

$$\omega = \frac{1+r/1+\beta}{y_2/y_1}$$

As long as transactions within the country are still voluntary, this wedge will be reflected in relative prices as people try to evade the quantitative restrictions. Either those who have access to foreign borrowing (presumably to roll over maturing holdings as net borrowing in the example was zero) could offload this right to do so and receive a return above r, or the price of consumption goods currently could rise relative to that in the future to induce an increased willingness to save.[11]

Alternatively, the government could apply a tax on foreign borrowing equal to T (or a tariff in an amount producing the same consequences for the intervention wedge) and thereby change incentives. A tax on foreign capital rotates the budget line in Figure 6, generating a voluntary outcome identical to the constrained one (and drawn by the more titled solid budget line). Unlike the quota, relative prices are directly affected and no private sector resources are wasted in the effort.

This leads naturally to proposition 3,

Proposition 3: Policy can influence the outcomes of individual choice by putting controls on quantities or by changing relative prices, but influencing prices tends to be less distorting than setting quantities.

Even more attractive to many economists is couching relative-price-based controls on capital in prudential terms and making them sensitive to the holding period of the instrument. For instance, as explained in World Bank (1997), the Chilean government taxes foreign interest income via a reserve requirement that effectively declines (in proportional terms) as the maturity of the instrument declines. Eichengreen and Wyplosz (1993) consider this issue from an industrial country perspective. A discussion of the various policy alternatives is given in Reinhart and Reinhart (1998) and a more specific treatment of reserve requirements in Reinhart and Reinhart (1999).

That said about the potential for policy, this simple framework also teaches an even more important lesson. Despite policy interventions that either shift or rotate the budget line, that constraint is anchored at one point—initial endowments. In a given period, a

---

[11] Those efforts may also involve resource cost as the private sector tries to work around the constraint, implying that some of the country's endowment will be wasted. That is the essence of rent seeking in the Krueger sense (Krueger, 1974), which is typically applied to restrictions on the trade of goods but also applies with force to the trade in assets.

government imposing controls or taxes on capital does not alter what an economy has produced to trade on the world market, it has only altered the terms of that trade from the vantage point of its citizens. This is reflected in proposition 4:

Proposition 4: People have to live within their means—that is, fundamentals matter.

While policy can tilt returns in favor of consumption today or tomorrow, ultimately a nation's choices are limited by current and future income prospects. Quotas, taxes, and transfers may disguise that for a time, but not forever. Therefore, a key lesson that is as much rooted in common sense as in high theory is do not expect from policy what it cannot deliver.

Table 1. Correlations Among Home-Currency Returns on Broad Equity Indexes

(Weekly, January 1992 to March 2001)

	U.S.	Germany	U.K.	Canada	Japan	Mexico	Brazil	Hong Kong SAR
U.S.	1	0.55	0.55	0.71	0.25	0.48	0.28	0.35
Germany		1.00	0.63	0.49	0.24	0.39	0.21	0.43
U.K.			1.00	0.45	0.26	0.39	0.22	0.45
Canada				1.00	0.28	0.39	0.25	0.34
Japan					1.00	0.20	0.22	0.24
Mexico						1.00	0.35	0.36
Brazil							1.00	0.20
Hong Kong SAR								1.00

Source: Bloomberg. United States (S&P 500), Germany (DAX), United Kingdom (FTSE), Canada (TSE300), Japan (Nikkei), Mexico (Bolsa), Brazil (Bovespa), and Hong Kong SAR (Hang Sen).

Properties of Asset Prices and Flows

The next four propositions are empirical in nature and relate to the behavior of asset prices and flows. These properties are observed in many different markets, across many countries, and over long stretches of time. By way of example, Tab. 1 reports the correlation observed over the past nine years in the weekly home-currency returns from broad equity indexes in eight industrial and emerging market economies.

As is evident, equity prices covary closely, with correlation coefficients ranging from 0.2 to 0.71. Using more sophisticated techniques over a different sample, Calvo and Reinhart (1996) provide evidence that these comovements can be explained by a small number of common factors.

This simple evidence suggests an equally simple proposition:

Proposition 5: Asset prices move together internationally.

There are many potential explanations for these high correlations, including commonality in shocks in technology and confidence, the importance of commodities that are traded on world markets, the linkage of spending in each country through trade channels, and the presence of the same global investors in all these financial markets. Whatever the specific mechanisms explaining these correlations, policymakers have to take into account influences emanating from abroad and the potential that their own actions will echo offshore. More problematic, though, is the general property that these correlations, while high on average, are not stable over time.[12] So while these financial linkages are important, they are hard to bet on.

Beyond observing the correlations among financial prices, empirical researchers have been unable to identify systematic relationships explaining their underlying behavior. The finance and economics literature is chock full of anomalies where facts fail to accord with theory, including the equity-premium puzzle (in which the return on stocks over the long run exceeds what interest rate arbitrage would suggest), home bias (in which investors tend to hold fewer foreign assets than efficient diversification of risk would seem to call for), and the failure of the expectations approach to the term structure of interest rates (in which the slope of the yield curve

---

[12] Loretan and English (2000) address this phenomenon, emphasizing the differences in measures of association in small samples versus the general population.

routinely fails to predict the future direction of interest rates).[13] This work suggests the following:

Proposition 6: Asset prices are difficult to link to fundamentals.

Accumulating evidence of the inability of theory to fit the facts has led economists to develop models of contagion that put herding behavior by investors center stage (which also helps to explain proposition 5).

Data on either stocks or flows of financial assets are hard to come by and never sampled with the frequency of asset prices. But what is obvious in many different episodes and shows clear in the aggregate data is that capital flows can change quickly. By way of example, Reinhart and Reinhart (2001) examine movements in real capital flows to emerging market economies over the past 30 years. Figure 7 depicts capital flows to emerging markets (in billions of U.S. dollars in 1970 terms) in recession years versus recovery years for the 1970–1999 period. The picture shown in the first panel of Figure 7 reveals that net flows to emerging markets are almost twice as large when the United States is in expansion as when the United States is in recession. Furthermore, this vast gap between recession and expansion owes primarily to a surge in foreign direct investment (FDI) flows (which nearly go up fivefold from recession to expansion) and to portfolio flows (Figure 7, third panel). Indeed, other net inflows to emerging markets fall from about US$17 billion, when the United States is in recession, to about US$8 billion of net outflows in expansions.[14]

---

[13] Representative of the work in these areas is Prescott and Mehra (1982) (on the equity-premium puzzle), Tesar (1990) (on home bias), and Shiller (1988) (on term structure anomalies).

[14] This disparate behavior between FDI and portfolio flows importantly owes to bank lending, which accounts for a significant part of other flows. Apparently, banks tend to seek lending opportunities abroad when the domestic demand for loans weakens, as it usually does during recessions.

Figure 7. Real Capital Flows to Emerging Markets and the U.S. Business Cycle

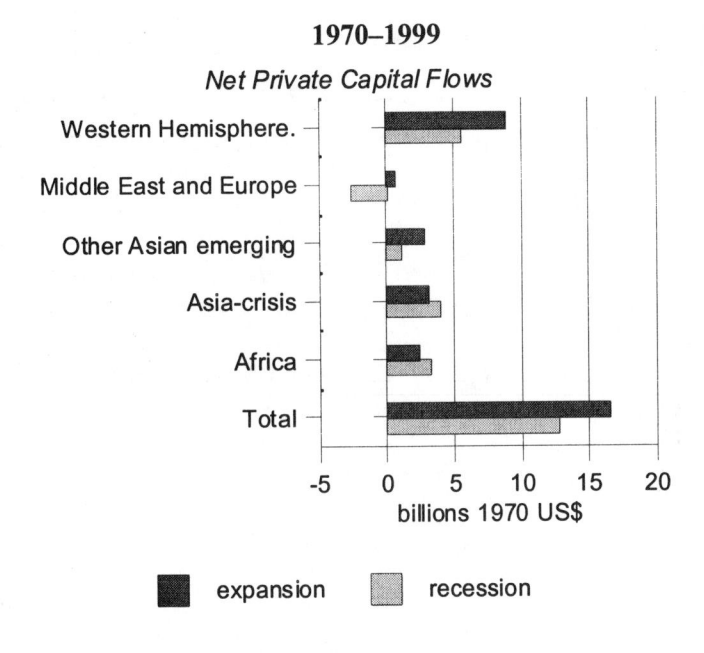

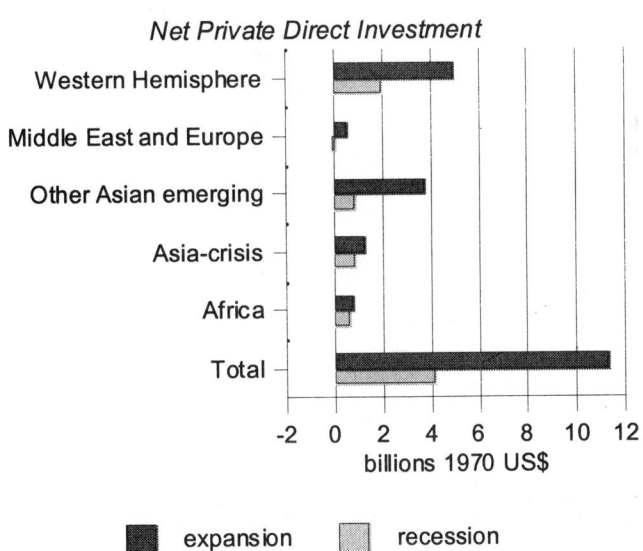

1970–1999

Net Private Capital Flows

- Western Hemisphere
- Middle East and Europe
- Other Asian emerging
- Asia-crisis
- Africa
- Total

-5 0 5 10 15 20
billions 1970 US$

■ expansion   ▢ recession

Net Private Direct Investment

- Western Hemisphere
- Middle East and Europe
- Other Asian emerging
- Asia-crisis
- Africa
- Total

-2 0 2 4 6 8 10 12
billions 1970 US$

■ expansion   ▢ recession

250 • Things to Love (or Hate) About Capital Flows

Figure 7 (continued)

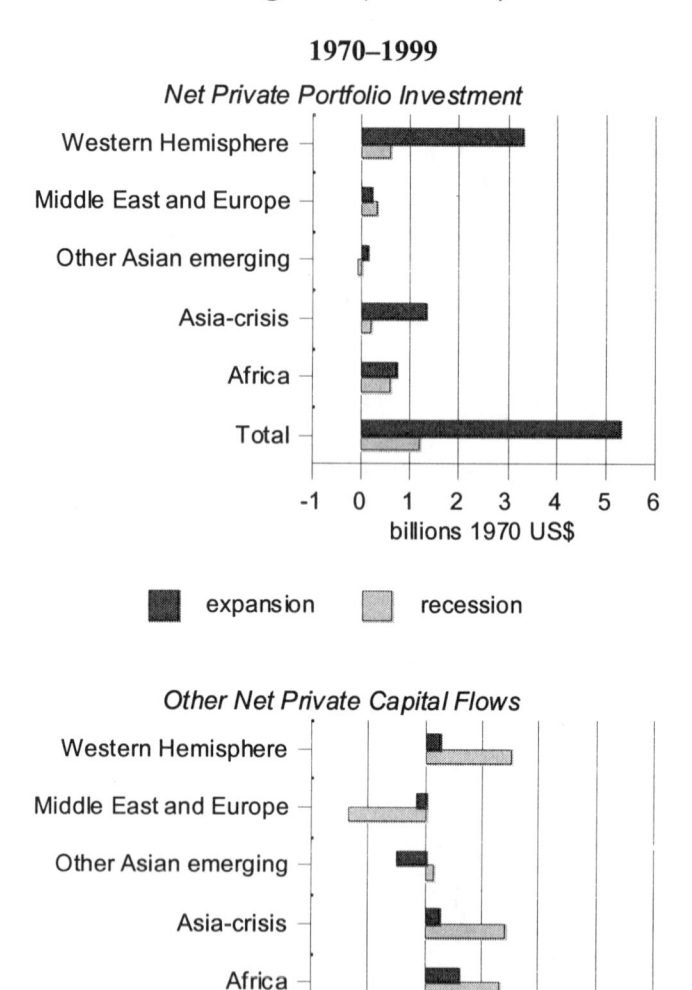

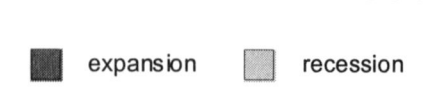

1970–1999

Net Private Portfolio Investment

- Western Hemisphere
- Middle East and Europe
- Other Asian emerging
- Asia-crisis
- Africa
- Total

-1 0 1 2 3 4 5 6
billions 1970 US$

■ expansion   □ recession

Other Net Private Capital Flows

- Western Hemisphere
- Middle East and Europe
- Other Asian emerging
- Asia-crisis
- Africa
- Total

-4 -2 0 2 4 6 8
billions 1970 US$

■ expansion   □ recession

The U.S. bank lending boom to Latin America in the late 1970s and early 1980s and the surge in Japanese bank lending to emerging

Asia in the mid-1990s are two clear examples of this phenomena. From a compositional standpoint, the more stable component of capital flows, FDI, does seem to contract during downturns—suggesting that emerging markets may wind up during these periods relying more heavily on less stable sources of financing short-term flows. Taken together, this evidence supports the proposition that:

> *Proposition 7*: Capital flows are changeable.

Moreover, while capital flows are generally quite volatile, they are especially so to and from emerging market economies. The typical industrial country has a track record of credible monetary policymaking, respect for the rule of law, deep domestic financial markets, and no recent history of debt repudiation. Unfortunately, that has not always been the case for many emerging market economies. As a result, global investors are more likely to flood in or retreat quickly as assessments of and attitudes toward risk change.[15] In this regard, size matters as well: the flow of capital to an emerging market economy in any given year can be quite large compared both to the pool of domestic saving and the outstanding stock of financial capital, especially relative to most industrial countries. This adds up to:

> *Proposition 8*: Emerging market economies are different than the economies of industrial countries.

Nowhere is this more evident than in the work on the macroeconomic consequences of a sudden reversal of capital inflows. For instance, the case studies provided by the World Bank (1997) document much more wrenching adjustments to income associated with large reductions in capital inflows to emerging markets than in the industrial country experience detailed in Freund (2000).

These four regularities admit a variety of interpretations that map into differing attitudes toward capital flows. That is, these same observations could be used to advocate liberalizing or restricting

---

[15] This is described in the work of Calvo, Leiderman, and Reinhart (1996) on what they refer to as the capital inflow problem, or the high degree of comovement in regional capital flows.

capital transactions. As to the former, the volatility of prices and flows could be taken as evidence that financial markets readily reprice assets when the assessment of risk or income prospects change. In that environment, such changes in relative prices send signals to redirect resources toward more appropriate uses. That asset prices are difficult to explain may only indicate that the process is complicated. But as a corollary, government intervention would only interfere with the signals sent by the market and have effects that could be difficult to predict. As to the latter view representing greater wariness toward free-flowing international capital, the inability to explain asset prices by fundamentals would suggest that markets are not obviously directing resources toward their best uses. Instead, prices and flows bear the imprint of the herd behavior of global institutions, introducing unnecessary volatility into domestic financial markets.

Propositions About Policy

Perhaps the most important message the literature on open-economy macroeconomics sends to national authorities in both developed and developing countries is that their policies are interconnected. In particular, as explained by Jeffrey Frankel (1999) in his Graham lecture, policymakers have only two degrees of freedom in their choice among three main policies. That is, the choice of exchange rate system (fixed versus floating), monetary policy (independent to achieve domestic objectives or dependent on foreign considerations), and treatment of capital flows (unrestricted or restricted) are linked. In particular, authorities cannot pursue both an independent monetary authority and fixed exchange rates while allowing capital to be mobile (which is why Frankel calls this the impossible trinity). Simply put, some sand has to be thrown in the gears of international finance for a nation to have simultaneously a monetary policy that is sensitive to the domestic economy and that delivers a fixed exchange rate. If not, potentially large flows of international capital will swamp efforts to defend the currency if a wedge opens up between domestic and foreign interest rates. Thus, authorities have been driven to imposing capital controls on occasion because, to them, it was the better alternative than giving up monetary autonomy or a stable exchange rate.

As a general proposition, then, we have:

> *Proposition 9*: The treatment of capital flows, monetary policy independence, and the exchange rate regime are inextricably linked.

Reinhart and Reinhart (1998) document the various efforts to deal with a surge in capital flows by authorities in emerging market economies.[16] Disciplined by the impossible trinity, sometimes those efforts include imposing restrictions on the mobility of international capital so as to preserve some degree of flexibility in domestic monetary policy and fixity of the exchange rate.

The remaining propositions concern how a market economy responds to policy interventions over time. They are shaped by the judgments that policy action influences market expectations, that markets are interconnected, and that the private sector adapts to any given regime. As was related in the first few propositions of this paper, economists generally believe capital flows can serve useful purposes. In particular, a nation expecting its income to increase has an incentive to borrow now to smooth consumption. Indeed, in our example of optimizing behavior, if the real interest rate equals the rate of time preference, consumption will be the same in both periods, implying that the country will borrow on world markets in the first period.

The problem becomes more complicated, though, when we introduce the reality that asset trades involve risk and depend importantly on expectations. In an example owing to Bartolini and Drazen (1994) and Pakko (2000), suppose that doubts arise among global investors about the country's ability or willingness to repay its loans next period. Presumably, the rate charged to borrowers will rise to reflect the assessment of a greater probability of default. Keeping the flow of foreign capital into the country at the same pace—that is, letting current consumption run above income—would require the government to subsidize foreign borrowing (or lower any existing

---

[16] A particularly relevant case after the writing of that paper is that of Malaysia, where, as explained in Haggard (2000), controls were explicitly imposed to preserve monetary autonomy and smooth exchange rates.

tax). But the act of doing so may well make investors more worried about repayment prospects, which would perversely raise borrowing costs and lower the flow of capital. This signaling aspect of policy decisions may raise the overall amplitude of the swing in capital flows. International capital flows would seem to be drawn to a country in good times, when it enjoys the favor of Wall Street and the City of London. At such times, official discouragement will not be viewed unfavorably. Indeed, official discouragement might even be interpreted as a sign of strength that implied lower default risks going forward. In bad times, when investors want to slow capital inflows, or even withdraw capital, they will be very sensitive to policy action in forming their expectations. Official encouragement will look like weakness and may worsen the situation. This leads to:

Proposition 10: Controlling outflows is hard.

Policymakers also have to appreciate that portfolio decisions of both global and domestic investors are not made in isolation. In such circumstances, a decision to restrict the flow of any one particular asset will have consequences for the prices of other assets. If one class of assets is blocked off to a global investor by capital controls, demand for other, unrestricted assets, will shift. The price consequences of those demand shifts, in turn, can induce changes in the portfolios of domestic investors not directly restricted by capital controls.

Reinhart (2000) provides a specific example in which a transactions tax on foreign borrowing has the effect of raising the volatility of domestic equity prices. Simply, the pressure of a shift in overall asset demand has to be released through changes in asset prices. The fewer asset prices permitted to adjust, the more those allowed to adjust will have to change.[17] This adds to our list of propositions:

---

[17] Put this way, the proposition is similar to the Le Chatelier principle, which was applied to economics by Samuelson (1947).

> **Proposition 11:** Controls in one market may shift volatility to other markets.

The obvious advice that flows from this is that policy makers need to be aware of the unintended consequences of their actions. Substitution across assets makes it difficult to intervene in financial markets with surgical precision.

The ability to shift across markets also suggests that the effectiveness of any particular set of restrictions can be eroded over time. As Alfred Marshall asserted in 1897 (in a quote repeated in Keynes, 1951),

> When one person is willing to sell a thing at a price which another is willing to pay for it, the two manage to come together in spite of prohibitions of King or Parliament or of the officials of a Trust or Trade Union.

With financial transactions, the problem is harder still. In the face of controls on one particular asset, market participants might simply move trading offshore or create a new instrument that mimics its risk and return characteristics within the domestic market. Indeed, over time, resources are used in the attempt to evade the controls. Garber (1996), for instance, argues forcefully that one form of a capital control—a tax on transactions—would be evaded over time. As Garber relates, a general principle of public finance is that a tax applied on an elastic market (where participants are quite sensitive to prices) delivers little revenue because it crowds out that taxed activity. This is formalized as:

> **Proposition 12:** Capital controls are evaded over time.

Given this property, policymakers are left in the uncomfortable position of either seeing the efficacy of their controls erode or making their regulations more complicated over time.

To be sure, the likelihood that capital controls interact with expectations, indirectly trigger responses in other markets, and directly lose their force over time is pointed to by advocates of free and open capital markets. But those propositions are convincing only to the extent that they can be read in the experience of countries imposing capital controls. And there the record is mixed. De Gregorio, Edwards, and Valdés (2000) find that the effects of Chilean capital controls were quite elusive and, at most, support the conclusion that controls shaped the composition, not the overall volume, of flows. Kaplan's and Rodrick's (2000) reading of Malaysian capital controls is considerably more favorable, while Haggard's (2000) is not.

A Summing Up

Table 2 summarizes the place of common ground among economists working on capital flows, sorting the dozen basic propositions advanced in this paper according to whether they are about theory, facts, or policy. While most economists would accept these propositions, the emphasis put on them varies considerably, and, as a result, so too do their policy recommendations.

Within that table are three points of truly common ground. As set out in bold type, most economists would accept that the marketplace provides benefits, that policies are interrelated, and that, if intervention is necessary, it should work through prices, not quantities. After that, consensus is harder to reach. The building blocks for those advising free-flowing international capital are the items in italics in the table, which combine to suggest that trade brings benefits and policy intervention has uncertain, and likely little long-run, net benefit. Economists in favor of limiting capital mobility put more stock in inconvenient facts of international finance—volatility and contagion—as implying that market inefficiencies abound and that the welfare gain to shaving interest-rate differentials may be small.

The current consensus, reflected among other places in the report by a working group of the Financial Stability Forum quoted in the introduction, recognizes that capital flows are volatile (proposition 7) and financial market prices can sometimes diverge from fundamentals (proposition 6). Moreover, it holds that there are probably some benefits to independent monetary policy and a smooth exchange rate, leaving the third in the impossible trinity at risk (proposition 9). But it also supports the view that open capital flows yield substantial long-run benefits (proposition 1), especially when compared to the

Table 2. A Dozen Properties of Capital Flows

About Choices:	About Facts:	About Policy:
Trade improves welfare.	Asset prices move together.	The treatment of capital flows, monetary policy, and the exchange rate regime are linked.
Smoothing income is more important than arbitraging interest rates.	Asset prices are hard to link to fundamentals.	Controlling outflows is hard.
Control through prices not quantities.	Flows are volatile.	Controls shift volatility.
Fundamentals matter.	Emerging market economies are different.	Controls are evaded.

resources that are wasted by the private sector as it tries to evade controls and misses important market signals (proposition 12). But that consensus appears willing to consider limited capital controls that are in price terms (proposition 3), on inflows but not outflows (proposition 10), and are not seen as a substitute for fundamental reform (proposition 4). Better still, those controls should be couched in terms of prudential terms and penalize short, rather than long, holding periods. That the consensus changed owes importantly to economists' willingness to learn from experience—and the experience of the past few decades has shown that capital flows can change abruptly and that financial market prices are often hard to explain.

References

Alston, Richard M., J. R. Kearl, and Michael B. Vaughan, 1992, "Is There a Consensus Among Economists in the 1990s?" *American Economic Review* 82 (May), pp. 203–209.

Bhagwati, Jagdish, 1998, "The Capital Myth," *Foreign Affairs* 77 (May/June), pp. 7–12.

Bartolini, Leonardo, and Allan Drazen, 1994, "Capital Account Liberalization as a Signal," IMF Working Paper 94/9 (Washington: International Monetary Fund).

Buiter, Willem H., 1981, "Time Preference and International Lending and Borrowing in an Overlapping Generations Model," *Journal of Political Economy*, Vol. 89, pp. 769–97.

Calvo, Guillermo, Leonardo Leiderman, and Carmen Reinhart, 1996, "Inflows of Capital to Developing Countries in the 1990s: Causes and Effects," *Journal of Economic Perspectives*, Vol. 10, pp. 123–39.

Calvo, Sarah, and Carmen M. Reinhart, 1996, "Capital Flows to Latin America: Is there Evidence of Contagion Effects?" in *Private Capital Flows to Emerging Markets*, ed. by Morris Goldstein (Washington: Institute for International Economics).

De Gregorio, José, Sebastian Edwards, and Rodrigo O. Valdés, 2000, "Controls on Capital Inflows: Do They Work?" *Journal of Development Economics*, Vol. 63, pp. 59–83.

Dooley, Michael P., 1996, "The Tobin Tax: Good Theory, Weak Evidence, and Questionable Policy" in *The Tobin Tax: Coping with Financial Volatility*, ed. by Mahbub al Haq, Inge Kaul, and Isabelle Grunberg, (New York: Oxford University Press).

Dornbusch, Rudiger, 1986, "Flexible Exchange Rates and Excess Capital Mobility," *Brookings Papers on Economic Activity*: 1, pp. 209-226.

———, 1998, "Capital Controls: An Idea Whose Time Is Gone" (unpublished: Cambridge, Massachusetts: Massachusetts Institute of Technology).

Eichengreen, Barry, and Charles Wyplosz, 1993, "The Unstable EMS," *Brookings Papers on Economic Activity*: 1, pp. 51–124.

Feldstein, Martin,1999, "A Self-Help Guide for Emerging Markets," *Foreign Affairs* (March/April), pp. 93–109.

Financial Stability Forum, 2000, "Report of the Working Group on Capital Flows," April.

Fisher, Irving, 1930, *The Theory of Interest* (New York: The Macmillan Company).

Frankel, Jeffrey A., 1999, "No Single Currency Regime Is Right for All Countries or at All Times," NBER Working Paper No. 7338 (Cambridge, Massachusetts: National Bureau for Economic Research).

Freund, Caroline, 2000, "Current Account Adjustment in Industrial Countries," Board of Governors of the Federal Reserve System International Finance Discussion Paper No. 692 (Washington: Federal Reserve System).

Garber, Peter M., 1996, "Issues of Enforcement and Evasion in a Tax on Foreign Exchange Transactions," in *The Tobin Tax: Coping with Financial Volatility*, ed. by Mahbub al Haq, Inge Kaul, and Isabelle Grunberg (New York: Oxford University Press).

Kaplan, Ethan, and Dani Rodrick, 2000, "Did the Malaysian Capital Controls Work?" prepared for an NBER conference on currency crises, (December).

Keynes, John Maynard, 1951, *Essays in Biography* (New York: W.W. Norton).

Krugman, Paul, 1996, *Pop Internationalism* (Cambridge, Massachusetts: Massachusetts Institute of Technology).

Loretan, Mico and William B. English, 2000, "Evaluating Correlation Breakdowns during Periods of Market Volatility," Board of Governors of the Federal Reserve System International Finance Discussion Paper No. 658 (Federal Reserve System).

Obstfeld, Maurice A., 1982, "Aggregate Spending and the Terms of Trade: Is There a Laursen-Metzler Effect?," *Quarterly Journal of Economics*, Vol. 97, pp. 251–270.

―――, and Kenneth Rogoff, 1997, *Foundations of International Economics* (Cambridge, MA: MIT Press).

Pakko, Michael R., 2000, "Do High Interest Rates Stem Capital Outflows?" *Economic Letters*, Vol.67, pp. 187–192.

Reinhart, Vincent Raymond, 2000, "How the Machinery of International Finance Runs with Sand in Its Wheels," *Review of International Economics*, Vol. 8 (February), pp. 74–85.

Reinhart, Carmen M., and Vincent Raymond Reinhart, 1985, "Some Lessons for Policy Makers Who Deal with the Mixed Blessings of Capital Inflows," in *Capital Flows and Financial Crises*, ed. by Miles Kahler (Ithaca, NY: Cornell University Press), pp. 93–127.

―――, 1999, "On the Use of Reserve Requirement in Dealing with Capital Flow Problems," *International Journal of Finance and Economics*, Vol. 4 (January), pp. 27–54.

Ricardo, David, 1973, *The Principles of Political Economy and Taxation* (New York: Dutton).

Rogoff, Kenneth, 1999, "International Institutions for Reducing Global Financial Instability," NBER Working Paper No. 7265 (Cambrige, Massachusetts: National Bureau of Economic Research).

Samuelson, Paul A., 1947, *Foundations of Economic Analysis* (Cambridge, Massachusetts: Harvard University Press).

Tesar, Linda, 1995, "Evaluating the Gains from International Risk Sharing," Carnegie-Rochester Conference Series on Public Policy No. 42, pp. 95–143.

Tobin, James, 1978, "A Proposal for International Monetary Reform," *Eastern Economic Journal*, Vol. 4 (July/October), pp. 153-59.

World Bank, 1997, *Private Capital Flows to Developing Countries* (Washington: Oxford University Press for the World Bank).

Chapter 15 | Tax Aspects of Offshore Financial Centers

VICTOR THURONYI

Recently, the G-7 countries (together with institutions such as the Organization for Economic Cooperation and Development (OECD), the Financial Stability Forum, and the Financial Action Task Force) have expressed concern over money laundering, inadequate banking supervision, and unfair tax practices in offshore financial centers.[1]

Some of the concerns expressed relate to the promotion of tax avoidance and evasion, but other elements (not solely relevant to tax) are also involved, such as bank secrecy. Given the multidisciplinary nature of the concerns expressed, this paper discusses the tax aspects, with a view to providing greater clarity and understanding for those interested in offshore centers, particularly for those who are not tax specialists.

The recent OECD-led effort to curb tax havens makes this discussion timely. It appears that the current anti-tax-haven efforts have developed some momentum, but such efforts are hardly new: the same concerns were expressed 20 years ago, and even earlier. In 1980, the International Fiscal Association held a seminar on tax havens "in consequence of the ever-increasing importance of tax havens in international taxation as well as of the fact that a growing number of states have enacted legislation aimed at combating the

---

[1] See OECD, *Harmful Tax Competition: An Emerging Global Issue* (1998); Statement of G-7 Finance Ministers and Central Bank Governors, para. 10 (Tokyo: Jan. 22, 2000). *See generally* Bruce Zagaris, "The OECD Report Identifying Harmful Tax Practices and Tax Havens Solidifies the Momentum of the Harmful Tax Competition Initiative," *2000 Tax Management International Journal 521. See also* Robert Goulder, "Financial Action Task Force Reports Cooperation from Blacklisted Jurisdictions," *Tax Notes Int'l* 1736 (Oct. 16, 2000).

excessive use of tax havens."[2] The use of tax havens was also the subject of a study by the U.S. Internal Revenue Service in 1981.[3] In the United States, the legislation on controlled foreign corporations[4] dates to the early 1960s, in response to President Kennedy's attack on "the unjustifiable use of tax havens,"[5] but the first measures to combat tax avoidance by establishing pocket-book corporations in low-tax jurisdictions were the foreign personal holding company rules, enacted in the Revenue Act of 1937.

I. HARMFUL TAX COMPETITION

Identification of Harmful Tax Practices

In its 1998 report on harmful tax competition, the OECD focused on two types of what it called harmful tax practices: tax havens and harmful preferential regimes. Tax competition arises whenever one country tries to attract part of the tax base of other countries by offering a favorable tax regime. This problem is quite pervasive; the tax systems of virtually all countries contain some tax competitive elements. Instead of tackling the tax competition problem as a whole, the OECD has taken a narrower approach, concentrating on those aspects of tax competition that are perceived as particularly harmful. This approach is of course consistent with the consensus decision making that applies at the OECD.

The OECD has followed up on its report by establishing a Forum on Harmful Tax Practices. Among other things, the Forum is to identify preferential tax regimes and tax havens. On June 26, 2000, the OECD released a list of 35 tax havens identified by the Forum, together with a report.[6] A half-dozen jurisdictions were excluded from the list because they made a public commitment to cooperate in

---

[2] Vogel, "Preface," in *Recourse to Tax Havens: Use and Abuse* (Paris: 34th Congress, IFA, 1980).
[3] Internal Revenue Service, "Tax Havens and Their Use by United States Taxpayers—An Overview," in A Report to the Commissioner of Internal Revenue, the Assistant Attorney General (Tax Division) and the Assistant Secretary of the Treasury (Tax Policy) (1981).
[4] *See* "Measures That May Be Taken Against Harmful Tax Practices" *infra*.
[5] *See* H.R. Rept. No. 1447, 87th Cong., 2d Sess. 57 (1962).
[6] OECD, "Toward Global Tax Cooperation: Report to the 2000 Ministerial Council Meeting and Recommendations by the Committee on Fiscal Affairs" (2000).

removing harmful practices. Inclusion on the list of tax havens has therefore involved an element of negotiation, because the classification of countries has depended on the attitude of the authorities toward eliminating the harmful aspects of their regimes. Sanctions against countries on the list might be applied by OECD member countries starting July 31, 2001.[7]

An interesting factor for bank regulators is that the OECD's concept of a tax haven is not satisfied merely by the existence of a low or zero income tax rate. In determining whether to consider a country as a tax haven, the OECD applies four key factors: (1) low or zero tax rate, (2) no effective exchange of information, (3) lack of transparency, and (4) facilitation of the establishment of foreign-owned entities without the need for a local substantive presence.[8] Thus, for example, a decision by a country to broaden the circumstances in which tax authorities of other countries may obtain information on bank accounts may bring a country out of the tax haven classification.[9] In order to avoid inclusion on the "List of Uncooperative Tax Havens", a country needs to make a commitment "to eliminate its harmful tax practices."[10] Precisely what this requires is not spelled out in the OECD report, and presumably needs to be worked out with the OECD by countries that wish to come off the list of tax havens.

The OECD report notes that the degree of harmfulness of a tax practice can vary, but identifies as particularly harmful cases where there is a failure to provide information, since this "facilitates tax evasion and money laundering."[11] The report notes that even some tax havens allow information to be released when criminal tax fraud is involved, but that "these tax haven jurisdictions do not allow tax administrations access to bank information for the critical purposes of detecting and preventing tax avoidance."[12]

---

[7] *See id.* at 18.
[8] *See id.* note 4 at 10.
[9] This may not, however, be sufficient if the country is considered as having a preferential regime that attracts investment with no substantial domestic activity.
[10] *See* OECD, *supra* note 6, at 19.
[11] *See* OECD, *supra* note 1, at 24.
[12] Id.

Thus, it is clear that, at least from the point of view of the OECD report, merely facilitating tax planning by providing low tax rates does not make a tax haven: apart from cases of special preferential regimes, it is the facilitation of tax avoidance and tax evasion that is determinative.[13] This makes it important to understand the concepts of tax avoidance and tax evasion, which are discussed in the third section below.

Measures That May Be Taken Against Harmful Tax Practices

In the case of a tax haven deemed "harmful," the typical taxpayer using the tax haven will not be resident there (resident entities may be formed, but the ultimate owners will not be residents). The country of residence of these taxpayers can take measures against its taxpayers who use tax havens. In many cases, these are specifically designed to eliminate the tax benefits of using the haven. Often, the result is that the tax haven is not in a position to offer a *legal* tax benefit; in order to reduce their taxes, investors must break the law of their country of residence.

Thus, for example, in a number of countries, the income tax return form requires the taxpayer to report any interest in a foreign bank account (in some countries, only where the account exceeds a specified amount). By checking "no" falsely, the taxpayer commits an offense. Likewise, the willful failure to report interest income from a foreign bank account would generally constitute tax fraud.

A taxpayer wishing to engage in legal tax planning may therefore interpose an entity, instead of holding an account directly. By using an entity, the taxpayer can defer tax in the taxpayer's home country by not repatriating the entity's profits and in some cases can escape tax completely by converting the income to capital gains that are taxed at a low rate or not at all.[14] This technique will work if the

---

[13] This assumes that the jurisdiction does not have special preferential regimes, which can be a separate reason for classification as a tax haven.

[14] If the entity is nonresident in the taxpayer's home country, it will not be taxed there. The profits earned will be subject to zero or nominal taxation in the tax haven. The profits may be subject to tax in the taxpayer's home country upon repatriation, but this tax can be deferred by retaining the money in the entity. Instead of

(continued)

entity is subject to a low (or zero) rate of tax in the tax haven where it is incorporated, and if the taxpayer's residence country has not enacted anti-avoidance legislation that covers the case. A number of OECD countries have enacted such rules, but the scope of such rules differs—some countries have much more extensive rules than others. This area of tax law is also in an evolutionary stage, with changes in the rules (almost always in favor of more extensive rules) occurring relatively frequently. As a result of the gradual legislative approach in most countries, the rules are typically highly technical, and may be overlapping.

Initially, many OECD countries introduced controlled foreign corporation (CFC) legislation, which taxes certain income of a controlled foreign corporation to its owners. Passive investment income is typically included in the type of income subject to the CFC rules.[15] Because CFC rules apply only to corporations that are controlled by a small number of resident persons, it is fairly easy to plan around these rules. Accordingly, a number of countries have enacted rules attacking the use of foreign investment funds to defer tax, as a supplement or extension of the CFC rules.[16]

In the United States, if an entity is a foreign personal holding company (generally, a company with primarily investment income the majority of the shares of which are owned by 5 or fewer U.S. citizens or residents), then the U.S. shareholders will be taxed directly on the investment income.[17] If this rule is sought to be avoided by spreading the shareholdings among more individuals, then the non-U.S. corporation is likely to be treated as a passive foreign investment company (PFIC).[18] A company can be a PFIC even in the absence of

---

repatriating the profits, the taxpayer can sell his interest in the entity, thereby taking advantage of favorable tax treatment of capital gains (a low tax rate or, in a number of countries and situations, a zero tax rate—for example, in the United States, the tax on capital gains is zero if property is held until death, and in several European countries there is, in many situations, no tax on private capital gains).

[15] *See* OECD, *Controlled Foreign Company Legislation* (1996) (reviewing CFC legislation in effect in 14 OECD countries).

[16] *See* Brian Arnold, "The Taxation of Investments in Passive Foreign Investment Funds in Australia, Canada, New Zealand and the United States," in *Essays on International Taxation,* H. Alpert and K. van Raad, eds., (1993); Lee Burns and Richard Krever, Interests in Nonresident Trusts 79–128 (1997).

[17] U.S. Internal Revenue Code §551.

[18] *Id.* §1297.

a substantial U.S. shareholding. In the case of PFICs, a deferral charge applies to the deferred income of U.S. shareholders, unless an election for look-through treatment is made. Another possible device is to invest via a trust established outside the United States. Such an arrangement would likely run afoul of rules which impose an extra charge in the case of distributions from foreign trusts made on a deferred basis.[19]

France has recently adopted legislation under which individuals resident in France, who own a 10 percent or greater interest in a foreign entity which benefits from a favorable tax regime and the majority of the assets of which are investment assets, are taxed on their pro rata share of the entity's income.[20] For this purpose, both indirect ownership (through a chain of entities) and ownership by related persons are taken into account.

In the United Kingdom, several anti-avoidance rules may apply to prevent the deferral of income earned by a foreign trust or entity or the conversion of ordinary income to capital gains.[21]

Australia has provisions attributing to a resident transferor income of certain foreign trusts and imposing on beneficiaries an interest charge for tax deferral in cases where attribution did not previously apply.[22] Income of controlled foreign companies is attributed to their Australian owners, unless exceptions such as that for active business income or taxation in countries with a tax system similar to that of Australia apply.[23] Australian residents must also include in their income their attributable share of the income of a foreign investment fund (FIF).[24] FIF is broadly defined. Similar rules apply to foreign life insurance policies with an investment component.

The kind of anti-avoidance rules discussed above function, in a broad sense, by looking through foreign entities and taxing their

---

[19] Id.§668.
[20] See Code Général des Impôts, art. 123 bis.
[21] See Giles Clarke, Offshore Tax Planning 81-159 (1999).
[22] See ITAA 1936 §§102AAA–102AAZG.
[23] See Id. 1936, §§316–468.
[24] See ITAA 1936 §§469-624.

income to the shareholders or beneficiaries of the entities. Other anti-avoidance rules are possible. In the FY 2001 U.S. budget proposal, the Administration proposed to require taxpayers to report payments to identified tax havens. Also proposed is a denial of foreign tax credit for tax paid to such jurisdictions. The Secretary of the Treasury would determine which jurisdictions are tax havens. What is interesting about such proposals is that they are targeted to specific countries identified as tax havens. These could lend themselves to be used in conjunction with the efforts of the OECD—those tax havens that do not cooperate with the OECD in reducing the harmful aspects of their regimes may find themselves included in the U.S. Treasury Department's list.[25]

Another example of targeting specific listed tax havens is provided by a regulation issued in Argentina that would treat transactions with an entity resident in a tax haven as subject to the transfer pricing rules (regardless of whether the tax haven entity is related to the taxpayer).[26] In Ukraine, payments to a company resident in a tax haven are only 85 percent deductible.[27]

TAX EVASION AND MONEY LAUNDERING

Tax Evasion as a Predicate Crime for Money Laundering

The classic concept of money laundering is the conversion of proceeds of a crime ("predicate crime") into money that is apparently legal. Money laundering is usually thought of in the context of drug dealing, but in fact the criminal laws of a number of countries have a much broader definition of predicate crimes for money laundering purposes. In a number of countries, predicate crimes include tax evasion.

In the United Kingdom, money laundering offenses include: assisting another to retain the proceeds of criminal conduct; acquiring or using the proceeds of criminal conduct; concealing or transferring the proceeds of criminal conduct; or tipping another person off about

---

[25] *See* OECD, *supra* note 6, at 24–26.
[26] *See* Felicitas Arguello, *J. Int'l Banking L.* 15 (2000).
[27] *See* Richard Marshall, "Ukraine Publishes Official Tax Haven Blacklist," *Tax Notes International* 1955 (May 1, 2000).

a pending money laundering investigation.[28] For this purpose, "criminal conduct" means an indictable offense or conduct which "would constitute such an offence if it had occurred in England and Wales or (as the case may be) Scotland."[29] The common law crime of cheating the public revenue falls within this definition.[30] The intention of the statute seems to cover evasion of the taxes of a foreign country, even though it is not a crime in the United Kingdom to evade another country's tax.[31] The islands of Jersey, Guernsey, and the Isle of Man have adopted legislation similar to that in the United Kingdom.[32]

Other countries have generic provisions that would cover money laundering for any serious crime or, in some cases, any crime. For example, in France, it is a crime to conceal the origin of the proceeds of a crime or to assist in the investment, concealment or conversion of a direct or indirect result of a crime.[33]

On the other hand, it is quite clear under current U.S. law that tax evasion is not a predicate crime for money laundering purposes.[34] Tax evasion is relevant to money laundering in the sense that, where there is a predicate crime, and where a person knows that property represents the proceeds of some form of unlawful activity, if the person conducts the transaction for the purpose of facilitating tax evasion (i.e., evasion with respect to such proceeds) that will constitute money laundering.[35] The basic reason for introducing this rule is to prevent a possible defense against other parts of the money laundering laws, whereby the customer tells the banker that his motive is not to conceal criminal activity or proceeds, just to evade taxes.[36] The U.S. government is considering whether to add tax

---

[28] *See* Jonathan Fischer and Jane Bewsey, "Laundering the Proceeds of Fiscal Crime," *J. Int'l Banking L.* 11 (Jan. 2000); Leonard Jason-Lloyd, *The Law on Money-Laundering* (1997).
[29] Criminal Justice Act of 1988, sec. 93A(7).
[30] *See* Fischer and Bewsey, *supra* note 28.
[31] See id.
[32] *See id.* at 14.
[33] *See* Code Pénal, art. 324-1 (as amended by Law No. 96-392, May 13, 1996).
[34] *See* 18 U.S.C. §1956.
[35] *See* 18 U.S.C. §1956(a)(1)(A)(ii); B. Frederick Williams and Frank D. Whitney, *Federal Money Laundering: Crimes and Forfeitures* 147-51 (1999).
[36] *See id.* at 148–49.

evasion to the list of predicate crimes for money laundering purposes.[37]

For those countries considering whether to expand their anti-money laundering legislation to include tax evasion as a predicate crime, one issue may be the elasticity of the concept of tax evasion (see discussion in "The Meaning of Tax Evasion and Avoidance"). In principle, the evasion of even small amounts of tax is considered a crime, although prosecutions are almost never brought for very small amounts. One solution may be to include in the law a minimum threshold amount so that evading minimal amounts of tax would not trigger the money laundering laws. While this could give some certainty to bank officials, it should not hamper money laundering prosecutions, since these almost invariably focus on far larger amounts in any case. Including tax evasion as a predicate crime would not necessarily represent a deviation from the principal concern to combat drug trafficking and crimes specifically targeted by money laundering. Because these crimes may be difficult to prove, tax evasion has classically been used to prosecute them. The same can be said for the crime of official corruption. Assume that corruption is included as a predicate crime for money laundering. Corruption itself is notoriously hard to prove, given that corrupt transactions are often given the veneer of legitimacy. However, where, as is typical, the corrupt official fails to report the proceeds on his tax return, the inclusion of tax evasion as a predicate crime would enable a prosecution for money laundering, in cases where the proceeds of corruption are laundered.

Relevance of Money Laundering to Tax Haven Classification

Under paragraph 53 of the OECD report, the facilitation of "tax evasion and money laundering" is listed as "particularly harmful characteristics of a tax haven." Thus, it appears that jurisdictions wishing to avoid classification by the OECD as tax havens, or wishing to be considered "cooperative" and thereby to avoid tax

---

[37] See U.S. Treasury Dept., The National Money Laundering Strategy for 2000 (March 2000), at 20.

sanctions, would benefit from demonstrating vigilance against money laundering.

THE MEANING OF TAX EVASION AND AVOIDANCE

Tax Evasion

As emerges from the above discussion, tax avoidance and evasion are often of relevance in connection with offshore centers. In the case of money laundering, the distinction between the two may be critical in determining whether a crime has taken place. However, these terms are often used imprecisely or with varying meanings. Part of the problem is a linguistic one. In English, tax evasion is synonymous with tax fraud and means criminal activity. In French, *"évasion"* means avoidance. Tax evasion should therefore be translated into French as *"fraude fiscal."* The general meaning of tax evasion (activity that is considered criminal) should therefore be clear. Specifically, what behavior constitutes tax evasion, however, depends on the criminal laws of each country.

The vast majority of countries have very broad rules on what constitutes tax evasion or tax fraud.[38] This is probably due to the recognition by legislators that attempting to enumerate carefully the offenses punishable as fraud could be defeated by taxpayers who commit fraud in ways that are not listed. Nevertheless, as a practical matter, drawing the line between civil fraud and criminal fraud is not easy and almost invariably is a matter of judgment. For example, in the United States there is a broad definition of tax fraud.[39] While a conviction for tax fraud requires some willful commision, the filing of a false return[40] would seem to be such a commission and therefore even the declaration of a relatively small amount could be prosecuted as tax fraud. (If the amount is very small, the taxpayer could perhaps defend on the basis that he forgot.) Thus, for example, if an

---

[38] *See* "Tax avoidance/Tax evasion," 68a *Cahiers de droit fiscal international* 230 (Australia), 246 (Austria), 267 (Belgium), 285 (Brasil), 296 (Canada), 358 (Finland), 404-05 (Greece)(where unreported income exceeds a specified amount), 422 (Hong Kong), 583 (United Kingdom.), 603 (Sweden)(1983).

[39] "Any person who willfully attempts in any manner to evade or defeat any tax imposed by this title or the payment thereof." I.R.C. §7201.

[40] *See U.S. v. Bishop*, 412 U.S. 346 (1973) ("voluntary, intentional violation of a known legal duty").

individual has a bank account in a foreign jurisdiction and checks the box on the return denying that he has such an account, that would be fraudulent. The difficulty is that criminal tax fraud prosecutions are rarely brought. Most cases are dealt with as civil fraud. As a practical matter, therefore, the failure to report a modest amount of interest income from a foreign bank account would be most unlikely to lead to a fraud prosecution, even if detected by the IRS, but it may technically constitute a felony.[41]

Germany also has a broad definition of tax evasion.[42] It applies when a taxpayer furnishes incorrect or incomplete information. The penalty is imprisonment up to 5 years. A higher penalty (imprisonment for 6 months to 10 years) applies in "especially serious cases."

Likewise, in France, art. 1741 of the tax code broadly defines tax evasion ("*fraude fiscale*") as including the failure to report amounts subject to tax, with a penalty of F 5,000 to F 250,000 and imprisonment for one to five years.

Article 198 of the Criminal Code of Russia makes it a crime for a natural person to evade tax by failure to submit a declaration, by including in a declaration data known to be distorted, or by other means, if done on a "large scale."[43] Similar rules apply to tax evasion by legal persons.[44] Russian prosecutors do not seem shy to use these provisions. Indeed, criminal investigations have apparently been launched "where a company did not pay certain taxes solely because of a difference of opinion in the interpretation" of the tax laws.[45]

---

[41] IRS guidelines issued in 1989 set limits below which criminal cases will normally not be brought. These are $2,500 for cases where the "specific item" method of proof is used and $10,000 where indirect proof is used. *See* Richard Roberts et al., "Criminal Tax Procedure" (Tax Management Portfolio 162-2d).

[42] Abgabenordnung §370.

[43] *See Criminal Code of the Russian Federation,* William E. Butler, trans., 3rd ed. (1999). "Large scale" means tax in excess of two hundred minimum amounts of payment for labor.

[44] *See id.* art 199.

[45] E. Sergeeva, "Criminal Liability for Tax Evasion by Legal Entities," in *Law of the C.I.S.: The Bottom Line,* published by Chadbourne & Parke (Spring 2000).

In Argentina, it is a crime punishable by imprisonment from one month to three years to use any means to impede the assessment or collection of taxes by misstating the taxpayer's real economic situation.[46] There are also other penalties, including for more severe offenses where the tax evaded exceeds a specified amount.

Switzerland has a peculiar set of rules concerning tax fraud.[47] There is a general concept of tax evasion and a subset of tax evasion known as tax fraud. While the former is a criminal offense punishable with a fine, only the latter is punishable by imprisonment. Tax fraud means the use of "forged, falsified or substantively incorrect documents, such as business books, balance sheets, profit and loss statements and salary certificates or other third party certificates."[48] A false tax return is not a "false document" within the meaning of this provision.[49] This narrow definition of tax fraud is out of line with the approach of other countries. It furnishes part of the explanation why the Swiss authorities have been reluctant to share information with the authorities of other countries to enforce their tax laws, even where a tax crime may have been committed abroad.[50]

Tax Avoidance

Tax avoidance is a more ambiguous concept than tax evasion. It can be used in a general sense to refer to any activity aimed at reduction of tax that is not criminal in nature.[51] Often, however, tax

---

[46] *See* Law 23,771, B.O. Feb. 27, 1990. *See generally* Mirtha Elena Glatigny, Nuevo Regimen Penal Tributario y Previsional (1991).

[47] *See* Direct Federal Tax Law, art. 174-193. *See generally* Harvard Law School, International Tax Program, Taxation in Switzerland 998-1007 (1976).

[48] *Id.* art. 186.

[49] *See* Mario Kronauer, "Information Given for Tax Purposes from Switzerland to Foreign Countries Especially to the United States for the Prevention of Fraud of the Like in Relation to Certain American Taxes," 30 *Tax L. Rev.* (1974) at 47, 82.

[50] In the case of mere tax evasion (i.e., where a criminal offense is not involved), it is apparently not possible for the Swiss authorities to compel a bank directly to give information, although they can require information from the taxpayer. However, a judge has a right in a tax fraud case to lift banking secrecy. *See* Maurice Aubert, "The Limits of Swiss Banking Secrecy Under Domestic and International Law," 2 *Int'l Tax and Business Lawyer* (1984) at 273, 279-81.

[51] For example, "Globalisation and Tax Survey," *The Economist* (Jan. 29, 2000) at 6 states: "Tax avoidance is doing what you can within the law." The following distinction between tax avoidance and tax evasion is drawn in a manual for revenue

(continued)

avoidance is used (often as part of a phrase such as "tax avoidance scheme") to connote tax minimization behavior that skirts the limits of the law or that is in fact legally ineffective in reducing the taxpayer's liability. In this latter sense, one can distinguish between tax avoidance on the one hand and tax mitigation (tax planning, tax minimization) on the other:

> The hallmark of tax avoidance is that the taxpayer reduces his liability to tax without incurring the economic consequences that Parliament intended to be suffered by any taxpayer qualifying for such reduction in his tax liability. The hallmark of tax mitigation, on the other hand, is that the taxpayer takes advantage of a fiscally attractive option afforded to him by the tax legislation, and genuinely suffers the economic consequences that Parliament intended to be suffered by those taking advantage of the option.[52]

Although the precise contours of "tax avoidance" can be disputed, the following definitions of the terms "tax evasion," "tax avoidance," and "tax minimization" can be suggested:[53]

- Tax evasion[54] or tax fraud is an offense against the tax laws that is punishable by criminal sanctions.

- Tax avoidance[55] is behavior by the taxpayer that is aimed at reducing tax liability, but which is found to be legally ineffective (perhaps because of an anti-abuse doctrine or by construction of the tax law), but that does not constitute a criminal offense.

---

agents in the United States.: "Avoidance of tax is not a criminal offense. All taxpayers have the right to reduce, avoid, or minimize their taxes by legitimate means. The distinction between avoidance and evasion is fine, yet definitive. One who avoids tax does not conceal or misrepresent, but shapes and preplans events to reduce or eliminate tax liability, then reports the transactions. Evasion on the other hand, involves deceit, subterfuge, camouflage, concealment, some attempt to color or obscure events, or making things seem other than what they are." U.S. Internal Revenue Service, *Internal Revenue Manual, Audit Guidelines*, § 913.

[52] IRC v. Willoughby [1997] STC 995 at 1003.

[53] *See* Frans Vanistendael, *Legal Framework for Taxation*, in 1 *Tax Law Design and Drafting*, V. Thuronyi, ed. (1996) at 15, 44–46.

[54] In French, fraude fiscale; in German, Steuerhinterziehung.

[55] In French, évasion fiscale; in German, Steuerumgehung.

- Tax minimization (tax mitigation, tax planning) is behavior that is legally effective in reducing tax liability.

It should be borne in mind, however, that no satisfactory definition that can explain actual usage will be acceptable, given that the various terms have been used inconsistently and interchangeably, even within a single legal system.[56] Moreover, the classification of particular behavior as tax evasion, tax avoidance or tax minimization, even within one legal system, may be difficult, and the difficulty is compounded when one is working on a comparative basis.

BANK SECRECY

As part of its anti-tax-haven efforts, the OECD recently released a report entitled "Improving Access to Bank Information for Tax Purposes." A significant aspect of this report is that all OECD members (including Switzerland and Luxembourg) agreed with it, without lodging reservations. Given the process of reaching this consensus, the recommendations of the report are not as far-reaching as some of the OECD members would have liked, but they still represent a significant breakthrough in the debate about the proper confines of bank secrecy. The report states:

> Ideally, all Member countries should permit tax authorities to have access to bank information, directly or indirectly, for all tax purposes so that tax authorities can fully discharge their revenue raising responsibilities and engage in effective exchange of information.[57]

However, the report also recognizes that this "ideal" state may not be attainable overnight and proposes some specific recommendations to move toward that state. These include the recommendation to "undertake the necessary measures to prevent financial institutions from maintaining anonymous accounts and to require the identification of their usual or occasional customers, as well as those persons to whose benefit a bank account is opened or a

---

[56] For example, section 482 of the U.S. Internal Revenue Code refers to "evasion" of taxes in a context that clearly would call for the use of the word "avoidance" instead.

[57] OECD, "Improving Access to Bank Information for Tax Purposes" (April 2000) at. para. 20.

transactions is carried out"[58] and to "reexamine policies and practices that do not permit tax authorities to have access to bank information, directly or indirectly, for purposes of exchanging such information in tax cases involving intentional conduct which is subject to criminal tax prosecution."[59]

On the latter point, it is noteworthy that the report speaks of conduct "subject to criminal prosecution,"[60] rather than referring to criminal investigations. In other words, the intention appears to be to allow access to information for civil fraud cases if the type of conduct in question could also be prosecuted as criminal fraud. As discussed above, the intentional failure to report income constitutes tax fraud in most countries.

The OECD report of course has no legal effect, and it will take some time for OECD countries to adjust their laws and treaties on information exchange so as to give effect to its recommendations. The report, however, furnishes a potent weapon for the OECD in its discussions with tax havens because it enables the OECD countries to say that, in principle, they have all agreed to allow exceptions to bank secrecy in favor of the tax authorities, and that tax havens should agree to do the same.

WITHHOLDING ON INTEREST AND INFORMATION EXCHANGE

Information exchange can involve a number of alternative procedures. Information can be requested by the authorities of one country from those of another country under procedures specified by international agreement, in civil tax investigations as well as in tax and nontax criminal cases.[61] Often, however, the procedures involved can be cumbersome. The most powerful technique from the point of

---

[58] *Id.* at para. 21.
[59] Id.
[60] Id.
[61] In the case of the United States, the relevant international agreements include tax information exchange agreements, mutual legal assistance treaties, and treaties for the prevention of double taxation. *See* Richard Barrett, "Confronting Tax Havens, the Offshore Phenomenon, and Money Laundering," *Int'l Tax J.* 23 (1997) at 12.

view of a tax administration is automatic reporting by financial institutions of the income paid to their clients. The majority of OECD countries require such automatic reporting.[62] In a number of countries, the tax authorities have developed systems to match the information received from financial institutions to tax returns filed, thereby enabling them to verify the correctness of the information on the returns through the use of computers. Doing this domestically has been no small feat, but it is possible because the tax administration can control the uniformity of format that enables the matching to take place.

The challenge is much greater internationally, among other things, because identification numbers are not uniform and formats of information differ. Such problems should be solvable, however, if there is an international agreement on information reporting. At the moment, there is no such agreement, but it may develop as part of a European Union initiative to improve tax compliance with respect to interest income.

The EU proposal, which has been agreed upon in principle, but remains to be implemented, is "based on the so-called 'co-existence model'." Under such a model each Member State will operate either a minimum withholding tax or provide information on savings income to other Member States, in order to ensure at least some effective taxation of non-residents' income from savings within the Community. A Member State may combine the elements."[63] This proposal was agreed to in principle by EU finance ministers in June 2000, with implementation to take place by end-2002.[64] Under this agreement, withholding taxes could be applied for a transitional period, eventually to be replaced by information reporting. The EU intends to consult key third countries to promote adoption of similar measures, and may not move forward until assurances from these countries are received. Consultation with third countries is necessary, as unilateral action might just encourage investors to move their funds outside the EU. The interest of the EU in this matter

---

[62] *See* OECD report on Access to Bank Information for Tax Purposes, appendix.

[63] Commission of the European Communities, COM(97)564 final, annex 2 (May 11, 1997).

[64] *See* "EU Finance Ministers Agree on Savings Taxation," 2000 *WTD* 121-1 (Tax Analysts).

suggests that perhaps sufficient political will can be mustered for more concerted multilateral action to deal with the problem of evasion of tax on portfolio income.[65] Expanded information reporting is likely to be an important element of any such action.[66]

Afterword

A few developments occurring since this paper was delivered in 2000 have affected the course of the initiatives it describes and accordingly merit some comment, although the basics of what is said remain largely valid today.

With respect to the OECD's dialogue with tax havens, the OECD has now announced that, although the criteria for determining whether a country will be considered a tax haven remain unchanged, "commitments will be sought only with respect to the transparency and effective exchange of information criteria to determine which jurisdictions are considered as uncooperative tax havens."[67] In other words, tax havens can keep their regimes of low (or no) taxes aimed at companies with no substantial activities therein, as long as they commit to a transparent application of their laws and agree to a certain amount of information exchange. The thrust of the OECD's tax haven effort has therefore been directed to the area of exchange of information. This takes the focus away from tax policy and accentuates the close relation between the money laundering and tax haven efforts discussed above.

In the wake of the Sept. 11, 2001, terrorist attacks, interest in clamping down on sources of finance for terrorism has increased on the part of governments. This has accentuated the interest of

---

[65] *See, e.g.*, Reuven Avi-Yonah, "Globalization, Tax Competition and the Fiscal Crisis of the Welfare State," *Harv. L. Rev.* 113 (May 2000) at 1573, 1654–57, 166–70.

[66] *See Tax Notes Int'l* 1739 (April 17, 2000).

[67] *See* OECD, "The OECD's Project on Harmful Tax Practices: The 2001 Progress Report" (declassified by OECD Council, Nov. 14, 2001). This report extended the deadline for making commitments to cooperate until Feb. 2002, delayed the time when defensive measures would be taken against noncooperating jurisdictions, and clarified what kind of commitments would be required in the areas of transparency and exchange of information. A working group is further elaborating the operational details for exchange of information agreements.

governments in being able to obtain information on investments in other countries, in connection with an investigation. It also has led to enhanced anti-money-laundering efforts.[68] Enhanced international cooperation on the exchange of information is therefore likely.

---

[68] In the United States, among other changes, sec. 1956(c)(7)(B) of the money laundering law was amended in November 2001 to include as a predicate crime "the...theft...of public funds by or for the benefit of a public official" but the amending law did not otherwise expand the definition of predicate crimes to include tax evasion. Another way that tax fraud may indirectly become a predicate crime to money laundering in the United States is through the medium of wire fraud (*see U.S. v. Pierce*, 224 F.3d 158 (2d Cir., 2000)).

V. Central Banking

Chapter

16 Central Banks and International Financial Volatility

LUIS JÁCOME HIDALGO

In November 1990, the Central Banking Department of the IMF, now the Monetary and Exchange Affairs Department (MAE), held a seminar on the evolving role of central banks in the light of the economic events occurring in the world at that time. The focus of the seminar was on the transition to a market economy in the countries of Eastern Europe and the prolonged period of high inflation affecting many developing countries (see Downes and Vaez-Zadeh, 1991). The seminar was attended by central bankers from various regions, IMF officials, and members of its Executive Board. Interest focused on the role of central banks in the development of the financial system, their responsibility in clearing and payment systems performance, and the importance of limiting government financing. Discussions also dealt with the relationship between monetary and exchange rate policies, between monetary policy and the prudential supervision of the financial system, and the implications for monetary policy of the losses accumulated by central banks. Special importance was attached to the examination of the appropriate degree of central bank independence, and to the issues relating to the role of central banks in financial reforms and economic transition. Finally, consideration was given to the role of central banks in financial crises.

However, unexpected trends occurred throughout the 1990s, in particular the increased volatility of international financial markets—brought about by the sudden stops and reversals of external capital flows and the intensification of financial crises—giving rise to significant losses in the output and wealth of numerous countries. As a result, today central banks' agendas have incorporated issues that are relevant in the context of the new international environment. There is a renewed debate about the appropriate exchange regime that countries should adopt, with opinions mostly divided between those who favor the adoption of exchange systems based on currency board arrangements or systems based on the U.S. dollar (or another strong currency as legal tender), and those that prefer a flexible regime supported by an "inflation targeting" scheme. Another issue of discussion is the level of involvement and the role of central banks in banking crises resolution, given the adverse effects of such participation on monetary policy and the central bank's financial position. Finally, central banks are increasingly concerned about achieving greater levels of transparency and accountability in order to help strengthen monetary policy credibility and effectiveness.

The aim of this paper is twofold. First, it reviews the functions of modern central banking in the context of the autonomy granted to these institutions in a number of countries during the last decade. And, second, it examines some critical issues that are currently part of the agenda of central banks in a world of high volatility of external financial markets and frequent domestic banking crises. As a starting point, the following section reviews "best practices" in the design of central bank autonomy given the broad consensus that prevails today around this institutional reform. In the next section, a brief overview of the main functions assigned to autonomous central banks is provided. The final section is the core of the document and examines the main challenges facing central banks in an environment of increased international financial instability, banking crises, and contagion.

Modern Central Banks and Autonomy Reform

Today, the legal and economic framework governing central banks provides a wide-ranging autonomy to these institutions.[1] A large number of countries during the 1990s embraced the autonomy reform with the aim of providing monetary authorities with the instruments necessary to fight inflation. From a broader perspective, the autonomy of central banks was one of the components of the structural reform, and in particular, of the financial reform adopted in various countries as part of the dominant trend of stimulating a better functioning of market economies.

---

[1] In this paper, the terms *independence* and *autonomy* are used interchangeably, just as they are in most works on the subject. However, some authors distinguish between the two terms, linking autonomy to a central bank's operational freedom, and independence to the lack of institutional constraints (see IMF, 1998).

There is no single definition of the term *independence* applied to central banks. Broadly speaking, it may be understood as a legal and institutional arrangement that allows monetary authorities to adopt policy decisions and operational procedures aimed at achieving and preserving price stability apart from the government and private sector's interests. Grilli et al. (1991) distinguishes between *political* and *economic independence*. Political independence refers to the capacity granted to the central bank to select policy objectives without government interference. In contrast, economic independence relates to the legal basis that supports the central bank in the unrestricted use of monetary policy instruments, and this independence is determined by the limits on the government's access to central bank credit. Fisher and Debelle (1994) draw a similar distinction in terms of *goal independence* and *instruments independence*. The former relates to the central bank's authority to freely determine policy targets (i.e., inflation) while the latter refers to the central bank freedom to use all instruments necessary to achieve a given target, which is defined by—or in agreement with—a political authority.

Rationale for Central Bank Autonomy

The increasing trend toward having independent central banks is based on the criterion that inflation imposes high costs on society, which are measured in terms of lower economic growth.[2] The theoretical underpinnings of this reform are related to the history of the Phillips curve and the associated academic debate, which has led to the increasing consensus around the idea that, although money is neutral in the long run (i.e., there is no trade-off between output and inflation), it can affect growth and employment in the short run. As a result, a central bank that is dependent on a political authority could engage in practices of "dynamic inconsistency" giving rise to an "inflationary bias."[3] In contrast, an autonomous central bank that does not produce unexpected inflation (say, for reasons of reducing

---

[2] A review of the channels through which inflation affects economic growth and of the empirical evidence in that regard may be found in IMF (1996).

[3] The problem of "dynamic inconsistency" refers to the incentives that governments have to change economic targets and policies after the market has elaborated its expectations and taken their decisions in light of the original government announcements.

unemployment or financing the fiscal deficit) may well enjoy credibility regarding its commitment to price stability.

From a theoretical view, the independent central bank model has been discussed in the literature according to two different approaches. The first is that of the so-called conservative central banker proposed by Rogoff (1985), whereby society delegates the conduct of monetary policy to a person who assigns a more severe evaluation to the welfare costs generated by inflation than society's assessment. The second approach goes beyond the delegation arrangement and models an explicit contract between society and the central banker (Walsh, 1993), whereby inflation targets are negotiated with the government, such that the central banker's wage is negatively affected if the increase in prices deviates significantly from the negotiated target. The approach adopted in practice by most countries is based on the delegation model, with New Zealand being the closest example to the explicit contract approach.

Empirically, most studies show that in the case of industrial countries there is a negative correlation between central bank independence and inflation, although there is no evidence of causality. The index commonly used to measure central bank independence involves legal and institutional aspects associated with the central bank objective, the procedures used to appoint central bank governors, and the financial links between the central bank and the government (see Grilli et al., 1991; Alesina and Summers, 1993). At the level of developing countries, such negative correlation is not observed (Cukierman, 1992) unless a distinction is made between de jure independence and de facto independence. The latter is expressed in terms of the frequency of turnover of central bank governors as a proxy variable, and assuming that its greater stability is a measure of a greater central bank autonomy (Cukierman et al., 1992). If the sample is restricted to the economies in transition, Loungani and Sheets (1997) find a negative correlation between increasing autonomy of central banks and lower inflation. In turn, Lybeck (1999) obtains the same result for the former Soviet Union countries, incorporating a public accountability component into the indicator of central bank independence.

Although the majority of opinions favor the institutional strengthening of central banks aimed at ensuring price stability, some views attach less importance to this relationship. Posen (1994) argues that the political decision to fight inflation and the adverse sentiment of the banking system toward inflation is more important, insofar as the costs exceeds its benefits in an inflationary environment. Mas (1995) questions the efficiency in the selection of central bank directors, which he claims does not necessarily result in conservative central bankers—his belief being that since fiscal policy is the main source of inflation, it is in this area that corrective measures must be taken. In a similar vein, Worrel (2000) attaches priority to the coordination of monetary and fiscal policies, particularly in small open economies, as a more efficient tool to defeat inflation, while others, including Forder (1998) see the potential limitations to credibility in the policy announcements made by the central bank. A popular critique is provided by Stiglitz, who approaches the problem from a democratic philosophy perspective, asserting that "there is a rationale for a degree of independence of the central bank, even in a democratic society. But the central bank must be accountable, and sensitive, to democratic processes." He proposes that "there must be more democracy in the manner in which the decision makers are chosen and more representativeness in the governance structure" (see Stiglitz, 1998). Empirically, Posen (1995) questions the negative correlation between central bank independence and inflation in industrial countries, when the sample period is extended to 1950–1989. A study of the IMF (1996) also finds that the negative correlation between inflation and increasing central bank independence, although valid for industrial countries, may be subject to changes depending on the sample period defined for the analysis.

Main Components of the Autonomy Reform

After several years of experience with the central bank autonomy reform in a number of countries, the IMF's MAE Department has drawn lessons, which have been used in providing technical assistance to member countries interested in reforming central bank laws (see IMF, 1998). The main components of the recommendations provided by the IMF can be grouped in four major categories: first, the definition of objectives and targets for the central bank; second, the modality of political autonomy; third, central bank economic and financial autonomy; and, fourth, the need for public accountability as a counterpart to the autonomy granted. These four recommendations are summarized in Table 1 and discussed hereafter.

The conventional wisdom favors central banks assigned with the primary objective of preserving price stability, based on the criteria that inflation is a monetary phenomenon and therefore falls within the natural scope of action of central banks. This is considered the best contribution that central banks can provide to the superior goal of improving living standards, given that price stability is considered a necessary, although not sufficient, condition for achieving a sustainable economic growth. On the other hand, assigning priority to price stability, or having it as a single objective, facilitates the definition and monitoring of targets and holds the central bank accountable, thereby enhancing the credibility and effectiveness of monetary policy. An example of a clear mandate is that of the European Central Bank, which states that "the primary objective of the European System of Central Banks shall be to maintain price stability." In the event the central bank is assigned multiple objectives—for example, price stability and the stability of the financial system, which may conflict with one another in the short term—a conflict resolution mechanism should be established and disclosed.

Table 1. Main Recommendations for the Central Bank Autonomy Reform

Principal Criteria	Main Guidelines
Clarity of objectives	Establish a primary objective, namely, to preserve price stability. In the case of more than one objective (for example, price stability vs. stability of the financial system), the first should prevail where disputes arise. A specific target—for instance, a given rate of inflation—should be defined and disclosed to allow better monitoring and accountability.
Political autonomy	Most countries give central banks instrument independence. Members of the central bank's board of directors should be nominated and appointed by the executive branch and parliament in a dual process, without government and private sector direct representation. Terms of office should be longer than that of the executive branch, while grounds for dismissal of board members should be strictly legal in nature and clearly established, avoiding any political interference.
Economic and financial autonomy	Prohibition or limitation of credit to the government should be established and disclosed. While the exchange regime should be defined by the government or agreed upon with the central bank, the execution of the exchange rate policy should be solely a central bank responsibility. Rules must clearly state the relations and functions between the central bank and the government, including the treatment of central bank losses/profits and the maintenance of central bank capital on the part of the government.

Table 1. (continued)

Accountability	Central banks must be held accountable and their governors should appear periodically before a designated political authority (Congress) to report on the conduct of monetary policy and the achievement of policy objectives. The report must be widely disseminated and explained. Financial statements must be published at least once a year under international accounting standards while summarized versions must be published more frequently.

Source: IMF (1998).

Regarding political autonomy, it is recommended that central banks should have operational or instrument independence rather than goal independence. This implies that the central bank must design and execute interest rate policy and, in general, have the freedom to use all monetary instruments that are required to achieve the inflation target, while inflation is defined by the government or is mutually agreed upon with the central bank.[4] Should the government have the right to overrule a decision adopted by the central bank, there should be a disclosed mechanism of conflict resolution. In addition, the members of the central bank board should be nominated and appointed respectively by both the Executive Branch and Parliament in a dual process to reinforce political independence. They must not represent the government or the corporate private sector in order to avoid conflicts of interest, for example, in relation to interest rate policy.[5] Moreover, their nomination and appointment should be staggered over time, to limit the link between the central bank board

---

[4] This recommendation is based on the idea that goal independence involves a definition of the short-run inflation-unemployment trade-off, which incorporates political matters. However, in some countries, like Chile, the definition of the policy goal (i.e., inflation) has been successfully assigned to the central bank.

[5] This is the case of Guatemala, where the members of the Monetary Board—the head of the central bank—are directly appointed by the government and the corporate private sector, including one that represents the private banks, forming a decision-making body that is naturally conducive to conflicts of interest.

and the government. Equally important, the grounds for dismissing directors must be strictly legal in nature and clearly stipulated by law in order to reduce the central bank's political vulnerability, while the process of dismissal should be overseen by the Judicial Branch.

Economic autonomy must be based on the prohibition or a severe legal limitation on the central bank for providing the government with financing, since this has been the recurrent cause of inflation in various countries. Regardless of who defines the exchange regime—the government, the central bank, or both in agreement—the central bank should have independence to conduct exchange rate policy, given its strong link with monetary policy. Financial autonomy implies that the central bank's solvency is legally guaranteed and maintained, so that if capital shortfalls occur, the government must be obliged to restore them.[6] This is because the persistent accumulation of central bank losses restricts monetary operations and limits the central bank's ability to comply with its fundamental objective of preserving price stability. The counterpart to this mandate is that the central bank must transfer its annual profits to the government budget once the required provisioning for legal reserves has been completed.

Accountability is the other side of the coin to the autonomy granted to the central bank. Although accountability is usually prescribed in central bank laws, the modality for executing it is often vague. As a result, a marked imbalance results between accountability and autonomy in favor of the latter. The modern trend points to central banks presenting open public reports on their operations before the Parliament (or a designated commission within the legislature). The report should include an assessment of the achievement of the policy target announced for a relevant period, and the policies and actions adopted to reach this target. When inflation is the target, "escape clauses" or measures of "core inflation" should be used and explained to the public in order to evaluate correctly central bank efforts, in particular, when the economy is vulnerable to adverse external shocks. In addition, central banks must publish their financial statements audited by an independent firm or authority at least once a

---

[6] In Korea, for example, any loss of the central bank should be initially covered by its own legal reserves, and the difference compensated by the government, while profits are transferred to the government after accumulating central bank legal reserves.

year, and summarized versions of this information should be published on a more frequent basis. Accounting and disclosure of central bank transactions and financial statements should follow international standards.

Toward the Consolidation of Central Bank Autonomy

Notwithstanding the success in reducing inflation in most countries during the past years, the central bank autonomy reform is still in the process of consolidation. This consolidation depends largely on future central bank ability to preserve and maintain price stability, so that markets can rely on an autonomous institution with sufficient reputation to guide expectations about long-term stability and economic prosperity free of political cycle disruptions. However, it is also important that reduction in inflation should be accompanied by long-term economic growth that is sufficiently high and sustainable to help improve the overall standard of living. Although promoting growth is typically a government responsibility and, hence, does not fall within the scope of central bank objectives, a protracted period of low economic growth—which does not allow welfare improvement—may raise unjustifiable criticism against central banks, claiming that the anti-inflationary stance is restraining economic activity. At the extreme, some voices may even suggest the reversal of central bank autonomy, creating uncertainty and eventually an "inflationary bias." Several Latin American countries just experienced adverse reactions against the central bank during the 1998–1999 recessionary period.

The history of a country's inflation is also relevant for the purpose of consolidating the central bank's autonomy reform. A country with a record of moderate inflation—where the society has become accustomed to living with a 15 to 30 percent rate per year—tends to voice little criticism of the accompanying social costs and to inappropriately identify the root of the inflation problem. As a result, the community, and in particular governments, will be reluctant to support an institutional reform that delegates the design and execution of monetary and exchange policies to a group of technocrats with no democratic representation. On the contrary, countries that have experienced triple-digit inflation, or hyperinflation, attach a high value to the loss in well-being resulting from the fall in real income and the generalized uncertainty caused by rapid increases in prices.

In general, these societies are more aware of the damaging effects of political influence in the conduct of monetary policy.

In addition, the economic conditions prevailing during the first years of the reform are very important. This is particularly true if they run counter to the central bank's assigned objective of preserving price stability, given that the central bank may still be engaged in the process of consolidating its credibility and reputation. Three types of threat to central bank autonomy are worth mentioning—namely, the fragility of the financial system, the weakness of public finances, and the emergence of adverse external shocks—which may even occur simultaneously. The potential negative impact of these events manifests itself in a combination of capital flight, exchange rate depreciation, interest rate hikes, and ultimately in inflation.

The most serious problem is usually the existence of a fragile financial system. In this environment, market sentiments often turn negative, reflecting the perception of an eventual future banking crisis, which makes it more difficult for central banks to achieve inflation targets. Central banks face the difficult dilemma of whether to abandon, at least temporarily, the original inflation target by relaxing monetary policy to allow lower levels of interest rates to limit adverse effects on impaired financial institutions, or instead to continue pursuing the original objective, at the risk of aggravating financial instability. The dilemma is all the more complicated if the financial fragility entails a systemic risk and, in addition, if the banking crisis is likely to result in a simultaneous currency crisis, which could exacerbate costs in terms of economic activity and inflation. The potential limitations for monetary policy imposed by a situation of financial fragility can be lessened as a result of obtaining compensatory external credits or the adoption of fiscal adjustment.

A second potential problem arises as a result of a persistent expansionary fiscal policy that requires a compensatory monetary restraint, leading to high interest rates and thereby to a lower economic activity. Although the inflation target may be achieved, economic recession may raise adverse reactions against the central bank as long as fiscal policy is not identified as the source of the inflation problem. The observed policy mix might send signals to the market about a lack of coordination between monetary and fiscal policies, a situation that may give rise to uncertainty and expectations of future higher inflation (Worrel, 2000). Additional uncertainty may result if the government accumulates high and increasing ratios of public debt associated with fiscal deficit financing. As a result, capital outflows and interest rate increases may take place, leading to a balance of payments crisis as the market anticipates that the fiscal deficit is not sustainable.

Adverse external shocks are common events in small open economies. In addition to restricting the availability of foreign currency—and sometimes of fiscal revenues as well—they often trigger capital flight with the resulting upward pressure on the exchange rate and inflation. In order to lessen these effects, central banks tend to raise interest rates at the cost of lowering employment and growth. However, the central bank's response must, insofar as possible, be sufficiently balanced to avoid an eventual "overadjustment." This is a complex task, given the difficulty of anticipating with a reasonable level of approximation the intensity and length of the external shock. Of greater difficulty still is for the market to identify the appropriate policy response. As a result, the central bank and its autonomy reform will be exposed to criticism in an environment of economic recession, in particular if the institution has yet to establish a solid reputation.

Traditional Functions of Autonomous Central Banks

Given the fundamental objective of preserving price stability, the basic functions assigned to an autonomous central bank are the following: the formulation and execution of monetary policy; the conduct of exchange rate policy and the management of international reserves; the role of lender of last resort (LOLR) in the financial system; the coordination of the payment system in the economy; and the role of fiscal and financial agency on behalf of the government. In some countries, the central bank also carries out banking supervision functions, when no other institution has been independently established to carry out such responsibility, as well as the production of certain economic statistics.

The conduct of monetary policy is based on a financial program elaborated for a given period, typically one year, which is aimed at preserving the value of the domestic currency as its ultimate goal. Central banks must choose monetary instruments that are consistent with the selected operational or intermediate targets and the exchange regime in place. Consistency enables the central bank to send clear signals regarding the direction of monetary policy in the short-run, and thereby to achieve greater effectiveness in meeting its final target. On a daily basis, monetary policy should facilitate liquidity management in the banking system in order to reduce interest rates' volatility in the interbank market and the associated financial costs that tend to be reflected in higher interest rates, and lower economic activity and employment. The management of exchange rate policy must also be consistent with other macroeconomic policies, so as to ensure stability and foster confidence among market participants. Market confidence depends to a great extent on the central bank having international reserves at levels that are adequate to sustain the exchange regime in place and to strengthen the country's external financial soundness. The central bank is responsible for managing the country's international reserves safely and efficiently under conditions of liquidity, profitability, and security.

Typically, central banks are given the responsibility of acting as LOLR.[7] This support should be considered part of a broad financial safety net, which may also include a well-designed deposit insurance system and flexible mechanisms for banking crises resolution, generally provided and executed by other institutions. LOLR mechanisms are generally aimed at providing liquidity support to impaired but solvent institutions, and comprise basically a central bank automatic liquidity window and an emergency loan facility. In the liquidity window, the automatic resource transfer is usually pursued in exchange for government securities, which minimizes risk to the central bank. Emergency loans are short-run liquidity facilities that are granted in return for high quality collateral and, in many cases, are coupled with an action plan imposed on the recipient bank until its current difficulties are overcome. In some countries, LOLR facilities are also provided to an insolvent institution, insofar as its failure may trigger a systemic crisis (the "too-big-to-fail" argument).

Regarding other functions, the central bank is usually the main protagonist in the functioning of a country's payment system. It

---

[7] The "last resort" criterion refers to a situation in which a bank suffering from a liquidity shortage has already exhausted all mechanisms for obtaining resources from the market before turning to the central bank.

develops policies for operating and modernizing the payments system and acts as settlement agent for the transactions carried out, while limiting its exposure to the risks inherent in these types of transactions. At the same time, the central bank ensures that the payment clearing mechanisms operate properly and provides incentives ensuring mutual cooperation between the parties involved. The modern trend in payment systems is to build real-time gross settlement (RTGS) systems in order to deal with large-value payments in a secure and efficient manner, thereby strengthening the development of interbank markets.

There is no agreement on whether or not central banks should also conduct banking supervision responsibilities. There are pros and cons—their analysis is outside the scope of this document—in this respect that do not allow a conclusive recommendation. In practice, either an independent supervision institution or a central bank in command of this task has succesfully worked.

In addition, the central bank usually provides the government with banking functions for managing its accounts, for receiving deposits—from tax collections, for example—and settling domestic and international liabilities, and for distributing, when necessary, public resources between different state entities. On occasion, the central bank acts on behalf of the government in handling the operational aspects of domestic and foreign credits, and provides advisory support on public debt policies and management. Also, in most developing countries central banks produce key macroeconomic studies that guide not only their own decisions, but also most government economic policies. The elaboration of economic statistics is frequently a responsibility of central banks as well, in particular, in countries where institutional development is still weak, such that reliable and solid statistics cannot be produced by other government entities.

New Challenges for Autonomous Central Banks

While today, countries worldwide are undergoing a period of low inflation in comparison with the two previous decades (Table 2), the global economy has become more prone toward financial instability. Financial crises have increased at the country level, such that they are now the main source of macroeconomic volatility and welfare losses.

This situation has prompted the international community to propose a "new international financial architecture" in order to forestall and lessen the high costs of the recent currency and banking crises, and the associated spillover and contagion to other countries.[8] The exposure of the global economy—and in particular of the emerging markets—to the volatility of international capital flows and the increase in the number of banking crises in various regions have presented central banks with new challenges, which may affect their traditional functions. Three important issues are briefly analyzed in this section, namely the renewed debate between fixed and flexible exchange regimes and its effects on central bank functions, the role of central banks in banking crises resolution, and the necessity of improving central bank accountability and transparency.

Table 2. Inflation in Various Regions of the World

(Annual percent)

	1981–1990	1991–2000	2000[1]
Industrial Countries	5.6	2.3	1.7
Developing Countries	39.0	23.3	5.8
Africa	15.1	21.5	6.9
Asia	7.1	8.2	3.5
Western Hemisphere	145.4	63.5	7.6

Source: *World Economic Outlook*, October (1999).
[1] Projections

Fixed or Flexible Exchange Rates Once Again

Perhaps the most important issue on central banks' agendas today is the debate on the appropriate selection of the exchange regime to help countries to cope with the volatility of international capital flows. The discussion has been updated in line with the new environment. Most experts are divided between the use of rule-based fixed regimes—also known as "super-fixed" exchange rates—such as currency board arrangements, and the adoption of flexible regimes in

---

[8] Eichengreen (1999) presents a fully documented discussion of this very timely issue.

the context of "inflation targeting" schemes. Intermediate arrangements, including pure fixed–exchange rate systems, exchange rate bands and crawling peg systems, which were more accepted in previous decades, are increasingly less popular in view of their greater vulnerability in the current circumstances. As an extension of the "super-fixed" regimes, some countries are evaluating the establishment of "dollarization" schemes (a few nations like Panama, and more recently Ecuador and East Timor, have already adopted them), whereby the use of the home currency as legal tender is replaced by the currency of the country's largest trading partner. The main benefits of "super-fixed" and "flexible/inflation targeting" regimes, including the implications of each of these regimes for central banks' traditional responsibilities, are discussed below. An assessment of the cost associated with each regime is not included, since it goes beyond the scope of this paper.[9]

As claimed by its adherents, the benefits of flexible regimes are enhanced by the adoption of "inflation targeting" schemes, since this strengthens central bank commitment to price stability and accountability.[10] In the current environment of international financial instability, flexible regimes play the role of shock absorbers—reducing the effects on the real sector of the economy, in particular on growth and employment, caused by adverse shocks—and encourage market participants to hedge foreign exposures in the event of sudden exchange rate variations. A well-designed "inflation targeting" scheme increases market confidence in the central bank's ability to confront adverse effects stemming from unexpected exogenous shocks through the adjustment of the exchange rate, coupled with a policy of central bank intervention, if necessary.

However, the implementation of this scheme requires the existence of favorable preconditions. For instance, the central bank must already have earned some reputation in the fight against inflation, so that the new scheme is initiated under a credible basis that will help to accomplish the inflation target. It is recommended

---

[9] For a recent cost-benefit analysis of the exchange regimes considered in this chapter, see the recent paper by LeBaron and McCulloch (2000).
[10] The "inflation targeting" scheme has been adopted in particular in industrial countries such as Canada, Germany, New Zealand, and the United Kingdom, as well as in some developing countries, such as Brazil and Israel.

that the new scheme be adopted when inflation levels are relatively low or showing a marked downward trend, while having strong fiscal conditions and a sound financial system is strongly advised. Similarly, the central bank should possess a high level of technical sophistication, allowing it to compile and manage information and data, and to build relevant macroeconomic models. Of course, solid central bank autonomy—in terms of clarity of the anti-inflationary objective, and political and economic independence—is essential if the desired results are to be achieved.

Traditional arguments in support of fixed exchange regimes are strengthened when a currency board arrangement is established, limiting or eliminating discretion in monetary policies. Although the central bank loses control over monetary policy as a result of the creation of a monetary rule,[11] having a less discretionary policy enhances credibility regarding its fundamental objective of achieving price stability.[12] As a result, inflation tends to decrease in the short term, as observed in countries that have adopted currency boards. In addition, the risk of devaluation is lower, compared with the pure fixed–exchange rate system, and interest rates tend to move downward. However, the establishment of this monetary-exchange arrangement also requires certain prerequisites. The first and most obvious is that the central bank must have sufficient international reserves to support the amount of currency issue. It is also recommended that public finances should be solid so as to favor the expected fall in interest rates, and that a sound financial system should be in place, given the limits that central banks face to provide liquidity support under a currency board arrangement.

Recently, the popularity of currency boards is increasingly giving way to "dollarization" schemes, in which the very existence of the central bank is called into question.[13] The proponents of such

---

[11] In general, under a fixed–exchange rate regime money supply tends to adjust passively to money demand.

[12] The popularity of currency boards increased in the 1990s in different regions, such that countries like Argentina, Bulgaria, Bosnia and Herzegovina, Lithuania, and Estonia adopted this monetary and exchange arrangement.

[13] In addition to the recent experiments of Ecuador and East Timor, some Central American countries, in particular El Salvador, are evaluating seriously the adopton of a "dollarizaton" scheme. In Argentina, "dollarization" has been under consideration for a number of years.

schemes tout their greater benefits by arguing that, with the introduction of the dollar as a legal tender, the risk of devaluation disappears completely, together with the possibility of costly currency crises, so that a country remains insulated from the contagion generated by international financial crises. As a result, it is expected that interest rates will be lower, compared with currency board arrangements, favoring growth and employment. In practical terms, those who support "dollarization" schemes point out that many countries are already de facto "dollarized," insofar as their assets and liabilities are mostly denominated in foreign currencies. This is the case with countries such as Bolivia, the Philippines, Peru, and Turkey. These arguments add to those that support the existence of a small number of currencies in the world as a means of achieving a better functioning of international economic relations.

The adoption of one exchange regime or another imposes different responsibilities on the central bank. While the introduction of an "inflation targeting" scheme strengthens the described functions of an autonomous central bank and focuses their role around the objective of preserving price stability, the adoption of a currency board arrangement gives rise to significant changes in the functioning of the central bank. The establishment of a monetary rule eliminates the central bank's capacity to flexibly manage monetary policy, as well as to execute exchange rate policy. In addition, it changes the nature and restricts the use of traditional monetary instruments, reduces the functions associated with the management of the payment system, and requires building unconventional LOLR facilities.

Under "inflation targeting," the central bank must optimize the use of indirect instruments of monetary policy to maintain a stable and adequate amount of money that is consistent with the target of inflation. The central bank authorities are also obliged to redouble their efforts to compile the information required for the construction of a structural model of the economy and, in particular, a comprehensive analytical framework that allows broad understanding of the dynamics of inflation. As a result, monetary authorities might be able to better anticipate future inflation performance and to adopt the measures required to ensure the achievement of the announced inflation target. The central bank should expand the disclosure of information to educate the market about inflation performance by means of pamphlets, press releases, seminars, and public appearances by the monetary authorities. The success of "inflation targeting" schemes is also predicated on the transparency of the central bank's policies and practices, including a higher degree of accountability, which is expected to strengthen its reputation and credibility.

With the introduction of a currency board, the independence of monetary policy is lost, in the sense that an automatic monetary mechanism is chosen to ensure price stability. Hence, the central bank is basically responsible for ensuring compliance with the monetary rule, which also supports the maintenance of the exchange system. Open market operations, if at all, are restricted subject to the availability of liquid international reserves—in excess of the amount of money base, for example. Central bank liquidity management remains important in order to prevent large monetary imbalances and interest rate volatility. This is more important in an environment where liquidity fluctuations are common as a result of financial instability, and interest rate arbitrage does not always work efficiently to lessen volatility, in particular, in countries where the monetary market is not well developed. The management of reserve requirements in the central bank also acquires an alternative emphasis, as compared to the approach under a flexible–exchange rate system, since under a currency board arrangement deposits with the central bank may be converted into a "buffer" to confront liquidity shortages. To this end, a higher level of reserves is recommended— than if a flexible exchange regime were in place; remunerating deposits in the central bank at market interest rates to avoid imposing costs on financial intermediaries that eventually will lead to an increase in interest rate spreads is also recommended.

Similarly, central bank assistance as LOLR is limited to the availability of foreign reserves in excess of the amount required to ensure the convertibility of its domestic currency obligations. Thus alternative forms of liquidity support must be sought in order to deal with runs on deposits and with temporary liquidity shortages in the financial system. The case of Argentina is illustrative in this regard, where four unconventional instruments have been established, namely, a central bank fund comprising international reserves in excess of those required by the convertibility law; a deposit insurance fund to which banks contribute according to risk-adjusted criteria; an external fund created with dollar-denominated financial assets— working as a put option against a foreign bank in the event of a liquidity need—contributed by domestic financial institutions as a substitute for reserve requirements in the central bank; and the resources available from a set of contingent repurchase contracts with foreign banks that allow the central bank to obtain liquidity in exchange for government debt denominated in dollars. Together, these mechanisms provide coverage to nearly 40 percent of deposits in the Argentinian financial system.

At the same time, central banks would continue carrying out duties on behalf of the government as a fiscal and financial agency, as well as managing international reserves. Coordinating and monitoring the functioning of the economy's payment system is still possible, although some restrictions may emerge as long as the currency board arrangement is unable to provide LOLR support. The central bank's involvement in the payment system is also important since it enables monetary authorities to observe and assess the liquidity conditions of all participants, which may serve as an early-warning indicator of potential difficulties experienced by financial institutions.

Should a central bank exist in countries that have adopted a foreign currency as legal tender? The experience of Panama suggests that a central bank is not required under "dollarization." However, the situation may differ for the transition period, insofar as the adoption of "dollarization" is preceded by a crisis situation that has impeded the timely design of the institutional framework required for the appropriate functioning of the new monetary arrangement. Indeed, not only did the majority of countries that have adopted currency board arrangements in the past few years do so in the midst of severe economic crises—Argentina, Bulgaria, Lithuania, and even Hong Kong SAR are clear examples—but also the recent "dollarization" scheme in Ecuador was adopted under a deep banking and currency crisis.

Under "dollarization," potential central bank responsibilities are fewer than those described for a currency board arrangement. For example, in Ecuador, the central bank continues issuing temporarily fractional currencies, while at the same time managing the payment system and producing macroeconomic statistics. In general, a central bank under "dollarization" could carry out short-term monetary operations for the purpose of smoothing liquidity fluctuations and interest rate volatility—at least while the financial system is strengthened and the money market developed—and administer a fund under the same parameters used to invest international reserves, which is aimed at confronting eventual liquidity shortfalls. The scope for central banks' involvement in these responsibilities—including the monitoring of the payment system—will be negatively correlated with the degree of foreign banks' participation in the domestic market. Other nontraditional functions that central banks can still perform under "dollarization" are the supervision of the financial system, the production and compilation of economic statistics, and the elaboration of macroeconomic studies, which are fundamental to monitoring and projecting economic behavior. In most developing countries, central banks have become a valuable public good that can hardly be replaced in the short run, considering the lack of solid institutions in the rest of the public sector.

The Role of the Central Bank in Banking Crisis Resolution

Central banks' potential degree of involvement in banking crises was not anticipated appropriately when monetary legal frameworks were reformed during the 1990s to grant central banks greater autonomy. While the reform's emphasis was placed on reducing inflationary government financing, clear rules were not established for limiting central bank functions as LOLR, nor were basic criteria set forth for central banks on their participation in resolving banking crises. However, the experience of the past few years demonstrates that banking crises are a major cause of the acceleration in inflation in various countries, and that central banks have difficulties in fighting inflation and maintaining their autonomy under these circumstances.

The frequency and the potential costs associated with banking crises have led central banks to become more and more involved in the response to and resolution of financial crises. This is not surprising, in that in most countries central banks remain the most important (if not the only) source of funds available to cope with problems of liquidity shortfalls and, on occasion, of insolvency of financial intermediaries. Also, governments feel tempted to shift to central banks, at least partially, the costs of banking crises with the expectation of hiding these costs within central banks' balance sheets. In general, central banks' involvement in banking crises is more frequent in countries that lack an appropriate institutional and legal framework to confront these crises. As a result of central banks' involvement in financial crises, a monetary expansion is generally expected, in particular when the magnitude of the crisis entails a systemic risk. In this scenario, central banks tend to lose credibility with regard to their ability to maintain control over monetary policy and meet announced inflation targets.

Although the prevention and resolution of banking crises are not direct responsibilities of monetary authorities, in practice central banks have been involved under at least three broad modalities. A first set of operations is linked to conventional LOLR facilities. Problems arise when LOLR mechanisms are not appropriately regulated, in particular in terms of the volume, collateral, and maturities of the loans provided. As a result, the monetization effect may be significant and the quality of assets received in exchange from the impaired banks tends to deteriorate as liquidity assistance increases, adversely affecting a central bank's financial position. In addition, excessive discretion in the management of LOLR facilities makes central banks vulnerable to political pressures to favor one institution over another, postpone the resolution of the financial crisis, and raise the associated fiscal cost.

A second group of transactions go beyond common LOLR facilities and are intended to facilitate banking crisis resolution. These are observed, for example, when central banks issue securities in exchange for low quality assets of an impaired bank in order to make attractive the bank's auction or absorption. Several sources of undesirable monetization and quasi-fiscal deficit generation are identified under this arrangement, although their impact will not be observed in the short run. On the one hand, the payment of the interest associated with the bonds issued by the central bank will produce a persistent monetary expansion. On the other hand, there is a potential loss if the value of such bonds (including interest) is not covered by the revenues obtained from the realization of the assets acquired by the central bank. A related case may take place as a result of the discount in the central bank of government securities granted to an impaired bank that is "too big to fail," in order to allow its continued operation while a restructuring process is under way. In this situation, there is an immediate monetary effect resulting from the injection of liquidity, as well as potential losses for the central bank depending on the financial conditions of the discounted government securities. In particular, losses may occur if these securities are issued at below-market interest rates, while the central bank discounts those securities at nominal value. A more extreme situation may take place if the central bank directly absorbs an impaired bank through a subordinated loan to capitalize the troubled institution, which in addition may require liquidity to ensure its continued operation. In this case, the central bank will end up conducting responsibilities that may conflict with its fundamental goal of preserving price stability.

A third modality arises when central banks are called to execute deposit insurance in exchange for assets of the banks in liquidation. As a result, monetary expansion takes place, which could be significant in the case of a systemic crisis. In addition, central banks may incur a potential loss if the present value resulting from the sale of the assets of the impaired bank is smaller than the value of the resources provided. A related type of operation stems from the direct capitalization by the central bank of deposit insurance funds. In this event, although a monetary impact is produced only when the deposit insurance is activated, the financial position of the central bank may be affected if the resources provided by the central bank are not canceled a posteriori, either by the government or by the contributions of the financial institutions.

The type of transactions previously described are not always correctly reflected in the central banks' financial statements, limiting the recognition of asset values and risks. As a result, quasi-fiscal deficits tend to emerge, hampering the conduct of monetary policy and leading to the deterioration of a central bank's credibility with respect to the fulfillment of policy targets. In order to correct these distortions, sooner or later the adoption of a restrictive fiscal policy is required, aimed at compensating the central bank's financial burden that has been inappropriately assumed. A transparent involvement of central banks in banking crises should follow the principle of placing the costs of the crises in the government budget, which implies accounting a central bank's transactions at market values according to international best practices.

The Challenge of Improving Central Bank Accountability and Transparency

After several years of experience with the autonomy reform of central banks, accountability still is a factor that has not been appropriately executed, especially in developing countries, in spite of the independence granted to monetary authorities. In many cases, central banks' authorities do not inform the executive branch or the legislature about the actions and policies conducted through a given period or, if they do, the report is not appropriately focused on relevant central bank responsibilities. The most common accountability procedure is the publication of a broad annual report, covering all central bank activities, including monetary policies, which is normally published with a significant lag.

The insufficient practical accountability observed in many cases has strengthened opinions that consider that the autonomy reform of central banks is not consistent with democratic practices. Stiglitz (1998) argues that although monetary policy is a key determinant of the economy's macroeconomic performance, the decisions adopted by the central bank involve trade-offs—mainly between inflation and unemployment—and the most important decisions are discussed in secrecy by a group of people in the central bank that is not representative of the general public. In the end, the head (of the country) "is held accountable for how the economy performs—whether or not he has much control." Stiglitz's proposal points to strengthening central bank accountability and to increasing transparency in policy decisions and formulation.

The enhancement of accountability and transparency is today a common trend in most central banks. Central banks' governors are required to appear before a designated public authority to report on the conduct of monetary policy—as well as other activities developed by the central bank—and to assess the achievement of the announced policy target. The improvement of accountability is required not only in relation to monetary policy but also in terms of the financial statements of the central bank. The enhancement of transparency is based on the hypothesis that it will strengthen credibility and reinforce reputation. In addition, it is believed that transparency will underpin monetary policy effectiveness, as long as the market knows and understands the goals and instruments of policy and, in particular, if there is a public and credible commitment of monetary authorities to fight inflation. Macroeconomic performance is also expected to improve, given that the market will be able to elaborate expectations and adopt decisions in a more informed environment conducive to better results. In many industrial countries, the implementation of "inflation targeting" schemes has strengthened accountability, since this policy requires public, long-term commitments and abundant disclosure of information, including monthly inflation reports. This course of action has been followed by some developing countries, although not all countries are ready yet to implement "inflation targeting" as explained above.

The international financial community also favors better transparency on central bank policies as part of the building of the New International Financial Architecture. The former Interim Committee recently called on relevant international financial institutions and the IMF to build a code of transparency practices for monetary and financial policies. The Code of Good Practices on Transparency in Monetary and Financial Policies: Declaration of Principles was approved in September 1999, and currently serves as a basis for IMF's technical assistance missions to member countries. It is also a key component of the Financial Sector Assessment Program (FSAP) conducted jointly by the IMF and the World Bank, which is aimed at identifying financial system strengths and vulnerabilities and helping develop appropriate policy responses.[14]

The Code is increasingly a guide for transparency enhancement worldwide. In its monetary component, the Code emphasizes the following central bank policies and procedures: (i) the clarity of roles, responsibilities, and objectives of central banks for monetary policy; (ii) an open process for formulating and reporting monetary policy decisions; (iii) the public availability of information on monetary policy; and (iv) the accountability and assurances of integrity by the central bank. Although the principles behind this code of good practices are an appropriate guide for policymakers in the central bank, they are not a straightjacket that should be identically applied in all countries. They provide enough flexibility to consider particular

---

[14] The FSAP was launched in May 1999 and has been applied up to now in about a dozen countries. It is intended to cover most of the industrial and developing economies in the next few years.

situations where increased transparency could endanger the effectiveness of monetary policy and threaten market stability.

References

Alesina, Alberto, and Lawrence Summers, 1993, "Central Bank Independence and Macroeconomic Performance: Some Comparative Evidence," *Journal of Money, Credit and Banking*, (May), pp. 151–62.

Cukierman, Alex, 1992, *Central Bank Strategy, Credibility, and Independence: Theory and Evidence* (Cambridge, Mass.: MIT Press).

———, Steven B. Webb, and Bilib Neyapti, 1992, "Measuring the Independence of Central and Its Effect on Policy Outcomes," *The World Bank Economic Review*, Vol. 6, No. 3, pp. 352–98.

Downes, Patrick, and Reza Vaez-Zadeh, 1991, *The Evolving Role of Central Banks* (Washington: International Monetary Fund).

Eichengreen, Barry, 1999, *Toward a New International Financial Architecture* (Washington: Institute for International Economics).

Fischer, Stanley, and Guy Debelle, 1994, "How Independent Should a Central Bank Be?" in *Goals, Guidelines, and Constraints Facing Monetary Policy Makers*, Federal Reserve Bank of Boston, Conference Series No. 38, pp. 195–221.

Forder, James, 1998, "Central Bank Independence, Conceptual Clarifications and Interim Assessment," *Oxford Economic Papers*, Vol. 50, No. 3 (July), pp. 307–34.

Grilli, Vittorio, Donato Masciandaro, and Guido Tabellini, 1991, "Political and Monetary Institutions and Public Financial Policies in Industrial Countries," *Economic Policy: A European Forum*, Vol. 6 (October), pp. 342–91.

International Monetary Fund, 1996, *World Economic Outlook* (October) (Washington: International Monetary Fund).

———, 1998, "Elements of Central Bank Autonomy and Accountability," Monetary and Exchange Affairs Department, IMF Operational Paper 98/1 (Washington: International Monetary Fund).

LeBaron, Blake, and Rachel McCulloch, 2000, "Floating, Fixed, or Super-Fixed? Dollarization Joins the Menu of Exchange Rate Options," *American Economic Review*, Vol. 90, No. 2, pp. 32–37.

Loungani, Prakash, and Nathan Sheets, 1997, "Central Bank Independence, Inflation and Growth in Transition Economies," *Journal of Money, Credit and Banking*, Vol. 29, No. 3 (August), pp. 381–99.

Lybeck, Tonny, 1999, "Central Bank Autonomy, and Inflation and Output Performance in the Baltic States, Russia, and Other Countries of the Former Soviet Union, 1995–97," IMF Working Paper 99/4 (Washington: International Monetary Fund).

Mas, Ignacio, 1995, "Central Bank Independence: A Critical View from a Developing Country Perspective," *World Development*, Vol. 23, No. 10, pp. 1639–52.

Posen, Adam, 1994, "Why Central Bank Independence Does Not Cause Low Inflation," *Finance and the International Economy*, No. 7, pp. 51–63.

———, 1995, "Central Bank Independence and Disinflationary Credibility: A Missing Link?" *Federal Reserve Bank of New York Staff Reports* (May).

Rogoff, Kenneth, 1985, "The Optimal Degree of Commitment to an Intermediate Monetary Target," *Quarterly Journal of Economics* (November), pp. 1169–90.

Stiglitz, Joseph, 1998, "Central Banking in a Democratic Society," *The Economist*, Vol. 146, No. 2, pp. 199–226.

Walsh, Carl, 1993, "Is New Zealand's Reserve Bank Act of 1989 an Optimal Central Bank Contract?" *Journal of Money Credit and Banking*, Vol. 27, No. 24 (November), pp. 1179–91.

Worrel, DeLisle, 2000, "Monetary and Fiscal Coordination in Small Open Economies," IMF Working Paper 00/56 (Washington: International Monetary Fund).

COMMENT

GEORGE IDEN

Luis Jácome Hidalgo, as a former central bank governor of Ecuador, is uniquely well suited to provide us with an excellent overview of, and perspective on, recent trends in central banking—and he has done that in this paper. Mr. Jácome begins by observing that the focus of central banks is continuously evolving. At the beginning of the 1990s, the focus was on establishing central banks in transition economies in Eastern Europe and the former Soviet Union, and on taming inflation through greater focus on price stability as the main goal of monetary policy. During the decade, attention has shifted to dealing with the increased volatility of international financial markets, including periodic financial crises, in the context of more independence on the part of central banks. Specifically, Mr. Jácome directs our attention to the choice of exchange rate regimes, the role of central banks in resolving financial crises, and achieving more transparency and accountability in monetary policy. As a starting point, however, he reviews "best practices" with respect to central bank independence.

Mr. Jácome follows current convention in distinguishing between instrument independence and goal or political independence for central banks, and notes that there is more consensus for central banks having autonomy in the use of monetary instruments than in the establishment of goals for monetary policy.[1] He observes that conventional wisdom favors central banks be assigned, at least with respect to monetary policies, a single and clear mandate, namely, preserving price stability. In this regard, it may be useful to draw a distinction that the consensus pertains to there being a preeminent goal for monetary policy. Mr. Jácome acknowledges that central

---

[1] Instrument independence may be difficult to achieve in practice. One reason is that central banks may lack a portfolio of marketable securities with which to conduct open market operations. In addition, there may be coordination problems with the ministry of finance if treasury bills are used as the primary instrument for mopping up liquidity, or the central bank may lack the financial capacity to issue central bank bills for that purpose.

banks typically are given other responsibilities, such as being financial agent and advisor to the government and banking supervisor, and I would add protecting against systemic vulnerability—that is, ensuring that the financial system functions smoothly without significant interruption or crisis. One of the difficulties is that the consensus in current thinking about the goals of the central bank may only pertain to monetary policy. The central bank should focus on controlling inflation, rather than on, say, running and owning other financial enterprises, economic development, or lowering unemployment. It is all right for the central bank to promote the development of financial markets or lower unemployment, but only to the extent that this does not conflict with its primary goal of maintaining price stability. However, the course is less clear concerning how the central bank should deal with conflicts among its objectives for monetary policy (typically price stability) and its other financial roles, including in particular maintaining the stability of the financial system. I agree with Mr. Jácome that clear rules have generally not been established for how central banks should operate in resolving a financial crisis, nor in how they should balance their responsibilities in avoiding crises and maintaining price stability, which is the primary responsibility of monetary policy.

With respect to the goal of price stability, Mr. Jácome presents data indicating that tremendous progress was achieved on that score during the 1990s, especially at the end of the decade—both in industrial and in developing countries. Monetary policy had two strong allies, however, low and falling oil prices and rapid productivity growth. The recent tripling in oil prices will once again present monetary authorities with a difficult test. Let us hope that much has been learned since the 1970s, and that those mistakes will not be repeated.

With respect to the choice of exchange/monetary regime, Mr. Jácome calls attention to the growing popularity of "inflation targeting," on the one hand, and "super-fixed" exchange rates—such as currency board arrangements or dollarization—on the other hand. Intermediate arrangements, such as crawling peg systems, have become less popular due to their greater vulnerability to current circumstances involving increased globalization and volatility of financial markets.

The role of the central bank in banking crisis resolution is difficult, to say the least. One reason is that the lender-of-last-resort (LOLR) function can conflict with the objective of maintaining price stability. In this regard, it is important to distinguish the role of the central bank with its routine lending to banks that are temporarily short of liquidity for overnight clearing, which is also sometimes referred to as LOLR. The context in which LOLR is used here is much more serious. Because LOLR can involve the commitment of substantial sums of public funds, decisions to undertake such lending may be made jointly with the government or ministry of finance. An important point that Mr. Jácome makes is that the extent of central bank involvement in banking crises was not anticipated appropriately when monetary legal frameworks were established (including those reformed during the 1990s), and appropriate guidelines for their involvement are generally lacking. For example, if the central bank is too aggressive in its LOLR role, it could become financially weakened to the point that its independence and capacity to conduct monetary policy would be seriously undermined.[2] In addition to crisis resolution, I would argue that the central bank generally has an important role in preventing financial crises and overseeing the smooth operation of the financial system, which is specifically mandated in some central bank laws.

Mr. Jácome points to two factors that are leading to more accountability and transparency in monetary policies: the fact that more central banks have been granted at least instrument independence; and an attempt on the part of international financial leaders to erect a "New International Financial Architecture" in the wake of the recent financial crisis of 1997–98. With independence comes an obligation for accountability. In addition, it is thought that transparency plays a constructive role in avoiding financial crises, or in minimizing their effects once they occur. The case for enhanced transparency is also based on the belief that it increases the effectiveness of monetary policy and promotes good governance.

---

[2] See Peter Stella, "Do Central Banks Need Capital?" IMF Working Paper 97/83 (July 1997); and Alfredo M. Leone, "Institutional and Operational Aspects of Central Bank Losses," IMF Paper on Policy Analysis and Assessment 93/14 (September 1993).

Mr. Jácome notes that the IMF has taken a leading role in the efforts to improve transparency in monetary and financial policies, particularly in its adoption of the Code of Good Practices on Transparency in Monetary and Financial Policies: Declaration of Principles, which was adopted by the Interim Committee of the Fund on September 26, 1999. Assessing observance of this code has become a standard part of the combined IMF/World Bank Financial Sector Assessment Program (FSAP), which seeks to identify financial sector vulnerabilities, in particular countries at their invitation, and to recommend corrective actions. In addition, the Executive Board of the Fund adopted on July 24, 2000, a Supporting Document to the Code of Good Practices on Transparency in Monetary and Financial Policies, which explains and amplifies the provisions of the Code, and provides examples of how different countries implement the broad principles of the code.[3] Production of the Supporting Document involved a detailed survey of transparency practices by members of the Fund and extensive consultation with monetary and financial institutions, including seven regional consultative meetings held around the world.

Mr. Jácome rightly notes that in many cases the modalities for executing greater accountability and transparency are vague—and in some cases unsatisfactory. How to achieve more transparency and how much transparency to strive for are areas where central banks are still exploring and finding their way. While it is no doubt correct, as Mr. Jácome says, that there is a trend toward more transparency in monetary policy, there is still a great deal of controversy over the specifics and in particular over implementation. Moreover, representatives from some countries argue that the Code is based on a particular style or system of economic management—political democracy and liberalized market capitalism.

In general, observance of the Code of Good Practices on Transparency in Monetary and Financial Policies seems to be correlated with a country's stage of economic development and form of government. Transparency of monetary policies may be quite limited in countries in the early stages of development, especially

---

[3] Both the Code and the Supporting Document to the Code can be found on the IMF's external website: www.imf.org/external/np/mae/mft/index.htm.

those where democracy has not been strongly established. In some countries, transparency may be viewed as counter to secrecy provisions of the central banking laws or may present a risk to the job security of the central bank's employees. In such countries, it may be useful to distinguish between information about individual firms and households, where confidentiality is a keystone, and information about monetary policy where transparency has an important role. In addition, some countries that have the legislative and other structural aspects of transparency in place have difficulty with implementation, particularly with providing substantive and timely explanations of changes in monetary policy.

In sum, Mr. Jácome has given readers an excellent overview of the dynamic landscape of central banking. A decade from now, future participants in this seminar series will refer to Mr. Jácome's paper as a reference point for describing the important central banking developments and issues at the beginning of the twenty-first century.

Chapter 17

Responsibility of Central Banks for Stability in Financial Markets

GARRY J. SCHINASI

There are four main questions I would like to address in this seminar.

- What is financial stability?

- Do central banks have a natural role in ensuring financial stability?

- What does a central bank need to execute this role effectively?

- How far have central banks actually gone in safeguarding financial stability?

Before attempting to provide answers to these specific questions, it is worth highlighting the controversies surrounding the general subject of central banking and financial stability. Although there is a long history of central banking and of financial crises and how they have been managed, there remains considerable controversy over the role of central banks in ensuring financial stability. The following two examples illustrate this point.

First, the United Kingdom recently moved responsibility for banking supervision from the Bank of England to the Financial Services Authority as part of the process of creating a single financial regulator. The creation of a single financial regulator is one way of rationalizing or merging together disparate organizations that are responsible for parts of the financial regulatory or supervisory framework. This rationalization can be justified for several reasons, but it is useful to observe that the Bank of England, which is the lender of last resort and the ensurer of financial stability, no longer has responsibility for banking supervision. An important issue raised by this example is, what kind of information does a central bank need in order to fulfill its mandate for ensuring financial stability and effectively providing lender-of-last-resort protection against instability?

A second example is the European Central Bank (ECB). This newly created central bank, which is supranational, manages a currency of eleven countries. In many ways, the Deutsche Bundesbank is the model used for designing the European Central Bank, both in statute and in practice. As will be explained more fully later, the Bundesbank can be characterized as a central bank based on a "narrow" concept of central banking. The Bundesbank had a single objective, the stability of the deutsche mark, which in domestic terms meant price stability. In practice, the Bundesbank was a "de facto" bank supervisor as well, even though there was, and still is, a separate Federal Supervisory Office. In effect, the Bundesbank was responsible for collecting all of the information required for good banking supervision, and it provided that information to the Federal Supervisory Office, which legally is the supervisor. In effect, the Bundesbank had a very direct and central role in banking supervision. By contrast, the ECB does not. The ECB appears to be the ultimate narrow central bank; it literally has a mandate for price stability and a very small role in ensuring financial stability, confined to ensuring the smooth functioning of the TARGET payments system, not the financial system.

What Is Financial Stability?

Given that this is a controversial subject, consider the first of the four questions: what is meant by financial stability? It is instructive to first consider what is meant by monetary stability: the stability of either the price level or of the inflation rate over some well defined, medium-term horizon—a year, 18 months, or two years. Over shorter horizons, it also entails the stability of overnight interest rates, for example, or of monetary aggregates.

The definition of financial stability is, in general, more controversial. What it generally means is the joint stability of the key financial institutions operating within financial markets and the stability of those markets. For the financial institutions, this generally means that they are sound, meaning they have sufficient capital to absorb normal, and at times abnormal, losses and sufficient liquidity to manage operations and volatility in normal periods of time. Market stability, generally, does not mean steady asset prices—even stable markets can have high volatility in asset prices. But it generally does mean the absence of the kind of volatility that could have severe real economic consequences. There is controversy about what is meant by "too much" volatility, for example, and about which asset prices, when volatile, would constitute general financial market volatility or instability. Is it just one sector, like real estate prices, or does it have to be a more widespread phenomenon?

The concept of financial stability is most often thought of in terms of avoiding financial crises but one can also think of it in terms of managing systemic financial risk. If systemic risk is managed reasonably well, including by market participants through their private risk management (the first line of defense) and the authorities through their banking supervision, market surveillance, and systemic risk management—then systemic financial crises will most likely not occur. It is necessary to have a working definition of systemic financial risk. A study by the G-10 provides the following definition:

> Systemic financial risk is the risk that an event will trigger a loss of economic value or confidence in, and attendant increases in uncertainly about, a substantial portion of the financial system that is serious enough to quite probably have significant adverse effects on the real economy. Systemic risk events can be sudden and unexpected, or the likelihood of their occurrence can build up through time in the absence of appropriate policy responses. The adverse real economic effects from systemic problems are generally seen as arising from disruptions to the payment system, to credit flows, and from the destruction of asset values. Two related assumptions underlie this definition. First, economic shocks may become systemic because of the existence of negative externalities associated with severe disruptions in the financial system. If there were no spillover effects, or negative externalities, there would be, arguably, no role for public policy. In all but the most highly concentrated financial systems, systemic risk is normally associated with a contagious loss of value or confidence that spreads to parts of the financial system well beyond the original location of the precipitating shock. In a very highly concentrated financial system, on the other hand, the collapse of a single firm or market may be sufficient to qualify as a systemic event. Second, systemic financial events must be very likely to induce undesirable real effects, such

as substantial reductions in output and employment, in the absence of appropriate policy responses. In this definition, a financial disruption that does not have a high probability of causing a significant disruption of real economic activity is not a systemic risk event.

The study notes that this definition encompasses much of what is in the literature but it is stricter in two respects. One is that the negative externalities of a systemic event extend into the real economy. They are not confined to the financial system. The second is that this extension into the real economy occurs with relatively high probability. The emphasis on real effects reflects the view that it is the output of real goods and services and the accompanying employment implications that are the primary concern of economic policymakers.

Finally, in answering the question, what is financial stability, it is useful to have a working definition of a financial crisis. Professor Anna Schwartz defines a financial crisis in the following way:

> A financial crisis is fuelled by fears that the means of payment will be unobtainable at any price and in a fractional reserve banking system leads to a scramble for high-powered money. It is precipitated by actions of the public that suddenly squeeze the reserves of the banking system. . . . The essence of a financial crisis is that it is short-lived, ending with a slackening of the public's demand for additional currency.[1]

Do Central Banks Have a Natural Role in Ensuring Financial Stability?

This section argues that they do. Specifically, there are features of central banking that make central banks a natural contender for ensuring financial stability. Consider the traditional definition of monetary stability from Henry Thornton's classic monograph, *An Enquiry into the Nature and Effects of the Paper Credit of Great Britain*, published in 1802.

> To limit the amount of paper issued, and to resort for this purpose, whenever the temptation to borrow is strong, to some effectual principle of restriction; in no case, however, materially to diminish

---

[1] Schwartz (1986), p. 11.

the sum in circulation, but to let it vibrate only within certain limits; to afford a slow and cautious extension of it, as the general trade of the kingdom enlarges itself; to allow of some special, though temporary, enquiries in the event of any extraordinary alarm or difficulty, as the best means of preventing a great demand at home for guineas; and to lean to the side of diminution, in the case of gold going abroad, and of the general exchanges continuing long unfavorable; this seems to be the true policy of the directors of an institution circumstanced like that of the Bank of England. To suffer either the solicitations of merchants, or the wishes of government, to determine the measure of the bank issues, is unquestionably to adopt a very false principle of conduct.[2]

In this definition, one can see the traditional monetary policy role of a central bank. It has all of the ingredients of managing monetary aggregates and interest rates. It has embedded in it the monetary transmission mechanism, and references to monetary targets, or maybe interest rate targets.

Let me now turn to Thornton's views on what may be interpreted as the role of the Bank of England in ensuring financial stability at that time. In particular, three passages from Thornton's classic appear relevant.

If any one bank fails, a general run upon the neighbouring ones is apt to take place, which if not checked in the beginning by pouring into the circulation a large quantity of gold, leads to very extensive mischief. . . .[3]

If the Bank of England, in future seasons of alarm, should be disposed to extend its discounts in a greater degree than heretofore, then the threatened calamity may be averted through the generosity of that institution.[4]

It is by no means intended to imply that it would become the Bank of England to relieve every distress which the rashness of country banks may bring upon them: the bank, by doing this, might encourage their improvidence. There seems to be a medium at which a public bank should aim in granting aid to inferior

---

[2] Thornton (1802), p. 259.
[3] *Id.*, p. 180.
[4] *Id.*, p. 188.

establishments, and which it often must find it very difficult to be observed. The relief should neither be so prompt and liberal as to exempt those who misconduct their business from all the natural consequences of their fault, nor so scanty and slow as deeply to involve the general interests. These interests, nevertheless, are sure to be pleaded by every distressed person whose affairs are large, however indifferent or even ruinous may be their state.[5]

The first passage describes a process of contagion that is likely to occur with a run on one bank. The second describes the role of the Bank of England. The third passage describes the concept of moral hazard, which is taken up below. All three passages together show clearly that Thornton had a working definition of the role of central banks in financial stability.

Consider a more modern view of the role of central banks in ensuring financial stability, which is consistent with Thornton's view. The following view was expressed by Paul Volcker in 1984, when he was Chairman of the U.S. Federal Reserve System:

> A basic continuing responsibility of any central bank—and the principal reason for the founding of the Federal Reserve—is to assure stable and smoothly functioning financial and payments systems. These are prerequisites for, and complementary to, the central bank's responsibility for conducting monetary policy as it is more narrowly conceived. To these ends, the U.S. Congress has over the last 70 years authorized the Federal Reserve (1) to be a major participant in the nation's payments mechanism; (2) to lend at the discount window as the ultimate source of liquidity for the economy; and (3) to regulate and supervise key sectors of the financial markets, both domestic and international. These functions are in addition to, and largely predate, the more purely "monetary" functions of engaging in open market and foreign exchange operations and setting reserve requirements; historically, in fact, the "monetary" functions were largely grafted onto the "supervisory" functions, not the reverse.[6]

According to Paul Volcker, the Federal Reserve system was *first* the ensurer of financial stability and *then* the manager of monetary stability. It is helpful to draw on some key points made by Thornton

---

[5] *Id.*
[6] Volcker (1984), p. XX.

and by Paul Volcker in order to characterize the reasons why there is a natural role of central banks in financial stability.

First, the central bank is the only provider of the legal means of payment, referred to by Anna Schwartz, and of immediate liquidity. That is, only the central bank provides the "finality of payment." Attorneys have played an important role in defining what the finality of payment really means and in setting up clearance, payments, and settlement systems to put into practice payments finality.

The second natural role is for the central bank to ensure the smooth functioning of the national payment system. It is within the context of the soundness and stability of national payments systems that policymakers have traditionally and naturally thought about and considered systemic risk. Traditionally, systemic risk has been viewed as the possibility that problems at one bank would create problems at other banks and, in particular, banks that make up the core of the national payment system. In this view, problems at one bank would cascade through the payments system and perhaps lead to bottlenecks in payments and the possibility of a widespread domino effect. The payment system, being the core of the financial market, has been the subject of much discussion, policy, and reform. Through G-10 efforts, there now exist real-time gross payments settlements systems that try to prevent the failure of one institution from cascading through the payments system and affecting other institutions within the payments system. So, again, the central bank has a natural role to play in financial stability—in this case, even if it is confined to the payments system.

The third natural role is that the banking system is the transmission mechanism through which monetary policy has its effect, in the first instance, on the real economy. To the extent that the banking system is experiencing distress, it will be more difficult for the central bank to provide whatever liquidity it thinks is necessary to achieve its monetary objectives. For this reason alone, central banks have a natural interest in sound financial institutions and stable financial markets. Central banks have, therefore, an interest in maintaining the stability of the banking system, in having the ability to see problems at an early stage and in being in a position to influence corrective actions.

Finally, there is an explicit link between monetary stability and financial stability. If we go back to the definition by Anna Schwarz of a financial crisis, she refers to the propensity for the money supply to collapse. One simple equation makes this very clear. In basic money-and-banking courses in college, one comes across an equation called the money multiplier, which establishes a relationship (some would even say an identity if these parameters are fixed) between central bank money (B) held as bank reserves by the banking system and the broader money supply (M). Formally:

$M = mB$,

or, in words, the money stock is equal to high powered money or the monetary base times the money multiplier (m). This can be written explicitly as follows:

$$M = \left[\frac{1 + \frac{C}{D}}{\frac{C}{D} + \frac{R}{D}} \right] B,$$

where C/D is the currency/deposit ratio of the public, and R/D is the cash/deposit ratio of the banks.

It has not been made clear in the above discussion whether M is a narrow monetary aggregate or a broad monetary aggregate: that will depend on what these ratios C/D (the ratio of currency to total deposit liabilities) and R/D (the ratio of required bank reserves to total deposits) are. Regardless, there is a direct link between what the central bank provides in the way of central bank money and the money supply of the economy. In the midst of a financial crisis, there could be a run on liquidity. Everyone will demand liquidity (and the finality of payment), and everyone in the system understands that the only liquidity that really exists is central bank money—base money (B). In this rush for central bank money, the money supply shrinks because the ratio C/D increases very rapidly as everyone increases C and reduces D. If the money supply is shrinking very rapidly in the presence of financial instability, then it will not take long before the central bank will have to supply liquidity (B) in order to restore monetary stability as the monetary aggregates collapse, as monetary stability objectives are less likely to be achieved, even in the short run. So when there is financial instability, there is likely to be monetary instability. This establishes a link between the natural role of the central bank as the provider of payments finality and its role in financial stability.

What Does the Central Bank Need to Execute This Role Effectively?

Even if one is not convinced that the central bank has a central role to play in financial stability, it is useful to consider this third question. This is probably the most controversial part of this subject. There are competing views. The first view might be characterized as the "open market operations view," which strongly believes that there is an inherent conflict between the conduct of monetary policy and the conduct of broader financial policies. If a central bank has responsibility for achieving monetary objectives (e.g., keeping inflation in some target range) and if it also has the responsibility for banking supervision, the question that arises is whether or not the central bank will face a situation of having several large banks whose viability importantly depends on interest rates and at the same time be faced with the possibility of having to tighten monetary policy to achieve its monetary objectives. What then does the central bank do? Does it raise interest rates by 300 basis points in order to achieve its monetary objectives, thereby risking the viability of some large banks or does it relax its commitment to its monetary objectives, thereby saving these banks and presumably the financial system.

The open market operations view argues that the central bank should maintain its commitment to its monetary objectives, because it believes the tools that the central bank has to implement monetary policy—open market operations—can also be used to inject liquidity into the financial system that would be appropriate for safeguarding the financial system from the collapse of large banks and any contagion that might occur.[7] The argument rests on (1) the central banks' ability to take good collateral in return for its central bank money provided to the market and (2) the belief that the market itself can distinguish quickly between solvent and insolvent institutions; that is, the market can distinguish between those institutions that have

---

[7] See Prati and Schinasi (1999) for a fuller discussion of these views and references to original sources.

liquidity needs but are otherwise solvent and viable institutions, and those institutions that are having difficulties obtaining liquidity because they truly are insolvent. The importance of collateral in this argument is that if a bank has good collateral then it is not insolvent and if it is insolvent it will not have good collateral. That is roughly the open market operations view.

The second view is the banking policy view. An interpretation of the banking policy view is that it too recognizes this inherent conflict between achieving monetary objectives and the broader financial policy objectives. But it takes a more pragmatic view about how difficult it is to distinguish illiquid from insolvent institutions and, in particular, how difficult it is for the private sector to discriminate between illiquid and insolvent institutions. For example, a bank may have collateral but it may be illiquid collateral. In this case, even a solvent bank may not be able to trade its collateral for the cash that it needs to conduct its business. Therefore, the banking policy view believes that the central bank has a role to play in helping the market to distinguish between illiquid and insolvent institutions. In the banking policy view, the central bank has a banking supervisory function. This function helps the central bank know the banking system, know the banks through which it conducts its monetary policy so that when a crisis does occur, it has current and useful information about the strength and soundness of each of the institutions that it supervises. In this view, open market operations are not sufficient to deal with bank runs and financial crises and there is a natural role for the central bank in banking supervision and the broader financial policy/financial stability function.

Even if one ignores the role of the central bank in managing or ensuring financial stability, it is still possible to identify the key elements of preventing crises. Regardless of what role the central bank plays, a financial system should have in place the mechanisms for identifying vulnerabilities, preventing those vulnerabilities from leading to crises and for dealing with crises if those two lines of defense fail. One can identify some of the key elements of prevention:

- Market Discipline

    - Internal incentive systems within financial institutions

- Risk management and control systems
- Stakeholder governance (shareholders, counterparties)

- Banking Supervision
- Market Surveillance (both on-exchange and over-the-counter markets)

Market discipline is a key element of prevention and is the first line of defense against systemic problems. If market discipline is working, individual financial institutions that make mistakes will pay for those mistakes very early on. There are three key elements to market discipline identified above, and they all play an important role.

Are there reasons to believe that private market discipline alone would be insufficient to prevent problems from arising? There are, and one of the most important is the existence of a financial safety net. In return for access to the financial safety net, each institution is required to hold a minimum amount of capital and to conform to best practices regarding accounting standards and business practices. The required capital acts as a cushion to absorb losses, losses that the taxpayer will not have to pay for. The second element of prudent management is adhering to strict accounting standards. The accounting standards are in place so that whatever losses are suffered will be reported and disclosed immediately. In some cases, disclosure occurs within a month—in most cases, within a quarter. Shareholders will have access to that information and can act as a disciplining force on the institution.

An example of how market discipline can work is how some financial institutions were paralyzed after the crisis in the autumn of 1998. Internationally active financial institutions were the major counterparties of the hedge fund Long Term Capital Management (LTCM) in the autumn of 1998. Even though no one really understood fully how large or small the losses of these institutions would be, the behavior of stock prices was telling. Some of these institutions' share prices declined by up to 40 percent within a week. The institutions that suffered those equity price losses got a clear message from shareholders about their behavior in the period leading up to the Long Term Capital Management problem. So shareholders have a role, and the only way that shareholders can really exact an accurate penalty from firms is if there is good accounting disclosure. There are other aspects of market discipline, and they include internal incentive systems, risk management and control systems, and financial stakeholder governance.

In the IMF's 1999 *International Capital Markets* report, there is a chapter on managing global finance, which tried to step back from the turbulence in the mature markets in the fall of 1998 to draw lessons. There were failures in private risk management and shortcomings in disclosure and other aspects of market discipline. However, in the view of the authors of the *International Capital Markets* report, there were also failures in banking supervision and in market surveillance. How is it that the kind of vulnerabilities that built up—in the two years preceding the Russian default and the LTCM crisis—were not detected at individual institutions through banking supervision and in the markets through market surveillance? The report does not provide definitive answers, but it does provide analyses about how to think about what banking supervision and market surveillance can do to identify these vulnerabilities before they build up to the point where a crisis occurs. In particular, more proactive banking supervision and more proactive market surveillance can be useful in identifying vulnerabilities before they become financial crises.

There are key elements of crisis resolution as well.

- legal framework for bankruptcy and closeout procedures for financial contracts;

- exit strategies for insolvent institutions (large and small); and

- lender-of-last-resort function in the central bank.

First, there is the need for a very clear and effective legal framework for bankruptcy and, in terms of financial markets and contracts, for closeout procedures. Closeout procedures are, in effect, a last resort, private, credit-risk mitigation technique. If all else fails, and you have a defaulting party, closeout procedures allow you to make good on (part of) the claim. One of the lessons from LTCM was that even in what many people consider to be the most advanced financial markets in the world, closeout procedures could not be relied upon. Nor could netting arrangements be relied upon. Attorneys at central banks *do* have a contribution to make in this important area.

The second part of any crisis resolution strategy is an exit strategy for insolvent institutions. To the extent that fiscal and monetary authorities become engaged with insolvent institutions, exit strategies for public agencies are required as well. As is well known, Japan has supplied a significant amount of public funds to its banking system in return for restructuring. It has structured those injections of public monies so that it can exact governance, either by ultimately taking over the banks and its management or by selling its shares in the market. Whenever a government intervenes in a bank directly, it needs to have an exit strategy. One of the most practical exit strategies would be holding shares in the company that are publicly traded.

Another key element of crisis resolution, and this is where the central bank comes in, is the lender-of-last-resort function in the central bank.

On prevention and resolution, and the role of the central bank in prevention and resolution, there are several issues that are still being debated. Some of this is being debated in the context of the operations of the European Central Bank; some of it is being discussed in the context of working out the details of the relationship between the Bank of England as lender of last resort, but not banking supervisor, and the U.K. Financial Services Authority, the new single regulator and supervisor. Some of this is even being debated within the United States with the new banking law, the Gramm-Leach-Bliley Act, which seems to shift the emphasis of supervision and regulation for conglomerates in the direction of the Federal Reserve System.

One can identify three key issues that focus on the role of the central bank. One key issue is, can market participants who are the agents of market discipline distinguish illiquid from insolvent institutions during a crisis and thereby continue to perform a useful market-disciplining role during a crisis? A conclusion that can be drawn from the turbulence that followed the collapse and private rescue of LTCM is that in a panic, there is no discipline—there is no market discipline whatsoever. It is a situation which is akin to a thousand people being in a movie theatre that has capacity for 750 people with three or four exit doors and they all smell smoke and rush for the exits at the same time! Even if there was not a fire, some people would get bruised because they are all rushing for the exits. During the LTCM crisis, there was good reason for everyone to be trying to exit the markets.

Given that there seems to be a role for some official participation in crisis resolution, and given that the central bank is the only provider of payments finality—of central bank money—the central bank is the only practical lender of last resort. Even if it is not the lender of last resort, which might ultimately be a treasury, it is the immediate provider of liquidity during a crisis. This leads to the second key issue. In fulfilling its role as lender of last resort, can the central bank in the middle of a crisis clearly distinguish illiquid from insolvent institutions? A corollary to that question is whether it really needs to distinguish between illiquid and insolvent institutions? Going back to the open market operations view, the central bank often only needs to provide liquidity to the markets, rather than to specific institutions. The market will then sort out how to distribute that liquidity. It can be argued that this would be the case where a relatively small number of smaller institutions are experiencing difficulties in which case liquidity provided to the market might be sufficient. In the case where there are larger institutions, then institution-specific injections of liquidity, not capital, might be required. In these cases the central bank would need to have information to identify illiquid from insolvent. If it is known that a bank is insolvent, the authorities would probably use an alternative mechanism to resolve the problem. It does not want to rely on a lender-of-last-resort role.

What kind of information does a central bank need in order to effectively execute its role as lender of last resort, and does it need to be directly involved in banking supervision? In thinking about this question, it is helpful to study the actual practices of central banks, which vary across countries. Consider three examples. First, there is the concept of central banking adopted by the U.S. Federal Reserve System (as discussed above). One could identify the U.S. Federal Reserve's responsibilities in both its monetary and financial policymaking mandates to be a broadly conceived central bank. It has many mandates, only one of which relates to the conduct of monetary policy.

The second example, at the other extreme—and it is difficult to discuss tangibly because it has only been in existence since January 4, 1999—is the European System of Central Bank (ESCB). If one takes the ECB as the central organ, which is composed of six votes of 17, then the ECB has no responsibility for ensuring financial stability. The following four passages describe the ESCB's functions related to prudential supervision and the stability of the payments and financial systems.

First, Article 25(1) of the ESCB Statute envisions a specific *advisory* function for the ECB in the field of Community legislation related to the prudential supervision of credit institutions and the stability of the financial system.

Second, Article 105(5) of the Maastricht Treaty stipulates that "the ESCB shall *contribute* to the smooth conduct of policies *pursued by the competent authorities* relating to the prudential supervision of credit institutions and the stability of the financial system" (emphasis added).

Third, Article 105(6) of the Treaty states that "the Council may, acting unanimously on a proposal from the Commission and after consulting the ECB and after receiving the assent of the European Parliament, confer upon the ECB specific tasks concerning policies relating to the prudential supervision of credit institutions and other financial institutions with the exception of insurance undertakings."

Fourth, the ECB is given a more explicit role in relation to the working of the payments system. Article 105(2) of the Treaty stipulates that one of the basic tasks of the ESCB "shall be to promote the smooth functioning of the payments system." Article 22 of the ESCB Statute is more specific, stating that "the ECB and national central banks may provide facilities, and the ECB may issue ECB regulations to ensure efficient and sound clearing and payments systems within the Community and with other countries."

As expressed in the first passage, Article 25(1) envisions an advisory function for the ECB. Whenever the EU comes up with legislation that directly bears on financial stability issues, a draft of the legislation goes to the ECB for comment. The ECB can exert whatever influence it has, but it has no specific role.

As noted in the second passage, Article 105.5 of the Maastricht Treaty stipulates that the ESCB is *not* the competent authority, either for prudential supervision of credit institutions or for the stability of the financial system.

The third example, again from the Maastricht Treaty, is a mechanism in the Treaty for the EU Commission to recommend to national parliaments and the European Parliament in consultation with the ECB that they provide responsibilities for banking supervision to the ECB, if it decides it is necessary. This confirms that the ECB has no banking supervision or financial stability mandate. This deserves qualification.

The European system of central banks is composed of the ECB and 11 national central banks. Some of these national central banks have responsibility for banking supervision, and some do not. There are separate national agencies for banking supervision that are independent of the central bank. The ESCB decision-making body has 17 votes, 11 of which are distributed among the national authorities, and only six of which are distributed to the center, the ECB. Even if all national central banks had responsibility for banking supervision, there might be a conflict in the presence of a crisis. What to do? Who gets the information? How quickly does the ECB get it, so that its votes can carry accurate information to the board table? So there are some unresolved issues, even though some of the national central banks that make up part of the European system of central banks have banking supervision responsibility.

As the fourth passage indicates, the ECB has a mandate for ensuring the smooth functioning of the target payment system within Europe. A rigorous reading of the Maastricht Treaty and the ECB statute or the ESCB statute would suggest that this is the only tangible mandate that the ECB has in the area of financial stability—that is, of ensuring the smooth functioning of the payments system. This mandate is not insignificant, but it does not encompass financial markets' stability per se.

To summarize, there exists a sharp contrast between a broad central bank in the United States and a narrow central bank in the Economic and Monetary Union. The U.K. system is presently somewhere in between in that the central bank has the lender-of-last-resort role and has a role in ensuring financial stability, but it does not have a mandate for banking supervision. There is a memorandum of understanding with the U.K. supervisor and Her Majesty's Treasury indicating that whatever information the Bank of England needs to carry out its mandates, it shall have free and open access to it. But it is a memorandum of understanding and thus an important question is what legal standing it would have in a court of law.

How Far Have Central Banks Gone to Ensure Financial Stability?

The final question is how far have central banks gone in safeguarding financial stability? Three examples serve to shed some light on this question. The first example is the case of Barings. In that case, the Bank of England, along with other official bodies, including Her Majesty's Treasury, probably decided that Barings was not systemically important. It was a small, at best medium-sized bank, and it was not central to the U.K. payments system. The Bank of England, because of its then banking supervisory role, apparently understood the relationships Barings had with U.K. and other European counterparts and over the weekend was able to determine, and then to decide, that Barings could be allowed to fail. If a ready and able buyer had bought Barings over the weekend, the Bank of England probably would have been very happy for that to happen. In this case, the financial stability role of the central bank was to decide how important this institution was for the U.K. financial system and the European financial system, and it decided it was not important enough to save.

The second example is LTCM, a $4 billion hedge fund, which was relatively small for advanced markets, certainly relatively small for the U.S. financial market. The notional value of outstanding derivative contracts in the world, as of the end of last year, was estimated to be $80 trillion. The U.S. repo market has an outstanding value daily of $1 trillion. So this $4 billion hedge fund was not very big. It was not bailed out because no public monies were used; it was a private rescue. There apparently was a coordination failure among the 15 or 17 major counterparties of LTCM; the Fed became involved to facilitate the rescue. As it were, 17 did not participate in the rescue, 14 did. There appear to be two main reasons why the Fed may have acted the way it did. One was for financial stability; certainly, even with the private rescue, even with the 75 basis point reduction in interest rates, there was tremendous turbulence in the deepest and most liquid markets in the world. The other reason why the Fed may have intervened and, in particular, the reason why the Fed lowered 75 basis points, is that there was a real future threat to monetary stability in that if risk taking was not restored to at least a normal level, then it is conceivable that even small businesses, viable businesses, thriving businesses, would not have been able to receive the credit they needed to conduct their day to day business. This is a threat to monetary stability. In short, one can make the argument that the Fed acted for both monetary and financial stability reasons.

The third example is the case of Hong Kong intervening in the Hong Kong equity markets. One possible reason for the intervention was for financial stability in the face of attacks on currencies, sometimes through the equity markets, double plays, and the like. The second reason was for monetary stability. The Hong Kong economy was likely to be subject to a widespread systemic problem if the equity market collapsed.

A key issue in deciding how far central banks can go in intervening in financial markets is how much risk a central bank should take in its activities with the market, either in its balance sheet or in its off-balance-sheet activities.

References

Bagehot, Walter, 1873, *Lombard Street* (London: Paul Kegan, 14th ed.).

———, 1848, "The Currency Problem," *Prospective Review*, pp. 297–337, reproduced in Vol. 9, *Collected Works*, ed. by Norman St. John-Stevas (Cambridge: Harvard University Press).

Bordo, Michael D., 1990, "The Lender of Last Resort: Alternative Views and Historical Experience," in *Economic Review*, Vol. 76, No. 1. (Richmond: Federal Reserve Bank of Richmond).

Capie, Forrest, 2000, "The Evolution of the Lender of Last Resort: the Bank of England"(unpublished; London: *City University Business School*).

Crockett, Andrew, 1997, "Why Is Financial Stability a Goal of Public Policy?" paper presented at the Federal Reserve of Kansas City's 1997 Symposium, "Maintaining Financial Stability in a Global Economy," Jackson Hole, Wyoming, August.

———, 1999, "Promoting Stable and Efficient Financial Systems for the 21st Century," remarks to IOSCO's 24th Annual Meeting, Lisbon, May.

Fetter, F.W., 1978, *Development of British Monetary Orthodoxy, 1797–1875*, (Fairfield, New Jersery: Augustus Kelley).

Group of 10, *Consolidation of the Financial Sector*, January 2001 available via Internet: http://www.bis-org/publ/gten05.

International Monetary Fund, 1999, *International Capital Markets: Developments, Prospects, and Key Policy Issues* (Washington: International Monetary Fund).

Kindleberger, C.P., 1989, *Manias, Panics and Crashes* (New York: Basic Books).

Prati, Alessandro, and Garry Schinasi, 1999, "Financial Stability in European Economic and Monetary Union," in *Princeton Studies in International Finance*,No. 86 (Princeton, New Jersey: Princeton University Press).

Schwartz, Anna J., 1986, "Real and Pseudo Financial Crises" in *Financial Crises and the World Banking System*, ed. by Forrest Capie and G.E. Woods (London: Macmillan).

Thornton, Henry, 1802, *An Enquiry into the Nature and Effects of Paper Credit of Great Britain* (New York: Augustus Kelley, reprinted 1978).

Volcker, Paul A., 1984, "The Federal Reserve Position on Restructuring of Financial Regulation Responsibilities," *Federal Reserve Bulletin*, Vol. 70 (July), pp. 547–57.

COMMENT

CYNTHIA LICHTENSTEIN

My comments will be confined to the topic addressed by Garry Schinasi and touched on by Jennifer Johnson-Calari and Peter Fisher: the role of the central bank in maintaining stability in the financial markets. Mr. Schinasi has surveyed in excellent fashion the propositions concerning central banks' role in this area that are debatable and pointed out that many central banks are not given lender-of-last-resort power under their statutory authority—and in many systems, bank supervision is given to another authority. In his opinion, a central bank must have bank supervision authority to fulfill adequately its lender-of-last-resort (LOLR) function, and I understood him to believe that the latter function, in addition to a central bank's monetary policy function, is critical to a central bank's responsibility to maintain stability in the financial markets. Mr. Schinasi does believe, apparently, that it is possible for a lender of last resort to distinguish between a financial institution which is illiquid—and should be aided by the LOLR—and one which is insolvent and should be closed up, thus reducing the risk of "moral hazard" so much discussed in the banking literature.

However, the discussion of this topic was focused on the central bank LOLR function in the context of aiding banks, not market participants, although Peter Fisher expressed his view that market risk is really credit risk, a view with which I would heartily agree. In this comment I want to address this much less discussed question, the LOLR function to add liquidity to the markets—and in effect by so doing, to aid illiquid securities firms at the time of extreme volatility in the equity markets, such as the experience of the United States in October 1997 when the Dow Jones fell steeply.

Now, obviously, here we are discussing the role of the central bank in highly developed economies with highly developed capital markets which have systemic implications. However, given the globalization of capital markets, the time is not far off when the development of a sophisticated finanzplatz or financial center will be seen as the hallmark of movement from emerging market status to emerged, if such a term may be used. At the time of this writing, the most recent issue of *Foreign Affairs* contained an article by Robert C. Pozen on "securitization in Europe," which, while not at all addressing the role of the central bank in this movement, stresses what Pozen calls "the securitization of finance" in the United States in the 1990s and surveys the extent to which the same process has been taking place in Europe in the last five years and states that it will grow exponentially in the next decade if Europe successfully integrates its capital markets. His definition of "securitization of finance" points out that in the United States in the 1990s, "[m]oney markets, corporate bond markets, venture capital, and publicly traded equity substantially displaced bank deposits and loans as both savings vehicles and sources of corporate finance."[1]

If indeed Mr. Pozen's predictions are fulfilled, the issue of the implication of securities firms or banks doing primarily an investment banking business for an economy's stability and the concomitant need for prudential supervision of such firms will come to the forefront as will the question of whether the central bank should provide liquidity to such firms in the event of a very sharp and unexpected market break. The U.S. Federal Reserve did intervene, reportedly, in the U.S. market crash of October 1987, and the New York Federal Reserve orchestrated the rescue by its lenders of the hedge fund Long Term Capital Management (LTCM) in 1998 on the ground that the systemic effects of a disorderly liquidation of the fund could not easily be quantified.

An official study was made afterwards of the LTCM rescue and other aspects of the market volatility at the time.[2] The study has an Appendix B, which discusses in detail SEC oversight of broker-dealers who may act as creditors of, or counterparties to (i.e., acting like bankers), these funds. The SEC imposes on broker-dealers both capital requirements (including capital to be held against the position risk of the institutions' own proprietary investments) and margin requirements against funds borrowed by the broker-dealers to carry their proprietary positions and their inventory. As the report notes,

---

[1] *Id.*
[2] *See* "Hedge Funds, Leverage and the Lessons of Long-Term Capital Management," Report of the President's Working Group on Financial Markets, April 1999.

the purpose of the capital cushion is "to help [the broker-dealers] withstand the failure of a counterparty or periods of system-wide stress."[3]

The report stresses that under the SEC's net capital rule, the broker-dealer must deduct from its net worth 100 percent of all loans not collateralized by liquid securities: "[in] this way, the net capital rule helps to insulate broker-dealers from credit risk posed by counterparties, such as hedge funds."[4]

Unfortunately, liquid securities as collateral have a great drawback: if the equity market takes, say, a 30 percent drop in one day, the loans are no longer fully collaterized. The prudential measure is failing when most needed.

The report went on to survey the risk management practices of the broker-dealers reporting to the SEC and how those practices held up in the third quarter of 1998 when LTCM was failing. The report concludes: "Stress testing, an essential component of risk management, was not thoroughly performed at all firms. While most firms were stress testing their proprietary positions with parallel volatility curve shifts and correlations, aggregate counterparty credit exposures were not always routinely stress tested. Furthermore, believing that credit exposures were protected by collateral, some firms did not formally review or limit their exposure to market movements based on an analysis of aggregate firm and customer positions."[5] The Commission, according to the report, is issuing "non-public inspection findings to several large broker-dealers addressing the strengths and weaknesses of their particular credit risk management structure, credit control procedures, and firms' implementation of credit policies."[6] The possible need for a central bank in a country where a major proportion of the finance is securitized to stand ready to oversee the supervision of the investment banking firms (whether domestic or foreign) and to lend to the markets if necessary becomes obvious.

---

[3] *Id.*, Appendix B, p. B-4.
[4] *Id.*, pp. B-4–B-5.
[5] *Id.*, p. B-11.
[6] *Id.*

The final significant document illustrating this thesis is the Memorandum of Understanding (MOU) between Her Majesty's Treasury, the Bank of England, and the U.K. Financial Services Authority (FSA), the lead regulator in the United Kingdom for firms that are primarily investment banks rather than banks of deposit.[7] This document in a very real sense raises many of the issues touched on by Mr. Schinasi: the Bank of England, the U.K. central bank, does not have prudential supervision of banks, building societies, investment firms, insurance companies, and friendly societies; the FSA does. To ensure the participation of the central bank in the supervision of these entities, the Deputy Governor (financial stability) is a member of the FSA Board. But it is the Bank that is to be the LOLR in the language of the MOU, "being able in exceptional circumstances to undertake official financial operations . . . in order to limit the risk of problems in or affecting particular institutions spreading to other parts of the financial system."[8]

This latter function the Bank is to carry out under arrangements set out in paragraphs 11 to 15 of the MOU. Those arrangements include the nomination of representatives by each institution (the Bank, the FSA, and the Treasury) who can be contacted and meet at short notice. If the Bank or the FSA identifies "a problem" that might require a "support operation" (code for LOLR), "they would immediately inform and consult with each other." The FSA will be in the lead of the support operations for an institution which it supervises (the "lead institution" to "manage the situation and coordinate the authorities' response"). The Chancellor of the Exchequer gets the option of refusing support action, so it is the political authority, not the central bank which gets the decision as to whether one has a situation of illiquidity or of insolvency. All that one can say is that, since the MOU envisions a support operation happening "very rarely and . . . normally only . . . in the case of a genuine threat to the stability of the financial system," we can only wait to see if, when such a crisis arises, as it will given the nature of modern capital markets, the system will work.

---

[7] For the text of the Memorandum, see www.bankofengland.co.uk/legislation/main.htm.
[8] *Id.*, para. 2 (iv).

Chapter 18

Central Bank Responsibility for Exchange Rate Policy and Implementation

KAREN H. JOHNSON

There is no simple, unique answer to the question of what is/what should be the responsibility of the central bank for exchange rate policy and implementation. Rather, there is a range of practices, determined largely by the interplay of several factors in a given country: the legal provisions governing international economic relationships; the degree of central bank independence; and the choice of exchange rate regime. In many respects, these elements are the result of deliberate decisions on the part of governments. However, inherent in this issue are some fundamental economic linkages. The exchange rate is an asset price; it is the foreign currency price of a unit of the domestic currency. As such, it is linked to monetary policy in inescapable ways. Thus the implementation of monetary policy and exchange rate policy cannot be separated, and the central bank cannot be excluded from exchange rate policy.

Legal Provisions

One straightforward place to start thinking about this topic is which governmental entity has legal title to the country's foreign exchange reserves. Those reserves are whatever foreign-currency-denominated assets are owned by the public sector. Various alternative arrangements are possible and are in use. It may be that ownership is concentrated in the hands of one public sector entity. That may be the central bank. It may be the executive branch, typically controlled by the Finance Ministry or Treasury but basically on the balance sheet of the executive branch. Or, ownership may be split between two or more public sector entities.

Note: The views in this paper are solely the responsibility of the author and should not be interpreted as reflecting the views of the Board of Governors of the Federal Reserve System or any other member(s) of its staff.

Table 1. Foreign Currency Holdings of U.S. Monetary Authorities Based on Currency Exchange Rates

(Changes in balance by source)

	Balance as of December 31, 1999	Investment Income	Currency Valuation Adjustments	Balance as of March 31, 2000
System Open Market Account (SOMA)				
Euro	6,870.6	67.8	(341.1)	6,597.4
Japanese yen	9,221.5	1.0	(51.1)	9,171.4
Subtotal	16,092.1	68.8	(392.2)	15,768.8
Interest receivables	48.0			34.3
Total	16,140.1			15,803.1
U.S. Treasury Exchange Stabilization Fund (ESF)				
Euro	6,868.5	67.0	(340.9)	6,594.5
Japanese yen	9,221.5	1.0	(51.1)	9,171.4
Subtotal	16,090.0	68.0	(392.0)	15,765.9
Interest receivables	78.6			59.8
Total	16,168.6			15,825.7

Table 1 shows the current situation in the United States. Ownership of foreign exchange reserves is split between the Federal Reserve and the Treasury, about evenly. Holdings of the Federal Reserve are in the System Open Market Account (SOMA). Those of the Treasury are in the Exchange Stabilization Fund (ESF). The latter is an account specifically created to hold such reserves. The creation of such an account is a common way to structure foreign exchange holdings. As you can see, the United States now limits its holdings to euro and yen; but many countries hold a greater number of foreign currencies in their reserves, and in the past the United States has held others. The fact that the holdings are equal in the two accounts, for each of the currencies, is a relatively new development that was deliberately brought about by transactions between the two.

Ownership of reserves creates a presumption that some actions related to foreign exchange rate policy could be undertaken. Ownership also likely reflects how decision-making authority has been allocated and how it has been executed in the past. In the case of the United States, ownership accurately reflects some degree of shared responsibility for exchange rate policy between the Fed and the Treasury.

Of primary importance, however, is the allocation of authority to decide upon the exchange rate regime that will be put in place. Before specific policy steps and implementation can come into play, there has to be a decision of where in the spectrum of possible regimes the country will choose to operate. At one extreme are fixed-rate regimes, of which there are more than one kind; at the other extreme, a freely floating exchange rate regime. And there are many possibilities in between. I will discuss below how this decision bears on the conduct of monetary policy and thus on the interaction of monetary policy and exchange rate policy. My point here is that this decision of regime is important in determining the role of the central bank in exchange rate policy and that this decision is inherently a political one. Thus, it is lodged with governments.

Central bank officials are generally consulted, particularly at times when a decision to make a change is under consideration in the context of some kind of crisis. Indeed, in some cases central banks might have the authority on their own to modify the regime from one kind of mixed regime (somewhere between fixed and floating) to another. But the choice of regime requires the kind of political authority that resides within governments and therefore not solely the central bank. Some regimes require active cooperation between two or more countries. That kind of international commitment is really only possible at the level of government. The choice of exchange rate regime can be imbedded in legislation. Alternatively, it can be an executive branch prerogative, delegated to a particular official in the executive branch or the head of government.

Once the exchange rate regime has been determined, there follows a need to formulate and implement policy on a day-to-day basis. For some regime choices, as will be discussed below, that policy is essentially fully implied by the regime choice. For others, there are significant decisions to be made over time. Responsibility for those decisions is a complex matter. The political authorities may wish to reserve that responsibility for themselves and may do so in some legal sense. However, the economic links between monetary policy and exchange rate policy imply that if the central bank has any control over and responsibility for monetary policy, it will inevitably have an impact on the exchange rate and therefore some role in exchange rate policy.

Central Bank Independence

The issue of central bank independence is framed in terms of monetary policy. If a central bank is empowered to make the decisions that govern its instruments of monetary policy without interference from other branches of government, then it is independent.

Different political systems imply some variation in what it means to be independent of other government authorities. In the United States, with the executive and legislative branches separate, independence is most importantly independence from the executive branch. The Federal Reserve System was created by Congress and could be changed by Congressional legislation at any time. However, both legally and in practice, the decisions of Federal Reserve officials are not subject to review or overturn by officials of the executive branch. In a parliamentary system, the line between executive and legislative is less sharp. However, independence implies that the cabinet in the normal course of governing does not have authority over monetary policy. Clearly, the parliament could legislate changes in the central bank structure and function if it chose.

In the past, we have observed a range of experience across countries. Prior to 1997, the Bank of England was an example of a central bank that did not have the final authority for monetary policy. The Chancellor of the Exchequer, i.e., the finance minister, made the decisions and was the official responsible to parliament for them. Over time, various arrangements were used for securing input from the central bank for these decisions, and the central bank clearly had an advisory role. It also had a major role in implementation of monetary policy and exchange rate policy. But if the central bank lacks final authority with respect to monetary policy, then its role with respect to exchange rate policy will be limited as well.

Examples of countries that have functioned with substantial independence throughout most of the post–World War II period include the Bundesbank, the Swiss National Bank, and the Federal Reserve. Independence is more importantly a question of practice rather than of legal provision. As a consequence, it is to some extent a question of degree. Many central banks have operated in a middle range where they exercised some independence but were at times subject to the influence of government officials.

Over the past decade or so, there has been a significant shift toward empowering central banks with greater independence. The creation of the European Central Bank (ECB) is perhaps the most extreme example. That institution was created by treaty among the countries participating in the European Union and was given by that treaty total independence from the governments of those countries with respect to monetary policy. Because of evidence that the inflation outcome in countries tends to be improved when the central bank is independent, moves to grant such independence have been common in recent years. Examples of countries that have changed central bank legislation to do this include (in addition to those in Europe) Japan and Mexico.

Because central bank independence is a question of practice and of degree, it can be divided into elements. A common distinction is between independence with respect to the setting of the ultimate goal of monetary policy and independence with respect to decisions about particular policy actions. The legislation establishing the central bank, perhaps subsequently modified, typically states or implies the objectives for the central bank in order to define its responsibilities. But that provision can be quite general or can be multifaceted. In that case, considerable discretion remains within the central bank to define for itself the specific objectives of monetary policy. The more narrowly stated the goal or mandate of the central bank by legislation, the less independence in this element of monetary policy it has. In the extreme, the goal can be stated so narrowly that the central bank effectively loses all independence with respect to monetary policy and exchange rate policy.

In those cases where the goal is stated more generally, even including a specific inflation target over some horizon, central bank authorities can retain independence with respect to settings of policy instruments. Implementation of policy measures generally results in changes to short-term interest rates (either directly or indirectly). The change in these interest rates in turn have an impact on the exchange rate (discussed further below). It is this linkage that unavoidably involves the central bank in exchange rate policy.

Exchange Rate Regime

As noted above, the choice of exchange rate regime is a political step, the ultimate responsibility for which rests with governments. The nature of the link between the central bank and exchange rate policy depends upon the exchange rate regime. Regimes range from fixed, of which there are several variations, to freely floating.

Of the fixed regimes, a multilateral currency union is among the most binding and absolute. It involves a decision by two or more countries to share the same currency. In 1999, we saw the initiative of the European Economic and Monetary Union (EMU) move to the third stage. Eleven members of the European Union now share one currency, the euro. One can draw an analogy with the 50 U.S. states. They form a currency union and share the U.S. dollar. However, EMU is unique in that the 11 remain independent sovereign states and previously had distinct currencies. Within the currency union, the commitment is so tight that in fact there are no exchange rates and no exchange rate policy. With respect to other currencies, together the 11 face the range of choices from fixed to floating. They have only one central bank, the European System of Central Banks, but many governments.

Currency union can also be unilateral. This results when a given country decides for itself to use the currency issued by another country and its central bank as the domestic currency in circulation. Today we frequently hear reference to dollarization, but in principle other currencies could be chosen for such use. Dollarized countries include Panama and, in a recent move, Ecuador. Liechtenstein uses the Swiss franc. For the country choosing to dollarize, domestic currency ceases to exist (although some retain domestic coinage). As a consequence, the country has in essence no exchange rate policy once it has chosen this regime. If a central bank continues to function, it has no monetary policy responsibilities. Both versions of currency union are extreme in that within the currency union, exchange rates and central bank functions have been eliminated.

The regime of a currency board implies a slightly less rigid commitment in that domestic currency continues to exist. Its exchange value, however, is fixed exactly to a particular foreign currency. The country retains a central bank, but its behavior is determined by the "rules" of being a currency board. Those rules state that the currency board, i.e., central bank, stands ready to swap domestic currency for the named foreign currency at the fixed rate. Argentina is an example of a country operating under a currency board regime.

The gold standard is a variation of a fixed exchange rate system in which the domestic currency is pegged not to another currency but to a fixed amount of gold. If other countries also peg their currencies to gold, then the various currencies are in effect fixed with respect to one another. The central bank, and/or the government, is pledged to maintain the value of the currency at the stated gold price. But of course it is possible to announce a change in the peg to gold, and in the history of the gold standard that happened fairly frequently. It is also possible just to announce a suspension of the system and to no longer promise that the currency is worth any stated amount of gold. That happened from time to time as well in history. When the gold standard was being adhered to, it offered some degree of flexibility as it is expensive to present currency to a central bank or government, demand the promised amount of gold, and ship it back to your home country. As a consequence, some flexibility in the implied cross exchange rates was possible under the gold standard.

The term "pegged exchange rate" implies an exchange rate regime in which the monetary authorities announce a promise to maintain the exchange value of the country's currency with respect to some other country's currency within a narrow band. They may "peg" their currency to the dollar, as was the case with rates generally under the Bretton Woods System before its breakdown and as some countries choose to do now. During the 1980s and 1990s the Exchange Rate Mechanism of the European Monetary System was a system of simultaneous bilateral commitments to maintain the exchange rates of the participating countries in terms of each other. These commitments defined a matrix of cross rates that was the mutual responsibility of the participating countries. Alternatively, the authorities may peg to a "basket" of currencies, i.e., to maintain the average value of the domestic currency in terms of specified amounts of several other currencies, usually those of important trading partners. One feature of any pegged system is that the pegs, having been set by governments, can be changed by them. Generally the system defines a narrow band of permitted variation that is viewed as consistent with the peg.

Managed floats are exchange rate regimes where some explicit statement has been made about the exchange value of the currency, but it is not fixed. This alternative is intended not only to permit more day-to-day flexibility in the rate, but also to provide some guarantee about its value. A crawling peg system is one in which a path of rates is announced ex ante, rather than a single pegged value, in terms of another currency or a basket. Thus some continuous change is built into the process. Typically, there is a permitted band around the pre-announced path as well. Variations of crawling peg systems have been used for intervals by several emerging market countries.

Target zones specify a range around a stated rate, but with bands sufficiently wide that some significant fluctuation is expected and allowed. However, the authorities are committed to keeping the exchange rate from moving beyond the range. Target zones have been suggested as an alternative for limiting the fluctuation of the major currencies in terms of each other, but have not yet been implemented for that purpose.

"Dirty float" is the term applied when there is no single peg, no band, no range, no commitment—the exchange rate is determined in the market each day—yet the authorities are not indifferent to the exchange value of the currency and may at a time of their choosing try to influence the market rate. One form of influence is to make public statements and hope that market participants react to those statements (verbal intervention). Another is for the finance ministry and/or the central bank to sell domestic currency for foreign currency in the market or vice versa in an attempt to alter the market price (market intervention). This regime is the one now used for the dollar, the euro, the yen, and many other currencies.

Logically, there is also the extreme regime of a freely floating exchange rate. Such a rate would be determined in the market at each moment, with the authorities committed never to intervene. But how could a government today make a promise that would bind not only itself but all future governments?

Policy Implementation

A tightly pegged exchange rate regime defines monetary policy. It completely determines what the central bank is to do in response to alternative market developments. The central bank is pledged to maintain convertibility to gold at a stated amount or to keep the market exchange rate equal to the announced pegged rate. Such a system precludes the central bank from using its policy tools to achieve some other goal at the same time. How then do we think about the central bank's role in this case?

The central bank typically functions as the fiscal agent for the government, but this relationship does not by itself determine the role of the central bank in formulating or implementing exchange rate policy. As fiscal agent, the central bank transacts on behalf of the government. But it can also do so for its own account. The government typically has a domestic-currency-denominated account at the central bank. When the government transacts, this account is debited or credited. But it can also have accounts at commercial banks or other financial institutions. The fiscal agent relationship does not define how decisions are made within the central bank or for exchange rate policy.

In a tightly pegged system, the central bank must use its tools to fulfill the commitments made to those in the market about the exchange rate. The central bank can do this directly by maintaining a pool of foreign exchange reserves and standing ready to transact with market participants on the promised terms. It can do so indirectly by instead exercising control over a very short-term interest rate and changing that rate so as to bring about a market exchange rate consistent with the peg. By bringing about changes in the interest rate, the central bank makes the currency more or less attractive to investors. Market participants trade with each other, not the central bank. The central bank watches the exchange rate and moves interest rates to achieve the exchange rate peg.

The central bank is in an entirely reactive role. It reacts to buying or selling of the currency from whatever source. Usually, it is the institution that has the tools needed to implement the exchange rate policy. But as a consequence of the exchange rate regime, the central bank has no scope for monetary policy directed at domestic objectives and no discretion. It may be at the center of the process, but it has little or no real power.

Capital controls are the one instance when it may be possible for a time to peg or manage an exchange rate and practice a separate monetary policy. This is the extreme exception to the basic framework presented so far. The imposition of capital controls makes certain transactions or investor behavior illegal. As long as they can be enforced, it would be possible to have an exchange rate objective and to implement that with external transactions while at the same time having a domestic objective that is not consistent with that exchange rate. The domestic objective can be pursued using domestic transactions. The capital controls attempt to prevent someone from doing essentially simultaneous transactions to take advantage of a price difference for a given asset, say the domestic currency or a domestic-currency denominated security, in a market within the country and one outside of it. The capital controls prevent price arbitrage. As a consequence, evading them is profitable. Market participants will expend resources to find a way to make those profits. After a time, it is generally the case that evasion begins to undermine the controls, and they become ineffective. Moreover, while they are in place, the capital controls distort prices and contribute to inefficient use of resources.

Eventually the various forms of fixed rates, except for those in which the domestic currency ceases to exist, encounter conditions that create a conflict between the exchange rate objective and domestic economic conditions. In some cases, there may be upward pressure on the exchange rate. In order to counter that pressure, the central bank has to expand the domestic money supply and in so doing put in place a monetary policy that is too expansionary for current economic conditions. Alternatively, there may be downward pressure on the exchange rate. In that case, the central bank would need to raise domestic interest rates and to sell foreign currency reserves in exchange for the domestic currency. The tight monetary conditions could damage economic activity. In any event, the available supply of foreign exchange reserves could be exhausted. Because the central bank is the one implementing the exchange rate policy, it is often the central bank that sounds the alarm that reserves are being depleted or that interest rates cannot stay high enough indefinitely. Such a development may require that the country change the peg, i.e., depreciate the currency, modify the system, i.e., widen the bands, or perhaps even abandon a fixed regime and move to a floating regime. The central bank may participate in such decisions, but once again we are essentially talking about a decision with respect to exchange rate regime, a decision in the end made by the government.

Implementation of Floating Rate/Monetary Policy

The role of the central bank is significantly different when the exchange rate regime is that of a loosely managed or floating rate. In this case, the central bank's responsibilities and daily decisions are directed toward one or more domestic objectives. The exchange rate in this case is one of many financial variables that play a role in the monetary policy process, but it is no longer the central variable.

First, the exchange rate is a channel of monetary policy. It reacts to policy actions taken by the central bank. Because it reacts, and because in turn participants in the economy react to the exchange rate, some of the effects of the monetary policy measure are transmitted through the exchange rate.

Second, the exchange rate is information. By monitoring changes in the exchange rate, central bank officials can anticipate some developments within the economy. In addition, they can infer to some extent market participants' views on the domestic economy and prospective monetary policy.

Third, the exchange rate is a source of shocks. Because every exchange rate by its nature relates to two economies, not one, the exchange rate is influenced by developments outside the domestic economy and can transmit the effects of those developments into that economy.

In a regime of a floating exchange rate, the central bank can process the information in exchange rate movements and assess the shocks hitting the economy through the exchange rate. It can decide to alter monetary policy in response—not to achieve a particular exchange rate objective, but rather to offset or to reinforce the impact of the exchange rate on domestic variables. The central bank can decide how it perceives the exchange rate having an impact on its final objectives. It still cannot independently choose a domestic objective and a goal for the exchange rate, but it can determine the priorities of reacting to the exchange rate or trying to influence the exchange rate or not as it seeks to achieve its domestic objectives.

What determines the exchange rate in the market? How is it linked to monetary policy? A floating exchange rate responds at each moment to offers to buy or sell domestic currency for foreign currency in the market. What are the incentives behind such offers? An investor is weighing the alternatives open to him to earn the highest possible return on his investment. Everything else being equal, the higher the domestic interest rate is, the more attractive domestic assets in the domestic currency will be to that investor. However, for a given domestic interest rate, the higher the foreign interest rate is, the more attractive a foreign asset denominated in some other currency would be. But the foreign asset, when it matures, will repay the investor in foreign currency. Each investor must choose a single currency in which to make the comparison of which assets yield more return. In order to compare alternatives in more than one currency, the investor has to form a view as to future exchange rates, so that he can determine total returns in one currency. But, of course, future exchange rates cannot be known now with certainty. So this calculation inevitably entails risk. The investor has to make an assessment of how much risk he believes is embedded in each investment strategy and how much risk he is willing to bear. Whatever the outcome of that evaluation, with everything else held constant, higher domestic interest rates tend to attract investors to the domestic currency and cause it to appreciate; higher foreign interest rates tend to do the reverse.

We might ask whether, under a floating rate regime, it is possible to separate the exchange rate from domestic monetary policy. That would permit some other part of the government to retain authority for exchange rate policy. The exchange rate reacts to monetary policy steps, but it also reacts to a variety of other economic events, including the other country's monetary policy. The authorities may not be indifferent to the exchange rate value that results from these forces. Such was the case for the dollar in 1979 and 1985, for example.

One tool that is thought by some to offer a way to influence the exchange rate other than through monetary policy is exchange market intervention. Intervention occurs when government authorities enter the market and buy one currency for another; they do this in order to have an impact on the market price. So in a floating rate regime, responsibility for exchange rate policy would seem to reside with that part of the government that has authority over foreign exchange intervention. However, foreign exchange intervention can be done in two ways: sterilized and unsterilized. In the case of unsterilized intervention, interest rates as well as the exchange rate are permitted to move in response to the transaction. In the case of sterilized intervention, a secondary transaction is done in domestic markets to keep interest rates unchanged.

If the intervention is unsterilized, it is in effect monetary policy. As noted above, we would expect monetary policy to be able to influence the exchange rate. If the intervention is sterilized, there is considerable debate as to whether it will have any effect on the exchange rate, or at least any lasting effect on the exchange rate. Much evidence would suggest not.

So the question of exchange rate policy can swing on who has the authority to make decisions about intervention: the central bank or some other part of government, usually the finance ministry. Often, in the case of a floating rate regime, the government will attempt to retain a role for itself by controlling intervention decisions. But if the central bank is independent, it can by itself always undertake the transactions that would transform the intervention from unsterilized to sterilized. So the government may have authority over intervention and may exclude the central bank from participating in setting that policy, but it may end up being sterilized intervention. And sterilized intervention may have little effect.

There have been extended times when the yen/dollar rate has continued to move down despite dollar purchases, which would be thought to strengthen the dollar and raise its value in terms of yen. This happened during much of 1994 and early in 1995. It happened again in 1999. Conversely, the value of the dollar in terms of the yen continued to rise somewhat further in 1998 despite dollar sales. There are episodes that would suggest some effectiveness of sterilized intervention. During mid-1995, dollar purchases occurred at the time of a rising dollar. In early 1999, dollar purchases marked the end of a period of dollar depreciation and the start of a short episode of dollar appreciation. This evidence is very partial and does not attempt to control for other effects on the exchange rate at the time of intervention. We can infer, however, that sterilized intervention is clearly not a dominant, alternative tool that gives officials the ability to control the exchange rate regardless of monetary policy stance or measures in the two countries.

For some intervals, the movement in three-month market interest rates for the United States and for Japan is consistent with the expectation that a widening interest rate differential in favor of dollar rates should contribute to a strengthening of the dollar. Such is the case during the final three quarters of 1995 and on balance during 2000. However, the dollar fell in 1994 while U.S. rates rose relative to Japanese rates. And over much of 1996 through mid-1998, the dollar rose substantially while the interest differential changed little. The exchange rate fluctuations over this period clearly were influenced by other factors.

Conclusions

Central bank responsibility for exchange rate policy and implementation depends crucially on the choice of exchange rate regime. That choice is generally made at a political level, although the central bank may be consulted.

The closer the exchange rate regime is to a tightly pegged alternative, the less scope for discretionary monetary policy there is for the central bank. In such a regime, the exchange rate is at the center of central bank responsibilities, which focus on implementing that exchange rate decision. However, the central bank's role is reactive. It has little real authority in the determination of either monetary or exchange rate policy.

The closer the exchange rate regime is to a freely floating alternative, the more monetary policy is framed around domestic objectives. In this case, the exchange rate reacts to monetary policy as well as to other economic developments. The central bank can decide in what ways it chooses to incorporate exchange rate movements into its decision making with respect to monetary policy. There may still be a role for other government officials to attempt to set exchange rate policy independently of the central bank through sterilized intervention or by putting in place capital controls. Empirical evidence casts doubt on whether sterilized intervention can have a lasting impact on the exchange rate. Capital controls may work for a time but in most cases introduce distortions and eventually succumb to substantial evasion.

Chapter 19
Current Challenges in Foreign Exchange Reserves Management

JENNIFER JOHNSON-CALARI

Emerging Market Challenges in Assets/Liability and Portfolio Management

Quite recently, I had the privilege of meeting with central bankers from many different countries to discuss current challenges in managing reserves. In this paper, I would like to present in detail some of these challenges—their origins, directions currently being explored by central bank management, and implications for governance and risk management.

In speaking about central banks as a class, please allow me to generalize in a way that veils the actual diversity among central banks in their portfolio objectives and reserves management practices. In reality, a central bank's portfolio objectives will depend on a unique set of macroeconomic conditions, which includes the foreign exchange regime, the level of reserves relative to liquidity needs, and the country's access to capital markets. Reserves management practices also differ dramatically along a continuum, which ranges from cash management operations to highly sophisticated portfolio management.

Despite these differences, however, there have been common pressures on many central banks, which are forcing them to reassess their operations. These pressures have been

- the global financial and liquidity crises of 1997 through 1998;

- improved access by emerging market borrowers to global capital markets; and

- technical market conditions regarding the supply of high grade fixed income assets.

Asset/Liability Management and the Emerging Markets Crisis of 1997–1998

Everyone is familiar by now with the commonly attributed causes of the Asian crisis of 1997 to 1998, namely the underlying structural weaknesses in the banking and corporate sectors. Exacerbating these weaknesses were large open foreign exchange positions at the microeconomic and sovereign level as well as poor asset/liability management practices. These included, inter alia, undisclosed forward sales of reserves, extensive maturity mismatches between assets and liabilities, and failure to manage reserves in such a way that they were available during crisis periods. Moreover, liquidity crises spread quickly to even healthy economies, in part because investors were unable to assess individual creditworthiness due to the lack of reliable and timely information on an individual country's external position. Foreign investors thus divested of emerging market assets as a class.

These crises have pressured central banks to better manage their asset/liability positions in terms of both debt rollover risk and market exposures. For most countries, this challenge is more difficult than for a financial institution because the foreign exchange assets are generally on the central bank's books while the debt is the liability of a government agency. The objective of asset/liability management is to structure assets and liabilities to be able to meet ongoing and unexpected liquidity needs as well as to minimize any exposure arising from changes in currency and interest rates. Immunization of net exposures across balance sheets, however, can lead to misleading earnings and valuation effects because of accounting rules. To effectively manage liquidity, it is critical that there is coordination at the highest levels across institutions and that accounting rules do not drive financial management decisions. In some countries, notably in Eastern Europe, senior management from the debt agency and the central bank effectively manage external exposures at the national level, but this is still the exception rather than the rule.

Financial contagion was also exacerbated by the lack of market data. To alleviate this systemic risk, the IMF has introduced a template for reporting on a country's reserves and a new external debt category as part of its Special Data Dissemination Standards. This is a voluntary standard designed for market borrowers. The reserve template provides a comprehensive format for reporting a country's official foreign currency external assets and those liabilities falling due over the coming year. To the extent countries subscribe to and meet this reporting standard, the volatility historically associated with emerging market investments is expected to decline as investors can make sounder decisions and authorities implement earlier adjustment.

Cost of Financing Reserves

The second point relates to increasing emerging market access to global capital markets. This has resulted not only in the need for better asset/liability management, as discussed, but also has changed the way in which central banks finance accumulation of reserves. Increasingly, reserves are being financed through external borrowings, at times at a quite significant cost. Generally, emerging market governments borrow in strong currencies and pay a risk premium, which is determined by the market's perception of their creditworthiness. Foreign currency reserves, on the other hand, have typically been invested in only the highest quality government obligations and in shorter maturities. The direct cost of financing these reserves equals the negative yield differential times the size of the financed reserves. As an illustration, over the last two and a half years, benchmark emerging market debt has yielded an average of 4.2 percent over U.S. Treasuries. If reserves of $10 billion had been financed at this average yield and invested in U.S. Treasuries, the annual cost would have been $420 million. This direct cost, which can be considered as an insurance premium for crisis protection, is forcing central bankers to focus more on portfolio return as part of their primary investment objectives.

Finally, the third condition causing central banks to reassess their operations is the shrinking supply of sovereign debt, particularly in the United States. As can be seen in Figure 1, there is a double-edged squeeze on the sovereign market as central banks increase the level of their reserves, while the supply of sovereign debt is simultaneously declining. While the reduction in debt is to date most pronounced in the United States, similar trends are evident in the other OECD countries, many of which have just announced large buybacks of their sovereign debt. This technical condition is forcing central banks increasingly into a world of riskier assets and a reassessment of their risk tolerance.

Figure 1.

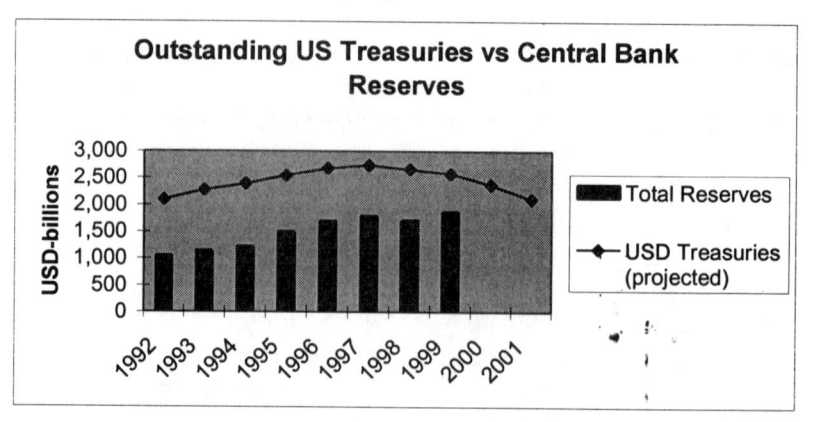

Outstanding US Treasuries vs Central Bank Reserves

[Bar chart showing Total Reserves (bars) and USD Treasuries projected (line) in USD-billions from 1992 to 2001, ranging from 0 to 3,000.]

In response, central bankers are under pressure to find acceptable alternatives to sovereign debt, as well as to restructure their investment portfolios to increase the portfolio return. As increased return generally requires increased risk taking, this solution will, in turn, place new burdens on central banks in quantifying and managing these risks, which I will discuss shortly.

Improving Portfolio Return

At this point, I would like to turn to the nature of the risk/reward trade-off and implications for governance and risk management. There are essentially three ways for central banks to try to improve the return on their portfolios:

- extend the portfolio maturity or duration;

- assume more credit risk; and

- engage in "directional" trading in an attempt to earn superior returns from anticipating future market price changes.

Of these three strategies, the third rarely produces consistent superior returns even among market experts and is equally likely to produce inferior returns. If it is difficult for investment banks and proprietary traders to "beat market expectations," it is even more so for central banks as they do not have the institutional culture or incentive structure for this type of risk-taking activity. I will thus limit my remarks to the first two strategies, the risks of which can be reasonably well calculated within a given degree of confidence.

Improving Portfolio Return: Extending Duration

Extending the portfolio duration, or average maturity of a portfolio, will tend to improve the expected portfolio return as a "normal" yield curve is upward sloping. This does not mean, however, that a longer duration portfolio will have a higher return over any given period and, in fact, will quite distinctly underperform shorter duration portfolios during periods of rising interest rates. The probable size and frequency of this underperformance is the risk associated with longer duration strategies.

Studies of the U.S. dollar market have shown that lengthening the portfolio duration increases the incremental return on a bond portfolio over time. It also, however, increases the risk, as measured by the volatility of total return. Up to the 18 month point on the yield curve, the incremental return of extending duration is significant and higher than the incremental risk. Many central banks thus tend to have a constant target portfolio duration in the range of 12 to 24 months, particularly if management wants to avoid a negative total return over any one-year accounting period. While it is questionable whether central banks should be managing their portfolio investments in a one-year accounting cycle, avoiding negative total returns on an annual basis is frequently considered to be a binding political constraint. Table 1 gives the incremental return and risk associated with extending duration.

Table 1. Risk/Return of U.S. Treasury Portfolios with Increasing Duration

(Average annual data from May 1991 to February 2000 in percent)

Duration	3 months	12 months	20 months	40 months
Return	4.77	5.16	5.86	6.91
Risk	0.40	0.80	1.87	3.60

I would like to make one additional point regarding duration versus liquidity, which is sometimes confused. Extending duration increases market value volatility but it does not, per se, impact liquidity. Liquidity is measured by the cost and timeliness with which one can sell or repo an asset to realize cash. In this context, a *five-year* U.S. Treasury note is more liquid than a *one-week* bank deposit as it can be transformed into cash on a next-day or even same-day basis. This can be done either through selling the asset or through lending it against cash in the repo market.

Improving Portfolio Return: Declining Creditworthiness

The second way to improve portfolio return, or minimize the cost of holding reserves, is to incur more credit risk by investing in asset classes with lower credit risk ratings. In this case, the higher expected return implies higher total return volatility as well as lower liquidity. Table 2 illustrates the long-term returns and volatility associated with asset classes of increasing credit risk.

Table 2. Mean Return and Risk of U.S. Dollar Fixed Income Asset Classes

(March 31, 1999 to March 31, 2000)

	Return	Risk
U.S. Treasury Index	7.99	4.24
AAA Corporate	8.28	4.7
A Corporate	8.46	4.81
High Yield	10.61	7.15

Source: Lehman Brothers Indices.

Based on modern portfolio theory, mathematical models can be used to create an optimal asset allocation whereby the actual risk/return trade-off for the portfolio is superior to any individual asset class. Central banks are increasingly using this technique to determine what should be their neutral portfolio position, or benchmark portfolio. As the benchmark portfolio represents the best long-term portfolio strategy given the risk constraints, any deviation from the benchmark represents an open or risk position.

Liquidity Analysis

While credit diversification can improve return, the liquidity of credit instruments must be carefully analyzed. Generally, credit instruments bear lower levels of liquidity in normal times and liquidity can disappear altogether during crisis periods. It is critical that governments conduct scenario analysis and stress testing for periods of crisis to understand: (i) their potential external liquidity needs; (ii) the behavior of funding sources during periods of crisis; and (iii) the liquidity of the asset class markets. This type of scenario analysis, while accepted among financial institutions, is not yet fully understood or applied among countries. Looking at the recent behavior of even high quality credit instruments, it is critical that central banks do this type of analysis when diversifying out of sovereign instruments. During the Asian crisis and the bail-out of the Long-Term Capital Markets (LTCM) hedge fund, markets for even high quality U.S. government agencies seized up and market bids disappeared to a disturbing and unprecedented extent.

Governance and Risk Management

Finally, I would like to discuss governance issues relating to effective liquidity and risk management. The most critical and difficult challenge to effective liquidity management is to ensure that fundamental policy decisions, which will drive the investment process, are taken at the highest levels. Reserves management is by nature a technical subject, and it is not uncommon to find communication gaps between executive directors, who ultimately are responsible for the risk profile of the central bank or the country, and portfolio managers, who are more focused on the market and take decisions at a micro level. Also, the government may put pressure on the central bank for annual earnings from the foreign reserves portfolio, which further encumbers the optimal investment of the reserves.

This challenge has been successfully addressed by many central banks, but the inherent difficulties should not be underestimated. In an effective structure, policy decisions will be institutionalized in an investment policy or authority, in which the executive directors specify their investment objectives and risk tolerance. Portfolio objectives typically include some combination of the following: maintenance of external stability, preservation of capital, immunization of liabilities, maximization of liquidity or maximization of return. As no single portfolio can simultaneously achieve all of these objectives, the executive directors also need to define acceptable levels of risk in terms of market value volatility, liquidity, and credit risk.

The objectives and constraints set up in the investment policy should be embodied in a benchmark portfolio. The benchmark portfolio is a notional or "paper" portfolio that provides the best return while meeting the risk constraints of the central bank. It represents a long-term investment strategy based on the structural conditions of the central bank and should not incorporate any market views as to the expected direction of currency, interest rates, or any other market prices. Rules regarding replication of the benchmark portfolio are set out and these rules provide a guide for the actual investment of the reserves. As the benchmark is defined as the "best" long-term portfolio, any deviation of the actual reserves from the benchmark portfolio is a risk position. If deviation is allowed, strict risk limits and frequent, if not daily, performance should be calculated. Performance is the difference between the benchmark return and the portfolio return on a mark-to-market basis. Performance calculation and reporting are critical both to understand whether risk taking has added value and, perhaps most importantly, to control accumulated losses.

Finally, governance entails an institutional structure where authority and accountability are carefully delegated to ensure that the portfolio objectives are met. Some recent organizational innovations have been the establishment of a senior asset/liability management committee (ALCO), which transcends institutional boundaries; the establishment of dedicated information technology and legal units to support the highly specialized needs of the market operations units; and the establishment of a "middle office" to manage benchmarks, risk measurement compliance, and performance.

What does all this mean for central banks' legal counsel? Firstly, new asset classes may require legal opinions regarding eligibility under the investment policy. Secondly, the increased use of repurchase agreements, swap transactions, and other instruments to manage risks will require a thorough understanding of the nature of these transactions, risks, and liquidation provisions under the governing legal system in order to draft and duly execute the contractual agreements. Increasingly external managers are also being used and legal counsel needs to understand the nature, risks, and accountability of these relationships to ensure that the legal contract and investment guidelines protect the funds under external management from undue risks.

Conclusions

In conclusion, recent financial shocks have highlighted some of the prevalent risks, which are currently being addressed. It is important, however, that the solutions to these past crises do not create new, unexpected problems. The international community, including the IMF, the Bank for International Settlements (BIS), and central banks, are working in many different fora to address policy issues and develop standards of best practice relating to liquidity and reserves management.

In summary, I would like to make the following points:

- liquidity management is increasingly an asset/liability management issue;

- market disclosure is critical to improving the risk profile of emerging market debt;

- return is an increasingly important portfolio objective for leading central banks into higher risk portfolios;

- risk management needs to quantify market value and liquidity risks under probable adverse scenarios; and

- policy decisions at the highest levels need to drive the investment process.

VI. Supervision and Regulation of Financial Institutions

Chapter 20

Selective Bank and Environmental Developments: Supervisory Trends upon Entering the Twenty-First Century

JOSEPH NORTON

As often "discretion is the better part of valor," this speaker has taken the liberty of refining and more specifically focusing the originally suggested topic for this presentation: "Banking Trends and Developments in the Twenty-First Century." Not only is "crystal ball gazing" a hazardous and uncertain task at best, but, in our current world of exponentially advancing technology and financial innovations, perhaps, such prognostication has been rendered meaningless, particularly when the time frame is a century. As such, I more timidly propose to narrow the subject matter by addressing *selective* bank *supervisory* trends and developments as we enter the twenty-first century. Also, though I will appreciate the theoretical and practical distinction between *regulation* and *supervision*, I am taking another liberty in using these terms interchangeably in this presentation unless the context otherwise specifically indicates.

In Part I of this presentation, I will propose, for general consideration, a series of what I view to be core "environmental" factors facing the banking industry and bank supervisors, namely, the debate over the structural context of bank supervision; the increasing law-based nature of modern financial sector reform; the overriding globalization process; and the pursuit of a new international financial architecture. Then in Part II, a set of specific supervisory trends will be explored. These trends include the notion of a supervisory "public-private partnership," the elusive and ongoing redefinition of the "business of banking," and the regulatory issues entailed with "large complex banking organization," "highly-leveraged transactions" and derivatives products. Part III then provides a more detailed discussion of the pressing supervisory issues surrounding the

---

Note: Appreciation is expressed to the author's SMU/CCLS colleague, Mr. Christopher Olive, for his substantive comments and input. This paper speaks as of May 1, 2000.

desire to develop more sophisticated and relevant "portfolio credit risk" approaches. Part IV contains some modest concluding observations.

I. Selective Core "Environmental" Developments

Shaping the overall context of "trends in bank supervision" and fundamental to any such matters, certain core "environmental" developments for bank supervisors/regulators stand out: (i) the ongoing debate over the role, if any, of central banks (CBs) in bank supervisory matters and the overall desired structural supervisory/regulatory framework; (ii) the implications of the increasing law-based nature of modern financial sector reform; (iii) the relevance of the relentless processes of globalization and financial innovation vis-à-vis modern bank supervision/regulation; and (iv) the relationship of domestic bank supervision/regulation to "the new international financial architecture" (NIFA).

Central Banks and Bank Supervision

One could build a viable proposition that there is a growing trend for divorcing CBs from bank supervision: recent structural reform efforts in the United Kingdom, Australia, and Korea could be cited as supporting examples.[1] However, this author would prefer that, on a global basis (particularly as to emerging, transition, and developing economies), the prevailing model of CB involvement in bank supervision will most probably remain the dominant model. Even in the highly developed United States, some of whose representatives abroad often are viewed as supporters of the bifurcated model, the new omnibus financial modernization legislation in fact substantively enhances the supervisory function of the Federal Reserve Board (FRB) of Governors of the Federal Reserve System. Further, even

---

[1] *See, e.g.*, Australia—Committee of Inquiry and the Australian Financial System, Financial System Inquiry Final Report (March 1997) (Wallis Report); and United Kingdom—Securities and Investments Board, Report to the Exchequer on the Reform of the Financial Regulatory System (July 1997).

where a structural separation is effected, the involvement of the CB in bank supervision will not, and should not, be fully eliminated.[2]

The Separation Issue in General

As we are well aware, modern central banks have two core functions, monetary and financial stability. These core functions underpin a commitment to preserve stability—stability in the value of money and stability in the country's banking system. However, the objective of financial stability does not necessarily imply that the central bank should be in charge of banking supervision and regulation.[3] In recent years, as alluded to above, a number of countries have moved prudential banking supervisory and regulatory responsibilities outside the central bank.[4]

There are arguments for and against the separation of monetary and supervisory policy. The argument traditionally favored by the German Bundesbank is based upon the potential conflicts of interest. For instance, the central bank may be perceived to have the incentive to loosen monetary policy to support the banking industry in times of trouble to safeguard its reputation as a prudential supervisor at the expense of inflation.[5] Other arguments for separation might include the need to protect the reputation of the CB (if price stability is the CB's primary objective) from public criticism often arising in controversial or sensitive supervisory situations (e.g., BCCI, Barings, etc.) and from the questioning of a CB's ability to effectively

---

[2] *See*, inter alia, J. Norton, "Structuring the Bank Regulators and Supervisors: Developed Country Experiences and Their Possible Implications for Latin America and Other Developing Countries," 4 *NAFTA Rev.* 5 (1998). For reference to and discussion of the new U.S. 1999 "Gramm-Leach-Bliley Act" legislation, *see* note 94 *infra*, and accompanying text.

[3] *See generally*, R. Lastra, 1996, *Central Banking and Banking Regulation* (London: London School of Economics and Political Science).

[4] *See*, inter alia, C. Goodhart and D. Schoenmaker, "Institutional Separation Between Supervisory and Monetary Agencies," *LSE Fin. Mkts. Group* (April 1993).

[5] *Cf.* T. Baums and M. Gruson, "The German Banking System—System of the Future," 19 *Brook. J. Int'l L.* 101 (1993).

supervise in an increasingly divergent financial institution/market environment.[6]

The case against separation of monetary and supervisory responsibilities is based upon a number of arguments, including inter alia the oversight of the integrity of the payment system, the effective operation of lender-of-last-resort functions (given the need for timely information about the health of the banking industry in times of crises), and the overriding need for consistency between monetary policy and bank supervision.[7] However, these weaknesses can be alleviated if there is sufficient authority for requiring coordination and information sharing between the supervisor and the central bank.

In developing, emerging, and transitioning economies—countries that are most in need of good banking supervision given their financial fragility in times of crises—the case for having both monetary and bank supervisory responsibilities within the central bank is supported by other arguments (in addition to the ones mentioned above). In particular, there are advantages of synergy in placing banking supervision under the umbrella of the central bank due to the scarcity of qualified economists and financial experts, the shortage of financial instruments to hedge financial risks, the lack of sophisticated accounting standards and practices, and the difficulties in establishing appropriate coordination between various agencies (in this case between the central bank and a separate supervisory agency).[8]

In all events, there is no one "right" regulatory structure for financial services—whether with respect to developed or developing economies. Different histories, cultures, domestic political dynamics, capabilities, etc., most often will dictate the particular shape and character that a regulatory structure will take. A framework that has

---

[6] *See* J. Norton and C.D. Olive, "Globalization of Financial Risks and International Supervision of Banks and Securities Firms: Lessons from the Barings Debacle," 30 *Int'l Law.* 301 (Summer 1996).

[7] *See* R. Lastra, Lenders of Last Resort, in Bank Failures and Bank Insolvency Law in Economics of Transition, ed. by R. Lastra and H. Shiffman (1998).

[8] *See* Norton, *supra* note 2, at 28.

been proven to be effective in one country might not be so successful (or successful at all) if adopted in another country.[9]

Mega or Multiple Financial Regulators

A related issue to whether the CB should conduct banking supervision is what should be the relationship between the central bank (or whoever is the banking regulator) and other financial regulators, in particular securities and insurance regulators? The answer is not straightforward and has several dimensions.[10]

In the United States, regulatory competition among various financial regulators is considered to be a good institutional solution to the increasing complexity and sophistication of financial transactions and financial actors.[11] The United Kingdom, on the other hand, has opted for a mega-regulator for all financial services and markets, and considers that the single regulator is the best option to deal with financial conglomerates and the increasing blurring of frontiers between different types of financial businesses.[12] This model appears to have influenced recent reforms in countries such as Japan and Korea. Some smaller countries, such as Norway, have also adopted the single regulator model.[13] Whenever this mega-model has been adopted, the central bank (or the supervisor) has relinquished its supervisory powers, *i.e.*, the single regulator has been typically placed outside the central bank. In a recent survey conducted of 123 countries, only the Netherlands Antilles, Singapore, and Uruguay had supervision of banking, insurance, and securities within the central bank.[14]

---

[9] *Id.* at 29.
[10] *See generally*, C. Goodhardt et al., *Financial Regulation*, Ch. 8 (1998).
[11] *See generally*, J. Norton and S.C. Whitley, *Banking Law Manual*, Chs. 1–3 (1998).
[12] *See generally*, W. Blair, G. Walker (et al.), 1998, *Banking and Financial Services Regulation* (London: Butterworths); and Michael Blair and G. Walker (et al.), *Blackstone's Guide to Financial Services and Markets Act*, 2000, ed. by M. Blair (London: Blackstone).
[13] Cf. M.J.B. Hall, Banking Regulation and Supervision: A Comparative Study of the U.K. and Japan (1993).
[14] This 1999 survey was conducted by Professor David Llewellyn.

There are economic and political reasons for having the single financial supervisor—if that is the preferred institutional arrangement—outside the central bank. On the economic front, the central bank would need to develop skills of conduct of business and consumer protection rules that go beyond its core competence of monetary policy and systemic oversight (challenges that do not seem to faze the U.S. central bank). On the political front, the granting of excessive power to the central bank may be viewed as undesirable and potentially dangerous if not matched by appropriate mechanisms of accountability. Oddly enough, in the United States, the federal legislature appears to be more amenable to granting the FRB increased powers and responsibilities rather than the Office of the Comptroller of the Currency, a part of the Executive Branch's Treasury Department.[15]

Institutional or Functional Regulation

Another dimension of this broader issue is the relationship of different financial regulators where there is no mega-regulator. With the expansion of activities of banks beyond the confines of what could be termed "traditional," countries have begun to consider whether their financial regulatory structures, which were formulated in a seemingly outdated era, are still adequate (if not relevant) in today's financial marketplace. Debate more often than not involves a discussion over "functional" versus "institutional" regulation.[16] This debate is even relevant in the case of a mega-regulator as to how it should organize internally and coordinate its different departments.

In the simplest of terms, institutional regulation places the supervision of certain institutions under the charge of a specified regulator or regulators. For instance, under this theory banks would be regulated by a specified banking agency, securities firms would be regulated by a specified securities agency, and insurance companies would be regulated by a specified insurance agency. This has been the historic method of financial regulation.[17] A simple and

---

[15] *See*, inter alia, M. Taylor, *"Twin Peaks": A Regulatory Structure for the New Century*, Centre for the Study of Financial Innovation (1995).
[16] *See, e.g.*, Melanie L. Fein, "Functional Regulation: A Concept for Glass-Steagall Reform?" 2 *Stan. J. L. Bus. & Fin.* 89 (1995).
[17] *See* R. S. Karmel, "Functional Regulation," 501 *PLI/CORP* 9 (1985).

straightforward approach, this theory fails to comport with modern realities which involve, for example, banks engaging in securities and insurance activities.

Functional regulation has been seen as an alternative approach. This theory separates regulatory responsibilities among agencies according to common activities or products, "so that financial products, services and markets delivering similar benefits and risks can be subjected to substantially equivalent regulation and so that economic competition, rather than jurisdictional barriers or differences in supervision, can determine which products, services and markets succeed in the marketplace."[18] In other words, functional regulation postulates that similar functions should be regulated similarly. Accordingly, banking activities would be regulated by a banking agency, securities activities would be regulated by a securities agency, and insurance activities by an insurance regulator.

Even though functional regulation promises to promote, inter alia, reduced duplication among regulators and increased fairness for regulated activities, it harbors serious shortcomings which render it problematic and prevent it from being incorporated wholesale as a *modus operandi* of financial marketplace supervision. First, the functions, much like institutions, are becoming increasingly difficult to distinguish.[19] As the business of finance becomes ever more intertwined, the meshing of functional distinctions could make functional regulation as obsolete as strict institutional regulation seems to have become. Furthermore, in relation to financial conglomerates, functional regulation would have the effect of

---

[18] *See* Chicago Mercantile Exchange, *Model for Federal Financial Regulation*, at 2 (1993). In the proposal by the Chicago Mercantile Exchange (CME) for the restructuring of the federal financial regulation regime, a consolidation was proposed that would envelop the Securities and Exchange Commission (SEC), the Commodity Futures Trading Commission (CFTC), the Office of the Comptroller of the Currency (OCC), the Office of Thrift Supervision (OTS), the Federal Deposit Insurance Corporation (FDIC), and the Securities Investor Protection Corporation (SIPC), in addition to parts of the Department of Labor and the Federal Reserve Board. *See* John C. Coffee, Jr., "Competition Versus Consolidation: The Significance of Organizational Structure in Financial and Securities Regulation," 50 *Bus. Law.* 447, 451 (1995).

[19] Alan Greenspan, Remarks at the Conference on Bank Structure and Competition of the Federal Reserve Bank of Chicago (May 1, 1997) (available at 1997 WL 217630).

(i) subjecting these institutions to multiple regulators, thereby increasing their cost of compliance, and (ii) preventing any single regulator from gaining a "full picture" of the institution and its operations, which would have the potential effect of allowing certain regulatory issues to "fall between the cracks." As a result, functional regulation cannot exclusively provide an adequate, efficient, or, even, feasible method of supervision for these entities.[20]

The Basel Core Principles do not provide essential guidance in this area, but in terms of prudential regulations and requirements, they lay down the traditional Basel focus on capital adequacy, with the proviso that "such requirements should reflect the risks that banks undertake."[21] Accordingly, what is needed is a method that would allow a fusion of the two regulatory approaches (i.e., institutional and functional). In other words, effective regulation of today's financial marketplace may require a combined approach that would allow the benefits of each respective approach to merge.

In any event, as the level of development of the financial markets and/or institutions in developing countries differ from country to country and certainly substantively differ from counterparts in developed countries, the "functional versus institutional" debate may be premature as to many emerging economies.[22]

Within this overall debate of institutional versus functional regulation also lies the issue as to what role "private actors" should play in the overall regulatory process.[23] Key here is the future role of the banking and financial services industries themselves in devising, implementing, and monitoring effective internal risk management

---

[20] *See* Karmel, *supra* note 17, at 12.
[21] *See* Basel Committee on Banking Supervision, *Core Principles of Effective Banking Supervision* (Sept. 1997), at Principle 6.
[22] *See* Norton, *supra* note 2, at 28.
[23] *See generally*, J. Norton and C. Olive, "The Ongoing Process of International Bank Regulatory and Supervisory Convergence: A New Regulatory Market 'Partnership'," 16 *Ann. Rev. Banking L.* 227 (1997).

systems[24] and the role of independent auditors in providing oversight and greater accountability in the supervisory processes.[25]

Countervailing Considerations

The countervailing balances to any reaffirmation of bank supervisory and regulatory authority within the CB structure should include a high degree of (i) independence from undue political influence, (ii) accountability, (iii) transparency and information sharing, (iv) rule-orientation, and (v) resource sufficiency.

Independence and accountability

The delegation of responsibility in the supervisory arena neither implies nor requires that the CB should be independent from government in the exercise of these supervisory responsibilities.[26] It is perfectly possible to restrict independence exclusively to the monetary policy functions of a central bank, leaving other central bank functions—e.g., banking supervision—under political control.

Additionally, some central bank laws (e.g., Spain and France) have depoliticized monetary policy but not banking supervision. In contrast, the U.S. Federal Reserve System is independent both in its monetary policy and banking supervisory responsibilities. The arguments for depoliticizing banking supervision are similar—though not identical—to those put forth in the case for central bank independence in monetary policy: technical expertise, the insulation from the short-term views of politicians worried about re-election, and the importance of the goal of sound banking. In developing countries, there might be an additional argument for independence in

---

[24] See T. Padoa-Schioppa, "Globalization of Risks: Cooperation Between Banking and Market Regulators," in Public Docs. of the XXth IOSCO Annual Conference, Tome I, No. 24, 63-64 (1995).

[25] See C. Hadjiemmanuil, Banking Regulation and the Bank of England, 165–173 (1996).

[26] The discussion presented in this subsection is largely derived from the various works of this author's CCLS's colleague, Dr. Rosa Lastra, who has kindly granted the author permission to make such derivations. Dr. Lastra's numerous writing on central banks include *Central Banking and Bank Regulation* (1996).

the exercise of prudential supervision if politicians are subject to temptations of corruption or nepotism.[27]

The next question is what does it mean to be independent in supervision? An analogy with the independence of the central bank in monetary policy is helpful to understand this issue. In order to carry out these responsibilities, a central bank must have control over monetary policy. Control in this context has two senses. First, it must have the technical capacity and the resources (human and otherwise) to meaningfully control or influence monetary conditions. Secondly, there is control in the sense of being able to exercise the bank's own best judgement, which in turn is linked to the rules regarding appointment and dismissal procedures, terms of office, budgetary autonomy and liaisons with the other relevant government authorities (e.g., a Ministry of Finance). A central bank is truly a central bank, and not just the monetary agent of government, when it is free to make and implement decisions.

However, in a democratic community independence is only one side of the coin, for accountability is also necessary. To begin, it is important to point out that authority is not given away, but "delegated." A clearly specified mandate is often given by a parliament or other legislative body, and the agency to whom the mandate is given, be it the central bank or another agency, is then left to get on with carrying it out. In addition, it should be stressed that accountability requires, at the very least, that the central bank explain and justify its decisions and actions and account for the decisions made in the execution of its responsibilities. Lawyers and economists tend to emphasize different issues in attempting to measure accountability. Lawyers emphasize the institutional dimension, i.e., the placing of the institution (the independent central bank) within the existing system of checks and balances, in relation to the three branches of the State: legislative, executive, and judiciary.

The concept of *accountability*—from a *legal perspective*—should be "diversified" to include parliamentary accountability as well as judicial review of the central bank's acts and decisions, and a degree

---

[27] *See* J. Norton and M. Yokoi, "Banking Reform in Emerging Economies: In General and In Reality—The Case of Thailand," Remarks presented to the LSE Conference on Banking Reform and Enforcement Issues (May 26, 2000).

of cooperation with the executive branch to ensure consistent overall economic policymaking.

In a national context, a parliament or other legislature remains sovereign in its legislative decisions, and one statute proclaiming central bank independence can always be removed by another one revoking it. Legislative accountability should be exercised through a variety of procedures and mechanisms, including annual reports and appearances of the Governor and other CB officials on a regular basis, and also in the case of an emergency situation.

Judicial review of CB's decisions and actions (conducted by an independent and depolitisized judiciary or special and independent administrative judicial committee) also is essential to prevent and control the arbitrary and unreasonable exercise of discretionary powers. This is a fundamental element of the rule of law. The discretion of central bankers—or any other officials—should never remain unfettered but instead should be subject to legal controls.[28]

Economists, while accepting this "institutional" articulation of accountability, in particular parliamentary accountability, tend to put the emphasis on two other forms of accountability: disclosure and performance control. Disclosure or transparency in the operation of monetary policy is a "market-based" form of accountability and is typically favored in Anglo-Saxon countries, such as the United States and the United Kingdom, where competition and transparency are considered to be the two main pillars of a market economy.[29]

Performance control, the other key form of accountability, is, in turn, conditional upon the objectives and targets imposed upon the central bank. Performance control is facilitated first by the existence of one rather than multiple goals or by their unambiguous ranking and, secondly, by the existence of a clearly stated and narrowly

---

[28] *See* Lastra, *supra* note 26.
[29] The publication of the minutes of the U.S. Federal Open Market Committee (the monetary policy arm of the Federal Reserve System in the United States) or of the Monetary Policy Committee of the Bank of England are examples of this form of accountability.

defined goal.[30] Finally, the support of public opinion is another form of de facto accountability.

As suggested by Dr. Lastra, a further twist to comprehension of the notion of accountability is the distinction between ex ante accountability and ex post accountability. The former typically implies scrutiny and the latter control.[31]

Independence and accountability can be seen as opposite ends of a continuum. While too much independence may lead to the creation of a democratically unacceptable "state within the state," too much accountability threatens the effectiveness of independence, and in some instances (particularly in the case of the exercise of a government override) may actually nullify independence. The optimal trade-off between independence and accountability varies from country to country. While it is fair to say that the Deutsche Bundesbank tilted on the side of independence (with weak parliamentary accountability though strong popular support), the Reserve Bank of New Zealand tilts on the side of accountability (because of ministerial control and the possibility of government override). The European Central Bank tilts on the side of independence, with weak parliamentary accountability and less than cohesive popular support amongst the Member States participating in European Monetary Union. The debate about independence and accountability resembles, as Dr. Lastra has pointed out, the philosophical debate about freedom and responsibility: independence without accountability would be like freedom without responsibility.[32]

Transparency and information sharing/gateways

One traditional model for a bank supervisory/regulatory style of administration centers largely around the perceived superior institutional wisdom of the supervisor/regulator, the need for a high degree of flexibility (i.e., largely unfettered discretion), and the desire

---

[30] *E.g.*, the case of New Zealand and the United Kingdom.

[31] *E.g.*, the appointment procedures of central bank officials and the debate of inflation targets are ways of exercising accountability through scrutiny. The reporting requirements and the appearances of the CB chairman or governor in front of parliamentary committees are ways of exercising accountability through control.

[32] *See* Lastra, *supra* note 26.

for secrecy and confidentiality (e.g., as to these combined factors, the so-called classic "moral suasion" approach of the Bank of England or traditional approach of the Japanese bank supervisor). The clear trend today, however, is for greater transparency in the supervisory/regulatory process and (as discussed below) for a more rule-orientated framework. This entails the movement toward the following:

- a more open process in the formulation of administrative rules (e.g., public pre-notification and the solicitation of relevant comments from affected or involved governmental agencies; and

- greater information-sharing, cooperation, and coordination by and between the supervisor/regulator and other relevant parties, such as other domestic financial agencies, international counterpart agencies in countries or regions where financial institutions of the home jurisdiction may have a presence, and appropriate regional and international financial institutions involved in financial sector monitoring/surveillance.[33]

The experiences of Germany are instructive in this regard. In Germany, banking supervision is undertaken by an agency external to the Bundesbank (the German central bank). However, in the German system, all supervisory information passes through the Bundesbank before going to the supervisory authority, which is conveniently located in the same building. (Supervision is actually undertaken by a system of external auditors who report to both the supervisors and the central bank, although actual supervisory functions are not undertaken by the Bundesbank.)[34]

The German system has two implications for supervisory structures. First, regardless of whether a formal separation exists between the central bank and the supervisory authorities, a system must exist whereby the central bank has immediate access to all supervisory information in order to allow it to perform its role as

---

[33] *See, e.g.*, IMF Annual Report—1999, Part III, 5 and 6.
[34] *See generally*, Baums and Gruson, *supra* note 5.

lender of last resort. Second, in a universal banking system such as Germany's where most financial assets do in fact flow through the banking system, information is much more readily available to the central bank in regard to both its monetary policy and its lender-of-last-resort roles.

The meaningful and timely existence of "information gateways" regarding transfer of information in appropriate circumstances has become an important aspect of financial institution regulation and supervision. In a particular jurisdiction, domestic information gateways should be established by law, regulation, and/or Memorandum of Understanding (MOU) between the CB, Ministry of Finance, securities regulators and insurance regulators, and with criminal prosecution and police officials respecting money laundering and financial fraud activities. These gateways should attempt to establish precisely when information regarding financial institution affairs is to be disclosed outside of the bank supervisor/regulator and the instances in which economic or financial information on other entities not regulated by the bank regulator should be disclosed to the bank regulators. This is especially pertinent to financial business groups that could well include nonfinancial institutions subject to the functional regulation of another regulatory agency, and that troubled financial institutions close to being placed in receivership may be addressed in a manner using public funds under a deposit insurance scheme, which may necessarily involve the countries' Ministry of Finance and Executive Government.[35]

With regard to international and regional arrangements, information gateways should be established which expressly authorize the CB/bank regulator to disclose certain information and otherwise coordinate with regulatory counterparts in other nations with interests relevant to the domestic financial institutions or markets. The Basel Committee and IOSCO have provided ample guidance in this area.[36]

---

[35] *E.g., Memorandum of Understanding Between HM Treasury,* The Bank of England Financial Services Authority (UK).

[36] *See* respective websites for these "organizations."

Rule orientation

As discussed more fully below, the current trend is toward a more rule-orientated supervisory/regulatory process.

Resource sufficiency

An effective bank supervisory infrastructure requires a significant financial commitment of government for ensuring sufficient (in terms of numbers and training) administrative, enforcement, and judicial personnel. In a time of increasingly stretched governmental budgets, resource sufficiency is and will remain a fundamental issue as to the ultimate effectiveness of a bank regulatory/supervisory structure.[37]

Law-Based Nature of Modern Financial Sector Reform

As mentioned above, a classic model of a non-rule-based regulatory/supervisory system was the United Kingdom. Historically, there was no legal basis for the activities of the Bank of England, either in regard to central bank functions or supervisory issues. Rather, the English banking system was managed as a small gentlemen's club of bankers through the practice of "moral suasion." In many ways, this can be seen to be a system that was largely *sui generis* to the peculiarities of the London financial markets (although a similar system was in effect in Hong Kong for most of its existence under British rule), which have now ceased to exist. The historical English system represented essentially a *laissez faire*, free market system, based on the Bank's practical powers of "moral suasion." Significant changes in the institutional composition of the London financial markets, the development of the EC single market, and certain financial scandals have led to the restructuring and greater legal formalization of this historical system.[38]

Clearly, our modern banking and financial markets call more and more for a greater movement to a law-based regulatory/supervisory systems. Such systems are seen as providing greater transparency, a

---

[37] *See* Norton and Yokoi, *supra* note 27.
[38] *See*, J. Norton, "The Bank of England's Lament: The Struggle to Maintain the Traditional Practice of Moral Suasion," in *Bank Regulation and Supervision in the 1990s* (J. Norton ed., 1992).

more level playing field, greater fairness, a reduction of undue governmental interference and abuse of discretion, and more effective enforcement. Also, the intersecting requirements of the expanding WTO system as to financial services envision a more rule-based approach.[39]

A law-based approach invariably should entail a broad rule-oriented framework where unfettered discretion, non-transparency, and cronyism must give way. But not only should such a framework be broad in its scope, it should be deep in its implementation. As such, a comprehensive and coordinated framework will need to entail and to interconnect the legislative, administrative, supervisory, examination, enforcement, and judicial administration processes of the country.[40]

Yet, a law-based approach to the economic regulation of the financial sector is not simply about laws and legal processes: law is merely one societal *means* to achieving and legitimizing appropriate policy objectives. In the area of financial sector reform, this chapter suggests that a law-based approach should also be an interdisciplinary approach, where law is the thread that weaves together economic, political, and social objectives with a transparent and fair implementation process and where the lawyers should work closely with the economists, policymakers, operational people, and the accountants.

Where the new rules of reform will derive from is a rather complex proposition. On the one hand, they have been evolving, over the past two decades, through a complex matrix of "soft-law" initiatives by and among a variety of international financial organizations and institutions. On the other hand, they have been shaped by the particular realities of economic law efforts in individual

---

[39] See *Trade Liberalisation and Financial Services*, Centre for Commercial Law Studies (London), Research Seminar (May 1997).

[40] This paragraph and the following ones of this subsection are derived from J. Norton, "A 'New International Financial Architecture'—Reflections on the Possible Law-Based Dimension," 33 *Int'l Law.* 891, 896–897 (1999)

countries. Associated with all this has been the varying influences of varying regional and subregional configurations.[41]

In any event, the commitment to a law-based financial sector reform program needs to be a *long-term societal commitment* whereby the notion of a process based upon a *"rule of law"* becomes ingrained within and throughout the fabric of civil, political and economic societies in emerging economies, in a substantive manner and not merely as a facade.

To achieve and to sustain this long-term commitment will depend, in large part, on the development of a strong and vibrant educational infrastructure involving new university educational approaches to the teaching of financial law-related subjects on an interdisciplinary basis, and to new approaches to bureaucratic and judicial training. In a sense a new "working partnership" needs to be forged among the academic, bureaucratic, judicial, and practical business and financial worlds in order to ensure that this interdisciplinary educational infrastructure comes into being and becomes an integral part of the overall financial sector reform process—a process that embodies not simply an enactment stage, but an effective administrative implementation stage, an effective administrative and judicial enforcement stage, and meaningful monitoring and readjustment mechanisms.

The significance of all this for bank regulators/supervisors are several. For instance, the bank regulators/supervisors need to take a forward-looking and proactive part in this ongoing law-reform processes in order to ensure relevancy and coherence. In addition, this new rule-orientation needs to permeate the way the regulators/supervisors implement and enforce this reform (e.g., as to their administrative processes and the need for meaningful judicial review): in effect, they need to play an integral part in this "rule by law/rule of law" process. Moreover, effective enforcement will depend to a large extent on the legal intersection of the supervisory

---

[41] *Id.*

and administrative and judicial enforcement components of the reform process.[42]

Overriding Globalization Processes

Now, what of this "unruly horse" called "globalization" that seems to pervade so many aspects of our modern economic and financial lives?

In General

Certainly, the term "globalization" has become a much overused and misused term—so much so that the word appears to have been rendered largely devoid of any critical substantive meaning and to have been transformed into a media sound-bite and marketing hype.[43] As insightfully noted by one observer:

> "[W]e are living in a globally integrated and interdependent world. And that what happens in one country could easily have a contagious effect on the rest of the world."[44]

As my colleague in London, Professor Emeritus Roy Goode, is prone to comment: "No island can any longer afford to remain an island." Certainly, this is most apropos for any emerging or transitioning economy today.

What makes "globalization" qualitatively different from conventional notions of "internationalization" are these elements of *interconnectedness* and *interdependence*. Globalization is not an end result but entails a complex series of linked, and at times competing and opposed, processes and changes that began to arise over the past several decades.[45]

---

[42] *See* Norton and Yokoi, *supra* note 27.

[43] *See*, inter alia, A. Giddens, Globalisation (BBC Reith Lecture Series 1999) (available at http://news.bbc.co.uk).

[44] Y.C. Cheng, 2002, "Preface," in *International Financial Sector Reform: Standard Setting and Infrastructure Development*, ed. by S. Goo, D. Arner, and Z. Zhou (The Hague: Kluwer Law International).

[45] This section is based, in part, upon the author's Inaugural Lecture at the University of Hong Kong (Oct. 1999).

These processes and changes have embraced the collapse of the Bretton Woods monetary system beginning in the early 1970s; global and ongoing debt crises of the 1980s that continue today and most probably into the future; the relentless expansion and increased sophistication and competitiveness of multinational enterprises; a relatively general worldwide embrace of the "Washington Consensus" promoting greater liberalization and deregulation of economic and financial markets; privatization or corporatization (as our People's Republic of China brethren are prone to say) of large sectors of what were previously state-owned and controlled economic activities; the demise of the Soviet Union and its satellites throughout Central and Eastern Europe; the decline of the Welfare State; exponential innovations in electronic, computer, telecommunications, and transportation technologies; and, of course, the advent of a "global information highway" from what 30 years ago in October 1969 was a very modest experiment by two research institutions in California to communicate with each other through a rudimentary "alpha-net." All this has come to question traditional patterns of international business, investment, and finance and related governmental and regulatory approaches.

But, globalization is about more than economic, business, and financial markets and activities: it touches the political, social, cultural, technological, and even religious "soul" of society. Yet, not all societies nor all parts of society may be impacted by globalization in the same way or same degree, or, if impacted, are not affected in the same way or degree.[46] Globalization does not mean necessarily "global order." To a large extent, to date at least, it has meant global disorder—not a global system, but a global non-system. This makes the new regulatory and supervisory challenges most intimidating.

Yet notwithstanding conventional wisdom to the contrary, the sovereign state is not necessarily in decline as a result of these processes: it is being reconfigured whereby political and social governance structures will need to be reinvented to deal with the new and rapidly changing realities and demands of modern life. While the state can no longer realistically expect to function under an

---

[46] *See generally* UNDP, Human Development Report (1999) (available at http://www.undp.org/hdro/report.htm).

eighteenth- or nineteenth-century framework, the domestic state will remain the central political focal point. But, this new governance will need to draw upon the individual, local, national, regional, and international layers of our society. And this "new governance" will have to mesh the political not only with the economic, business, and financial, but with the human and social dimensions of our society.[47]

This globalization process or processes may lead a state to undertake a number of new approaches and activities, which (at least superficially) may appear to be at the expense of the nation-state: new roles in furthering global competition, in denationalizing laws and moving more toward international standards; in pursuing greater and different types of "public-private partnerships" (e.g., see "The Supervisory Public-Private Relationship" below); and in seeking greater interstate, regional, and international cooperation in a broader range of areas of common interest and concerns. These new approaches/activities are most germane to bank and other financial regulator/supervisors.

Globalization is about a race for knowledge, not simply for information—which translates into a race for power and wealth. How will that power and wealth be harnessed and shared? Who will be the winners, the losers?

There will be no easy and one answer to any of these questions. The challenge is to determine in what ways a particular society and its political subdivisions can come to take positive, directional control over the "dialectic"—i.e., over the very "pushes and pulls" of the unleashed globalization processes. Will the traditional nation-states be strengthened or weakened? Will they become more efficient or chaotic? More democratic or more authoritarian? More secure or less safe? Will there be more benefits and opportunities than burdens and detriments; and will the benefits and opportunities be shared widely or narrowly? Will the individual become more enriched or alienated? Will legal systems be more about technical rule making than about social justice? Will our environment become more sustainable or increasingly threatened? The answer to each of these

---

[47] *See*, inter alia, A.C. Aman, Jr., "The Globalisation State: A Future-Oriented Perspective on the Public/Private Distinction, Federalism, and Democracy," 31 *Vand. J. Transn. L.* 769 (1998).

questions will have particular repercussions for financial markets and the various actors within these markets—including the regulators/supervisors.

Law and Financial Markets

Globalization, most certainly, will bring enormous challenges and discomforts to traditional legal notions. To illustrate the infrastructural role of law, in the globalization process, just consider the area of global financial markets. Now, the fundamental relationship of legal infrastructure to sustainable economic and financial infrastructure has not always been recognized. In fact, it is only in very recent years, that international institutions such as the IMF and World Bank have incorporated infrastructural legal reform into their adjustment and technical assistance programs. But, it has become evident, particularly with the recent East Asian financial crises, that issues of economic and commercial law reform are a primary political and societal concerns. This sustainability of economic growth of enhancement of the quality of life, and of the stability of the economic and financial systems must be a driving imperative for the twenty-first century for all economic systems, whether the lessor developed, developing, emerging or transitioning, or industrialized. As argued above, all this will require viable (and "safe and sound") financial and commercial law systems of considerable sophistication and of high integrity and transparency— that is, as argued above, a "law-based" approach.[48]

Moreover, it has become apparent since the breakdown of the Bretton Woods (International Monetary) System in the early 1970s that financial markets around the world have become and are becoming more and more interconnected and interdependent—that is *"globalized."* As such, many countries, especially developing, emerging, and transitioning economies are finding themselves in a state of major transformation as to the nature and requirements of their economy and its financial markets. The modern reality is that political and economic power comes, in part, from developing and

---

[48] *See* note 40, *supra*, and accompanying text.

sustaining viable and economic financial markets—markets that are becoming increasingly internationalized.[49]

Several preliminary observations on the critical importance of the future development of financial law and regulation can be drawn upon, particularly as to the issues that will be subject to considerable external, regional and international pressures. The recent financial crises in East Asia, Russia, Brazil, and elsewhere bring this point home.[50]

A first observation is that the relationship of law to financial markets, financial institutions, and financial innovation is an evolving and diverse process entailing a rich matrix of *private* and *public* laws, of domestic, regional, and international laws (including "soft law") and a mix of statutes, administrative regulations, and case law. This unfolding legal framework covers both traditional and segregated notions of particular type of financial institution and broader, more integrated notions of "financial services" and "financial institutions."[51] As such, "financial law" (domestic and international) will be a blend of private and public law. In all events, this developing area of law needs to become attuned and receptive to these dramatically and vastly changing notions, to the new legal and economic realities of individual countries and to the general growing and economic interdependence within various regions of the world, and to more general international financial market developments.[52]

A second related observation suggests that the future of domestic financial institutions and markets will and should continue to be influenced and shaped in a significant measure by external, international, and regional supervisory developments. These external pressures may well come to provide the strands for a gradual

---

[49] *See*, inter alia, J. Norton & D. Arner, "International Co-Operative Efforts and Implications for Law Reform," in *Bank Failures and Bank Insolvency Law* in *Economics in Transition*, Ch. 9 (R. Lastra and H.N. Schiffman eds. 1999).

[50] *See* J. Norton, "Financial Sector Reform and International Financial Crises: The Legal Challenges," *Essays in International Financial and Economic Law, No. 16* (J. Norton ed. 1998).

[51] See generally R. Cranston, Principles of Banking Law (1998).

[52] *See, e.g.*, J. Norton, "The Korean Financial Crises—Reform and Positive Transformation: Is a Second 'Han River Miracle' Possible?" 2:2 *Global Econ. Rev.* 3–36 (1998).

integration and convergence by "small steps" respecting the financial systems and markets of individual sovereign nations, and otherwise (notwithstanding the recent East Asian financial crises) should help foster, generally, greater transparency and stability in financial markets—domestically, regionally, and internationally.[53]

All this of needs to be effected within a system that embraces a strong "rule of law" and that fosters sound constitutional underpinnings.

International Convergence and International Standards

In coming to terms with these dilemmas, states will need increasingly to move toward greater economic and monetary convergence and coordination: we already see this through the onslaught of the "Gs"—G-3, G-7, G-8, G-10, and now G-22—and their related organizations such as the new Financial Stability Forum, and through regional endeavors such as the European Union and its Economic and Monetary Union and (as to emerging regions) the MERCOSUR common markets efforts in the Latin American "Southern Cone." There will also be a need for redirection of technology, global efforts and security, a reorientation of current international organizations, an invigorated commitment to a democratic architecture, and a great sharing of responsibilities with non-state actors such as nongovernmental organizations (NGOs).

But even more fundamental and more immediate than this overall convergence process, and what is a key catalytic factor to convergence, is the ongoing development and transmission of "international bank supervisory standards" as primarily articulated through the Basel Committee on Banking Supervision. Illustrative are the recent Basel Core Principles and Compendium.

The basic pillars of an effective regulatory and supervisory system can be seen on five levels: (i) adequate entry requirements, (ii) minimum prudential regulations, (iii) effective ongoing

---

[53] *See, e.g.*, S. Fischer (IMF Economic Counsellor and Director), "Reforming World Finance: Lessons from a Crisis," *The Economist* (Oct. 3-9, 1998).

supervision, (iv) adequate enforcement mechanisms, and (v) channels for international cooperation.

At an initial level, there must be an adequate licensing process. Licensing allows the regulatory authority to control and define the number and types of institutions that it is responsible for. Permissible activities of institutions and the licensing requirements need to be clearly defined.[54] Further, the licensing authority must have the right to set criteria and reject applications, assessing at a minimum, ownership structure, qualifications of directors and management, operating plans and controls, and projected capital base.[55] In addition, in case of an application from a foreign financial institution, approval should be sought from the home regulatory authority.

Beyond initial entry requirements, the authorities must be able to monitor and reject transfers of ownership or major acquisitions.[56] Such controls are essential to maintaining the initial level of standards set for entry and to maintain an accurate picture of the institutional population. Despite this basic level of control, however, financial innovation is vital to economic success and should not be unduly deterred through bureaucratic impediments.

At a second level, prudential regulations and requirements are necessary as a precursor to successful ongoing supervision. Today, financial regulation is turning increasingly to a process of risk-based supervision and therefore the authority must establish requirements appropriate to the risks that banks are likely to face in their ongoing operations. It is at this level that the Basel Committee has historically been very constructive and, arguably, effective in establishing standards and methodologies.[57]

Within the context of supervision, prudent minimum capital adequacy requirements are essential,[58] not only from a regulatory viewpoint, but more importantly from the standpoint of international investors. Beyond minimum capital requirements, supervisors need

---

[54] *See* Basel Core Principles, *supra* note 21, at Principle 2.
[55] *Id.* at Principle 3.
[56] *Id.* at Principles 4–5.
[57] See J. Norton, Devising International Bank Supervisory Standards (1995).
[58] *See* Basel Core Principles, *supra* note 21, at Principle 6.

to be able to evaluate policies, practices, and procedures related to the granting of loans, the making of investments, and the ongoing management of both (the process of monitoring credit risk).[59] While obviously supervisors cannot and should not subject each individual decision to scrutiny, they should make sure that banks have in place prudent written policies for such activities and internal information capabilities, as well as follow concentration limits to single borrowers and prohibitions against connected lending.[60] In addition, banks must establish and implement policies and procedures for asset quality maintenance and provisioning.[61]

In addition to credit risk (which itself is becoming an increasingly complex and important topic of supervision, as discussed below), supervisors must ensure that banks have adequate policies and procedures to deal with country risk,[62] market risk,[63] and other risks such as interest rate and liquidity risk.[64] Finally, banks must establish procedures and policies to deal with operational risks, such as fraud, corruption, and money laundering, including internal controls and "know-your-customer" rules.[65]

At a third level, once prudential requirements are established, supervisors must have clear and effective methodologies for ongoing supervisory efforts. Such a system should include both on-site and off-site supervision,[66] along with regular contact with bank management and understanding of each institution's operations[67] as part of a comprehensive means of gathering and analyzing information from institutions, on both a solo and a consolidated basis.[68] Beyond information gathering and monitoring, supervisors must have a means of independent validation of information, either through on-site examination or the use of effective and accountable

---

[59] *Id.* at Principle 7.
[60] *Id.* at Principle 8.
[61] *Id.* at Principles 9–10.
[62] *Id.* at Principle 11.
[63] *Id.* at Principle 12.
[64] *Id.* at Principle 13.
[65] *Id.* at Principles 14–15.
[66] *Id.* at Principle 16.
[67] *Id.* at Principle 17.
[68] *Id.* at Principle 18.

external auditors.[69] Finally, if financial groups are allowed, supervisors must be able to supervise such banking groups on a consolidated basis.[70] As one significant aspect of this process, banks must maintain and publish fair and accurate financial statements in accordance with consistent accounting policies.[71]

At a fourth level, banking supervisors must be able to enforce prudential regulations and cause banks to undertake appropriate corrective action, up to and including de-authorization and liquidation.[72] Internationally, there is an increasing focus on varying levels of supervision for institutions based on their financial health, under the doctrine of "prompt corrective action" developed in the United States following the S&L crisis in the 1980s.[73] If a supervisory authority is not given powers to implement its authority, then its effectiveness is effectively eliminated. Further, these powers should be clear and non-discretionary to the extent possible.[74]

Finally, banking supervisors must be able to operate in the international arena for financial institutions that continues to develop worldwide. Home supervisors of internationally active financial institutions should practice global consolidated supervision,[75] at a minimum establishing contact and information exchanges with other relevant foreign supervisory authorities.[76] In terms of foreign banks operating domestically, such institutions must follow the same standards required for domestic institutions and supervisors must be able to share information with the institutions' home supervisors in order to ensure effective supervision.[77]

---

[69] *Id.* at Principle 19.
[70] *Id.* at Principle 20.
[71] *Id.* at Principle 21.
[72] *Id.* at Principle 22.
[73] J. Norton and S. Whitley, *Banking Law Manual* §§ 3.11[8], 5.08[3][a] (1998).
[74] *See* R. Helfert (former U.S. Federal Deposit Insurance Corporation (FDIC) Chairman), "Rules Versus Discretion in the Intervention of Troubled Financial Institutions—The United States Perspective," Doc. No. SPIRANSRSF/II 1 Di. No. 2 of 1997 SELA Caracas Conference Proceedings.
[75] *See* Basel Core Principles, *supra* note 21, at Principle 23.
[76] *Id.* at Principle 25.
[77] *Id.*

Technology/Innovation: Challenges for Regulators

How can legal rules and systems and the relevant regulators cope with new innovative dimensions in economic/business/informational technology, intellectual property, dramatically new and different social, human rights and environmental issues, and in global financial markets?

To regulate or not to regulate; how to regulate and/or self-regulate; how to be proactive with and supportive of financial market developments and innovations, while preserving a "safe and sound" and stable financial system; how to protect rights and interests of involved parties (e.g., issues of security, privacy, adequate disclosure)? As will be discussed more fully in Part III, all these seemingly geometrically unfolding issues will bring into question the very nature of "the business of banking" and of banks themselves. In turn, this will bring into question the nature and role of bank supervision itself.

Bank Supervision/Regulation and the New International Financial Architecture (NIFA)

Another fundamental and related "environmental" factor is whether the recent and expanding web of international standards and principles, referred to above, respecting financial law being formulated and transmitted through a loose matrix of intergovernmental and regional groupings, institutions, and arrangements, constitutes a "new international financial architecture." Whatever the immediate answer, the initial enquiry is of long-term global significance and is one that touches upon a fundamental restructuring of existing international economic and financial institutions: a further evolvement of international "soft law," practices, and standards; a reconfiguration of varying regional and subregional arrangements; and, above all, a robust and sustained efforts of domestic systems to effect fundamental and long-term legal, economic, political, social, and educational reform processes.[78]

---

[78] *See* Norton, *supra* note 41.

Recent discussions and formulations concerning the (NIFA) have largely (but not exclusively) directed themselves to banking and financial sector reform issues related to emerging and transitioning economies. This "architecture" is not entirely "new," is not traditionally "international," is not exclusively "financial," is not in any real sense an architectural plan or design, and is not solely directed at emerging and transitioning economies.[79] However, as becomes evident in a careful reading of the recent G-7 Finance Ministers Report, the NIFA should address at least the following subject areas:[80]

- Strengthened Macroeconomic Policy for Emerging Economies

- Strengthened and Reformed IFIs

- Accurate and Timely Informational Flows and Transparency

- Strong Financial Regulation in Industrial Countries

- Strong Financial Systems in Emerging Markets

- Exchange Rate Policies

- Sound Accounting Standards

- Legal Infrastructure

- Corporate Governance

- Anticorruption/Money Laundering

- Technological Innovation/Adaptation

- Risk Management

---

[79] *See* generally "Symposium on the New International Financial Architecture," *Int'l Law* (Winter 1999).

[80] *See* generally Report of G-7 Finance Ministers (June 1999) (delivered at the G-7 Summit in Cologne, Germany). A subsequent, reaffirming G-7 meeting was held in Okinawa, Japan, in July 2000.

An integral component of all this will be a significant "law-based dimension" evolving around "global principles and standards setting as to the following."[81]

- Banking Regulation
- Capital Markets Regulation
- Insurance Supervision
- Corporate Governance
- Financial Conglomerates
- Payment, Settlement, and Custody Mechanisms
- Pension Funds and Collective Investment Schemes
- Accounting and Auditing Standards

The NIFA at this stage is somewhat incomplete, however, as there remains a large "unfinished agenda" including matters such as[82]

- Financial Conglomerates
- Offshore Centres
- Highly Leveraged Institutions (HLIs)
- Moral Hazards
- Exchange Rate Stability
- Short-Term Capital Flows

---

[81] *See generally*, International Financial Sector Reform: Standard Setting and Infrastructure Development, 2002, ed. by S. Goo, D. Arner, and Z. Zhou (The Hague: Kluwer Law International)..

[82] *See* generally R. Lastra, *Reform of the International Financial Architecture* (Kluwer/London 2000).

- Regional Responses to Financial Crises
- Reform of the IFIs
- Interaction of International Standards and the WTO/GATS Financial Law and Process
- An Educational Infrastructure
- The Social Safety Net Component
- Supervision of Global Banks and Banking/Financial Organizations

In a practical sense, there will be no one comprehensive and defined "new financial architecture," but a loose, yet complex construct for seeking long-term domestic, regional, and international stability and equilibrium in financial and other economic markets.[83] Looked at it another way, the NIFA terminology, while vague, serves as a critical "code word" or point of reference for coherency, meaning, effectiveness, and some semblance of structure within what essentially has become a highly fragmented, volatile, yet interconnected network of financial markets/systems (i.e., a "non-system").

More particularly, the period from 1986 to the present has been one of strengthening of regulation and supervision of financial institutions and markets, with the overriding goal of achieving "international standards." Further, in this author's view, the period from 1986 to 1995 was really a period of modernization and search for best practices worldwide. Moreover, the period since the Mexican financial crisis in 1994-95 has seen the beginning of a new period centered on the establishment of minimum internationally acceptable

---

[83] *See* generally *G-7 Cologne Report, supra* note 80, at 7. *See also* Basel Committee on Banking Supervision, *Supervisory Lessons to be Drawn from the Asian Crises* (June 1999); U.N. Executive Committee on Economic and Social Affairs, Toward a New International Financial Architecture (Jan. 21, 1999) (available at http://www.un.org./esa/ coordination/ifa.htm). Cf. D. Folkerts-Landau & P.M. Garber, *The New Financial Architecture: A Threat to the Markets?*, Deutsche Bank Global Research (Apr. 1999) (highly critical review of the NIFA).

standards of public financial law through a process centered on the Group of Seven, the Group of Ten, the Basel Committee on Banking Supervision ("Basel Committee"), the International Organization of Securities Commissions (IOSCO), the International Association of Insurance Supervisors (IAIS), the Joint Forum, the recently formed Financial Stability Forum, and even the largely private International Accounting Standards Committee (IASC)—what may be called the new "international financial groupings"—and the traditional "international financial institutions" such as the International Monetary Fund (IMF), World Bank, and the regional development banks.

Following the recent Asian, Russian, and Brazilian financial crises, attention respecting financial sector reform in emerging economies has focused even more on the importance of developing such standards and upon their implementation into domestic legal systems and regulatory and supervisory practices. The question of whether all of this focus, coupled with the broader ongoing global convergence processes, amounts to a "new international financial architecture" remains an open one.[84] Nonetheless, it is clear that domestic bank regulatory authorities must remain not only the primary subjects and beneficiaries of any NIFA, but these authorities must also take a correspondingly proactive role in the evolving formulation and implementing of this new financial architecture.

II. Selective Supervisory/Regulatory Trends

Supervisory Public-Private Partnership

Global banking supervision has necessarily evolved in a revolutionary but reactionary sense to global and regional crises and systemic market events over the past decade. One common theme of this banking supervision evolution is that as financial institutions, products, and markets become inherently more complex and volatile, the supervisory framework has also become increasingly more complex and interventionist in methodology. As discussed above, the

---

[84] *See* generally A. Sheng, "The New Financial Architecture: Is There a Workable Solution?" 33 *Int'l Law.* 855 (1999); J. Norton, "A New International Financial Architecture: Reflections on the Possible Law-Based Dimensions," 33 *Int'l Law.* 891 (1999).

supervisory initiatives of the Basel Committee and U.S. banking authorities and have generally sounded in "supervisory guidance" on complex activities and structures, and "roadmap frameworks" for the implementation and enforcement of risk management and internal control systems for those activities. This supervisory guidance has increasingly incorporated the concept of "public-private partnership" into bank supervision. This "partnership approach" generally vests the leading commercial banks (i.e., a new "elite corp" of financial institutions) with greater independence and discretion to identify, measure, monitor, and manage the material risks arising from trading book and banking book activities, subject to compliance with qualitative and quantitative parameters. Thus, banking supervision as a paradigm increasingly guides the commercial banks to develop and implement comprehensive risk management and internal control frameworks that are suitable for their particular institutional risk profiles (i.e., a form of "qualified self-regulation"), subject to prudential standards.

The U.S. "risk-focused supervision" approach to large bank supervision has apparently developed in recent years to enable banking authorities to carry out consistent and timely supervisory oversight and understanding of the total bank and bank business line risk management and internal control systems, which arguably has a "risk mitigation" effect in and of itself.[85] This partnership approach correspondingly provides bank supervisors with direct access to review critical information generated by the risk management and internal controls within their constituent banks in a deliberate movement towards "real-time" supervision. Bank authorities increasingly gain access to otherwise "proprietary information" of the bank, including internal and external audits of its most complex activities, and consistent access to senior bank management. In fact, the U.S. banking authorities generally assign "specific supervisory teams" to review and assess the largest and most complex banks,

---

[85] *See* U.S. Comptroller of the Currency, "Large Bank Supervision," in *Comptroller's Handbook for Bank Examination and Supervision* (Dec. 1995); U.S. FRB Division of Banking Supervision and Regulation, *Risk-Focused Framework for Supervision of Large Complex Institutions*, SR 97-24 (SUP) (Oct. 27, 1997).

some of whom are actually resident in domestic and foreign offices of such banks.[86]

There is little question that the leading commercial banks that engage in active and substantial credit and market risk activities, particularly those involving complex OTC derivatives and other off-balance-sheet activities, are increasingly separating themselves from the rest of the global banking community as an "elite class" of banking institutions. The separation is evident in terms of the breadth and complexity of on- and off-balance-sheet activities, as the leading U.S. banks have utilized advances in theoretical finance and information technology to implement more efficient risk management systems across their global business lines and indulge in complex derivatives for dealing profits and hedge accounting benefits. Moreover, as discussed below, these institutions have consolidated through consistent acquisitions of bank and nonbank financial institutions to form "banking conglomerates" with substantial degrees of influence (if not dominance) over the U.S. and global bank supervisory processes. This "public-private" partnership (i.e., this new tier of "qualified self-regulation") between banking authorities and large banks in particular is fairly subtle in scope and application, but nonetheless vastly important for bank regulators/supervisors in both developed and developing countries for establishing effective regulatory and supervisory frameworks for the activities and risks covered by these institutions.

Deregulation, "Reregulation," and the "Business of Banking"

The ability to reasonably define "the business of banking" in the modern global banking context, for business and regulatory purposes, is becoming increasingly difficult, as the characteristics of different types of banks and NBFIs continue to blur. The fact is that, on a global basis, commercial banks are authorized to conduct a wide range of complex financial activities and transactions either directly, through bank subsidiaries, or indirectly as part of larger "holding company" type organizations. For example, in the United States, the perseverance of the commercial banking industry, and bank

---

[86] *See* generally U.S. General Accounting Office, "Risk-Focused Examinations: Regulators of Large Banking Organizations Face Challenges," GAO/GGD-00-48 (Jan. 2000).

regulatory activism, gradually eliminated the substance of the more meaningful restrictions imposed on nonbank activities, such as securities and derivatives activities, over the past 30 years. The banking industry's expansion into new activities was critical to its survival, as foreign bank and NBFI competition generally eroded the significance of traditional credit market activities. Thus, in conducting new activities, U.S. and foreign banks have increasingly attempted to smooth out their income cycles by moving away from interest income and debt securities income to other income sources, particularly syndicated lending, OTC derivatives dealing activities, mergers and acquisitions advisory fees, and proprietary trading income. These banks have also become significant participants in securities and securities-related activities through mergers and acquisitions with NBFIs.[87]

The leading commercial banks are increasingly engaging in complex securitization, OTC derivatives, and other off-balance sheet activities, many of which are designed to implement "regulatory arbitrage" objectives related to capital requirements or specific accounting treatments. These banks also engage in significantly leveraged and complex relationships with highly leveraged institutions (HLIs) such as hedge funds and other counterparties, through OTC derivatives, repurchase agreements, and other credit-related facilities. These complex activities and counterparty relationships render nontransparent the largest banks' balance sheets and financial conditions at any given point in time and subject to the most complex of risks, particularly credit risk, market risk, and operational risk. It is difficult to surmise whether or how banking authorities can actually maintain a comprehensive understanding of the changing risk profiles of their constituent banks in a consistent and timely manner, given that such risk profiles can be significantly altered through off-balance-sheet transactions in a matter of days or even hours. The banking authorities could generally verify that the appropriate risk management and internal control systems are in place "on paper" and perhaps even "in practice" to some extent, but a closer supervisory partnership is necessary to facilitate convergence of bank

---

[87] *See, e.g.*, discussion by J. Norton, 2000, "Conjuring an Elite Corp of Banking Institutions Within a Public-Private Partnership," in *Corporations, Capital Markets and Business in the Law*, ed. by T. Baum, K. Hopt, and N. Horn (London; Boston: Kluwer Law International).

risk management practices with supervisory objectives. Thus, the principal question is no longer whether banks should engage in certain activities or organizational forms, but whether these elite banks are actively and successfully managing the complex risks arising out of the complex activities which dominate the new "banking business."

The clearly ongoing deregulatory trends (especially when combined with trends discussed below respecting banking consolidation and financial conglomeration) have expanded significantly the scope of "banking business" to the point where it is more reasonable to identify what is not within the scope of "banking business." The evolution of "banking business" to financial products and services far beyond deposit-taking and lending activities is the result of fundamental changes which have occurred over a period of years, such as

- the decline in core deposits and proportionate increase in nondeposit liabilities;

- the disintermediation of highly rated corporate borrowers from banks to the capital markets (CP markets);

- the increased lending to smaller and potentially riskier firms and consumers;

- technological advancements that result in enhanced electronic product delivery;

- the significant increase in off-balance sheet (OBS) activities, particularly OTC;

- derivatives activities and securitization techniques;

- the continuous search for fee-generating activities to expand and diversify income sources;

- the gradual reduction of statutory barriers and limitations to engaging in securities and insurance activities through deregulatory activism;

- the gradual inclusion of activities considered by the banking agencies to be as "incidental to" the business of banking or "closely related to banking so as to be a proper incident thereto";

- the sustained efforts to reduce operating costs and compete more efficiently; and

- the increased intra-banking industry and nonbank competition in the U.S. and global credit markets.

The "banking business" has expanded even further through the removal or reduction of many legislative and regulatory restrictions and burdens on bank operations in many jurisdictions, particularly in the United States under the Gramm-Leach-Bliley Act of November 1999 (GLBA).[88]

The advances in information technology, financial engineering, and risk management expertise have also accelerated expansion of the "banking business" in the past decade. The plethora of new electronic payment technologies, global electronic linkages of financial markets, financial derivatives, and asset securitization structures, as well as the rise of internet technologies, e-commerce and e-finance, all challenge the traditional perceptions and functions of banks and other nonbank financial institutions. The question remains whether the future nature of the banking business will be linked to the creation of a symbiotic and efficient series of "portals" for the harnessing, processing, and implementation of such new technologies. These mutually reinforcing trends will consequentially require continued supervisory enhancements and based on the foundations of, among other things, the Basel Committee's New Capital Adequacy Framework: minimum capital requirements, supervisory review of bank capital, and market discipline.

---

[88] *See* Pub. L. No. 106-102, 113 Stat. 1338 (1999). The new organizational structures and financial service activities authorized under the GLBA present the opportunity for banks, insurance companies, and securities firms to make cross-industry and cross-border acquisitions to establish financial conglomerates subject to the umbrella supervision of the FRB and functional regulation of respective regulatory agencies for different component activities (discussed further *infra*).

M&As and Consolidations (Domestic and Cross-Border)

One of the more visible and significant dimensions of the ongoing "globalization onslaught" manifests itself in the increasing globalization of financial markets and capital flows.[89] An integral consequence of and further stimulus for this expanding phenomenon has been the rise of major domestic and cross-border mergers and acquisitions (M&As) of banking organizations. The recent major domestic bank M&As also have substantial cross-border, regional, and global implications.[90]

The global bank "urge to merge" may emanate from a number of specific catalysts, particularly as reactions to financial sector crises and restructuring.[91] However, the major catalyst appears to be more in terms of strategic posturing in an increasingly globalized sector of the world economy. One effect of the cross-border bank M&A trend is the consolidation of global banking institutions (GBIs) into a small category of elite institutions. Another effect is the dramatic reconfiguration of the actual global playing field for GBIs, other global financial institutions (GFIs), and global financial conglomerates (GFCs).[92] The ongoing series of bank M&As has also facilitated a "push" for greater international cooperation among banking and nonbank financial regulators and supervisors, and for appropriate and applicable international regulatory/supervisory standards for financial conglomerates. In this sense, the relevant regulatory/supervisory processes are becoming "globalized" as opposed to national in application.[93]

---

[89] *See, e.g.*, B. Eichengreen, *Globalizing Capital* (1997); Group of Seven, Statement of G7 Finance Ministries (June 1999) (Cologne G7/G8 Summit).

[90] *See, e.g.*, J. Norton, "A Slice of the Global 'M&A' Mania: Cross-Border Bank Mergers and Acquisitions—A View from the U.S. Regulatory and Supervisory Perspective," presented at the International Conference on "Cross-Border Mergers and Acquisitions" (RIL Institute, Cologne, April, 2000).

[91] *Cf.* J. Norton & D. Arner (eds.), *Financial Crises in the 1990s* (London/Kluwer, to be published in Winter 2000).

[92] See generally J. Norton, Devising International Banking Supervisory Standards (1995).

[93] This is primarily evident from the ongoing regulatory and supervisory focus on GFIs and GFCs of the "Joint Forum," consisting of the Basel Committee on Banking Supervision (Basel Committee), the International Organisation of Securities Commissions (IOSCO), and the International Association of Insurance Supervisors

(continued)

However, banking systems, for regulatory and supervisory purposes, still "sound" largely in domestic legal, regulatory, and supervisory frameworks. The tensions and interconnections between domestic and international elements, factors, and concerns thus become readily apparent. The question arises as to whether the domestic regulators should establish a domestic "level playing field" for domestic and foreign banking institutions by the legal and practical imposition of a "national treatment" approach, or apply an international-standard based (but domestically applied) "gateway" for foreign banking institutions to initially enter a jurisdiction (i.e., the supervisory notion of "consolidated supervision"). The related question facing the domestic regulator/supervisor includes, but is not limited to, how should national regulatory processes address foreign bank M&As? What is the appropriate post-M&A supervisory overlay for foreign bank acquisitions, which necessarily involves a mix of domestic and international aspects?

In many ways, the current hype about the cross-border bank M&A trend is "old wine in new bottles," in that similar business, legal, structural, and accounting concerns are being raised that have been raised previously in the United States and other jurisdictions on several occasions over the past several decades. However, the financial values involved today are substantially larger; the driving forces and determining contexts are markedly different; the penetration across traditional geographic and market boundaries seemingly have no limits; and issues such as market interconnections, market valuations, and market discipline are being driven by global forces with significant global implications and consequences. This is clearly the case with the current and continuing "wave" of bank/financial institution M&As.

Thus, in the context of cross-border bank M&A and otherwise, the prevailing pressures and trends today are toward international standards and convergence, whether it is with respect to company law, taxation, accounting, antitrust, or regulatory treatment. These pressures for greater international cooperation and convergence are bringing corresponding pressures for changes to domestic legal, tax,

---

(IAIS) (the "Joint Forum"). *See, e.g.*, Joint Forum, Risk Concentration Principles (Dec. 1999); Intra–Group Transactions and Exposures Principles (Dec. 1999); Supervision of Financial Conglomerates (Feb. 1999).

and accounting systems. Yet the importance of domestic legal and regulatory systems remain primary. As such, there is an increasing importance of the role of conflicts of law (i.e., private international law) for cross-border transactions. Further, an improved and more sophisticated understanding and usage of the comparative methodology will be critical for effective lawyering. Moreover, a comprehensive understanding of the increased complexities of the modern M&As will require a sound interdisciplinary approach which understands business and financial markets, finance and accounting principles, and the dynamics of divergent cultures and enterprises.

Finally, the competent legal analyses of cross-border M&As will require a sound understanding of the evolving trade and investment liberalization framework under the World Trade Organization (WTO). This will be particularly true as to the financial services area respecting the inevitable tensions to arise under the WTO's General Agreement on Trade in Services (and its role as to financial services) vis-à-vis the need to maintain respectable prudential standards.

Regulation and Supervision of Large Complex Banking Organizations

The consolidation of the banking industry through aggressive mergers and bank acquisitions of NBFIs has been quite evident in the United States, Europe, and Japan, and includes both domestic and cross-border M&As. These transactions have occurred for various reasons. For instance, in Japan, the relatively recent mergers and alliances between domestic banks is arguably understood as a "survival response" to ongoing inherent weaknesses in the banking industry. The banking industry consolidation has given rise to a concentrated group of large complex banking organizations (LCBOs, a term coined by the U.S. Federal Reserve Board) that gives true meaning and depth to the term "financial conglomerate" and requires a special form of supervision.[94]

The regulation of LCBO activities and capital adequacy and consolidated supervision of the LCBO proper raises interesting global

---

[94] *See* FRB Division of Banking Supervision and Regulation, *Risk-Focused Supervision of Large Complex Banking Organizations*, SR 99-15 (SUP) (June 23, 1999).

supervisory issues, particularly given the existence of two "diverse" structural models of supervision referenced previously in this paper: the U.K. "single regulator" approach and the U.S. "financial holding company" (FHC) approach enacted under Title I of the GLBA. The U.K. "single regulator" approach is fairly well known, but the GLBA is a relatively new phenomenon that eliminates decades of statutory restrictions among and between banks and NBFIs and various financial service activities. The GLBA authorizes, among many other things, broad affiliations between banks and other NBFIs through the FHC construct. The FHC approach essentially authorizes existing U.S. bank holding companies (BHCs) and foreign banking organizations (FBOs) qualifying as such to elect to convert to FHC status, subject to various "capital," "management," and "community investment" parameters. Upon approval of FHC status, the FHCs may conduct a range of nonbank activities, both including and in addition to those currently permitted for BHCs, such as unlimited securities activities, certain insurance activities, and most importantly "merchant banking" activities (i.e., private equity investment activities).[95]

The GLBA designates the FRB as "lead supervisor" of the FHC consolidated entity, but requires coordination and consultation with the U.S. Treasury Department on implementing certain issues, such as approval of additional activities under the GLBA framework, implementing the "merchant banking" authority, and in determining whether banking or other agencies are the appropriate regulatory authorities for certain financial products containing banking, securities, and/or futures attributes. Perhaps most importantly, the GLBA imposes a "functional regulation" scheme on *other entities* owned and controlled by the FHC. These *other entities* may include national banks and their subsidiaries (including new "financial subsidiaries" owned by national banks that may engage in, among other things, activities not otherwise permitted of the parent bank), regulated and supervised by the OCC; broker-dealers; investment advisers and investment companies; futures commission merchants; and insurance companies. These entities are generally subject to functional regulation by their respective authorities in the securities, commodities, and insurance arenas. The GLBA addresses issues of

---

[95] *See* S.900/H.R. 10 Conference Report, at 2-4 ("GLBA Conference Report").

supervisory "command and control" between the FRB and functional regulatory agencies over the FHC entities by restricting FRB influence over those agencies on most points. The GLBA also raises interesting issues of risk management and capital requirements for the consolidated FHC, particularly noting that functional regulatory agencies impose somewhat different capital and risk management schemes for their respective entities, although some convergence is apparent in certain respects. Notably, the number of U.S. BHCs and FBOs converting to FHC status and taking advantage of the expanded opportunities for new activities was quite substantial at the outset and continues at this time.[96]

Thus, increasingly complex activities and organizational structures will greatly complicate bank supervision and give rise to LCBO supervision as a new component of financial institution supervision in the near future. The leading LCBOs will assert a global dominant presence in both developed and developing financial markets. The sheer size, complexity, and influence of these LCBOs and their cross-border activities raise the issue of whether the discretion and independence vested in them by the Basel Committee and other authorities to develop, implement, and more importantly enforce their own risk management and internal control systems, without closer monitoring and supervisory enforcement, is appropriate. There is little question that financial markets events over the past two years and their negative impact on certain LCBOs and emerging market banks have underscored the challenges involved in adapting risk management systems to new products, customers, and business lines in global and increasingly interrelated markets, and in trusting these organizations to enforce their own risk management and internal control systems.

Supervision of Complex Counterparty Credit Risk

The Basel Committee supervisory guidance following the Asian Financial Crisis of 1997, and the Russian Financial Crisis and Long-Term Capital Management (LTCM) debacle and ensuing financial market turbulence of 1998, has arguably been "reactionary," in observance of incredible and universal breakdowns in LCBO risk

---

[96] *Id.*, at 5–6.

management and market "outlier" volatility events that now seem to periodically define the modern financial markets. The Asian financial crisis, Russian financial crisis, LTCM debacle, and the financial market turbulence arising from these episodes, have generated significant Basel Committee guidance in particular on increasingly complex counterparty credit risk issues. The notion of "counterparty credit risk" in this sense is the credit risk that a lending, trading, or derivatives counterparty will not fulfill its obligations in full on the due date or at any time thereafter. With traditional instruments such as loan assets, investment (debt) securities bonds, or foreign currency forward contracts, the amount that the counterparty is obligated to repay is the full or principal amount, such that for these instruments, the amount at risk is equivalent to the principal amount.

The counterparty credit risk inherent in OTC derivatives, repurchase agreements, and other securities and commodities lending and borrowing arrangements, however, is somewhat different from that of traditional instruments. The OTC derivatives generally "derive" their value from an underlying asset or index. The derivatives credit risk is not equal to the principal amount of the trade, but the cost of replacing the contract if the counterparty defaults. This replacement value changes over time and consists of the current replacement and future (potential) replacement costs. The current replacement cost is fairly straightforward to measure, given the Basel Committee recommendation of using the current mark-to-market value of the contract. The future replacement cost is more difficult to estimate because it is generally a function of the time left to maturity, and the expected volatility and price of the underlying asset, both of which may change considerably over the life of the contract.

The Basel Capital Accord introduces capital requirements for credit risk inherent in categories of loans and other credit exposures, including counterparty credit risk for OTC derivatives. In determining capital requirements under the current Basel Capital Accord, the Basel Committee recommends multiplying the notional principal of an OTC derivatives transaction by a "percentage," called the "add-on," to determine potential replacement value. In 1995, the Basel Committee released a revised "add-on" formula that recognized the risk reduction benefits of "netting," which generally allowed banks to set aside less capital for credit risks.[97] The leading derivatives dealing LCBOs argue that the potential replacement cost is best measured by statistical models that estimate the volatility of the underlying variables, and the effect of movements on these variables on the value of the derivatives contract, to generate "expected exposure" or "worst case" exposure. In any event, following the determination of derivatives credit risk exposures, derivatives dealer banks may or may not require the counterparty to submit to "haircuts" or provide collateral as a means of mitigating this credit risk.

The losses generated by the episodes of financial market stress episodes in 1997–1998, particularly those arising from bank-HLI counterparty relationships, demonstrated that basic credit risk management policies, procedures, and internal controls were insufficient or simply not enforced at the most sophisticated LCBOs. The complexities arising out of these incidents are legion, but the fact is that, particularly in terms of the LTCM debacle, certain LCBO risk management failures, coupled with extreme financial market volatility, unexpected credit spread divergence and market correlations, excessive leverage, and nontransparent counterparty linkages, nearly jeopardized the global banking and financial system. The excessive reliance of LCBOs on certain market paradigms and functions resulted in relative failures to enforce, among other things, bank counterparty credit risk management systems and internal control systems in product, customer, and business lines that experienced significant growth and profitability. In these cases, competition and the pursuit of earnings apparently generated counterparty risk exposures for which existing risk management and internal control infrastructures were neglected or unenforced.

For instance, in the 1997 Asian financial crisis, excessive reliance by LCBOs on implied sovereign guarantees likely caused them to become vulnerable to the deteriorating financial condition of their individual sovereign and private counterparties. The result was substantial losses arising from various credit-related activities. In the 1998 Russian Financial Crisis, excessive reliance on the Russian

---

[97] See Basel Committee on Banking Supervision, The Treatment of Potential Exposure for Off-Balance Sheet Items (Apr. 1995).

government and domestic banks to act as rational counterparties, and on the IMF to rectify unsustainable financial conditions, guided LCBOs and hedge funds to establish an elaborate framework of derivatives trading activities. The derivatives trading largely involved exotic and potentially illiquid products such as credit derivatives and nondeliverable ruble forwards. This framework was based on the unstable Russian currency and interest rate markets, and all but disintegrated with the Russian dollar debt moratorium, which precluded Russian counterparties from paying dollars to other counterparties on their derivatives and repurchase agreements. This in turn caused leading LCBOs to largely renege on their credit-derivatives-related obligations to hedge funds and other banks. This resulted in the immediate recognition of hundreds of millions of dollars in counterparty credit and trading losses.

Finally, in the LTCM episode, overreliance on the use of collateral and counterparty reputation severely compromised the due diligence processes for LCBO credit risk and market risk management. The effective collapse of LTCM, an enormous hedge fund with positions/exposures in many different markets and wide ranging and multifaceted OTC derivatives and leverage relationships across LCBOs and investment banks, could potentially have collapsed financial markets if not for the FRB-arranged "private bailout" of LTCM by its counterparties. These compromises generated yet another elaborate framework of exotic leveraged derivatives trading activities across financial markets that generally unraveled as financial market conditions exhibited dynamic risk characteristics following the Russian crisis.

The Basel Committee and U.S. guidance following these episodes examined the complexities of risk management and recommend "best practices" or "general principles" for implementation at the bank or national supervisory level. The policies and procedures used by LCBOs for counterparty credit risk management and disclosures of such risks were addressed in the following regulatory guidance:

- The Basel Committee guidance following the Long-Term Capital Management (LTCM) episode on highly leveraged institutions in January 1999[98]

- The FRB supervisory guidance issued on counterparty credit risk management in February 1999[99]

- The report issued by the U.S. President's Working Group on Financial Markets on Hedge Funds in April 1999[100]

- The Basel Committee guidance on the management of credit risk issued in July 1999[101]

- The guidance issued by the IOSCO Hedge Funds Task Force in November 1999[102]

- The Financial Stability Forum Report on Hedge Funds and HLIs issued in April 2000[103]

This "public sector" guidance has been visibly supplemented by the development of private sector guidance focusing on, among other things, collateral management practices between HLI counterparties to derivatives and other transactions of the Counterparty Risk Management Policy Group (CRMPG)[104] and International Swaps and

---

[98] *See* Basel Committee on Banking Supervision, *Banks' Interactions with Highly Leveraged Institutions* (Jan. 1999); Basel Committee on Banking Supervision, "Sound Practices for Banks' Interactions with Highly Leveraged Institutions" (Jan. 1999).

[99] *See* FRB Division of Banking Supervision and Regulation, *Supervisory Guidance Regarding Counterparty Credit Risk Management*, SR 99-3 (SUP) (Feb. 1, 1999).

[100] *See* President's Working Group on Financial Markets, Hedge Funds, Leverage, and the Lessons of Long-Term Capital Management (April 1999).

[101] *See* Basel Committee on Banking Supervision, *Principles for the Management of Credit Risk* (July 1999).

[102] *See* Report of the Technical Committee of IOSCO, *Hedge Funds and Other Highly Leveraged Institutions* (Nov. 1999).

[103] *See* Financial Stability Forum, *Report of the Working Group on Highly Leveraged Institutions* (Apr. 2000) (available at http://www.fsforum.org/).

[104] *See* Counterparty Risk Management Policy Group, *Improving Counterparty Risk Management Practices* (June 1999).

Derivatives Association (ISDA).[105] The issues addressed in these reports and guidance include recommendations that LCBOs and banking authorities should undertake to enhance counterparty credit risk management and disclosures. These recommendations also bring focus upon several critical issues: the enhancement of collateral management practices and the implementation of "market discipline" factors to mitigate opportunities for excessive leverage. One of the more important aspects of counterparty credit risk is the ability to obtain information on and measure credit risk inherent in complex counterparty relationships, particularly for OTC derivatives. The effectiveness of counterparty credit risk management systems for OTC derivatives transactions, particularly collateral management as a credit risk protection strategy, were tested to the limits by some of the most volatile financial market conditions ever experienced during 1997–1998.

Thus, credit risk measurement may well be one of the most critical elements in managing complex counterparty credit risk. The only way that banks may meet this challenge is through advances in credit risk measurement techniques and enhanced credit risk disclosure by their counterparties. The only way that banking authorities will understand significant bank counterparty credit risk exposures is through enhanced bank supervisory disclosures of their exposures. These observations are not necessarily mutually exclusive. The banking authorities have adopted the position, through frequent public dialogue and the Basel Committee proposal for a *New Capital Adequacy Framework* (discussed further *infra*), that greater reliance on market discipline, as supported by efforts to improve public disclosures, should be viewed as part of a comprehensive approach to supervising and regulating LCBOs. The utilization of effective market discipline through improved public disclosures will arguably result in greater accuracy of regulatory and market assessments of credit risk and related capital adequacy.

The Basel Committee has recently surveyed "actions taken" by leading LCBOs following its January 1999 papers addressing counterparty credit risk in light of the LTCM episode, and surmised

---

[105] *See* International Swaps and Derivatives Association, *ISDA 1999 Collateral Review* (1999).

that such banks have considerably reduced their exposures to HLIs.[106] The U.S. banking authorities clearly have the authority to require such disclosures for regulatory purposes, and the SEC may develop regulations to effectuate similar disclosures to the "public investor" community. The question is simply whether forcing enhanced disclosures of counterparty credit risk information will be politically feasible, given the proprietary nature of this information.

The issue of enhanced HLI counterparty disclosures of nontransparent items affecting creditworthiness, such as liquidity risk and leverage risk, as a part of market discipline is quite another matter. The LCBOs may utilize effective contractual provisions in credit/derivatives transactions to require HLI counterparties to disclose such information, except that relationship and proprietary information concerns will likely militate against detailed and meaningful disclosure requirements through contract in this respect. The other approach, recently introduced in the United States, is to develop federal legislation designed to effectuate such disclosures, which targets the infamous group of HLI investment vehicles, "hedge funds." In the United States, hedge funds are simply private investment companies or partnerships, typically incorporated in tax haven/bank secrecy jurisdictions (such as the Cayman Islands, Ireland, and Luxembourg), which are structured to be exempt from direct regulation and supervision under relevant financial laws, except to the extent of their exchange-traded activities.

The U.S. Congress introduced the *Hedge Fund Disclosure Act*, H.R. 2924, which rests on the proposition that market surveillance and transparency are the preferred mechanisms mitigating risks posed by hedge fund activities. Hedge funds are indeed significant bank counterparties in OTC derivatives and repurchase agreement transactions, and other credit facilities. The Act purports to require disclosure of high levels of leverage by hedge funds on the assumption that such activities have the potential to affect third parties when such leverage, coupled with significant trading activities and nontransparency, generate conditions that may result in events such as those of September–October 1998. The Act purports to

---

[106] See Basel Committee on Banking Supervision, Banks' Interaction with Highly Leveraged Institutions: Implementation of the Basel Committee's Sound Practices Paper (Jan. 2000).

enhance the market's ability to self-regulate by allowing investors to have access to "timely and accurate" information so that market participants may determine when an HLI becomes "excessively leveraged."

The legislation apparently has the endorsement of the Financial Stability Forum, whose report identified measures to enhance the transparency of all HLIs, including hedge funds, as a key requirement for enhancing market discipline.[107] The Act implements some of the recommendations issued in the President's Working Group Hedge Fund Report, which concluded that the principal policy issue to be addressed involved the use of excessive leverage, and that several measures could be undertaken to reduce excessive leverage among market participants. Under the Act, large unregulated hedge funds would be required to make additional public disclosures regarding their use of leverage. Second, the Act would require all public companies to disclose additional information about their material financial exposures to significantly leveraged institutions, including commercial banks, investment banks, finance companies, and large unregulated hedge funds.

The question is whether such legislation is an appropriate role of government in facilitating "market discipline," and if so, whether the legislative provisions actually implement the Act's official purpose. If the Act implements an appropriate interventionist objective, the problem becomes in defining the nature, scope, and timing of disclosures to be made, and the counterparties to make them (or more importantly the counterparties not excluded from the Act). Notably, the Act excludes pooled funds that are registered with the SEC or operated as Commodity Pool Operators (CPOs) regulated by the CFTC, or subject to the supervision or reporting requirements of a federal banking agency. Aside from political considerations on which counterparties are covered or excluded from the Act, the real question is whether bank supervisory guidance requiring banks to obtain relevant, real-time, and ongoing disclosures from counterparties and introducing limitations on leverage to those counterparties would be more productive than legislation requiring relatively infrequent

---

[107] *See* Statement of Congressman Richard H. Baker, before the Committee on Banking and Financial Services, *Hearing on Over-the-Counter Derivatives, Hedge Funds and Netting Proposals*, U.S. House of Representatives (Apr. 12, 2000), at 3.

regulatory/public disclosure of leverage levels by otherwise unregulated entities would be more appropriate.

OTC Derivatives

The OTC derivatives industry continues to evolve and proliferate at a mind-boggling pace. For instance, the Bank for International Settlements and U.S. Comptroller of the Currency (OCC) recently released their reports detailing the size and diversity of derivatives activities, and these reports represent several significant issues. According to OCC figures, the notional measure of U.S. commercial bank derivatives transactions is nearly US$35 trillion, nearly US$31 trillion of which represents OTC derivatives activities. These activities generate nearly US$2.5 billion in revenues. Bank credit exposures from OTC derivatives exceeds US$395 billion.[108] In a recent speech, FRB Chairman Alan Greenspan, relying on statistics of the Bank for International Settlements, indicated that U.S. commercial banks are the "leading players in the global derivatives markets."[109] The growing size and complexity of banking organizations render banking authority mandates increasingly difficult to achieve, and nearly impossible to understand and evaluate bank OTC derivatives positions and operations.

Thus, OTC derivatives, particularly interest rate, foreign exchange, and credit derivatives, have become essential to bank risk management strategies, proprietary trading activities, international operations, and counterparty relationships. Additionally, the sheer size and leverage involved in OTC derivatives markets has uncertain implications for the global financial system. These implications are certainly demonstrated by the periodic financial market episodes occurring in both emerging and developed financial markets, where financial assets become subject to extreme swings in volatility and value.

---

[108] *See* Opening Statement of Rep. James A. Leach, Chairman, Committee on Banking and Financial Services Committee, *Hearing on Over-the-Counter Derivatives, Hedge Funds and Netting Proposals*, U.S. House of Representatives (Apr. 11, 2000), at 2.

[109] *See* Statement of Mark C. Brickell, J.P. Morgan & Inc., to the Committee on Banking and Financial Services, *Hearing on Over-the-Counter Derivatives, Hedge Funds and Netting Proposals*, U.S. House of Representatives (Apr. 11, 2000), at 2.

There is little question that periods of extreme volatility are accentuated by nontransparent and leveraged OTC derivatives activities. The regulatory concerns to be addressed in this regard include, at the very least, obtaining a clear idea of the nature and scope of bank derivatives dealers' OTC derivative products, particularly those based in exotic instruments and/or illiquid market sectors. The more illiquid and leveraged derivative structures create opportunities for nontransparent "liquidity holes" in financial markets and instruments that lead to periods of extreme market volatility, as well as opportunities for significant counterparty credit risk given the inherent leverage in structures such as the "total rate of return swap." The banking authorities undoubtedly have difficulties in keeping pace with the rate of financial innovation, and its implications for the global banking and financial systems.

Thus, banking authorities may, in the context of market discipline, have the incentive to prod leading bank derivatives dealers to disclose the exact nature and scope of their OTC derivatives activities on a more frequent basis, not just in terms of dollar amounts for given categories. In particular, banking authorities may require bank derivatives dealers, in the spirit of Basel Committee guidance, to disclose the exact amount and nature of more exotic products incorporating leverage and pricing characteristics that could have significant effects on underlying cash and exchange-traded markets. For instance, in the United States, banking authorities could require their LCBOs conducting significant OTC derivatives operations to render such disclosures. The majority of OTC derivatives activities is certainly concentrated in a small number of U.S. commercial and investment banks, so imposing this measure as an aspect of supervisory guidance seems logical at this time. There is little question that requiring such disclosures would represent a significant step toward implementing the regulatory notion of "market discipline."

In the United States, however, such issues have been subsumed by the continuing emphasis of the OTC derivatives industry on legislation to close the remaining "vulnerabilities" in the U.S. financial law framework. The notion of "legal uncertainty" has always been an issue with OTC derivatives, even as these markets developed on the basis of, among other things, regulatory arbitrage and the avoidance of regulation. The "legal uncertainty" primarily relates to certain ambiguous provisions of the Commodity Exchange Act (CEA) which may or may not provide the relevant enforcement agency, the Commodity Futures Trading Commission (CFTC), with jurisdiction to regulate or supervise certain OTC derivatives. The CFTC, in exercising jurisdiction, could potentially declare that certain swaps and other OTC derivatives are actually futures contracts subject to an "exchange-traded" requirement, thus rendering them illegal and unenforceable. The CFTC answered early calls for regulatory clarity by issuing policy statements and exemptions, particularly following the Futures Trading Practices Act of 1992 (FTPA), particularly the Swaps Exemption of 1993, to clarify that certain transactions were not covered by the CEA. The CFTC Swaps Exemption is merely an administrative provision that could be revoked or revised by the CFTC at any time. There are other aspects of "legal uncertainty," such as swaps involving securities prices. If the CFTC were to determine that swaps involving equity prices of individual equities were futures contracts, the Shad-Johnson Accord would preclude the CFTC from issuing an exemption, resulting in such derivatives being deemed as illegal and unenforceable OTC futures contracts. Finally, there remains some legal uncertainty regarding foreign exchange transactions under the so-called Treasury Amendment (a statutory exemption under the CEA), notwithstanding the U.S. Supreme Court decision in *Dunn v. CFTC* excluding OTC foreign currency options from the CEA.

These actions reduced legal uncertainty for some time, but recent occasions under prior CFTC leadership revived the issue in a dramatic sense, including a "concept release" in May 1998 that raised many regulatory and supervisory issues regarding OTC derivatives. The U.S. Congress ultimately introduced "moratorium" legislation preventing the CFTC from taking regulatory action in the OTC derivatives realm, but the "risk posed by legal uncertainty" theme and its threads resurfaced as the principal focus of the industry with renewed vigor.

The President's Working Group on Financial Markets issued an extraordinary report on OTC Derivatives in November 1999.[110] This

---

[110] See President's Working Group on Financial Markets, Over-the-Counter Derivatives Markets and the Commodity Exchange Act (Nov. 1999).

report addressed aspects of this "legal uncertainty" by recommending to, among other things, increase the legal certainty for swaps; revise the so-called "Treasury Amendment" to bring certainty to the scope of the exclusionary language; reform the Shad-Johnson Accord provisions (particularly those limiting single-stock futures contracts); clarify that certain electronic trading systems for excluded swaps and derivatives would not be covered by the CEA; and provide a comprehensive regulatory framework for OTC derivative multilateral clearing systems. The report has been supplemented by proposed legislation, the *Over-the-Counter Derivatives Systemic Risk Reduction Act of 2000*, introduced by Chairman Leach, which incorporates many of the Working Group's recommendations, which include:[111]

- Provide for the establishment of multilateral clearing organizations for OTC derivatives.

- Place all OTC derivatives clearing not performed by a futures exchange or securities clearinghouse under the supervision of the FRB or OCC.

- Provide for uniform resolution of OTC derivatives clearing in the event of insolvency.

- Provide that the regulatory status of or jurisdiction over a given OTC derivatives transaction with any of the institutions defined as "financial institutions" in the GLBA or the Federal Deposit Insurance Act (FDIA) will not render the transaction unenforceable.

- Authorize electronic trading of OTC derivatives by "financial institutions" as defined in the GLBA and FDIA.

- Eliminate "legal uncertainty" by exempting OTC derivatives with financial institutions from conflicting state laws.

---

[111] *See* Statement of Michael A. Watkins, on behalf of the ABA Securities Association, on H.R. 1161, H.R. 2924, and the Regulatory Structure Affecting Over-the-Counter Derivatives Transactions, before the Committee on Banking and Financial Services, U.S. House of Representatives (Apr. 11, 2000), at 5.

Although this legislation arguably focuses on aspects of the "legal uncertainty" debate most suited to implementation under the U.S. banking laws, there seems to be little question on the need or desire to achieve one or more aspects of "legal uncertainty" on these issues in short time. Perhaps the real question is not necessarily whether such legislation should be enacted, but rather to thereafter focus on amending financial laws to provide more regulatory flexibility to the derivatives exchanges. In this regard, the new report of the CFTC Staff Task Force, entitled *A New Regulatory Framework*, argues that the CFTC exemptive powers under the FTPA should be used to establish a regulatory environment that will permit derivatives exchanges to implement "self-regulatory" changes to ensure they remain competitive under real world conditions. The objective of the Report was to shift the CFTC towards an "oversight standard" that limits direct regulation to achieve a degree and scope that is directly related to the characteristics of the derivative product and the type of customer that has direct or indirect access to the market.[112]

The House Banking legislation is supplemented by proposed legislation to amend the insolvency provisions of the FDIA and U.S. Bankruptcy Code with respect to enforcement of OTC derivatives and repurchase agreement transactions for bank and nonbank derivatives dealers and end users. This legislation, entitled *The Financial Contract Netting Improvement Act of 1999*, H.R. 1161, implements certain recommendations set forth in the President's Working Group Hedge Funds Report to address statutory ambiguities concerning, among other things, the netting treatment of certain innovative financial contracts, such as credit derivatives. The proposed Act also removes legal uncertainties regarding the ability of market participants to net one type of exposure against another (i.e., "cross product netting," such as swaps against repurchase agreements) under ISDA "master netting agreements." Similar legislation has been proposed before, largely at the incentive of the banking authorities themselves, on reduction of systemic risk. In reality, such legislation may be necessary, but clearly favors OTC derivatives dealer LCBOs,

---

[112] *See* Testimony of Terrence A. Duffy, on behalf of the Chicago Mercantile Exchange, before the Committee on Banking and Financial Services, *Hearing on Over-the-Counter Derivatives, Hedge Funds and Netting Proposals* (Apr. 11, 2000), at 6–7.

perhaps to the detriment of other counterparties affected by the insolvency process.

III. Portfolio Credit Risk Capital Requirements

The concept of portfolio credit risk management and proposed revisions for a New Capital Adequacy Framework encompass swift financial innovations in the primary and secondary credit markets. The avoidance of large concentrations of credit exposure is a critical aspect of loan portfolio management; most experienced lenders would undoubtedly agree that successful portfolio management involves more than ensuring diversification across a significant number of borrowers. The accepted premise among major LCBOs is that credit risk must be actively managed not only at the individual borrower/counterparty level, but also at the portfolio level. This "public-private partnership" supervisory trend will be given special elaboration in this section.

Evolution of Credit Intermediation

Technological advances have forever changed the "intermediation" aspect of "banking business" with respect to risk management and prudential supervision of large commercial banks. The term "intermediation" used to describe a process in which banks and nonbank financial institutions received depositor and investor funds, and then onlent the funds to businesses and individuals. The loans were held on the books of the bank or NBFI until they matured, rolled over, or entered default/nonperforming status. The term "credit risk" was the primary risk incurred by the bank or NBFI, as interest rate risk was easily managed by ensuring that the contractual interest rate floated with the cost of funds. Over the past 20 years, however, technological and other advances have changed the traditional "intermediation" dramatically at the largest U.S. banks and NBFIs.

The principal financial innovation in this respect is the employment of bank-sponsored "securitization" techniques, which account for a significant percentage of large bank credit activities. Banks securitize a vast range of bank loans, including short-term commercial loans, trade and credit card receivables, auto loans, first and second mortgages, commercial mortgages, lease receivables, and small-business loans. The securitization process has generally transformed traditional intermediation. Of course, securitisation techniques may result in either as much or more credit risk being absorbed by banks than when they engage in traditional bank lending, from bank-sponsored securitization processes, and their participation in providing credit enhancements or "direct credit substitutes" (DCSs), to the special purpose bankruptcy-remote vehicle, or securitization conduit. The DCS value is necessarily derived from the value of the loan asset pool underlying the securitization. The securitization may result in credit risk that is highly "concentrated" within fairly small positions on or off balance sheet of the sponsoring bank. Large banks have developed very sophisticated procedures for measuring and managing credit risks flowing from securitizations, some of which have been modified for use in more traditional on-balance sheet lending (such as credit scoring, a statistical procedure which generates an estimate of default probability for potential loans).

The use of statistical credit scoring is becoming closely related to securitization for various reasons, primarily because it provides consistency in loan underwriting standards and allows the estimation of loss probability distributions for pools of loans being securitized. The estimates of such probability distributions are necessary for ratings agencies to determine the amount of credit enhancement required to achieve a given rating on securities created from securitized loan pools. The banks, in order to develop credit scoring models, need to utilize historical loss data on an appropriate number of homogeneous loan documents. Securitization processes require good data on loss probabilities, and these data require the use of standardized loan documents. Thus, securitization is a widely used application by banks with expertise and information technology capable of measuring and managing credit risk in a sophisticated manner using credit scoring models, and various cost-reduction benefits may be generated by such increasing sophistication. Moreover, the credit scoring and standardization processes will necessarily result in increasing certainty on the estimates of loss probability distributions associated with various loan and asset pools. The increasing certainty of risk is equivalent to increased opportunities to manage and mitigate credit risk. Indeed, as securitization markets evolve and refine for standardized loan products, similar markets will evolve for nonstandardized loan products. Nonetheless, as securitization revolutionizes the bank intermediation process, the sponsoring banks themselves still assume substantial credit risk on the loan pools through credit enhancements.

The introduction of credit derivatives several years ago has spawned dramatic innovations in the securitization market. Credit derivatives are, in a nutshell, on- and/or off-balance-sheet financial instruments that authorize banks to assume or to transfer credit risk on a specified or "referenced" asset or pool of assets. Banks are increasingly using credit derivatives as end users (purchasing credit protection from or providing credit protection to third parties) or as dealers intermediating credit protection. Banks use credit derivatives to reduce credit concentrations and manage overall credit risk exposures.[113]

The credit derivatives market, while fledgling only several years ago, is exploding in growth and diversity, particularly given the state of the Japanese banking system, and Asian and Russian financial crises. Moreover, after years of being a mere subcomponent of asset-backed finance, collateralized bond obligations (CBOs) and collateralized loan obligations (CLOs), have become a significant aspect of the innovations in credit intermediation. Most CBOs and CLOs are cash-flow transactions involving the repackaging of corporate loan or bond pools into one or more securitized tranches of debt securities, and primarily directed toward regulatory capital arbitrage.

The advent of credit derivatives has allowed CBO and CLO issues to overcome various obstacles towards completing these transactions, such as circumventing covenant restrictions that preclude or inhibit loan assignments. Credit derivatives are also being used to synthetically replicate CLOs. In all, the proliferation of credit-based financial innovation among banks, and one of the principal motivating factors of such innovation, regulatory capital arbitrage, has reached the point where credit risk, risk-based capital treatments, and other supervisory issues are now primary concerns of the banking authorities.[114] The top LCBOs have invested heavily in

---

[113] *See* FRB Division of Banking Supervision and Regulation, *Supervisory Guidance for Credit Derivatives*, SR 96-17 (GEN) (Aug. 12, 1996).

[114] *See, e.g.*, Office of the Comptroller of the Currency, Federal Deposit Insurance Corporation, Board of Governors of the Federal Reserve System, and
(continued)

technology and expertise to refine these techniques in various respects, one of which is to measure portfolio credit risk.

Basel Committee Guidance on Portfolio Credit Risk and Capital Requirements

The leading banking authorities conduct supervisory oversight on a number of aspects of banking business credit risk. These aspects include capital requirements, credit-granting standards, and the credit monitoring process; the assessment of asset quality and the adequacy of loan loss provisions and reserves; risk concentrations and large exposures; and connected lending and country and transfer risk.[115] The Basel Committee has issued substantial guidance addressing problematic practices on various aspects of portfolio credit risk management (including but not limited to the HLI counterparty credit risk context) and derived "principles" to address those practices. This guidance is largely derived from poor credit risk management and "regulatory arbitrage" practices that generated significant bank exposures arising from the Asian Financial Crisis.[116] This guidance addresses, among other things, Loan Accounting and Disclosure[117] and Credit Risk Disclosure.[118]

The more important Basel guidance, of course, arises from the proposed revisions to the Basel Capital Accord, introduced in June 1999 as the *New Capital Adequacy Framework*.[119] The problems associated with and usefulness of the current Basel Capital Accord, a relatively simplistic approach to capital requirements for credit risk

---

Office of Thrift Supervision, *Interagency Guidance on Asset Securitization Activities* (Dec. 1999); FRB Division of Banking Supervision and Regulation, *Capital Treatment for Synthetic Collateralized Loan Obligations*, SR 99-32 (SUP) (Nov. 17, 1999).

[115] *See* Basel Core Principles, *supra* note 21, at Principles 7–11.

[116] See, *e.g.*, Basel Committee on Banking Supervision, Supervisory Lessons To Be Drawn from the Asian Crisis (June 1999); Basel Committee on Banking Supervision, Capital Requirements and Bank Behavior: The Impact of the Basel Accord (Apr. 1999).

[117] *See* Basel Committee on Banking Supervision, *Sound Practices for Loan Accounting and Disclosure* (July 1999).

[118] *See* Basel Committee on Banking Supervision, *Best Practices for Credit Risk Disclosure* (July 1999) (consultation paper).

[119] See Basel Committee on Banking Supervision, Consultative Paper on a New Capital Adequacy Framework (June 1999).

derived from political compromise, have been well documented over the past several years. The credit-risk-based requirements of the Basel Accord were developed on the bases of establishing minimum capital requirements after a long decline in bank capital levels, and without the technology of credit risk measurement and complex securitisation and credit activities that are prevalent at this time. The "standardised framework" approach originally proposed (but soon disregarded for market risk that is still effective for credit risk) is becoming fairly problematic as banks, using their own internal capital allocation procedures, account for the vast range of credit risk characteristics of different credit instruments.

The new capital framework consists of three "pillars": *minimum capital requirements*, which endeavor to develop and expand on the standardized rules established in the 1988 Capital Accord; *supervisory review* of a bank's capital adequacy and internal credit risk assessment process; and the effective use of *market discipline* to enhance disclosure and otherwise promote safe and sound banking practices. These three elements are to be the critical "pillars" of an effective bank capital framework. The Basel Committee also sought to develop an alternative approach for establishing minimum capital requirements at certain banks, based on the banks' internal credit rating systems.

The objective of the first pillar, minimum regulatory capital requirements, is to establish a more comprehensive and risk-sensitive treatment of credit risk. The Committee considered a modified version of the current Accord, the use of banks' internal rating systems, and portfolio credit risk models, in this process. The Committee proposed to replace the current approach with a system using external credit assessments for determining risk weightings for sovereign credit risks, and, either directly or indirectly and to varying degrees, the risk weightings of exposures to banks, securities firms, and corporations. This approach would result in reducing risk weightings for high quality credits, and increasing risk weightings for certain low quality credits.

The Committee also introduced, among other things, a new risk weighting mechanism for asset securitization exposures. The Committee further recognized that the current Capital Accord does not incorporate appropriate incentives for *credit risk mitigation techniques*, such as collateral management programmes, and further that the Accord may not have enhanced the development of certain forms of mitigation by imposing restrictions on the type of *hedging activities* that may be acceptable for reduction of capital requirements. The Committee, therefore, proposed to establish an approach for capital treatment of credit risk mitigation techniques.

Notably, the Basel proposals generally formulate a *revised standardized approach* for establishing capital requirements at most banks. The Committee also recognized that the *internal credit rating systems* at certain banks may be an acceptable basis for establishing capital requirements, subject to supervisory approval and compliance with certain quantitative and qualitative standards. The Committee proposed to set forth a more rigorous analysis of these issues and others not addressed herein in its proposals and in future "consultative" documents.[120]

The second pillar of the new framework, the *supervisory review of capital adequacy*, seeks to ensure that a bank's capital position and strategy is consistent with its risk profile and encourages "supervisory intervention" if the capital position and strategy do not provide sufficient protection against credit risk. The Committee opined that supervisory authorities should have the unilateral authority to require banks to reserve capital in excess of the minimum capital ratios. The Committee emphasized that development of an internal capital allocation and assessment process, and the establishment of capital targets reflective of the bank's specific risk profile and internal control environment, should be addressed by senior management, and thereafter subject to supervisory review and intervention as appropriate.

The third pillar of the framework, *market discipline*, is offered by the Basel Committee as an important lever in strengthening banking systems. The Committee asserted that effective market discipline

---

[120] For instance, the Basel Committee also sought to expand coverage of the Capital Accord to incorporate other significant risk categories. The interest rate risk in the banking book and other risks, such as "operational risk," have not been specifically addressed in the Accord to date. The increasing significance of these risks resulted in their proposed incorporation into the New Capital Adequacy Framework.

requires authorities to develop a framework for the disclosure of reliable and timely information on capital structure, risk exposures, and capital adequacy, to enable market participants to conduct meaningful risk assessments. The Basel Committee has recently augmented discussion on incorporating the "market discipline" pillar into the new capital framework.[121] The Basel Committee is expected to introduce subsequent guidance on various other aspects of the New Capital Adequacy Framework, including the treatment of securitization transactions, and more focused guidance on internal credit ratings following its comprehensive review of current bank practices in this area.[122]

The regulatory questions, therefore, become how banks should measure credit risk for banking and trading book activities, on a portfolio basis. The measurement variable is critical for determining the process by which banking authorities will impose credit-risk-based capital requirements in the near future. The measurement variable necessitates, among other things, consideration of measurement on *portfolio(s)* of credit risk on a bank-wide, business line, or product basis. Methods of credit risk "hedging" methodologies, through credit derivatives or other risk mitigation techniques, will be acceptable for measurement and capital adequacy purposes.

Credit Risk Measurement

The credit risk of a loan or other exposure over a given period generally will involve the *probability of default* (PD) and the percentage of the loan's value that may be lost for a given *default event* (DE). The DE is usually specific to a given credit transaction or facility because it necessarily depends on the structure of the transaction or facility. The PD is generally associated with the borrower, instead of the transaction, on the basic assumption that the borrower will default on all credit obligations if it defaults on an individual obligation. The end product of PD and DE is the expected loss (EL) on the exposure, which represents an estimate of the

---

[121] *See* Basel Committee on Banking Supervision, A New Capital Adequacy Framework: Pillar 3—Market Discipline (Jan. 2000).
[122] *See* Basel Committee on Banking Supervision, *Range of Practice in Banks' Internal Ratings Systems* (Jan. 2000) (discussion paper).

average percentage loss rate over time on a pool of loans having the given expected loss.

Starting with the above points as a beginning premise, leading LCBOs are using increasingly sophisticated statistical techniques to measure credit risk. Banks are using these techniques to design and voluntarily implement consistent rule-based frameworks for allocating capital to cover the measured credit risks in a "risk-adjusted return on capital" (RAROC) format similar to the RAROC framework developed by institutions such as Bankers Trust for market risk in the 1990s. The banks are necessarily utilising RAROC processes for credit risk for internal business purposes.

In understanding how much capital should be internally allocated to any particular credit activity based on the measured risk level for that activity, a bank may determine the rate of return on that allocated capital to cover the associated risk. If the rate of return is insufficient, the bank may take appropriate actions from the capital deployment perspective.

The RAROC processes are also helpful in pricing credit activities and products, although the decision to follow RAROC in making a particular decision may be biased in favor of market share or competitive pressures. There is little question that the internal RAROC processes of banks often differ to the extent of resulting in a range of different internal capital allocations, even for specific categories of credit product or activity. The differences in internal capital allocations necessarily lead to "regulatory capital arbitrage" (RCA) activities, often through the evolution of credit products, such as credit derivatives and DCSs, which themselves raise complex issues of properly measuring credit risk and allocating capital to cover those risks.[123]

In the pursuit of increasingly sophisticated capital requirements to address these issues, banking authorities will likely not be able to encapsulate the complex risk positions that banks actually engage.

---

[123] *See* Remarks by Janet L. Yellen, Board of Governors of the Federal Reserve System, *The "New" Science of Credit Risk Management at Financial Institutions*, Conference on Recent Developments in the Financial System, Jerome Levy Economics Institute of Bard College (Apr. 11, 1996) (on file with author).

The complexity of credit risk positions and diversity among banks in measuring and managing credit risk leads to the presumption that a "standardized framework" for credit-risk-based capital requirements is inappropriate. The banking authorities are increasingly moving towards implementation of a "large bank supervision" framework. These frameworks focus on each individual bank, whereby teams of regulatory experts are assigned to each bank, obtain access to "proprietary information" (senior management, internal records, and reports), examine its risk management and internal control systems, and supervise its activities and compliance with legal and regulatory requirements, including capital requirements. The critical focus of this supervisory framework is risk management, and ensuring the effective measurement of credit risk. The risk management examinations must necessarily focus on, among other things, the techniques used to measure credit risk, and engage in efforts to remain on the "cutting edge" of, and be able to articulate what generally constitutes the "best practices" of credit risk measurement. This may be difficult, given the newly evolving technologies for quantifying bank portfolio credit risk across all credit activities and products.

Of course, as the recent Basel Committee capital proposal and industry reviews suggest, internal credit ratings are becoming increasingly important in credit risk management at large complex global banks. The bank internal ratings are similar to those developed by credit rating agencies, in addressing the risk of loss due to borrower payment defaults. The bank rating systems are somewhat different from those used by rating agencies, however, in both design and application, particularly because these ratings are used for internal purposes as opposed to public benchmarks. The rating systems used by banks differ markedly among banks as well, in terms of the number of grades and risks associated with each grade, and the assignment and review of ratings.[124]

The question posed is whether principles may be articulated for the "appropriate" or "best" design and application of credit rating systems by banks. The critical aspect of this question may well be

---

[124] *See, e.g.*, William F. Treacy, *Credit Risk Rating at Large U.S. Banks*, Federal Reserve Bulletin (Nov. 1998), at 897.

whether the rating process will substantially involve elements of human judgment, statistical models, or both, and what the limitations of these elements are for different types of exposures. The more direct question is the role that bank internal credit rating systems will play in the evolving regulatory apparatus for credit risk management, particularly capital requirements.

In the *New Capital Adequacy Framework*, the Basel Committee articulated its intent to address credit risk mitigation techniques in the banking book, and in particular to develop an improved approach to cover collateral, guarantees, credit derivatives, and on-balance-sheet netting. The Basel Committee held a series of discussions with large active global banks on credit risk mitigation techniques, their treatment under the Accord, and other individual issues, and issued substantive guidance on credit risk mitigation techniques.[125] The Committee observed that various "national characteristics" such as legal, accounting, and regulatory treatments are significant determinants in the use of credit risk mitigation techniques.[126]

The Committee further observed that bank internal analyses of the adequacy of economic capital allocations, as opposed to minimum regulatory standards, are key determinants in this regard. The Committee ultimately determined that collateral and guarantees are the most widely used credit risk mitigation techniques by banks, but that marked differences exist between banks in applying these techniques. The Committee also established that the use of credit derivatives as a technique, such as in providing "maturity mismatched credit protection," will likely become a far more meaningful component of credit risk management in the near future. The factors in selecting credit risk mitigation techniques are inherently focused on "legal enforceability, price, liquidity, credit quality, available of products and counterparties, historical recovery data, ease of structuring and regulatory treatment."[127]

The credit derivatives market may well prove to be the most challenging and complex derivatives market, from legal and

---

[125] *See* Basel Committee on Banking Supervision, *Industry Views on Credit Risk Mitigation* (Jan. 2000).
[126] *Id.*, at 2.
[127] *Id.*

regulatory perspectives. United States banking authorities have issued guidance concerning the regulatory capital treatment of certain products and applications, and use of certain products for risk management purposes.

The end result may approach the development of a framework underscored by the implementation of one or more models for estimating the bank-wide credit loss probability distribution at any given point in time, similarly to the "Value-at-Risk" (VaR) models underlying the Basel Committee Market Risk Amendment of January 1996. As banking authorities begin to accept banks' ability to quantify and manage credit risk, the impetus will be to explore methods to incorporate these abilities into regulatory and supervisory capital standards such as the Market Risk Assessment.

The regulatory position at this time is that credit risk measurement methodologies are apparently not nearly as refined and tested as those for market risk. The Basel Committee did not incorporate the use of credit risk models to measure credit risk in the new capital adequacy framework proposal, but endeavored to continue reviewing this all important issue, which will have a decisive effect on the new framework, in the future.[128] The principal reasons for this include the relative absence of (i) a highly liquid secondary market for commercial loans and other credit products resulting in the inability to reliably estimate loss distributions by directly observing changes in "credit asset" or "credit liability" prices and (ii) historical loss/default data for commercial loans and credit products.

Notwithstanding the regulatory position at this time, there is little question that the increasing emphasis on internal credit ratings will soon merge into the allowance of fully internal credit risk models as leading LCBOs continue investing in advanced credit risk measurement tools and portfolio management techniques that set them apart from the banking industry at large. These LCBOs, armed with statistical expertise, information technology, and sophisticated models, will continue forging new approaches to commercial credit activities that will likely spur the rest of the banking industry to catch

---

[128] The Basel Committee previously conducted a review of leading bank practices in the credit measurement arena. *See* Basel Committee on Banking Supervision, *Credit Risk Modelling: Current Practices and Applications* (Apr. 1999).

up, and introduce even greater uncertainty and complexity in the emerging science of banking supervision.

IV. The Future of Bank Supervision/Regulation

The Basel Committee's guidance on counterparty credit risk and other complex issues, discussed above, illustrates the level of supervisory expertise and implied regulatory powers and resources properly required of our bank regulators/supervisors today in order to implement and enforce a modern supervisory framework. This raises the further question of whether the majority of developed and developing bank supervisors actually possess the expertise and more importantly the authority to develop the "partnership" approach necessary to implement and to enforce this complex and detailed Basel Committee guidance (which largely reflects evolving U.S. banking agencies' doctrine).

The leading bank authorities, particularly the U.S. FRB and OCC, have substantial resources and expertise at their disposal and would probably come the closest to implementing and enforcing the Basel guidance in any meaningful sense. However, the leading banks remain consistently plagued by credit and market risk management failures, and undoubtedly provide significant transactional leverage through OTC derivatives, repurchase agreements, and other credit facilities for other "highly leveraged institutions" (HLIs) to conduct complex trading activities across financial sectors and markets. Finally, as the Basel Committee has repeatedly noted, these banks consistently engage in "regulatory arbitrage" activities, which raises the question of whether banks, which work together in partnership with the Committee in developing guidance, are acting in good faith in implementing their own risk management and internal control systems. There is little question that, given appropriate attention to detail and proper resources, these banks could arguably implement and enforce global risk management and internal control systems to manage such credit, market, and other risks.

From the emerging markets perspective, the complex activities and products and aggressive expansion into new markets by such banks underscores several important concepts. First, the complex "science" of counterparty risk management requiring legal, financial, accounting, and tax expertise is fast becoming an overwhelming component of bank supervision. The emerging market banking institutions and banking authorities themselves need to obtain significant expertise in complex financial structures and products, valuation, and hedge accounting techniques in order to remain competitive and viable in the global financial markets (institutions) and to avoid becoming rendered irrelevant or otherwise overcome by regulatory arbitrage (authorities).

Notably, the Basel supervisory guidance requires close working relationships between banks and their supervisors in a "public-private partnership" that exists in the United States but may not be culturally feasible in many other domestic regimes. Moreover, banking authorities will necessarily require, through legislation or otherwise, the vesting of legal authority to implement and enforce much of the Basel Committee guidance. The bottom line is that emerging market banks and their authorities should develop and achieve working "partnership" arrangements to harness the powers of financial innovation. If this does not happen, leading LCBOs and financial market complexity may well dominate one or both factions. This may relegate domestic emerging market banks to "community bank" status in the global banking community, and leave their authorities unable to cope with future banking or financial crises, which are a near certain by-product of the ever-increasing financial market volatility.

COMMENT

MARK A. CYMROT

Managing for Uncertainty in Central Bank Immunity

The United States welcomes deposits from foreign central banks. In order to encourage these deposits, U.S. law exempts from attachment and execution, "property . . . of a foreign central bank . . . held for its own account" unless this immunity has been waived.[1] Central bank immunity supplements the immunity given by U.S. law to all agencies and instrumentalities of foreign states. Generally, government instrumentalities are subject to U.S. lawsuits only for commercial activity performed in or having a direct effect in the United States; they are immune for governmental conduct.[2] The only property of a foreign state or instrumentality subject to attachment or execution is property used for commercial activity in the United States.[3] Central bank reserves, therefore, have several layers of protection.

U.S. officials are very protective of central bank immunity. The foreign central bank reserves currently on deposit in U.S. banks are a great benefit to the U.S. economy and provide stability to the world economy. In supporting one central bank's claim for immunity, a Federal Reserve Bank official said that if central bank funds were subject to attachment by private litigants, central bankers "might withdraw their dollar assets from this country, thereby destabilizing the dollar and the international monetary system."[4] The lightning speed at which migrating funds destabilized Asian economies recently serves to highlight this threat.

---

[1] *See* Foreign Sovereign Immunities Act, 28 U.S.C. §1611(b)(1).
[2] 28 U.S.C. §§ 1609–1611.
[3] *Id.*
[4] Affidavit of Anthony M. Solomon, President of the Federal Reserve Bank of New York in *Banque Compafina v. Banco de Guatemala*, 583 F. Supp. 320, 321 (S.D.N.Y. 1984).

436 • Comment

Despite these serious concerns, U.S. law of sovereign immunity lacks clarity in some important respects. The Foreign Sovereign Immunities Act "is a marvel of compression," one court said, but then quickly added that the economy of words has led to "considerable confusion in the district courts."[5] In the 24 years since the FSIA was enacted, relatively few cases have been brought against central banks. As a result, the parameters of the sparsely worded immunity section have not been fully defined.

In the zones of imprecision, central bank property can be threatened with attachment or execution. As Thomas C. Baxter, Jr., General Counsel and Executive Vice President of the Federal Reserve Bank of New York, said, a prudent central banker will assess the scope of immunities available. Yet, despite the uncertainties, central banks can engage in most transactions in the United States without risking the immunity to their national reserves, if they take practical measures to avoid problems.

Central Bank Immunity

A key provision in the immunity law is the phrase "held for its own account." In enacting the law, Congress said that funds held for a central bank's own account are "funds used or held in connection with central bank activities, as distinguished from funds used solely to finance the commercial transactions of other entities or of foreign states."[6] In a recent case involving the central bank of Ecuador, the court summarized the evolving rule of immunity as follows:

> Property of a central bank . . . is immune from attachment if the central bank uses such property for central bank functions as such functions are normally understood, irrespective of their commercial nature. . . . Conversely, if an activity is to be regarded as commercial, as distinguished from a central bank activity, it should

---

[5] *Texas Trading & Milling Corp. v. Federal Republic of Nigeria*, 647 F.2d 300, 306 (2d Cir. 1981), cert. denied, 454 U.S. 1148 (1982).

[6] H.R. Rep. No. 94-1487, 94th Cong., 2d Sess. 31, reprinted in 1976 U.S. Code Cong. & Ad. News 6604, 6630.

be an activity of the foreign central bank not generally regarded as a central bank activity.[7]

Applying this distinction, however, is not easy. Central bank activities are not specifically enumerated in the U.S. statute and many of the bedrock central bank functions may be commercial in nature.

For instance, parties seeking to attach central bank property may argue that depositing government reserves in an interest-bearing account in the United States is a commercial activity. No court has specifically addressed this issue. In determining whether an activity is commercial, the courts look to its nature, not its purpose.[8] The U.S. Supreme Court, for instance, has held that Argentina and its central bank engaged in commercial activity when the bank issued government bonds as a component of a program designed to control the country's critical shortage of foreign exchange.[9] In deciding that the bonds were commercial in nature, the Supreme Court said that:

> the question is not whether the foreign government is acting with a profit motive or instead with the aim of fulfilling uniquely sovereign objectives. Rather, the issue is whether the particular actions that the foreign state performs (whatever the motive behind them) are the type of actions by which a private party engage in "trade and traffic or commerce."[10]

The court, thus, reasoned that since Argentina's bonds were "garden-variety debt instruments," the government and central bank had engaged in commercial activity.[11] A party attempting to attach central bank funds thus may assert that since private parties deposit funds in interest-bearing accounts, depositing central bank reserves constitutes a commercial activity.

---

[7] *Weston Compagnie de Finance et D'Investissement, S.A. v. La Republica del Ecuador*, 823 F. Supp. 1106, 1112 (S.D.N.Y. 1993) (quoting from Ernest T. Patrikis, "Foreign Central Bank Property: Immunity from Attachment in the United States," 1982 *University of Illinois Law Review* 265, 277).

[8] 28 U.S.C. §1603(d) states: "The commercial character of an activity shall be determined by reference to the nature of the course of conduct or particular transaction or act, rather than by reference to its purpose."

[9] *Republic of Argentina v. Weltover, Inc.*, 504 U.S. 607 (1992).

[10] *Id.* at 614.

[11] *Id.*

Even property found to be used for commercial activities will be immune if it is used for a central bank function. Courts, however, have not definitively enumerated the scope of central bank functions. Court precedents and commentators provide guidance in developing a list of generally accepted central bank activities. They include supervising the banking system, making loans or acting as the lender of last resort to depository institutions, acting as fiscal agent for the government, holding deposits or managing reserves of the government, acting as the government's bank, including making and receiving payments, issuing, redeeming, and paying interest on government bonds, issuing legal tender currency, formulating and implementing monetary policy, and imposing credit controls and exchange restrictions.[12] This list is not exhaustive; many central banks have additional functions.

Some transactions are easier for courts to categorize than others. There is no doubt that maintaining the national reserves in U.S. bank accounts is a protected function. It is the very reason for central bank immunity. In enacting the immunity law, the Congress stated that, "if execution could be levied on [central bank deposits] without an explicit waiver, deposit of foreign funds in the United States might be discouraged. Moreover, execution against the reserves of foreign states could cause significant foreign relations problems."[13] This rule is not difficult to apply. An account in the name of the central bank is owned by the central bank.[14] The funds in a central bank account generally belong to the bank and not its depositors.[15] In a dispute

---

[12] Ernest T. Patrikis, "Foreign Central Bank Property: Immunity from Attachment in the United States," 1982 *U. Ill. L. Rev.* 265, 274 (1982); *Finanz AG Zurich v. Banco Economico SA*, 192 F.3d 240 (2d Cir. 1999); *Bank of China v. Wells Fargo Bank & Union Trust Co.*, 209 F.2d 467 (9th Cir. 1953); *Republic of Panama v. Citizens and Southern International Bank*, 682 F. Supp. 1544 (S.D. Fla. 1988); *Republic of Panama v. Republic National Bank of N.Y.*, 681 F. Supp. 1066 (S.D.N.Y. 1988).

[13] H.R. Rep. No. 94-1487 *supra* note 6 at 31, reprinted in 1976 U.S. Code Cong. & Ad. News at 6630.

[14] *Bradford v. Chase Nat'l Bank of City of New York*, 24 F. Supp. 28, 37 (S.D.N.Y. 1938), *aff'd*, 309 U.S. 632 (1940).

[15] *Bank of Credit and Commerce International (Overseas) Limited v. State Bank of Pakistan*, 46 F. Supp.2d 231, 238 (S.D.N.Y. 1999); *Banque Compafina v. Banco de Guatemala*, 583 F. Supp. 320, 321 (S.D.N.Y. 1984).

where competing governments in Panama sued U.S. banks holding the central bank deposits, the court said:

> While BNP [Panama's central bank] as an entity certainly owes certain fiduciary duties to those private individuals and entities which have deposited funds in the bank, this does not change the fact that the defendants are holding funds "from or for the account of the central bank." . . . The defendants are not holding funds in BNP's name "from or for the account"of each of BNP's private depositors.[16]

Thus, unless central bank immunity has been waived, a creditor holding a judgment against the government cannot collect from central bank accounts in the United States, even if the only funds in the account came from government deposits.

Courts may have more difficulty when the central bank is conducting commercial operations for the government or private parties. A case brought by a creditor against the Ecuador central bank illustrates the point. The court lifted an attachment order on funds received by the central bank for the Ecuadorian telephone company in payment of its worldwide services.[17] The court found that "the performance of general banking and agency services for its government is a function of a central bank."[18] The court, however, refused to lift the attachment on funds received as an intermediary for private parties in Ecuador. The court said that "the Central Bank is acting, with respect to such funds, just as would any ordinary bank in transmitting the funds of one private party to another."[19] Many central banks, however, perform this same function for private parties and consider it a central bank activity. For instance, ALADI is an association of Latin American central banks to facilitate payments among private parties in their countries.

---

[16] *Republic of Panama v. Citizens and Southern International Bank*, 682 F. Supp. 1544, 1547 (S.D. Fla. 1988).
[17] *Weston Compagnie de Finance et D'Investissement, S.A.*, supra, 823 F. Supp. at 1115.
[18] *Id.* at 1113.
[19] *Id.* The court ordered additional briefing on the issue of whether the Uniform Commercial Code, § 4-A-503, prohibited the attachment of funds in an intermediary bank. *Id.* at 1115.

One court held that Banco de Guatemala's funds in a New York bank were used for central bank activities even though the bank was negotiating loans from several nations' export-import banks and from foreign commercial banks.[20] Another court held that the central bank of Nicaragua did not engage in commercial activity when it stopped payment on a check that it issued to provide foreign exchange to honor a certificate of deposit issued by a Nicaraguan commercial bank. The court found that the central bank was acting to conserve foreign exchange during a crisis, which was a central bank function.[21]

The challenge presented in defining central bank functions is shown by the treatment of letters of credit. At least one court has held that making and receiving payments seem to be central bank activities.[22] However, the Committee on International Law of the New York City Bar commented during the legislative hearings that "a central bank which issues letters of credit in commercial transactions should not be granted immunity for its assets used for that purpose."[23] One court has now agreed with this opinion.[24]

Thus, until the courts or Congress more fully enumerate central bank functions, some uncertainty will remain in the breadth of central bank immunity. The prudent approach is to structure central bank activities to minimize risk.

Practical Measures to Avoid Problems

Central bankers can avoid threats to their immunity by recognizing the problem areas and constructing their transactions to

---

[20] *Banque Compafina v. Banco de Guatemala, supra*, note 15,. 583 F. Supp. at 321.

[21] *De Sanchez v. Banco Central de Nicaragua*, 515 F. Supp. 900 (E.D. La. 1981). The logic of this decision was criticized by the U.S. Supreme Court in *Republic of Argentina v. Weltover, Inc., supra*, note 9.

[22] *Weston Compagnie de Finance et D'Investissement, S.A., supra*, note 7 823 F. Supp. 1106. *See also Republic of Panama v. Citizens and Southern International Bank*, 682 F. Supp. 1544, 1547 (S.D. Fla. 1988).

[23] Hearings on H.R. 11,315 Before the Subcommittee on Administrative Law and Government Relations of the House Committee on the Judiciary, 94th Cong., 1st and 2nd Sess. 76 (1976).

[24] *Werner Lehara International Inc. v. Harris Trust Savings Bank*, 484 F. Supp. 65 (W.D. Mich. 1980).

avoid problems. Problems can arise when the central bank (1) acts in a commercial transaction for the government or private parties; (2) mixes funds from different activities in one account; (3) acts as custodian or trustee for the government or third parties; and (4) waives its immunity.

The area fraught with the most uncertainty is when the central bank acts in a commercial transaction for the government or third parties. If the government or third party has unsatisfied creditors, they may seek to attach the funds of the government or the third party through the central bank's accounts in the United States. There are several ways to mitigate this problem.

One approach taken by some countries is to separate the government's banking functions between a central bank and a national bank. The central bank supervises the banking system, conducts monetary policy, and invests the national reserves abroad—functions that are universally accepted as those of central banks. The national bank takes deposits from government agencies and instrumentalities and from private parties, and conducts commercial banking transactions for them abroad. This approach provides a greater assurance that the property used for central bank activities will fall within traditional central bank functions and therefore will be protected by immunity.

The problem with this approach is that it gives the government less protection during a financial crisis. The national bank may not enjoy central bank immunity. As the international financial structure has evolved, some developing countries have found that they face rogue creditors who are aggressive litigants and not interested in negotiating debt restructurings.[25] They insist upon being paid in full for debts that they purchase at substantial discounts. One group has sued countries in Latin America and Africa 15 times in the past six years.[26]

---

[25] *See* Mark A. Cymrot, "What Peru's Brady Deal Means for Rogue Creditors," *Latin Finance*, No. 90 (September 1997).
[26] *Elliott Associates, L.P. v. The Republic of Peru*, 12 F. Supp. 2d 328 (S.D.N.Y. 1997), *rev'd*, 194 F.3d 363 (2d Cir. 1999) (rehearing pending).

Panama recently faced one such creditor during its Brady debt restructuring. A rogue creditor purchased Panamanian debt after Panama announced the term sheet for its Brady debt restructuring and then filed suit prior to the closing. The rogue promptly obtained summary judgment.[27] When Panama undertook a Yankee bond offering, the rogue obtained an order of attachment from the New York courts and successfully collected $70 million on debt purchased for less than half that amount. Against these aggressive creditors, the maximum immunity provided by the central bank may be essential to protect the government's assets and its efforts to negotiate reasonable restructuring agreements with commercial creditors.

A second approach to protect immunity is for the central bank to use multiple bank accounts for different activities. Funds used to invest the national reserves can thereby be segregated from funds used for commercial activities. If the funds used for commercial activities are later found to fall outside of the immunity, the central bank reserves will remain unaffected. This approach is advisable because mixing the funds in a single account may result in the loss of immunity for all funds in the account. In a case involving Tanzania, a court held that funds held in an account used for mixed purposes lost its immunity when some of the funds were not immune.[28] Two other courts have rejected this finding, holding instead that only the non-immune funds can be attached even when mixed with immune funds in the same account.[29] However, even this finding raises serious accounting and tracing issues that may make it difficult to segregate protected reserves from other funds. Clearly, the safer approach is to use separate accounts for different purposes.

Yet another approach is to structure transactions, where possible, so that property, as defined by U.S. law, remains outside of the United States. The term "property" has a very specific meaning in U.S. law. An extensive body of law identifies the location of an intangible asset, such as a bank account, certificate of deposit, or a

---

[27] *Elliott Associates, L.P. v. The Republic of Panama*, 975 F. Supp. 332 (S.D.N.Y. 1997).

[28] *Birch Shipping Corp. v. Embassy of United Republic of Tanzania*, 507 F. Supp. 311, 313 (D.D.C. 1980).

[29] *Liberian Eastern Timber Corp. v. Government of Republic of Liberia*, 659 F. Supp. 606, 610 (D.D.C. 1987); *Weston Compagnie, supra.* 823 F. Supp. at 1114.

debt. Many commercial transactions can be structured so that a foreign state or central bank's property never comes into United States, even when the transaction is conducted with U.S. parties.

A few years ago, we assisted the Republic of Peru to privatize $1 billion of stock of the Peruvian telephone company in an international public offering.[30] At the time, Peru was attempting to complete a Brady debt restructuring. Two rogue creditors, who were insisting upon full payment, represented threats to attach the proceeds of the stock sale in New York. If they were successful, Peru's Brady restructuring probably would not have closed because its major creditors were not willing to accept a 50 percent discount if these two creditors were paid in full. Yet, the stock sale could not be delayed without damaging Peru's IMF economic program. With a novel approach, the sale of American Depositary Receipts listed on the New York Stock Exchange was structured so that no Peruvian property entered New York.

Using J.P. Morgan Securities, Inc. and Merrill Lynch & Co. as lead underwriters, the telephone stock was transferred and paid for in Peru. The underwriters sold American Depositary Receipts to their customers in New York and elsewhere. Had the underwriters purchased the telephone company stock in the usual manner, the "debt" that the underwriters owed Peru to pay for the stock would have been attachable at their home offices in New York. The transaction was structured, however, so that Letters of Credit on behalf of the underwriters were issued by London banks and confirmed by a private commercial bank in Peru. As a result, the underwriters never had a debt to Peru; instead, they owed a debt to the originating banks on the letters of credit. This debt due the originating banks was not attachable to recover Peru's debts to its creditors. All obligations to pay Peru, therefore, were located outside of New York and could not be affected by attachment orders in New York.

---

[30] See *Pravin Banker Associates, Ltd., v. Banco Popular Del Peru*, 9 F. Supp. 2d 300 (S.D.N.Y. 1998).

A similar approach or other creative approaches may be used to protect central bank reserves in circumstances where immunity is unclear.

Central banks can also take advantage of the immunity provided to all commercial banks that act as the intermediary in a funds transfer. Under the Uniform Commercial Code, Article 4A, the law in most U.S. jurisdictions, intermediary banks in funds transfers can not be attached. Section 4-A-503 states:

> For proper cause and in compliance with applicable law, a court may restrain (i) a person from issuing a payment order to initiate a funds transfer, (ii) an originator's bank from executing the payment order of the originator, or (iii) the beneficiary's bank from releasing funds to the beneficiary or the beneficiary from withdrawing funds. *A court may not otherwise restrain a person from issuing a payment order, paying or receiving payment of a payment order, or otherwise acting with respect to a funds transfer.*[31]

This section has been interpreted to mean that the intermediary bank in a funds transfer cannot be attached or otherwise restrained from transferring funds.[32] Thus, if the central bank makes payments or receives payments directly for private parties, its account in New York may be attached because it is acting as an originating or beneficiary bank.[33] However, if the third party acts through an account in a local commercial bank, which sends funds abroad through the central bank, the central bank's account in New York cannot be attached.[34] The structure of the transaction, therefore, can protect the central bank's deposits in the United States.

In a recent case, a creditor of the Government of Ecuador and its central bank successfully attached funds in the central bank's account in New York that the central bank had received for private parties in Ecuador.[35] The private parties apparently had accounts directly with the central bank, and therefore, the central bank was the beneficiary's

---

[31] Emphasis added. *E.g.,* N.Y. U.C.C. § 4-A-503 (McKinney 1991).
[32] *Weston Compagnie de Finance et D'Investissement, S.A. v. La Republica del Ecuador,* No. 93 Civ. 2698, 1993 WL 267282, *2–3 (S.D.N.Y. July 14, 1993).
[33] *Id.* at *3.
[34] *Id.*
[35] *Id.*

bank. Since the funds in New York belong to the central bank, the court found that the creditor could attach the funds to satisfy its debt.[36] In the same case, the court held that the creditor could not attach funds when the central bank was acting as an intermediary bank.[37]

Another area of danger for central banks is custodian and trustee accounts. Funds deposited by a government or private party in the central bank belong to the bank.[38] The bank has a debtor-creditor relationship with its customer. The situs of that asset is in the country where the deposit is made. When the central bank takes these funds abroad, they are the funds of the central bank held for its own account and thus protected by immunity.[39] A creditor of the government cannot attach the central bank's account as a means of satisfying a debt of the bank's customer. However, when the bank becomes the trustee or custodian of its customer, title to the funds remain with the customer. These same funds deposited abroad, therefore, are not for the bank's "own account." In that circumstance, the customer's creditor can attach funds in the hands of the central bank.

Waivers are another area of concern. Central bank property loses its immunity from attachment and execution when the central bank or its government explicitly waives the immunity. Waivers of central bank immunity were common prior to the international debt crisis of the early 1980's. Banks routinely demanded waivers and governments gave them in order to obtain credit. However, some governments have recognized the long-term importance of protecting their national reserves. With the growth of the secondary market for emerging market debt, this precaution has become more important. More countries now face rogue creditors who will not negotiate reasonable restructuring terms.

Some governments have attempted to make use of competitive market forces to negotiate loan agreements without central bank waivers. In other cases, the governments have offered other security to avoid the need to waive. For instance, the Brady Plan provides for

---

[36] *Id.*
[37] *Id.*
[38] *Republic of Panama v. Citizens and Southern International Bank*, 682 F. Supp. 1544 (S.D. Fla. 1988).
[39] *Weston Compagnie, supra*, 823 F. Supp. at 1112.

security in the form of U.S. Treasury bonds held at the Federal Reserve Bank of New York. Central banks have not been asked to waive their immunities as part of Brady bond offerings.

Conclusion

The national reserves deposited by central banks in the United States are immune from attachment or execution unless the bank or its government has waived the bank's immunity. Central banks, however, should be familiar with U.S. immunity laws in order to avoid structuring transactions in a way that threatens this immunity. Most transactions can be conducted in the United States, if the bank considers the limits of U.S. immunity statutes.

Chapter 21
Legal Issues Incident to Holding Central Bank Assets Abroad

THOMAS C. BAXTER, JR., AND ROBERT B. TOOMEY

Holding Central Bank Assets Abroad: Why and Where

A primary role of a central bank or monetary authority is the management of its country's foreign exchange reserves. While a central bank may hold foreign reserves for a number of reasons, generally, a central bank retains foreign reserves so that it may be able to move quickly to support exchange rate policies or to redress imbalances in imports/exports. Foreign reserves also allow central banks to diversify their (and their government's) overall reserves into different currencies to permit broader (or, in some cases, safer) investment opportunities. Some central banks may use foreign reserves to influence domestic monetary policy. In any event, threats to quick liquidation of foreign assets threaten this fundamental rationale for holding such assets.

Any investment of the reserves of a central bank, either in a foreign jurisdiction or domestically, should meet the twin goals of security and liquidity. A central bank's foreign currency reserves may be held in a number of different currencies and the choice of currency will reflect the twin goals. Many central banks hold foreign reserve assets denominated in the generally recognized reserve currencies (dollar, euro, yen). The reason for this is obvious: the reserve currencies provide central banks with money markets that are deep and liquid so as not to hamper the implementation of policy objectives. The home jurisdictions of these currencies have active markets in financial trading centers that offer a broad array of safe investment products. The currency of other assets may be determined by local or regional concerns, but any choice of currency must be made on the basis of security and liquidity. Central banks will also pick currencies in jurisdictions with stable political climates and few foreign exchange controls. These characteristics contribute to necessary liquidity. Once the currency is chosen, central banks, like other financial institutions, put their reserves to work by investing in obligations, usually (although not exclusively) in the financial center for that currency. Generally, these financial centers allow the central bank the greatest flexibility by providing a number of safe investment opportunities in deep and liquid markets.

Types of Assets

The types of assets that a central bank may hold are generally limited by domestic statute. These statutes reflect the need for conservative central bank investment policies consistent with the goals of security and liquidity. As a result, many central banks invest currency balances in deposit accounts at either central banks of the country of the chosen currency, at the Bank for International Settlements (BIS), or, depending on credit evaluations, at large commercial banks. Other foreign currency assets may include sovereign debt, certificates of deposit (from central or commercial banks), certain kinds of derivative instruments, repurchase agreements (either with the central bank or with private counterparties), and other liquid investments. A central bank may also hold banknotes of its own currency in offshore centers to provide for the international demand for the currency. This latter asset, while not technically speaking a foreign reserve, does represent an asset held outside the home jurisdiction and may be subject to the legal risks discussed below.

How Assets May Be Held

Use of Intermediaries

Foreign assets may be held in a number of different ways and with different types of intermediaries. As noted above, funds may be held on deposit with other central banks, commercial banks, or the BIS. Central or commercial banks may also act as custodian for sovereign securities owned (either outright or pursuant to a repo or securities lending arrangement) by other central banks.

The type of intermediary presents specific risks to the central bank. A central bank may be exposed to the credit of the institution if the assets are held as a deposit. Because of this risk central banks should be particularly careful about deposits in commercial banks.

The risks when assets are held by a custodian are different and central banks should be aware of the legal characterization of these assets as in custody, and, in particular, the local jurisdiction's insolvency protections.

In addition to the different types of counterparty risk, each of these methods of holding assets also presents specific legal risks. The nature of the intermediary and the service provided implicate a number of legal issues, including capacity and authority of the intermediary, sovereign immunity, the insolvency protections available to an investor in the event of counterparty or custodian insolvency, the possibility of attachment, and choice of law. Aside from sovereign immunity, these issues are the same any financial institution would have to address when holding assets outside of its home jurisdiction and due diligence should be at least as thorough as that performed by other financial institutions active in the same market.

Capacity of Central Bank

Central banks must consider in what capacity assets are to be held. In particular central banks must consider how to hold assets that are, in fact, beneficially owned by another party. Often central banks that are organized as entities independent of their governments may serve as fiscal agent for their governments and be entrusted with the management of government foreign reserves that may be distinguished from central bank reserves. The government, in these cases, may have investment discretion with respect to its assets and the central bank may merely be in the position of executing governmental instructions. Alternatively, the central bank may exercise a fair amount of discretion in the investment of government assets even if it is not the beneficial owner of such assets. Central banks may also serve as fiscal agents for other entities (governmental agencies and other quasi-governmental or government-sponsored entities) and may (as has been the case with the Federal Reserve Bank of New York) serve as collateral agents in connection with public sector bond restructuring. It is therefore important for central banks to determine whether, and to what extent, they should disclose the capacity in which assets are held. There are different legal risks to each method and the treatment of the assets may be different under local law.

Legal Issues

Issues Identified

A number of legal issues confront central banks holding assets abroad. The legal risks are minimal in some jurisdictions, while in others the risks may be significantly greater or the legal protections available are uncertain. The significant legal risks are (1) attachment and execution; (2) asset freezes; (3) uncertainties surrounding sovereign or central bank immunity; (4) notice of litigation involving assets; (5) specific counterparty and custodian legal risk; and (6) choice of law.

Attachment and Execution

A significant legal risk facing central banks with respect to holding assets overseas involves attachment and execution in connection with judgments rendered in that jurisdiction. Litigants may also attempt to attach or execute against central bank assets on a judgment rendered in a jurisdiction foreign to that jurisdiction in which the assets are held.

Attachment refers to the formal seizing or freezing of property to bring it under the control of a court. Litigants may seek to attach assets prior to judgment (prejudgment attachment) in order to ensure that assets are available in the jurisdiction to satisfy an eventual judgment. Attachment of assets after judgment (postjudgment attachment) provides a means of executing on the judgment. Execution on assets after receiving a judgment results in a total loss of those assets and title moves to the claimant. Obviously, any attachment, either prejudgment or postjudgment, largely defeats the liquidity objective. Furthermore, while attached assets may after a time become unencumbered, assets which are executed on become lost and unrecoverable. If a central bank's assets were subject to attachment or execution in a jurisdiction, the twin goals of security and liquidity would be defeated. A central bank that does not assess this risk and appropriately plan for it and minimize it could jeopardize its ability to fulfill its policy mandates and, indeed, subject its assets to permanent loss.

Asset Freezes

In addition to judicial attachment or execution, central banks need to be aware of governmental action that could result in assets held abroad being frozen. The most notable example of this occurred in the late 1970s when President Carter issued an Executive Order freezing all Iranian assets in the United States and abroad. Some $12 billion in assets were frozen, thus diminishing their liquidity to zero. The problems associated with the freeze (from the Iranian perspective) were further exacerbated as judicial attachments of a large portion of the frozen assets were put in place. Freeze orders may lawfully be followed by banks, including a central bank, situated in the country issuing the freeze.[1] As noted below in the context of sovereign immunity, central banks take on certain political risks of the countries in which they hold assets.

Sovereign or Central Bank Immunity

In order to evaluate the particular legal risk to assets held abroad posed by attachment/execution risk, a central bank needs to assess the scope of any immunities that may be available. Particularly relevant, given the functions performed by central banks, is sovereign immunity. In some important financial centers, statutory protections have been provided for most of the typical functions performed by central banks, and for central banks specifically. These protections extend to assets held in those jurisdictions as well as to protection from suit. Statutes in the United States and United Kingdom are the most notable examples of this approach. Note also that Swiss law provides specific statutory protections for central bank assets held at the BIS.[2] Other jurisdictions appear to rely on developing international law precedents that appear to allow for some central bank immunity, although the scope and strength of these precedents in any given jurisdiction may be unclear and subject to judicial review. A final group of jurisdictions have older internal precedents denying central banks immunity if the central bank is organized as an entity separate and independent of the government, and it is not clear whether courts in these jurisdictions would rely on more recent

---

[1] *Bank Markazi Iran v. Federal Reserve Bank of New York*, Award No. 595-823-3 (Iran-U.S. Claims Tribunal, Nov. 16, 1999).

[2] Statutes of the Bank for International Settlements, Article 55, Section 3.

international precedent granting limited immunity to central banks. Finally, central banks need also to be aware of the political risk, particularly the stability of the political system in any jurisdiction and the possible impact of foreign policy considerations, on immunities that might be available. An evaluation of the approaches to immunity, and the risks they pose in a jurisdiction may cause central banks to relocate assets to jurisdictions that provide the safer and more certain environment.

Note that there are two types of sovereign immunity that need to be considered: immunity from suit and immunity from attachment. Immunity from suit protects a central bank from being sued in the courts in a jurisdiction without the consent of the central bank. Immunity from attachment protects assets from actions based on judgments received either in that jurisdiction or in some other forum. While these types of immunities may overlap, they are not always the same.

What Is a Central Bank?

Central banks vary in both their form and function so it is not always evident when an institution qualifies as a central bank eligible for either sovereign or central bank immunity. Even the statutory provisions for immunity described below do not clearly define what qualifies as a central bank. A number of activities have been attributed to central banks but few institutions that are thought of as central banks perform all these activities. The traditional central bank activities, in addition to the holding of domestic and foreign reserves, include (1) issue of notes, coin and legal tender; (2) custody of cash reserves of depository institutions; (3) discounts and advances to depository institutions; (4) receipt of deposits from the government, international organizations, and depository institutions; (5) open market operations; (6) credit controls; and (7) supervision of banks.[3]

---

[3] *See* Ernest T. Patrikis, "Foreign Central Bank Property: Immunity from Attachment in the United States," 1982 *U. Ill. L. Rev.* 265.

Statutory Approach

The two most comprehensive statutory approaches to central bank immunity are contained in the United States Foreign Sovereign Immunity Act (FSIA)[4] and the United Kingdom State Immunity Act 1978 (SIA).

FSIA

The FSIA specifically protects central bank property from prejudgment attachment and, unless the immunity is explicitly waved, from attachment in aid of execution and from execution. In order for the immunity to apply three major conditions must be met: (1) the entity must be a central bank; (2) the property in question must be held for the foreign central bank's own account; and (3) there must be no waiver of immunity. Assuming that criteria (1) and (3) are met, central banks must be concerned that the assets are held for their own account within the meaning of the FSIA. There is little judicial guidance on this point. While many central bank assets should fit within this provision, questions may be raised about assets that are, in fact, those of the central bank's government or of another agency within the government. This characterization may be important because the protections for government assets and central bank assets in the FSIA are different.

More significantly for purposes of the FSIA, funds held for a central bank's own account are those that are used or held in connection with central bank activities. Unfortunately, these terms do not clearly indicate the scope of the concept of central bank activities, although presumably many activities of central banks will be obvious as central bank activities. The legislative history of the FSIA provides limited guidance on the phrases "held for its own account" or central bank activities, but courts that have dealt with these issues have attempted to take a pragmatic approach by looking for activities that may be "normally understood" as central banking activities.[5] Note also, that a United States court has held the regulation and supervision of a nation's foreign exchange reserves is a sovereign

---

[4] 28 U.S.C. §§ 1330, 1332 (a) (2)–(4), 1391 (f), 1441 (d), 1602–1611.

[5] See, e.g., Weston Compagnie de Finance et d'Investissement v. La Republica del Ecuador, 823 F. Supp. 1106 (S.D.N.Y. 1993) ("Weston").

activity, being one aspect of a government's sovereign function of regulating the money system, and one of the intrinsically governmental functions of a central bank.[6]

There is also some question under the FSIA whether a central bank may waive its pre-judgment attachment immunity. The cases that have addressed this issue have taken the approach that while central banks may explicitly waive post-judgment attachment and execution, pre-judgment attachment may not be waived.[7]

SIA

The approach under the United Kingdom's SIA is similar to that adopted in the FSIA, and it also codifies the restrictive approach. In practice the property of a State's central bank will only be liable to process of execution if it has waived, in writing, its immunity from execution. The SIA provides that central banks are immune from the jurisdiction of the courts of the United Kingdom if the action of the central bank relates to anything done in the exercise of sovereign authority and the circumstances are such that a state would have been immune. The test of what constitutes a governmental act is whether the act was of its own character a governmental act as opposed to an act which any private citizen could perform.[8] Note that this test is not the picture of clarity in that many acts that are governmental in purpose may be done by private citizens for an entirely different purpose.

With respect to attachment of property, subject to waiver, a central bank's property is not subject to any process for the enforcement of a judgment or arbitration award. This is true even if the central bank had no jurisdictional immunity from suit as described above.

Developing International Case Law Approach

Results in jurisdictions without statutory guidelines may be similar to those in the United States or United Kingdom, although

---

[6] *De Sanchez v. Nicaragua*, 770 F.2d 1385 (1985).
[7] See Weston.
[8] Kuwait Airways Corp. v. Iraqi Airways Co. [1995] 1 WLR 1147.

without specific statutory guidance there is less certainty. The courts in these jurisdictions have recognized, in differing ways, the restrictive theory of sovereign immunity. Restrictive sovereign immunity contrasts with absolute immunity and represents an attempt by courts to provide for the multiplicity of agencies and instrumentalities that have developed in recent years engaging in activities fairly characterized as sovereign in nature. The absolute theory of immunity provides immunity for all activities (and assets) of the sovereign notwithstanding that the activities and assets of the sovereign were arguably commercial in nature. The absolute approach looks at the nature of the institution to determine immunity eligibility rather than at the nature of the activities. Activities of a clearly commercial nature are treated the same as sovereign acts. Under this approach central banks with a juridical existence separate from the government do not receive immunity because they are not part of the government. It matters little that the central bank performs functions that traditionally have been thought of as those of a sovereign. Under this approach assets that the central bank invests as agent for its government may enjoy the immunities available to the government, but such assets should be clearly earmarked as governmental assets in order to get any protections available. Even if assets are not earmarked, an attachment may be voidable upon a showing that the assets are in fact those of the government.

The restrictive approach looks at the nature of the activity and pays less attention to the type of institution. Under the restrictive approach, a central bank will be immune so long as the activities in which it engages may not be characterized as commercial in nature. Just as in the FSIA situation noted above, what constitutes a commercial activity is not always clear and international case law provides a number of different approaches. It is important for central banks to assess the state of the law in a particular jurisdiction to determine whether an activity or the use to which its assets are put is commercial.

Determining whether assets are commercial or sovereign

While some activities of central banks clearly are of a sovereign nature, others fall into a gray area. As noted above, a court has held the regulation and supervision of a nation's foreign exchange reserves a sovereign activity, being one aspect of a government's sovereign function of regulating the money system, and one of the intrinsically governmental functions of a central bank.

Problems arise when the central bank engages in activities that are on their face commercial in nature but have some connection in their purpose to governmental or public function activities.[9] Investments or activities that provide financing for building or for some other governmental enterprise such as a governmentally owned public utility may be commercial activities. Because of these areas of doubt central banks should consider ways to more clearly earmark assets that are used for sovereign purposes. Whether accounts containing such assets should contain an identifying rubric and whether such a rubric or other identifying mark would be helpful in litigation should be investigated with counsel from the jurisdiction where the accounts are located.

Mixed-use assets

Note also that a central bank may hold assets in accounts that are for mixed purposes, both sovereign and nonsovereign. How a local jurisdiction approaches these situations is important to the security of the assets. A central bank should be aware of the best approach to protect mixed assets. Also, a central bank should determine whether a jurisdiction will treat an account with some nonsovereign use assets as somehow completely tainted and open to attachment. Alternatively, a court may seek to trace commercial assets into an account.

Other Approaches and Immunity Issues

Absolute theory of sovereign immunity

Some jurisdictions, particularly those in which the issue has not been formally addressed for some time, may adopt an approach to

---

[9] The most well-known example of this problem is discussed in *Trendtex Trading Corp. v. Central Bank of Nigeria* [1977] 1 All E.R. 881. In another recent case, funds in a central bank's account were deposited by a number of private banks to facilitate international monetary transactions. *LNC Investments, Inc. v. The Republic of Nicaragua*, 2000 U.S. Dist. LEXIS 5365 (S.D.N.Y. Apr. 26, 2000). These functions would seem to be classically commercial.

immunity for central banks which is based on the absolute theory. As noted above, the absolute approach may not provide any immunity for central banks that are organized as entities independent from their government, notwithstanding that the banks engage in activities that appear to involve sovereign functions. As a result, this lack of immunity protection may extend to assets that are foreign currency reserves. If this theory governs, it is doubtful that earmarking assets in a way to reflect their sovereign function would protect these assets.

Assets held as agent

Central banks that hold assets in jurisdictions adopting the absolute theory of immunity should also investigate the impact this theory would have on assets of the government held through the central bank. While those assets may receive absolute immunity if they are held directly by the government or governmental department in the foreign jurisdiction, query what impact holding such assets through the central bank would have on the available immunity. Would the assets be subject to jurisdiction or attachment if the central bank did not disclose that it acted as agent for its government? If the central bank identified its role as agent in all relevant account documentation and account designation would the outcome change? If it is not readily apparent what the answers to these questions are, local counsel should be in a position to describe the risks and the best approaches to minimize those risks.

Waiver

A central bank needs also to consider the impact, if any, on available immunities if it waives any part of its immunity. Of particular concern is the impact of submitting to jurisdiction, of submitting to jurisdiction with limitations, or permitting attachment or execution of assets. The enforceability of these waivers and the impact on the overall structure of immunities should be considered.

Notice of Litigation

Central banks that hold assets outside their home jurisdictions need also to be concerned about whether, how, and when they will receive notice of any attempts to execute into, freeze, or otherwise impair their assets. Litigants may be irreparably harmed during the period when immunity is considered. Of particular concern are those jurisdictions that may allow for a freezing of assets pending a disposition on the substance of any sovereign immunity claims. These latter jurisdictions follow the United Kingdom case of *Mareva Compania Naviera S.S. v. International Bulkcarriers*, 2 Lloyd's Rep 509 (1975) (*Mareva*). *Mareva* held that courts in the United Kingdom could grant interlocutory injunctions "in all cases in which it shall appear to a court to be just or convenient." The basic test is whether there is a real potential that a judgment debtor would move the assets out of the reach of the court and whether the judgment creditor appears likely to win on the merits. The *Mareva* injunction is recognized as a powerful tool for general creditors to restrain assets. Contrast the *Mareva* approach with that of the United States. The United States Supreme Court has pointedly refused to follow the *Mareva* approach and has denied preliminary relief even in the face of strong evidence of a potential movement of assets beyond the reach of the creditor.[10] The United States approach is that potential creditors should not be able to encumber a potential debtor's assets until that creditor has a judgment in hand. This result is recognized under New York State law as well.[11] Thus, central banks should be aware of the approach followed in the jurisdiction in which assets are located.

Frozen assets (either through a *Mareva* or similar injunction) leave the central bank without a liquid tool for its management of currency policy objectives. While the outcome of the jurisdictional question may ultimately be favorable, a court may feel compelled to freeze assets temporarily in order to protect all parties. But even short-term encumbrances, especially if they are publicized, could present the central bank with devastating burdens in managing their reserves. This problem may be particularly acute in those jurisdictions that do not have clearly developed statutory immunities for entities like central banks, where a court would be unlikely to raise the issue on its own.

---

[10] Grupo Mexicano de Desarrollo, S.A., et al. v. Alliance Bond Fund, Inc. et al., 527 U.S. 308 (1999).

[11] Credit Agricole Indosuez, et al. v. Rossiyskiy Kredit Bank et al., 2000 N.Y. LEXIS 508 (Court of Appeals 2000).

Counterparty and Custodian Legal Risk

Generally

All financial institutions, including central banks, need to understand the particular legal risks in dealing with different types of counterparties and custodians. Particularly with custodians, central banks need to develop enforceable contracts that clearly define the rights and obligations of the custodian with respect to the assets. The custodian's role with respect to the management of the assets should be spelled out and should be drafted carefully to protect the sovereign nature of the assets if the central bank plans to rely on sovereign immunity. If the custodian is to perform only ministerial functions (valuation and settlement duties) this should be clearly spelled out. Central banks also need, particularly with respect to commercial custodians, to be aware of any standard terms and conditions that govern the contractual relationships of the institutions with which they deal that may not be published or easy to find.

Central banks may provide limited services but may also be the most secure custodians for assets of other central banks. Assets held at other central banks may also contribute to a characterization of assets as sovereign rather than commercial. Private custodians may provide additional investment opportunities but central banks must perform heightened due diligence with respect to the insolvency regime in that jurisdiction for that type of entity. Even more so than other financial institutions, central banks need to ensure that their assets are not frozen and subject to bankruptcy proceedings and, indeed, are not deemed part of a bankruptcy estate subject to any stays. Care should also be taken to ensure that any products that the central bank invests in are given the appropriate protection under that jurisdiction's insolvency regime and to determine how those concerns impact the immunity analysis.

Drexel Insolvency

A number of lessons applicable to central bank dealings with market counterparties may be learned from the failure of Drexel Burnham Lambert in the early 1990s. A commodity dealing affiliate of Drexel approached a number of central banks seeking to manage some of those central banks' reserves, particularly gold reserves.

Some central banks, most notably the Bank of Portugal and the Bank of Yugoslavia, entered into a number of gold lending transactions with Drexel. Drexel, consistent with market practice, then engaged in transactions lending the central bank gold to other parties taking cash as collateral. The cash collateral taken in by the commodity affiliate was then lent to the Drexel parent company which, before the maturity of the loans, became insolvent and unable to repay its affiliate. As a result, the commodity firm was unable to make payments to get back the gold and, thus, was unable to repay the central banks. After the commodity firm went into bankruptcy, the central banks had to wait until their claims were adjudicated by the United States bankruptcy courts. Of particular note, at the time of the bankruptcy proceeding, the Portuguese bank alleged that the central bank customers of Drexel were targeted to be left unpaid because they were seen as less sophisticated, were farther away, and seemed less prone to sue. Also, from news accounts, the scope of investment discretion given Drexel by the central banks was unclear.

Choice of Law

Central banks need also to be aware of the law that will be applied to foreign custodial arrangements. Of specific concern should be the impact of the situs of the assets and the choice of law in any agreements. The location of assets may, for example, provide the relevant law for the assets and their treatment and disposition, notwithstanding that the central bank has chosen a different law to govern its dealings in those assets with a counterparty. The ownership of assets may be determined by the law of the situs rather than by the law chosen by the parties. In taking advantage of any immunities available to them, central banks should be aware also of what law the local jurisdiction will apply in determining whether the central bank qualifies as a central bank. This important threshold question must be answered before a central bank may assess its legal risks and potential immunities.

Conclusion: Reducing Legal Risk

Central banks should consider methods that might help to protect their assets under the legal regime of the jurisdictions in which assets are placed. As a first step, local counsel should be engaged so that the state of the law in a particular jurisdiction may be evaluated.

After consulting with counsel, consideration should be given to indicating clearly the central banking nature of both the institution and its assets and activities. Assets used for those activities normally associated with sovereign activities should be marked if possible. Also, a central bank should consider ways in which it might earmark assets so that a court faced with a litigant seeking to freeze such assets would be alerted to the sovereign issues before ordering an attachment. Of course, local counsel should be consulted to determine the extent to which a court would look to, and give effect to, any such earmarking.

Chapter

22 Assessing the Case for Unified Financial Sector Supervision

RICHARD K. ABRAMS AND MICHAEL W. TAYLOR

In recent years a number of countries have restructured their financial sector supervision to create a unified supervisory agency for the banking,[1] insurance, and securities sectors. A study of a sample of 72 countries (Llewellyn, 1999) classifies 10 of them as having adopted some form of unified supervision: Australia, Canada, Denmark, Iceland, Japan, Norway, the Republic of Korea, Singapore, Sweden, and the United Kingdom. It is perhaps significant that the majority of unified agencies have been formed only in the past decade, which may suggest that there is an increasing trend in the direction of this type of regulatory agency. Nevertheless, it is essential that each country consider the appropriateness of this organizational form to its own special circumstances. The aim of this paper is to provide a framework in which the arguments for and against the unification of financial sector supervision can be analyzed and assessed.

The paper begins by discussing a list of prerequisites for effective supervision which are intended to provide a set of criteria for assessing alternative regulatory arrangements. It then reviews the arguments for and against the unification of supervision in the light of these criteria. An important related issue is the role of the central bank in a country's regulatory arrangements, which we consider in the fourth section. Finally, we conclude that although in some circumstances the unification of supervision may enhance regulatory effectiveness, this will not always be the case. The central contention of this paper is that to be effective the structure of the regulatory system needs to reflect the structure of the markets that are being regulated. While appearing to provide a strong justification for

---

[1] Throughout this paper we take "banks" and "banking" to refer to any institution that performs the payments system and intermediation functions of a bank whether or not it uses the word in its name.

unification in some circumstances, this factor is only one of several that need to be taken into account; in some cases the balance of argument may tend to favor unification, whereas in others it will not.[2]

Prerequisites for Effective Supervision: A Summary

It should be stressed at the outset that changing the structure of regulation cannot of itself guarantee effective supervision. Institutional structure is a second order issue, to be considered once the various conditions for effective regulation, as discussed in this section, are in place. Hence maintaining and enhancing supervisory capacity and the effectiveness of supervision should be the primary goal of any proposed regulatory reform. As such, the development of regulatory capacity should be given prominence over the issue of regulatory structure, and the latter is only a matter of fundamental concern to the extent that it can assist in achieving this overarching objective.

There are a number of essential prerequisites which any regulatory structure should meet if it is to have a reasonable likelihood of success.[3] Furthermore, if these prerequisites are not met, steps should be taken to rectify these shortcomings before consideration is given to developing more complex forms of financial

---

[2] There are a number of subsidiary issues that also need to be considered, including whether other parts of the financial sector (*e.g.*, pension funds or finance houses) should also be included within the scope of a unified regulatory agency. A further issue of fundamental importance is whether the unified agency should be responsible for both prudential and business practice regulation. These issues are beyond the scope of this paper, and we will assume throughout that we are concerned with the formation of a unified prudential regulatory agency.

[3] Basel Core Principle 1 states: "An effective system of banking supervision will have clear responsibilities and objectives for each agency involved in the supervision of banking organizations. Each such agency should possess operational independence and adequate resources. A suitable legal framework for banking supervision is also necessary, including provisions relating to authorization of banking organizations and their ongoing supervision; powers to address compliance with laws as well as safety and soundness concerns; and legal protection for supervisors. Arrangements for sharing information between supervisors and protecting the confidentiality of such information should be in place." While referring specifically to banking, the prerequisites identified in this Core Principle are equally applicable to the regulation of any financial institution or activity. The Code of Good Practices on Transparency of Monetary and Financial Policies (Transparency Code) also contains a number of principles that are relevant to these issues.

sector regulation, such as the development of a unified supervisory function. The following list does not aim to be exhaustive, but nonetheless attempts to provide an indicative set of key features.

Clear Objectives

A regulatory agency must have clear objectives, preferably set out in statute.[4] Clear objectives assist the agency's senior management in making decisions on the efficient allocation of resources and in determining the appropriate policy response to a given problem. Well-formulated objectives can also help prevent regulation from expanding beyond the minimum necessary to correct clear instances of market failure. Finally, they also provide a mechanism by which the regulatory agency can be held to account for its decisions and policies.

Independence and Accountability

A regulatory agency must be able to take decisions which belong to its sphere of competence without undue outside interference, whether it be from ministers, parliamentarians, industry leaders, or other government officials (including, potentially, central bankers). In this regard, it is especially important that senior management be protected from arbitrary removal. The rules governing the removal of senior management must therefore be transparent and demanding, ideally set out in an act of parliament. Budgetary autonomy, in the sense of the existence of an earmarked source of funding for the agency and its ability to allocate resources according to its own internal priorities, is equally important, for otherwise efforts to develop an aggressive and effective regulatory body can be stopped by cutting the agency's budget. Because of this, it is generally desirable that the regulatory agency be funded by a levy on regulated firms, rather than being dependant on allocations from the general government budget.

The need for regulatory independence should be balanced by a corresponding need to ensure that the agency can be held to account

---

[4] See Transparency Code, Part V.

for its policies and actions.[5] Accountability in the first instance needs to be to government and to parliament, since these are the sources of the agency's powers. However, responsiveness to the regulated industry may also need to be taken into account. This might, for example, be accomplished by creating a mechanism of formal consultation with representatives of regulated firms. The statutory industry panel established as part of the United Kingdom's new regulatory arrangements provide one possible way in which this might be achieved.[6] These types of accountability mechanism are especially important when the regulatory agency is funded by an industry levy, since it provides some means by which the industry can check and balance the regulator's power to raise funds and prevent the costs of regulation from becoming excessive. On the other hand, care needs to be taken that in introducing accountability to the industry the regulatory agency is not exposed to the risk of regulatory capture by the industry.

Adequate Resources

Allied to the funding issue is the consideration that the regulatory agency needs to have adequate resources to discharge its task effectively. Especially important is the ability to recruit, train, and retain a cadre of experienced professional staff. Since the kinds of skills required to make an effective regulator are also likely to be in heavy demand in the private sector, it follows that the regulator must be able to offer its staff competitive remuneration. Similarly, the regulator must also be able to command adequate resources to ensure timely and effective data collection and processing.

---

[5] Transparency Code, Part VIII.

[6] The Practitioner Panel was also established in November 1998 and is now placed on a statutory basis by the Financial Services and Markets Act. Its membership comprises senior representatives of the businesses that are regulated by the Financial Services Authority. The Panel may make representations to the FSA, and the Act requires that the Authority "have regard" to such representations. By § 11, if the FSA disagrees with the view expressed or proposal made in the representation it must give the panel a statement in writing of its reasons for disagreeing, and this statement may be made public.

Effective Enforcement Powers

A regulatory agency must possess effective enforcement powers over the full range of the firms it is responsible for regulating. These powers should include, as a minimum, the ability to require information from regulated firms, to assess the competence and probity of senior management and the owners of the institution, and to take appropriate graduated sanctions against failure to comply with regulatory rules, including having the ultimate power to intervene in the institution if necessary. Ideally, the regulatory authority should have the ability to revoke licenses to conduct financial services business. However, in some countries this may not be compatible with constitutional provisions that require a strict separation of executive and judicial functions. In the latter case, the authority should have the ability to make recommendations on the revocation of licenses, with the decision-taker required to give reasons in the event that the authority's recommendation is not acted on. Enforcement powers are likely to remain more effective if the regulator has the ability to amend them quickly: for this reason it is generally preferable to set out only the broad framework of the regulatory agency's powers in legislation, leaving the details to be filled in by directives and guidelines that can be issued and amended by the regulatory agency itself. To effectively carry out their responsibilities, the staff of the regulatory agency should also have immunity from suit for actions taken in the discharge of their official duties.

Comprehensiveness of Regulation

Another essential feature of a regulatory system is that it should be comprehensive and free of regulatory gaps, i.e., there should be no scope for particular activities or types of intermediaries to escape effective regulation simply because there is doubt about which agency should be responsible for regulating it. A central component of comprehensiveness is that regulatory agencies should practice effective consolidated supervision of the institutions for which they are responsible. However, the case for comprehensiveness goes beyond this: all efforts should be made to eliminate gaps in the jurisdiction of the regulatory agencies, which could allow otherwise regulated activities or institutions to escape effective regulation. The regulators must also be in a position to respond quickly to market innovations to ensure that the regulatory framework remains up to date and does not become ineffective or act as a barrier to the legitimate evolution of the market.

Cost-Effective Regulation

Regulation imposes costs both directly and indirectly. The direct costs are those needed to sustain the activities of the regulatory agencies: they include staff salaries, administrative overheads (including accommodation costs), and the information technology budget. The indirect costs of regulation are more difficult to quantify, but are those incurred by the regulated industry as a result of the need to comply with regulatory requirements. These costs can take many different forms, ranging from the costs of employing specialist "compliance" staff to the costs of maintaining special systems for regulatory reporting that go beyond those necessary for an institution's own internal purposes. As a general principle a regulatory arrangement with lower costs, both direct and indirect, is to be preferred to one which imposes higher costs.

To Unify or Not

The effectiveness criteria will now be used to examine the case for the unification of supervisory functions. The starting point is to consider the appropriateness of merging the three core financial sector supervisory functions into a dedicated agency or commission. It is also necessary to consider those circumstances when unification may not be appropriate. Finally, it is important to consider the implications that the decision to unify will have for the role of the central bank, and in particular whether or not it would be appropriate to separate the monetary policy and banking supervision functions.

Arguments for Unification

A wide range of arguments have been advanced in favor of unification.[7] Some of the most persuasive are based on efficiency gains, in particular the economies of scale, which seem to be offered by unification of supervisory agencies. However, some of the most

---

[7] See Briault (1999) for a full discussion.

prominent recent arguments are based on either the need to revise supervisory coverage in light of the rise of financial conglomerates or to ensure competitive neutrality in light of the blurring distinctions between the various classes of financial institutions.[8] These latter arguments, which have been advanced in the context of a number of industrial countries, may not be as universally applicable as those based on regulatory efficiency.

Supervision of Financial Conglomerates

The rise of financial conglomerates, which operate diverse groups of financial institutions domestically,[9] and often internationally as well, has led regulators to seek to identify ways to efficiently and effectively oversee their operations. Fragmented supervision may raise concerns about the ability of the financial sector supervisors to form an overall risk assessment of the institution on a consolidated basis, as well as their ability to ensure that supervision is seamless and free of gaps. There are also group-wide risks that may not be adequately addressed by specialist regulators, which have oversight jurisdiction over only part of a diversified conglomerate. Among these risks are whether the group as a whole has adequate capital and whether it has adequate systems and controls for managing its risks. Financial sector supervisors must also be able to ensure that they are able to respond on an institution-wide basis should serious problems occur in any part of the conglomerate. Experience has shown that, while these firms generally claim to have financial firewalls between their various operations, they are often proven to be largely illusory when serious difficulties arise.

Ensuring effective supervision of diversified financial conglomerate groups places several requirements on the various financial supervisory bodies that are not usually present in more simple corporate structures. First, the supervisory bodies must have an effective and efficient system of rapidly sharing information with

---

[8] This literature is relatively extensive, given that the subject of regulatory structure has otherwise been under-researched. First to make this argument were Borio and Filosa (1994). Their work has been followed by Goodhart (1995), Taylor (1995), and Goodhart et al. (1998).

[9] These groups combine at least two of the activities of banking, insurance, and securities.

each other on each particular institution, while also ensuring the appropriate degree of confidentiality. Second, the supervisory bodies must have a close and ongoing working relationship to ensure that suspicions and findings are fully and promptly shared and that regulatory gaps are identified and closed. Third, and most importantly, steps should be taken to ensure that, for each institution, one supervisory agency is given the power, authority, and responsibility to take the lead in both forming an overall risk assessment and to lead the regulatory response, should problems arise; this agency is generally referred to as the lead regulator.

Financial institutions also seek to minimize the burden of supervision by demanding that supervision of their operations be carried out as efficiently and with as little duplication as possible. For conglomerates, this requires that some attempt be made to address the additional burden associated with fragmented supervision. This can be done by minimizing overlap and duplication in reporting and oversight, and by simplifying the process of seeking decisions on the part of the regulator. Having a single contact point for all requests on regulatory issues may allow regulators to respond more rapidly and flexibly, while reducing the risk of regulatory gaps developing.

Although it might be possible for a series of specialist regulators to cooperate in the supervision of a diversified financial group, for example, by using the lead regulator arrangement, a unified approach seems nonetheless to offer a better prospect of coordination and the exchange of information than would occur between separate agencies.[10] It can be argued that a unified supervisory function is best suited to deal with all of the above problems, for by placing all the financial sector supervisors for a given conglomerate under a single agency, one creates a single management structure that should be able to instruct—and if need be to force—the various operating divisions to closely cooperate and share information as it becomes available. Furthermore, cooperation in closing regulatory gaps and eliminating regulatory overlap can be more easily effected, as can binding decisions regarding the assignment of a lead regulator. Such an arrangement may also aid international cooperation, because foreign

---

[10] Achieving agreement on assigning a lead regulator has proved remarkably difficult in practice.

supervisors will be given a single contact point for all regulatory issues.

Competitive Neutrality

A related argument is based on the fact that the lines of demarcation between products and institutions have blurred as financial systems have evolved and matured. Thus, the situation may arise where financial institutions offering similar services or products are supervised by different authorities. In this case, there is a strong likelihood that there will be differences in their regulation and the associated costs of achieving compliance, which may, in turn, give certain institutions a competitive advantage in offering a particular service or product.

The existence of a range of supervisory authorities also poses the risk that financial firms will engage in some form of supervisory arbitrage. This can involve the placement of a particular financial service or product in that part of a given financial conglomerate where the supervisory costs are the lowest or where supervisory oversight is the least intrusive. It may also lead firms to design new financial institutions or redesign existing ones strictly to minimize or avoid supervisory oversight. If such attempts at regulatory arbitrage become widespread, these efforts may have second-round effects in which the various supervisory authorities "compete" to reduce the burden of their oversight in order to avoid a flight of their "clients" to other supervisory agencies. While some such competition is conceivably healthy, there is the risk that the authorities may allow prudential supervision to be weakened. A unified supervisory function is well designed to deal with all of the above-noted problems, for a single supervisory body is better able to iron out differences and inconsistencies, whatever their source. Having a single management structure directly overseeing all supervisory bodies is also probably the most effective way to ensure that the various bodies do not compete for customers.

On the other hand, complete regulatory neutrality should not be a primary objective of supervision. One of the main objectives of financial sector supervision is minimizing the risk of systemic difficulties. Thus, the potential social costs associated with financial difficulties in a participant in the payments system, whose failure might give rise to systemic problems, are very different from those associated with the failure of a mutual fund or a finance company. Accordingly, the optimal amount of oversight of a similar operation may vary markedly between different types of institutions. Thus, while supervisors may wish to closely examine a bank's activities in a potentially risky market, e.g., stock market derivatives, their attitudes toward the same operations being carried out by a mutual fund would be very different. Given these differences, supervisors can argue that it is proper to supervise the same operation differently depending on the nature of the institution in which carrying out the transaction. Thus, to a degree, supervisors should encourage a certain amount of regulatory arbitrage, insofar as it involves locating riskier operations in subsidiaries that are outside of the systemically important part of the conglomerate. Of course, if the conglomerate's firewalls are inadequate, this approach may be self-defeating.

Regulatory Flexibility

A potential advantage of the unified approach to supervision is that it may allow for the development of regulatory arrangements that are more flexible than can be achieved with separate specialist agencies. Whereas the effectiveness of a system of separate agencies can be impeded by "turf wars" or a desire to "pass the buck," these problems can be more easily limited and controlled in a unified regulatory organization. Specialist agencies can also be impeded from operating effectively where their respective enabling statutes leave doubts about their jurisdiction or locus for dealing with a particular matter, especially when a new type of financial product or institution emerges, which was not covered by the original legislation. As a result, a unified agency may offer a more effective way of responding to market developments or innovations.

While flexibility is useful in the context of the developed financial markets, where the rapid pace of financial innovation rapidly leads to the obsolescence of regulations and rules, it is also desirable in emerging and transition economiesl. Countries that have recently liberalized their financial systems often experience a process of rapid industry change, which may include the growth of certain types of nonbank financial intermediaries which can pose a significant threat to financial sector soundness.[11] Thus, having a regulatory agency with the scope and capacity to respond rapidly to these changes by extending its regulatory jurisdiction is a major benefit of a properly constituted unified agency. However, achieving this objective requires that the enabling statute for the unified agency be drafted with sufficient flexibility to permit it to rapidly respond to market innovations. If the range of products and institutions subject to regulation is too narrowly defined in the legislation, or the legislation cannot be amended quickly, then the benefits of a unified approach versus a set of separate agencies will be more limited.

Regulatory Efficiency

Although scale economies are difficult to measure in a regulatory organization, as a matter of general principle, a larger size of organization permits finer specialization of labor and a more intensive utilization of inputs. In a regulatory context, unification may permit cost savings on the basis of shared infrastructure, administration, and support systems. The existence of multiple, specialized regulatory bodies has generally resulted in the duplication of support infrastructures, for example, in data collection and processing, and personnel administration. These are areas where there would appear to have been significant scope for cost savings and economies of scale from unification. Unification may also permit the acquisition of information technologies, which become cost-effective only beyond a certain scale of operations and can avoid wasteful duplication of research and information-gathering efforts. A more unified approach to data collection may also lay the basis for a more efficient reporting system, which could result in significant cost savings for the regulated enterprises, particularly financial conglomerates. On the other hand, as discussed below, there are also important synergies between the data necessary for banking supervision and for monetary policy purposes which may outweigh the synergies between the data required for banking supervision and for the regulation of other financial intermediaries. Which factor should be given greatest weight to a large extent will depend on the structure of the financial system; one in which financial conglomerates form a significant element will

---

[11] This is so particularly when they are formed to evade effective supervision.

probably benefit to a greater extent from combining the data collection effort for all types of financial institutions.

The absence of hard data makes it difficult to assess the strength of the economies of scale argument, although it is worth noting that in all of the Scandinavian countries—which were the first to establish this type of regulatory agency—it is believed that the approach has made it possible to realize significant scale economies (see Taylor and Fleming, 1999). Britain's Financial Services Authority (FSA) has also reported substantial savings from the unification of support services. In most cases, the supervised institutions also seem to take the view that unification has eliminated unnecessary duplication and overlap (see Briault, 1999).

The economies of scale argument is most applicable in countries where supervisory agencies tend to be small, notably in small countries or those with small financial systems. In these countries, the benefits of merging the administrative and data processing functions of the various supervisory functions are difficult to dismiss. Such overheads can constitute a heavy cost for such functions, and the economies of scale in sharing these services can be great, particularly if the supervisory functions do not share these functions with some other larger institutions, such as the central bank or the finance ministry. In fact, one former head of a unified supervision function viewed this as the strongest argument for unification. On the other hand, similar benefits may be gained by having the supervisory functions share such services individually or as a group, even though they remain independent from one another in their management and all of their other operations. This approach may be taken a step further by having the supervision function(s) effectively subcontract administrative and EDP services from a larger body such as the central bank. This option is discussed in more detail later in this paper.

Developing a Body of Professional Staff

An essential requirement of effective regulation is that a regulatory agency should be able to attract, retain, and develop a body of skilled professional staff. Unification can assist in this process, especially in those countries where regulatory capacity is still being developed. As a single larger employer of financial regulators, a unified agency might be better placed to formulate a coherent human resources policy, including a career planning strategy for its personnel. It would be able to offer its staff a more varied and challenging career than they would enjoy in a specialist regulator and might be sufficiently large to develop its own tailored, in-house training programs.

Unification also makes it easier for supervisors to share specialized knowledge. First, it could allow supervisors for one group of financial institutions to borrow a specialist from another group, or even to hire a single specialist to support several different supervisory functions. Second, it may lay the basis for efficiency gains by having supervisors work together on issues of mutual interest, either with respect to particular financial conglomerates or on regulatory and reporting issues in general. Third, this arrangement may also help preserve scarce management skills, for in many countries finding a sufficient number of capable managers to lead their supervisory functions is problematic.

The shortage of supervisory resources is a serious problem in a number of countries, most notably in the Baltic States, Russia, and the Other Republics of the Former Soviet Union (BRO). But while most are clearly applicable in small countries or smaller financial systems, this argument also applies in larger financial markets, especially in those areas where developments in regulatory techniques have required regulators to recruit and retain human resources with highly marketable skills. Given that the public sector always has difficulties in competing with the private sector for these skills, one of the attractions of unification is that it enables these scarce human resources to be deployed to their greatest effect.

Improved Accountability

A final argument in favor of unification is that it improves the accountability of regulation. Under a system of multiple regulatory agencies, it may be more difficult to hold regulators to account for their performance against their statutory objectives, for the costs of regulation, for their disciplinary policies, and for regulatory failures. The existence of multiple agencies, perhaps with overlapping responsibilities and areas of jurisdiction, makes possible a blame disbursement strategy among the regulators, thus making it difficult to hold any of them accountable. One advantage of a unified agency is that by creating a single management structure, it should be clear to politicians, the industry, and the public who should be held to account for particular regulatory actions or failures.

On the other hand, the relationship between unification and improved accountability is essentially second-order. A unified agency might still be difficult to hold to account if its objectives are ill-defined, while multiple specialist agencies might be more easily held to account if their objectives are clearly specified. Hence, the fundamental consideration should be the clarity of regulatory objectives rather than the number of agencies involved in regulation.

Arguments Against Unification

Not surprisingly, the list of arguments against unification is almost as long as the list of arguments in favor. These include claims that unification will result in unclear objectives for the regulatory agency; economies of scope will prove hard to achieve as long as banking, securities, and insurance business are subject to different regulations; the agency will suffer from diseconomies of scale; and it will extend moral hazard concerns across the whole financial services sector. There is also the concern that the change process itself may be poorly managed or become politicized. As a result, it will be subject to unpredictable and possibly undesirable outcomes (see Box 1).

Box 1. Pandora's Box

A serious disadvantage of a decision to create a unified supervisory agency can be the unpredictability of the change process itself. This risk has a number of different dimensions.

The first risk is that opening the issue for discussion will set in place a chain of events that will lead to the creation of a unified agency, whether or not it is appropriate to create one. The problem is one of political power: powerful actors within the government and the public sector may see such a proposal as an opportunity to increase their influence within government by taking on important additional powers. Furthermore, the individuals that see themselves best placed to lead the unified agency will tend to push the issue aggressively and seek to rush the proposal through parliament quickly, before the internal balance of power shifts against them. In such circumstances, there is clearly a risk that mistakes will be made in the design of the agency and that the plan may be pushed forward even if it appears likely that the unified authority will be sufficiently flawed as to make its creation inadvisable. If the process of creation becomes tied into an internal battle for power, it would also increase the risk that the unified agency will have insufficient autonomy, or worse be highly politicized.

The second risk is legislative. The creation of a unified agency will generally require new legislation, but this creates the possibility that the process will be captured by special interests. As a result, issues that had previously been thought settled under existing financial services legislation—for example, decisions on the scope of activities subject to regulation or the appropriateness of exemptions from regulation—may be reopened. Thus, depending on the balance of parliamentary forces, the legislative outcome may be weaker than the original legislation under which the separate regulatory agencies had been established. One way to minimize this risk is to limit the need for legislation to a simple enabling act. This would establish the unified agency and effect a transfer of powers to it from the existing regulatory bodies, while leaving existing statutes otherwise unaffected. However, this minimalist approach has its disadvantages. One is that it does not permit the harmonization of legislation across the different financial services sectors, which is one of the primary advantages of regulatory unification. Another is that it may also fail to address the issue of regulatory gaps. It also does nothing to reduce the risks that the reorganization will result in a power grab that will undermine the autonomy of the individual agencies.

The third risk created by the change process is a possible reduction in regulatory capacity through the loss of key personnel. Many of the staff will view the unification process change with trepidation, while others may see this a difficult and trying period, which they would prefer to avoid. Thus, many staff who would be important or valuable members of the new organization may view this as a time to test the job market or retire. This has been a serious problem during the formation of a number of unified agencies, with staff turnover in some cases reaching unsustainable levels. It is likely to be compounded in the event that the change involves extraction of banking supervision from the central bank. Many of the best bank supervisors may prefer either to remain with the central bank or to move into the private sector rather than risk the perceived reduction in pay and/or status that joining a specialist regulatory body would involve. Thus, there is a real risk that many seasoned workers and highly qualified professionals may be lost, a very serious consideration if the supervisory function is not particularly strong or well-staffed. On the positive side, this is also a time when it may be particularly easy to weed out the weaker, less skilled staff within the old function.

The fourth risk is that the change management process itself will go off track. The process of creating a unified regulatory agency places heavy demands on management resources, often in environments where such resources are already in short supply. The management challenge of putting together a number of disparate regulatory agencies should not be underestimated, and there will be a need for a well-conceived and carefully monitored change management program to make it effective. During the transition process itself, this risk may be addressed by ensuring that the new supervisory body has—or hires—experts with the skills to bring about such a reorganization in an efficient, cost effective manner. However, the management issues, which will arise in the early years of the unified agency, cannot be dealt with in a similar way and are for the agency's own management to address.

Unclear Objectives

One of the most powerful arguments advanced against unified regulatory agencies is that it will be difficult for them to strike an appropriate balance among the different objectives of regulation. Given the diversity of these objectives—ranging from guarding against systemic risk to protecting the individual consumer from fraud—it is possible that a single regulator might not have a clear focus on the objectives and rationale of regulation and might not be able to adequately differentiate among different types of institutions. Indeed, rather than improving accountability, the creation of a unified regulator might diminish it because of the difficulty of designing a single set of objectives for it. As a result, its statutory responsibilities may be vague and ill-defined, which in turn can give rise to problems of holding the regulatory agency to account for its activities. Vague objectives may also provide little guidance for the regulator when (as inevitably will be the case) its different objectives come into conflict.

Specialist agencies with a clear focus on a specific regulatory objective are arguably both more easily held to account for their actions and less likely to extend regulation inappropriately.[12]

Diseconomies of Scale

Despite the strength of the economies of scale argument in favor of unified regulation, it has to be recognized that a single unified regulator may also suffer from some diseconomies of scale. One source of inefficiency could arise because a unified agency is effectively a regulatory monopoly, which may give rise to the types of inefficiencies usually associated with monopolies. A particular concern about a monopoly regulator is that the new function could be more rigid and bureaucratic than separate specialist agencies. This view is based on the premise that the larger the organization the more bureaucratic it is likely to be, particularly if its operations become so broad-based that the line managers are unable to fully understand the range of operations of the organization. However, this issue is more likely to hinge on the organization and management of the function than on its size. If the supervisory body is poorly managed, staffed, or organized, it is likely to be inflexible and bureaucratic, whether it is large or small. It must not be forgotten that a unified function in a small country may still be smaller than each of the main supervisory bodies in a large country and that many large countries have efficient and flexible financial sector supervisors.

Another source of diseconomies of scale is the tendency for unified agencies to be assigned an ever-increasing range of functions, sometimes called the "Christmas-tree effect." This may arise because the formation of a unified agency may tempt politicians and policymakers to require it to perform tasks that are only tangentially connected to its core functions. For example, in some Scandinavian countries, unified agencies have been required to take on the regulation of real estate brokers, although this arguably detracts from their primary function. Similarly, the U.K.'s FSA has already been the subject of several attempts to assign it new responsibilities that are beyond its already broad scope. These include the regulation of

---

[12] See Taylor (1997) for elaboration of this point.

mortgages (on consumer protection grounds) and encouraging competition in the financial services industry.

Limited Synergies

Some critics of unification argue that the synergy gains from unification will not be very large; in other words, economies of scope are likely to be much less significant than economies of scale. In this regard, it is true that the cultures, focus, and skills of the various supervisors vary markedly. For example, it has been noted that the sources of risks at banks are on the asset side, while most of the risks at insurance companies are on the liability side. Furthermore, the behavior of the various types of supervisors varies markedly, with some describing banking supervisors as being more like doctors examining the health of the patient, while securities supervisors are more like policemen trying to catch the miscreant securities dealers.[13] The evidence of unified authorities to date tends to suggest that even within a single organization these differences of style and culture will remain, and trying to create a single agency culture has been one of the most difficult tasks for management. To some extent the difficulty has been compounded—or at least not assuaged—by the fact that the internal organization of these agencies has tended to mirror traditional institutional lines—i.e., most have been established with separate departments for banking, securities, and insurance regulation. However, this is now changing, as some authorities are beginning to experiment more with matrix-based organizations, for example the Complex Groups division of the FSA, which specializes in the supervision of financial conglomerates. However, while there is a consensus that efficiency gains from unification can be substantial, the evidence to date that the unified agencies can achieve significant synergies between their different functions is mixed and difficult to quantify.

Moral Hazard

Perhaps the most worrisome of all the criticisms of unified regulation is the "moral hazard" argument. This argument is based on

---

[13] It may also be significant that international cooperation also tends to occur on institutional lines and in this respect the work of the Joint Forum is the exception rather than the rule.

the premise that the public will tend to assume that all creditors of institutions supervised by a given supervisor will receive equal protection. Hence if depositors, and perhaps other creditors, are protected from loss in the event of bank failure, then the customers and creditors of all other financial institutions supervised by the same regulatory authority may expect to be treated in an equivalent manner. Clearly this is an informational problem, and in the event of unification, the new supervisory body will need to clarify the rules of the game regarding the treatment of the various financial institutions.[14] Furthermore, it may be necessary for the supervisor to reinforce its position by treating any nonbank institutions that get into trouble strictly according to the preannounced rules of the game.

The Role of the Central Bank

A further dimension to the arguments for and against unification is the extent to which the central bank is, or should be, directly involved in banking supervision. The earliest examples of unified supervision, in Denmark, Norway, and Sweden, were established in systems where the central bank had not been the banking supervisor. This state of affairs remains exceptional in most of the rest of the world. Thus, in many countries, the decision to create a unified supervisory agency will probably necessitate the extraction of banking supervision from the central bank, as has occurred recently in Australia and the United Kingdom. Although an alternative possibility would be to combine all supervision within the central bank, as practiced in Singapore, moral hazard considerations may weigh heavily against this structure. (This option is discussed in more depth later in this section.) For the purposes of the present discussion, it will be assumed that the unification of supervision will involve the separation of the banking supervision and monetary policy functions.

The arguments for and against the separation between supervision and monetary policy have been well examined (Goodhart and Schoenmaker, 1995). The arguments against separation are strong. In particular, since banks are the conduit through which changes in

---

[14] In such circumstances, constructive ambiguity may not be all that constructive.

short-term interest rates are transmitted to the wider economy, the central bank needs to be concerned about their financial soundness as a precondition for an effective monetary policy. This argument is reinforced by a number of others, including these: the synergies between the information required for the conduct of monetary policy on the one hand and the supervision of the banking sector on the other; the central bank's need to assess the creditworthiness of participants in the payments system, which will inevitably involve it in forming judgments about the solvency and prudent conduct of banks; and the central bank's need to have access to information on the solvency and liquidity of individual banks in order to exercise its lender-of-last-resort functions. These arguments have traditionally been seen as making a powerful case for combining the banking supervision and monetary policy functions, and their strength is attested to by the fact that, as was discussed in the introduction, the practice in many countries remains for the central bank to be responsible for banking supervision.

In addition to these arguments, it is also possible to cite a number of operational considerations in favor of combination. First, the economies of scale obtained from the combination of monetary policy and banking supervision may be as substantial as those that arise from combining the regulation of the different financial sectors. The commonalities in the information requirements for these respective functions have already been mentioned. In addition, to the extent that there is an overlap in the knowledge and skills required for these different functions, a central bank may enjoy a comparative advantage in recruiting and retaining the best staff. This argument is particularly strong in countries where the absolute level of human capital with these skills is very small.

Another important consideration, especially in the countries of the BRO, is that many central banks now have a strong guarantee of their independence, sometimes even written into constitutional law. This degree of independence, established primarily for the purposes of ensuring a credible monetary policy, can also help to shield banking supervision from undue parliamentary or ministerial influence. Thus in transitional or emerging market economies there may be a case for retaining banking supervision within the central bank not only on the traditional grounds cited above, but also out of a concern to avoid the politicization of bank regulation.

On the other hand, it may be possible to develop governance and funding arrangements for the unified regulator that give it adequate political autonomy. Moreover, it should be borne in mind that there are several general arguments for the separation of banking supervision and monetary policy, irrespective of whether or not the separation arises out of the unification of supervision. First, a central bank that is also responsible for supervision may err on the side of laxity if it fears that tight monetary conditions may lead to bank failures.[15] Second, bank failures inevitably will occur and when they do they will be blamed on the supervisor. If the supervisor is the central bank its credibility will be undermined, and with it its credibility in the conduct of monetary policy. In addition, it has been argued that changes in payment system technology, most notably the move to real-time gross settlement, changes the nature of the oversight the central bank needs to exercise over participants in the system (Financial System Inquiry, 1997). Finally, as the financial system becomes less bank-centered and more dominated by financial conglomerate groups with banking as only one of their financial services activities, the moral hazard issues discussed above gain increased significance, and these may point to the need for a regulatory structure with comparative distance between the central bank—as provider of lender-of-last-resort assistance—and the agency responsible for routine supervision and regulation.

So far the discussion has concerned only the combination of banking supervision with monetary policy within the central bank. However, another option in structuring regulation would be to combine a wider range of regulatory functions within the central bank. Thus the central bank might be responsible for supervising the securities markets as well as banks, and possibly even insurance companies. This arrangement is likely to seem particularly attractive in some of quite specific circumstances: first, when the financial sector, and especially the nonbank financial sector, is relatively small, making it difficult to establish viable regulatory agencies outside the central bank; second, where banking is the main form of financial

---

[15] However, as Goodhart and Schoenmaker (1995) argue, the validity of this argument is to a large degree dependent on the structure of the banking and financial system; the more the system involves intermediaries financing maturity mismatch positions through the wholesale markets the greater the potential for conflict between monetary and financial stability goals.

intermediation and other financial sectors are dominated by groups with a bank at their head; third, where the central bank has a strong competitive advantage in attracting staff with the right skills and credentials, for example where central bank salaries are significantly above those available for other public officials; and finally, where the central bank has strong guarantees of its independence, thus providing a defense against the politicization of regulation. In circumstances where all, or most, of these conditions prevail, the option of centralizing all regulatory functions within the central bank may seem to have much to commend it.

However, this option also suffers from a number of serious disadvantages. Clearly, the moral hazard problem will be even more pronounced if the unified supervisory function is conducted by the central bank itself. It may be difficult for a central bank which also supervises a wide range of financial intermediaries to make sufficiently clear the differentiation among them. Thus it may give rise to a perception in the public mind that all types of financial contracts will receive the same degree of protection in the event of firm failures. While it may be possible for the authorities, through a campaign of public education, to explain the different levels of protection available to the holders of different types of financial claim, their attempts to do so may be undermined by the perception that holders of all financial claims will enjoy the prospect of central bank support.

A second difficulty is that this approach might be perceived as granting the central bank excessive powers. If all regulatory functions are combined within the central bank, this will result in the central bank having responsibility for the conduct of monetary policy and the regulation of all financial intermediaries, both banks and nonbanks. A related problem is the risk that particular regulatory failures may tarnish its reputation and credibility, especially in its conduct of monetary policy. Both of these objections might be minimized in the event that the supervisory function remains a legally independent agency, albeit one located within the central bank. But if this is done, it will be important to ensure that the supervisory agency is able to establish a distinct identity of its own in the public mind.

Conclusion

The main conclusion of this review of the issues raised by the unification of financial sector supervision is that no one model of regulatory structure will be appropriate for all countries. While fully unified supervisory agencies—those regulating banking, insurance, and securities—do offer certain advantages over separate agencies, the advantages appear to vary sharply among countries. Moreover, they must also be weighed against the disadvantages, the strength of which will also vary considerably from case to case. The same points apply to the other regulatory structures considered in this paper. Hence, in each case, it is essential to first perform a full assessment of the advantages and disadvantages of applying a particular model developed in one member country to the conditions of another.

The assessment of advantages and disadvantages should take into account two overarching factors. The first is that any change process involves risks, and the greater the proposed structural change the greater will be the risks. Many of these risks have been examined in "Pandora's Box," but perhaps the most important single factor is that the change process may result in a serious reduction in existing regulatory capacity unless it is well managed.[16] This concern is particularly great with respect to banking supervision, which is the key supervisory function in many developing and transition economies, given the centrality of banks to their financial systems. In these countries, great care will need to be exercised to ensure that banking supervisory capacity is not compromised by unification. Another important factor is the need to preserve (or enhance) the independence of the regulatory agency. If a proposal to create a unified authority threatens either agency capacity or independence, then it is probably not worth undertaking. In any case, the benefits of change should be relatively clear and unambiguous before embarking on a proposed unification. Where the evidence of the benefits of unification is more ambiguous, or the costs of change may be high, more modest institutional innovations should be considered, ranging from the formation of a unified oversight board to shared facilities with the central bank.

---

[16] This is likely to be a particular concern in transition or developing economies where regulatory capacity may, in any case, be already relatively weak.

The second overarching factor is that the institutional structure of regulation should reflect the institutional structure of the industry it is designed to regulate. For example, the combination of banking and securities regulation is most clearly appropriate where the system comprises universal banks. In countries where banks are not significant players in the securities markets, the case for a combination of function is much less strong. Similarly, the combination of banking and insurance regulation is most appropriate where linkages between banks and insurance companies are particularly significant. Combining the regulation of all three sectors within a single agency will, therefore, be most appropriate when the financial services industry of the country comprises a number of diversified, multiactivity groups or where the distinctions among different types of financial intermediaries have become blurred. In the latter case, a strictly institutional approach to regulation may no longer adequately reflect the distribution of risk in the financial system.

These various factors suggest that it will be important to differentiate the institutional structure of regulation based on the stage of development of the financial market and its degree of complexity. Ultimately, however, the question of regulatory structure should be regarded as a second order issue. It is important not to lose sight of the primary objective: the provision of effective supervision by a well-staffed, well-resourced, and independent regulatory agency.

References

Borio, C.E.V., and R. Filosa, 1994, "The Changing Borders of Banking: Trends and Implications," BIS Economic Paper No.43, December (Basel: Bank for International Settlements).

Briaut, C., 1999, "The Rationale for a Single National Financial Services Regulator," Financial Services Authority, Occasional Paper Series No. 2. (London: Financial Services Authority)

Financial System Inquiry, 1997: *Final Report*, (Canberra: Commonwealth of Australia).

Goodhart, C.A.E., 1995, "Some Regulatory Concerns," London School of Economics Financial Markets Group, Special Paper No.79 (London: London School of Economics).

———, P. Hartmann, D.T. Llewellyn, L. Rojas-Suarez, and S. Weisbrod, 1998, *Financial Regulation: Why, How and Where Now?* (London and New York: Routledge).

Goodhart, C.A.E. and D. Schoenmaker, 1995, "Institutional Separation between Supervisory and Monetary Agencies" in *The Central Bank and the Financial System*, ed. by C.A.E. Goodhart, (Cambridge, Mass: MIT Press).

Llewellyn, D.T., 1999, "Introduction: The Institutional Structure of Regulatory Agencies" in *How Countries Supervise Their Banks, Insurers and Securities Markets* (London: Central Banking Publications).

Taylor, M., 1995, *Twin Peaks: A Regulatory Structure for the New Century* (London: Centre for the Study of Financial Innovation).

———, 1997, *Regulatory Leviathan: Will Super-SIB Work?* (London: CTA Financial Publishing).

———, and A. Fleming, 1999, "Integrated Financial Supervision: Lessons of Northern European Experience," World Bank Policy Research Paper No. 2223 (Washington: World Bank).

Chapter 23

Supervision of Financial Institutions in the United Kingdom

WILLIAM BLAIR

Introduction

The opportunity to address the biennial meeting of central bank lawyers hosted by the International Monetary Fund is a pleasure and an honor. This paper seeks to contribute to the more general discussion on the merits, or otherwise, of the unitary approach to financial regulation, which has recently been adopted in the United Kingdom. I would like to begin by emphasising that the search for a single regulatory model is likely to be in vain. Financial regulation involves a balance between a large number of factors, economic, political, social, and cultural. These vary from country to country. It is not my purpose, therefore, to advocate the adoption of the unitary, or indeed any other, model of regulation. Each country has its unique circumstances and requirements. However, I do express the personal view that it is well suited to the particular circumstances of the United Kingdom, and that its adoption (which I shall describe) has generally been considered a success.

Continuing with some general comments, I would like to draw your attention to the fact that the case for financial regulation is not universally accepted among scholars. Some have explained economic regulation as a product. It is allocated in accordance with the laws of supply and demand, solicited by interest groups to advance their private interests.[1] The more general view is that regulation is supplied by government in response to public demand and aims at the correction of inefficient or inequitable market practices in the public

---

[1] George J. Stigler, "The Theory of Economic Regulation," 2 *Bell J. Econ.* 3 (1971).

interest.[2] Whatever the theoretical position, in practice it is universally accepted that financial activity in the form of banking, investment business, and insurance requires proper regulation and supervision. For the purposes of this paper, I draw no distinction between these two terms.

The Modern Regulatory Landscape

An important development we have witnessed over the last decade has been the accelerating degree of regulatory convergence. Cooperation between supervisors and harmonization of regulatory standards have been the raison d'être and the main product of international bodies/forums such as the Basel Committee and the International Organization of Securities Commissions (IOSCO). On the other hand, regulatory structures remain different from country to country, and there is no real impetus for the adoption of a uniform regulatory model. One significant exception relates to the European Union. The introduction of the single currency has led to demands by some for a unified system of financial regulation, although this appears at present as a very remote possibility. National regulators continue to apply their own rules, but there is a considerable degree of harmonization in the content of their rulebooks. The principle of the "single passport" means that an institution authorized in one member state is free to carry on banking, insurance, or investment business throughout the Union.

Since this paper is primarily about regulatory structures, I would like to provide a brief description of such structures from an international perspective. The instruments of regulation include government departments, independent agencies, and the Central Bank. Often the regulatory process is based on a combination of these bodies. Regulation is typically organized according to the nature of the business concerned. The three main divisions are banking business and in particular deposit-taking, securities business and other forms of investment activity, and insurance business. Speaking specifically of the responsibility of central banks, patterns again vary. In some countries, the central bank is the prime regulator

---

[2] Richard A. Posner, "Theories of Economic Regulation," 5 *Bell J. Econ. 335* (1974).

for banking and investment business generally. In others, it has regulatory responsibility for banking business alone. In others, it has no specific regulatory responsibility at all, save that a central bank is invariably regarded as having an overall mandate as regards the health of a country's economic and financial system. As one would expect, the structure of financial regulation in any particular country depends on a combination of planning and circumstance.

The first country to develop a modern system of financial regulation was the United States. The remarkably far-sighted reforms of the 1930s, contained primarily in two statutes,[3] constituted a considered response to the fact that uncontrolled speculation and financial abuse had caused financial collapse, followed by a calamitous depression. On the other hand, the regulation of banking and investment business (and the separation of the two types of business) was never an issue of the same importance in command economies organized along Marxist lines. Depressions were seen as ills inherent in the capitalist system itself. But with political reform and economic liberaliztion came the necessity to impose some sort of control over the financial forces that were being unleashed in the process. This point is not confined to the former socialist systems. It applies, for example, to Britain as well. The 1980s are often perceived as a time of economic deregulation. At one level this is true, but the very fact of deregulating economic activity led to the emergence of regulatory structures intended to impose constraints in the public interest. The modern regulatory framework for the prudential supervision of banks and investment firms is primarily the result of such concerns.

Regulatory structures must adapt and change to respond to the challenges of the modern times, and the process is an ongoing one. Nevertheless, in some countries, reform has been radical. Australia is one example, another is Japan. The reform of Japan's system of financial regulation is outside the scope of this paper. Suffice it to say that it has raised fundamental issues, which have not arisen in quite the same way in any of the other major international financial centres. Financial reform in Japan seems to go to the heart of the country's economic, political, and social system. By comparison,

---

[3] Securities Act 1933 and Securities Exchange Act 1934.

reforms in the United Kingdom have taken place against a much more modest background. Financial reform is seen as important, but in no sense of central concern. This may reflect in part the experience of the two countries, which has been very different. In Japan, reform of financial regulation is, in a sense, the culmination of massive economic growth over a number of decades. In the United Kingdom, the story has been one of continued relative economic contraction (though there has been a substantial reversal in the last decade). But at the same time, the United Kingdom hosts a significant part of the international financial services industry, which for a variety of reasons, continues to be based in the City of London.

The Development of Regulatory Structures in the United Kingdom

Like the United States, the United Kingdom experienced the full force of the Great Depression. Unlike its transatlantic counterpart, blame was not placed at the door of the domestic stock market. The results of this fundamental difference in perspective were twofold. First, there never was in the United Kingdom a legal bar dividing banking and securities business such as was imposed in the Glass-Steagall Act. In practice, banks and securities houses were separate, but this reflected business preference and nonstatutory impediments such as internal Stock Exchange Rules.[4] There never was a need to remove legal bars to integrated financial businesses, for the simple reason that by and large such bars did not exist. The comparison may be drawn with the Financial Services Modernization Act of 1999 in the United States. The second consequence was that, until comparatively recently, the United Kingdom had no corpus of regulatory law equivalent to that subsisting in the United States. The supervision of the banking sector was carried out by the Bank of England on a largely nonstatutory basis. There was legislation protecting investors against fraudulent activities, but it was on a modest scale compared to its United States counterparts. One historical footnote as to the effect of disparate regulation may be noted. Regulatory (including fiscal and monetary) restrictions in the United States led to migration of a series of international financial

---

[4] See generally Willliam Blair et al., Banking and Financial Services Regulation, Ch. 1 (2d. ed. 1998).

businesses to London. In particular, restrictions on interest-bearing accounts were a significant feature in the development of the eurodollar market. This had a significant impact on the reemergence and the strengthening of London's role as a leading international financial center (which was by no means either assured or predictable at the end of the second world war).

So far as the banking sector is concerned, the immediate catalyst for change was the First European Banking Directive. This led to the enactment in 1979 of a Banking Act, which contained the very first statutory framework for the regulation of banking institutions and the undertaking of banking business in the United Kingdom. The statute was re-enacted in expanded form in 1987, which at the time of writing is the current statute, though this will change when the reforms are fully in place.

The enactment of the Banking Act generally placed on a formal basis the existing system of regulation by the central bank (the Bank of England). The same was not true in the broader sphere of financial services. The factual background was the remarkable transformation of the financial sector in London affectionately known as "big bang."[5] Essentially, what was involved in this colorful phrase was enormous inward investment, the merging of brokers, market-makers, and other securities businesses into financial conglomerates with banks at their heart, and (it may be added) a rapid increase in foreign ownership. London is unique as a financial center in the sense that most of the banks and investment firms based there are in the hands of nondomestic institutions.

Inevitably a new structure had to be devised to deal with this financial explosion. Following the publication of the *Gower Report* in 1984 and the government's white paper for the regulation of financial services in the United Kingdom, a multilayered regulatory system emerged. This had a number of features. The statutory basis was provided by the Financial Services Act 1986, which for a short further period is still in force. Structurally, regulation was placed in the hands of a number of self-regulatory organizations acting under

---

[5] This term was initially used to describe the abolition in the same day of fixed commissions and dual capacity and the implementation of a series of other reforms in the operation and structure of the London Stock Exchange.

the general umbrella of an agency called the Securities and Investments Board (SIB). These organizations authorized firms to carry on particular types of business, and were the front-line regulator for the supervision of the business. They were organized along functional lines. One dealt with the securities and futures industry. Another dealt with investment management. The third dealt with personal investment at the retail level. The wholesale money markets, however, remained regulated by the Bank of England on a largely informal basis.

In keeping up with the United Kingdom's long history of self-regulation in the field of financial services, the new system was intended to enshrine this principle within a more formal regulatory framework. Thus, the regulatory system that emerged from the 1986 Act should (in theory) have been popular with the U.K. financial services industry. In practice, it was never much loved for a variety of reasons. Fundamentally, the proliferation of agents (including the Bank of England) and consequent proliferation of supervisors, rulebooks, regulatory standards, and so on was overly burdensome. The complication of the mixed system of regulation and tensions inherent in it led to a number of failures to tackle issues of great importance to the consumer such as inadequate provision of information on product prices and intermediaries' commissions. In addition, a number of events in this period such as the pensions' misselling scandal, the BCCI affair, and the collapse of Barings seemed to point to weaknesses in the regulatory system. The result was that the new system never had a chance to bed down, and change was in the air during most of the life of the 1986 Act. The "reform" debate was enriched by a number of valuable contributions.[6]

The Move to a Single Regulator

A narrow window of political opportunity opened in May 1997 for change of a fundamental nature. Over the space of two or three weeks, a plan was implemented for the complete overhaul of the

---

[6] *E.g.*, Michael Taylor, *Twin Peaks, A Regulatory Structure for the Next Century* (CSFI, December 1995); Charles Goodhart and Dirk Schoenmaker, *Institution Separation Between Supervisory and Monetary Agencies* (LSE Financial Markets Group, April 1993).

United Kingdom's regulatory structures. As a preliminary step, the Bank of England as central bank was given responsibility for monetary policy (a role which it will surrender if and when Britain joins the Euro). As regards regulation, the plan was for a single regulator: but it was not to be the Bank of England. Banking, investment business, and insurance business were all to be regulated by the same body. As was stated at the time, the catalyst for change was the changing nature of the markets:

> So there is a strong case in principle for bringing the regulation of banking, securities and insurance together under one roof. Firms organise and manage their businesses on a group-wide basis. Regulators need to look at them in a consistent way. This would bring the regulatory structure closer into line with today's increasingly integrated financial markets. It would deliver more effective and more efficient supervision, giving both firms and customers better value for money.[7]

A detailed plan was produced at the end of July 1997. It was clear from the start that the reforms were to be truly radical. Supervision of the banking sector was to be transferred from the Bank of England to the new regulatory body. It would take over the responsibilities of the four agencies charged with supervising investment business. In addition, it would take over the responsibilities of the agency supervising the savings and loans institutions (called building societies in the United Kingdom) and other saving institutions. It would undertake regulation of the insurance industry, including in due course the regulatory responsibilities of the Council of Lloyds of London. The new regulator, named the Financial Services Authority (FSA), was indeed to be a unitary body in practice as well as in theory.

Implementation

On any view, these proposals were ambitious. Equally remarkable, they had been implemented in large part by mid-2000 and were expected to become fully operational within the next year. The process has involved a number of steps.

---

[7] Gordon Brown, Chancellor of the Exchequer, May 20, 1997.

The FSA was established as a functioning body prior to the implementation of the full legal framework. This has been achieved by existing agencies "subcontracting" their operations to the FSA. In the case of banking supervision, legislation was required. This was enacted in the form of the Bank of England Act 1998. This is a relatively short statute, which has the effect of transferring regulatory functions from the Bank of England to the FSA.

A much more detailed piece of legislation has been required to provide the full legal architecture for the new system. The Financial Services and Markets Act 2000 is a mammoth piece of legislation. Together with the secondary legislation in the form of rules and regulations (not to mention the regulatory guides and handbooks) required to implement it, it represents a major investment in legislative and governmental time, and also on the part of the firms and institutions that have participated in the consultation process, and a considerable achievement on the part of the new regulatory body.

When the process is complete, the regulators will literally be under one roof—in their offices in London's Docklands' Canary Wharf.

Issues of Principle

Legislation aside, the creation of the unified regulator has been a large logistic task. Much of the work is on the level of detail but, perhaps not surprisingly, important issues of principle have had to be resolved. The process has forced to the front some very basic principles indeed.

- *The purpose of regulation.* The Financial Services and Markets Act 2000 contains specific regulatory objectives, namely market confidence, public awareness, the protection of consumers, and the reduction of financial crime. More generally, I believe that in an economy such as that of the United Kingdom, regulation has to take account of two very different components. As regards retail consumers, the regulator must to a considerable degree act as their champion. When it comes to savings, insurance, and pensions, individuals are absolutely dependent on the integrity and fair dealing practices of the providers of financial services.

Therefore, individuals depend largely on the regulator to protect their interests by acting as a counterweight to powerful financial institutions. A completely different approach is called for as regards wholesale financial operations. Sophisticated investors dealing in the securities markets, the futures markets, the OTC derivatives markets, the currency markets, and so forth are largely expected to evaluate risks themselves. Here, the regulators' concerns mostly refer to the preservation of market efficiency and market stability by guarding against systemic risk (e.g., capital adequacy measures) and ensuring market transparency. In summary, as regards the individual, there is a strong public interest in ensuring that investment services and products such as pensions are provided on a fair and reasonable basis. At the wholesale level, the focus is more upon the preservation of the efficiency, stability, and fairness of the market in order to facilitate and encourage healthy economic growth.

- *Accountability.* In practice, financial regulators are accountable to the market itself. Sometimes this is translated into timidity to impose strict sanctions in case of regulatory infractions and overt willingness to contain industry demands, creating fears of "regulatory capture." A strong argument for a single regulator is its ability to deal with even the largest international financial group on something like equal terms. As regards political accountability, the FSA board is appointed by the Chancellor of the Exchequer (Finance Minister). To date, parliamentary scrutiny has been monopolized by consideration of the new legislation. Now that this stage has been passed, it seems likely that the Treasury Select Committee of the House of Commons will wish to take evidence regularly on the FSA's discharge of its responsibility. As a means to increase regulatory accountability, calls have been made for the division of the posts of chairman and chief executive officer in the FSA. Arguably such division could lead to inefficiency in the FSA's decision making and it has been ruled out by the Treasury and the FSA.

- *Market abuse.* London has generally been less effective than New York in containing market abuse and especially insider trading. The 2000 Act seeks to remedy that situation by empowering the FSA to impose financial penalties for market abuse and providing an extended definition of what it consists of. In addition, the FSA is given the power to initiate criminal proceedings in the case of insider dealing and market manipulation. However, the appropriate scope of those activities which should be considered abusive in the sense of attracting criminal or civil penalties remains controversial.[8] As a result the definition of the offense of market abuse in the Act has changed several times and industry input has been valuable. Nevertheless, the offense lacks an intent test. Also, it overlaps significantly with existing criminal law offenses, exchange rules, and the rules of self-regulatory organizations such as the City Code of the Panel on Takeovers and Mergers.

- *Due process.* The new powers given to the FSA, and the wide scope of its regulatory responsibilities, prompted concerns that the powers might be used in an oppressive manner. The entry into force of the legislation coincides with introduction into U.K. law of the European Convention on Human Rights as of October 2000. The result has been a focus on issues of due process generally. In particular, a Financial Services and Markets Tribunal has been set up to provide an independent review of complaints by parties objecting to a proposed penalty. The Tribunal is administered by the Lord Chancellor's Department (equivalent to a Ministry of Justice) and it is independent of the FSA itself.

---

[8] *See* E. Avgouleas, "The Regulation of Fraud and Manipulation in Financial Markets and Its Reform: A UK-EC Perspective" (July 1999) (unpublished Ph.D. thesis, LSE). The thesis proposes the introduction in the United Kingdom of a right of action that could be exercised by after-market traders in the case of financial market fraud and manipulation.

- *Manner of regulation.* The FSA has promised a more focused and transparent approach to regulation,[9] but it remains to be seen how far that can be achieved in practice. However it is clear that substantial practical benefits will accrue from the unification of the previously fragmented regulatory regime. In particular, there will be a single unified rulebook governing conduct of business for all the different kinds of investment and financial institutions coming under the regulatory oversight of the FSA, and a single compensation scheme for investors and depositors. The system will be complemented with the financial services ombudsman, which will mainly consider consumer grievances. Furthermore, the manner the FSA will chose to discharge its regulatory duty will affect its relationship with industry. Inevitably, the FSA must work closely with industry in order to provide a well-regulated environment for the conduct of investment busines in the United Kingdom.

- *Cost of regulation.* Last but not least, is the question of the cost of regulation. Cost is both direct in terms of fees and levies, and indirect in terms of time required to ensure compliance by regulated firms. It is expected that the costs of compliance for financial institutions will increase during the transitional period. But the hope is that once industry becomes comfortable with the 2000 Act and the new FSA rulebooks, the benefits of focused regulation will exceed significantly any costs. The FSA itself is self-financed. It is not supported by fiscal revenues. That fact, together with the reference in the 2000 Act to the "desirability of maintaining the competitive position of the United Kingdom" will ensure that pressure is maintained to avoid the FSA developing into a costly, inefficient bureaucracy.

The Future

With the coming into force of the Financial Services and Markets Act 2000 and supporting secondary legislation, the establishment of

---

[9] Financial Services Authority, *A New Regulator for the New Millennium* (January 2000).

the structure of the United Kingdom's new regulatory regime will largely be complete. The whole process, from the time when the proposal was first put forward was about four years, which is an impressive achievement given the size of the task. Moreover, by then, in practice the FSA will have been operational for over two years under the transitional arrangements referred to above. The FSA's responsibilities will include:

- banks;

- markets, exchanges, clearinghouses, etc.;

- insurance companies;

- listing securities (this role was transferred from the London Stock Exchange on May 1, 2000, following moves for the demutualization of the latter and its merger proposals with Frankfurt Stock Exchange, proposals which were not pursued);

- building societies (equivalent to U.S. savings and loans institutions);

- friendly societies and industrial providence societies (another form of savings institution);

- stockbrokers, investment banks, derivatives, market makers;

- fund managers;

- life insurance and independent financial advice;

- provision of mortgages;

- lawyers and accountants doing mainstream investment business;

- Lloyds of London (the international insurance market); and

- credit unions.

In summary, the FSA will regulate and authorize all financial businesses in the United Kingdom together with unit trusts and open-ended investment companies, and it will recognize and supervise investment exchanges and clearinghouses.

What of the future? All in all, it is fair to say that the establishment of the United Kingdom's unified regulator has so far proved to be a bold but successful reform. Of course there are dangers inherent in an organization that becomes too powerful or unwieldy. For example, there are still doubts as to how well and how fast the regulatory cultures of the merging organizations will mesh within the new regulatory mold. In reality, however, international financial markets and the institutions which operate within them often dwarf in size and sophistication the regulatory bodies, with the possible exception of those in the United States, and in particular the Secutiries and Exchange Commission and the Federal Reserve. A powerful and credible regulator in the United Kingdom should be seen as an essential adjunct to good business. In the end, the litmus test of the reforms will be whether regulation is delivered more efficiently at a lower cost. The auguries are promising, and the reforms decisively resolved one central feature of modern financial markets: divisions based on securities business, banking business, and insurance business are increasingly blurred. The unitary approach may, or may not, provide a model for other regulatory systems. That depends on the particular system concerned, as I made clear at the outset. In the case of the United Kingdom, however, the formula appears to have worked.

Chapter 24 | Converging Standards for Evaluating Banking Supervision in Individual Countries

RICKI TIGERT HELFER

The evolving standards for banking supervision require assessments of the quality and effectiveness of banking supervision and regulation in individual countries. This paper notes a variety of circumstances in which these assessments have increasingly been required. It begins with an analysis of assessments in the context of three iterations of standards for cross-border supervision of banking organizations. It then turns to a discussion of the U.S. approach mandated by statute for judging the quality and effectiveness of consolidated supervision by home country banking authorities of banks seeking entry into the United States. The paper focuses on the implementation of international standards for banking supervision developed by the Basel Committee on Banking Supervision (BCBS) in the form of "Core Principles for Effective Banking Supervision."[1]

The paper emphasizes that assessments of the quality and effectiveness of banking supervision in other countries have real consequences for the individual countries whose bank supervisory systems are under review. The paper highlights the importance of ensuring the fairness and uniformity of the assessments. It notes that in a number of contexts assessments require a balancing that will yield different results depending upon who is making the assessment. The paper suggests that ensuring the objectivity of the assessments is critical to their credibility in the outside world and to their acceptance by political authorities in countries being evaluated. The paper contends that one way to ensure that objectivity is to establish a mechanism for identifying problem areas in the conduct and results of

---

[1] (September 1997) available from the BIS website at www.bis.org/publ (Core Principles). The BCBS is physically located at the Bank for International Settlements (BIS) in Basel, Switzerland, and its publications, including those cited in this paper, are available under the name of the BCBS from the BIS web site at www.bis.org/publ.

assessments, for discussing how to improve the assessment process, and for implementing suggested changes. This paper in particular suggests that central bank lawyers in individual countries should be more involved in the process of assessments and that they should meet periodically in regional and extraregional meetings, perhaps under the auspices of the BIS, to discuss problems and solutions in an effort to ensure the fairness and uniformity of assessments of banking supervisory systems in individual countries.

Assessments of the Quality and Effectiveness of Consolidated Banking Supervision

Consolidated banking supervision was probably the first area in which an assessment of the quality and effectiveness of banking supervision in individual countries was called for. In May 1983, the BCBS published its "Principles for the Supervision of Banks' Foreign Establishments" as a replacement to the Basel Concordat, which was the Committee's first major pronouncement in 1975 on cross-border supervision. The revised Concordat, which applied to countries that were members of the BCBS,[2] established "best practices," not "requirements." It called for individual countries to assess the quality of supervision in other countries in order to determine whether banks seeking to establish cross-border offices were being adequately supervised.[3] The Concordat created a presumption that "host authorities are in a position to fulfill their supervisory obligations adequately with respect to all foreign bank establishments operating in their territories" but noted that "this may not always be the case." That is where the obligation to assess another country's bank supervisory system came into play. In this regard, the Concordat stated:

---

[2] The BCBS consists of the senior representatives of bank supervisory authorities and central banks from Belgium, Canada, France, Germany, Italy, Japan, Luxembourg, Netherlands, Sweden, Switzerland, United Kingdom, and the United States. These are the Group of Ten countries, plus Switzerland and Luxembourg.

[3] The BCBS documents use the term banking "establishments" to refer to foreign bank offices and seem to include subsidiaries, branches, and agencies of foreign banks. For ease of language in this paper, I will use the term "offices" to refer to the same thing.

In cases where host authority supervision is inadequate, the parent authority should either extend its supervision, to the degree that it is practicable, or it should be prepared to discourage the parent bank from continuing to operate the establishment.

Thus there were potential consequences of an assessment that banking supervision in a particular country was not adequate, but it is not clear how many host countries applied the ultimate sanction of excluding the banks from a home country with ineffective cross-border banking supervision.

In an effort to provide guidance on improving bank supervisory systems in home countries, the Concordat identified a range of techniques that supervisory authorities could use to fulfill their responsibilities and noted that an important one was the principle of consolidated supervision in accordance with which

parent banks and parent supervisory authorities monitor the risk exposure—including a perspective of concentrations of risk and of the quality of assets—of the banks or banking groups for which they are responsible, as well as the adequacy of their capital, on the basis of the totality of their business wherever conducted.

It also called for the supervision of a bank's foreign establishments to be considered from three different aspects: solvency, liquidity, and foreign exchange operations and positions.

The new Basel Concordat was thus the beginning of an effort to place responsibility on the bank supervisory authorities in home and host countries for the effective supervision of foreign banks and also an early example of the BCBS's efforts to identify the standards for categories of supervision that make up a strong system of banking supervision.

This effort became considerably more serious in 1992 when the BCBS published "Minimum Standards for the Supervision of International Banking Groups and their Cross-Border Establishments" (1992 Standards). Thus the "best practices" of the previous directive became "minimum standards" that required that the supervisory authorities represented on the BCBS take "steps to ensure that their own supervisory arrangements meet the standards as soon as possible." Thus there was a time frame for compliance and a set of minimum standards that every country represented on the Committee was required to meet. Under the 1992 Standards, consolidated supervision by the home country authority became not just one of the techniques for supervision, albeit an important one, but an essential requirement of the standards. Moreover, the 1992 Standards set out the elements of consolidated supervision necessary for a country to meet the standards. In addition, these Standards required that a new cross-border banking office receive the consent of both the host country supervisory authority and the bank's and the banking group's home country supervisory authority (if they were different).

Even more significantly, the 1992 Standards introduced a firm requirement that the host country assess and act upon the results of the assessment of the quality and effectiveness of banking supervision in the home country. It mandated that a host country authority determine whether a bank or banking group seeking to enter the host country "is subject to consolidated supervision by an authority that has—or is actively working to establish—the necessary capabilities to meet these minimum standards." If the answer is "no" to both inquiries, the BCBS directs that the host country banking authority prohibit the bank or banking group from establishing an office in the host country, unless the "host country itself accepts the responsibility to perform supervision of the bank or banking group's local [offices] consistent with these minimum standards." For purposes of assessing the home country authority's bank supervisory skill, the 1992 Standards require that

> the host country authority should determine whether the bank and, if different, the banking group is supervised by a home country authority which has the *practical capability of performing consolidated supervision.* (Emphasis supplied.)

"Practical capability" clearly was intended to mean more than subscribing on paper to the principles of consolidated supervision. The 1992 Standards included minimum requirements for effective consolidated supervision:

> The home country supervisory authority should (a) receive consolidated financial and prudential information on the bank's or banking group's global operations, have the reliability of this information confirmed to its own satisfaction through on-site examination or other means, and assess the information as it may

bear on the safety and soundness of the bank or banking group, (b) have the capability to prevent corporate affiliations or structures that either undermine efforts to maintain consolidated financial information or otherwise hinder effective supervision of the bank or banking group, and (c) have the capability to prevent the bank or banking group from creating foreign banking establishments in particular jurisdictions.

Thus, in the context of the 1992 Standards, "practical capability" means having supervisory staff with the experience and knowledge to perform the necessary elements of consolidated supervision identified in the Basel document. It means deploying the staff worldwide, if necessary, to perform meaningful examinations on-site or to evaluate audit results; obtaining the necessary credible information to assess the bank or banking group's operations effectively and being capable of evaluating the information; and having the authority and being willing to take enforcement actions as necessary to sanction banks or banking groups that fail to meet necessary supervisory standards and/or fail to supply accurate information to allow a full and complete evaluation of their operations.

This emphasis on "effective" supervision through minimum standards has become the hallmark of more recent initiatives in the BCBS. In the 1992 Standards: (1) the BCBS required one country to assess the quality and effectiveness of banking supervision in another; and (2) there were consequences to such an evaluation that gave rise to additional responsibilities for the host country performing the assessment or to a prohibition on banks from the home country entering the host country.

Even so, the 1992 Standards were directed at the members of the BCBS. If the overall goals of reducing systemic risk and increasing the stability of the international system were to be achieved, it was necessary to look more specifically at the trouble spots around the globe. For that reason, in October 1996, the BCBS issued a report of the working group of members of the BCBS and the Offshore Group of Banking Supervisors entitled "The Supervision of Cross-Border Banking" (1996 Report). The Report identified two problems in the implementation of the 1992 minimum standards. The first problem identified was that home country supervisors had experienced difficulties in obtaining the information they needed to undertake effective consolidated supervision and the impediment was identified as bank secrecy laws. The Report was firm that bank secrecy laws should not be permitted to "impede the ability of supervisors to ensure safety and soundness in the international banking system." The second problem related to the directive that all cross-border operations should be subject to "*effective home and host [country] supervision*" (Emphasis in original.). In particular, the 1996 report stated that host country supervisors have "no common standards to judge what constitutes effective consolidated supervision by home supervisors" and whether such supervision is being "capably" executed. The report suggested that "in deciding how best to carry out effective consolidated supervision, home supervisors needed a mechanism to assess the standards of supervision exercised by host supervisors." In response to this need, the 1996 Report stated that the Offshore Group of Banking Supervisors had established minimum criteria for its members and had sought the help of the BCBS in determining whether individual offshore centers met those criteria.

The issue of how to judge whether a country is meeting its bank supervisory responsibilities is clearly a thorny one. Indeed, Appendix B of the 1996 Report stated:

> There can be no single set of criteria to determine whether or nor a home supervisor is performing "effective consolidated supervision," since supervisory techniques differ from country to country, due to institutional, historical, legal or other factors. The concepts of consolidated supervision can, however, be defined namely as a group-wide approach to supervision whereby all the risks run by a banking group are taken into account, wherever they are booked. In other words, it is a process whereby a supervisor can satisfy himself about the totality of a banking group's activities, which may include nonbank companies and financial affiliates, as well as direct branches and subsidiaries.

Thus, the difficulty of the task of assessing the quality and effectiveness of consolidated supervision in an individual country was brought to the fore. The 1996 Report essentially recognized it as a moving target in two respects. First, as noted in the quoted material above, the report recognized that "supervisory techniques differ from country to country, due to institutional, historical, legal, or other factors" and therefore how consolidated supervision is achieved would vary from country to country. Second, the report emphasized that consolidated supervision is a "process" by which the bank supervisory authority must satisfy himself or herself about the "totality" of the banking group's activity, but whether the process is adequate in the eyes of another supervisor and the results of that judgment will vary from supervisor to supervisor depending upon the capabilities of home and host country supervisors.

Let me explain. The 1996 Report makes clear that in some sense there is a zero-sum calculation being made by supervisors of their own capabilities and the capabilities of another supervisor:

> In reaching a decision as to the effectiveness of the consolidated supervision conducted by a home [country] supervisor, the host [country] supervisor will also need to take account of his own supervisory capabilities. If he has limited resources, greater demands will be placed on the home [country] supervisor than if host [country] supervision is strong. The host also has to judge the extent to which its supervision complements that of the home [country] supervisor, or whether there are potential gaps. Accordingly, one host [country] supervisor may decide that a given country is conducting effective consolidated supervision, whereas another host [country] supervisor with different capabilities may decide that it is not.

Assuring the reliability of the assessment process for determining the quality and effectiveness of banking supervision in an individual country is a complicated proposition with the kind of balancing described above involving one supervisor's assessment of its own and another supervisor's capabilities. These kinds of assessments are especially difficult when performed for the operational reason of determining which a host country supervisory authority will bear the lion's share of responsibility for consolidated supervision of a foreign banking group's offices. These assessments will not always be objective, given the fact that they involve a supervisor assessing his own capabilities and a balancing of his capabilities against another supervisor's capabilities, especially when finding another country deficient will automatically lead to the assessing country having to devote its own resources to making up the difference. In the case of a supervisor lacking in basic resources, the assessment is easier and more objective, but in the case of a supervisor that is on the borderline in terms of his capabilities, objectivity is harder to achieve, for himself and for the other supervisor who is making the judgment.

In contrast, if the assessment is not being made by the host or home country bank supervisory authority, but by some third party, the nature and results of the assessment will presumably vary from the balance described in the 1996 Report, but may not be any more definitively objective. To get some sense of how these country-to-country assessments are being made, it is useful to analyze how one country has chosen to evaluate the supervisory capabilities of other countries under a statutory mandate to perform such assessments in approving or disapproving new foreign bank offices.

U.S. Approach to Assessments of Consolidated Supervision in Other Countries

The United States enacted legislation in 1991, the Foreign Bank Supervision Enhancement Act (FBSEA),[4] that prohibits foreign banks from establishing branches, agencies, representative offices, and commercial lending company subsidiaries without the prior approval of the Board of Governors of the Federal Reserve System (Fed).[5] In particular, the statute provides that the Fed may not approve an application by a foreign bank to establish an office in the United States, including a subsidiary, unless it determines that

> (A) the foreign bank engages directly in the business of banking outside of the United States and is subject to comprehensive supervision or regulation on a consolidated basis by the appropriate authorities in its home country; and (B) the foreign bank has furnished to the Board the information it needs to adequately assess the application.[6]

According to the Fed's public information office, as of February 23, 2000, it had published 107 decisions approving applications by

---

[4] 12 U.S.C. §3101 *et seq.*, Public Law 102-242, Title II (1991).

[5] *See* 202(a) and 204 of the FBSEA amending the International Banking Act (IBA), 12 U.S.C. §3105 and §3107. At the time the FBSEA was enacted, the Bank Holding Company Act already prohibited any company, including a foreign bank, from acquiring ownership or control of a U.S. bank without the prior approval of the Fed. *See* 12 U.S.C. §1842(a).

[6] Section 202(a) of the FBSEA amending the IBA, 12 U.S.C. §3105(d)(2). The FBSEA also amends the Bank Holding Company Act to add these same criteria to the Fed's review of an application to acquire ownership or control of a U.S. bank. *See* section 202(d) of the FBSEA amending 12 U.S.C. §1842(c).

foreign banks from a diverse range of countries to establish representative offices, agencies, and branches in the United States and 24 decisions approving foreign bank acquisitions of U.S. banks since the FBSEA became effective.[7] Some of the foreign banks whose applications were approved already had offices in the United States, and some of the foreign banks were establishing U.S. offices for the first time. The statute does not require reapproval of foreign bank offices already in place in the United States at the time the FBSEA was enacted, but it did give the Fed for the first time the authority to terminate the offices of foreign banks in the United States if

> (A) the foreign bank is not subject to comprehensive supervision or regulation on a consolidated basis by the appropriate authorities in its home country; or

> (B)(i) there is reasonable cause to believe that such foreign bank, or any affiliate of such foreign bank, has committed a violation of law or engaged in an unsafe or unsound banking practice in the United States; and

> (ii) as a result of such violation or practice, the continued operation of the foreign bank's branch, agency, or commercial lending company subsidiary in the United States would not be consistent with the public interest or with the purposes of the [FBSEA and other relevant U.S. banking statutes].[8]

The Fed's regulations implementing the FBSEA set out the basis for determining comprehensive supervision on a consolidated basis. They state:

> The [Fed] shall determine whether the foreign bank is supervised or regulated in such a manner that its home country supervisor receives sufficient information on the worldwide operations of the foreign bank (including the relationships of the bank to any affiliate) to assess the foreign bank's overall financial condition and compliance with law and regulation.[9]

---

[7] *See* Appendix A for the Fed's list of foreign banks for which new offices have been approved and the countries in which the foreign banks are headquartered.

[8] Section 202(a) of the FBSEA amending the IBA to insert a new provision, 12 U.S.C. §3105(e).

[9] 12 C.F.R. §211.24(c)(ii).

The Fed's regulations set out five principal factors that the Fed will consider in assessing the quality and effectiveness of consolidated home country supervision related to whether the home country bank supervisory authority is (1) monitoring and controlling the bank's activities worldwide; (2) obtaining information on the condition of the bank and its offices outside the home country through regular examination or audit reports; (3) obtaining information on the dealings and relationships between the foreign bank and its affiliates; (4) receiving financial reports from the bank that are consolidated on a worldwide basis, or comparable information that permits analysis of the foreign bank's financial condition on a worldwide consolidated basis; and (5) evaluating prudential standards, such as capital adequacy and risk asset exposure, on a worldwide basis.[10]

On the face of these provisions, the Fed cannot permit foreign banks to open or maintain foreign bank offices in the United States unless the Fed finds the home country supervisor subjects the foreign bank to comprehensive supervision on a consolidated basis. Quite a few countries in the world could not meet this standard. For that reason, the Fed has applied a qualifier to the statutory standards. A review of the published decisions of the Fed shows that it will consider an intermediate position—to what extent a home country supervisor is in the process of "actively working to establish arrangements for the consolidated supervision of a bank"[11]—in deciding whether to permit a foreign bank to establish an office in the United States. This intermediate standard is comparable to the standard set out in the 1992 Minimum Standards, which permits a host country to evaluate whether the relevant supervisory authority is "not actively working to establish the necessary capabilities" before deciding whether to accept greater responsibility for supervising cross-border banking operations.

The Fed also established a hierarchy for banking offices in the United States depending upon whether the type of office for which application is being made can accept deposits from the public or engage in other retail banking activities. It is easier to get approval of

---

[10] *Id.*
[11] *See* "Order Approving Establishment of a Branch" by Kookmin Bank, Seoul, Korea, Federal Reserve Release, February 11, 2000 (www.federalreserve.gov/boarddocs/press/BHC/2000/20000211/).

a representative office (which cannot accept deposits or make loans to the public) than an agency (which can accept credit balances but not deposits from U.S. residents), and it is easier still to get approval to open an agency than a branch (which can engage in a full range of retail and commercial banking activities). Thus, the Fed requires less advanced supervisory capability of the home country supervisor of a foreign bank that seeks only to open a representative office in the United States. According to the Fed:

> [We have] stated previously that the standards that apply to the establishment of a branch or agency need not in every case apply to the establishment of a representative office because representative offices do not engage in a banking business and cannot take deposits or make loans....
>
> With respect to supervision by home country authorities, the Board to date has required foreign banks that proposed to establish a representative office to be subject to a significant degree of supervision by their home country supervisor as determined with reference to a number of factors....[12]

Even in the case of representative offices, the Fed applies a lower standard for home office supervision if the applicant bank will accept limitations on the activities the representative office may engage in. The Fed stated this standard in an order approving a limited representative office for a Russian bank:

> (i) The bank commits that the proposed representative office will engage only in a limited set of activities considered to pose minimal risk to U.S. markets or U.S. counterparties, and
>
> (ii) The bank is subject to a supervisory framework that is consistent with approval of the application, taking into account the limited activities of the proposed office and the operating record of the bank.
>
> In assessing whether a particular applicant would be eligible for this standard, a review of the home country supervisory system would be expected to indicate that the bank's home country supervisor is

---

[12] *See* "Order Approving Establishment of a Representative Office" for Promstroybank of Russia, April 8, 1996, 82 *Fed. Reserve Bull* 599 (June 1996).

taking definite action to implement a system of supervision containing the factors previously required in representative office applications.[13]

The Fed has also emphasized in its various orders related to approvals of foreign bank offices in the United States that it must have necessary assurances of access to information on the operations and affiliations of the applicant bank to determine compliance with applicable U.S. laws. In the case of the application of one Chilean bank, for example, the Fed's order stated that the bank had committed to cooperate with the Fed "to obtain any necessary consents or waivers that might be required from third parties in connection with disclosure of such information."[14]

The Fed has not rejected any foreign bank applications to open offices in the United States. However, based upon the Fed's assessment of the more limited capabilities of the home country supervisor, the Fed has actively encouraged some foreign banks to file applications for offices that are lower in the hierarchy of foreign bank offices than the office originally sought by the applicant foreign bank. The Fed has also not terminated a foreign bank office solely on the grounds that it is not supervised on a comprehensive consolidated

---

[13] *Id.* According to the Fed's order, under these standards permissible activities would normally include soliciting new wholesale, but not retail, business; acting as liaison between the bank's head office and U.S. customers; general marketing or promotional activities; developing and strengthening correspondent banking relationships; certain loan solicitation activities; or other such limited functions. They would not include making loan decisions, soliciting deposits from noninstitutional sources, or engaging in business with individuals acting personally. In the order related to the application of a Czech bank, the Fed also noted that the bank had committed that it would not conduct any activities related to trading of securities or foreign exchange. "Order Approving Establishment of a Representative Office," for Komercni Banka of Czech Republic, April 22, 1996, 82 *Fed. Reserve Bull.* 597 (June 1996). To ensure that these limitations are met the Fed also conditioned approval of the application of Promstroybank, *see* note 12 *supra*, for example, on restrictions on the number of employees in the representative office. In addition, the Fed also reviewed the financial and managerial resources of the bank, as well as its operating record, in order to determine the financial stability of the bank and whether it is capable of complying with applicable laws.

[14] "Order Approving Establishment of an Agency" for Banco de Credito e Inversiones S.A. of Chile, April 12, 1999 (www.federalreserve.gov/boarddocs/press/BHC/1999/19990412/).

basis;[15] however, it is reasonable to assume that if the Fed is concerned about the supervisory capabilities of particular home country supervisors, it will scrutinize the U.S. operations of foreign banks headquartered in that country more closely through more detailed on-site examinations of the offices. Moreover, it is certainly possible that the Fed may ultimately ask foreign banks that established an office in the United States prior to the date on which the requirements of the FBSEA became effective, or that established an office after that date but failed to meet the conditions or expectations of the Fed, to scale back the office to one lower in the hierarchy of offices, or even close the office, if the Fed's concerns become more significant. Finally, if need be, and with proof of serious consequences from a weak home country supervisor, the Fed may decide to take action to terminate the license of the foreign bank in the United States. For now, the Fed is focused on trying to encourage as many supervisory reforms as possible in other countries to ensure a sound international financial system. Allowing the foreign bank office to stay open, with the known option of closing it if need be, provides the leverage the Fed needs to encourage consequential reform.

Core Principles for Effective Banking Supervision

The Group of Seven Economic Summit in Halifax, Canada, in June 1995, focused substantial attention on the need for reform in the infrastructure of banking and financial regulation in emerging market countries. In particular, the summit of finance ministers and central bank governors called for the development of minimum standards for banking supervision that could be implemented in programs of economic and financial reform overseen by the International Monetary Fund (IMF) and the World Bank. The central bank governors of the BIS asked the BCBS to develop minimum standards for banking supervision.

The BCBS was reluctant to take on such a task because a number of its members were concerned that such an undertaking would distract the BCBS from its principal focus, which was to ensure sound

---

[15] Daiwa Bank's U.S. offices were terminated on the basis of violations of U.S. law.

banking supervision in the BCBS member countries. Some were also concerned that there would be a moral hazard associated with such an undertaking—that the rest of the world would view the BCBS as endorsing the conduct of banking supervision in countries that ostensibly adopted the minimum standards, even though the members of the BCBS were well aware that effective banking supervision had proved to be an ongoing effort—with the goal posts constantly moving—ever since the BCBS was formed in 1975. Nevertheless, the BCBS came to recognize that if it did not develop the minimum standards for banking supervision that the Group of Seven were seeking, the IMF or the World Bank or both would develop those standards out of necessity, and the recognized expertise in the field of banking supervision lay not with those institutions but with the BCBS.

The BCBS developed 25 principles of banking supervision in the areas of licensing, including the fit and proper test for directors and senior managers; approval for changes of structure; arrangements for ongoing banking supervision, including risk assessment, capital adequacy, credit and market risk management, internal controls, off-site surveillance, and on-site examination or use of external auditors; informational requirements including accounting and reporting standards; formal powers of supervisors for enforcement actions and liquidation procedures; and cross-border banking as it relates to the obligations of home and host country supervisors. To ensure the credibility of these standards outside the member countries of the BCBS, a draft of the standards was shared with eleven regional groups of bank supervisory authorities from around the world. In addition, supervisors from 16 countries were asked to participate more extensively in the development of the standards.[16] The "Core Principles for Effective Banking Supervision" were published in September 1997 and were endorsed at the annual meeting of the IMF and the World Bank in October 1997.

In the introduction to the standards, the BCBS states that the Principles "have been designed to be verifiable by supervisors,

---

[16] "Core Principles" at 3. Those countries were Chile, China, the Czech Republic, Hong Kong SAR, Mexico, Russia, Thailand, Argentina, Brazil, Hungary, India, Indonesia, Korea, Malaysia, Poland, and Singapore.

regional supervisory groups, and the market at large."[17] In addition, the BCBS agreed to "play a role, together with other interested organisations, in monitoring the progress made by individual countries" in implementing the Core Principles.[18] Moreover, it suggested that

> the IMF, the World Bank and other interested organisations use the Principles in assisting individual countries to strengthen their supervisory arrangements in connection with work aimed at promoting overall macroeconomic and financial stability.[19]

Thus, the Core Principles were developed in order to have a direct impact on financial and banking infrastructure reform in non-BCBS countries, and with the clear intention that there would be consequences from a failure to adopt the minimum standards for banking supervision contained in the Core Principles. Those consequences were directly implied by the reference to the work of the IMF and the World Bank in using the standards to promote economic reform and financial stability. Presumably, the consequences would be in the form of the decreases in the monetary incentives that the IMF and the World Bank have to encourage countries to accept necessary reforms.

Unlike other standards applied by the IMF and the World Bank, however, which are often developed internally by those agencies with little opportunity for the outside world to comment, drafts of the Core Principles were widely circulated to bank supervisory authorities from around the world and were the product of participation in their development by representatives of key non-BCBS emerging market countries. Moreover, they were discussed with approval at the International Conference of Banking Supervisors in October 1998 and, the BCBS committed, they would be discussed at that same conference biennially thereafter.[20]

Despite the BCBS's efforts to be inclusive in the development of the Core Principles and its commitment to play a role in monitoring

---

[17] *Id.*
[18] *Id.* at 2.
[19] *Id.*
[20] *Id.*

progress made by individual countries in implementing the Standards, ensuring consistency and reliability in their implementation proved to be difficult to achieve.

Core Principles Methodology

The BCBS came to recognize that the Core Principles "may be interpreted in widely diverging ways, and incorrect interpretations may result in inconsistencies among assessments."[21] To ensure that the assessments will be as objective and uniform as possible, the BCBS established a working group composed of representatives of the BCBS, the IMF, and the World Bank, with consultations with bank supervisors from Group of Ten and non–Group of Ten countries, to develop a methodology for implementing the Core Principles. The *Core Principles Methodology*, published in October 1999, sets out "all significant criteria which are relevant for compliance" with the Core Principles.[22] For each of the 25 Core Principles, it sets out the "essential criteria" for compliance and the "additional criteria" that "further strengthen supervision and which all countries should strive to implement."[23] According to the Methodology, "[t]o achieve full compliance with a Principle, the essential criteria generally must be met without any significant deficiencies."[24] The Methodology makes clear, however, that there is room for discretion in applying the criteria for compliance with the Core Principles:

> There may be instances, of course, where a country can demonstrate that the Principle has been achieved through different means. Conversely, due to the specific conditions in individual countries, the essential criteria may not always be sufficient to achieve the objective of the Principle, and therefore the additional criteria and/or other measures may also be needed in order for the aspect of banking supervision addressed by the Principle to be considered effective.[25]

---

[21] BCBS, "Core Principles Methodology" (October 1999) at 2, available at BIS website at http://www.bis.org/publ.
[22] *Id.* at 2.
[23] Id.
[24] *Id.*
[25] *Id.*

As an example, the Core Principles Methodology includes as an appendix the format developed by the IMF and the World Bank for conducting their assessments of the state of implementation of the Core Principles in individual countries. The examples, however, are not particularly helpful in directing when essential criteria will be enough for compliance and when additional criteria will be necessary. Although the BCBS is seeking to ensure that the assessments of supervisory capability in individual countries will be "objective and uniform," and the Methodology in the form of specific criteria will help achieve those goals, the guidance cannot ensure that "incorrect interpretations" will be avoided in the future.

Consequences of Assessments

A number of consequences of assessments of the capabilities of a bank supervisory authority in an individual country have already been discussed: a prohibition on banks headquartered in the home country being evaluated from engaging in banking operations in a host country and potential limitations on the availability of IMF and World Bank funding for noncompliant countries. The latter could include little or no funding for developing a deposit insurance system until essential bank supervisory reforms have been made.[26] In addition, the BCBS has stated it intends to enlist the market in encouraging compliance with the Core Principles.[27] That can only result if there are consequences in the marketplace for noncompliance. Rating agencies, such as Standard and Poor's or Moody's, may downgrade a noncomplying country and that may affect the willingness of foreign investors to make investments in, or credit available to, the country. These consequences will be increased, of course, to the extent there is transparency of information about noncompliance.

Political authorities will need to understand and appreciate what the consequences of being noncompliant with the Core Principles mean to the country. For these same political authorities to respond to the potential consequences by providing political support for achieving compliance with the Principles, they will have to accept

---

[26] *See* Ricki Tigert Helfer, "What Deposit Insurance Can and Cannot Do," 36 *Finance and Development* at 22 (March 1999, IMF).

[27] Core Principles at 2.

that the standards are being applied fairly, uniformly, and predictably. To achieve that goal will require more information than we currently have in the public domain and is likely to require more direct and regular monitoring of how the assessments are conducted and whether the results are consistent and reliable.

Proposal for Monitoring and Evaluating Assessments

To date, the Core Principles have been developed by bank supervisory officials and have been implemented with the assistance of financial officials and occasionally newly hired officials with supervisory experience at the IMF and the World Bank. To give the level of comfort to political officials in countries being evaluated to ensure support for compliance, in my view it makes sense to enlist the help of lawyers at the central banks. Lawyers are trained to apply legal rules and standards, and central banks are responsible for systemic risk and financial stability. The combination of skills and background mean that central bank lawyers are well suited to participate in ensuring the credibility of the assessment process and to prevent the objective of these assessments—to ensure international financial stability—from dropping off the radar screens of senior government officials around the world. Through regional groups, central bank lawyers could compare experiences, identify problems in the conduct of assessments, and ensure that standards applied in one country are applied in the same way in another country. Occasional extraregional meetings under the BIS's auspices could give greater visibility to the effort and could allow for even more uniformity in the way the standards are applied. Over time it may even make sense to develop standards for judging how the assessments are being performed and whether their results are fair and uniform.

Chapter 25 | Some Aspects of the Discretion of Bank Regulators in Addressing Banking Problems

TOBIAS M.C. ASSER

Most banking laws authorize the bank regulator to order a bank in distress to take corrective measures or to take control of the bank through provisional administration or a receivership.

As a rule, the scope of the powers of a public agency such as the bank regulator are limited by the statutory provisions (the banking law) granting those powers. Sometimes, the law prescribes more or less precisely when and how a certain authority is to be exercised. More often, however, the law grants the regulator a degree of *discretion* in deciding when and how a certain power is to be exercised. Discretion in this context means that the decision whether or not to take action and the choice of measures to be imposed on a bank depend to a greater or lesser extent on the judgment of the bank regulator.

Some banking law provisions grant the regulator a great deal of discretion. Others restrict the regulator's discretion, for instance by including a limited list of corrective measures from which the regulator must chose. In some cases the law goes even further and requires the regulator in circumstances defined by the law to take a particular action; then, the law is said to be *mandatory*.

The foregoing is illustrated by the following banking law provision:

> When a bank has failed to follow sound banking practices, the bank regulator, after having afforded the bank's managers an opportunity to explain such failure, may issue a warning to them.[1]

---

[1] France: Art. 42 of Law No.84-46 on the activities and supervision of credit institutions.

In analyzing the law, a distinction must be drawn between the *legal authority* to take such regulatory action, the *grounds* on which that authority may be exercised, and the *regulatory action* that may be taken pursuant to that authority. In the foregoing example, the legal authority to take corrective action is granted by the provision that the bank regulator may issue a warning. The ground for exercising that authority is that the bank has failed to follow sound banking practices. The action authorized by the law is the issue of a warning to the bank's managers.

Legal Authority to Take Regulatory Action

In the foregoing example, the legal authority to take corrective action is couched in permissive language: the provision says may issue a warning. This means that the bank regulator has discretion in deciding whether or not to exercise his authority under the provision. If, in contrast, the provision had used mandatory language and had said shall issue a warning, the regulator would have no discretion in the exercise of his authority: whenever the regulator determined that a bank had failed to follow sound banking practices, the regulator would be required to take the action prescribed by the law.

The permissive approach raises a serious issue. Assuming that all provisions of the banking law which authorize the bank regulator to take corrective action against a wayward bank are couched in permissive language—as is the case in many countries—would the regulator then be permitted not to take any corrective action at all against such bank? As, strictly speaking, the answer must be affirmative, the issue is whether this state of affairs is acceptable. Should the bank regulator not be required by law to address every infraction of the banking law?

Without opening a discussion of regulatory forbearance, the supporters of permissive treatment generally respond that there are circumstances in which the exercise of remedial authority on the part of the regulator would make little sense, for instance, when the violation at issue is insignificant or has been corrected already by the bank. This response is not very convincing, because the law can contain suitable exemptions. For instance, the law can explicitly require that the violation be significant before corrective action may be taken. This reduces discretion in the exercise of regulatory authority to address an infraction to a judgment as to the significance of the infraction. Situations in which an infraction has been corrected already can be covered in the law by requiring that the infraction be continuing when action is taken by the regulator.

There are provisions of banking law which leave the regulator no choice in the exercise of his authority and require him to take regulatory action. In *Switzerland*, for example, the banking law contains the following provision:

> When the bank regulator discovers violations of the law or other irregularities, it shall take the measures necessary to restore the rule of law and to remove the irregularities.[2]

The provision requires the regulator to do whatever is necessary to remedy the situation; if it had been phrased in permissive language and had said *may take the measures*, it would have permitted the regulator to abstain from corrective action altogether. The exercise of regulatory authority to take regulatory action is made mandatory. However, the choice of regulatory action is largely discretionary. This means that the provision is not strictly mandatory. It would be strictly mandatory if the provision also dictated the measures to be taken by the regulator.

Strictly mandatory provisions of banking law are usually reserved for special situations, where it concerns a particular regulatory act in narrowly defined circumstances. Thus, in England, the banking law requires the bank regulator to revoke a bank's banking license when a winding-up order has been made against the bank.[3] Another example would be the provisions of United States banking law which require the regulator to take prompt corrective action in the event that a bank fails to meet capital adequacy standards.[4]

There are banking laws which provide for a two-step approach in granting authority to take regulatory action. The first step usually

---

[2] Art. 23 (1) of the Federal Law on Banks and Savings Banks.
[3] Section 11(6)(a) of the Banking Act 1987.
[4] 12 U.S.C. §1831o, even though these provisions require banks to submit and carry out a capital restoration plan whose content is negotiated with the regulator, leaving considerable room for discretion as to the content of the plan.

consists of a guideline, recommendation, or order to the bank to correct a certain deficiency, often within a deadline specified by the regulator, while the second step consists of more rigorous action, such as the application of a sanction or taking control of the bank through provisional administration if the first step is not taken by the bank.[5] One would expect that, when a bank fails to comply with a guideline or order of the regulator, the law would require the regulator to follow up with stricter regulatory action. Instead, the banking law typically permits the exercise of the regulator's authority to respond to this failure and provides accordingly that the second step *may* be taken.[6] As noncompliance with a direction of the bank regulator is a serious matter that cannot be disregarded by the regulator, it is difficult to understand why the exercise of the regulator's authority at the second level would not be mandatory. Flexibility can be built into a mandatory two-step approach by allowing extensions of the deadline for completion of the remedial action to be taken by the bank as a first step, and by making the choice of remedial action imposed as a second step more or less discretionary.

The banking law may curtail the discretion of the bank regulator in exercising authority granted by the banking law by prescribing procedures whereby the bank or its owners are given prior notice of impending regulatory action and are afforded an opportunity to present their views to the regulator at a hearing before such action is taken.[7] Such procedures have the effect of delaying a regulatory response to banking problems and thereby restrict the discretion of the regulator in determining the time of such response. As a delay in regulatory action caused by such procedures could have serious adverse effects on the bank concerned or even the banking system as

---

[5] Belgium: Art. 57(1) of the Law on the Statute and Supervision of Credit Institutions; Canada: Sections 485(3)(a) juncto 648(1.1) of the Bank Act; France: Articles 43 juncto 45 of Law No. 84-46 on the Activities and Supervision of Credit Institutions; Luxembourg: Art. 59(1) and (2) of the Law of 1993 on the Financial Sector; Netherlands: Art. 28(2) and (3) of the Law on Supervision of the Credit System.

[6] *See* the provisions cited in the preceding footnote.

[7] Canada: Section 645(2) of the Bank Act; England: Section 13 of the Banking Act 1987; France: Art. 42 of Law No. 84-46 on the Activities and Supervision of Credit Institutions; United States: 12 U.S.C. §1818(b).

a whole, the law may permit the regulator, in matters of urgency, to take regulatory action without such prior notification or hearing.[8]

The discretion of the bank regulator in taking action can also be restricted by providing that the action may only be taken with judicial concurrence. Typical examples would be taking regulatory control of a bank through a provisional administrator [9] or a receiver[10] who may be appointed only by court order. As a result of such provisions, the regulator may not exercise authority without judicial approval, and regulatory discretion of decision making is shared between the regulator and the court.

The balance of discretionary power between the regulator and the court can be calibrated by statutory provision. For instance, if the law provides that judicial insolvency proceedings may be opened against a bank upon the application of a bank's creditors after consultation with the bank regulator,[11] most of the discretionary decision making power rests with the court. If, however, the law provides that judicial insolvency proceedings shall be opened against a bank that is unable to pay its obligations or that is insolvent, and that only the bank regulator may petition the courts for the opening of insolvency proceedings against the bank,[12] the balance of power has shifted somewhat towards the bank regulator. If in this example, the law would also provide that the inability to pay or the insolvency of the bank is to be determined exclusively by the bank regulator, the discretionary power of decision making would rest mostly with the regulator. In the previously mentioned case, the court would not materially participate in the decision-making process. Its role would be limited to protecting the interests of the bank and its owners by reviewing the petition in the light of, inter alia, procedural requirements of the banking law and general principles of administrative law, for instance, to ascertain that the petition is not

---

[8] Canada: Section 645(2) and (3) of the Bank Act; England: Section 14 of the Banking Act 1987; France: Art. 48(2) of Law No. 84-46 on the Activities and Supervision of Credit Institutions; United States: 12 U.S.C. §1818(c).

[9] *E.g.*, Austria: Art. 83 of the Austrian Banking Act.

[10] *E.g.*, Netherlands: Art. 71 of the Law on Supervision of the Credit System.

[11] France: Art. 46-3 of Law No. 84-46 on the Activities and Supervision of Credit Institutions; Netherlands: Art. 70 of the Law on Supervision of the Credit System.

[12] Germany: Section 46b of the Law on the Credit System.

unreasonable. It follows that the absence of discretionary power on the part of the judiciary in the decision-making process need not mean that the judiciary could not play an important role as watchdog over compliance with the rule of law by the bank regulator.

A subsidiary issue is whether taking control of a bank through provisional administration or receivership should not always be submitted to the prior review of the courts. From a normative perspective, it may be argued that taking control of a bank involves a seizure of assets and that, therefore, taking control of a bank should require judicial involvement to protect the rights of interested parties, unless withholding such protection is necessary to serve a public good exceeding the need to protect those rights. The need to protect individual property interests through the courts is well established in both law and economics. Generally, therefore, it is difficult to justify banking law provisions which authorize the bank regulator to take control of a bank without any form of prior judicial review in any circumstances.[13] So as to avoid the court from usurping the discretion of the bank regulator, the banking law could restrict the scope of judicial review of the decision of the regulator to take control of a bank, for instance, by providing that the decision be set aside by the court only

> if the court finds that such decision was arbitrary, capricious, an abuse of discretion, or otherwise not in accordance with the law.[14]

Nevertheless, from time to time there may be a public interest that outweighs the need for protection of individual property rights, such as a systemic interest in a banking crisis requiring the expeditious regulatory takeover of an important bank that is failing. For such fairly rare circumstances, the banking law could make a narrowly written exception permitting the bank regulator to take control of a bank without prior court review; the regulator's decision could then be made subject to a judicial review ex post.[15]

---

[13] This, e.g., is the situation in the United States: 12 U.S.C. §191 and §203.
[14] United States: 12 U.S.C. §203(b).
[15] In the United States, a bank for which a conservator has been appointed by the bank regulator may within 20 days after the appointment bring action for a court order to terminate the appointment; 12 U.S.C. §203(b).

Grounds for Regulatory Action

Typically, the banking law provisions granting authority to take regulatory action specify the concrete circumstances in which that authority may or must be exercised. Thus, the degree of discretion to be granted to the bank regulator to take regulatory action can be more or less controlled through the statutory grounds on which such action may be taken. Broad and vaguely defined grounds for regulatory action leave the regulator greater discretion in deciding whether the circumstances of a particular case before it comes within the scope of his authority to act than narrow and precisely defined grounds for regulatory action.

Sometimes, broad and narrow grounds are found side by side in the same section of the banking law. For example, the banking law of Australia contains substantially the following provision:

> The bank regulator may give a bank a direction of a kind specified in subsection (2) if the regulator considers that the bank has contravened a prudential regulation or a prudential standard, or the direction is necessary in the interests of depositors of the bank.[16]

The provision specifies two basic grounds for issuing a direction to a bank: (A) the bank has contravened a prudential regulation or a prudential standard and (B) a direction of a kind specified in subsection (2) is necessary in the interests of depositors of the bank. The ground described under (A) is fairly narrow, as there will not be much discretion involved in deciding whether a bank has or has not contravened the law, one would hope. The ground described under (B) is fairly broad and allows the regulator considerable room for discretion in deciding whether the interests of a bank's depositors require a direction of a kind specified in subsection (2).

This example also illustrates that the law can correlate the grounds for regulatory action to the action authorized. The ground described under (B) requires the regulator to determine whether the interests of a bank's depositors require regulatory action. By defining

---

[16] Section 11CA(1) of the Banking Act 1959.

what regulatory action may be required, the provision implicitly limits the ground on which such action may be taken.[17]

In the interest of transparency, bank regulators have issued regulations giving specific content to some of the broader grounds for corrective action that are found in their banking law. Thus, for instance, in the United States, where corrective action is authorized on the ground that a bank engages in an unsafe or unsound practice in conducting its business,[18] the bank regulator has issued safety and soundness standards as well as procedures for their enforcement.[19] This approach has several advantages. The banks are informed about the standards of banking practice and the procedures that the bank regulator will apply in determining whether a bank is in violation of the banking law. The standards are marginal standards defining the boundaries of tolerable banking practices; within these boundaries, the banks are free, although within the framework of his general supervision activities, the bank regulator should caution banks that are found moving close to the borderline. By further defining the grounds for taking corrective action, the regulator reduces his discretion and creates an expectation that the standards will be enforced, promoting predictability of regulatory action and enhancing his public credibility.

There are banking law provisions that grant authority to the bank regulator to take regulatory action without specifying any ground. For example, the banking law of France includes a provision that in substance reads as follows:

> The bank regulator may issue to a bank a recommendation to take appropriate measures to restore or strengthen its financial condition, to improve its management methods or to ensure that its organization is adequate for its activities or development objectives.

---

[17] In practice, however, this restriction will not place much of a restraint on the bank regulator. Section 11CA(2) of the Banking Act 1959 lists no less than 14 kinds of direction that may be given to a bank; the last kind of direction listed is especially broad, as it permits any other direction as to the way in which the affairs of the bank are to be conducted or not conducted.

[18] 12 U.S.C. §1818(b)(1).

[19] 12 U.S.C. §1831p-1 and 12 C.F.R. §30.

The bank concerned must respond within two months by describing in detail the measures taken pursuant to that recommendation.[20]

Although the discretion of the regulator in deciding *in what circumstances* to issue the recommendation may seem unlimited, in practice, his discretion will be restricted by principles of administrative law requiring that there be a need for regulatory action as permitted by the provision. It should be noted that, for obvious reasons, no mandatory provision of banking law was found which authorizes regulatory action without specifying the grounds on which such action must be taken.

Definition of Regulatory Action

Finally, the law may adjust the degree of discretion to be granted to the bank regulator by defining the action that the regulator may or must take. In doing so, the legislature defines the extent to which the regulator may intrude in the affairs of a bank. This is important, as the legislature may decide that regulatory action exceeding a certain level of intrusiveness requires judicial consent.

The degree of statutory specificity in prescribing what regulatory action may be taken differs considerably from country to country, and in some countries from provision to provision of the banking law. At one end of the spectrum are broad provisions that authorize the regulator to take whatever measures are necessary to remedy the infractions referred to in the grounds for exercising the authority.[21] At the other end of the spectrum are banking law provisions with exhaustive lists of the kinds of regulatory action that may be taken.[22] There are also banking law provisions where the open-ended provisions are combined with an illustrative list of remedial measures.[23]

---

[20] Art. 43 of Law No. 84-46 on the Activities and Supervision of Credit Institutions. Failure to respond may lead to punishment of the bank with a disciplinary sanction, pursuant to Art. 45 of Law No. 84-46.
[21] Netherlands: Art.14 of the Law on Supervision of the Credit System; Switzerland: Art. 23 (1) of the Federal Law on Banks and Savings Banks.
[22] France: Art. 45 of Law No. 84-46 on the Activities and Supervision of Credit Institutions.
[23] Germany: Art. 46 (1) of the Law on the Credit System.

Some banking laws cover both ends of the scale in a single provision. Thus, for example, the banking law of *Australia* lists 14 kinds of direction that the regulator may give to a bank, including, inter alia:

(f) a direction not to accept the deposit of any amount;

(j) a direction not to pay a dividend on any shares;

(n) any other direction as to the way in which the affairs of the bank are to be conducted or not conducted.[24]

The open-ended kind of direction last listed implicitly recognizes, and cures, the principal disadvantage attached to an exhaustive enumeration of regulatory action: as the legislature cannot foresee all kinds of measures that the bank regulator may need to respond adequately to an infraction of evolving prudential standards, writing an exhaustive list of regulatory action into the law risks omitting the very measure that is needed.

Rules of Administrative Law

As was noted before, the scope of authority of the bank regulator is defined by the statutory provisions that grant that authority. If the authority is granted in a strictly mandatory fashion leaving no discretion to the bank regulator in the exercise of his authority or in the choice of regulatory action, the scope of the regulator's authority is exclusively determined by the statute granting the authority. If, however, the law granting authority leaves the bank regulator a measure of discretion, there may be other rules of law that govern the use of that discretion by the regulator.

In many countries, the bank regulator is considered to be a state agency and as such is deemed to be bound by rules of administrative law. These rules, written in part to protect private citizens from the improper use of state power, aim inter alia at containing the exercise of regulatory discretion by state agencies within proper bounds. This restraining function of administrative law is particularly important in cases where the bank regulator imposes or takes action with respect to

---

[24] Section 11CA(2) of the Banking Act 1959.

a bank in difficulty, as often in such cases the intervention of the regulator is especially intrusive.

Administrative law pursues this objective in a threefold manner: by prescribing rules of procedure for administrative decision making, by establishing principles of good administration as substantive rules of law governing administrative acts, and by offering administrative appeal from administrative acts to interested parties. The first two categories of administrative law govern directly the exercise by the bank regulator of discretion to take or impose remedial action with respect to banks that violate prudential standards.

Administrative law of procedure includes requirements for state agencies to give prior notice to interested parties of impending administrative acts, to invite the parties to a hearing where they can present their views to the agency before a decision is made, to give decisions in writing including proper reasons therefore, and to publish decisions or to provide the parties with copies thereof. Generally, administrative law of procedure would not adequately address the special requirements of bank regulation. For instance, where for matters of urgency the banking law might have exempted regulatory action from prior notice and hearing requirements, administrative law may not provide for such exemption. It is preferable, therefore, to provide for special procedures in the banking law that supersede general procedures of administrative law.

Among the before mentioned principles of good administration is the *principle of proportionality*. It requires that regulatory restrictions on the rights of individuals not be disproportional to what is necesssary to the public interest by which such restrictions are justified. An example of the application of the principle of proportionality to banks is found in England where the the Financial Services Authority is required to have regard to:

> the principle that a burden or restriction which is imposed on a person, or on the carrying on of an activity, should be proportionate to the benefits, considered in general terms, which are expected to result from the imposition of that burden or restriction.[25]

---

[25] Section 2(3)(c) of the Financial Services and Markets Act 2000.

Generally, however, it is not the function of administrative law to dictate the manner in which the bank regulator must use the discretion granted him by the law. Generally, administrative law tells the bank regulator not *how* to use his discretion but rather *how not* to use his discretion. Thus, for instance, administrative law would indicate, not what would be a proportional or reasonable use of discretion by the bank regulator in particular circumstances, but what would be a *dis*proportional or an *un*reasonable use of discretion in those circumstances. In this sense, the substantive rules of administrative law establish the outer bounds of admissible discretionary behavior by the bank regulator.[26] They help determine when regulatory acts are ultra vires or where the regulator otherwise exercises his authority in an unlawful manner. Hence, the norms of administrative law setting these limits are often expressed as negative concepts: *abuse* of authority, *misuse* of authority, decisions that are *arbitrary and capricious* or *unreasonable*, or use of power that is *disproportional* to the deficiency addressed.

Upon judicial review or appeal, the discretion of the bank regulator should generally be respected. Accordingly, the judiciary should generally limit its involvement to an assessment of the legality[27] of the regulatory act under review and refrain from a review de novo whereby it takes the seat of the regulator and substitutes its discretionary judgment for that of the regulator. Normally, the judiciary lacks the special expertise required for proper discretionary judgments in cases demanding remedial action with respect to banks in difficulty; judicial errors of judgment in this area can have serious systemic consequences. Therefore, if administrative law generally permits the judiciary to replace decisions of state agencies with its own decisions, the banking law should exempt decisions of the bank regulator from this treatment and limit judicial intervention to a

---

[26] Otherwise, administrative law (lex generalis), would be allowed to negate in whole or in part the discretion granted to the regulator by the banking law (lex specialis), which would be inconsistent with principles of statutory hierarchy.

[27] Legality of a regulatory act means both that the act does not exceed the parameters of the law by which the authority for the act was given and that the act does not violate the boundaries set by rules of administrative law.

review of the legality of regulatory decisions and the annulment of regulatory decisions that are found to violate the law.[28]

Considerations in the Exercise of Discretion

The law governing the exercise of discretion by the bank regulator can be traced by two concentric circles. The outer circle sets the boundary line of proper banking regulation; regulatory acts that would fall outside that circle should be condemned as unlawful. Between the two circles lies the area of the law that addresses the manner in which regulatory discretion is to be exercised, including procedural law setting notice, hearing, and publication requirements.

Within the inner circle, the law largely defers to the bank regulator: Whereas the law outside the inner circle is enforced in the courts to overturn regulatory acts, the law that lies within the inner circle is not. In the inner circle, the law consists mostly of general principles and standards of good administration that do not rise to the level of enforceable rules of law whose violation should lead to the annulment of regulatory acts or damage awards against the regulator, even though they would be considered at the administrative and political levels where the bank regulator must account for his work. These principles and standards include, for instance, higher standards of care than the standards expressly imposed by the banking law. They may also include objectives of banking supervision when these are written into the law.[29] They also include, perhaps most importantly, the need to respect the freedom of regulated banks, based on the principle that bank regulation is justified only if and to the extent that it is required to serve the public interest in a safe and sound banking system and only insofar as that interest is of greater value than the loss of economic freedom that it inflicts on banks. A good bank regulator is guided by this principle in all its decisions. This does not mean that it would not be the principal task of the regulator to protect the banking system, if necessary at the expense of individual banks. It does mean, however, that in exercising discretion the bank regulator should treat the license to engage in banking activities as the rule and any restriction of that license as an exception

---

[28] *See, e.g.,* United States: 12 U.S.C. §203(b).
[29] *See, e.g.,* England: Section 2 of the Financial Services and Markets Act 2000.

that requires adequate justification. In doing so, a good bank regulator does not skirt the bounds of the permissible but occupies the center of the inner circle of norms of proper administration.

In exercising discretion, the bank regulator should primarily be guided by systemic considerations. These include two objectives of banking law which are of special significance where it concerns regulatory action to address banking problems. They are the objective to maintain a safe and sound banking system and the objective to maintain a level regulatory playing field where banks share equally in the burden of prudential regulation. The second objective is derived from two subsidiary considerations, namely, the administrative law principle of equality of treatment and the economic argument that inequality of regulatory treatment among banks has the effect of granting some banks a subsidy as compared to others, hurting competition between them and thereby the health and vigor of the banking system as a whole.

Preserving a safe and sound banking system does not normally require that each and every bank in difficulty must be rescued, especially not if bank depositors are protected by deposit insurance. Actually, the occasional bank failure helps combat moral hazard and reinforces accountability of banks to the public. Moreover, as is the case for insurance generally, some losses covered by the deposit insurance fund should be expected. One of the issues to be addressed here is whether the objective to maintain a level regulatory playing field for banks requires equal treatment of banks also where it concerns rescue efforts.

There may come a point where corrective action taken or imposed by the bank regulator proves ineffective and the regulator must decide whether the bank should be closed, whether the bank should be sold to or merged with another bank, or whether a final effort should be made to rescue the bank as a going concern by taking control of the bank through provisional administration or a receivership.

In some countries, a rescue effort by taking control of a bank will be reserved for banks whose size or position in the financial sector is deemed so important that their failure, sale, or merger must be ruled out for systemic reasons. The argument that the rescue of such bank, unlike others, is inconsistent with the administrative law principle of equality of treatment is answered with the observation that the systemic interests in saving the bank are so strong as to override that principle. Free ridership of bank owners can be avoided by requiring the owners to pay the costs of the rescue effort or by reducing their ownership interests. The moral hazard that a bank rescue would lead managers and owners of other banks into thinking that they may incur greater risk, and thus the possibility of greater gain, without consequences because their banks will be rescued as well can be reduced by imposing civil and criminal penalties on bank managers and owners whose reckless activities endangered their banks. A subsidiary reason for reserving bank rescues for banks deemed "too big to fail"[30] is that the scarce resources of the bank regulator do not allow the regulator to nurse every bank in difficulty back to health. Thus, in those countries, taking control of a bank through provisional administration or receivership is regarded as an extraordinary measure that is to be taken only if dictated by systemic considerations, and the bank regulator must exercise discretion in distinguishing between banks that are to be rescued and banks that are not. An issue is whether the banking law should delineate the scope of such discretion, for instance, by specifying bank rescue eligibility standards.

In other countries, however, the administrative law principle of equality of treatment of banks will be regarded as so important that all banks in difficulty would benefit from a rescue effort through administrative control, unless this would be patently inappropriate (criminal activities by the bank) or ineffective (the bank is too far gone). In these countries, the discretion of the bank regulator would be limited.

Concluding Observations

In considering the degree of discretion to be granted to the bank regulator, it is not unusual to find an inverse relationship between the generality of the grounds for authority to take corrective action and the variety or invasiveness of corrective action allowed to be taken

---

[30] The term "too big to fail" is misleading as it is often not a bank's size that determines the effects of its failure on the banking system. The banking system could be seriously damaged by the failure of several small banks.

under that authority. It is not uncommon for the law to combine broad grounds of authority with narrowly prescribed corrective actions and narrow grounds of authority with broader arrays of measures. Similarly, banking laws show a tendency toward more narrowly defined grounds of authority as the action which they authorize becomes more invasive. Examples of these tendencies are found in countries where the banking law grants the regulator discretionary authority to issue orders or restrictions concerning a bank's activities while requiring a court order for taking control of a bank through a receivership. Such a graduated approach to corrective action appears logical.[31]

In determining the scope of discretion to be granted to the bank regulator, a balance must be struck in two partly overlapping areas, namely: (a) between protecting the banking system as a whole and protecting the interests of individual banks and their owners; and (b) between protecting the banking system from both regulatory abuse and negligent forbearance and the need to avoid provisions that are so tightly written that they would unduly impair the ability of the regulator to address unexpected conditions or unforeseen innovations in banking services or financial products. The unprecedented rate of change in the financial markets and the banking industry experienced during the last decades has made it necessary to grant bank regulators greater regulatory discretion than previously was deemed desirable. This development has shifted the burden of providing safeguards against abuse of discretion to administrative law. Decisions as to the degree of discretion to be granted to the bank regulator may depend on these and other considerations, including the extent of accountability and functional autonomy of the bank regulator.

Regulatory discretion means that for certain measures the legislature relies more or less on the regulator's judgment. In bank regulation, there are generally good reasons for doing so. The bank regulator must be assumed to have unique expertise and experience in the area of its jurisdiction that justify making it solely responsible for decisions on matters that fall within its jurisdiction. Generally

---

[31] There are exceptions, however. In the United States, for cease and desist orders, the interests of banks are protected by notice and hearing requirements (12 U.S.C. §1818(b)), while the bank regulator may appoint a conservator or receiver for a bank without prior notice or hearings (12 U.S.C. §203 and §191).

speaking, laws granting discretion to the bank regulator are testimonials that the legislature has confidence in the regulator, whereas laws that are mandatory or otherwise prescriptive reflect a lack of trust in the regulator.

While a discretionary regime preserves flexibility for the regulator, it may create uncertainty concerning regulatory action. Moreover, a discretionary regulatory framework may raise concerns about the fairness of regulatory intervention, especially in countries where respect for the rule of administrative law on the part of the regulator is wanting. In contrast, while a mandatory regime is relatively inflexible, it offers greater transparency and certainty about regulatory action than a discretionary regime, and it promotes equality of treatment. The transparency and predictability of a discretionary regime may be improved by issuing definitions of circumstances that would trigger the authority of the regulator to take action.

The principal weakness of a strictly mandatory system is its methodology of eliminating regulatory discretion and prescribing in its stead uniform measures for all banks that have reached a certain state of noncompliance with the banking law, regardless of whether such measures are appropriate in the light of prevailing circumstances. A prescriptive regime of regulatory action that is too strictly mandatory puts the bank regulator into a straitjacket and may exclude or impede a flexible response. Theoretically, under extreme circumstances, a mandatory corrective system rigorously applied could produce a wholesale closure of the banking system. Such an outcome would violate the elementary objective of prudential banking regulation aiming at the preservation of a functioning banking system. Therefore, a mandatory regime may force the regulator, when faced with conditions unforeseen by the legislature, either to order measures that are not suitable for the problems to be corrected or to avoid taking the action prescribed by the law altogether; for instance, by denying that the statutory ground for the action exists and breaking the law. Obviously, this dilemma should be avoided.

There are conditions in which a strict mandatory regime should a priori be ruled out. For instance, such a regime is generally unsuitable for heterogeneous banking systems, because these banking systems require a fair degree of corrective differentiation by the regulator, due to differences in the conditions and needs of various categories of banks. Similarly, mandatory banking law provisions whose application depends on a valuation of marketable bank assets should be avoided in countries with less developed or illiquid financial markets that do not produce reliable asset values.

Logic dictates, therefore, that even a mandatory regime normally requires a minimum of discretion for the bank regulator. Such discretion may be provided by the law in the form of exceptions to mandatory provisions in order to address unusual circumstances.[32] Exceptions can be made to the regulatory action required, to the grounds on which such action is taken, or to both. However, where such exceptions undermine the objectives pursued in making the regime mandatory, they would normally be permitted only if the result of the application of the mandatory regime in a particular case would be incompatible with crucial systemic interests or would otherwise be unreasonable.

Does a mandatory regime moderated by suitable exceptions produce better results than one that is discretionary? It cannot be denied that discretion can easily turn into permissiveness and lax banking supervision, especially in societies with a club culture. In contrast, a mandatory regime creates an appearance of predictability and equality of treatment and thereby enhances the credibility of the bank regulator.[33] Mandatory systems of regulatory action have other advantages. These are chiefly that they require frequent monitoring of the bank and that, even though applying their trigger points may be more an art than a science, they force regulators periodically to collect and analyze evidence concerning the direction in which the bank's financial condition develops.

It may be concluded from the foregoing that a good banking law would generally require the bank regulator promptly to take

---

[32] See also Section 2.3.3 of the Report of the G-22 Working Group on Strengthening Financial Systems (October 1998).
[33] There are countries with emerging market economies where the certainties provided by a mandatory regime with firm statutory rules would compensate for a lack of trained bank regulators. In such countries, a mandatory system could also help keep the judiciary from reviewing discretionary decisions of bank regulators as to their merits and overturning them.

appropriate action to address violations of prudential standards by a bank, and would empower the regulator to do so by offering a balanced menu of options representing both a discretionary and a moderately mandatory approach, depending on the kinds of circumstances addressed, while generally submitting the most invasive regulatory measures to a prior review by the judiciary. For each country, its sociopolitical character and its experience with banking crises will help determine whether its banking law grants more or less discretion to the bank regulator in addressing banking problems.

Chapter 26
Key Legal Aspects of Bank Restructuring

JAN WILLEM VAN DER VOSSEN

The past years have witnessed extensive banking and financial sector problems in a range of countries. In Southeast Asia, for instance, countries that had strong and growing economies have suffered severe setbacks as a result of weaknesses in their financial systems, causing losses in the double digit percentages of GDP. In the Baltic states, Russia, and a range of countries in the Commonwealth of Independent States, the transition from a centrally planned economy to a market-based economy led to excessive growth of a commercial banking system, an insufficiently developed private sector, weak banking and banking supervision practices, and consequently extensive banking sector problems and restructuring needs. In Latin America, much damage was suffered, partly as a result of contagion of confidence loss in other regions, but also partly as a result of inherent weaknesses in the economic and financial systems.

The international financial institutions (IFIs) were often the first to respond to these issues, providing extensive technical assistance in restructuring banks, most often connected to programs of macroeconomic stabilization. In this context, the attention of the IFIs focused primarily on economic aspects. Recapitalization needs of individual banks or the system as a whole needed to be assessed, methods devised to finance recapitalization, estimates prepared of the impact of government finance for restructuring on the fiscal position, the effect of a disabled banking system on payment systems assessed, as well as the impact of diminished credit allocation on the real sector. Losses of financial institutions needed to be estimated and spread over owners, shareholders, managers, governments, creditors, and depositors.

Plans were designed for macroeconomic stabilization, and for restructuring of the financial systems in countries. Programs were developed for the overhaul of financial sector supervisory structures and methods devised for the operational and financial restructuring of individual institutions. For instance, how could a return to core activities, cost cutting, and better lending practices restore banks' viability? How much capital was needed up front to restore solvency and compliance with capital adequacy rules, in order to reduce the immediate threat to creditors and depositors? Where could this capital be obtained: from old and new shareholders, government, depositors, and other creditors? What form should recapitalization take? Injection of equity capital? Haircuts? Trading bad assets for government bonds? Gradual recapitalization through restored profitability and retained profits?

This article intends to review the key elements of the restructuring process, and identify some of the legal questions that need to be addressed, and for which rules must be in place if the process is to work. The next section will discuss the need to start a restructuring operation with a solid audit of the legal, regulatory, and judicial infrastructure for bank intervention and restructuring. The third section will discuss some of the impediments to establishing and/or implementing a legal and regulatory framework in a restructuring operation. In this context, the article will also discuss the appropriateness of intervention measures of increasing severity in a situation of deteriorating bank and banking system soundness. The fourth section will deal with the balance between, on the one hand, owner and shareholder rights and, on the other hand, depositors' rights, proxied by the authorities' rights to exercise supervision, take measures against the bank, and conduct terminal intervention.

The fifth section will outline the main elements of a restructuring exercise, focusing on some of the critical points in the restructuring process, starting with remedial measures, through imposition of temporary management, conservatorship, and closure and liquidation. The following section will briefly discuss aspects of bankruptcy and liquidation. The next section will address some remaining issues, and the last section will mention some of the other areas in this complex field, not to discuss them at length but to add to the checklist, and to illustrate the complexity of a "legal audit" of a country's framework for bank restructuring. The scope of the article does not allow for more detailed drafting suggestions. Each of the topics dealt with in the article would merit extensive further discussions. Indications for legal solutions mentioned in some of the sections are not intended to be proscriptive, but to contribute to a discussion.

The Need to Review Legal Infrastructure

Appropriate as the initial focus of the IFIs on the economic aspects of banking sector problems was, it was not complete. Early on, many weaknesses in the legal and regulatory framework came to light, as the process of restructuring came under way, causing delays, confusion, further erosion of confidence in the restructuring process, additional opportunities for asset stripping at the expense of the creditors and depositors of the financial institutions, and generally further loss of productivity.

Under normal conditions, many weaknesses could probably be worked around, if the authorities and the institutions cooperated effectively. However, in the pressure cooker environment of bank restructuring, threatened, on the one hand, by a complete loss of shareholders' investments and, on the other hand, depositors' interests, substantial cost to the budget, and slowed economic growth, the tools to resolve the strongly conflicting interests of the authorities and of the owners and managers of the financial institutions were not powerful enough.

For instance, banking supervisory authorities suddenly appeared to have insufficiently strong powers to take control over the banks. Shareholders in failed banks retained too much power, and could cripple any actions that were not in their immediate interests. Excessively strict confidentiality rules hampered establishing the true net worth of a bank, cooperation with external auditors, cross-border supervisory information sharing, and calculating the extent of offshore liabilities. Strong appeals clauses in banking legislation delayed supervisory action. Bank closure and liquidation rules were insufficiently effective, left loopholes for asset stripping and left too much power with shareholders. Examples of such difficulties can be seen in the bank restructuring exercises in Thailand, Russia, Indonesia, and even in the United States, where perceived deficiencies in the regulatory intervention mechanisms prompted introduction of the FIDICIA legislation on prompt corrective action.[1]

Therefore, dealing with problems of intervention, recapitalization, operational and financial restructuring, and bank closure and liquidation requires a thorough review up front of the enormously complex system of rules and regulations needed to run a bank restructuring operation in all its aspects. Additionally, effective court and judicial systems, as well as good quality legal, accounting, and auditing professions need to be in place to apply the legal framework effectively, consistently, and in proper sequence.

The best laid micro- and macroeconomic plans cannot be implemented without a suitable legal and regulatory framework. In many cases, emergency corrective legislation, often in the form of decrees, may be needed.

Impediments to Creating an Effective Legal Framework

Especially in the countries making the transition from a centrally planned economy, with their newly gained respect for, and protection of, private ownership and private enterprise, but also in the more market-based economies of Southeast Asia and Latin America, banks have been seen as fully autonomous, serving only the interests of the owners, and subject to as few government restrictions as possible. This conception, theoretically not incorrect but unacceptable without considerable limitations, and combined with close links between banks and political groups, often lay at the basis of an insufficiently strong supervisory and regulatory framework. It hampered introducing and taking sufficiently intrusive restructuring measures, limiting or even eliminating the rights of owners and shareholders, even if considerable risk existed for creditors and depositors, and for the effectiveness of financial intermediation.

However, the conception that banks, like many other types of private enterprise, are basically fully autonomous and only need to take account of owners' and shareholders' interests is subject to a number of limitations that flow from the nature of banking and its

---

[1] *See* Table 1.

role in the economy. These limitations need to become more strict as the financial condition of a bank deteriorates.

The Shift from Entrepreneurial Interests to Depositors' Interests

Banks, and other financial institutions, have a very profitable franchise, if properly used. They can collect money from the public, pay them a usually limited amount of interest, and subsequently use these funds to grant loans and make investments for the benefit of their owners and shareholders. The reward for the banks is justified by their ability to manage risk in a way that depositors are incapable of, or do not see as the best use of their time.

Banks' risk management needs to be of sufficiently high quality that the depositor does not need to doubt that the funds will be repaid according to contract. At the same time, there is a clear public interest in well-functioning banks, as they channel funds to the productive sector of the economy, to the benefit of all.

As risk management experts, and having access to privileged borrowers' financial information, banks have an advantage over their depositors and economic policymakers. This advantage can potentially undermine market discipline, as depositors and others cannot assess whether the bank is doing a good job of managing the risk. Consequently, banks are less pressed to manage the risks well, resulting in an inefficient and potentially unsafe intermediation process.

Therefore, there is a need to correct asymmetries of knowledge and power between the bank and the depositors, by means of a licensing process and banking supervision exercised by public authorities focused on reinforcing sound banking principles. When a bank shifts from being a safe and sound institution that is capable of meeting its obligations to financial weakness, posing a threat to depositors' funds, the franchise granted by the public authorities is being abused. At this point, the balance between ownership rights and the rights of other interested parties needs to be corrected, in order to limit the damage potentially caused by this abuse. The bank can no longer be relied upon to manage the risks safely and soundly, and to retain depositors' confidence.

Also, a counterweight is needed against the changes in the incentive structure for owners and management when the bank deteriorates. Owners and managers are generally aware of the deteriorating condition of the bank before others. Especially if they suspect that the bank is already insolvent, they have nothing to lose when taking extraordinarily high risks. If luck goes their way, they win; if it does not, the depositors lose. Therefore, as the bank deteriorates, interested parties are justified in being more intrusive in their demands upon the way the business of the bank is conducted.

This increasing intrusiveness is seen in the increasing degree of severity of the corrective and intervention measures that can be taken against a bank, corresponding to the deterioration of its financial condition. This basic principle should be at the heart of the design of an appropriate set of measures to restore bank soundness or intervene before damage becomes too great.

A good example of how the balance shifts toward public intervention is the prompt corrective action framework in the United States. Greater intrusiveness of supervisory action with regard to the way the bank is run will typically encounter strong opposition from the owners, managers, and possibly politicians. Owners will argue that the supervisors intervened too soon, that not all rescue possibilities had been exhausted, that unnecessary damage was done, that the existing owners and managers are best placed to rehabilitate the bank, and similar arguments. Therefore, when control over the bank is taken from the owners and managers, the legal structure for banking supervision, intervention, and rehabilitation is put under even more severe pressure. It needs to be capable of standing up to very strong resistance and allow rapid decisions. The robustness of the critical points in the legal and regulatory framework for restructuring therefore needs to be ascertained in advance as much as possible.

Table 1. United States FIDICIA System for "Prompt Corrective Action"

Capital Level Trigger	Mandatory and Discretionary Actions
10% > capital adequacy ratio > 8% or 5% > core capital ratio > 4%	Bank cannot make any capital distribution or payments that would leave the institution undercapitalized.
Capital adequacy ratio < 8% or core capital ratio < 4%	Bank must submit capital restoration plan; asset growth restricted; approval required for new acquisitions, branching, and new line of business.
Capital adequacy ratio < 6% or core capital ratio < 3%	Bank must increase capital; restrictions on deposit interest rates and asset growth; may be required to elect new Board of Directors.
Capital adequacy ratio < 4% or core capital ratio < 2%	Bank must be placed in conservatorship or receivership within 90 days; approval of FDIC required for entering into material transactions other than usual core business, extending credit for any highly leveraged transaction, changes in accounting methods, paying excessive compensation or bonuses.

Critical Points in the Restructuring Process

The restructuring process can be defined as the process of restoring a bank to operational and financial viability, and ultimately compliance with the prudential standards. This definition has a number of components that imply the need for legal and regulatory instruments. Restoring operational viability can require that the supervisory agency undertake a last attempt at corrective action, impose caretaker management over the bank, force the bank to take decisions that would otherwise be within the autonomy of the bank, for instance to terminate employment of managers and/or staff, to take long delayed legal action against delinquent borrowers, to issue stricter internal loan approval procedures, or to take higher provisions against bad assets.

To restore financial viability, the supervisory authority could order a bank to issue additional shares, possibly requiring changes in the bank's articles of association. This would require preparation and clearance with the stock exchange authorities of disclosure documents and prospectuses. It could require legal action against shareholders to collect unpaid share contributions, the sale of bad assets, the purchase of new, good assets, and similar actions. These are examples of actions that the bank needs to undertake itself, as a party to these arrangements, but with supervisory sanctions against noncompliance.

Restoration of compliance with prudential standards can for instance imply concluding a memorandum of understanding (MoU) with the supervisory authority. An MoU could address temporary forbearance of noncompliance with the full rigor of the regulations. As a result, the bank can be "considered compliant" so long as the agreed restructuring program remains on track. This "presumed compliance" can, for instance, play a role in protecting the bank from the actions of other regulatory bodies during the restructuring phase, for instance, when the bank is also subject to stock exchange regulations in jurisdictions that allow banks to be members of the stock exchange.

It will be noticed that measures such as described above all imply a greater or lesser degree of suspension or elimination of the powers of the incumbent management, and are thus already quite intrusive in limiting management autonomy.

Some key phases in bank restructuring are the following. It should be noted that in cases of systemic restructuring, i.e. when multiple banks need to be restructured, several additional phases can be distinguished, raising additional legal issues. Nevertheless, even in a systemic restructuring operation, in the final phases of the process it is individual banks that need to be dealt with. The systemic aspects relate mostly to the institutional framework. These will be identified as they appear.

Individual Bank Restructuring

Serious banking problems or crises typically come to light after a protracted process of financial deterioration. Although this is rarely a sudden development, the situation can be critically exacerbated by external developments, for instance a devaluation of the currency. An illustration of this can be found in Indonesia, where banking problems became much more severe when the currency collapsed. Several phases can be distinguished in the restructuring of a bank and of a banking system.

Track Record of Prior Supervisory Action

When it becomes apparent that an individual institution is in an unsafe and unsound condition, the supervisory authority often has difficulty showing conclusively that it has taken timely, less intrusive action and followed up appropriately. When the supervisory authority then takes sudden, more drastic measures such as the imposition of caretaker management, the bank might successfully argue that the supervisor had not tried to take less intrusive action; therefore it is not entitled to impose outside management, which would cause damage to the reputation of the bank. Additional effects could be a higher cost of borrowing, or risk of deposit withdrawal. As indicated above, owners will argue that the supervisor should first give the bank the opportunity to take corrective action autonomously, possibly in agreement with the supervisor, oriented toward meeting regulatory standards, rather than performing very specific actions, for instance firing managers or cutting staff.

In practical terms, the need to build a track record might be mitigated if the powers of the supervisory authority can be exercised "notwithstanding any appeals procedure against the measures undertaken." This allows rapid action, without prejudicing the rights of owners unduly. This implies that the appeals procedure cannot result in immediate rescission of the supervisory measures, but can result in a declaration by the judicial bodies that the supervisory action was unjustified, and that the agency can be held liable for damages, or restoration of the situation as prior to the actions, insofar as still possible. Supervisory powers should therefore be carefully drafted, and should allow action without waiting for the outcome of an appeal. Such provisions are key to an effective set of supervisory powers.

Many of the actions required by a supervisory authority may require that management be forced to take action. For instance, when the supervisor decides that a bank manager is no longer fit and proper and should be removed from the bank's management board, the supervisory agency cannot itself break off the contractual relationship between the bank and the manager, as it is not a party to that contract. The bank will need to do this itself.

Therefore, the supervisory agency needs the backing of additional legal provisions, specifying that the nonimplementation of an order of the supervisory agency is in itself subject to additional criminal or administrative proceedings, initiated by the supervisor, but actually prosecuted by a special body, and adjudicated before a tribunal. Such action would imply, for instance, that the confidentiality regime to which the supervisory body is subjected allows it to provide information to the prosecutors and judges.

Taking Control of the Bank

The essence of this phase is that the supervisory authority can set the agenda for, and implement changes needed to maximize chances of, recovery or minimize damage to the interests of creditors and depositors. Supervisors can take control by various mechanisms. Formal ownership of the bank can be left unaltered, but all management and governance powers placed with the supervisory agency, or with a caretaker or conservator appointed at the initiative of the supervisory agency. Alternatively, the owners can be forced to formally sell the bank to the supervisory agency or to a third party until further action is taken. Further action could consist of sale back to the owners, to a new set of owners, or liquidation. These are all very intrusive actions that need to be carefully legislated, and could require judicial review at certain stages.

Taking control is probably one of the most critical moments in bank restructuring. It involves limiting or taking away, temporarily or permanently, wholly or in part, the rights of the owners and managers of the institution to manage the enterprise as they see fit, within the boundaries of the laws and regulations. Several types of situations can be distinguished.

If the bank is not in good condition, but needs primarily some drastic turnaround actions which the management has been incapable of or unwilling to perform, and there is no unusual risk of failure, temporary control might be sufficient. The law would need to give the supervisory authority the powers to impose such temporary management. The decision to impose temporary management should specify the degree of autonomy of the interim manager vis-à-vis the existing governance bodies of the institution. In view of the high degree of intrusiveness of this action, these powers would need to be given by Act of Parliament, which should also broadly describe the conditions under which the supervisory authority could use them. The full legislative procedure to be followed in incorporating this mechanism into the law would ensure optimal safeguards against illegal, arbitrary, or bad faith actions by the supervisor. This type of control should be limited in time and the terms of reference should be focused on the remedy of the unsafe practices of the bank, or on correction of serious noncompliance, for instance with the capital rules.

If the institution cannot be brought back to safe, sound, and profitable operation, and needs to be dealt with in a more permanent way, two basic options are available. If the bank has any value left, which could be better exploited by a stronger partner, a merger could be considered, a sale of assets and liabilities, or license withdrawal, closure, and liquidation. These are options which can only be effectively exercised by a conservator appointed by the supervisory authority or the courts, if the latter can be relied upon.

The power to sell or close a bank by anyone other than the owners should only be given, again, on the basis of powers laid down in an act of the legislature, to be used in well-described circumstances, such as willful and repeated breach of regulations, irredeemable damage to the financial position of the bank, practices that pose a grave threat to the rights of depositors and other creditors, and the unlikelihood of improvement of the situation.

It is clear that the simple words "sell, close, liquidate" raise a whole host of legal issues. Aside from the specific legal problems related to the performance of these actions in relation to banks, they presuppose that a functioning civil, corporate, and securities law system is in place in a country and that the rights laid down in these laws can be applied properly, that they can be pursued in a court of law, and that judicial decisions can be implemented effectively.

The interim manager should have the power to decide to what degree existing governance bodies and individual managers can be retained. This would need to be at the discretion of the appointed interim manager, who might consider it useful to retain reliable and knowledgeable managers and to isolate those that are at the root of the problem. The interim manager would need to have discretion over hiring and firing, including of upper echelon officials.

Imposition of Temporary Administration

For the purposes of this article, temporary administration is to be seen as the imposition of caretaker management in a bank, with tasks falling short of those of a conservator (see next section), to be imposed when the situation is not quite as critical, and aimed primarily at restoring sound business practices in an institution that is still considered viable.

It is essential that the banking law clearly specify under what conditions the supervisory agency can appoint and install a temporary administrator in the bank. For instance, when the bank is repeatedly and seriously in breach of prudential standards, a serious threat exists to the interests of depositors and creditors, or the bank is manifestly engaging in unsafe and unsound banking practices, which are not likely to be corrected by management on its own accord. Here it can be useful to show noncompliance with earlier corrective orders. Also, imposition of caretaker management should be possible "notwithstanding any appeals procedure."

For temporary administration or caretaker management to be effective, clear rules are needed in the banking law on disclosure of the decision to impose temporary administration, on the extent of the powers of the temporary administrator, the extent to which the powers of the incumbent management and governance bodies are suspended or eliminated, the duration of the temporary administration, and the effects of the temporary administrator's actions on third parties. Such aspects need to be reinforced in the actual decision to impose temporary administration.

An option is to impose a form of "silent curatorship," which would be similar to temporary administration but would not be made public. Clearly, this option is only viable when realistic expectations exist that the bank will become viable again. As soon as the latter no longer appears to be the case, silent curatorship should be converted to temporary administration and publicly disclosed. In the alternative, if the bank should fail, causing damage to third parties, the supervisory agency could be held liable for having known of a dangerous situation and not having made its actions and concerns known to the markets and the public.

Imposition of Conservatorship

Conservatorship should be imposed in conditions of serious distress of the financial institution. The law would need to provide criteria of such a situation of serious distress, such as: consistent and serious breaches of key prudential standards; severe and potentially irreversible threats to creditors' and depositors' interests; consistent and serious breaches of standards for safe and sound banking; or engagement in criminal activities which are condoned or committed by the bank's management. The underlying justification for this very severe limitation of ownership rights is the degree of risk and the corresponding urgency to stop a slide into insolvency. The criterion of criminal behavior is of a different nature and need not depend on the prudential risks. Criminal behavior could, for instance, include money laundering and tax fraud. The decision to impose conservatorship needs to take immediate effect, "notwithstanding any appeals procedures against the decision." Without such protection, the measure would not be effective.

As in the case of temporary administration, it is important that the burden of proof for the supervisory authority when imposing conservatorship not be too heavy. For the decision as to whether the criteria are met, the law could refer to "the opinion of the supervisory agency." This relieves the supervisory authority from satisfying the judge of the highly technical facts on the bank's financial condition, or the unsafe nature of its practices, and could allow the judge to accept the opinion of the expert authority, barring gross deficiencies in the presentation of the case by the supervisory authority. Such an approach would speed the process and would make the outcome less dependent on the level of knowledge of the judge in accounting, prudential, and financial matters.

Also, in the case of conservatorship, the powers of the conservator relative to those of the management and Board need to be explicitly laid down in law, as should the extent to which the governance bodies of the bank retain any powers at all. The conservator should have full management powers, which should be confirmed in his/her appointment. These powers should include hiring and firing, selling parts of the bank or its assets and liabilities, purchasing assets and liabilities, and any other actions to serve the interests of the depositors and creditors.

The most important task of the conservator should be to take stock of the assets and liabilities of the bank, and to make an assessment of its viability. If this assessment is negative, the conservator should be able to take further measures such as preparation for sale, privatization, or bankruptcy and liquidation. If the assessment is positive, he could set conditions for the return of the bank to its owners, for instance, the conclusion of a memorandum of understanding with regard to the rehabilitation of the bank, additional capital contributions, and similar actions. In other words, the conservator should be able to exercise full rights as if he were sole owner of the institution, excepting the right to receive a share in any liquidation surplus.

The rules for the appointment of a conservator should be clear, set out in law, or possibly in a regulation, and parallel to criteria for the approval of managers. They should include what credentials are required, what fit and proper criteria are applied, who appoints the conservator, and how he/she can be removed, and who writes the terms of reference. Is it a judge or supervisory authority, subject to judicial review? Also a clear sunset clause is needed: when does the appointment expire, or under what conditions? Appointment or dismissal should not be subject to political interference.

An issue that arises frequently is whether the conservator needs to be an official of the supervisory agency. A balance needs to be struck here between the need for objectivity, which would argue in favor of appointing an outsider, and the need to bring the bank back to viability and compliance, which might argue in favor of a supervisor who would have more detailed operational knowledge of the bank. In many countries, the number of people that are qualified to perform the duties of a conservator is limited, which could argue in favor of the appointment of a supervisor. On balance, a nonsupervisor seems preferable. It is important that the conservator is seen to be independent, even if he/she is closely bound, for instance, by an MoU. His/her independence can lower resistance on the part of the owners and shareholders.

In the process of imposing conservatorship and his/her appointment, there is a clear need to take due account of the interests of the owners/shareholders, as these are about to be divested of their governance powers over their enterprise, possibly losing it forever. In light of the urgency of the need to take control of the bank, the proper balance needs to be found between due process and expediency. At least the process needs to be fully transparent, with the owners/shareholders being informed at all times of the status of the appointment procedure and further phases of the process, names of candidates, terms of reference, and other modalities. This right should be based in law, with precise modalities laid down in the decision to appoint the conservator. Basically, the owners/shareholders need to be in a position to follow what policies and actions the conservator is undertaking. They need to have sufficient information to give real substance to their right to appeals, even if any appeals procedures would not delay the implementation of the conservatorship. In light of the far-reaching powers of a conservator, a judicial authority could be charged with reviewing the appropriateness of the terms of reference to establish that owners' rights are not curtailed more than necessary.

The relationship between the conservator and the supervisory authorities needs to be made clear in the law. Should the conservator be fully subject to the normal supervisory regime? Should there be a periodic reporting requirement to the supervisory agency? It could be argued that so long as the bank is in operation the bank shall remain under the full rigor of the banking law. The supervisory authority should then have full access to information on the conduct of the conservatorship, the conservator should be fully subject to the fit and proper test, and the supervisory authority should be able to ask for removal of the conservator, for instance when the conservator is not meeting the objectives of the conservatorship.

Involvement of the judiciary is in principle an important component of due process. However, in countries where the judiciary is not yet considered equal to this task, it may be necessary to design the conservatorship differently, by providing more powers to the supervisory agency. This should then be balanced out differently with regard to owners' rights, for instance by providing an administrative appeals option to the Ministry of Finance, Central Bank Board, or similar bodies, even if these are less independent. Also, full transparency should be observed at all times.

Diagnosis

After taking control, the first priority of the conservator should be to diagnose the financial condition of the institution. This should go considerably further than normal supervisory off-site analysis and on-site inspection. The objective is to produce a strategic assessment of whether the institution is solvent, can still be made viable, and, if so, of what measures would need to be taken to rehabilitate the institution. On the basis of this review, the decision needs to be made whether or not the institution needs to be closed, sold, or rehabilitated. Such decisions go beyond normal supervisory decisions with regard to a bank.

As this diagnosis goes much further than normal supervision, the need for information goes beyond what the supervisor is normally entitled to ask. Where normally supervisors are empowered to obtain periodic reports, ask ad hoc information, perform on-site inspections, and discuss prospects with management, the conservator should be able to examine all aspects of the business, not only issues that are directly relevant to supervision. Therefore, the conservator needs to have explicit powers of investigation and needs access to all information about the bank, as any CEO should have. These powers should be laid down in the law and confirmed in the appointment of the conservator.

The conservator should also have the explicit power to bring in outside experts, for instance to address specific management concerns, e.g., how to manage the layoff of a large group of staff, review of the data processing systems, or the performance of due diligence with a view to establishing the bank's net worth. The conservator should be able to provide such experts with full access to information at his/her discretion, but on a "need to know" basis.

Importantly, the conservator should not be hindered by confidentiality restrictions, although disclosure of, for instance, client information should serve the overall objectives of the conservatorship, e.g., performance of due diligence, loan collection, cooperation with the supervisory agencies, external auditors, and regulatory agencies abroad and in general preparing the institution for sale, closure, or rehabilitation.

The conservator should have the power to compel owners and shareholders of the bank to provide any information they have with regard to the bank, such as the full extent of their dealings with the bank, as well as their outside business interests that have financial or management connections with the bank.

In view of the scope of their access to information, the position of outside performers of due diligence needs to be dealt with explicitly. Once duly appointed by the conservator, they should have the same access to information at all levels in the organization, and with regard to shareholders and owners, as the conservator.

The due diligence performed by or on behalf of the conservator needs to be distinguished from due diligence performed by or on behalf of a potential purchaser of the bank or parts thereof. The latter type of due diligence requires a different set of rules, involving a different confidentiality regime, different informational needs, and rules regulating the modalities of access to information, for instance by means of data rooms where potential buyers can inspect the books on a confidential basis.

Triage

After the performance of due diligence, or establishment by other means of the condition of the bank, the conservator needs to make a choice among three options: (i) closure and liquidation, (ii) rehabilitation under strict conditions, or (iii) restoration of the bank to its owners. The latter option should be very rare, as it would imply serious misjudgment in imposing conservatorship.

In jurisdictions where there is a likelihood of political interference with the process, a mandatory system for making this choice is to be preferred. Such a system would need to eliminate the discretionary element as much as possible, also in the way insolvency is defined and established. For instance, where the judiciary has weak financial expertise, requiring that the judge be convinced of the technical insolvency of the bank may be creating undue difficulties in actually having the bank closed. Here, insolvency could be defined as reduction of capital to below a statutory level or inability to pay obligations as they fall due. Both criteria would avoid giving the judiciary a technical assessment of the actual value of assets and liabilities of the institution in order to establish whether there is a negative difference between assets and liabilities.

The conservator should be empowered to make the triage decision and to take further action, such as filing for delicensing, bankruptcy, and liquidation or concluding a memorandum of understanding for rehabilitation. Such an MoU should bind the conservator, the bank, its owners, and the supervisory authorities. It should lead to the rehabilitation of the bank within a specified time.

Rehabilitation

Rehabilitation of a bank usually takes the form of a combination of operational restructuring and financial restructuring. Operational restructuring generally refers to improving the operations of the bank to make them safer and sounder, less costly, and more profitable. The legal issues involved would include the legal issues around cost cutting, dismissal of staff, coming to arrangements with creditors and debtors, negotiating with supervisory authorities with regard to temporary forbearance, and selling certain parts of the business in order to focus on core business. It could involve selling bank real estate, leasing office buildings instead of owning them, and similar measures. These actions should generally not be too difficult to achieve in most jurisdictions.

Financial restructuring in broad terms refers to the immediate improvement of the bank's balance sheet, i.e., increasing its capital.

This can be achieved through different means. As the net worth of a bank is the residual of the value of its assets and its liabilities, increasing capital can be approached through both sides of the balance sheet.

On the asset side, bad assets, requiring capital-diminishing provisions, can be sold, thereby freeing up provisions, generating income, and, through retained profits, increasing capital. Cash obtained from selling bad assets can be invested in better quality assets that do not require provisions, but generate cash flow and increase capital. Bad assets can also be traded for good assets, for instance government securities, with the same effect.

Another obvious channel for increase of capital is to require additional capital contributions from shareholders. This could take the form of payment on additionally issued shares, or collection of unpaid earlier contributions. Such an operation will require different steps. First, the articles of the bank may need to be changed to allow additional issue of shares. This will require a general shareholders' meeting, approval by the justice department and the regulator of the new articles, plus the whole preparation of the actual issue. If the shares are issued on the public market, stock exchange requirements will need to be met. Documentation will need to be prepared, and other logistical issues addressed by the investment bank preparing the issue.

A third possibility for increasing capital lies in a reduction in the value of liabilities: a "haircut." In a number of jurisdictions, conservators have the power, sometimes under judicial control, to apply haircuts if that would help make the bank more saleable, and thus serve the overall interests of depositors and creditors, who would stand to recover more than if the bank were liquidated. One form of this reduction of liabilities is a debt for equity swap. Especially deposits or the claims of shareholders are prime targets for such an approach. In order to be able to apply haircuts and other abbreviations of depositor rights, the conservator would need to be specifically empowered to do so by law. Possibly, judicial review would be required, whereby the conservator may need to show that the haircut is to the ultimate benefit of the depositor/creditor, before being allowed to proceed.

A key issue in the context of bank rehabilitation is whether the bank should be returned to the owners after rehabilitation. It could be argued that the former owners have proven themselves unfit to own and operate a bank and should therefore not be permitted to regain ownership. On the other hand, if the failure of the bank was not their fault, sale-back could be considered. In any case, it is key that at the end of the rehabilitation process the net worth of the bank is established once again as a basis for setting the sale price. This could serve as a basis for resale to any potential buyers, including former owners under certain conditions. In any case, prospective owners, old or new, should pay fair market value for the institution, as set by auditors. Thus the agency that conducted the rehabilitation could recoup its investment. Resale could involve due diligence by the potential purchaser, data rooms, possibly share issues, and similar aspects.

Mergers, Sale, and Purchase and Assumption Transactions

In the context of most bank restructuring operations, there will be a need to transfer deposits and assets to other institutions. This implies that the civil code of the jurisdiction needs to have adequate rules to transfer claims and obligations reliably. In the case of transfer of deposits, i.e., claims on the bank, a mechanism must exist to obtain the permission of the depositors for debtor substitution. For the transfer to be valid, permission of the creditor/depositor is generally required. Depositors may not agree, and may consider the new debtor an unacceptable risk. Less complications tend to arise in the case of creditor substitution, or the transfer of liabilities. Borrowers generally have less interest in who they need to pay, and will generally only require that they know to whom they should pay their obligations in a valid manner. This is also a civil law matter. Restructurers will need to be aware how the civil code in the jurisdiction in question deals with these issues.

A merger will typically involve two licensed entities. The following options appear with regard to licensing. The acquiring bank retains its license, the merged bank loses its license, and the assets and liabilities of the latter are purchased by the absorbing bank. No new license is needed and one license is withdrawn. Typically, the acquiring bank will need to obtain supervisory permission for the purchase and assumption transaction. In a case where both banks are merged into a new entity, two licenses will be withdrawn, and one new license will be issued. The new entity will require a license and supervisory permission to acquire the two former entities. It is good supervisory practice to require that the acquiring bank shows that it is capable of absorbing the other bank, managerially as well as financially, without putting its own depositors and creditors at risk and may thus be required to present a business plan.

Systemic Bank Restructuring

Asset Management

Asset management is a part of individual bank rehabilitation, but the creation of a separate corporate entity, an asset management company (AMC), to undertake this task is more frequently seen in cases of systemic bank restructuring. Asset management can be defined as increasing the value of assets and lowering the required provisions by improving the chances of repayment. This can involve obtaining better security for repayment, better revenue through more aggressive collection efforts, retaining the assets for later sale after market prices improve for instance, in the case of real estate or equity holdings. When a separate corporate body has been created, it will frequently purchase the bad assets off the books of the bank in return for cash or better assets and perform the asset improvement actions outlined above.

These functions, certainly in the case of systemic restructuring, when large volumes of assets need to be managed, can usually best be performed by a separately created AMC. In case the AMC is created by the supervisory agency, this agency needs to have been authorized by law to create corporate bodies to assist it in the performance of its tasks. The law should then be sufficiently flexible to allow the creation of a specific AMC, which may need to be financed by the supervisory agency, and which will need to absorb bad assets from banks. The law needs to be examined in advance to establish whether these function can be performed.

Outside funding may be available, but that would imply that the AMC is able to show its commercial orientation and likelihood of profit. Also, a guarantee may be needed from the agency creating the AMC for the liabilities of this corporate entity. It will need to be ascertained that the supervisory agency is authorized to perform these actions. The AMC may need to sell shares to the agency that created it, which will need to be able to purchase them. Creation of the agency will involve aspects of, for instance, corporate law, stock exchange law, and labor law.

If, in the case of individual bank rehabilitation, the bank itself is creating the agency, the supervisory authority will be required to give permission for the creation of this corporate entity by the bank, and may also be required to participate in its funding, e.g., by granting loans. Again, should the supervisory agency participate in the funding, this would need to be clearly permissible under the banking law. In a jurisdiction where the supervisory agency is not permitted to grant loans to commercial entities, an exception may need to be created to allow this. It will need substantial working capital in order to be able to finance the bad asset buyouts at sufficiently high prices to provide capital relief to the banks it deals with and to finance its operations.

In a systemic restructuring, when many banks need to be dealt with, an AMC could be appointed as the liquidator for banks that are to be closed. Asset management and liquidation of assets are related activities, as both intend to maximize the income from the assets. In such cases, the bankruptcy and liquidation rules would need to allow that an AMC be appointed liquidator.

What should be the relationship between the conservator and the AMC? Should the conservator play an active role in running the AMC? It is suggested that the conservator should focus on reestablishing profitable business practices in the bank and regard the AMC as convenient outsourcing of the asset management function.

Restructuring Agency

Banking systems in a country can be in such poor overall condition that systemic restructuring, i.e., the removal, recapitalization, or rehabilitation, of many banks is needed. A banking system can be considered to be under systemic stress when its capital level has decreased to the point where it no longer has the confidence of the markets and thus can no longer sufficiently perform the basic functions of a banking system: intermediating deposits to the productive sector and performing payment services.

Systemic banking problems are often the result of a combination of factors, including poor macroeconomic policies, poor banking regulation and supervision, poor accounting and auditing practices, connected lending, government directed lending, and weak loan enforcement laws and practices. For many of these factors, the government must take at least part of the responsibility. Thus, it is appropriate that government take at least part of the responsibility for rehabilitation of the banking system and provide public funding.

The actual restructuring can be undertaken by a special unit, a bank restructuring agency (RA), wholly or partially funded by government, budgeted and staffed by, for instance, supervisory personnel, investment bankers, accountants, and lawyers. Clear oversight and accountability structures would need to be created when setting up this RA. The government should appoint the head and the members of the oversight body. The RA should most likely report either directly to Parliament or to the Minister of Finance.

It would be responsible for developing a restructuring strategy, developing a vision on the state and function of the banking system after the crisis, but also setting concrete policies for the conduct of the restructuring, for instance setting criteria for triage of banks, initiating bankruptcy or liquidation of banks that cannot be restored to viability, assessing rehabilitation plans, overseeing the implementation of rehabilitation plans, and providing an account of its activities and how public funds were used.

A jurisdiction will rarely have created the authority to set up an RA in advance. Therefore, when a crisis hits, the country may need to introduce emergency legislation to be able to create such an agency. Often, time will not permit the full rigor of the procedure for an act of Parliament, and emergency decrees by government may be needed, at least temporarily. This aspect will need to be investigated at the very first stages of a systemic banking problem. An emergency budget appropriation may be needed to finance the RA, requiring specific action by the Ministry of Finance.

In a number of financial crises, RAs were used alongside AMCs, which took responsibility for managing the assets of a number of weak banks. Funds for these AMCs could come from the restructuring agency. The laws or decree creating the RA would need to allow it to create an asset management subsidiary and to provide it with capital.

Bankruptcy and Liquidation

Bank restructuring, individually or in a systemic crisis, will often imply the need to "close" banks. In both situations, basically similar rules apply. In order to liquidate effectively, without undue dissipation of assets, the supervisory authorities must have the authority to immediately take control of the bank, when the need to liquidate becomes clear. Next, the supervisory authority must order the bank to cease taking on additional liabilities, and, simultaneously, bankruptcy proceedings must be initiated before the bankruptcy court. Some jurisdictions have separate bankruptcy regimes for banks.

Once bankruptcy is declared, the license of the institution must be withdrawn by the supervisory authority. The decision of the bankruptcy court should include the appointment of a liquidator, set his/her terms of reference, and outline reporting requirements. The bankruptcy law, whether it be a special law for banks or not, is assumed to comprise the normal components of an equitable liquidation procedure and, for instance, have rules for preparing an inventory of claims and liabilities, notification of depositors and other creditors, procedures for the presentation and verification of claims, and procedures for the adjudication of claims that the liquidator considers unfounded.

A system of oversight over the activities of the liquidator needs to be in place, for instance in the form of periodic reports to the judge in charge of the bankruptcy, reports to creditors' meetings, and reports to the supervisory agency.

The banking law should specify that the bank remains under supervision for the duration of the liquidation, in order to allow the supervisory authority to verify that the interests of the depositors are appropriately respected. The law should require that the supervisory agency agree with the final list of liabilities to be paid from the liquidation proceeds and the amounts to be paid. The supervisory agency should also be given a role in decisions about how the liquidation should be conducted, i.e., should the emphasis be on speed of the process (fire sales) rather than maximum proceeds, and whether assets should be sold through private transactions or through auctions, and similar issues.

The legal provisions on bankruptcy and liquidation should contain a "cram-down" clause, enabling the bank and its creditors that have come to a settlement to overrule dissenting shareholders or creditors, to the benefit of the larger group.

Other Issues

Asset Stripping

A major problem to be addressed when taking over control of a bank or preparing it for closure or liquidation is to prevent asset stripping by the owners and shareholders. A normal bankruptcy law will contain provisions allowing the liquidator to reverse transactions performed within a certain time before bankruptcy was declared, if these transactions were performed in order to withdraw assets from the estate in light of the impending failure of the institution, and were not conducted against fair consideration. Existing legislation may not always provide such powers to a caretaker manager or conservator. It is essential that the conservator have such powers, comparable to those of a liquidator, and that he/she take full control of the institution. It is important that this control extend itself to the subsidiaries and other entities previously controlled by the bank, in order to prevent bank assets that had been parked in subsidiaries or controlled entities to disappear.

This area should be included in the inventory of the legal framework undertaken at the beginning of the restructuring exercise.

Write-Down of Share Values

In the context of bank rehabilitation, rules are needed for the write-down of share values. Existing shareholders will have seen the intrinsic value of their shares decrease as the net worth of the bank decreased, although the nominal value of the shares will remain the same. In the course of rehabilitation, in many cases involving sacrifices by depositors, public funds, and new shareholder funds, the real value of the shares of the "old" shareholders would increase as the net worth of the bank increased as a result of the rehabilitation process. Clearly it would be unfair to allow the former shareholders, who had proved themselves incapable of operating the bank profitably, to profit from the financial and managerial efforts of others.

Therefore, one of several options could be followed, all requiring specific legal provisions. First, the old shareholders could be disenfranchised by being forced to sell the bank to the supervisory authority or a restructuring or asset management agency. A provision to this effect would need to be included in the banking law or restructuring law. This approach could be considered when the bank is insolvent. Second, the nominal value of their shares could be permanently reset at the level of their—very low—intrinsic value at the time of intervention. When the bank subsequently increases its net worth as a result of the rehabilitation, the old shares would then not grow in value. The lower value would need to be specified on the share documents, or new, lower-denominated shares could be issued in exchange for the old.

In such a construction, care should be taken to include legal provisions that also reduce the governance rights of the old shareholders and prevent their resurgence when the bank is released from caretaker management or conservatorship. Governance rights can take the form of, for instance, voting rights in the shareholders' meeting or rights to appoint managers. The only right the old shareholders should retain is a right to a share in the liquidation surplus, if available. Such measures basically eliminate the rights of shareholders of the bank and are justified only in the extreme case of rehabilitation by third parties.

Cram-Down Provisions

In the phase prior to full supervisory, caretaker, or conservator control of the institution, implying full decision-making power, and notwithstanding any shareholder governance rights, it may still be necessary to deal with the existing management bodies of the bank and its shareholders. In such situations the issue arises of obtaining minority shareholder consent with certain actions the bank has been ordered to perform, e.g., firing a manager. To be able to deal effectively with such cases, corporate law containing provisions on overruling specific minority shareholders (cram down) may be needed, in order to enable compliance with the supervisory order. This seems a preferable route to forcing the supervisory agency to take full control of the institution. Cram-down provisions may also be needed when a liquidator attempts to obtain a settlement between the bank and its creditors in order to abbreviate bankruptcy proceedings and thus cut costs and maximize proceeds. Minority shareholders should not be allowed to block such an agreement, provided it has been established to be fair, for instance by the judge overseeing the liquidation.

Confidentiality

Until the point where a financial institution is declared bankrupt, issues of confidentiality play an important role in the restructuring process. Breaches of confidentiality can damage any remaining confidence the institution may enjoy, lower the value of the assets, and encourage withdrawal of deposits, calling of guarantees, and similar actions. It is therefore important that the legal provisions on caretaker management, conservatorship, and terms of reference for due diligence create confidentiality regimes along the lines of those applicable to the supervisory authority.

Such regimes should also have the appropriate exceptions, however, permitting disclosure to law enforcement agencies, other financial sector supervisory agencies, anti-money-laundering bodies, supervisory agencies abroad, and external auditors in the same way as these exceptions should be available to supervisory agencies.

Care needs to be taken that the confidentiality regime is not abused to hide supervisory failings. In cases of bank distress, the supervisory agency is typically under severe scrutiny, in order to establish why institutions failed, whether better supervision could have prevented this, and whether there is a case to sue the supervisory agency for damages. Defensiveness on the part of the supervisory agency is therefore to be expected, and confidentiality regimes may be invoked as protection, not always justifiably.

The balance to be struck lies between the need to protect any chances of limiting the damage to the institution and the need for full transparency of the supervisory approach to the institution.

Accountability

In cases of individual bank restructuring or closing, there may not be a need for specific accountability rules going beyond the normal arrangements. These could imply that the supervisory agency present periodic reports to Parliament or the Minister of Finance, in which cases of individual bank restructuring could be discussed and the actions of the agency explained. In case of a major bank, there may be a need for ad hoc, additional information, possibly directly to Parliament, a specific report, or similar higher profile accountability arrangements. In case of systemic restructuring, clearly a much more prominent set of arrangements is appropriate, which would need to be a part of the legislation setting up the institutional arrangements for the systemic restructuring operation.

In all cases, the supervisory agency should be accountable before a court of law, either an administrative tribunal, in appeals cases, or before a civil court, in case of damage claims. As indicated above, urgent actions of the supervisory agency should not have to wait until the appeal has been decided upon.

Some Other Relevant Areas of Law and Regulation

The restructuring process is a very complex set of legal actions. Many of these are based on the banking law, insofar as they relate to supervisory action against banks, caretaker management, and conservatorship. They can involve central bank law, for instance, relating to the ability to create central bank subsidiaries to further the restructuring process and lend to AMCs. Special bank restructuring law may be involved for setting up the institutional framework for a systemic restructuring operation. Corporate law is involved when setting up corporate entities such as RAs and AMCs. Also, many aspects of civil law come into play, for instance relating to the transfer of assets and liabilities, mortgages, securities and guarantees, contracts and contract enforcement law, and many other aspects. Clearly, bankruptcy laws and liquidation rules are key in bank restructuring. For a proper functioning of the process, other laws are also needed, such as labor law in case bank staff needs to be cut in the context of rehabilitation; criminal law if bank managers have been found criminally negligent or have engaged in criminal activity; securities law, when new shares need to be issued; and accounting law, when better accounting rules need to be introduced.

The complexity of the legal aspects of bank restructuring underscores the need to involve legal expertise at the very beginning of the process to explore fully in advance whether the framework can perform all the legal actions needed for effective bank restructuring, and whether emergency legislation is needed to remedy, even if only temporarily, the major deficiencies. RAs and AMCs will need strong legal staff to assist them, and central banks and supervisory agencies may consider hiring outside lawyers to support the activities of the legal staff to conduct effectively the high-pressure litigation often connected to different aspects of the restructuring operations.

Chapter
27 | Five Observations About Banking Failures

ROSS S. DELSTON

1. Every Bank Failure Is a Regulatory Failure

Certainly banks do not fail *only* because regulators fail in their oversight responsibilities. Many other failures are typically involved in any bank failure, including failures of governance, internal controls, loan execution, and credit review. The impact of local, regional, and national economies is always a factor. Yet it is rare indeed for a bank failure, even in a banking crisis, not to have been preceded by numerous warning signals, such as excessively high levels of (i) connected (insider) lending; (ii) risk, including foreign exchange, interest rate and investment risk; (iii) direct investments in real estate; (iv) fraud and other criminal activity; and (v) spending on a headquarters building, typically with palatial executive suites and board rooms.

In many cases, bank regulators exercise regulatory forbearance, a wink and a nod in the other direction, while the bank sinks toward and then past the point of insolvency. In fact, it is atypical to find insolvent banks at zero capital, but more often than not at a significant negative net worth, which, for large banks around the world, can amount to billions of dollars. Timidity in enforcement, supervision, examination, and regulation may have the effect of encouraging management to engage in the high levels of risk noted above, and therefore may result in greater losses by the bank.

Bank failures are also a failure of external auditors, who may be negligent or engage in deliberate attempts to mislead the regulators and the public to protect their clients, as well as of negligent or willful

---

Note: The author wishes to express his appreciation to José Benjamín Escobar of the IMF Legal Department and Elizabeth Milne of the IMF Monetary and Exchange Affairs Department for their thoughtful and thought-provoking comments.

acts by the bank's management, its consultants, advisors, investment bankers, and yes, even lawyers.

Banks that are already insolvent are often unmasked by a banking crisis, leading some to think that their insolvency was brought about by the crisis itself. The insolvent condition is sometimes mistakenly thought to be a result of the crisis (the fallacy of *post hoc ergo propter hoc*: after, therefore, because of), when, in fact, the insolvency often preceded the crisis but was never brought to light, either by regulators, external auditors, or the bank management itself.

2. Banks Experiencing Runs on Deposits Are Almost Always Insolvent

On an accounting basis, a run is a symptom of illiquidity, which means in the banking context that the long-term assets of the bank—loans—can't be liquidated fast enough to pay the bank's short-term liabilities—deposits. As a result, the bank runs out of cash and must often borrow on the interbank market or from the central bank's liquidity window.

In theory, when a bank is illiquid prior to or as a result of a depositor run, the bank is not necessarily insolvent, since it may simply be experiencing a short-term inability to liquidate long-term assets to pay short-term liabilities, an asset-liability mismatch. In practice, it is rare indeed to find a bank that is experiencing a run that is not subsequently found to be insolvent.

It is almost always the case, however, that once a depositor run is in full sway, and banking regulators examine the bank on an emergency basis, the bank turns out to be insolvent on a book basis, that is, its assets (primarily loans) are less than its liabilities (primarily deposits). In a number of crisis countries, external auditors (typically not the auditors that were previously associated with the bank) were brought in to examine insolvent banks to determine the extent of the losses. Typically, the losses calculated by the new auditors in these cases exceed everyone's expectations.

If in fact it is almost always the case that a bank experiencing a run is insolvent, even in the case of a systemic banking crisis, a more interesting question is why banking regulators and external auditors were unaware of the bank's problems, while members of the public know enough to line up outside a bank to withdraw their deposits. Or perhaps regulators and auditors knew and did nothing, hoping that the problem would go away, or they were negligent in doing their job and didn't know the severity of the problem or, worse, colluded with owners to deceive the public.

3. Lender-of-Last-Resort Financing May Have Unforeseen Consequences

Typically, central banks have the authority either explicitly, or implicitly (as is the case in the United Kingdom), to provide emergency liquidity financing (ELF) outside of the normal liquidity window, with or without the pledge of assets by the bank. However, when central banks provide ELF without adequate security, or with the pledge of assets by the illiquid bank that are sufficient based on book value but not on market value, the potential exists for the financing not to be repaid when the bank fails.

This possibility has at least two outcomes, both bad: the first is that the central bank becomes the largest creditor of the bank, since it has replaced deposits with ELF. The nonpayment of this financing can result in a charge against the capital of the central bank. Given enough such financing or a large enough bank that receives it, central banks themselves can become insolvent. The second possible outcome is that the central bank or banking regulator decides not to close the bank since to do so would result in nonpayment of the financing. Hence, banks are kept open that would (or should) otherwise be closed.

It is an article of faith among central bankers that ELF financing should not be provided to insolvent banks, but only to those experiencing short-term liquidity shortfalls. However, this policy (sometimes required by law) presumes that banks undergoing depositor runs will *not* be found to be insolvent later. If in fact the presumption were to be changed so that such banks were presumed to be insolvent, then ELF should only be provided, if at all, to banks that are "too big to fail." At the very least, this would eliminate the need to fund the myriad of smaller, nonessential banks that typically receive ELF. While the concept of "too big to fail" is a controversial one, in every crisis country there are banks that were considered too big or too essential to be allowed to close, and therefore regulators acted in some manner to prevent them from failing.

This suggests that the rules for providing ELF in many countries should be revisited and the tilt toward providing financing for every bank experiencing a run addressed. It should be noted that under many bankruptcy laws around the world, illiquidity, typically defined in banking laws around the world as the "inability to pay debts as they become due" is one of the grounds for the appointment of a bankruptcy receiver. This test is also one of the grounds for closure of a bank under some banking laws, such as those of the United States. The adoption of a ground for closure such as this would eliminate at least in part the need to provide ELF. At the same time, there should be sufficient flexibility in the law to allow a central bank to provide ELF on an unsecured basis when needed in a banking crisis. In the case of a banking crisis, such financing should be provided by the government, using the central bank as its agent, since the health of an essential part of the economy is at stake, rather than the liquidity needs of a particular bank, which is the normal province of any central bank.

4. Without Effective Laws, Bank Restructuring Agencies Are Doomed to Failure

It is virtually impossible to have a successful bank restructuring agency without the passage of a new law by the legislative branch to create the agency. When presidential or executive decrees are used to create the agency and endow its legal powers, such decrees rarely if ever have the force of law necessary to overcome existing statutory law, even in transitional countries or countries without a fully functioning democracy. Typically, existing laws, such as those relating to banking, bankruptcy, companies, securities, and taxation must be amended in some way to provide sufficient authority for the new agency to fully address a banking crisis. In some cases a law is necessary to provide the new agency with appropriate "super powers," powers usually reserved for court-appointed receivers or administrators in bankruptcy cases, such as the power to repudiate contracts that have not been fully executed, as well as to keep contracts in force that would otherwise be terminated.

It is also virtually impossible to have a successful outcome without a political consensus that involves not only the executive and legislative branches of government, but also the major political parties, and not just the ruling party, but the opposition as well.

Three principles—autonomy, adherence to the rule of law, and transparency—are useful analytic tools in examining whether a bank restructuring agency law has been properly drafted. It is virtually impossible for a bank restructuring agency to function effectively without a law that conforms to these principles.

"Autonomy" in this context means that a bank restructuring agency should be created as an independent agency of the government and, in particular, should be separate and distinct from the central bank, banking regulator, and ministry of finance.

"Adherence to the rule of law" means that there should be clear and unambiguous restrictions on the exercise of power by the state, particularly where the taking of private property through the termination of ownership interests is concerned. Constitutional limitations on government takings of private property should also be taken into account.

"Transparency" means that any bank restructuring agency law should contain clear, comprehensive, and unambiguous language that is comprehensible to bank owners and management, potential investors in restructured banks, and buyers of assets, as well as the public at large.

Examples of successful bank restructuring agencies, such as the Swedish Bank Support Agency, or the Resolution Trust Corporation (RTC) and Federal Deposit Insurance Corporation (FDIC) in the United States, suggest that adherence to all three principles is essential to a good outcome.

5. Lawsuits Against Banking Regulators Increase When Banks Fail

Legal protections against civil lawsuits that may be brought against employees of central banks and banking regulators are always a good idea, but never more so than when banks fail. Once a bank fails and is closed, owners, shareholders, directors, managers, depositors, and creditors all have a greater likelihood of bringing suit against regulators, typically alleging that either the bank was solvent and the regulators were negligent in closing the bank, or the bank was insolvent and the regulators were negligent in not closing it earlier. Often, such lawsuits are not only brought against the central bank, banking regulator, or national government but also government employees in their personal capacity. This means that the costs of defending the suit, as well as any settlement or judgment rendered by a court, must be borne by the employee, and not the government.

Principle 1 of the Basel Core Principles provides that "[a] suitable legal framework for banking supervision is necessary, including . . . legal protection for supervisors." The explanation of this provision is found in the commentary to Principle 1, which states that a suitable legal framework requires a number of components to be in place, including "protection (normally in law) from personal and institutional liability for supervisory actions taken in good faith in the course of performing supervisory duties."[1]

Public disclosure of statutory protections is considered an international best practice. See the Code of Good Practices on Transparency in Monetary and Financial Policies: Declaration of Principles, adopted on September 26, 1999. Sections 4.4.1 and 8.4.1 of the Code refer to the need to publicly disclose information about statutory protections for employees of banking and financial regulators. The text of the Code is available on the IMF's website at www.imf.org/external/np/mae/mft/code/index.htm. The Code is available in a number of languages in addition to English, including Russian and Chinese.

A research paper by the author entitled "Statutory Protections for Banking Supervisors," Financial Sector Website Paper No. 4 (1999), is currently available on the World Bank's website at www1.worldbank.org/finance/html/policy_issues_debates_pubs.html. The study surveys the laws of 20 jurisdictions, including Australia,

---

[1] The full text of the Basel Core Principles and commentary is set forth as item no. 30 (www.bis.org/publ/index.htm).

Ecuador, Germany, Hong Kong, the Philippines, Sweden, Switzerland, the United States, and the United Kingdom.[2]

---

[2] The paper is also available in Russian from the author.

Chapter 28 | Impact of Bank Secrecy on the Rule of Law in the World

JOHN W. MOSCOW

In considering the rule of law in the world, I bring to bear a perspective that is uniquely my own, with a background that not everyone here shares. I am not a banker, nor a bank regulator. I do not work for a Fortune 500 company, a trade association, or an international law firm.

Rather, I am an assistant district attorney in Manhattan—New York County, to use its official name—charged with prosecuting those crimes and offenses committed in the 22 square miles of the county, or within the county's jurisdiction as defined, a very different matter indeed. Although I have little experience with the rule of law in the world, I have gained a good deal of experience with unlawful and criminal conduct.

From my perspective, dealing with what I call "Economic Crime in the Global Village," I have been intimately acquainted with financial disorders. More recently, I have been prosecuting securities frauds, as well as looking at some of the events uncovered by what is referred to as the "Bank of New York" case.

Since 1977, I have been prosecuting economic crimes, sophisticated and simple, which make up the criminal side of the white-collar world in Manhattan. I have dealt with securities frauds, frauds against government agencies, tax shelter frauds, and corruption cases. Since 1989, I have dealt with the Bank of Credit and Commerce International (BCCI), certain aspects of the collapse of the Venezuelan banking system, and a number of substantial international securities frauds involving victims from around the world. It is

---

Note: The author wishes to acknowledge Robert M. Morgenthau, the District Attorney of New York County and leading opponent of money laundering for many years.

apparent that the world economy has become a global economy, in which some countries are better able to participate than others.

The Role of Rule of Law in the Business World

The April 18, 1998, edition of the *Financial Times* asserted editorially that, at the national level, the emerging global standard consists of liberal trade and open financial markets. It demands a high quality of regulation, and independent legal processes, to protect private property and handle bankruptcy. It calls for noncorrupt government. Within this framework, prosperity is generated by free competition among profit-seeking companies.

Whether we will obtain the utopia of prosperity through free competition among profit-seeking companies is something that time will tell. Experience teaches me, as I will share with you, that high-quality regulation, independent legal processes, including independent prosecutors and honest judges, and noncorrupt government are necessary to avoid disaster, even if they can not generate prosperity. What the *Financial Times* proposed, and what appears to me beneficial, is establishing the rule of law in the worldwide economy. That requires a certain amount of change.

Simply put, in the 20-odd years since the Reagan-Thatcher era started, there has been a revolution in the roles of government and business. Power has shifted at an incredible pace from government to business, especially with the end of the Cold War and the diminished need for "National Security" to be preeminent. The needs of international business for government are relatively few; they are concerned with everyone getting a level playing field. I do not suggest that any business wants a level playing field; they each want the edge over their competitors. Collectively, that means the field should be level.

How does this relate to central banks? Central banks and their customers are creating value in the world or owning companies that do so. They represent banks, which are creatures of law and which, by and large, with inevitable exceptions, follow the laws of the countries in which they do business. Banks live by, and rely on, the rule of law in every commercial transaction in which they engage. The honest businesses with which banks deal rely on it as well. But there are business interests in the world other than those that are honest.

Being successful in the global economic village makes a businessman the target of thieves—of people who want to undercut an established manufacturer's prices without incurring their costs. Under the law, they can not do this, so they break the law. (I focus on business here, because that is where the money is.) Whether the issue is patent, or trademark, or copyright, a manufacturer who does not pay royalties can easily undersell one who does.[1]

Necessary Legal Evidence

The rule of law involves the use of legal mechanisms to defend property rights. And the clearest way I know to accomplish that end—to protect production and creation of goods—is to put in jail the people who steal property and to seize or forfeit the proceeds of their crimes. Such actions require the use of courts and, to be successful in court, the gathering of valid, accurate evidence. Having said that, let me add that collecting such evidence is a daunting task, requiring intensive investigation into the source of goods, and requiring a more complicated, if less manpower-intensive investigation, to trace the proceeds of the crime.

Identifying the originators of contraband goods by tracing goods backwards starts at the level where the goods are sold. The goods could be drugs, or stolen goods, or counterfeit goods; it does not matter. I refer to them all as contraband. One can, theoretically, follow the trail of invoices backwards to the point of original manufacture if the goods are counterfeit or stolen; if, as may well be the case, the invoice trail is false, one can, theoretically, accomplish the same end with street-level surveillance. But the repeated seizure of street peddlers' wares makes no more of a dent in the illicit commerce in contraband goods than repeated arrests of street dealers stops the flow of narcotics into the United States, and that has not worked. However necessary it is for social purposes to combat street-

---

[1] And, of course, without the royalties or licensing fees there is little economic incentive for inventors, designers, composers, authors, or even software writers to work. The condition of man in a state of nature, wrote Thomas Hobbes, is solitary, poor, nasty, brutish, and short. The rule of law is an improvement—for everyone.

level distribution, it is more effective to deter crime at its source—with the wholesalers and manufacturers. To prove by evidence in a court of law who the wholesalers and manufacturers are, there exist two choices.

One can attempt to follow the goods backwards from the point of sale to the point of origin, or one can follow the money from the point of sale back to the beneficiaries. There is a serious problem with tracing the origin of goods, aside from the investigative difficulty, and that has to do with the fact that certain goods, at some point in their origination, are legal until they are mislabeled, and hence are immune from effective seizure.[2] Proof of the receipt of profits, however, is evidence on which one can act. The money, by definition, is the proceeds of the sale of contraband, and hence is the proceeds of crime. By tracing the money to its ultimate beneficiaries, one can both seize the money and make a legal case against the human beings who profit from the trade in counterfeit goods (or contraband weapons or drugs).

In that sense, following the profits from contraband is far more lucrative and productive—financially and in terms of evidence obtained—than is the tracing of the goods themselves.

That solution, however, has a major failing, and it is one which needs to be addressed and remedied.

The problem with tracing money to identify the people engaged in profiting from contraband is that there exist hurdles to obtaining valid, legal evidence. Key among the hurdles are bank secrecy laws and corporate secrecy laws. To hold accountable in the world economy those people benefitting from economic crime, such laws must be abolished.

---

[2] I have in mind, for example, watches, which can be manufactured inexpensively and legally and do not acquire their counterfeit characteristics until a brand name is falsely attached. That step, which can be late in the process, leaves the expensive capital-intensive part of the manufacturing process immune from forfeiture. "How was I to know that the other scoundrel would add a false brand name?" will be the defense offered by a shipper, even if he is corrupt and secretly pays the man who adds the false brand name to the watches.

Keeping Up with Technology

As the world economy becomes more like a global village, we must adjust. We can not afford the peculiar legal quirks of places such as Grand Cayman, Cyprus, the Cook Islands, or the Netherlands Antilles, which operate as havens of secrecy, whether for bank transactions or corporate ownership. The impact—indeed the purpose of those laws—is to facilitate what we call money laundering for the purpose of concealing criminal activity. It is necessary to adjust our view of equal sovereignty, with which we have dignified many nations unworthy of equal treatment in world financial markets.[3] We need to provide for adequately staffed modern legal systems, adjusting to new technologies as technologies change. We need independent and honest prosecutors. We can not afford local corruption anywhere if it impacts on the world economy. As times change, we must change with them.

Simply put, with our current technology it is possible to move money in and out of bank secrecy jurisdictions so fast that investigation becomes almost impossible. In the case of BCCI, the bank secrecy statutes of the various jurisdictions in which BCCI operated were such that no one—no auditor, no regulator, indeed, no one outside the circle of thieves—knew the true identities of the owners of the bank or of its various borrowers. Without that knowledge, it is impossible to evaluate whether transactions are with related parties, or are arm's-length deals in which a banker is putting his own money at risk, and is presumably using his best judgment in doing so. Old fashioned secrecy is out of date. We must adapt.

I suggest that we do so by eliminating bank secrecy statutes as a factor in international trade and finance. In this age of multibillion-dollar-a-year narcotics trafficking, of 24-hour-a-day securities

---

[3] For example, there is a proposal adopted that *all* financial transactions through one notorious money-laundering nation be deemed suspicious, which requires any U.S. licensed financial institution to fill out Suspicious Activity Reports for every transaction involving that country. This tends to make their dealings very expensive, and highlights them all for law enforcement. That country has responded by paying millions of dollars in a highly focused effort to enlist the support of key U.S. political leaders, who are in a political position to defeat the law enforcement efforts of the Department of State, the U.S. Treasury, and the Department of Justice. Whether the paid-for lobbying will be successful is not clear, but it looks likely.

markets with international securities frauds as easy to accomplish as lifting the phone and calling abroad, and "asset protection programs," which is a euphonious way of describing frauds on creditors and courts, it is inappropriate for international lawyers and bank regulators to defend in the abstract that which is in reality used to corrupt the public and private lives of the major industrial and financial nations or the world.

Money Laundering and Narcotics

The problems of violent crime, economic crime, and official corruption with which the District Attorney's office deals every day are massively inflated by narcotics. The District Attorney's office is on Centre Street, due south of Park Avenue in Manhattan. Park Avenue at the north of the island has a large population of narcotics addicts who must burglarize, rob, and steal to feed their narcotics addiction. The money they get goes to drug dealers, to larger drug dealers, and then into the banking system. South from Harlem on Park Avenue are a large number of the world's banks; BCCI was there, at 320 Park, laundering narcotics money from the junkies committing crimes of theft and violence. Due south of our office is the Federal Reserve Bank of New York, where the dirty money is transferred. When we started investigating, District Attorney Robert M. Morgenthau and I decided that bankers laundering narcotics money should be derailed by our office and, if possible, sent to jail.

The money that went to BCCI had to get into the banking system, and then be invested, for the drug dealers to profit. Likewise, the proceeds from the sale of counterfeit goods has got to get into the banking system for the counterfeiters to benefit. To keep their profits safe, and to keep you from getting legal evidence against them, the counterfeiters, like the narcotics dealers (who, after all, are merely dealing in unlicensed pharmaceutical products based on cocoa leaves and poppies) need secrecy, which means that they need to launder their money through a bank secrecy jurisdiction—Grand Cayman, Cyprus, Cook Islands, Netherlands Antilles, or the like—before sending it back to Park Avenue for investment. And what we have learned—and it is frightening—is that the money, once back in New York, is respectable, and can be used to buy influence over the law enforcement and foreign policy decisions of this and other nations.[4] The ancient concept used now to validate bank and corporate secrecy is that bank secrecy must be preserved to keep a gentleman's financial affairs confidential. That concept dates back to the days when only "gentlemen" had checking accounts. That concept is archaic, and must give way to the current reality. Bank secrecy statutes in international trade and finance are used by crooks, tax evaders, securities fraudsters, counterfeiters, and capital flight fellows; they are used by narcotics dealers, but they are not needed by honest folks engaged in honest transactions.[5]

Bank Secrecy in Global Terms

I have said that bank secrecy in international finance must give way to the harsh realities of life. There is no reason why the people on Grand Cayman can not have rigid bank secrecy laws. I, for one, do not care what they do among themselves, so long as they are consenting adults. I do care, however, when they try to merchant their sovereign status and impose their sovereignty on the rest of us to protect narco-dollars or other proceeds of contraband from detection. If the people of Grand Cayman, the Cook Islands, or the other countries selling their sovereignty for cash were to have bank secrecy statutes relating only to local residents—not corporations—doing business in their local currency, and not involved in international trade and finance, their laws would be of concern only to themselves. But we are not dealing with that.[6] Banks in such countries are taking deposits from people they have never met, and from brass-plate companies with no assets except the bank account, and inserting the

---

[4] *See* footnote 5.

[5] There are three levels of bank "secrecy" which warrant discussion. There is an obvious interest in privacy—in that no one wants his financial affairs to be open to his competitors, his neighbors, or perhaps, his family. At that level, only bona fide criminal investigators and bank regulators can get access to the data. At the next level of secrecy, only bank regulators can get access to the identifying information on bank accounts and financial transactions; police officers can not. At the third level, not even bank regulators can obtain the identifying information necessary to see if transactions involve relating parties or are being conducted at arm's length.

[6] For example, when a Liechtenstein entity launders payments from the French government-owned oil company through North African nations and into the coffers of a political party in Germany, Liechtenstein becomes of concern to us all.

money into the world monetary system. Most of this is in dollars, and most of it goes through Manhattan.

Two-thirds of the world's trade is conducted in dollars. Far more than 99 percent of the international dollar transactions clear through New York County in any given day. The current volume, I understand, is about $2.7 trillion on a normal day. One can move that volume of money only by moving it so quickly that it is instantaneous. I remember my shock when I learned that the fastest way for two banks in Hong Kong to settle a dollar transaction was to wire the money from Hong Kong to New York and back again. What that means is that, from an evidentiary point of view, money in New York can be wired to Grand Cayman, sheltered from further identification, and wired back to New York as an arm's-length transaction, when in fact it is not. That money's trip to Grand Cayman, economically harmless a century ago when it required a sailboat, gold coins, and handwritten entries, is infinitely mischievous when it can be done electronically, instantaneously, from a distance, with no one ever going to the island at all. Technology has changed world trade and world finance irrevocably in recent years, and we must adjust to that change.

One final note on the economic utility of tax havens. Countries which exist to shelter in untaxed form profits earned from the world's industry and commerce provide an exceptionally mischievous service which should not be tolerated. The following example comes to mind. A man owns a factory in London that produces widgets. He establishes a sales company offshore in the Caribbean and sells his widgets through that company. Before he established the sales company, he made a profit, let us say of a million pounds a year, on which he paid taxes. After he established the sales company he sold goods at almost no profit from the factory to the sales company and sold the goods at whatever profits he could realize from the sales company to the world market. He paid no taxes. The factory in London still requires fire protection; the garbage must be collected; and he very much expects that the police will protect his premises from depredation by street criminals. His contribution to the cost of those services, however, is nil. To make matters worse, the offshore company is audited, if at all, by accountants who care only about their audit and not about the expenses of the firm. The hiring of public servants working for countries offshore to the tax havens for nominal work at high pay—which might be construed by independent observers as bribes—attracts no scrutiny and the tax laws continue to permit this sort of behavior.

The amount of wealth in offshore tax havens is enormous, liquid, immune from audit and most criminal investigations, and available to malefactors of great wealth for malicious use without fear of retribution. Given the constant need of politicians the world over for money, this pool constitutes a constant temptation to corrupt governments throughout the world while allocating the tax burden of the cost of governments to people without the ability to hide their wealth. The anti-democratic implications and the morally corrupting aspects of this behavior are just becoming known.

What is clear is that, here too, times change. The old idea that one country does not care about the fiscal offenses of another has outlived its usefulness; it is now dangerous. Last year, you will recall, the Russian government was so strapped for revenue that it had to go to the oligarchs, asking them to pay their taxes. The billions of dollars laundered through the Bank of New York were tax evasion or tax avoidance, and not really a problem. Unless you realize that the Russian government has nuclear, chemical, and biological weapons, that the people guarding those weapons need to be paid, and that there are terrorists in the world willing to buy the weapons. All of a sudden, one understands that the collapse of the Russian government due to nonpayment of taxes would be a disaster with worldwide consequences. Or simply, as one of our Supreme Court justices wrote three quarters of a century ago, "Taxes are what we pay for civilized society."

Privacy of Banking vs. Anonymity of Crime

Just as bank secrecy is a criminally malevolent anachronism, so too have secretly owned corporations and anonymous trusts become tools of the trade for the criminal parasites on the world economy. It is only slightly useful to be able to trace funds if the beneficiaries of those funds can conceal their identities.

But, following the huge amounts of money involved in the narcotics trade, we have found an entire cottage industry of professionals—lawyers, accountants, and so-called financial planners—establishing ostensibly legal mechanisms for people to conceal the ownership of money from the courts of the nations in which they choose to live.

In one case, a British part-time magistrate and his former partner, a lawyer in London, established a whole series of companies to facilitate securities fraud in New York.

The way the scheme worked, a securities fraudster in New York hired the judge to set up offshore companies, which had to be owned by someone who was not a U.S. citizen or resident. The judge and his partner incorporated the companies in Liberia, which worked for a while. Then the U.S. SEC came looking around to see who owned the companies. The magistrate thereupon hired a Liberian diplomat to falsely state that he was the beneficial owner of the companies. As the diplomat had diplomatic immunity, one could reasonably assume that his statement would end the inquiry.[7]

These companies, having been established with no owner, could transfer ownership quite readily; one could transfer their entire assets (a bank account) by "selling" the company without anyone knowing that a transfer had occurred. That transaction, in slightly different form, takes place routinely in the laundering of money that we believe originates in the drug trade, but the technique is clearly transferable. In fact, British police, following a narcotics money launderer, found much of the evidence about the Liberian companies. When we got together, by good fortune, the British police provided the evidence to convict our securities fraudsters: they, in turn, promptly gave evidence against the magistrate, whom the British police proceeded to arrest. It turned out that he had performed his "secret corporation" trick for a large number of people, including a number of New Yorkers. Cases such as this, against many parties, are pending on both sides of the Atlantic at this time.

In another case, one of the big accounting firms established a corporation in the Caribbean and acted as its managing agent. My office served the accounting firm with a subpoena, and the firm

---

[7] That it did not is due partly to luck and mostly to the skill of the detectives working on the case, who persuaded the diplomat to cooperate with law enforcement authorities.

fatuously asserted that the Caribbean partnership was not the U.S. partnership and that it had not been served. Of course, both partnerships have the same name, the same signature, the same telephone book—internal—and the Caribbean partners who took direction from New York. So the firm agreed to accept service of the subpoena, but then responded that it did not know who owned the company and would have to ask the person with whom it dealt.

Such behavior by professionals is designed to make money out of crime. The lawyers and accountants are establishing formalistic structures specifically designed to defeat those very laws which your companies need to establish a level playing field. If thieves can hire accountants and attorneys to shield the proceeds of crime, there is a problem with the law.

To trace the proceeds of counterfeiting (and, again, the same goes for contraband weapons or drugs) you need legal, competent, valid evidence.[8] To the extent that contraband is, as it surely is, an attack on legitimate commerce, laws protecting the proceeds of contraband commerce are bad for the economy of the world. And, quite frankly, to the extent that professionals assist this conduct by establishing structures designed prospectively to defeat valid legal claims, they too are your enemies.

Times change. The world economy is in flux, and will continue to be. The value of goods and services will vary over time. But if we are to establish a rule of law in the global economic village we must forbid the bank secrecy and corporate secrecy which are so inimical to legal, honest, competent evidence—that is, inimical to the truth. Corporations such as international banks, which are creatures of law and are themselves law-abiding, must work together to eliminate the use of bank secrecy, corporate secrecy, and other anachronistic legalisms used to shield the proceeds of crime from its victims.

---

[8] I say legal because you can, by paying money or otherwise, unlawfully obtain the information from a "bank secrecy" jurisdiction. You just cannot use it in court. The rule of law providing for secrecy becomes a rule protecting only the guilty.

Chapter
29 | Internet Banking: Some Recent Legal Developments

JOHN JIN LEE

Like other manifestations of the Internet revolution that has altered our lives as we know it, retail banking over the Internet has ridden the crest of a major wave of customer service, the likes of which have not been seen before. It is not so much that the nature of the services is unusual; in fact, virtually all of the services are the same ones that have been made available by banks for some time. Rather, what is unique about Internet banking is the fact that the services are available in as ubiquitous a manner as possible; there has never been a medium for distribution of information that costs so little and yet provides such a limitless reach with no constraints of time or space.

The ubiquitous nature of the Internet can be broken down into several discrete components, which individually and together have spawned a set of unique developments generating new areas of competition among purveyors of retail banking services. These components include the following characteristics.

The Internet Is a Unique Electronic Medium

Since the Internet exists in the electronic world, information that is disseminated over the Internet constitutes a form of electronic communication. The printed word, which prior to the Internet was distributed only through paper instruments like books, magazines, newspapers, and the like or through electronic mass media channels constrained by time, such as radio and television, could now be distributed in electronic form with no constraint on time. All that is required for access to such electronic communication is a computer hooked up to the World Wide Web, along with appropriate access to either a particular bank's website or e-mail address. In light of this, should electronic communication be deemed equivalent to the more traditional printed or written communication?

The Internet Has No Geographic Borders

Since any informational content distributed over the Internet is not bound by any geographic boundaries, the traditional notions of jurisdictional reach by governmental bodies must now be analyzed differently. Among other considerations, should Internet banking be subject to the same traditional jurisdictional restraints imposed on banking in the more traditional world of brick and mortar, or should these services be made available without such restraints?

The Internet Is an Interactive Medium

In contrast to other media such as books, magazines, newspapers, radio, and television, the Internet offers the opportunity for one or more parties to interact through electronic communication. This interactivity presents the opportunity for an endless array of banking services limited only by creativity, operational practicality, and policy considerations. One central question is the extent to which banking services should be permitted, along with the degree of security that must be established to ensure that the integrity of the services is not compromised by "computer hackers" (computer experts who assume a somewhat perverse sense of pride in their ability to break into whatever security shroud has been cast on Internet access to particular informational content).

The Internet Maintains Extremely Low Barriers to Entry

The ability to transact business over the Internet is relatively inexpensive when weighed against its limitless reach, so almost anyone interested in entering into the banking business over the Internet may do so with virtually little capital investment. As such, the traditional differences between financial services offered by banks and "nonbanks" became more blurred with the advent of the Internet.

The Internet Provides for Anonymity

Since interactivity over the Internet takes place through interaction of one or more computers, participants in the interaction may remain anonymous. In light of this anonymity, how can banks operating over the Internet assure themselves of the identities of those with whom they interact without compromising the privacy and confidentiality afforded by the medium?

The Internet Provides for Facile Transport Between Websites

Since the World Wide Web allows for facile transport from one website to another through various forms of "links," it becomes easy for an operator of a website to exist as a central repository of information on any given category of interest or services. The appeal of such Internet "portals" to potential Internet users is immediately obvious, so for banks the challenge is to create the right "portal" to attract the greatest number of customers.

The above elements have created many novel developments in Internet banking, and some of these developments have created some very interesting legal issues for consideration. Some of the principal developments and associated legal issues are addressed below.

Use of Electronic Communications in Consumer Disclosures

Retail banking in this country is characterized by the high degree of regulatory controls imposed on various aspects of depository and lending operations. In addition to the multitude of state laws governing retail banking, particularly in the consumer lending context, numerous federal laws and regulations exist to govern various aspects of retail banking operations. These laws include the following:

- Electronic Fund Transfer Act (15 U.S.C. §1693, *et seq.*) (EFTA) and its enabling Regulation E (12 C.F.R. Part 205): this law "establishes the basic rights, liabilities, and responsibilities of consumers who use electronic fund transfers and financial institutions that offer these services," 12 C.F.R. Section 205.1(b).

- Truth in Savings Act (12 U.S.C. §4301, *et seq.*) (TISA) and its enabling Regulation DD (12 C.F.R. Part 230): this law establishes, among other things, deposit account disclosures "to enable consumers to make informed decisions about accounts at depository institutions," 12 C.F.R. Section 230.1(b).

- Equal Credit Opportunity Act (15 U.S.C. §1691, *et seq.*) (ECOA) and its enabling Regulation B (12 C.F.R. Part 202): this law was enacted "to promote the availability of credit to all creditworthy applicants without regard to race, color, religion, national origin, sex, marital status, or age" and "prohibits creditor practices that discriminate on the basis of any of these factors," 12 C.F.R. Section 202.1(b).

- Truth in Lending Act (15 U.S.C. §1601, *et seq.*) (TILA) and its enabling Regulation Z (12 C.F.R. Part 226): this law was passed "to promote the informed use of consumer credit by requiring disclosures about its terms and cost," 12 C.F.R. Section 226.1(b).

- Consumer Leasing Act (15 U.S.C. §§1667–1667f) (CLA) and its enabling Regulation M (12 C.F.R. Part 213): this law aims "to ensure that lessees of personal property receive meaningful disclosures that enable them to compare lease terms with other leases and, where appropriate, with credit transactions," 12 C.F.R. Section 213.1(b).

One common thread woven through all the above retail banking laws is the requirement for written disclosures to be made to consumers in order to provide consumers with the proper information regarding a proposed transaction with the financial institution. For instance, under Regulation E, a financial institution is required to make detailed written disclosures regarding an electronic fund transfer service, such as that offered through use of an "automated teller machine," otherwise known as an ATM, either at the time the consumer contracts for the service or before the first electronic fund transfer occurs on the consumer's account; see 12 C.F.R. Section 205.7. Similar written disclosure requirements exist in each of the other regulations; see 12 C.F.R. Section 230.4 for Regulation DD, 12 C.F.R. 202.9 for Regulation B, 12 C.F.R. Sections 226.5–226.6 and 226.17–226.18 for Regulation Z, and 12 C.F.R. Sections 213.3–213.4 for Regulation M.

On May 2, 1996, the Board of Governors of the Federal Reserve System (Fed), which is the governmental agency charged with the authority and responsibility for issuing regulations under each of the above laws (see 15 U.S.C. §1696 for EFTA, 12 U.S.C. §4308 for TISA, 15 U.S.C. §1691b for ECOA, 15 U.S.C. §1604 for TILA and

15 U.S.C. §1667f for CLA), published a Regulation E proposal identifying the use of "electronic communication" as a potential vehicle for providing the mandatory written disclosures to alleviate undue regulatory burden on the financial services industry without undermining consumer protection.[1] The proposal required, among other things, that the Regulation E standard for the disclosures be in a "clear and readily understandable" form and not be adversely affected by the use of "electronic communication.[2] In addition, the disclosures must be in a form that a consumer may retain, a requirement which may be satisfied by placing the disclosures in a format allowing them to be downloaded into a consumer's computer for printing.[3] However, the financial institution must provide a paper copy of the required disclosures if a consumer makes such a request within one year of receipt of the "electronic communication."[4]

Following its review of this Regulation E proposal, the Fed issued an interim regulation on March 25, 1998.[5] Since the vast majority of the comments received on the proposal were favorable, the Fed believed that an interim regulation was appropriate to permit the use of an "electronic communication" to serve as a legal equivalent for written disclosures mandated under Regulation E.[6] Although the Fed addressed specific issues in the "Supplementary Information" section of the rule, the interim regulation itself was relatively brief, consisting only of a definition of "electronic communication" and an operative provision authorizing the use of "electronic communication" where written disclosures are required:

(c) Electronic communication.

(1) Definition. For purposes of this regulation, the term electronic communication means a message transmitted electronically between a consumer and a financial institution in a format that allows visual text to be displayed on equipment such as a personal computer monitor.

---

[1] *See* 61 *Fed. Reg.* 19696 (1996).
[2] *See* 61 *Fed. Reg.* at 19697.
[3] *Id.*
[4] *Id.*
[5] *See* 63 *Fed. Reg.* 14528 (1998).
[6] *Id.*

(2) Electronic communication between financial institution and consumer. A financial institution and a consumer may agree to send by electronic communication any information required by this regulation to be in writing. Information sent by electronic communication to a consumer must comply with paragraph (a) of this section and the applicable timing and other requirements contained in the regulation.[7]

Among the matters addressed in the "Supplementary Information" section of the interim regulation were the following important issues.

Agreement Between Financial Institution and Consumer

Many of those commenting on the proposal requested the Fed to clarify when an agreement between a financial institution and a consumer exists. In response, the Fed merely stated that "[w]hether such an agreement exists between the parties is determined by applicable state law."[8] Although such a response might be appropriate in the traditional physical world of paper documents, in a virtual world where geographic boundaries do not exist, reliance on state law seems somewhat misplaced.

Requirement to "Send" Disclosures Through Use of an "Electronic Communication"

Current technology allows Internet users to obtain information in two primary ways. One is to view and, if desired, download information placed on a particular website. The other consists of an e-mail message sent by one party to another. In the context of the interim regulation an issue arose with respect to whether the Regulation E disclosures could be deemed "sent" to consumers by making the disclosures available on the website of the financial institution, or whether some type of e-mail message had to be sent to the consumer by the financial institution. The Fed opined that the requirement can only be met by issuing some type of notice to the consumer, since the mere posting of disclosures on a website without notifying the consumer would not permit the consumer to be aware

---

[7] See 63 Fed. Reg. at 14532.
[8] See 63 Fed. Reg. at 14529.

when a disclosure became available.[9] Of course, where the disclosures were particularly lengthy or otherwise too cumbersome for ordinary issuance by e-mail, the Fed recognized the appropriateness of making the disclosures available on their website, coupled with a brief e-mail note sent to inform the consumer of their availability on the site.

Requirement for Disclosures to Be "Clear and Readily Understandable"

In stating that the requirements of paragraph (a) of the section must be met, the interim regulation was referring to two key disclosure standards of Regulation E. One is that the disclosures must be "clear and readily understandable." The Fed was quick to point out, however, that adherence to this standard did not require the financial institution to ensure that the consumer possessed the proper equipment to meet this standard, although such a responsibility did exist for equipment maintained by the financial institution in its place of business for use by consumers.[10]

Consumer Ability to Retain Disclosures

The other key requirement of paragraph (a) of the section was the need for the financial institution to provide disclosures "in a form the consumer may keep." The Fed stated that the only responsibility imposed on the financial institution is to ensure that the disclosures may be printed by or downloaded onto a consumer's computer.[11] The institution had no responsibility to ascertain whether the consumer's equipment in fact had the ability to print or download, nor to verify that the consumer in fact retained a copy of the disclosures. Of course, where the financial institution maintained equipment at its place of business for use by consumers, the institution would be required to ensure the disclosures could be printed or otherwise sent to the consumer's e-mail address for retention.

---

[9] *See* 63 *Fed. Reg.* at 14529.
[10] *See* 63 *Fed. Reg.* at 14530.
[11] *Id.*

Use of Paper Disclosures

The Fed assumed an interesting stance on the use of paper disclosures in the context of Internet banking. First, it dropped the original requirement in the proposal for allowing the consumer to request a paper disclosure upon demand.[12] In so doing, it believed that, as a practical matter, financial institutions would in fact issue paper disclosures when so requested by consumers. On the other hand, financial institutions would be permitted to require paper confirmations of notices sent by a consumer to the financial institution in connection with an alleged error involving an electronic fund transfer.[13] Although the basis for the requirement was based on the concern for greater security with regard to paper confirmation, such an approach seems inconsistent with the one embraced for disclosures sent to consumers.

At the same time that the interim regulation was published, the Fed issued similar proposals to permit disclosures to be sent in the form of an "electronic communication" under Regulation DD, 63 Fed. Reg. 14533 (1998); Regulation M, 63 Fed. Reg. 14538 (1998); Regulation Z, 63 Fed. Reg. 14548 (1998); and Regulation B, 63 Fed. Reg. 14552 (1998). Like the interim regulation on Regulation E, the proposals for the other retail banking regulations were noteworthy for the brevity of the revisions, particularly with respect to the requirement for the financial institution and consumer to agree to the use of an "electronic communication" for issuing disclosures. Although the Fed justified its approach on the thought that it would permit financial institutions much flexibility in designing the manner in which the disclosures would be issued to the consumers in electronic form,[14] it was clear from the numerous comments made on these proposals that the financial services industry preferred more detailed guidance from the Fed.

In response to these comments, the Fed reissued the "electronic communication" proposals for Regulation B, 64 Fed. Reg. 49688 (1999); Regulation M, 64 Fed. Reg. 49713 (1999); Regulation Z, 64 Fed. Reg. 49722 (1999); and Regulation DD, 64 Fed. Reg. 49740

---

[12] *Id.*
[13] *See* 63 *Fed. Reg.* at 14531.
[14] *See, e.g.*, 64 *Fed. Reg.* at 49688.

(1999). The Fed also issued a new Regulation E proposal consistent with the detailed nature of the other regulatory proposals.[15] Finally, in recognition of the limited usefulness of the interim regulation under Regulation E due to the fact that Regulation E disclosures are frequently issued along with the Regulation DD periodic statement disclosures provided for deposit accounts, the Fed issued an interim regulation on Regulation DD to permit deposit account disclosures required for periodic statements to be made to consumers in the form of an "electronic communication."[16] The language and rationale used for issuing this interim regulation were similar to that used for the Regulation E interim regulation.

By far the most important issue contained in the reissued "electronic communication" proposals was the requirement for the financial institution to obtain consent from the consumer before any disclosures can be sent in electronic form.[17] Those commenting on behalf of the financial services industry were concerned that the validity of a consumer's consent would remain in doubt if the consent were governed by applicable state law, both because state laws vary as to the standard for determining consent as well as to the question of which state law would apply. These respondents suggested that the Fed adopt a federal standard for consent. Those representing consumers, however, expressed concern that the ease with which consent could be procured would induce consumers to commit to receipt of electronic disclosures without complete understanding of its implications. Many consumer advocates were particularly concerned about the use of electronic disclosures in mortgage and other loans that are normally consummated in person. In addition, these respondents were skeptical about the integrity of electronic disclosures, given the ease with which any document in electronic form may be altered.

In response to these concerns, the Fed established more detailed guidance on the requirements for procuring consumer consent and was particularly careful to specify rules that addressed the concerns of both the industry and consumer respondents. Central to its approach was the adoption of a standardized disclosure statement and form for

---

[15] *See* 64 *Fed. Reg.* at 49699 (1999).
[16] *See* 64 *Fed. Reg.* at 49846 (1999).
[17] *See* 64 *Fed. Reg.* at 49689, 49700–01, 49713–14, 49723–24, 49740–41.

procuring a consumer's consent.[18] By utilizing a standardized form, the Fed hoped to strike a fair balance between the federal standard advocated by the industry respondents and the consumer safeguards proposed by the consumer advocates.

Another aspect of the Fed's approach was the adoption of different treatment for the various disclosures required under each of the regulations. This treatment, of course, required considerably more thought to be given to each disclosure, a process that resulted in considerably more lengthy proposals. This, in turn, provided many more areas for possible comment. It is beyond the scope of this article to identify even the majority of such possible comments. However, one can best appreciate the unique effect of the Internet on retail banking by noting some of the more interesting issues:

- Consent must be affirmative: One consumer safeguard incorporated into the standardized consent form is the requirement for the consumer to provide an affirmative indication of his or her decision to receive electronic disclosures.[19] This represents a clear departure from a frequent approach used by credit card issuers when sending initial disclosures, where issuers send a statement indicating that the consumer's use of a credit card constitutes the consumer's agreement to be bound by the terms and conditions of the disclosure.

- Combined disclosures under multiple regulations: The introduction of a detailed disclosure statement and form to evidence the consumer's consent under each of these regulations poses the obvious question as to whether a single disclosure and form may be used where a consumer transaction triggers the application of more than one of these regulations. It would seem practical to permit such a practice, although the proposals are silent on this issue.

- Broker or other third party participation: The use of a broker by consumers to assist in shopping for retail banking services has become more prevalent in recent years. For instance, many consumers use brokers to find a new home or automobile, in

---

[18] See 64 Fed. Reg. at 49691, 49703, 49716, 49729, 49743.
[19] See 64 Fed. Reg. at 49692, 49704, 49716, 49729, 49744.

which financing services are also involved. It seems quite plausible to argue that the Internet would promote increased use of such brokers, so that where these brokers assist consumers in finding appropriate financing, it would seem practical for these brokers, and not the financial institutions, to provide the necessary consent disclosure and form to the consumer. However, the proposals are silent with respect to this point.

- Relation to in-person and telephone disclosures: If viewed as yet another distribution channel for retail banking services, the Internet prompts the need for establishing the boundary line between disclosures that are required to be given on paper because a person is physically present in the offices of the financial institution and those which may be provided through an "electronic communication." For instance, may a financial institution choose to direct a consumer appearing in its office to a computer housed in that office for certain of its retail banking services? The proposals indicate that such a process cannot be used.[20] There is also a question as to whether consent to electronic disclosures may be provided through use of the telephone. The proposals are silent on this issue.

- Relation to state law: Each proposal states that the Fed sees no inconsistency between the requirements in the proposal for providing electronic disclosures, on the one hand, and any state laws requiring paper disclosures on the other hand.[21] However, one can argue to the contrary, given the obvious disincentive for financial institutions to provide an electronic disclosure if in fact applicable state law imposed a paper disclosure requirement.

At the time of writing,[22] the Fed had not acted on any of the proposals, although it originally stated its intention to issue the final regulations by March 2000. Even though it did not acknowledge any reason for its delay in promulgating these regulations, the Fed was perhaps concerned over the possible passage of a federal law governing the use of electronic signatures, especially since the two principal legislative bills being considered by the U.S. Congress on

---

[20] *See* 64 *Fed. Reg.* at 49703, 49716, 49728, 49743.
[21] *See* 64 *Fed. Reg.* at 49693-94, 49706, 49717, 49732, 49746.
[22] May 2000.

the subject both incorporate a form of consent provision; see S. 761 (The Millennium Digital Commerce Act)(1999) and H.R. 1714 (The Electronic Signatures in Global and National Commerce Act)(1999). If a final law on electronic signatures is passed with a consent provision, there is a possibility that the consent provision would apply to transactions targeted by the "electronic communications" proposals, which would, of course, preempt any contrary consent provision contained in these proposals.

COMMENT

BRIAN W. SMITH

A Clear View, a Steady Hand, and a Firm Resolve: A Practitioner's Perspective on the Issues Facing E-Commerce in Financial Services and How to Address Them

I will first identify and discuss several pressing legal issues confronting the providers of e-commerce in financial products and services and then offer some practical suggestions for how practitioners and policymakers might address these issues in a manner intended to facilitate the further development of e-commerce.

I will focus on an area in which I am privileged to counsel dozens of clients in many countries: e-commerce in financial services, i.e., employing the Internet to take deposits, lend money, sell insurance, distribute securities, manage invested assets, or pay for goods or services. I see clients of all sizes and at all levels of familiarity with the myriad of legal and regulatory issues potentially applicable to their services. From dot-com "start-ups," to experienced technology providers, to the most sophisticated financial services behemoths, the issues which I find most pressing and about which we labor to develop "best practices" are the same all over the world.

The issues I view as most pressing are:

- Forming the commercial relationship—i.e., ensuring the identity of a customer, or trading partner and creating a valid and enforceable contract,

- Privacy and data protection—i.e., obtaining and using the wealth of information available in an Internet transaction yet protecting both the customer's privacy and the transaction's security.

- Global interoperability—i.e., providing a transborder (multi-jurisdictional) operational and legal framework to take the fullest advantage of Internet technology.

Let's briefly examine each in turn.

Forming the Commercial Relationship

Essential to the establishment of a binding commercial relationship is authenticating the parties' identity and their authority to complete a transaction. Much technology exists to create and recognize digital or other electronic signatures, as well as to assign and present electronic certificates confirming the identity and authority of an individual. There is much legislation being crafted—in the states and abroad—to encourage the use of digital signatures and certificates by confirming the validity of contracts formed and signed by these technologies.

Setting aside for a moment the lack of uniformity in these internal (i.e., 50 states) or national laws, a topic better left for the global interoperability discussion, the issues surrounding the creation of the legal relationship are most vexing.

Despite the existence of suitable technology and even, in some instances, encouraging laws, millions of transactions take place on the Internet and very few of them do so with a form of electronic authentication and/or digital certification appended to them. Why?

I think there are basically two reasons: one, there exists no real incentive to seek or issue certificates. They are not yet required in commerce. Consumers and commercial traders are each able to transmit their business on the Internet and then authenticate and document the transaction in more traditional ways off-line. The business environment is only just starting, e.g., business-to-business on-line purchasing consortia, to establish transaction rules which require trading partners within the environment to employ authentication and certification technology. Until this becomes a more universal requirement of on-line transactions, the uncertainties, inefficiencies, and costs of using off-line certification and documentation for on-line transactions will continue. Two, there continues to be an appalling lack of uniformity of the legal in requirements and processes. There is still a good deal of uncertainty about how each jurisdiction's laws will interact with each other in both defining how and when a contract is formed and even less clarity as to the rights a party possesses and the processes a party must follow to assert those contractual rights.

It is almost a tautology that all commentators and policymakers must decry the absence of more uniform and workable international rules directed at Internet transactions and I am no exception. It is also almost axiomatic that the same persons always find some parochial concern to cause them to shy away from reaching agreement. Clearly, if we wish to fully exploit the promise of the Internet, we cannot be allowed to continue this situation much longer.

Despite the uncertainties in forming the commercial relationship, some self help—best practices—are emerging to give Internet-based businesses more comfort in their Internet business arrangements.

A few suggestions which our clients have found useful are

- Use the technology to facilitate legal goals. The majesty of the Internet-related technology is that it affords creative ways to achieve legal results. Pop-up screens, bold or colored text, highlighted lines or paragraphs, and text-framing techniques all provide a means to enhance the clarity and availability of disclosure and essential contract terms. Sequencing the transaction so that a party must answer by click-through questions such as: Did you understand the terms of the agreement? Do you agree to the terms? etc. and preventing the completion of the transaction until all these answers are provided go a long way to confirming a legal meeting of the minds.

- Make *all* disclosures and terms of agreement clear and meaningful. Avoid wordy and ambiguous discussions.

- Empower the other party to both agree and to decline so that the parties' arrangement is unambiguous.

Policymakers attempting to develop comprehensive legal rules for conducting business on the Internet will badly miss the mark. The speed with which Internet-based business is developing and the fact that the technology to support it is ever-changing almost guarantee that attempts to detail how business will be conducted will be too late to deal with actual practices and will only impede the conduct of the business and therefore frustrate the policy goals. It reminds me of the story about the dog who each day raced into the street to try to "catch" the speeding cars. After many frustrating attempts, one day the dog dashed into the roadway, clamped his jaws on the wheel of a speeding Volkswagen and only then realized he didn't know what to do with the monster he had "caught."

A better policy model would be to attempt to bring a minimal level of clarity to the uncertain legal and regulatory environment (e.g., giving certainty to contracts electronically formed to build bridges over the gaps in conflicting or disharmonious laws, and iron out differences in choice of law provisions) and to minimize the impediments or hurdles institutions must go over in order to operate (e.g., set up a watchful but nonintrusive regulatory scheme).

Privacy and Data Protection

Protection of customer data and the requisite use and sharing of such data are rapidly becoming cornerstones of Internet financial services. The prospect of unfettered technology-enabled access to this data has, I believe, always been a fiction created by uninformed marketeers, promulgated by pundits, and demonized by public interest watchdog groups. In reality, most financial institutions have long been aware of their responsibility to protect the privacy of their customers' information and the security of their systems.

Nonetheless, the subject of privacy has become a touchstone for all that is believed to be "evil" about big business, and the debate over the precise contours of how to define the frontier between the customers' and the institutions' rights and responsibilities rages worldwide. A particularly politically charged dispute has centered around whether a financial institution must give its customers "opt in" protection—meaning a customer must give permission for the sharing of customer data (even among commonly owned/affiliated companies) or if it is sufficient for an institution to provide its customers with the opportunity to "opt out" of such sharing. In the latter case, the silence of the customer is typically seen as consent to share. You can readily see how the battle lines form over these approaches.

For my part, the debate is more about perceptions than about reality. Using the elastic capabilities of technology, financial services firms can unambiguously describe to customers what data are gathered and how they are used by the institution. The institution can clearly describe the data-sharing arrangements it wishes to utilize and the protections it will employ to assure confidentiality and data integrity. At that point, if clearly given the opportunity to do so, a consumer can say *no* to the sharing arrangements.

The keys are responsible, good-faith business practices; clear and meaningful disclosures; and customer empowerment. Sure, there will be abusers—not every institution always acts responsibly or in good faith or in the clear light of day. But a legal and regulatory scheme which exhibits the minimum performance criteria, backed up with decisive enforcement is a model which has been tested and proven many times and ought to work here.

A few suggestions our clients have found useful are:

- Develop a comprehensive and *accurate* (it's what is accordingly done) privacy policy.

- Employ internal audit and outside consultants to review compliance with the articulated privacy policy.

- Develop customer service capacity to respond accurately to customer concerns or complaints on the enforcement of the privacy policy.

Perhaps a more pressing problem is the protection of data, especially in an "open system" environment. By open system, I mean the free trading environment we commonly identify with the Internet, i.e., any party may contact another and transact e-business. This, I distinguish from a "closed system" or "branded" system in which parties that "belong" to the system also transact with the parties within the system. The principal difference between the two are carefully crafted business rules defined by and subscribed to by the participants in the closed system which delineate the manner of their dealings with each other, including the data security, encryption, or other techniques for data protection required to "play" within the system. The open system lacks these extra business rules and typically relies on the lowest common denominator approach to data security.

It is my belief, formed by my experience at MasterCard and several more immediate client projects, that the branded or closed environment is the engine for growth of the Internet in financial services. The branded approach will provide guidelines of data security, even data sharing; it will provide a minimum level of assurance to all participants—financial institutions and customers—as to the manner in which business will be conducted, their rights and responsibilities. The closed network can develop business protocols which provide a good measure of reliability in the transaction of business.

Examples of this abound: MasterCard and Visa are obvious ones. But Identrus—a consortium of leading banks around the world, including several of our clients—is attempting the same thing for the provision of business-to-business certification authority services to the participating banks' customers. Industry-specific groups, e.g., auto or airline industry purchasing consortia, are also emerging.

The open system appeals to the "technos" who envision the Internet as a free marketplace for all to transact business at will. The closed system need not prevent the continued development of unfettered Internet access and transactions. Rather, it would seem that, especially in financial services, there are business models which might benefit from coordinated and branded business rules.

Antitrust and competition authorities are apparently considering how these industry-specific groups are formed, how they operate, how they regulate who can participate, and their perceived effect on competition. We will be hearing more on this, I'm sure.

Global Interoperability

As we speak, financial services firms are attempting to speed their products and services, via the Internet, across the globe. While the business-to-business model is more likely to gain widespread reach before business-to-consumer applications, both are beginning their tentative stretch.

Frustrating developments on both fronts is the absence of a legal and business rules structure.

Earlier, I offered the view that Internet contract formation would be greatly aided by the use of digital certificates but that, so far, there were no obligations imposed by law or by business rules that certificates must be used. To counter this, there are developing "Trusted Marketplaces" where groups of companies are coming together to establish business rules for their Internet interactions with each other. Central to those rules is the use of digital certificates. Energizing examples of these marketplaces are the national or even regional chambers of commerce, the industry-specific groups mentioned earlier, and professional groups (architects, engineers, etc.).

To achieve interoperability—which is more readily accomplished from a technology perspective—the legal and regulatory environments across which the transactions take place must be harmonized. This can partly, but not entirely, be done by business rules and procedures among the trading partners.

Interoperability encompasses many interrelated concepts in addition to technology issues. These include on the institution/customer level uniformity of contract terms, a specific choice of law, accommodation of local law variants on business rules, disclosure, dispute resolution, and, in consumer transactions, pricing models. On the institution-only level they include risk management, currency exchange, tax, security, corporate governance, and doing business issues.

The Internet's demand for global interoperability will present both the financial services institutions and the policymakers with significant challenges. Capital requirements and risk identification and assessment will be of major importance to both constituencies.

This is where the "tires hit the road." Technology makes this possible *now*. Many institutions will, with their partners, take advantage of the technology and responsible, get-creative business rules to launch into this global environment. Policymakers could provide some assistance by expediting the consideration and resolution of some of the emerging international solutions being offered to the legal and supervisory concerns we all have discussed.

Conclusion

There are many issues relevant to e-commerce in financial services. The trick is to attempt to discern the real issues from the academic or theoretical and then to get a very clear understanding of them and the approaches available to solve them.

This is not for the faint of heart. It is, however, much like exploring a new world. My wife, of Norwegian descent, reminded me the other day that the Smithsonian Institution is hosting an exhibition on the Vikings and their many exploits and contributions to our present-day world. Not least among them, it seems, was their great exploration—even of North America 500 years before Columbus!

When I now attempt with my Internet clients to navigate the rough seas of legal risks or the uncertain waters of unclear legal precedent, I often console myself by thinking it could be worse—I could have been asked to row an open boat several thousand miles to nowhere!

VII. Monetary Areas and Exchange Arrangements

Chapter
30 Dollarization: A Primer

TOMÁS J.T. BALIÑO

Dollarization refers to the use by residents of one country of assets (or liabilities) denominated in another country's currency.[1] Dollarization may be partial or full—these categories are sometimes also known as de facto and de jure dollarization—depending on whether a domestic currency circulates in parallel with the foreign currency.

This phenomenon has attracted a lot of attention recently, partly because a large number of economies are partially dollarized, and partly (and perhaps more importantly) because some countries have contemplated or have decided to move to full dollarization. The aim of this paper is to summarize the key issues that both partial and full dollarization entail and draw some tentative conclusions.

Partial Dollarization

Domestic use of a foreign currency is a widespread phenomenon.[2] Table 1 shows that in 18 out of 52 countries that had borrowed from the IMF, the share of financial assets held in foreign currency exceeded 30 percent as of 1995. A caveat is in order in analyzing these figures: owing to the practical impossibility of having reliable estimates of foreign cash in circulation in a country, the data in the table comprise only deposits. However, this data problem distorts the picture. In many highly dollarized countries cash is more important than deposits for transactions and often also as an asset because of mistrust in the domestic banking system or to conceal wealth from the authorities. Thus, the information used in dollarization analyses—

---

[1] The use of the term dollarization to refer to the general phenomenon is due to the fact that the dollar is the foreign currency most commonly used in other countries.

[2] For a detailed discussion of partial dollarization, see Baliño, Bennett, and Borensztein (1999).

613

including that reported in Table 1—underestimates the degree of dollarization, particularly as regards economies where cash makes up a large part of money balances.

Table 1. Reported Ratios of Foreign Currency Deposits (FCD) to Broad Money in Countries with IMF Arrangements Since 1986

Country	1990	1991	1992	1993	1994	1995
Highly dollarized economies (FCD/broad money > 30 percent) 1/							
Argentina	34.2	35.1	37.1	40.4	43.2	43.9
Azerbaijan	...	...	...	14.8	58.9	50.3
Belarus 2/	...	...	...	40.6	54.3	30.7
Bolivia	70.8	76.8	80.8	83.9	81.9	82.3
Cambodia	...	...	26.3	38.8	51.8	56.4
Costa Rica	...	37.7	31.9	29.5	30.3	31.0
Croatia	...	...	...	53.8	50.2	57.4
Georgia	...	...	...	...	80.1	30.8
Guinea-Bissau	41.5	34.7	31.6	30.9	31.1	31.2
Lao P.D.R.	42.0	39.4	36.8	41.4	34.4	35.6
Latvia	...	...	...	27.2	27.5	31.1
Mozambique 3/	...	11.8	16.7	23.2	25.3	32.6
Nicaragua	...	28.7	37.4	45.6	48.6	54.5
Peru	...	59.9	65.0	70.2	64.2	64.0
São Tomé and Príncipe	...	...	...	...	38.3	31.9
Tajikistan	...	...	...	...	...	33.7
Turkey	23.2	29.7	33.7	37.9	45.8	46.1
Uruguay	80.1	78.5	76.2	73.3	74.1	76.1
Median	41.7	36.4	36.8	40.4	48.6	39.7
Average	48.6	43.3	43.0	43.4	49.4	45.5

Sources: IMF, IMF Staff Country Reports, and *International Financial Statistics (IFS)*. (Table reproduced from Baliño, Bennett, and Borensztein, 1999.)

1/ Classification based on observations for 1995; countries in bold are those selected for review.
2/ Latest year's observation for March.
3/ Latest year's observation for June.

In analyzing partial dollarization, economists have generally distinguished between asset substitution and currency substitution as the two broad forms of dollarization. The former refers to the holding of wealth in the form of assets denominated in foreign currency; the latter refers to the use of foreign currency as a means of payment.

While less discussed in the literature, dollarization can also take the form of borrowing in foreign currency, i.e., liability dollarization.[3]

Why Does Partial Dollarization Happen?

People wish to hold foreign currency assets chiefly for the following reasons: (a) rapid or unpredictable depreciation of the national currency; (b) portfolio diversification; (c) fears of confiscation; and (d) convenience.

Rapid or unpredictable depreciation of the national currency is a major reason. Many of the countries listed in the above table have been afflicted by rapid inflation, and the public has resorted to asset substitution as a way to protect the value of its wealth.[4] Asset substitution generally comes first, and need not be accompanied by currency substitution.

However, if there is currency substitution, there will be asset substitution. In most countries where the foreign currency eventually displaced the domestic currency as a means of payment, that happened only after a long period of time. This suggests that it is difficult (and costly) to switch from one currency to another to make payments. However, in many cases, even after stabilization efforts succeeded, economies remained highly dollarized. Explanations of this phenomenon have varied. Some economists have suggested that hysteresis was the reason; that is, once people have switched to a currency, it is too costly for them to switch back—thus, even after stabilization they are likely to hold a significantly larger proportion of their assets in foreign currency than they did before the switch. Another explanation, though, suggests that such persistence can be merely a statistical artifact: data on dollar holdings generally exclude assets held overseas or in the form of cash. Thus, if a country succeeds in stabilizing its currency, there will be portfolio reshuffle as people move funds deposited abroad or held in cash into the domestic financial system. Since the latter are typically captured in the statistics

---

[3] For a discussion of liability dollarization, *see* Calvo (1999).

[4] Indexation, or the holding of real assets, has been another means for the public to protect its wealth in high-inflation countries. Thus, Brazil and Chile, where indexation has been widespread, did not become dollarized economies despite the high inflation they suffered.

while the former are not, even if the total amount of foreign currency assets has fallen, the data will show an increase.

Costs and Benefits of Partial Dollarization

Having a partially dollarized economy has both costs and benefits. The balance between these will depend on the specifics of each case.

Costs of Partial Dollarization

From the point of view of policymakers, partial dollarization makes monetary policy implementation more difficult, as it is harder to predict the composition of the monetary aggregates in the country, and shifts from one to the other have important consequences in the economy. For instance, even if the demand for a broad money aggregate (which includes foreign currency) remains unchanged, a shift in the demand from national currency to dollars will tend to depreciate the exchange rate and raise prices in national currency. Moreover, while monetary authorities can alter the volume of domestic money—if they are prepared to float the exchange rate—they cannot control the volume of the foreign money.

Insofar as dollar deposits are closer substitutes than domestic currency deposits for cross-border deposits, dollarization can make an economy more vulnerable to capital flows. Reversals of such flows can have a significant impact on the domestic economy.[5]

The circulation of a foreign currency also deprives the government of a source of revenue. Insofar as banks and the public are prepared to hold base money at zero (or below market) interest rates the government obtains free (or below cost) financing. That benefit is called seigniorage. To the extent that base money is replaced by foreign money, it is the issuer of that money (the foreign government or bank) that collects seigniorage.

Partial dollarization can make domestic financial systems vulnerable in case of a currency depreciation. Even if a bank has fully

---

[5] However, as amply proved most recently by the 1997 crises in Asia, such reversals can be very severe also in nondollarized economies.

matched its foreign currency liabilities with foreign currency assets, it can still incur losses in case of a devaluation if its borrowers default on their loans because their income and wealth are denominated in domestic currency. Also, it is harder for the government to provide financial support to the domestic banking system, in case of difficulties. While the government (more precisely, the central bank) can provide unlimited support in domestic currency to a troubled bank (albeit that would lead to inflation), it cannot provide liquidity in foreign currency beyond what it holds in usable international reserves and what it can borrow.

If wages are dollarized, the use of devaluation as a tool for regaining competitiveness will lose effectiveness, which can mean losing a tool of macroeconomic management, or require a larger devaluation (and inflation) to achieve the desired result.

For the public, dealing with two or more currencies involves transaction costs incurred when converting assets denominated in one currency into the other(s) and when doing other necessary tasks, such as having to calculate prices in more than one currency and to record operations separately by currency. Also, economic agents often need to incur costs in hedging and diversifying their positions, which would not happen in a single-currency environment.

Also, mindful of the problems of devaluing in a dollarized economy,[6] the government may be reluctant to resort to devaluing the currency even when there is a strong case to do so, which can lead to such a measure being undertaken too late.

Benefits of Partial Dollarization

But partial dollarization has benefits—which of course is why it exists. In an environment where people do not wish to hold financial assets in domestic currency, dollar-denominated assets can be one of the few vehicles for the public's savings. It can be argued that holding such assets is also more efficient—from the point of view of using resources—than vehicles such as accumulation of unproductive real assets or gold, which have a higher social cost of production and

---

[6] These problems include, for instance, those arising from an increased default rate on dollar-denominated liabilities.

which cannot be easily converted into productive assets as foreign currency assets can. Thus, dollarization can encourage financial intermediation in cases where there is little appetite for holding domestic currency nominal assets.

Also, dollarization can be beneficial in providing a means of payment and unit of account in cases where the domestic currency has largely ceased to perform those functions. Clearly, in cases of currency substitution is which the public is unwilling to use the domestic currency for transactions—e.g., because of a high rate of inflation—it is more efficient to use a foreign currency as the means of payment than to resort to barter. Also, in some cases, even if the domestic currency is still used in transactions with residents, it may be more efficient for an economic agent to conduct part or all of its transactions in a foreign currency. That can be the case, for instance, in cases of enterprises that do a large part of foreign trade. For instance, some firms in European countries outside the euro area, but which do a large volume of business with euro area countries, are likely to hold euros as part of their normal liquidity management; similarly, hotels and other businesses that deal with foreign tourists are likely to do the same.

The government itself may benefit in some cases of dollarization. That happens, for instance, if the alternative is to have transactions shifted to the black economy—which is harder to tax. Moreover, if dollarization makes it possible for the economy to operate more efficiently than would otherwise be the case (e.g., because the alternative would have been a higher degree of bartering), the government will be able to collect more tax revenue. In addition, the government will be able to collect taxes from financial institutions, which it would not be able to get otherwise.

In addition, if domestic residents have the possibility of holding foreign exchange balances, in case of fears of devaluation they may still keep their funds in the domestic financial system—albeit switching from domestic to foreign currency balances, instead of moving them abroad or into foreign cash. Finally, if the government has been issuing debt in foreign currency, having such debt may encourage fiscal discipline insofar as the government will not be able to erode the outstanding debt's value through inflation.[7]

Policymaking in Partially Dollarized Economies

Policymakers in partially dollarized economies need to take dollarization fully into account in their decisions. Experience has shown that policies specifically oriented to reduce dollarization—beyond what can be expected from a sound macroeconomic management—tend to be of limited value and often too costly.[8] However, policymakers need to adopt measures to better manage dollarization.

Monetary Policy Implementation and Payment Services

In partially dollarized economies, policymakers need to take into account the possibility that domestic prices are influenced not only by domestic currency money balances but also by foreign currency balances. Berg and Borenzstein (2000a) carried out several tests for some countries, which suggested that the answer to that question depends crucially on how broad is the aggregate chosen, and also varies across countries, and subsample periods.

Also, policymakers need to decide whether to conduct monetary operations solely in domestic currency or in foreign currency as well. While using foreign currency assets for that purpose tends to further encourage dollarization, in cases where such assets are the predominant component of monetary aggregates it would be problematic to conduct monetary operations solely in domestic currency.

Similar considerations apply to the provision of payments services. In dollarized economies, foreign banks overseas or their domestic branches may be willing to provide settlement services in foreign currency. However, the central bank may decide to provide such services (as it has done for instance in Bolivia, Lebanon, Peru, and Uruguay). By doing so, the central bank obtains some seigniorage

---

[7] A similar argument applies to the issuance of indexed debt.
[8] Some of these experiences are discussed in Baliño, Bennett, and Borensztein (1999).

(on the settlement balances that banks must keep with the central bank) and can avoid systemic risk in situations in which a commercial bank lacks enough funds to settle and the clearing bank refuses to provide the necessary credit.

The choice of exchange regime needs also to take dollarization into account, and in particular whether it reflects currency or asset substitution. In the former, the case is stronger for a fixed exchange rate regime because otherwise the easy substitutability between the two currencies will make a floating exchange rate highly volatile. In the latter, a floating exchange rate will tend to reduce the destabilizing effects of portfolio shifts (see Baliño, Bennett, and Borensztein, 1999). However, these authors—as well as Berg and Borensztein, 2000—indicate that broader considerations than just the degree of dollarization should be brought to bear on the choice of exchange rate regime.

Prudential Considerations

The prudential concerns outlined above as well as the fact that the central bank has limited means to act as lender of last resort make it especially important that measures be adopted to limit systemic risk in dollarized economies, and to ensure that if such risk materialized there are sufficient means to deal with it with minimal disruption.

Thus, in dollarized economies, the supervisory authorities need to monitor carefully the level of risk that financial institutions take on. This will involve a thorough assessment of the quality of the internal risk management arrangements that those institutions have in place. It will also involve setting and monitoring foreign exchange exposure limits, limiting the mismatch of maturing assets and liabilities, and monitoring foreign exchange derivatives. Supervisors will need to be especially vigilant to ensure that banks thoroughly evaluate the repayment capacity of borrowers in case of a devaluation. It may also require banks to keep a certain part of their portfolios in liquid form to deal with unforeseen liquidity needs. For instance, Argentina has required banks to hold such assets in a form that is easy to liquidate and which would not be affected by a systemic crisis in Argentina.

Full Dollarization

Full (or de jure) dollarization refers to the replacement of the national currency by a foreign one, which becomes legal tender. While there have been many economies (most very small)[9] that have used a foreign currency as their own for many years, the issue has recently attracted a lot of attention.

Why Is Full Dollarization Currently Being Debated?

Several reasons explain why dollarization has become a topical issue. First, the success of currency board arrangements (initially Argentina's and Estonia's but later also others, like Bulgaria's) in rapidly bringing down high inflation rates began to focus attention on the benefits of a strong peg to a foreign currency. Second, turmoil in the wake of the Asian and Russian crises of 1997/98 further encouraged discussions on how many currencies were likely to exist in the future. Some authors began to argue that in a world of liberalized capital movements only two polar exchange arrangements could survive in the medium term: flexible exchange rates or strong pegs—a currency board or adoption of a strong foreign currency as the domestic currency.[10] Third, the creation of the euro, whereby some of the oldest countries in the world have given up their monetary sovereignty in favor of a supranational currency, has helped to make the abandonment of a national currency politically more acceptable.[11]

Interest in the issue was further heightened when the then-President of Argentina announced in January 1999 that his country was considering going from the existing currency board arrangement to full dollarization. Similar discussions took place in other countries such as El Salvador and, at the private sector level, in Mexico. Finally, in the midst of a virtual collapse of its currency and a major economic crisis, the Ecuadorian government announced in January

---

[9] Bogetić (2000) lists 21 economies that are fully dollarized.

[10] For a recent discussion of the broad issue of choosing exchange rate regimes, *see* Mussa, et al. (2000).

[11] The issue of a single currency for a region has also come up in policy discussions in other economic areas, such as South America's Mercosur.

2000 that the national currency would be replaced by the dollar; Congress approved dollarization on March 13, 2000.

Reasons for Full Dollarization

There are three main reasons for countries to consider full dollarization. In some cases, like Ecuador, dollarization can quickly give to the economy a stable currency, following a poor track record of stability. In the case of countries with a successful currency board (e.g., Argentina), the objective can be to strengthen stability by making a stronger (and more irreversible) commitment to non-inflationary policies than is entailed by a currency board. The third is to get the benefits of having the same currency as an economy's main trading partners or sources of capital. Full dollarization has costs and benefits similar to the case of partial dollarization.[12]

Benefits of Full Dollarization

Economies that consider dollarizing typically expect the move to lead to greater confidence in the stability of the value of the currency, as compared to the old one. In turn, this is expected to help lower interest rates and make long-term finance possible.[13]

Moreover, it may encourage residents to keep their financial savings domestically, rather than placing them abroad, thus increasing the availability of finance to domestic borrowers.

Dollarization also entails lower costs of transaction, chiefly for foreign-orientated businesses but also for other economic agents who prefer to hold at least part of their liquidity in foreign currency (e.g., because they mistrust the domestic currency). These lower costs arise

---

[12] Berg and Borensztein (2000) discuss the pros and cons of dollarization as compared to its closest alternative, a currency board.

[13] This argument has been forcefully made in particular by Calvo (1999) and Fernández-Arias and Hausman (2000). The latter argument has suggested that currencies in many developing countries suffer from "original sin," which the authors define as a bad reputation (caused by past high inflation rates) which makes it impossible for residents to take on long-term liabilities in domestic currency. In their view, this is a major disadvantage domestic firms face in Latin America and in other developing countries.

from: less need to effect currency exchanges; less need to hedge currency risk.

An additional benefit is a stronger integration with other members of the currency area. For instance, it has been argued that the fact that Canadian provinces have stronger commercial links with each other, rather than with the geographically closer United States, is related to the fact that they share the same currency.

Finally, it can be argued that by removing the possibility of devaluation as a means to lower the real value of nominal variables—in particular wages—dollarization can strengthen the case for fiscal soundness and structural reforms, which become the main policy tools that remain available to change relative prices.

Costs of Full Dollarization

Full dollarization also entails costs. The loss of seigniorage, discussed for the case of partial dollarization, is total. The revenue from issuing reserve money accrues to the foreign issuer, rather than to the national monetary authority. The amounts involved can be significant. For instance Bogetić (2000) has estimated them as equivalent to ½ percent of GDP per year in the case of Argentina. However, in countries ravaged by hyperinflation, economic agents' holdings of reserve money are likely to be small—and so would be the seigniorage lost because of full dollarization. In addition, the loss of seigniorage can be mitigated—or even fully eliminated. This could happen if the government of the country that decides to dollarize comes to an agreement with the issuer of the foreign currency on sharing the seigniorage. Full dollarization makes such an agreement more likely than partial dollarization. In fact, during the preliminary discussions between Argentina and the United States, there was less opposition (and some support in Congress) to such a possibility as compared to other possible accommodation to the Argentine side—such as Argentina having representation on the Fed's Board or access to the Fed's lender-of-last-resort services.[14]

---

[14] For views expressed in the United States Congress, see, for instance, U.S. Congress (1999a and 1999b).

Dollarization entails a loss of monetary independence—the monetary policy stance will be determined by the issuer of the currency. This can be considered another cost, since the economy of the issuing country may be at a different point in the cycle than the dollarized country. For instance, the issuing country's economy may be in a boom—and hence its central bank may adopt a tight monetary policy—while the dollarized economy may be in the midst of a recession. However, the same problem would occur if a country that had its own economy had a fixed exchange rate arrangement—the difference would be that it is easier to devalue a currency than to create a new one. This is another way of saying that the countries sharing the common currency are not an optimal currency area.[15]

Another potential difficulty is that real price adjustments—except to the extent that they originate in the economy issuing the currency—will require nominal adjustments. In particular, if real wages need to be lowered, that can only be done by reducing nominal wages. If nominal wages are sticky downwards, that implies that the adjustment will take longer than in the case where real wages could be adjusted by an increase in the price level. This in turn will lead to unemployment. However, it can also be argued—and evidence from currency board arrangements such as Argentina's tend to support the argument—that downward price rigidity can help in encouraging structural reforms that it would have been difficult to implement otherwise.

Also there are political considerations that make it harder to give up the national currency. In fact, issuing a national currency has traditionally been an attribute of sovereign states: countries that became independent made that one of their first steps.

Benefits and Costs of Dollarization for the Issuing Country

Dollarization also entails benefits and costs for the country that issues the currency. The main benefits are the seigniorage gains (the exact counterpart of the seigniorage cost for the dollarized economy) and the trade and other benefits that may accrue from a closer

---

[15] On the issue of optimal currency areas, the classical reference is Mendell (1961).

integration with the dollarized economy, particularly in terms of more trade and larger capital flows.[16]

The major costs for the issuing countries arise from the likely pressure to adjust monetary policy to the needs of the dollarized country.[17] There will also be pressure to share seigniorage—which would be harder to exert in a case of a partially dollarized economy. Moreover, the currency issuer could be pressured to act as a lender of last resort vis-à-vis the dollarized country's financial sector, which could be particularly costly if that sector is weak.

In the discussions that took place in the United States on these issues, particularly at the time when the possibility of Argentina adopting the dollar was in the news, the U.S. administration and the Federal Reserve indicated their unwillingness to consider giving Argentina representation on the Federal Reserve Board, providing lender-of-last-resort services, or even sharing seigniorage.

Preconditions for Dollarization

Countries contemplating dollarization must be willing to make their policies consistent with such a decision. In particular, they need to ensure that they have the means to finance government expenditure without resort to currency issue. They also need to be willing to adopt policies that facilitate price and wage flexibility; this is particularly important, given the usual downward stickiness of nominal prices and wages.

Also, the country that dollarizes needs to have the reserves (or borrowing capacity) to be able to buy back the outstanding stock of reserve money. Thus, the conversion rate must be such as to make that buyback financially possible.

---

[16] A strong case for dollarization appears for instance in Calvo (1999) and in the paper presented to the Joint Economic Committee of the U.S. Congress (U.S. Congress, 1999a and 1999b).

[17] This would be particularly the case if the dollarization was in the form of a monetary union—like the euro area—rather than of a unilateral decision.

Dollarization eliminates the possibility of a central bank acting as a lender of last resort simply by issuing reserve money.[18] However, preventing systemic financial distress would still be a priority of the dollarized economy's authorities as it is in other economies. Therefore, having a sound banking system or taking decisive measures to make it sound rapidly becomes an even more pressing priority for policymakers that wish to dollarize.

Finally, a strong political commitment will be needed to reap the benefits of dollarization. Little would be gained if people believe that the measure may be revoked in the future. For instance, long-term borrowing and lending are key benefits that some propounders of dollarization have espoused. Such operations are unlikely to develop if people are afraid, e.g., that a domestic currency might be reintroduced before the maturity of a contract and that outstanding dollar-denominated contracts will be forcibly converted into that currency.[19]

Conclusions

Deciding to give up a national currency to adopt another country's is a momentous decision that countries need to think through carefully. It has several benefits: it can yield price stability; it facilitates international trade (at least with the countries that use the adopted currency in international transactions); and it can help lengthen the maturity of financial instruments. It has costs: loss of seigniorage and need for nominal wage/price flexibility to effect real wage/price changes. Moreover, dollarization should not be seen as a panacea: sound policies—particularly fiscal and prudential—still are essential. Experience with dollarization is still too short in cases like Ecuador's to fullly weigh its merits and drawbacks and even more so to attempt to draw general conclusions. It is, however, a valid option

---

[18] However, issuing reserve money to deal with a banking crisis will entail serious consequences (devaluation, higher inflation) also in a nondollarized economy. But it is still true that, in the latter case, the authorities can provide the funds to allow a troubled bank to honor its obligations in nominal terms, even if the cost of doing so falls on the whole society in the form of inflation or devaluation. Moreover, as noted in Calvo (1999), dollarized economies can set up stabilization funds or obtain private contingent credit lines to deal with bank emergencies.

[19] In some countries (such as Argentina), dollar deposits were mandatorily converted into local currency.

for policymakers to keep in mind, together with other schemes for exchange rate and monetary policy implementation currently in use.[20]

References

Baliño, Tomás J.T., Adam Bennett, and Eduardo Borensztein, 1999, *Monetary Policy in Dollarized Economies*, IMF Occasional Paper No. 171 (Washington: International Monetary Fund).

Berg, Andrew, and Eduardo Borensztein, 2000a, "The Choice of Exchange Rate Regime and Monetary Target in Highly Dollarized Economies," IMF Working Paper 00/29 (Washington: International Monetary Fund).

———, 2000b, "The Pros and Cons of Full Dollarization," IMF Working Paper 00/50 (Washington: International Monetary Fund).

Bogetić, Željko, 2000, "Full Dollarization: Fad or Future?" *Challenge*, Vol. 43, No. 2 (March–April), pp. 17–48.

Calvo, Guillermo, 1999, "On Dollarization," University of Maryland. Available via Internet: www.bsos.umd.edu/econ/ciecalvo.htm/.

Fernández-Arias, Eduardo, and Ricardo Hausmann, 2000, "Is FDI a Safer Form of Investment?" IDB Working Paper Series 416 (Washington: Inter-American Development Bank).

Mendell, Robert A., 1961, "A Theory of Optimum Currency Areas," *American Economic Review*, Vol. 51, No. 4, pp. 657–65.

Mussa, Michael, et al., 2000, *Exchange Rate Regimes in an Increasingly Integrated World Economy*, IMF Occasional Paper No. 193 (Washington: International Monetary Fund).

Schaechter, Andrea, Mark Stone, and Mark Zelmer, 2000, *Practical Issues in the Adoption of Inflation Targeting by Emerging Market*

---

[20] For a clear discussion of some of these options, see Mussa et al. (2000) and Schaechter, Stone, and Zelmer (2000).

Countries, IMF Occasional Paper No. 202 (Washington: International Monetary Fund).

U.S. Congress, Joint Economic Committee, 1999a, "Encouraging Official Dollarization in Emerging Markets," *Staff Report*, April.

———, 1999b, "Basics of Dollarization," *Staff Report*, July.

Chapter

31 | Dollarization and Euroization

MICHAEL GRUSON

The adoption of a foreign currency by a country is not a new phenomenon. At least, the adoption by means of a currency board has a long history.[1] A currency board is an authority that issues notes and coins that are fully backed by a foreign currency and are fully convertible on demand into the foreign currency at a fixed rate.[2] The legal tender, however, still remains the country's own domestic currency. As experience with currency boards in developing countries has shown, currency boards are more likely to sustain a sound currency than a central bank does.[3] However, as the recent exchange rate crises in the emerging markets over the last two years made clear, currency board regimes with pegs that are less than absolute are vulnerable in today's globalized high-volume financial markets and are not likely to protect the currency against international monetary speculation.[4]

Another method of adopting a foreign currency is the full or official adoption of a foreign currency.[5] Because the adopted currency

---

Note: The author thanks Irene Baur for her contribution to this paper.

[1] See, e.g., Kurt Schuler, Currency Boards (Virginia, 1992).

[2] For a short introduction to currency boards see Kurt Schuler, *Introduction to Currency Boards* (visited Sept. 29, 2000) (http://users.erols.com/kurrency/intro.htm). For detailed information see Steve H. Hanke and Kurt Schuler, *Currency Boards for Developing Countries: A Handbook* (updated Web version of 1994 publication, visited Sept. 29, 2000) (http://users.erols.com/kurrency/iceg.htm).

[3] See Hanke and Schuler, *supra* note 2, at 13–36.

[4] Jeffrey Frankel, *Remarks at the IMF Economic Forum on Dollarization: Fad or Future for Latin America*, at 2 (June 24, 1999) (transcript available at http://www.imf.org/external/np/tr/1999/TR990624.HTM, visited Sept. 28, 2000); Miguel Kiguel, *Remarks at the IMF Economic Forum on Dollarization: Fad or Future for Latin America*, at 11 (June 24, 1999) (www.imf.org/external/np/tr/1999/ TR990624.htm, visited Sept. 29, 2000).

[5] The adoption of a foreign currency mainly occurs in two varieties: unofficial and official adoption. Whereas unofficial adoption occurs when individuals hold foreign currency bank deposits to protect against high inflation in the domestic

(continued)

is frequently the U.S. dollar, this method is usually discussed under the heading "dollarization." However, since the introduction of the euro, euroization also has become an issue. In the case of dollarization and euroization, not only is the exchange rate fixed to a foreign currency, but the foreign currency (the "anchor currency") has the exclusive status as legal tender and the country's own domestic currency is given up. In addition, neither a currency board nor a central bank is necessary. The main expectation of being dollarized is that the dollarized country can wholly eliminate the risk of sharp exchange rate adjustments, because by giving up its own domestic currency it receives a stable, largely trusted "world" currency which is not subject to monetary speculation. This would finally benefit the economy of the adopting country, encourage foreign investments, and contribute to economic growth.[6] Dollarization has recently attracted much attention because several large Latin American countries have contemplated making the dollar their official legal tender, i.e., to become officially "dollarized."[7] Never before, have large and independent countries such as Argentina seriously considered giving up their own currency and adopting the dollar as official legal tender.[8]

---

currency, full or official adoption occurs when a government adopts a foreign currency as the exclusive legal tender. *See* Connie Mack, *Basics of Dollarization*, at 2–6 (visited Sept. 28, 2000, http://www.senate.gov/~jec/basics.htm); Hanke and Schuler, *supra* note 2, at 10. Since unofficial adoption is widespread and, therefore, to a certain extent beyond legal control, this comment will focus on the official adoption of a currency.

[6] *See* Andrew Berg and Eduardo Borensztein, "The Pros and Cons of Full Dollarization," at 5 (IMF, Working Paper, March 2000); Steve H. Hanke and Kurt Schuler, "A Dollarization Blueprint for Argentina," at 11 (Cato Institute, Foreign Policy Briefing, No. 52, 1999).

[7] At the the time of writing, Ecuador was in the process of dollarization, whereas Argentina, El Salvador, Guatemala, and Costa Rica were contemplating dollarization. *See* Senate Committee on Banking, Housing, and Urban Affairs, Report to Accompany S.2101 Together With Additional Views, 106th Congress, 2nd Session, S. Rep. No. 106-354, at 8 (2000); Alan M. Taylor, "Dollarization as a Technology Import," at 1 *et seq.* (Federal Reserve Bank—San Francisco, Economic Letter, No. 2000-16, 2000). In addition, economists are discussing dollarization for Indonesia. *See* Kurt Schuler, *Dollarizing Indonesia* (visited Sept. 29, 2000) (http://users.erols.com/kurrency/indodollr.htm). In general, an agreement with the United States is not a prerequisite to legal dollarization, even though it might be advantageous because of political or economic benefits; *see* Mack, *supra* note 5, at 2; Kiguel, *supra* note 4, at 13.

[8] *See* Frankel, *supra* note 4, at 2 *et seq.*; Hanke and Schuler, *supra* note 6, at 10–21; Mark M. Spiegel, "Dollarization in Argentina" (Federal Reserve Bank—San Francisco, Economic Letter, No. 99-29, 1999). At the time of writing, the following

(continued)

However, dollarization is not a miracle solution for economic or fiscal problems. The adoption of a foreign currency may make sense for certain countries at certain times.[9]

The success of an official adoption of a foreign currency depends on two main conditions. First, the adopting country must have totally lost trust and confidence in its own monetary policy and must be willing to admit this publicly. Second, the country must have confidence in the central bank of the anchor country, i.e., the country whose currency is adopted, in order to submit itself to the decisions and the policies of that central bank.[10] This requires a shift of trust. Additionally, some economists think that it is necessary that the domestic economy of the adopting country be compatible with that of the anchor country. This condition is based on the view that in particular an expansionary domestic public finance policy of the adopting country could contravene the benefits of dollarization, i.e., might cause a considerable increase in the inflation rate.[11]

---

five independent countries used the U.S. dollar as their legal tender: East Timor, Marshall Islands, Federated States of Micronesia, Palau, and Panama. In Cuba, both the U.S. dollar and the Cuban peso were legal tender until 1951. Since then, only the Cuban peso is legal tender. See Johansen v. Confederation Life Association, 447 F. 2d 175 (U.S. CA, 2nd Cir, 1971). Except for Panama and Cuba, these are all countries with small economies. Another eight independent countries use other foreign currencies as their legal tender. See, for a table as of January 2000, Mack, supra note 5, at 6.

[9] A critical view is expressed by Frankel, supra note 4, at 3, and Kiguel, supra note 4, at 14. The choice of the most appropriate exchange rate regime, be it just a fixed exchange rate regime or combined with a currency board or the outright adoption of a currency, depends on the particular economic circumstances, such as the degree of integration with its trading partners. See Report by G-7 Finance Ministers on Global Financial Structure, at paragraph 33 (June 18, 1999, www.state.gov/www/issues/economic/summit/99_summit_report.html).

[10] See Mack, supra note 5, at 7; Spiegel, supra note 8, at 3. The loss of monetary sovereignty which is still thought to be one of the basic elements of state sovereignty is a high hurdle for dollarization. Indeed, in 1983, Israel's Finance Minister had to abandon plans for Israel to become dollarized because of extreme opposition from the population. See Frankel, supra note 4, at 4.

[11] The need for economic convergence was seen by the European countries that formed the European Monetary Union (EMU). Thus, in the process of setting up the EMU, achieving a sound government financial position in the participating countries was a big issue. To enforce the continuance of the budgetary discipline, which had to be present when joining the EMU after the start of the EMU, regulations were enacted alongside a Resolution of the European Council: Council Regulation (EC)
(continued)

Currently, the central bank of the United States, the Federal Reserve System, is widely trusted because the U.S. economy is strong and there is practically no inflation.[12] The Federal Reserve System is credited with being the engineer of this happy situation. Thus, at this time, it may be argued persuasively that a country with high inflation and with a central bank that is not politically independent would be better served by abandoning its own monetary authority and submitting to the policies of the Federal Reserve System.[13] Such submission would not have been acceptable at other times in the recent history of the United States when inflation was high or when interest rates were skyrocketing.

The adoption of the currency of another country has become more acceptable because of a shift in the philosophy of monetary policy. In the past it was the accepted aim of monetary policy to balance price stability, economic growth, and unemployment. This balance might call for moderate inflation. Today, price stability seems to be the only accepted aim of monetary policy.[14] The reason for this change is the assumption that price stability is a precondition for strong long-

---

No. 1466/97 of July 1997 on the strengthening of the surveillance of budgetary positions and the surveillance and coordination of economic policies (1997 O.J. (L 209/1)), Council Regulation (EC) No. 1467/97 of July 1997 on speeding up and clarifying the implementation of the excessive deficit procedure (1997 O.J. (L 209/6)), and the Resolution of the European Council on the Stability and Growth Pact of June 1997 (1997 O.J. (C 236/1)). *See* Hugo J. Hahn, "The Stability and Growth Pact for European Monetary Union: Compliance with Deficit Limit as a Constant Legal Duty," 35 Comm. Mkt. L. Rev. 1998, at 77–100; ECB, "The Implementation of the Stability and Growth Pact," 45–72, at 45–61 (ECB, *Monthly Bulletin*, May 1999). *See generally* Mack, *supra* note 5, at 17.

[12] A situation with no inflation corresponds to price stability. The price stability is measured by means of consumer price indices. Since such indices cannot always be fully corrected, they are likely to overstate slightly the "true" rate of inflation by approximately 2 percent. Thus, price stability can be considered achieved up to an inflation rate of 2 percent. *See* ECB, "The Stability-Orientated Monetary Policy Strategy of the Eurosystem," 39–50, at 46 (ECB, *Monthly Bulletin*, January 1999). Therefore, the Governing Council of the ECB, for instance, adopted the following definition for price stability: "price stability shall be defined as a year-on-year increase in the Harmonised Index of Consumer Prices (HICP) for the euro area below 2%." *See* ECB, at 46.

[13] Hanke and Schuler, *supra* note 6, at 10–14, discusses the pros and cons for Argentina; Spiegel, *supra* note 8, at 2–4.

[14] Stanley Fischer, "Central Banking: The Challenges Ahead—Maintaining Price Stability," at 2 *et seq.* (IMF, *Finance & Development*, No. 4, December 1999).

term economic growth and increasing standards of living.[15] The most recent example of this development is the constitution of the European Central Bank (ECB), whose first and foremost goal is to protect price stability (EC-Treaty art. 105(1)).[16] This obligation is not only a political goal but is "constitutionally" anchored in the EC-Treaty, which can only be amended under certain circumstances set forth in the EU-Treaty art. 49.[17] Only as a second objective shall the ECB "support the general economic policies in the Community."[18] If price stability is seen as the only aim of monetary policy, the country adopting the currency of another country with a high degree of price stability may feel it does not give up much for what it gains. The adopting country has an even better chance of achieving a continued good performance in the future regarding price stability, if the central

---

[15] *See,* for instance, the findings of the International Monetary Stability Act of 2000, S.2101, 106th Cong., 2nd Session, §2 (a) (2000); ECB, *supra* note 12, at 39–41; William J. McDonough, "A Framework for Pursuit of Price Stability," at 2 *et seq.* (Federal Reserve Bank—New York, *Economic Policy Review,* 1997).

[16] Treaty Establishing the European Economic Community (newly renamed the European Community) of Mar. 25, 1957 (commonly called the Treaty of Rome, effective Jan. 1, 1958), 298 U.N.T.S. 11, as amended by the Single European Act of Feb. 28, 1986, 1987 O.J. (L 169/1). The Treaty of Rome, as amended by the Maastricht Treaty of Feb. 7, 1992 (effective Nov. 1 1993), 1992 O.J. (C 224/1), as amended by the Amsterdam Treaty of Oct. 2, 1997 (effective May 1, 1999), 1997 O.J. (C 340/145), is herein referred to as the EC-Treaty. The consolidated version of the EC-Treaty is published in 1997 O.J. (C 340/173). *See also* the Protocol on the Statute of the European System of Central Banks and of the European Central Bank, 1992 O.J. (C 224/104) [hereinafter Protocol] art. 2. In order to clear the mandate of the Federal Reserve System so that it is bound by the primary goal of price stability, Senator Mack introduced the Economic Growth and Price Stability Act (S.1492, 106th Cong., 1st Session (1999)).

[17] Treaty on the European Union of Feb. 7, 1992 (commonly called the Maastricht Treaty, effective Nov. 1, 1993), 1992 O.J. (C 224/1), as amended in 1997 by the Amsterdam Treaty, 1997 O.J. (C 340/145) [hereinafter EU-Treaty]. The Maastricht Treaty established the "European Union" as denoting the overall political entity which comprises the three existing European Communities (i.e., the European Community, the European Coal and Steel Community, and the European Atomic Energy Community). The amendment procedure set forth in EU-Treaty art. 49 also applies to the Protocol, since pursuant to EC-Treaty art. 311 the Protocol is an integral part of the EC-Treaty, and the simplified amendment procedure (EC-Treaty art. 107 (5), Protocol art. 41) is not applicable.

[18] EC-Treaty art. 105 (1); Protocol art. 2; *see* Hugo J. Hahn, "The European Central Bank: Key to Monetary Union or Target?", 28 Comm. Mkt. L. Rev. 1991, at 797-798.

bank of the anchor currency is a politically independent institution[19] like the Federal Reserve System,[20] the Deutsche Bundesbank,[21] or the European Central Bank.[22]

A far more legal than economic question is whether the anchor country, the country whose currency is adopted by another country, is forced to tolerate such adoption. This question is covered by public international law. Under this law the anchor country certainly has to tolerate the adoption when it has given its consent. In case there is no consent of the anchor country, it could force the adopting country to refrain from dollarizing if the unilateral adoption would be a "breach of duty" under public international law.[23] As already mentioned, the adoption of a foreign currency, at least by way of currency boards, has a very long history and is thought to be consistent with public international law.[24] This may lead to the conclusion that adopting a foreign currency has become customary international law.[25] Consequently, an adoption, even without the consent of the anchor country, cannot be considered as a breach of international public law and, therefore, the anchor country has to tolerate the adoption. However, in terms of political courtesy, it might be advisable to ask

---

[19] For detailed information about the connection between an independent central bank and the maintenance of price stability, *see* Mark M. Spiegel, "British Central Bank Independence and Inflation Expectations" (Federal Reserve Bank—San Francisco, *Economic Letter*, No. 97-36, 1997); Otmar Issing, "Central Bank Independence and Monetary Stability," at 14 *et seq*. (Institute of Economic Affairs, *Occasional Paper No. 89*, 1993).

[20] Federal Reserve Bank—San Francisco, *U.S. Monetary Policy: An Introduction* (visited Sept. 22, 2000) (www.frbsf.org/system/fedsystem/monopol/structure.html).

[21] Gesetz über die Deutsche Bundesbank § 12 v. 16. Juli 1957 (BGBl. I S. 745) (current version BGBl. I 1992, S. 1782); *see* Issing, *supra* note 19, at 20–29.

[22] EC-Treaty art. 108; Protocol art. 7; *see* René Smits, "The European Central Bank: Institutional Aspects," at 152–178 (Kluwer, The Hague and London, 1997).

[23] Under public international law, all states are responsible in law for their internationally illegal acts, i.e., for a breach of a treaty or a customary obligation. The breach of such an obligation will in general give rise to remedies. On the law of state responsibility *see, e.g.*, Lord Templeman, Public International Law, at 138–191 (Old Bailey Press, London, 1997); Ian Brownlie, Principles of Public International Law, at 435–478 (Clarendon Press, Oxford, 5th ed. 1998).

[24] A unilateral adoption of a foreign currency is widely thought to be legal. *See, e.g.*, Berg and Borensztein, *supra* note 6, at 14; Mack, *supra* note 5; at 2; Kiguel, *supra* note 4, at 13.

[25] On customary international law, *see generally* Ian Brownlie, *supra* note 23, at 4–11.

the anchor country for consent or at least to notify it of the intention to dollarize.

The United States and the European Community, for instance, are taking different positions about dollarization and euroization.

The United States seems to be neutral or even in favor of dollarization by other countries. Especially regarding the dollarization of Latin America, the United States expects that export markets which have been until now a source of volatility and slow growth because of bad monetary policy and devaluations abroad will strengthen.[26]

Therefore, there are even voices in the United States that actively support dollarization. A Senate bill, the "International Monetary Stability Act of 2000," encourages dollarization by sharing the seigniorage of the transferred currency with the dollarizing country.[27] However, it does not pressure any country into dollarization nor take a position about whether or not a country should dollarize. The bill proposes a rebate of 85 percent of the seigniorage to the dollarizing country calculated by a formula in the Act[28] and uses the balance of 15 percent to finance rebates to countries that have officially dollarized before the enactment of the bill.[29] Precondition for the rebate is a certificate issued by the Secretary of the Treasury stating that the country is officially dollarized. The Secretary will begin making payments ten years and three months after certification for newly dollarized countries,[30] and for previously dollarized countries payments will start as soon as 10 percent of the payments to other

---

[26] Senate Committee on Banking, Housing and Urban Affairs, *supra* note 7, at 9.

[27] The International Monetary Stability Act of 2000, S.2101, 106th Cong., 2nd Session, § 4 (2000). The loss of seigniorage is thought to be one of the biggest obstacles to dollarization. *See* Hanke and Schuler, *supra* note 6, at 10; Mack, *supra* note 5, at 10–11; Berg and Borensztein, *supra* note 6, at 15–18. The International Monetary Stability Act was not introduced in the 107th Congress.

[28] The International Monetary Stability Act of 2000, *supra* note 27, §4(a)(2).

[29] The International Monetary Stability Act of 2000, *supra* note 27, §5(b). *See* Mack, *supra* note 5, at 22–23.

[30] The International Monetary Stability Act of 2000, *supra* note 27, §4(a)(2). The ten-year delay is enacted to ensure that countries only get payments when they are sufficiently committed to dollarization. *See* Senate Committee on Banking, Housing and Urban Affairs, *supra* note 7, at 6.

countries under this Act are equal to or larger than the payments that would be made to previously dollarized countries.[31]

The Secretary of the Treasury may make the issue of the certificate conditional on the fulfillment of 11 listed factors plus any additional factors that the Secretary of the Treasury deems relevant.[32] The compliance with these factors seems to be a high hurdle for applying countries. But, in fact, the absence of any one or more of the described considerations does not preclude the Secretary from issuing the certificate.[33] The bill gives the Secretary of the Treasury broad discretion in issuing the certificate. Lastly, it should be pointed out that the certification does not represent an endorsement by the United States of the policies of a dollarized country, but a judgment by the Secretary that rebating seigniorage to a country is in the interest of the United States.[34] The bill also provides measures to decertify and cease making payments.

Nevertheless, there are possible risks for an anchor country like the United States in encouraging dollarization. The Federal Reserve System might be expected to conduct a monetary policy that benefits the officially dollarized country to the detriment of the United States. However, according to Chairman Alan Greenspan, the Federal Reserve System is accustomed to international pressure and is not likely to take such actions.[35] In addition, there may be pressure on the Federal Reserve System to act as a lender of last resort for banks in the officially dollarized countries.[36] However, the bill makes it clear

---

[31] The International Monetary Stability Act of 2000, *supra* note 27, §5(a); *see also* Senate Committee on Banking, Housing and Urban Affairs, *supra* note 7, at 8.

[32] The International Monetary Stability Act of 2000, *supra* note 27, §3(a) and (b). The list contains conditions such as whether the country has in fact officially dollarized, opened its banking system to foreign competition or complied with internationally accepted banking principles, cooperated with the United States on money-laundering and counterfeiting issues, and consulted with the Secretary prior to certification.

[33] The International Monetary Stability Act of 2000, *supra* note 27, §3(c).

[34] *See* Senate Committee on Banking, Housing and Urban Affairs, *supra* note 7, at 4.

[35] Alan Greenspan, Testimony in Baliño, T., Bennett, A., and Borensztein, E., *Monetary Policy in Dollarized Economies*, March 15, 1999, at 14–15 (IMF, Occasional Paper No. 171, 1999).

[36] Since official dollarization causes the loss of monetary policy and therefore impairs the lender-of-last-resort function of the central bank, the dollarized country has to take other provisions, such as establishing a lender-of-last-resort facility

(continued)

that the Federal Reserve System is not the lender of last resort for countries that have chosen dollarization, that it must not take the economic conditions of the dollarized countries into account when setting monetary policies, and that it will not be the supervisor of the financial institution of the dollarized countries.[37]

However, euroization may face far more problems. The introduction of the euro is regulated in EC-Treaty art. 121(4), 122(2) and depends on the fulfillment of certain criteria, known as convergence criteria, set out in EC-Treaty art. 121(1). A Member State that adopts the euro without meeting these criteria will certainly violate the EC-Treaty and can be sued according to EC-Treaty art. 230 before the European Court of Justice. The situation differs when the adopting state is not a member of the European Community but an accession country.[38] Accession countries are not bound by the EC-Treaty and therefore by the convergence criteria. Only the international public law would be applicable that would allow euroization as outlined above. This would lead to the strange situation that a candidate could introduce the euro without meeting the convergence criteria, would act lawfully under international public law, and might enter the European Community with the euro already being adopted.

The ECB is aware of this problem and is discussing the theoretical and practical pros and cons in the relevant committees and working groups. Thus, it hasn't yet reached a specific point of view.[39]

---

outside its central bank. In addition, dollarization diminishes the risk of bank crisis, so that the establishment of a lender-of-last-resort facility does not have to be given priority. *See* Mack, *supra* note 5, at 9; Kiguel, *supra* note 4, at 13.

[37] The International Monetary and Stability Act of 2000, *supra* note 27, §2(b); *see* Mack, *supra* note 5, at 9.

[38] At the time of writing, there were 13 applicant countries, namely Bulgaria, Cyprus, Czech Republic, Estonia, Hungary, Latvia, Lithuania, Malta, Poland, Romania, Slovak Republic, Slovenia, and Turkey. *See* European Commission, Directorate for Enlargement, Introduction (visited Oct. 4, 2000, http://www.europa.eu.int/ comm/enlargement/intro/index.htm). Indeed Bulgarian economists are discussing the adoption of the euro before Bulgaria's accession to the EU. They propose a unilateral introduction with or without consent of the EU and the European Central bank, *see* Nikolay Nenovski et al., *Transition from Lev to Euro—Early Step to the EU* (visited Sept. 18, 2000, http://www.capital.bg/old/weekly/00-06/17-6htm).

[39] E-mail from Nils Bünemann, Press Officer, European Central Bank, to Irene Baur, member of the International Associate Program, Shearman & Sterling (Sept. 19, 2000) (on file with the author).

As the ECB outlines in its monthly bulletin, it basically considers the introduction of the euro as an ongoing process that encompasses three stages: pre-accession to the EU, European Monetary Union (EMU) membership with a derogation as defined by EC-Treaty 122(1) and 122(3),[40] and finally full EMU membership.[41] Although meeting the convergence criteria does not constitute a condition for joining the EU, it is a prerequisite for becoming a full participant in the EMU.[42] Furthermore, the new Member States will have to "treat . . . exchange rate policy as a matter of common interest" (EC-Treaty art. 124(1)). Therefore, the new Member States are expected to participate in the exchange rate mechanism II (ERM II).[43] Lastly, in the view of the ECB, the new Member States shall "regard their economic policies as a matter of common concern" (EC-Treaty art. 99). This means that the new Member State will participate in the EU policy coordination and surveillance procedures under the same conditions as current Member States with derogation in the EU. This relates particularly to the provisions of the excessive deficit procedures and the Stability and Growth Pact.[44] Accordingly, for instance, Poland, once it has

---

[40] Pursuant to EC-Treaty art. 121(1) and 122(2), Member States that do not fulfill the necessary conditions for the adoption of the euro, i.e., the convergence criteria, are to be given a "derogation." The derogation provides that most of the articles that govern the EMU do not apply to these Member States. Member States with a derogation do not fix their currencies irrevocably to the other Member States nor do they adopt the euro as their legal tender. They still enforce their own monetary policies. At the moment, Sweden is a Member State with a derogation, whereas Denmark and the United Kingdom have a special position, i.e., an opt-out. However, in fact, Denmark and the United Kingdom are treated as Member States with derogation. *See* Council Decision of May 3, 1998, in accordance with EC-Treaty 109j(4) (EC-Treaty, as amended by the Amsterdam Treaty (*see* footnote 16), art. 121(4)), 1998 O.J. (L139/30); Smits, *supra* note 22, at 134–139.

[41] ECB, "The Eurosystem and the EU Enlargement Process," 39–51, at 46 (ECB, *Monthly Bulletin*, February 2000).

[42] ECB, *supra* note 41, at 46.

[43] The ERM II is governed by the Resolution of the European Council on the establishment of an exchange rate mechanism in the third stage of economic and monetary union, June 16, 1997, 1997 O.J. (C 236/5). The Resolution provides the main features as well as principles and objectives of the exchange rate mechanism. Whereas the operating procedures will be set forth in an agreement between the ECB and the national central banks of the Member States outside the euro area. In addition, the Resolution states that "participation in the exchange rate mechanism will be voluntary for Member States outside the euro area. Nevertheless, Member States with derogation can be expected to join the mechanism."

[44] ECB, *supra* note 41, at 46.

become a Member State, will achieve the same rights and duties that presently the United Kingdom has.

These provisions intend to ensure and encourage policies by the new Member States to be oriented towards price stability and economic convergence. The ECB has expressed the view that the outlined process should be followed closely in order to enable the ECB to fulfill its statutory mandate of price stability in an enlarged euro area.[45]

In addition, it is the view of the European Commission that the accession countries must first join the EU before they can be eligible for the adoption of the euro.[46] The European Commission considers this procedure necessary for the accession countries to achieve a high degree of sustainable convergence with regard to fundamental economic grounds within the EU.[47] Since this catching-up process is likely to take time, the status of the accessing country should be determined in the Accession Treaty as a Member State with a derogation as defined by EC-Treaty art. 122(1) and 122(3).

The accession countries are basically agreeing with the accession procedures as outlined by the European Commission and the ECB. At the Helsinki seminar that was held on November 11 and 12, 1999, the governors and deputy governors of the central banks of the accession countries and the representatives of the Eurosystem reached important conclusions about the outlined procedures. However, they mainly contain informal agreements of the accession countries with respect to adjusting their economic structures to those within the EU, to implementing a price stability oriented monetary policy, and to participating in the ERM II.[48]

In conclusion, dollarization or euroization has changed from being an idea to a frequently discussed issue. Apparently, it has

---

[45] ECB, *supra* note 41, at 46.

[46] "European Commission, Directorate General for Economic and Financial Affairs, Accession To the EU and Implications for EMU," at 36 (European Commission, Directorate General for Economic and Financial Affairs, Enlargement Papers, No. 1, May 2000).

[47] European Commission, Directorate General for Economic and Financial Affairs, *supra* note 46, at 36.

[48] ECB, *supra* note 41, at 48–50.

begun a process of currency consolidation which may end in a few currency blocs. However, whether this process will lead to a sound international monetary system has yet to be proven. Today it can be said that the benefits of the adoption of a foreign currency need the support of an economic and public finance policy that is based on the maintenance of price stability. Therefore, regarding euroization in accession countries, the EU and the ECB will enforce the above outlined process with political pressure, if an accession country adopts the euro without meeting the convergence criteria.

Chapter 32
Strongly Anchored Currency Arrangements

ALAIN IZE

The discussion of the benefits of currency board arrangements (CBAs) and other strongly anchored currency arrangements, such as full dollarization, has intensified in the wake of the recent currency crises in Latin America and East Asia. Indeed, a currently popular (although not universally shared) view is that, in a world of increasing real and financial globalization, only rule-based exchange rate regimes, such as pure floats or strongly anchored currency arrangements, are resilient enough to sustain the large shocks in capital flows and interest rates that are typical of the new international monetary system.

This paper reviews the motivation, experience, pros and cons, and implementation requirements of CBAs and discusses the relative benefits of currency boards and full dollarization. Section I briefly reviews some of the pitfalls of conventional exchange rate arrangements; Section II defines and explains CBAs; Section III retraces their historical roots and examines their performance; Section IV examines their pitfalls. Based on this review, Section V discusses the conditions under which the introduction of a CBA may (or may not) be appropriate while Section VI compares the relative merits of CBAs and full dollarization. Section VII concludes by briefly examining some implementation issues.

I. Pitfalls of Conventional Exchange Rate Arrangements

Except in very small, open economies, the sustainability record of conventional fixed-peg arrangements has been dismal. For example, a study of 61 pegged exchange rate regimes in Latin America since the 1950s finds that they had a mean duration of 32 months and a median of only 10 months.[1] This limited duration may, in some cases, have

---

[1] *See* Klein and Marion (1994).

reflected desirable traits of flexibility and adaptability to changing economic environments. All too often, however, the collapse of fixed-peg regimes has been associated with speculative attacks on the currency.[2] While these attacks have generally taken place in the context of weakening economic fundamentals (including rising fiscal or external imbalances), the resulting collapse of the exchange-rate regime was imposed on the monetary authorities by market forces. Thus, while in some cases a realignment of the exchange rate may in fact have been the best course of action, in most other cases maintaining the parity would have been preferable in view of the high economic costs associated with a sudden, large collapse of the peg and the fact that the deterioration of economic fundamentals was perceived to be reversible and/or of a limited magnitude.

A perceived lack of commitment to defend the peg can lead to inefficient outcomes. The awareness that an exchange rate realignment will be used, if needed, to correct a currency overvaluation caused by inflation may undermine monetary and fiscal discipline, as well as market discipline in setting prices and wages. On the other hand, the authorities may find it optimal to abandon the peg under market pressure although they would have preferred maintaining it in the absence of such pressures. This encourages speculative attacks and exposes the economy to sustained periods of high interest rates induced by a large currency risk premium. When attacked, the monetary authorities must choose between a sterilization-based strategy and an interest rate-based strategy. Both have severe pitfalls, as illustrated by the recent experience of Mexico and Colombia.

Mexico, in 1994, chose the former strategy. Out of concern for the adverse implications of high interest rates on a weak banking system, the Mexican authorities dealt with falling confidence through portfolio reallocations rather than price adjustments. They substituted dollar-denominated short-term debt ("tesobonos") for maturing peso public debt. At the same time, they systematically sterilized capital outflows by reinjecting through open market operations the liquidity

---

[2] The literature on speculative attacks and self-fulfilling currency runs has expanded dramatically in the last decade, following the seminal contribution of Krugman (1979). An extensive recent survey can be found in Flood and Marion (1998).

taken away by depositors. Thus, incipient reductions of banks' reserves due to purchases of dollars by banks' customers were offset by systematic purchases by the central bank of treasury bills held by the banks. This strategy did not recognize that the equilibrium interest rate should have risen to incorporate the increase in the currency risk component. Moreover, it systematically reinjected in the economy the liquidity needed by speculators to continue attacking the currency. The accompanying decline in international reserves can, in such cases, become so large in relation to the monetary base that the exchange rate ceases to be credible and a collapse becomes unavoidable. This situation was reached in Mexico in December 1994. The inevitability of the collapse was compounded by the fact that large further claims on the dwindling international reserves were made by tesobono investors who refused to roll over their investments.

Colombia, in 1998, chose instead an interest rate defense. When pressures built up on the capital account of the balance of payments, the monetary authorities let the interbank interest rate rise to whatever level was necessary to limit the loss of international reserves. While the strategy was at first successful (conditions in the foreign exchange market initially stabilized), the deterioration of the banking system's soundness that followed the increase in lending rates weakened the effectiveness of monetary policy in dealing with further shocks. Partly as a result, the exchange rate was ultimately allowed to float in late 1999.

However, the transition to a pure float (or quasi-pure float) also faces important hurdles. One such well-known pitfall is excess exchange rate volatility, as illustrated by the very large and seemingly inexplicable fluctuations of the U.S. dollar against other reserve currencies after the abandonment of the Bretton Woods Agreement.[3] In light of such volatilities, the Mexican peso bilateral exchange rate against the dollar was, at first sight, surprisingly stable in the late 1990s. However, Mexico experienced a very high volatility in interest rates, as the monetary authorities allowed interest rates to offset much

---

[3] For a recent discussion of this issue, see Clarida (1999).

of the impact on the exchange rate of shocks in market sentiment.[4] Thus, volatility was channeled into a different market but did not disappear.

At the same time, real interest rates in Mexico have remained quite high, at least until very recently. Thus, notwithstanding the lack of an interest rate defense, as in Colombia, the Mexican banking system has nonetheless been similarly affected by high interest rates, the only difference being one of timing. Interest rates rose before the collapse of the exchange rate regime in Colombia and after the collapse in Mexico.

The high risk premiums in Mexico have reflected the difficulty of establishing a credible money-based nominal anchor following the collapse of the exchange rate anchor. Such reputational costs were mostly the legacy of the Bank of Mexico's mixed record in controlling inflation and ensuring the stability of the peso during the past three decades. In such cases, trust needs to be gradually reestablished through a sustained record of low inflation and stable economic conditions. In addition to strong commitment, however, this also requires effective monetary management and a smooth communication of monetary policy intentions to the public, i.e., an effective inflation-targeting framework. While many of the larger emerging countries have recently made notable strides in introducing and perfecting such a framework, its complexity remains an important obstacle to its introduction in the smaller and less sophisticated central banks.

The benefits of exchange rate bands were widely touted in the early 1990s as a regime that combined the advantages of fixed and floating rates. The wave of currency crises that has affected countries with such regimes suggests otherwise. Starting with the collapse of the European ERM system in 1992, countries with exchange rate bands that experienced currency crises and eventually were forced to abandon the band included Mexico (1994), Thailand (1997), Indonesia (1997), Russia (1998), Brazil (1999), Colombia (1999), and Ecuador (2000). Chile (1999) and Poland (2000) made orderly exits

---

[4] This reflected, to a large extent, the choice by the Bank of Mexico of a quantity-based (rather than price-based) operational target for monetary policy during this period.

and Israel has broadened the width of its band to the point where it has ceased, for all practical purposes, to be meaningful.

II. What Is a CBA?

A CBA is a rule-based monetary system. The first rule is a so-called "commitment technology." The central bank, through an explicit legislative act, commits to exchange its monetary liabilities against foreign exchange at a fixed exchange rate. In many countries, this commitment is asymmetric: the central bank commits itself to *sell* foreign exchange at a fixed rate but not to buy. Thus, exchange rate revaluations are, in principle, allowed. The second rule is a backing rule designed to ensure the credibility of the exchange rate rule. The central bank only issues monetary liabilities by purchasing foreign exchange and holds sufficient international reserves to fully back its monetary liabilities at all times.

Taken together, these two rules form a currency arrangement that is both strong and consistent. The commitment technology, if adequately embedded in the law, rules out, for all practical purposes, the possibility of an unexpected devaluation. Indeed, as devaluing requires changing the law, it is unlikely that the public can be taken by surprise. In view of the political costs incurred in a legal reform, even a preannounced devaluation becomes unlikely, except perhaps under truly exceptional circumstances. Thus, tying one's hands limits the scope for the inefficient outcomes mentioned in the previous section. At the same time, the backing rule boosts the credibility of the central bank's commitment to sell foreign exchange on demand against its monetary liabilities.

Interest rates play a fundamental equilibrating role in CBAs. A capital outflow leads to contraction of domestic liquidity that forces interest rates up. Indeed, sterilization is not an option under a CBA. Interest rates must continue to rise until the attractiveness of holding domestic assets is such that outflows stop. Similarly, a current account deficit leads to a loss of international reserves that also contracts monetary conditions until a new equilibrium is reached with either larger capital inflows (attracted by higher interest rates) or an improved current account balance (induced by the decline in economic activity brought about by the monetary tightening).

III. How Successful Have CBAs Been?

The roots of CBAs go back to the English colonies in the 1840s. The first CBA was introduced at that time in the Mauritius Islands, mostly to satisfy local interests. The main benefit was a gain in seigniorage. The colonists no longer needed to purchase British pounds nor pay for the costs of shipping the currency from England. At the same time, this arrangement resolved many of the problems faced by previous similar attempts to issue local currency. It limited the scope for inflationary money creation, which had been a serious problem when the currency was issued by the local authorities. It also limited the risk of fiscal losses when a private currency issuer failed and had to be rescued in order to prevent a currency crisis. Following the success of the Mauritius currency board, CBAs multiplied in the British and other colonies and successfully operated thereafter for more than a century.

The end of the colonial era, following World War II, marked the demise of CBAs. In part, this resulted from the newly independent countries' claim for autonomy and national identity. At the same time, the success of Keynesian economics led to the widespread belief of the primacy of discretion over rules. In this context, central banks that "fine-tuned" monetary policy were perceived to be better off than those that followed preestablished rules. The fact that the international reserves that backed the CBAs were constrained to earn a relatively low return was another important factor in their demise. The rise of development economics led to the belief that those reserves could be more usefully utilized to fund the country's development effort. Indeed, central banks came to be perceived as public deficit-financing and development-oriented institutions.

CBAs have experienced a strong revival in the last 15 years. This revival followed in part the need for rapid stabilization in countries that experienced bouts of hyperinflation linked with a breakdown of monetary discipline and a collapse of the central bank's monetary credibility. In some cases, such as in Argentina, the collapse of monetary credibility was a direct result of attempts to use the central bank as a development and fiscal deficit oriented institution. CBAs that were introduced under such conditions include, in addition to Argentina (1991), Bulgaria (1997), and, arguably, two of the Baltic countries, Estonia (1992) and Lithuania (1994). In Hong Kong

(1983), the CBA was introduced as a means to stabilize the foreign exchange market in the wake of the announcement of the reincorporation of the former British colony with mainland China. In other cases, particularly Djibouti (1949), Brunei (1967), and Bosnia (1997), the main motivation for the CBAs was operational simplicity. In Bosnia, the political environment made the rule-based arrangement particularly attractive.

CBAs have, so far, a remarkable survival record. Arguably, there have been only two cases so far in history where CBAs had to be abandoned under hardship conditions. Both episodes took place in Argentina and resulted from a sharp, sudden deterioration of the international economic environment linked in the first case (1914) to the start of World War I and, in the second case (1929), to the onset of the Great Depression. Moreover, in both cases, the authorities opted out of the arrangement rather than incurring the hardships that would have been associated with maintaining the CBA.

CBAs' record in terms of inflation stabilization is mixed. In Argentina, Estonia, and Lithuania, stabilization was already well on its way before the introduction of the CBA and the latter did not bring about an inflexion point in the downward path of inflation. Moreover, in the Baltic countries, the inflation record of Latvia, which did not introduce a CBA, matches that of Estonia and Lithuania. But not so, of course, in Latin America if one compares Argentina's post-CBA inflation record to that of Chile and Mexico. In Bulgaria, the announcement of the CBA's future introduction at the ongoing market exchange rate, which removed all nominal anchors, may have accentuated the outburst of inflation that preceded its introduction. At the same time, this enhanced the credibility of the CBA by eroding monetary liabilities in relation to international reserves, hence raising its backing.

Hong Kong's post-CBA inflation record compares unfavorably to that of Singapore, which let its currency float. The discrepancy was due to the fact that real exchange rates were pressured to appreciate in both cases. While Singapore allowed its nominal exchange rate to appreciate, Hong Kong's real exchange rate appreciated through higher inflation. The main culprit was the "Balassa-Samuelson effect" according to which productivity growth in the tradable sector caused wage increases that, under a rigid nominal exchange rate, translated into price increases in the nontradable sector.

This being said, the long-term inflation record of CBA countries is, by and large, enviable compared to that of their neighbors. For example, a comparison of price indices over the period 1970–1992 for some of the Caribbean countries clearly shows that the countries under the Eastern Caribbean Central Bank arrangement (ECCB), a currency board-type arrangement, fared better than any of their neighbors, in some cases by a considerable margin.

CBAs' record on interest rates is also generally quite impressive, reflecting their credibility. For example, interbank rates in Estonia (whose exchange rate was pegged to the deutsche mark) fell very rapidly to levels comparable to that in Germany. In contrast, interest rates in Latvia remained much higher, notwithstanding the fact that, as noted above, Latvia had a similar inflation record. Interestingly enough, Lithuania's interest rates (whose exchange rate was pegged to the U.S. dollar) remained (initially) high despite the introduction of its currency board. The main culprit was a lack of credibility resulting from a weak perceived initial commitment to the new regime. In particular, the monetary authorities initially maintained a discretionary capacity to alter the peg.

Argentina's record on interest rates under the CBA is also quite favorable, compared to that of other Latin American countries or to that of previous attempts made by Argentina to peg its exchange rate. Thus, as already noted, Mexico's real interest rates have been much higher in recent years under a floating rate than Argentina's under a CBA. If one compares Argentina's CBA experience with an earlier attempt at stabilization under the "tablita" system, it is clear that the credibility gains from the CBA were permanent, unlike those of the tablita.

Nonetheless, interest rates under a CBA may still incorporate a residual currency risk premium and be affected by changes in market sentiment. Indeed, due to currency risk Argentina's local currency deposit rates remain significantly above those on foreign-currency-denominated deposits and have been substantially affected by shocks such as the "tequila crisis." Even foreign-currency-denominated rates have, on such occasions, deviated substantially from U.S. rates due to an increase in country risk.

IV. Potential Pitfalls of CBAs

While the benefits of CBAs clearly show up in the data, particularly as regards interest rates, CBAs also have important potential pitfalls whose relevance is harder to quantify but that need to be carefully considered by countries envisaging the adoption of such arrangements.

The weaknesses of CBAs are the flip side of their strengths. In particular, while the commitment to preserve the parity is an asset in times of currency instability, it can become a liability in the presence of large real exchange rate misalignments. Correction of a large real exchange rate misalignment may require prolonged periods of tight liquidity and high unemployment that could cast doubts on the CBA's sustainability. Owing to limited price arbitrage, countries with substantial nontradable sectors are particularly vulnerable, which explains why most CBAs, with the notable exception of Argentina's, have been established in small open economies. If one compares the evolution of Argentina's real exchange rate to that of Mexico and Chile, Argentina's appears to have appreciated substantially more during the period 1985–1996. While this, of course, does not necessarily mean that Argentina's exchange rate has become overvalued, it does illustrate an important potential risk associated with CBAs.

Exchange rate misalignments can also occur because the exchange rate of the reserve currency country (i.e., the exchange rate against which the local currency is pegged) fluctuates against other major reserve currencies. Thus, to prevent its currency from depreciating along with the pound sterling in the wake of the abandonment of the Bretton Woods agreement, Singapore initially pegged its currency to the dollar in June 1972. In June 1973, it exited its CBA altogether as the dollar weakened against gold. Countries with limited trade relations with the reserve currency country are particularly exposed to such shocks. Thus, the pegging of Djibouti's currency to the U.S. dollar has led to wide fluctuations in inflation and competitiveness in relation to the European countries, which are Djibouti's natural trading partners.

Changes in monetary conditions in the reserve currency country may also be inopportune to the CBA country if the business cycles of the two countries do not coincide. Thus, Hong Kong's inflation during the early 1990s was partly the result of low nominal interest rates imported from the United States at a time when a rapid economic expansion (driven by China's business cycle) and an asset price boom would have called for higher rates. Moreover, the high domestic inflation resulted, with a fixed nominal exchange rate and near-interest-rate parity, in severely negative real interest rates that exacerbated the asset price boom.

While the inability to allow the exchange rate to float discourages systemic runs on banks motivated by expectations of an exchange rate realignment, it also increases the vulnerability of the banking system to runs when they occur. Under a pure floating rate system, the immediate depreciation of a pressured exchange rate promptly reduces the expected return from buying foreign currency, thereby discouraging further deposit withdrawals (and later conversion into foreign exchange). In contrast, in a CBA, depositors can only be induced to hold the local currency if interest rates become sufficiently high. However, as stressed earlier, such a defense may lack credibility if it is perceived to be undermining the solvency of the banking system.

Indeed, the convertibility of the monetary base in a CBA does not guarantee that of bank deposits. Thus, banks may be hard-pressed to honor requests for withdrawals of deposits if they are unable to obtain lender-of-last-resort support from the central bank. However, unless the latter holds international reserves in excess of those needed to back the monetary base, it will find itself unable to support the liquidity of the banking system. Thus, banks may have no alternative but to ration deposit withdrawals. A severe lack of liquidity resulting from a crisis of confidence in the sustainability of the CBA can thus put the payment system at risk.

V. When Are Strongly Anchored Exchange Rate Arrangements Advisable?

CBAs are clearly not a panacea. They should only be introduced in countries where their benefits clearly outweigh their potential drawbacks. In particular, the credibility of CBAs appears to be a determinant in countries that have squandered (or that never had the opportunity to acquire) their monetary credibility. In such cases, the sacrifices required for the central bank to recover its reputation may be so large that they are outright unviable. Arguably, this was the case of Argentina in the early 1990s.

Countries with weak institutions or post-chaos countries that do not have the human resources (nor the political will) to put in place strong, independent central banks also a priori qualify for such arrangements. Some of the eastern European countries that have adopted CBAs in recent years probably belong to this group. Countries undergoing periods of political turbulence or political uncertainty, such as Hong Kong during the late 1980s and the 1990s, may also be well served by a CBA.

CBAs also can make eminent sense in countries that are too small and open to have their own currency, or in countries whose trade links make them naturally part of an optimum currency area. Indeed, countries with large, well-diversified trade and small nontradable sectors do not benefit as much from exchange rate flexibility as large closed countries. Most of the existing CBA countries, with the notable exception of Argentina (and, arguably, Hong Kong), fall in some way in this category.

Inversely, countries in which it would probably not be advisable to introduce a CBA include those countries in the midst of a banking crisis and those that have limited international reserves (such as Indonesia in 1998) or countries that are large and subject to substantial terms of trade shocks. Those countries are probably better served by a freely floating rate regime.

Countries with weak public finances may use the introduction of a CBA as an opportunity to introduce fiscal reforms and strengthen their fiscal balance. However, continued fiscal weaknesses in such countries may severely undermine the sustainability of the arrangement or raise its costs. Large fiscal deficits can lead to a public debt crisis or contribute to overvaluing the exchange rate. Instead, in the absence of monetary policy capability, the importance of a flexible countercyclical fiscal policy increases in CBA countries.

The question arises of whether highly dollarized countries, such as Peru and Bolivia, would benefit from CBAs. There does not appear to exist an obvious answer at this stage. Peru has opted for maintaining a floating currency, notwithstanding the high dollarization of its economy and has been so far quite successful in reining in inflationary pressures. Bolivia has followed the route of a heavily managed, albeit flexible, nominal exchange rate. By accelerating the rate of crawl of the exchange rate in periods of economic slowdown and adverse movements in the terms of trade, it appears also to have maintained a small but significant capacity to affect real wages over time, thereby gradually altering its real exchange rate to maintain its international competitiveness.

VI. CBA or Full Dollarization?

An ample debate has arisen in the past five years as to whether full dollarization was preferable to a CBA. Proponents of full dollarization have pointed out that because CBA countries retain the option of exiting the arrangement, expectations of an exchange rate arrangement continue to be present, thereby unnecessarily driving a wedge between interest rates in local currency and foreign currency, particularly for longer maturities. In turn, this wedge raises the cost of capital, inhibits financial development, depresses capital formation, and slows down economic growth. Moreover, the presence of an exit option comes back to haunt the economic debate in times of stress in international capital markets, thereby increasing the vulnerability of the economy to external shocks. Finally, the use of a national currency imposes nonnegligible exchange conversion costs and may hamper financial development by increasing market segmentation and unnecessarily multiplying the number of financial instruments (thereby contributing to more shallow markets). For such reasons, new entrants to the realm of strongly anchored currency arrangements, such as El Salvador, have opted for full dollarization over a CBA.

However, CBAs leave more room, at least in principle, for residual exchange rate flexibility. Leaving aside the potential benefit of maintaining an outright exit option under severe shocks, which—for the reasons explained above—may be more of a curse than a benefit, CBAs also allow the exchange rate to be pegged to a basket of currencies rather than to a single currency. In view of the wide volatility of the major reserve currencies with one another, this option may be relevant in some countries, particularly those with diversified trade that do not clearly belong to a major currency and trade zone. Arguably, CBAs also allow for opportunistic switches in anchor currencies. Thus, a CBA country that is pegged to the euro and wishes to depreciate its currency over time could conceivably switch to the dollar when the latter has strengthened against the euro. This assumes, however, that the bilateral exchange rate between the major reserve currencies systematically falls out of balance while being mean-reverting over the long run. While widely accepted, there is no uniformity of views among economists on this issue.

CBAs also have seigniorage benefits as they allow the central bank to earn interest income on the international reserves that back the currency. Under stable prices, this source of income is not negligible. However, it is typically small. For example, if currency holdings constitute around 3 percent of GDP, an average figure for middle-income countries, the yearly interest income is 0.15 percent of GDP with a 5 percent nominal interest rate. Moreover, cash holdings around the world are rapidly declining with the advent of electronic means of payment. Thus, the relevance of economic seigniorage is likely to decline over time. In fact, "emotional" seigniorage, i.e., the ability to conserve a national currency as part of a national identity and cultural heritage, could constitute a more important and lasting benefit of CBAs compared to full dollarization.

VII. Some Implementation Issues

Because CBAs renounce using the exchange rate as a shock absorber, it is essential that they be designed with built-in alternative buffers that enhance their resilience to shocks. These may be divided into three types, liquidity-oriented buffers, solvency buffers, and real buffers.

CBAs need to have liquidity buffers to smooth out day-to-day interest rate volatility. While in traditional, colonial-type CBAs, the international reserves that backed the currency provided sufficient liquidity to oil the workings of the CBA, this is no longer true in modern CBAs as the importance of currency in the payments system has shrunk dramatically in favor of bank-based instruments and the depth and complexity of financial markets has grown explosively. While global financial integration has simultaneously facilitated interest rate arbitrage through capital flows (the basic liquidity adjustment mechanism in CBAs), the experience of Hong Kong and other CBAs with sophisticated money markets, such as Argentina, shows that such flows have not been sufficient to adequately smooth out day-to-day liquidity. Instead, the volatility of money market rates in Hong Kong became very high after the introduction of the CBA.

To limit such volatility, a number of CBA countries, such as the Baltic countries and Bulgaria, have opted for maintaining high, averaged reserve requirements. These reserves, which are fully backed, automatically accommodate the ebbs and flows of liquidity in the domestic money market. Other countries, such as Argentina, have asked their banks to hold their liquidity in the form of liquid reserves with a private bank abroad rather than in required reserves at the central bank. After the introduction of its real time gross settlement system (RTGS), which centralized settlements at the central bank, and in the wake of the Mexican "tequila" crisis, Hong Kong introduced a repo facility that allows banks to obtain end-of-day settlement funds at a moderately penal rate against their holdings of central bank bills. As these bills are themselves fully backed by international reserves, this reform amounted to broadening the definition of the monetary base to include central bank bills. In addition, both Argentina and Hong Kong stand ready to conduct traditional open market operations as needed to offset well-identified liquidity shocks.

CBA countries also need liquidity buffers to protect their financial systems from systemic shocks and ensure the convertibility of bank deposits. The key to maintaining such a capability is, of course, securing the access of local banks to external liquidity, through the central bank (as in Hong Kong) or with foreign banks (as in Argentina). When banks must access this liquidity through the central bank, the latter must hold sufficient excess international reserves and put in place lender-of-last-resort arrangements. By conducting limited open market operations, the central bank must also stand ready to use part of its excess reserves to help maintain the liquidity of the local money market and relieve pressures on public debt instruments. The alternative, as in Argentina, is to induce banks to use foreign short-term money market instruments and prenegotiate contingent credit lines from foreign private banks to help maintain the liquidity of the longer-term public debt market. Building up a sufficient deposit insurance fund, invested abroad, can provide an important additional cushion to help absorb systemic liquidity shocks that lead to the closure of the marginally less solvent banks.

Prudential norms, such as on maturity mismatches, can also help reduce the vulnerability of banks to liquidity shocks.

To strengthen the resilience of the banking system to shocks that may affect its solvency, a prudent and sound supervisory framework is, of course, essential. This should include an effective bank resolution framework that ensures that troubled banks can exit smoothly and with minimum impact on the overall stability of the system. A well-designed safety net, including, as already noted, a deposit insurance fund with sufficient resources and an appropriate mandate and legal powers for facilitating expedient bank resolutions (particularly closed-doors resolutions) is particularly relevant for CBA countries in view of their limited lender-of-last-resort capability.

In addition, capital requirements should be high enough to ensure a sufficient solvency buffer. However, the experience of many countries experiencing accentuated output and credit cycles shows that banks' capital, unless much above minimum requirements, does not always function as an effective buffer during the cycles. In good times, banks often fail to build up extra cushions while they increase their lending aggressively, thereby contributing to deepening the upward phase of the credit cycle. In bad times, their capital may rapidly become constrained by the minimum prudential requirements. In view of the difficulties of raising new capital during downturns and the adverse impact on market perceptions of incurring losses and allowing capital to dip below minimum standards, banks try to avoid provisioning at any cost and cut down aggressively on new lending to reduce the risk weighting of their portfolios. As a result, bank accounts lose their transparency, the supervisory authorities become hard-pressed to look the other way (thereby providing implicit forbearance), and the credit crunch accentuates the economic downturn, with further adverse effects on banks' soundness.

To address these problems, several countries have introduced (or are in the process of introducing) preprovisioning requirements that induce banks to build up their general provisions during the good times and allow them to convert these provisions into specific provisions during the bad times. While more work is needed to perfect such arrangements and obtain a consensus view at the international level, there is little doubt that they can provide a more effective (and less costly) solvency buffer that should be of particular relevance to CBA countries.

To limit the vulnerability of their financial systems to economic downturns, CBA countries must also be prepared to use fiscal policy as a flexible countercyclical instrument. Flexibility is also needed on the supply side. In particular, the labor market legislative and regulatory framework must be such as to facilitate labor mobility and limit wage inertia. Measures to promote productivity growth can also play an important role in building up a sufficient cushion against risks of currency overvaluation.

References

Baliño, Tomas, Charles Enoch, Alain Ize, Veerathai Santiprabhob, and Peter Stella, 1997, *Currency Board Arrangements: Issues and Experiences*, IMF Occasional Paper No. 151 (Washington: International Monetary Fund).

Clarida, Richard, 1999, "G3 Exchange Rate Relationships: A Recap of the Record and a Review of Proposals for Change," Group of Thirty Occasional Paper No. 59 (Washington: Group of Thirty).

Flood, Robert, and Nancy P. Marion, 1998, "Perspectives on the Recent Currency Crisis Literature," *International Journal of Finance and Economics*, Vol. 4, No. 1, pp. 1–26.

Klein, Michael W., and Nancy P. Marion, 1994, "Explaining the Duration of Exchange Rate Pegs," NBER Working Paper No. 4651 (Cambridge, Massachussetts: National Bureau for Economic Research).

Krugman, Paul, 1979, "A Model of Balance-of-Payments Crises," *Journal of Money, Credit, and Banking*, Vol. 11, pp. 311–25.

Chapter 33 | Common Currencies, Single Currency, and Other Forms of Currency Arrangements

JEAN-VICTOR LOUIS

Members of the IMF are following different ways for managing the issue and circulation of money in their territory.

The regime adopted depends on the kind of exchange regimes one country establishes with one or other currencies. From free floating to the participation to a single currency regime there are a lot of intermediary regimes (Eichengreen and others, 1999, pp. 3–4), including various modalities of pegging one's currency with one or a basket of currencies. "The rationale for pegging a country's currency to an anchor currency is based on two major policy concerns: the minimisation of exchange rate risk, and the stabilisation of inflation"(Beckx, 1998, p. 20). As the same author indicates, "the choice of a particular currency as an exchange rate anchor depends on three major factors: the importance of the trade relations with the anchor currency country, the importance of the financial flows with that country, and the stability of the anchor currency" (Beckx, 1998; see also Noyer, 2000, p. 7). The same is true for currency board systems or "dollarization" processes. An additional factor for deciding in favor of "dollarization" could be the high level of currency substitution, i.e., a high level of *de facto* "dollarization" (Noyer, 2000, p. 7), which is sometimes also called "partial dollarization."

"Dollarization" tends to avoid some negative elements of currency board arrangements: it removes the currency risk from the liabilities of commercial banks, it dampens expectations that the exchange rate peg might be changed, and eliminates the negative effects of high interest rates in the domestic currency (necessary for defending the peg; Hadjiemmanuil, 2000, note 63).

To organize a currency board system has been in the past (nineteenth century) a solution aimed at avoiding practical problems and losses induced by the circulation of a dominant (metropolitan) currency in a large area (Walters and Hanke, 1992, p. 559); more recently, it has been and it is still used by some countries of Latin America, and Eastern or Southeastern Europe.

A currency board has the main characteristic of being ready to exchange domestic currency for the foreign currency at a specified and fixed rate (Walters and Hanke, 1992, p. 558). The issue of banknotes is fully backed by external reserves. Currency boards may be useful in small economies that are heavily dependent on large trading partners (Walters and Hanke, 1992, p. 561). They are also viewed as an intermediate stage before the adoption of a full "dollarization" regime, called, in relation to the euro, "euroization," in (private) reports for the Balkans (Emerson and Gros, 1999, pp. 80–81; see also Cucic, 2000, p. 47).

"Dollarization" is a generic term used to describe the system in which a dominant international currency is adopted directly as the transaction medium (Canto, 1992, p. 843). "In general terms, dollarisation is a response to economic instability and high inflation, and to the desire of domestic residents to diversify their asset portfolios" (Eichengreen and others, 1999, p. 5). It may concern either the U.S. dollar or any other international currency. In the literature, "euroization" appears as a possible development in some countries of Central, Eastern, and Southeastern Europe, prior to—or, for some authors, as a temporary or permanent substitute for—their accession to the European Union and their full participation in the Economic and Monetary Union.

It is not possible to enter into all the details of situations because each situation is specific. Joseph Gold has made an interesting description of the various currency regimes adopted by members of the IMF, in a book called *Membership and Nonmembership in the International Monetary Fund*, published by the Fund in 1974. This book will be for us an essential source on the post–Second World War currency regimes. After a brief analysis of these different situations, I will look in particular to the external projection of the European Monetary Union (EMU).

A Description of Some Currency Regimes

Common Currencies

The expression "common currencies" has been used in the context of monetary unions, either bi- or multilateral. Gold mentions, for example, the Syria and Lebanon convention, these two countries possessing currencies that nominally were distinct from each other but were in fact a common currency. The Bank of Syria and Lebanon was the bank of issue, the foreign assets were managed by this bank, and the notes—marked either Syria or Lebanon—circulated and were freely accepted in both countries (Gold, 1974, pp. 105–106). Other historical examples of that kind are mentioned (Malaya-Malaysia, Tanganyika-Tanzania, later forming with Uganda and Kenya the ephemeral East African Community).

A more lasting regime is the one uniting seven countries of Western Africa and six of Central Africa (and the Comoro Islands), with France, known as the CFA Franc zone. The features of this area are well known. Each group of countries has one central bank. The Central Bank of West African States (commonly referred to by its French acronym, BCEAO) serves as the central bank for the UMOA (Union monétaire ouest africaine, known as the UEMOA after economic union), while the Central Bank of Equatorial States and Cameroon (commonly referred to by its French acronym, BCEAC) serves as the central bank for the UDEAC (Union douanière des Etats de l'Afrique centrale)—renamed the CEMAC (the Central African Economic and Monetary Community). The BCEAO issues one single currency: the CFA franc, which has a fixed exchange rate with the French franc (now the euro). The BCEAC issues a separate currency for each of the six states of Central Africa and has an agreement among the six states and with the French authorities (see Berrigan and Carré, 1997, p. 130). The regime is based on a cooperative agreement with France, which includes a commitment by France to the area ensuring a free and unlimited convertibility of its currency, that convertibility being guaranteed by the fact that the French Treasury (and not the central bank) offers an unlimited drawing right guarantee in French francs (now in euros) on the operations accounts opened in its books, where at least 65 percent of the exchange reserves of the central banks are pooled (Berrigan and Carré, 1997, p. 131); a fixed parity between the currency of the area and the French franc (now the euro), a guarantee of the outstanding amounts on the operations account by reference with the SDR, in case of depreciation of the French franc (now the euro), the outstanding amount of the operations account being multiplied by a coefficient in order to maintain the external value of the CFA franc in SDR and the participation of the French authorities in the formulation of monetary policy in the CFA zone (including a veto right for the representative of the French Treasury, in the governing bodies of the central banks).[1]

All these situations are clearly a legacy of special relations that have existed and sometimes are maintained in another form with a bigger economy. For the CFA franc zone, it has resulted in "a much better record of price stability than do neighbouring countries" but "they have experienced a similar mediocre economic growth rate" (Berrigan and Carré, 1999, p. 133). Eichengreen and others (1999. p. 67) observe that "[d]uring all but one of the fifty years that members of the two francophone [sic] African monetary unions have been pegging to the French franc, there has been no significant change in the bilateral rate" but, they observe, it is rather an exceptional situation, "most developing-country pegs are short lived."

The appellation "common currency" is used in these cases of monetary unions. Some have proposed the same denomination for the euro. They take the view that the common currency of a monetary union has a dual nature. For each member of the union, it is both a "national" and a "foreign" currency, since each of them is responsible for its issuance and accepts it as legal tender, but none of them has full control over it and it may be used as a medium of payment to discharge international liabilities at least among the members of the union.

I will not discuss the validity of such a view for every kind of monetary union that has developed. I would only say that such view is not in line with the allocation of competencies among the European Community and those of its Member States that participate in the

---

[1] France has been authorized to maintain its agreements with the countries of the French franc area by a decision of the EU Council 98/683/CE of November 23, 1998, *OJ*, L320, Nov. 28, 1998. France will have to report to the EU Council and to consult the ECB in case of modification of these arrangements. On this decision, see Zilioli and Selmayr (1999, pp. 326 *et seq.*), and Cafaro (1999, pp. 255 *et seq.*).

single currency, the euro. The power exercised by the European Central Bank in the EMU may not be compared with the exercise of a "foreign" power. This qualification gives a wrong view of the integration process, no matter if one explains it by the joint exercise of competencies (sovereignty) or the transfer of powers (sovereignty) to common institutions. The central bank is one of them and, without doubts, the more supranational. On the other hand, if national central banks (NCBs) are in charge of the issuance of the euro-denominated banknotes, and if, during the transition period (from 1999 to 2002), before that issuance, national legislation on legal tender is still in force, it is by virtue of European Community legislation that could have opted for another solution. With the complete substitution of national monetary signs by euro-denominated ones, legal tender will become a European Community concept, to be interpreted uniformly by the European Court of Justice. That will be clearer, I hope, when I will try later on to analyze the status of the euro, as it derives from the Treaty on the European Community and of the so-called euro-regulations.

Dollarization, Euroization, and Currency Boards

The longest lasting case of "dollarization" is the one of *Panama*. Under law No. 84 of June 28, 1904, the monetary unit of Panama is the balboa but "the present gold dollar of the United States of America and its multiples shall be legal tender in the Republic for its nominal value, equivalent to one balboa" (Gold, 1974, p. 94).

The Panamanian authorities could only issue gold or silver currency, and the issuance of silver coinage had to be guaranteed by gold deposited in the United States, all coins being mint in the United States with the cost of transport inherent to this process. As it has been pointed out, "it was more economical to use U.S. currency instead." As a result, "U.S. dollar notes and coins have consistently furnished most of Panama's circulating medium" (Hernandez, 1982, p. 800). The Constitution of Panama of 1972 took that into account by providing that "[t]here shall be no paper money of compulsory tender in the Republic" (article 231, quoted by Hernandez, 1982, p. 801, n. (2)).

Gold mentions also the case of the *Dominican Republic*, an original member of the Fund, that had only silver coins in its currency up to 1947, and the role of the U.S. dollar in Liberia. Since 1974, when Gold wrote his book, there have been other examples, especially in *Latin America* [2] and, after the fall of the Berlin Wall, in 1989, in the *countries of Central and Eastern Europe* (CEECs). I will have a look at the situation of those countries that are candidates to the accession to the European Union and, as such, that should be able to assume all the obligations of membership and, in particular, to subscribe to the objectives of political, economical, and monetary union (see the conclusions of the European Council meeting in Copenhagen, June 21–22, 1993, *EU Bulletin*, 6-1993, N 1-13).

Among the 12 CEECs and the Mediterranean countries engaged in the process of accession to the EU, Bulgaria and Estonia have had a currency board pegged to the euro/deutsche mark, since 1997 and 1992, respectively, and one country—Lithuania—has had a currency board pegged to the U.S. dollar since 1994, but the Bank of Lithuania has announced its intention to repeg the litas to the euro in the second half of 2001 (ECB, 2000, p. 42–43). The currency regimes of the others include a variety of formulas from managed floating (the euro serving informally most of the time as the reference currency) to crawling pegs or pegs to the euro (see Table 3 for monetary and exchange rate policies of accession countries, in ECB, 2000, pp. 42–43).[3]

At its meeting of April 13, 2000, the Governing Council of the ECB deliberated on its position toward the appropriateness of currency board arrangements (CBAs) as a strategy to be used by accession countries with regard to adopting the euro. It has concluded

---

[2] The press has recently announced the approbation by the IMF of a stand-by credit agreement to Ecuador, after the adoption of an economic program for the next 12 months. The central element of this plan is a dollarization at the fixed rate of 25,000 sucres for a U.S. dollar. For a cautious but rather positive assessment on dollarization in Ecuador, see the declaration by Stanley Fischer, Dow Jones Newswires, May 16, 2000. The current interest of Argentina for total dollarization, replacing the currency board system, existing since 1991, is also often mentioned (see Emerson, quoted in note (5). On the Cavallo Plan and the Convertibility Law of March 1991, see Hadjiemmanuil (2000), p. 16.

[3] The situation described in the *ECB Bulletin* is evolving. For example, Poland has decided to let the zloty float freely, renouncing the regime of a crawling fluctuating band, against a currency basket, comprising the euro and the U.S. dollar; see *Reuters,* April 11, 2000. The President of the central bank justified the decision by the will to realize a better score in the fight against inflation.

that the appropriateness would be assessed on a case-by-case basis. In the words of Vice President Noyer: "the Governing Council neither encourages nor discourages the adoption of euro-based CBAs. In any event, such arrangements cannot be regarded as a substitute for two years' participation in ERM II (the exchange rate arrangement between the euro and the currency of a non-participating Member State). Accession countries, which have operated an euro-based CBA, deemed to be sustainable, might not be required to go through a double regime shift in their strategies to adopt the euro. Thus such countries may participate in ERM II with a CBA as a unilateral commitment augmenting the discipline within ERM II. However, it should be clearly understood that a *common accord* would have to be reached on the central parity against the euro."[4] This confirms the attitude taken by the ECB after a seminar held in Helsinki, on November 12, 1999, to which the ECB, the 11 NCBs of the Eurosystem, and the NCBs of the accession countries participated, in favor of "a plurality of approaches":

No common path should be prescribed to all 12 accession countries with regard to the orientation of their exchange rate policies prior to accession, the inclusion of their currencies in ERM II or the latter adoption of the euro." On the other hand, after the latest statement of the ECB, it seems clear that a CBA is not to be seen as a substitute for the two years' participation in ERM II, but, to take on board the expressions used by T. Padoa-Schioppa, in his press conference of November 1999, presenting the results of the early mentioned Helsinki seminar, "as a special additional constraint," "a peg with zero fluctuation band." If the ECB has somewhat clarified its position on CBAs, it has refrained to express itself directly on "euroization" processes although the reference to the common accord as far as the parity of the accession member currency against the euro could be seen also as a warning that the adoption of the euro could not be the result of a unilateral decision.[5] In a speech made in the US,

---

[4] Introductory Statement, ECB Press Conference, Frankfurt-am-Main, April 13, 2000; available at www.ecb.int.
[5] A "Europa South-East Forum,"constituted in July 1999 by policy institutes of the region, working in cooperation with the CEPS in Brussels and the network of Open Society Foundations, has proposed a program to be realized progressively, which includes a radical banking reform, a euro-deutsche mark currency board, with the initial required backup of foreign exchange reserves provided by a loan of the European Union, where needed, a "European monetary association agreement" for
(continued)

at the beginning of the year, Christian Noyer opposed the de facto "unilateral monetary union" which official dollarization in Argentina would imply to "the process which led to EMU and the present negotiations for EU accession" (Noyer, 2000, p. 7). Political institutions of the EU have not publicly expressed a specific position on this topic, other than the necessity to stick to the Copenhagen criteria.

It is not for the jurist to judge on the merits and feasibility of a CBA or euroization solutions. But nevertheless, in legal terms, it seems clear that for the countries aspiring to full membership in the EU, there is no short way to participation in the final stage of EMU, and, if the CBA could help to induce stability, it does not dispense at least the accession country concerned to respect all the criteria for the full membership to the EU, including the EMU.[6] That supposes not only the respect of the convergence criteria, but also, among other requirements, adaptations of the banking sector, a modernization of the financial markets, and a serious improvement of the statistical apparatus. CBAs could help in realizing these objectives by introducing an external constraint. For some, who consider the situation of CEECs in general, this constraint is not sustainable, at least in the medium term (Bernard, 1999, p. 105; Berrigan and Carré, 1997, advise a "cautious approach," p. 126). Others insist on the necessity of a stable currency for economic recovery and point out the good results of full dollarization schemes in Panama and Puerto Rico. They insist on euroization being an alternative to convergence for countries with very weak institutions (Gros, in Emerson and Gros, 1999, pp. 80–81 and annexes 3 and 4; see also Hadjiemmanuil, 2000, p. 17: "A CBA provides for a more robust linkage to the euro than the simple participation to the Exchange Rate Mechanism II, or an

---

those countries interested in going beyond the currency board to full euroization, and from January 1, 2003, full euroization, either under the new association agreement or as full Member States of the EU (e.g., maybe, Slovenia) (Cucic, 2000, p. 47). Bosnia has adopted a currency board regime in relation to the deutsche mark.

[6] Hence the reaction attributed to the EU, as often called "Brussels," to the process of euroization, as the *Wall Street Journal* of August 12, 1999 observes: "Brussels may well see the process as a way of getting the single currency by the backdoor, without any of the hardship that Member States have gone through."

informal policy of shadowing the euro," and Hernandez, 1982, p. 815).[7]

The situation of *Luxembourg* is often mentioned as an example of a country where the notes and coins of another country, in this case, Belgium, are legal tender. This original regime of dual currency is sometimes presented as a demonstration that monetary union can exist without coordination of economic policies. It is perhaps interesting to analyze briefly this situation resulting from the creation some 70 years ago of the Belgium Luxembourg Economic Union (UEBL). The Convention of July 25, 1921, creating the UEBL, was very discrete on monetary questions. It provided for the substitution of the marks, issued by the German government and circulating in Luxembourg, by Belgian notes and a limited power for the Luxembourg to issue banknotes (articles 22 and 23). It was only on May 23, 1935 that a convention concerning financial and monetary questions was concluded between the two countries. This convention provided that Belgian banknotes would be legal tender in Luxembourg and settled rules for the issuance of Luxembourg notes (articles C and E), but it was only through the protocol on the monetary association of January 29, 1963, that the regime found a complete regulation. First of all, it is defined as a monetary association and not as a monetary union. There was no legal commitment of the two parties to maintain the parity of their currency. Both countries were only bound to modify the parity of their currency by common agreement, taking over, as an "ultimate guarantee," for the relations between the two francs, the commitment included in the Benelux Treaty of 1958 on economic union between Belgium, the Netherlands, and Luxembourg. The parties to the 1963 Protocol could well remember that Luxembourg had not followed the 25 percent Belgian devaluation of 1936 and it was clear, for the Luxembourg partner, at least, that in the absence of agreement on a parity move, both parties would be allowed to go ahead unilaterally, because no "abdication" of sovereignty was involved in the so-called

---

[7] The Centre of European Political Studies in Brussels has engaged in a campaign for a "quick euroization" of the countries of "Post-war Southeast Europe," which started with a green paper, circulated April 4, 1999, and knew successive versions, the final one being published in Emerson and Gros (1999); *see* in addition: Michael Emerson, "Cosmos, Chaos and Backbone for a Wider European Order," CEPS Working Document No. 130, 1999, specially, pp. 11–13, where the situations of all potential accession countries are looked at.

association agreement. Second, the parity between the currencies of the two countries resulted from a unilateral decision of Luxembourg confirmed in 1979, by a Decree of the Grand Duke, taken for the application of the Law of March 15, 1979 concerning the monetary status of Luxembourg. Third, the association was based on the existence of the National Bank of Belgium, which held a branch in Luxembourg, for the exercise of the main functions of central banking: lender of last resort and intervention on the exchange markets. Fourth, there was no pretension of irrevocability in an arrangement (a possibility of unilateral denunciation was provided every ten years) that lasted for so long because it was generally considered as profitable for both parties.

The association has lapsed with the development of European monetary integration.[8] It has solved specific problems existing between two neighboring countries different in size, which now find in a larger context a solution better adapted to the present and future developments of their economy. Any temptation to see in it a precedent for the realization of the European monetary integration is bound to fail. The EMU arrangements are definitely of another nature than the monetary association between Belgium and Luxembourg.

The Eurosystem as a Single Currency Regime

The Maastricht Treaty on the European Union has laid down the basis for the progressive establishment of economic and monetary union (EMU). This is not the place to recall the process that led 11 Member States to enter into the third and final stage of the EMU at the beginning of 1999. The key provision on the substitution of the euro (called in the Treaty, the ECU) to national currencies, is article 123.4 (ex article 1091.4) of the EC Treaty providing that

> At the starting date of the third stage, the Council shall, acting with the unanimity of the Member States without a

---

[8] The two countries have nevertheless decided, in an intergovernmental agreement on a common interpretation of the monetary protocol, concluded on November 23, 1998, *Mémorial* 1998, A, 3010, to continue the circulation of Belgian notes and coins in Luxembourg until the introduction in 2002 of euro-denominated notes and coins. This avoids the need for Luxembourg to issue a sufficient amount of its own currency, only to be obliged to recall it in less than three years later to replace it with euro notes and coins.

derogation, on a proposal from the Commission and after consulting the ECB, adopt the conversion rates at which their currencies shall be irrevocably fixed and at which the ECU shall be substituted for these currencies, and the ECU will become a currency in its own right. This measure shall by itself not modify the external value of the ECU. The Council shall, acting according to the same procedure, also take the measures necessary for the rapid introduction of the ECU as the single currency of those Member States.

The so-called Madrid scenario adopted in December 1995 by the European Council has provided for a transitory period of three years from the start of the third stage and the introduction of euro-denominated notes and coins. During that period, the euro would not have the quality of money if one follows the classical definition of F.A. Mann for whom "in law the quality of money is to be attributed to all chattels which, issued by the authority of the law and denominated with reference to a unit of account, are meant to serve as universal means of exchange in the State of issue" (Mann, 1984, p. 8). It has been the task of two regulations adopted by the EU Council to conciliate the situation of the transition period with the requirement of the Treaty that provides, right from the beginning of the third stage the substitution of the euro for the national currencies of the participating Member States. The drafters of the legal texts had also to consider the clear political will of the European Council, expressed in Madrid in 1995, that the single monetary policy would be defined in euro, that the money market would operate in euro, that the payment system infrastructure would have to be adapted to ensure the proper functioning of a money market in euro, and that the public debt would be issued in euro, right from the start of the transition period. How to translate that economic reality into legal texts and make of the euro a monetary reality in the absence of monetary signs denominated in euro?

That was the challenge the European Community legislature had to face. Two regulations are the seat of the matter: EU Council Regulation (EC) No. 1103/97 on certain provisions relating to the introduction of the euro [1997] OJ L162/1, and EU Council Regulation (EC) No. 974/98 on the introduction of the euro [1998] OJ L139/1.

The first regulation, based on article 308 (ex article 235) of the EC Treaty—a clause allowing the EU Council to act in the absence of any specific legal basis—states the equivalence 1 to 1 between the euro and the ECU (a unit of account based on a basket of currencies),[9] under the official definition, the continuity of legal instruments after the introduction of the euro (article 3), and some practical rules concerning the conversion and rounding.

The most important regulation, as far as monetary law is concerned, is the second one based on article 123.4 of the EC Treaty, quoted above. This regulation states unambiguously that "as from 1 January 1999, the currency of the participating Member States shall be the euro (article 2)." The regulation rejects firmly the hypothesis of a monetary dualism based on the coexistence of parallel currencies. We find in the same provision the affirmation usual in modern monetary legislation: "the currency unit shall be one euro" and "one euro shall be divided into hundred cents." To make matters clearer still, article 3 states that "[t]he euro shall be substituted for the currency of each participating Member State at the conversion rate" from January 1, 1999. During the transition period, "the euro shall also be divided into the national currency units according to the conversion rates." National currencies are no more than nondecimal divisions of the euro. As confirmed by the preamble of the regulation, "the euro unit and the national currency unit are units of the same currency," a supranational currency.

The euro-denominated notes and coins will be issued from January 1, 2002. The euro will then take the form of a physical currency, which will serve as a means of payment imposed by the law. Euro banknotes "shall be the only banknotes which have the status of legal tender in all these [the participating] Member States" (EC Treaty, article 106, ex article 105a; regulation 974/98, article 10) and article 11 of the regulation includes a similar provision for the coins that will be issued by the Member States, under the control of the ECB. Notes and coins denominated in the national currency units will cease to be legal tender on June 30, 2002 at the latest.

---

[9] The basket included all the currencies of the Member States, except these of the last three acceding countries: Austria, Finland, and Sweden. The ECU was the monetary unit of the European monetary system, created in 1979. Each currency had a central rate defined in ECU.

Before 2002, the euro remains a bank money and its use by private persons is limited by the principle that has been coined as the principle of "neutrality." During the transition period, "where in a legal instrument a reference is made to a national currency unit, this reference shall be as valid as if reference were made to the euro unit according to the conversion rates" (article 6(2)) and that "subject to anything parties may have agreed" (article 8(2)). Two related "principles" derive from the regulation. They reflect an orientation of the Madrid scenario. They are referred to, in the practice, as the rules of "no compulsion" and "no prohibition" in the use of the euro. It means that parties are free to stipulate the use of either the euro or the national currency unit but that the use of the euro unit cannot be imposed upon them (see article 8(1) and 8(5)). Exceptions have been provided to the "no prohibition" rule. They concern first the possibility to discharge an obligation in euro, under article 8(3) of the regulation:

> ... any amount denominated either in the euro unit or in the national currency unit of a given participating Member State and payable within that Member State by crediting an account of the creditor, can be paid by the debtor either in the euro unit or in the national currency unit. The amount shall be credited in the denomination of his account, with any conversion being effected at the conversion rates.

The inspiration for this provision came from an article of the new Dutch Civil code (vol. VI, article 114), which permits a debtor to discharge the amount of the debt by transfer to a bank account in the country in which the payment is to be made, unless the creditor has expressly excluded this method of payment. If such a possibility has not been excluded, the debt is validly discharged from the moment the sum owed is entered on the creditor's account.

Article 8(3) needs some comments on its precise content. First, and despite its wording, it does not exclude cross-border payments, as it is fortunately clarified by recital 13 of the preamble. Second, the units mentioned are either the euro unit or the creditor's national currency unit. Third, the financial institution holding the creditor's account is obliged to make the necessary conversion if the currency of the account is not the same as the currency of payment. Fourth, it remains unclear whether the provisions of paragraph 3 cover payments by check. It seems that one should conclude that at least crossed checks are included.

Article 8(4) provides for another exception to the noncompulsion rule by allowing the Member States the possibility of redenominating both public and private debt without having to seek the consent of creditors (see Lambrecht, 1999, p. 271). With respect to public debt, the redenomination appears as a logical consequence of the decision taken of issuing the new debt in euro. A public issuer will be able to redenominate his debt under two conditions: if the debt is denominated in its national currency and if it has been issued under the issuer's national legislation. Other issuers will be able to redenominate their debt issued in the national currency of another Member State if this State has redenominated part or the whole of the debt denominated in national currency. Redenomination in the meaning of the regulation is understood as the simple change of monétary unit. National legislators may provide additional measures like "renominalization" of debt, for example in order to eliminate unusual figures arising of conversion after rounding, or "reconventioning" of debt, for example, by amending rules on the calculation of interest or other issues relating to debt servicing.

The monetary union in the EU includes a single currency, the euro, a single monetary policy, and a single exchange rate policy (EC Treaty, articles 4.2, ex article 3a.2 and 105). A European System of Central Banks (ESCB), with a European Central Bank, has been established, in which every national central bank of the EU participates. Only the NCBs of participating countries participate integrally and form with the ECB what is called for practical reasons, the "Eurosystem." The ECB is responsible for the determination and implementation of monetary policy, the NCBs being normally in charge of the operations, in accordance with the principle of decentralization, which characterizes the regime of indirect application of European Community law. The monetary policy appears as the sole responsibility of the ECB, the NCBs acting under the guidelines and instructions of the ECB (Statute of the ESCB and the ECB, articles 12.1 and 14.3). This constitutes a particularly developed form of the so-called "dédoublement fonctionnel," used in the past to explain the process of application of public international law in the legal order of the state. In that measure, NCBs are functionally branches of the ECB and only secondarily national organs. The same is not true as far as other fields of competence of central banks are concerned. NCBs still have an important role to play in the functioning of the payment system and many of them are in charge of the prudential control of credit institutions, without mentioning other attributions, not typical of central banking, that are exercised by them on the request of the government or the legislature (see Trichet, *Le Monde*, April 12, 2000) and submitted to the tutelage of the ECB (Statute, article 14.4).

Could the quality of central bank be contested to the NCBs of Member States participating in the single currency? Charles Goodhart defines the functions of a modern central bank as the discretionary monetary management and the regulation and support, for example, through the lender of last resort function, of the banking system (Goodhart, 1992, p. 321). Considering the erosion of the possibility for individual countries to define an independent monetary policy in an interdependent World, this definition could perhaps lead to the conclusion that the only "modern" central bank in the world is the Federal Reserve System. It is nevertheless clear that the ECB is freer to decide on interest rate than the individual NCBs before the monetary union, considering the importance of trade relations among the countries concerned.

The new article 56 of the charter of the Bank for International Settlements (BIS), defines the word "central bank" as "the bank or banking system in any country to which has been entrusted the duty of regulating the volume of currency and credit in that country; or, in a cross-border central banking system, the national central banks and the common central banking institution which are entrusted with such duty." This definition of cross-border central banking intends to take into account the reality and the originality of the existence of a System, such as the ESCB. It is difficult to appreciate now the kind of balance of power that will prevail, not only in law, where things are clear, but also de facto, between the center and the periphery. Governors of NCBs, when seated in the Governing Council of the ECB with the members of the Executive Board, are deemed to be independent experts taking decisions, with one vote each (except for financial questions), in the interest of the Eurosystem as a whole, but they are nevertheless the heads of their central banks. The overlapping nature of these roles gives rise to a mutation of the activities of the NCB—participation in the ESCB influences all their activities, their staff, and their financial policies. Some of their traditional functions are put at risk. Definitive answers have not been given to such problems as the organization of prudential control on credit institutions and financial markets, which are becoming more and more global. Whatever the evolution of the respective role of the ECB and the NCBs within the system, one thing is clear: the irrevocability of the transfer of competences to the ECB in the field of monetary policy.

The External Projection of Currency Regimes

The IMF and Currency Regimes

In his famous book, already quoted, Sir Joseph Gold observes that "It is probable that the drafters of the Articles had in mind as the norm a member with a currency of its own that was subject, at least legally, to regulation by no other country." Nevertheless, "there were departures from that norm even among the countries listed in Schedule A" (original members). In addition, the Articles recognize that a country may have no central bank of its own" (Gold, 1974, pp. 90–91). Apart from the cases mentioned in the first part of this paper, Gold analyses a lot of other situations that the IMF has had to appreciate and on which it has concluded that the prospective member met the criterion of ability to perform the obligations imposed by the Articles.

As Gianviti has noticed, the Fund is a country-based and not a currency-based institution (Gianviti, 1997, p. 539). This author underlines also that the arrangements entered into by members for the management of their currencies or the conduct of their policies do not exempt them from their obligations under the Fund's Articles. A third principle is also pointed out by Gianviti: the participation in a common currency, with a common central bank, does not prevent the participants from exercising their membership rights under the Articles (Gianviti, 1997, p. 540).

The three principles listed by Professor Gianviti are evidently correct[10] from the standpoint of the Articles of Agreement of the Fund

---

[10] One should nevertheless observe that it would be possible, as suggested by René Smits (1997, pp. 442–443), to consider that the European Community has

(continued)

and coherent with the general principles of international law. It is also possible that considering the size of the economies and of the international reserves concerned by the past and present experiences of common currency regimes, no difficulty has arisen in the practice. The situation of the EMU, including neither an express nor an implicit exit clause, presents an undeniable specificity, legally, but also economically and politically, with respect of currencies that the authoritative *New Palgrave Dictionary of Money and Finance* still qualifies in its 1992 edition as "Exotic currencies." In the context of the present paper, law matters more than economics and politics but it is difficult to refrain from noting the part, in international trade, of the European countries participating in the single currency, the volume of their GDP, and the resulting amount of their cumulated quotas, from which derives their role in the life of the Fund and in the functioning of the international monetary system.

The Euro and Its Insertion in the International Context

It has been suggested that the states participating in the EMU are not able to comply *uti singuli* with their obligations toward the IMF (Martha, 1993, p. 749 *et seq.*, pp. 754–55; Smits, 1997, p. 448, Louis, 1997, p. 201 *et seq.*, p. 204). It is the case for the obligations listed in Article IV, sections 1 to 3 and Article VIII, sections 2a, 3, and 4 of the Articles of Agreement of the IMF. It is true that article 31.1 of the Statute of the ESCB and the ECB provides that NCBs are allowed to effectuate operations linked to the accomplishment of their obligations towards international organizations but one should take note that the authors of the statute had in mind a period of irrevocably fixed exchange rates preceding the single currency and that nobody could reasonably envisage an immediate substitution of the European Community and the ECB to the Member States in international organizations. The Member States are no more competent as far as exchange rate arrangements are concerned. Under Article 111 (ex article 109) of the EC Treaty, it is the EU Council that is responsible for the adoption, the modification, the implementation of, or the renunciation of exchange rate arrangements concerning the euro. It is for the ECB to comply with the obligation of conversion of amounts

---

assumed the competences of the states for the purposes of Article II, section 2 of the Articles of Agreement of the IMF. So the European Community should be seen as a "country" within the meaning of these Articles.

in euro detained by foreign central banks. NCBs are not responsible for the practice of discriminatory exchange rate regime. Individual Member States have lost their competence to determinate the value, either internal or external, of the currency circulating in their territory and this transfer is irrevocable (Protocol N 10 to the EC Treaty). Only the ECB and, for some aspects, the Council of the EU are in command.

It is true that the same loss of competences cannot be observed as far as economic policies are concerned. The economic policy of the Community consists in the close coordination of the economic policies of the Member States (article 4.1, (ex article 3a.1) of the EC Treaty). The coordination process and the multilateral surveillance are organized by article 99 (ex article 103) of the EC Treaty. There is no transfer of competences within the economic union part of EMU comparable to the allocation of competences to the Community institutions and the ECB in monetary matters. It is nevertheless not in line with the allocation of competences at the Community level that the process of coordination of economic policies could be dictated by the action of an international forum without the participation of representatives of the Community in this forum. It is the reason why, for example, the problem of an adequate representation of the European Union at the level of the "G-7 Finance" is so important.

The adequate representation of the new currency area raises questions in relation to the Articles of Agreement of the IMF but also within the EU context. The euro area does not include all the Member States of the Union,[11] and the prospect of accession of the United Kingdom to the third stage of the EMU still appears to be a remote one, considering the state of public opinion in Britain regarding this. That is an important handicap to a coherent projection of the EMU in the external sphere, not only on the legal standpoint but also and perhaps more so, politically. Member States reluctant to make the substitution find this situation encouraging. Precisely, this reluctance is an important trend that explains why a unanimous vote (of the participating Member States) in the EU Council has been provided for deciding on the modalities of the representation of the EMU in

---

[11] The United Kingdom and Denmark have opt out clauses, meaning that they are not obliged to adopt the euro. Sweden will join the the euro area as soon as it has fulfilled all the conditions.

international forums (see article 111.4, ex article 109.4). On the other hand, the same provision alludes to the allocation of competences between the Member States and the Community in the economic and the monetary sphere and that is a pretext used by some in order to maintain the status quo as far as their presence in international economic institutions is concerned. There are also different views on the respective role of the Council, the Commission, and the ECB. The ECB has indeed an international legal capacity and may participate to international monetary institutions, under article 6 of the ESCB Statute. It became a member of the Bank for International Settlements in November 1999 and has an observer on the Executive Board of the IMF. The greatest obstacle of the adequate representation of the EMU in the outside world is, to be sure, the lack of an (economic) government of the European Union. The Council of Economic and Finance ministers and the informal grouping, constituted by the ministers of the euro area, called the Euro 11 Group, cannot pretend to be a substitute for it. The result of this lack of progress on the political field, corresponding to the federalization process in the monetary field, is an endemic cause of weakness of the EU, in comparison with its partners. In other words, the second most important currency of the world is a currency "without a State" (Padoa-Schioppa, 1999, note 27) or, in order to avoid a statomorphic reference, a currency without a polity.

Some Concluding Remarks

After this short presentation, it is perhaps possible to propose some general comments. They will bear on the so-called "monetary sovereignty," the concept of money and the role of central banks.

The development of currency arrangements gives contrasting views on the reasons why one or more countries have adopted a specific regime. Economic, financial, and political links with a (often dominant) country, relations of proximity, or the will to resist to globalization have been and still are the reasons for the selection of monetary arrangements. Except in the case of the EMU, the preoccupation to restore the conditions of autonomous decisions in monetary affairs does not play a role in decisions led by pragmatism and, often, as the consequence of the impossibility to maintain stable conditions for the economy without an external constraint. In some other cases, it appears as a transition toward full participation in a bigger area. "Monetary sovereignty" appears in all these contexts as a very relative phenomenon in an increasingly interdependent world.

The concept of money is also an evolving one. The growing trend toward dematerialization has made it possible to define as money something that does not have the physical appearance of a chattel, as under the traditional definition. The importance of monetary signs in the payments is continuously decreasing in favor of scriptural and electronic money. The legal status of the euro during the transition period from 1999 to 2002 denotes it as only an abstract unit of account. However, it is a reality in financial and exchange markets.

Central banks also see their role decreasing in the context of regimes based on CBAs or when they are part of a monetary union. They have lost their (apparent) discretion in monetary policy and they are challenged in their traditional functions as prudential control authorities or for the management of public debt. They evidently are on the defensive. It seems that the condition for them to keep something of their former position is in the participation in larger groupings.

References

Beckx, P., 1998, "The Implications of the Introduction of the Euro for Non-Euro Countries," *Euro Papers*, No. 26 (Brussels: European Commission).

Bernard, L.D., 1999, "What Impact Will the Euro Have on the Candidate Countries of Central and Eastern Europe?" in *The Euro-Zone: a New Economic Entity?* ed. by A. Lamfalussy, L.D. Bernard, and A.J. Cabral (Brussels: Bruylant), pp. 87 *et seq*.

Berrigan, J., and H. Carré, 1997, "Exchange Arrangements Between the EU and Countries in Eastern Europe, the Mediterranean, and the CFA Zone," in *EMU and the International Monetary System*, ed. by P. Masson, Th.H. Krueger, and B.G. Turtelboom (Washington: International Monetary Fund), pp. 122 *et seq*.

Cafaro, S., 1999, "I primi accordi della Comunità in materia di politica monetaria e di cambio," in *Il Diritto dell'Unione Europea*, pp. 243 *et seq*.

Canto, V.A., 1992, "Exotic Currencies," in *The New Palgrave Dictionary of Money and Finance*, Vol. I, ed. by P. Newman, M. Milgate, and J. Eatwell (London: Macmillan), p. 843.

Cucic, L., ed., 2000, *A New Croatia: Fast-Forward into Europe* (Brussels: CEPS).

Eichengreen, B., P. Masson, M. Savastano, and S. Sharma, 1999, "Transition Strategies and Nominal Anchors on the Road to Greater Exchange-Rate Flexibility," Essays in International Finance, No. 213 (Princeton, New Jersey: Princeton University).

Emerson, M., and D. Gros, eds., 1999, *The CEPS Plan for the Balkans* (Brussels: CEPS).

European Central Bank, 2000a, "The Eurosystem and the Enlargement Process," *Monthly Bulletin* (February), pp. 39 *et seq.*

European Central Bank, 2000b, "Introductory Statement," ECB Press Conference, Frankfurt-am-Main, available at www.ecb.int.

Gianviti, F., 1997, "Comments on Polak and Thygesen," in *EMU and the International Monetary System*, ed. by P.R. Masson, Th.H. Krueger, and B.G. Turtelboom (Washington: International Monetary Fund), pp. 539 *et seq.*

Gold, Sir J., 1974, *Membership and Nonmembership in the International Monetary Fund* (Washington: International Monetary Fund).

Goodhart, C., 1992, "Central Banking," in *The New Palgrave Dictionary of Money and Finance*, Vol. I, ed. by P. Newman, M. Milgate, and J. Eatwell (London: Macmillan), p. 321 *et seq.*

Hadjiemmanuil, C., 2000, "The Choice of Institutions for Monetary Stability in an Emerging Economy: Independent Central Bank or Currency Board?," in *Transnational Finance and the Challenge of Law,* ed. by Mads Andenas and Chizu Nakajima, (: Kluwer International).

Hernandez, M.T., 1982, "Financial System in Panama," in *Emerging Financial Centres*, ed. by R.C. Effros (Washington: International Monetary Fund), pp. 799 *et seq.*

Louis, J.-V., 1997, "Union monétaire européenne et Fonds monétaire international," in *Währung und Wirtschaft. Das Geld im Recht*, ed. by A. Weber (Baden-Baden: Nomos) pp. 201 *et seq.*

Lambrecht, P., 1999, "Redénomination et renominalisation des obligations émises par les Etats et par les entreprises de l'UEM," in *The Euro and Non-Participating Countries*, ed.by L. Thévenoz and M. Fontaine (Zürich-Brussels: Schulhess, Bruylan), pp. 271 *et seq.*

Mann, F.A., 1984, *The Legal Aspect of Money*, 4th ed. (Oxford: Oxford University Press).

Martha, R.S.T., 1993, "The Fund Agreement and the Surrender of Monetary Sovereignty to the European Community," *CML Rev.*, Vol. 30, pp. 749 *et seq.*

Noyer, C., 2000, "The International Impact of the Euro," speech delivered during his visit in the United States, European Central Bank, January. Available via the Internet: www.ecb.int.

Padoa-Schioppa, T., 1999, *Moneta, Commercio, Istituzioni: Esperienze e Prospettive della Costruzione Europea*, (Trieste: European Central Bank). Available via the Internet: www.ecb.int.

Smits, R., 1997, *The European Central Bank. Institutional Aspects*, (The Hague; Boston: Kluwer Law International).

Walters, A., and S.H. Hanke, 1992, "Currency Boards," in *The New Palgrave Dictionary of Money and Finance*, Vol. I, ed. by P. Newman, M. Milgate, and J. Eatwell (London: Macmillan), p. 558 *et seq.*

Zilioli, C., and M. Selmayr, 1999, "The External Relations of the Euro Area: Legal Aspects," *CML Rev.*, Vol. 36, pp. 273 *et seq.*

Chapter 34
Legal Tender: A Notion Associated with Payment

KAZUAKI SONO

Legal tender is money that, if tendered by a debtor in payment of his monetary obligation, may not be refused by the creditor. Thus, the legal tender is a notion associated with the discharge of monetary obligation by "payment." When the banknote of a currency is designated as legal tender, it will ordinarily be accompanied by nominalism. This paper considers how confusing the role of national currency has become by examining how the legal tender, a traditional core concept of national currency, has lost its importance at present.

The Supreme Court of the United States considered the authority of determining legal tender as a component element of currency power (in the Legal Tender Cases [*Knox v. Lee* and *Parker v. Davis*], 79 U.S. (12 Wall.) 457 (1871). Since the power is within the exclusive jurisdiction of the state issuing a particular currency, a monetary obligation expressed in that currency cannot escape from the reach of this regulation (*lex monetae*). The state can also replace the currency by a new one and fix the conversion rate of the old currency in relation to the new as has been done recently in the European Union.

However, the utility of the concept of legal tender may have to be reassessed because monetary obligations are now increasingly discharged by account settlement without any "tender" of currency.

Traditional Role of National Currency

Traditionally, monetary sovereignty was an important element of a nation's sovereignty. The economic well-being of a nation rested in part on the stability of the currency which the nation maintained. Its monetary authority controlled the supply of credit and geared the economy to its maximum potential. The legal tender rule, therefore, accompanied the mandatory nominalism. Regardless of a change in the purchasing power, the monetary obligation expressed in the domestic currency was discharged by tendering the same amount.

Thus, for example, the insertion of a gold clause in a contract, which indexed the amount to be paid to the amount of gold that was obtainable at the time of the accrual of the monetary obligation, was regarded as an unacceptable challenge to the governmental authority to gear the national economy.

In 1933, the Congress of the United States adopted a joint resolution declaring that the gold clause was against public policy and that monetary obligations expressed in U.S. dollars would be discharged by tendering the same amount in U.S. dollars (48 Stat. L. 113, 31 U.S.C., §§ 462, 463 (1933)). This resolution was broadly respected internationally for monetary obligations payable in U.S. dollars: in essence a philosophy similar to art. 8(2)(b) of the Articles of Agreement of the International Monetary Fund prevailed.

Forgery of national currency was a serious offense. Wherever committed, it was a challenge not only to the monetary sovereignty of a nation but also to the foundation of the international monetary order. Thus, the U.S. Supreme Court even assumed it to be an international obligation of sovereign states to enact penal provisions against counterfeiting and other crimes regarding foreign money (*United States v. Arjona*, 120 U.S. 479, 7 S. Ct. 628 (1887)). In 1929, under the auspices of the League of Nations, the International Convention for the Suppression of Counterfeiting of Currency was adopted to cope with international counterfeiting bands (112 Treaty Series 372 (1931)). The legislative jurisdictional reach of a nation could be extended against an offender abroad regardless of the nationality of the offender (e.g., Japanese Criminal Code, art. 2 (4)). The monetary sovereignty was very strong.

Since the national currency was closely linked to the national economy, the use of a foreign currency for domestic transactions, whether as a unit of payment or as a unit of account, was, as a matter of principle, incompatible with the role of the national currency. For international cases where monetary obligations were expressed in foreign currencies, some countries even insisted that all monetary claims of foreign origin had to be asserted in domestic currency in court, while others prescribed that the obligor had an option to pay in domestic currency at the exchange rate on the day of payment. The home currency rule was particularly strong in common law countries, e.g., *Manners v. Pearson & Son*, [1898] 1 Ch. 581 (C.A.); *Re United Railways of Havana & Regla Warehouses Ltd.*, [1961] A.C. 1007; and *Die Deutsche Bank filiale Nurenburg v. Humphrey*, 272 U.S. 547 (1926).

Changes After the Floating Exchange Rate System

However, under the floating exchange rate system coupled with the penetration of a philosophy in support of the freedom of capital transfers, commercial concerns realized that the protection of their transactional value is left to themselves in this unpredictable world of exchange rates. This reality was recognized by court. For example, a clause in a "domestic" loan agreement in pounds sterling which indexed the amount to be repaid to the Swiss franc was sustained in the United Kingdom in *Multiservice Bookbinding Ltd. and Others v. Marden*, [1978] 2 All E.R. 489 (Ch.D., 1977). In this loan agreement, which was payable after 10 years, it was provided that, if the exchange rate between pounds and Swiss francs differed more than 3 percent on the day previous to the date when the repayment was due, the amount repayable in pounds would be adjusted accordingly. When the due date came, the exchange rate of the pound to the Swiss franc was about one-third (i.e., from about 12 Swiss francs to about 4 Swiss francs). This meant that the borrower had to pay about three times as many pounds on the principal alone. The court did not accept the argument that this clause was against public policy, being unequitable and unconscious, and emphasized that the person providing the financing was entitled to ensure that the real value of what he financed would be maintained.

In 1977, the United States quietly repealed the 1933 Congressional Resolution which prohibited the gold clause (Public Law 95-147, 91 Stat. 1227).

Germany prohibited indexation clause by Law (No. 3) of 1948 but abolished the law in 1998 on the ground that the monetary sovereignty has been transferred to the European Union. Note that Germany had also prohibited the use of the ECU clause domestically until then. The combined use of a unit of account and unit of payment in international transactions is of course an indexation. A creditor often wishes to secure the value of his monetary claim by linking the determination of its sum due at the time of payment to a certain unit whose value may be more stable than the currency of payment. As well known, until recently, ECU was often used as such a unit of account in order to minimize the risk of volatility in the foreign exchange rate.

However, in reality, private ECU became to be used as if it were a unit of payment (hence a currency) in transactions which called for monetary settlement through bank accounts. That development was a beginning when the legal tender rule started losing its significance.

Moreover, parallel to the freedom of international capital transfers under the floating exchange rate system, domestic account holding in foreign currencies has become permitted in major countries. To this reality, courts of major countries responded by abandoning the home currency rule for international cases. In a leading case in the United Kingdom, *Milangos v. George Frank (Textiles) Ltd.*, [1976] A.C. 443 (1975), the court upheld the claim to pay in Swiss francs as agreed in the contract after emphasizing the parties' need to adapt to changes in the international monetary system and to the necessity of commerce. Meanwhile, the traditional breach day rule for determining the exchange rate for conversion has also been shifted to the actual payment date rule, thus leaving the determination of the exact amount to be paid in pounds to the foreign exchange rate on the day of actual payment.

In the United States, Restatement 3rd, Foreign Relations Law of the United States, § 823 (1987), still maintained the home currency rule as the principle, only permitting to a court the discretion to render judgment in a foreign currency. However, the 1989 Uniform Foreign Money Claims Act, § 7(a) provides that the judgment in a foreign currency is the principle when the parties previously agreed to a foreign currency as the unit of payment, and in *Mitsui & Co. v. Oceantrawi Corp.*, 85 Cir. 8008 (MGC) (S.D.N.Y. 1995), the federal court entered judgment in foreign currency for the first time, and emphasized the policy considerations of freely permitting parties to international commercial contracts to select the currency in which to transact business and bear currency fluctuation.

France still maintains the home currency rule for judgment, but since the court has already changed the rule on the conversion date of a foreign currency claim to the French franc from the breach date to the actual payment date, it can be regarded as tantamount to the practical abolition of the home currency rule.

In Germany, money debt expressed in a foreign currency may be payable in domestic currency and the payment date rule applies for conversion (BGB, § 244). In Japan, the Supreme Court, in *obiter dictum*, also confirmed that the rule in article 403 of the Civil Code, which provides an option to the obligor to pay in domestic currency at the exchange rate then prevailing, meant the option to convert on the actual payment date (29 *Minshu* 1029, July 15, 1975). However, the main issue in this Japanese case was whether a foreign creditor who held a claim in foreign currency could make the claim in Japanese yen in Japanese court. Since the yen was rapidly gaining strength, the earlier the foreign currency was converted to yen, the greater the amount in yen was than the amount in yen which the creditor would have obtained on the actual date of payment. Under such circumstances, the court held that the creditor in foreign currency may make a claim in Japanese currency under an expanded interpretation of article 403 and that the conversion date was the date when the trial was concluded. It may have been that, in order to tackle the delicate question of how to calculate the proper amount of damages in case of breach, particularly when the exchange rate was significantly changing, the court considered an equitable path to be the middle way, i.e., between the date when the claim was made and the date when payment was actually made.

In this context, it may be noted that the Principles of European Contract Law of 1998 provides, after stating a rule similar to German BGB art. 244, "[i]f the debtor has not paid at the time when payment is due, the creditor may require payment in the currency of the place where payment is due according to the rate of exchange prevailing there either at the time when payment is due or at the time of actual payment" (art. 7:108(2)(3)). The UNIDROIT Principles of International Commercial Contracts of 1994 also takes a similar approach (art. 6.1.9). It may be of interest that these provisions were modeled upon article 41 of Geneva Uniform Law on Bills of Exchange of 1930, and article 36 of Uniform Law on Cheques of 1931.

Impact of Globalization on the Money Market

In the days when economic interaction among states was mostly through traditional trade in goods, each state could determine its monetary and fiscal policies primarily based on their impact on the domestic economy. The foreign exchange policy was, of course, important for the maintenance of a favorable balance of payments position for current payments, but it could be formulated as relatively distinct from other policies. However, under the present system, monetary and fiscal policies, such as on taxes, public expenditures, and the prime rate, would be immediately interwoven into the exchange rate before their impact was felt within the confine of the nation's boundaries. Consequently, the effect on domestic economy which previously could have been anticipated by a proper implementation of those policies is no longer assured. The scope of a government's maneuverability in the management of its economy has thus been seriously narrowed.

Meanwhile, the development of electronic fund transfers has revolutionized the means for discharging a monetary obligation. People now tend to include the application of such accounting techniques in the definition of "payments," and this is called the "global payment system." The European Union completed this picture by nonissuance of paper money but allowing the euro to circulate in the virtual world at present and be settled in bank accounts.

Traditionally, it was explained that control over the supply of credit in an economy was in the hands of its monetary authority. The amount of currency which was placed in circulation was important because of its direct link to "payment." Even in account settlements, if they were confined within the national boundary, the monetary authority could maintain their grip. This was the basis on which nations' monetary authorities could exercise their control over the supply of credit. However, the overwhelming spread of account settlements on a global scale now often bypasses central banks.

Moreover, since the settlement of monetary obligations is now mostly through adjustments in accounts not requiring any settlement in cash, it is no longer necessary to be expressed in any national currency unit as long as an agreed formula exists on how it will be recalculated into other currency units when such need arises. Thus, for example, the ECU, a monetary but noncurrency unit of account, was constantly used as a unit of account until recently, and now EC regulations attempts to shift this unit of account to the monetary status, i.e. euro.

The UNCITRAL Model Law on International Credit Transfers of 1992 provides in its definitional section that "funds" or "money" include credit in an account kept by a bank and include credit denominated in a monetary unit of account that is established by an intergovernmental institution (art. 2(h)). Envisaged at the time of its adoption was, of course, a private ECU account. Therefore, the new EC regulation that assimilates ECU designation in a contract to the money designation is not a surprise. Reflecting upon such development, the 1998 resolution of the International Law Association confirms that the matter is within the confine of *lex monetae*, hence no new legislation is necessary even in non-European countries to attain the same result in that regard.

Traditionally, it was conceptually inconceivable to consider the domestic currency, which is the legal tender, able to become an object of purchase or sale. On the other hand, foreign currencies were commodities in the foreign exchange market. Only when foreign currencies assumed a payment function in the international transaction were they treated as money. However, such foreign exchange transactions now take place in a third country which is a part of the global money market. Moreover, the liberalization of financial services with unrestricted capital movement will make it difficult even to identify, for legal purposes, the location (*situs*) of an account when a bank maintains branches throughout the world and the account is accessible from any place. The traditional approach to legally identify (or designate) the location of an account and to subject the account to the *lex situs* have already invited many confusing judicial decisions. As the presence of currency becomes more and more virtual, the traditional thinking that a bank account has a physical location may have to be abandoned as unnecessary and misleading. The world seems to continue to suffer from the residue of the territoriality based traditional jurisprudencial thinking. This is also a hotly debated issue in relation to pledging of securities kept in registers by Euroclear.

The present tendency for national currencies to lose their important function at each of their home countries and the consequent decline of the home currency rule in courts seem to have already reduced the importance of posing the question of whether foreign currencies are commodities. Today national currencies themselves are speculated on in exchange markets as if they were commodities together with securities. Governments accordingly intervene in the markets by selling or purchasing their own currencies in an endless game with banks, dealers, and speculators. This occurred as the legal tender rule and the accompanying nominalism have become less meaningful.

In the transactional law sphere, this state of affairs constantly calls for a new analysis of the relationship between the manner of calculating damages resulting from the breach of a monetary obligation, the currency to be used for the measurement, and its conversion date.

The Principles of European Contract Law simply indicate that "[d]amages are to be measured by the currency which most appropriately reflects the aggrieved party's loss" (art. 9:510). The UNIDROIT Principles of International Commercial Contracts states that "[d]amages are to be assessed either in the currency in which the monetary obligation was expressed or in the currency in which the harm was suffered, whichever is more appropriate" (art. 7.4.12). Thus, the courts will continue to be confused. The court nevertheless has to maneuver under traditional legal formulae one way or another influenced by the residue of nominalism. They are not to be blamed because the courts have no jurisdiction to speak out on the appropriateness of the monetary system itself.

The prevalence of "account settlements" also makes obsolete the traditional meaning of the "legal tender" rule since the credit and debit of an account need no longer be in any national currency unit. Moreover, as the account settlements in the fund transfers in multi-country locations increase and as shifting the location of financial activities from one jurisdiction to another becomes easier, traditional money aggregates have lost information value to national monetary authorities. This phenomenon also has implications for the control of liquidity, a traditional concern of central banks. This challenge is further strengthened by the increase in the number of countries that honor "a foreign currency clause" in purely domestic contractual arrangements.

If we are really committed to the healthy development of the globalization of the economy, one of the first enquiries we have to make is how to reestablish a reliable measure of monetary value. This can start with a serious reexamination about the raison d'etre of each national currency perhaps before concentrating on "dollarization or not."

VIII. Payment Systems

Chapter 35

CPSS Core Principles for Payment Systems

GREGOR HEINRICH

There are a number of international initiatives that have the goal of improving or maintaining financial stability by strengthening financial infrastructure. The Committee on Payment and Settlement Systems (CPSS) of the central banks of the Group of Ten (G-10) countries is contributing to this process through its work on developing Core Principles for systemically important payment systems (Core Principles).

At the time of this presentation, the Core Principles are not yet finalized. In December 1999 a consultative report was published, containing a set of Core Principles. At its meeting in Mexico in May, the CPSS approved the current draft of the Core Principles and also encouraged continuation of the work on Part 2 of the report, which explains the principles in more detail and provides guidelines for their implementation.[1]

The principles are expressed in a deliberately general way to help ensure that they can be useful in all countries and that they will be durable. They do not represent a blueprint for the design or operation of any individual system, but suggest the key characteristics that all systemically important payment systems ("SIPS") should satisfy.

The CPSS established a Task Force on Payment System Principles and Practices in May 1998 to consider what principles should govern the design and operation of payment systems in all

---

[1] Almost 300 comments and suggestions were offered in the first consultative phase. In summer 2000 a revised text, taking account of the comments received was again made available for public comment, and the final version was published in January 2001 (www.bis.org/cpss). This article reflects the state of discussions at the time of the presentation.

countries.[2] The Task Force is seeking to develop an international consensus on such principles. It comprises representatives not only from G-10 central banks and the European Central Bank, but also from 11 other national central banks of countries in different stages of economic development from all over the world and representatives from the International Monetary Fund and the World Bank. In undertaking its work it has also consulted groups of central banks in Africa, the Americas, Asia, Pacific rim, and Europe.

The CPSS and General Concern for Risk Reduction

The CPSS is one of the permanent central bank committees reporting to the G-10. The G-10 Governors established the CPSS in 1990, as a follow-up to the work of the Committee on Interbank Netting Schemes, which produced the "Lamfalussy Report,"[3] and more generally to take over and extend the activities of the earlier Group of Experts on Payment Systems, in 1990.

The CPSS serves as a forum for the G-10 central banks to monitor and analyze developments in domestic payment, settlement, and clearing systems as well as in cross-border and multicurrency netting schemes. It also provides a means of coordinating the oversight functions to be assumed by the G-10 central banks with respect to these private netting schemes. In addition to addressing general concerns regarding the efficiency and stability of payment, clearing, settlement, and related arrangements, the CPSS pays attention to the relationships between payment and settlement arrangements, central bank payment and settlement services, and the major financial markets which are relevant for the conduct of monetary policy.

The CPSS, under the auspices of the Bank for International Settlements (BIS), has published various reports in recent years covering large-value funds transfer systems, securities settlement systems, settlement mechanisms for foreign exchange transactions,

---

[2] Chairman of the Task Force is Mr. John Trundle, Head, Market Infrastructure Division, Bank of England; see Annex 3.
[3] "Report of the Committee on Interbank Netting Schemes of the Central Banks of the Group of Ten Countries," BIS, November 1990.

clearing arrangements for exchange-traded derivatives, and electronic money.[4]

The CPSS has long been at the forefront of efforts to reduce risks in payment and settlement systems. This has been motivated by concerns that the credit and liquidity risks inherent in payment and settlement systems have the potential to contribute to systemic problems if not properly managed and controlled. In this connection, the CPSS has considered it important to cooperate with other groups, including the International Organization of Securities Commissions (IOSCO), the Basel Committee on Banking Supervision, and the G-10 Deputies, to address issues of common concern. In the context of its activities the CPSS maintains contact with many global payment system providers, industry associations, and other regulatory authorities.

The work of the CPSS has consistently emphasized the importance of large-value interbank funds transfer systems, which are used by banks to execute payments among themselves for their own account or on behalf of customers. More recently, the CPSS has also embarked on a more detailed study of retail payment instruments and related settlement systems. Payment systems, their risk management arrangements, and implications for central bank policy have often been a focus of the CPSS discussions, and over time it has compiled substantial information on their main characteristics both in G-10 and in non-G-10 countries. This experience has laid the groundwork on which the new Core Principles can build.

Why Core Principles for Payment Systems?

Safe and efficient payment systems are critical to the effective functioning of the financial system. Payment systems are the means by which funds are transferred between banks, and the most significant payment systems, which the Core Principles refer to as "systemically important payment systems," are a major channel by which shocks can be transmitted across domestic and international financial systems and markets. Robust payment systems are,

---

[4] Most publications are available online at the website of the Bank for International Settlements (BIS) at http://www.bis.org/cpss.

therefore, a key requirement in maintaining and promoting financial stability.

As regards the Core Principles in particular, several influences are of relevance: international consensus for promoting internationally accepted standards, the objective need to reduce payment system risk, the request from many emerging market economies for particular guidance in their payment system reform process, and the existing body of policies and recommendations emanating from the CPSS.

The Consensus for Promoting Internationally Accepted Standards

Over the past few years, a broad international consensus has developed on the need to strengthen payment systems by promoting internationally accepted standards and practices for their design and operation. The consensus for promoting internationally accepted standards was perhaps first formulated in 1997 by the ad hoc Working Party on Financial Stability in its report on "Financial Stability in Emerging Market Economies."[5]

In response to an initiative at the Lyon summit in June 1996, representatives of the countries in the Group of Ten and of emerging market economies had jointly sought to develop a strategy for fostering financial stability in countries experiencing rapid economic growth and undergoing substantial changes in their financial systems.[6]

---

[5] "Financial Stability in Emerging Market Economies—A strategy for the formulation, adoption, and implementation of sound principles and practices to strengthen financial systems," Report of the Working Party on Financial Stability in Emerging Market Economies, April 1997; (www.bis.org/publ/gten02.htm).

[6] Representatives of Argentina, France, Germany, Hong Kong, Indonesia, Japan, Korea, Mexico, the Netherlands, Poland, Singapore, Sweden, Thailand, the United Kingdom, and the United States participated in the work, which was carried out under the chairmanship of Mario Draghi, Chairman of the Deputies of the Group of Ten. In the course of the work, representatives of these economies consulted with officials from other countries in order to take account of their views on the matters being considered. Representatives of the Basel Committee on Banking Supervision, the International Accounting Standards Committee (IASC), and the International Organization of Securities Commissions (IOSCO) and staff members of the Bank for International Settlements (BIS), the European Commission, International Monetary Fund (IMF), Organization for Economic Cooperation and Development (OECD), and the International Bank for Reconstruction and Development (World Bank) attended

(continued)

This enterprise had been prompted by the recognition that banking and financial crises can have serious repercussions for these economies in terms of heightened macroeconomic instability, reduced economic growth, and a less efficient allocation of savings and investment.

The Working Party formulated a concerted international strategy to promote the establishment, adoption, and implementation of sound principles and practices needed for financial stability. The strategy has the following major components:

- Development of an international consensus on the key elements of a sound financial and regulatory system by representatives of the G-10 and emerging market economies;

- Formulation of norms, principles, and practices by international groupings of national authorities with relevant expertise;

- Experience such as the Basel Committee, the International Association of Insurance Supervisors (IAIS), and IOSCO;

- Use of market discipline and market access channels to provide incentives for the adoption of sound supervisory systems, better corporate governance, and other key elements of a robust financial system; and

- Promotion by multilateral institutions such as the IMF, the World Bank, and the regional development banks of the adoption and implementation of sound principles and practices.

Financial stability requires sufficient political and social consensus supporting the measures needed to establish and maintain that stability. A financial system that is robust is less susceptible to the risk that a financial crisis will erupt in the wake of real economic disturbances and more resilient in the face of crises that do occur.

---

the meetings and provided crucial input. The working party also consulted with other international groupings, received contributions from a number of regional development banks, and had the benefit of market participants' views.

Although reforms are in many cases urgent, the time required for their implementation will differ considerably depending on the nature of the reform and the need for appropriate sequencing.

The working party thus established that the international community could be of assistance by developing in a consultative manner a corpus of sound principles and practices bearing on financial system robustness and supporting their adoption and implementation.

As the existing examples of standards issued by various standard setting bodies show,[7] these "high-level" recommendations by the Working Party on Financial Stability have resulted in a number of detailed initiatives, each geared toward plugging particular gaps in the global financial stability framework.

Such standards, including the Core Principles, are important as "the widespread adoption of high-quality internationally accepted standards, or codes of good practice, can make an important contribution to effective policymaking, well-functioning financial markets and a stronger international financial system."[8]

The Need to Reduce Payment System Risk

Stable and healthy payment systems are the essence of a well functioning market economy. The need for a well-founded body of principles which all countries can look to for guidance is ever more important, given the developments in payments and payment systems in particular during the past 20 years.

Probably most important is the phenomenal growth in financial market activity. Estimates compiled by the CPSS indicate that these systems transfer the equivalent of over 6 trillion U.S. dollars per day in the G-10 countries,[9] a large portion of which is related to the settlement of financial market transactions. Since financial

---

[7] *See* the Financial Stability Forum's "compendium of standards" at (www.fsforum.org, and at footnote 35).

[8] (www.fsforum.org/Standards/WhyImportant.html).

[9] Bank for International Settlements, Statistics on Payment Systems in the Group of Ten Countries, 1998.

transactions almost invariably involve some form of payment, one product of this market growth has been growth in the values that have to be handled by payment systems—many of which were originally ill equipped to handle the activity. The result: a substantial increase in risks.

This growth has occurred in terms of both the total number of individual payments and related messages as well as of the total amounts involved in payments. For instance:

- CHIPS, the New York Clearing House's net settlement system and, along with the European Central Bank's real-time gross settlement system TARGET, the system with the largest turnover, is a good example for the volumes settled in one single system, and for its cross-border impact: 87 financial institutions from 27 countries create an average daily volume of 234,000 payments valued at a total of US$1.3 trillion; its peak day, so far, was November 28, 1997, when 457,012 payments were settled, with a total value of US$22,236 trillion.[10] As regards TARGET, transnational payments within TARGET reached a daily average of 350 billion euro in July 1999.

- Within the European Union (EU) the volume of cross-border payments is bound to increase as the internal market establishes itself and develops toward full economic and monetary union,[11] in particular as the European Central Bank has urged the providers of payment services to develop an infrastructure that allows payments from one EU country to another to be made as fast and cheaply as within any given national/domestic framework.

- S.W.I.F.T. was considered very successful in 1978 when it linked about 500 banks in 16 countries and had achieved an annual traffic volume of almost 25 million financial messages. Today S.W.I.F.T. handles the same number of messages in a few weeks,

---

[10] Nelson, "Proposed changes to CHIPS," *Int'l PaySys*, London: ibc, 1999.

[11] In March 1992 the volume of retail payments below ECU 2,500 was estimated at 200 million transactions: "Payment systems in Europe," opening address by Commissioner d'Archirafi at the European Finance Convention, December 3, 1993. In the EU, the Commission typically focuses on retail payments, whereas work on large-value payment systems has been undertaken by central banks.

and its users, who now exceed 6,500 in number, are located in roughly 130 countries; traffic totalled 937 million messages in 1998.[12]

Payment systems involve many risks. The prime concern here—i.e., from the point of view of regulation—is counterparty risk. That is, credit and liquidity risks arising from the interbank exposures which exist in many payment systems.

More specifically, the concern is with counterparty risk where it is extreme enough to cause systemic risk—namely, the risk that, because of these interbank exposures in payment systems, the failure of one bank participating in a payment system will cause the failure of others.

Request from Emerging Markets

Emerging markets have themselves been requesting guidance—in the same measure as awareness of payment system risk increases, central banks worldwide have been active in reducing perceived risks. One tendency is certainly the increased introduction of real-time gross settlement (RTGS) systems.[13] RTGS is particularly important, partly because it comes as close to eliminating payment system risk as you can get and partly because it is an important platform for other system improvements—namely, mechanisms to deal with the "exchange of value" risk that occurs when settling financial market transactions.

But also netting systems have undergone constant improvements towards greater safety and towards reducing to a very large extent payment system risk.

---

[12] S.W.I.F.T.—1998 Annual Report, p. 14. As a systems operator for the private ECU Clearing and Settlement System, S.W.I.F.T. started in 1986 with 7 clearing banks and about 1,700 daily transactions (average), and terminated these services in December 1998 with 62 clearing banks and on average 7,308 daily transactions (information provided by the BIS as former Agent for the Private ECU Clearing and Settlement System, January 4, 1999).

[13] We are not aware of a list containing all existing RTGS systems, but we know of over 40 countries where RTGS systems, or systems with similar risk reduction effects, have been introduced or which are about to introduce such a system.

While the industrialized countries have led the pace in payment system reform, countries and institutions that are at the beginning or in the middle of a payment system reform process are eager to "do the right thing" and to be assured that the major investments they are putting forward will result in an own modern payment system infrastructure that is in line with agreed international best practice and yet compatible with the country's particular needs.

Making Good Use of the "Acquis"

The CPSS and previous related groups have over the years developed a rich body of analysis of relevance to payment systems,[14] the best known being probably the 1990 Report to G-10 Governors of the Committee on Interbank Netting Schemes (the Lamfalussy Report).[15] The report analysed issues affecting cross-border and multicurrency netting schemes and established minimum standards and more general goals for the design and operation of such schemes as well as principles for their cooperative oversight by central banks.

But in the context of establishing minimum standards for relevance in promoting financial stability worldwide, i.e., for establishing standards that would address any type of system of systemic relevance, the Lamfalussy standards are suitable only to a degree.

On the one hand, the Lamfalussy standards were designed for netting arrangements in large-value payment systems in a cross-border context and did not as such contemplate the new RTGS developments or entirely national systems or, for that matter, retail payment systems. Nevertheless, the standards proved to be extremely useful in assessing risk reduction measures in payment systems and the Lamfalussy standards have been accepted and applied increasingly widely, not only in the specific field for which they were

---

[14] The past work of the CPSS and related groups has included detailed analysis of payment and settlement system infrastructure in both developed and emerging economies. Although most of the earlier work has been analytical rather than prescriptive, in some areas—notably in its work on cross-border and multicurrency netting and on foreign exchange settlement risk—more specific guidelines and strategies have been developed to reduce risk, particularly systemic risk.

[15] *See* footnote 3.

developed, but also to payment, clearing, and settlement systems of many other types, even where they did not entirely "fit" the scope of the standards. The Lamfalussy standards were instrumental in encouraging designers, operators, and overseers of netting systems to consider and address risks and to achieve certain minimum standards. "Best practice," however, as one of the goals of the CPSS Core Principles, is more demanding than the minimum and an increasing number of systems have recognized the benefits of, for example, being able to withstand the failure of more than the single largest net debtor to the system.

On the other hand, the Lamfalussy standards were developed entirely in a G-10 environment, as the only potential participants in multicurrency or cross-border netting systems at the time were from G-10 countries. Even if the Lamfalussy standards are regarded as convincing and serve as a guideline for many payment systems overseers, new standards and "core principles" for payment systems required a wide consultation with as many relevant parties as feasible.

The CPSS Core Principles thus build on the existing work; they use to a large extent standards of the Lamfalussy Report, but they also extend the Lamfalussy standards in that they do not apply only to netting systems and in that a much wider circle than only G-10 central banks participated in their creation.

Who Is the Audience?

The Core Principles are directed both at public bodies as well as the private sector. On the one hand, they will be of relevance to system *operators and designers*. In many countries, the operator of a payment system will be the national central bank, but that is not necessarily the case. Designers of payment systems will also have an interest in the Core Principles as they will help the designers to avoid certain, noncompatible design features in SIPS.

The Core Principles are also directed at payment *system overseers*, mainly the central banks. The overseer will need to monitor on a regular basis the compliance of any systemically important payment system with the Core Principles. This applies both to systems that are operated by the central bank and also to systems that are operated by the private sector.[16]

Finally, the Core Principles are directed at *participants and users* of SIPS as they have a justified interest to know which minimum criteria to expect from overseers and operators of such systems. Also, the requirements, expectations, and expertise of participants and users in payment systems are an important element in the continuing dialogue between operators, overseers, and users that is essential for the success of any payment system.

The Scope of the Core Principles

"Systemically Important" Payment Systems

How does a country know which of its payment systems should comply with the Core Principles?

The consultative report sets out Core Principles for the design and operation of systemically important payment systems and defines central bank responsibilities in applying these principles. It is noteworthy that the Core Principles do not distinguish between "large-value" and "low-value" or "retail" payment systems as such, and application of the principles also does not depend on whether such systems involve a credit or debit mechanism and whether they operate electronically or involve paper-based instruments. Rather, the new term "systemically important" refers to systems that could trigger or transmit systemic disruptions in the financial area because of the size or nature of individual payments that they handle or because of the aggregate value of the payments processed. In practice the boundary between payment systems that are systemically important and those that are not will not always be clear-cut and the central bank will need to consider carefully where that boundary should be drawn.

It should be noted that it is well possible that a given country may not have a systemically important payment system. But even for

---

[16] *See* Annex I, "Responsibilities of the Central Bank in Applying the Core Principles."

payment systems that are not "systemically important," the principles may also be useful in assessing and understanding the characteristics of systems which pose relatively little systemic risk and it may be desirable for such systems to comply with some or all of the principles.

Universal Coverage

The Core Principles are not a set of rules that are addressed only to developed countries nor only to certain regions of the world. Rather, they are geared toward SIPS in all countries. At the same time, the principles do not propagate a certain type of system, nor do they propagate a given system of a particular country, as being the one model other countries should follow.

They are thus a general framework giving payment system overseers and other relevant institutions a guideline, and some minimum standards, for the design, operation, and oversight of payment systems.

Not Addressed to Securities Systems

The focus of the Core Principles is on *payment systems*, that is, systems that provide for the transfer of funds. The most direct application is for systems which involve only funds transfers, but the principles can also apply to the payments aspects of systemically important systems in which transfers of other financial assets, such as securities, and related transfers of funds are both settled. Such systems can raise financial stability issues in their own right, so the report states that it is important too that their overall design and operation should be safe and efficient.

The Core Principles may also provide some help in evaluating the arrangements for settling other types of financial assets, such as securities settlement systems, but a full consideration lies outside the scope of the Core Principles report.

Rather, CPSS and IOSCO have embarked on a project to examine the specific issues involved in securities settlement and to draft recommendations for such systems.[17]

The Requirement of a Well-Founded Legal Basis

As mentioned above, the Core Principles retain the essential elements of the Lamfalussy principles, as they are of relevance to SIPS.

In particular Principle I, *"The system should have a well-founded legal basis under all relevant jurisdictions,"* is identical to Principle I, taken from the Lamfalussy Report.[18]

When looking at the Core Principles, one will notice that not only Principle I has legal implications. In fact, a number of principles have legal implications and will require particular attention when implemented in a national environment:

- Well-founded legal basis under all relevant jurisdictions (I).

- Clear rules and procedures on the system's impact on financial risks incurred through participation (II).

- Clear rules and procedures on management of credit risks and liquidity risks (III).

- Prompt final settlement on the day of value (IV).

- High degree of security and operational reliability (VII).

---

[17] The objective of this project is to promote the implementation by securities settlement systems of measures that can reduce risks, increase efficiency, and provide adequate safeguards for investors by developing recommendations for the design, operation, and oversight of such systems. The recommendations will cover both individual systems and the cross-border linkages between systems. To this end, the two committees have set up a joint task force on securities settlement systems, comprising about 20 central banks and securities regulators, in addition to the co-chairmen, from both industrialized and emerging market economies. A first international consultative meeting with more than 50 public institutions was held at the BIS on January 19, 2000.

[18] *See* Annex II.

- Access criteria (IX).

- Governance (X).

The legal basis for a payment system is critical to its overall soundness. The term "legal basis" as such does not mean that a specific law is required that will address payment system issues or, in the context of the Core Principles, systemically important payment systems.

The foremost goal of a sound legal basis is to achieve predictability for all parties that participate in a given system. The parties therefore need to know their obligations and liabilities to a degree that they can reasonably predict the outcome of a regular transaction, and also the risks they incur in the event of a disruption of the system itself or of a failure of another participant in the system. Since most risk management systems ultimately must make assumptions about the rights and obligations of parties to payment transactions, the analysis of risk management systems almost always leads back to questions about the soundness of legal assumptions.

The "legal basis" typically consists of framework legislation as well as specific laws, regulations, and agreements governing payments and the operation of the system, and of course any binding court decisions that need to be taken into account. Framework legislation will be legislation that is of relevance to payment systems, even if not specifically addresses payment systems. Examples of framework legislation include public law rules that cannot be altered by agreement (e.g., insolvency law, public law of banking, or in some cases also competition and consumer protection laws), or general legislation whose rules may apply in the absence of particular agreements between the parties to a contract. Specific laws governing the central bank, payments including electronic payments, payment finality, payment netting, and related topics are especially relevant. In addition, laws from countries other than the host country may be relevant to the robustness of the system, where their effects can be identified.

The drafters of the Core Principles were well aware of the legal complexities and of the differences in the various national legal frameworks. Although sound legal underpinnings are very important, absolute legal certainty is seldom achievable. Recognition of this fact, however, should not deter payment system operators, participants, and authorities from seeking to establish a sound legal basis for payment systems.

In this context, a number of important elements of the "legal basis" can be identified.

(a) *Finality*: It is particularly important to establish the timing of final settlement of payments made through the system in order to define when key financial risks are transferred in a payment system and to provide an important building block for risk management systems.

(b) *Insolvency law*: Insolvency law is very relevant, as system designers and relevant authorities must ask themselves what would happen if a participant in the system were to become insolvent. Would transactions be honored as final, or could they be considered void or voidable by liquidators and relevant authorities? In some countries, for example, so-called "zero-hour rules"[19] may cause payments not to be final even if they appear to have been settled in a payment system (even in a real-time gross settlement system) prior to the insolvency of a participant on the day of value.

Furthermore, insolvency statutes may not yet recognize the netted value of payments or related obligations as binding on the liquidator in the event of insolvency. For example, it can be relevant to consider whether a liquidator might be able to successfully challenge the netted value of payments in a payment system involving net settlement. In such cases, it is not safe to rely on netted amounts for credit or liquidity risk management purposes.

---

[19] When applied in the context of a payment system, "zero-hour rules" make all transactions by the bankrupt participant null from the start ("zero hour") of the day of the bankruptcy (or similar event). In the case of a system with deferred net settlement, such a clause could cause the netting of all transactions to be unwound. This would entail a recalculation of all net positions and could cause significant changes to participants' balances, with possible systemic consequences. In a real-time gross settlement system, the effect could be to reverse payments regarding the bankrupt participant that have apparently already been settled and were thought to be final.

In particular, following the analysis undertaken for the Lamfalussy Report, a number of countries have therefore undertaken programs of legal change years to strengthen greatly the legal underpinnings of netting and to remove the risk of adverse effects from "zero-hour rules," particularly on systemically important payment systems.[20]

(c) *Collateral and rights in rem*: The law of secured interests (whereby, for example, collateral can be accepted as security for lending)[21] may also be highly relevant to the design of risk management systems for payment systems. For example, many central banks provide credit to participants in a payment system subject to some type of collateralization agreement. Many privately operated netting systems adopt collateralization mechanisms to back up lending facilities to help ensure settlement in the event of initial failures to settle. The law of secured interests is typically the foundation of the collateralization or security agreement, and must be scrutinized carefully to ensure that a security agreement will be enforceable in a timely manner as envisaged.

(d) *Technological neutrality*: As a general principle, it is desirable for laws not to differ in their effect according to the type or level of technology used in a payment system. Where electronic processing is

---

[20] *See*, for instance, the EU Settlement Finality Directive, which obliges EU countries to remove "zero-hour rules" and to uphold certain netting and collateral arrangements also in the event of the insolvency of payment system participants: Directive 98/26/EC of the European Parliament and of the Council of May 19, 1998 on settlement finality in payment and securities settlement systems—*Official Journal L 166. 11/06/1998 p. 0045–0050*; Devos, "Specific cross-border problems regarding bank insolvencies and European harmonization efforts," in Giovanoli/Heinrich (ed.), *International Bank Insolvencies: A central bank perspective,* London: Kluwerlaw International, 1999, pp. 311–36. On the issues in general, *see*, for instance, Giovanoli, "Legal issues regarding payment and netting systems," in: *Cross-border electronic banking—Challenges and opportunities,* (ed. by J. Norton), London: Lloyd's of London, 1995, pp. 205–31; Le Guen, "Netting and legal protection for interbank settlement systems," *Banque de France Bulletin Digest*, No.10, Oct. 1994, pp. 33–44.

[21] A collateral transaction is typically subject to three main bodies of law: the law of secured interests, insolvency law, and contract law. The main areas of concern are the conditions under which a pledge or repo will be valid and also the procedures that have to be followed if the transferor defaults and the collateral has to be realized by the transferee. However, the most likely reason for a default by the transferor is insolvency, and thus the realization of the collateral is also likely to be directly affected by the relevant *insolvency law*.

involved, or whether the underlying instruments the system handles are electronic or paper-based, it will be necessary to ensure that the relevant law (particularly where it is not very modern) is compatible with the methods used. New legislation might indeed be needed to achieve clarity and predictability of interpretation if the existing legal system is too restrictive and/or does not allow for the parties to agree on relevant issues by contract.[22]

(e) *Public law of banking*: Banking and central banking laws can play an important role. Banks and central banks may need authority in law to establish and participate in payment systems and to design effective and well-managed systems, including adopting sound risk management principles.[23]

(f) *Foreign law*: Laws from outside the domestic jurisdiction can be relevant where there is a cross-border element to the system. At one extreme this is particularly the case where a system provides a cross-border service. The laws of the participants' home jurisdictions are likely to be relevant, as well as the laws of the jurisdiction under which the system operates. Many laws are potentially relevant, but of particular importance will be insolvency laws in the different jurisdictions. It may be relevant to consider whether, in the event of a foreign participant's insolvency, the insolvency procedure in the foreign country will have a direct effect in the country where the payment system is located or whether the foreign liquidator might be

---

[22] *See* UNCITRAL Model Law on Electronic Commerce/Loi type sur le commerce électronique, June 14, 1996, (www.uncitral.org/english/texts/electcom/ml-ec.htm). Also, even though not directly applicable to payment systems as such, the standard contractual arrangements contained in the S.W.I.F.T. handbook or the model standard contract between two or more trading partners developed by the United Nations and the European Union, respectively, may be of interest: United Nations Economic and Social Council (ECE), Model Interchange Agreement for the International Commercial Use of Electronic Data Interchange, of September 20, 1995, ECE Recommendation No. 26, adopted by the Working Party on Facilitation of International Trade Procedure in March 1995, UN DOC. TRADE/WP.4/R.1133/Rev.1, June 23, 1995; Bertrand, "EDI—The final draft of the European Interchange Agreement," *Int'l Computer Law Adviser* 5 (1991) 4–15.

[23] *See* Banca d'Italia, White paper on payment system oversight: Objectives, methods, areas of interest, Rome, November 1999.

able successfully to challenge the netted value of payments in a national payment system.[24]

Furthermore, foreign law may need to be considered when evaluating the validity of any collateral agreement in a cross-border context.

There have been a number of regional and international initiatives to reduce the risks of legal uncertainties or conflict. These include various European Union directives, such as the Settlement Finality Directive,[25] aimed in particular at setting legal certainty for operations with the TARGET system, the United States' Uniform Commercial Code[26] (on which the New York Commercial Code is based and which is of relevance for the CHIPS system) and the UNCITRAL Model Law on Cross-Border Insolvency.[27]

---

[24] *See* Giovanoli/Heinrich (ed.), *International Bank Insolvencies: A central bank perspective*, London: Kluwerlaw International, 1999.

[25] *Supra* footnote 20.

[26] The New York Commercial Code follows—in its articles relevant to payment systems—Article 4A of the Uniform Commercial Code. The relevant section in the New York State Uniform Commercial Code Article 4-A [N.Y. U.C.C. § 4-A-403(2)], practically identical in every U.S. state, reads: "Section 4-A-403. Payment by Sender to Receiving Bank. (1) ....; (2) If the sender and receiving bank are members of a funds-transfer system that nets obligations multilaterally among participants, the receiving bank receives final settlement when settlement is complete in accordance with the rules of the system. The obligation of the sender to pay the amount of a payment order transmitted through the funds-transfer system may be satisfied, to the extent permitted by the rules of the system, by setting off and applying against the sender's obligation the right of the sender to receive payment from the receiving bank of the amount of any other payment order transmitted to the sender by the receiving bank through the funds-transfer system. The aggregate balance of obligations owed by each sender to each receiving bank in the funds-transfer system may be satisfied, to the extent permitted by the rules of the system, by setting off and applying against that balance the aggregate balance of obligations owed to the sender by other members of the system. The aggregate balance is determined after the right of setoff stated in the second sentence of this subsection has been exercised" (http://assembly. state.ny.us/cgi-bin/claws?law=122&art=38). Also note the general deference within the law to funds transfer system rules contained in Article 4-A-501: Section 4-A-501. Variation by Agreement and Effect of Funds—Transfer System Rule (http://assembly.state.ny.us/cgi-bin/claws?law=122&art=39).

[27] Although not geared at specific issues related to payment systems. *See* UNCITRAL Model Law on Cross-Border Insolvency/Loi-type sur l'insolvabilité transnationale, of May 30, 1997; UNCITRAL, Official Records of the General

(continued)

As regards the law for security interests in goods, an international convention unifying substantive rules governing security interests appears does not appear to be feasible, in particular in view of the wide divergences existing among legal systems and the complexity of the issues involved in secured credit law; however, a number of international bodies are working at harmonizing applicable rules—at least for certain types of commercial transactions.[28]

What Are the New Principles?

Principle IV, requiring at least same-day settlement, preferably intraday:

> The system should provide prompt final settlement on the day of value, preferably during the day and at a minimum at the end of the day.

This principle is one of two that stipulates a *minimum standard*, i.e., it establishes a measurable threshold that a given system will either achieve or not achieve.

Principle IV relates to daily settlement in normal circumstances. Between the time when payments are accepted for settlement by the payment system (including satisfaction of any relevant risk management tests, such as the application of limits on exposures or availability of liquidity) and the time when final settlement actually occurs, participants may still face credit and liquidity risks. These risks are exacerbated if they extend overnight, in part because a likely time for the relevant authorities to close insolvent institutions is between business days. Prompt final settlement helps to reduce these

---

Assembly, Fifty-second Session, Supplement No. 17 (A/52/17, annex I) (UNCITRAL Yearbook, vol. XXVIII: 1997, part three); *Idem, Guide to Enactment of the UNCITRAL Model Law on Cross-Border Insolvency*" (A/CN.9/442). The Model Law and Guide to Enactment are also available at http://www.uncitral.org/english/texts/insolven/ml+guide.htm; Sekolec, "The UNCITRAL Model Law on Cross-Border Insolvency," in Giovanoli/Heinrich, *supra* footnote 24.

[28] For an overview of initiatives at both government and nongovernment level, see United Nations/UNCITRAL, "Security interests—Current activities and possible future work. Report of the Secretary-General," Doc. A/CN.9/475, April 27, 2000.

risks. As a minimum standard, final settlement should occur at the end of the day of value.

The Core Principles do not recommend a particular type of system that would fulfill this minimum standard, and in particular, they do not explicitly recommend the introduction of RTGS systems, as the desired goal may be achieved by several different system designs that are not necessarily "RTGS."

Nevertheless, the Core Principles report emphasizes that in most countries it should be a goal for at least one payment system to exceed this minimum standard by providing real-time final settlement during the day.[29] This is particularly desirable in countries with large volumes of high-value payments and sophisticated financial markets.

Principle VI, calling for safe settlement assets, preferably claims on a central bank or otherwise assets that pose little or no credit risk:

> Assets used for settlement should preferably be a claim on the central bank; where other assets are used, they should carry little or no credit risk.

Most systems involve the transfer of an asset among system participants to settle payment obligations. Most systemically important payment systems settle across the books of a central bank, as the most common and preferable form of a settlement an asset is an account balance at the central bank, representing a claim on the central bank.[30] In contrast, settlement via an account at a commercial financial institution always involves the credit and liquidity risk relating to the solvency of that institution.[31] When that central bank is the central bank of issue for the currency used by the payment system,

---

[29] Core principles report, at Principle IV, 2.

[30] *See* Giovanoli, "Bargeld-Buchgeld-Zentralbankgeld: Einheit oder Vielfalt im Geldbegriff?," in: *Banken und Bankrecht im Wandel* (Festschrift Beat Kleiner), Zürich: Schulthess, 1993, 87–123 (121).

[31] Credit risk: the risk that a party within the system will be unable to fully meet its financial oblications within the system currently or at any time in the future. Liquidity risk: the risk that a party within the system will have insufficient funds to meet financial obligations within the system as and when expected, although it may be able to do so at some time in the future.

there is no credit risk for the payment system participant holding that balance, and the liquidity risk to the system and its participants is also virtually nonexistent. Such central bank balances are therefore the most satisfactory settlement assets.

There are, however, examples of other forms of settlement asset, representing claims on other supervised institutions, as exemplified in the account with a commercial bank. If settlement is completed using such assets, the Core Principles require that the assets must pose little or no credit risk. The Task Force's latest thinking is that account should also be taken of whether such an asset involves significant liquidity risk.

As all participants in the system must accept the asset, the system's safety depends in part on whether the asset leaves the holder with significant credit risk. If there were more than a negligible risk that the issuer of the asset could fail, the system could face a crisis of confidence, which would create systemic risk.

Principle VII, stipulating that a SIPS needs to be practical for users, efficient for the economy:

> The system should provide a means of making payments which is practical for its users and efficient for the economy.

Operators, users (that is participants, such as banks and their customers), and overseers of systems all have an interest in the efficiency of a system. "Efficiency" is a however a very commonly used term—not just in payment systems. In the context of payment systems, the term relates to achieving an acceptable level of safety and service at the minimum cost. There will typically be a trade-off between minimizing resource costs and other objectives, such as maximizing safety. It may be conceivable to design a system that is absolutely risk free in a given environment, but the cost may be so high that noone uses it. This may be an issue in any environment where several payment systems compete with each other or where a system design that was suitable for one country was introduced into another without taking account of the country's specific factors such as geography, its population distribution, and its infrastructure.

The costs of providing payment services will depend on the quality of service and the features demanded by users, and on the need for the system to meet the Core Principles limiting risk in the system. A system which is consistent with the demands of the markets it serves is likely to be more heavily used and so will spread more widely the risk-reducing benefits of satisfying the other principles and the costs of providing the services.

But a given system that is efficient today may not be so tomorrow. Systems should therefore be designed and operated so that they can adapt to the development of the market for payment services both domestically and internationally. Their technical, business, and governance arrangements should be sufficiently flexible to respond to changing demands, for example, in adopting new technologies and procedures.

The report discusses these concepts in more detail, and sets out an analytical framework for system design. This should encompass:

- the identification of efficiency requirements;

- the evaluation of costs (social and private, including not only those that are passed on to participants directly through system charges but also indirect costs, such as cost of liquidity and collateral);

- the determination of technological and infrastructure constraints (e.g., telecommunications, energy availability, transportation, and banking structure); and

- the definition of the safety constraints imposed by the core principles.

Principle X, requiring effective, accountable, and transparent governance arrangements:

The system's governance arrangements should be effective, accountable, and transparent.

Payment system governance arrangements[32] encompass the set of relationships between the payment system's management and its governing body (such as a board of directors), its owners, and its other stakeholders. These arrangements provide the structure through which the system's overall objectives are set, how they are attained, and how performance is monitored.

Effective governance provides proper incentives for management to pursue objectives that are in the interests of the system, its participants, and the public more generally. It also ensures that management has the appropriate tools and abilities to achieve the system's objectives. Governance arrangements should provide accountability to owners (for example, to the shareholders of a private sector system) and, because of the system's systemic importance, to the wider financial community, so that those served by the payment system can influence its overall objectives and performance.

An essential aspect of achieving accountability is to ensure that governance arrangements are transparent, so that all affected parties have access to information about decisions affecting the system and how they are taken.[33]

Because systemically important payment systems have the potential to affect the wider financial and economic community, there is a particular need for effective, accountable, and transparent governance, whether the system is owned and operated by the central bank or by the private sector. And good governance provides the foundation for compliance with the Core Principles as a whole.

Principles A–D, spelling out the responsibilities of central banks in applying the core principles:

Different aspects of the safety and efficiency objectives for SIPS may be pursued by a variety of different public sector agencies. Central banks have a leading role, particularly because of their strong

---

[32] For banking institutions, *see*, for instance, Basel Committee on Banking Supervision, *Enhancing corporate governance in banking organisations*, September 1999 (www.bis.org/publ/bcbs56.htm).

[33] *See* IMF Code of Good Practices on Transparency in Monetary and Financial Policies, September 26, 1999 (www.imf.org/external/np/mae/mft/code/index.htm).

interest in financial stability, their role in providing settlement accounts for payment system participants, and their concerns with the functioning of money markets for the implementation of monetary policy and with maintaining confidence in the domestic currency both in normal circumstances and in a crisis. The expertise they have developed through carrying out these functions means that central banks have a leading role to play in respect of SIPS. In many cases they have been given explicit responsibilities in this area, e.g., in central bank legislation, or their role is part of an undisputed tradition. Most central banks now recognize the oversight of systemically important payment systems as a core function, contributing to financial stability and complementing the implementation of monetary policy.

The four central bank responsibilities in applying the Core Principles to SIPS[34] stem from this leading role. A distinction is drawn (in Responsibilities B and C) between those systemically important payment systems which are operated by the central bank and those which are not. The central bank has different responsibilities in these two cases but, in both cases, the central bank's objectives are safety and efficiency and the obligation to see that the Core Principles are applied.

Implementation

Finally, the question arises how the Core Principles should be implemented, and who will enforce implementation.

As an international standard of best practices, the Core Principles are intended to be applied. They are part of the "Compendium of Standards" compiled the by the Financial Stability Forum (FSF).[35]

---

[34] *See* Annex I.
[35] This compendium provides a common reference for the various economic and financial standards that are internationally accepted as relevant to sound, stable, and well-functioning financial systems. As the compendium is posted on the FSF's website (http://www.fsforum.org), it serves as a gateway or point of entry for financial authorities and market participants to access the sites where the complete standards, supporting documents, and assessment methodologies referenced in the standards are located. The compendium aims to signal the importance attached by the international community to the implementation of these standards and sound
(continued)

However, there is no absolute "recipe" how a country should go forward in applying the principles, nor is there an absolute method how the international community will see to it that the Core Principles are respected.

As any document or recommendation produced under the auspices of the BIS, the Core Principles do not have the power of law; at best they are "soft law."[36] As the BIS and the CPSS have no regulatory powers, any guidance has to be of high quality in order to be relevant. The Core Principles—like other work of the CPSS—have to be relevant and useful in helping designers, operators, and overseers of payment systems decide what to do.

However, other international financial institutions like the IMF and the World Bank can and do encourage, within their mandate, adoption and implementation of such guidance as part of the assistance they provide.

This shows two facets of implementation of the Core Principles: the "pull" and the "push" method. In the first instance, the countries that will apply the principles will want to do so entirely on their own motivation, because they find the principles convincing and because they want to be part of the international consensus that was achieved. In the second instance, implementation may be seen as occurring through "pushing," as the World Bank and the IMF will use the principles in financial sector assessments or in technical assistance programs aiding those institutions that wish to bring their systemically important payment systems to the level recommended in

---

practices, and facilitate the dissemination of information on them. An FSF document listing ongoing and recent work relevant to sound financial systems is available at http://www.fsforum.org/Reports/RepORW.html. At an FSAP follow-up meeting held in spring 2001, the IMF and World Bank also recognize the Core Principles as being one of 11 key standard areas, together with the CPSS/IOSCO recommendations for Securities Settlement Systems (Consultative Report, January 2001, http://www.bis.org/cpss).

[36] *See* Giovanoli, "A new architecture for the global financial market: Legal aspects of international financial standard setting," in: Mario Giovanoli (ed), *International Monetary Law—Issues for the New Millennium*, Oxford, 2000, pp. 3–60.

the Core Principles and call on these institutions for guidance and assistance.

For instance, IMF staff, in conjunction with the relevant authorities of the respective countries, has embarked on a series of experimental "Reports on the Observance of Standards and Codes" (ROSC).[37] These reports summarize the extent to which countries observe certain internationally recognized standards, focusing primarily on the areas of direct operational concern to the IMF.[38]

In practice, the "pull" and "push" approaches will need to be distinguished, even though they will necessarily influence each other. In the context of the international community's desire to strengthen financial stability, the Core Principles are one of many existing standards. Therefore, a prioritization of standards will be necessary, and such prioritization will necessarily vary from economy to economy, taking into consideration their current legal and institutional framework, their status in observance of standards, economic circumstances, financial structures, and policy priorities. As concerns the Core Principles, a balance would also need to be struck between national and domestic considerations, which could be achieved through national authorities working closely with the international financial institutions (such as the BIS, the IMF, or the World Bank) and standard-setting bodies, such as the CPSS.

In the context of a particular country's—or central bank's—desire to implement the Core Principles, this can of course be accomplished independently of the other international standards that are not related to payment and settlement systems. Also in such event it should be recalled that the Core Principles do not propagate any particular model. In particular Principle VIII comes into play here as it specifically mentions that a system should be "practical for its users

---

[37] At their inaugural meeting in Berlin on December 16, 1999, the Group of Twenty Finance Ministers and Central Bank Governors agreed to undertake the completion of the "Reports on Observance of Standards and Codes" (ROSC) and of the "Financial Sector Assessments" (FASP)—both elaborated jointly by the IMF and the World Bank—within the context of continuing these efforts. Similarly, Western Hemisphere Finance Ministers have encouraged their members to participate in FSAPs and have agreed to participate in ROSCs.

[38] Access to country reports and general information on ROSCs is available at http://www.imf.org/external/np/rosc/index.htm.

and efficient for the economy." In some countries this will require thorough analysis of the needs, possibilities, and also limitations of the payment system participants and the economy as a whole, and may also require the building of particular payment system expertise.

In this, cooperation is of essence. Cooperation does not mean copying what the neighbor has done, and it also does not mean following blindly the advice of experts and consultants. In implementing the Core Principles, a multifaceted approach is desirable, like in any major project.

In some central banks, specialized offices or teams have taken on the task of bringing forward a country's payment system reform project.[39] In others, those responsible for payment system oversight have been grouped into a special division in the central bank, separate from the department that is responsible for the operations, or even, a special authority may be created, with certain own regulatory powers and an own annual report.[40]

Within the institution, or among institutions, it is important that all relevant experts, economic analysts, technicians, and lawyers cooperate from the outset of a project. As experience has often shown, it would be a mistake to bring in lawyers only at the end of a project, shortly before planned implementation of a new system; likewise it would be a mistake if only technicians, accountants, and information technology experts worked together without consulting the economists on issues such as the cost of collateral, expected participation, pricing, etc. This may require that the lawyers gain more knowledge of the concerns of payment system experts. And, as Principle I of the Core Principles shows, the payment systems experts need to be aware of the importance of legal issues and need to be aware of the solutions that the lawyers can find in order to achieve a "well-founded legal basis." On a national level, it will be beneficial that the authorities that are taking the lead in a payment system reform project—most likely the central bank—engage from the outset in a dialogue with the anticipated users of the systems—the banking

---

[39] *E.g.*, at the central banks of Peru and Brazil, at the BCEAO in Dakar, or at Bank Indonesia (National Payment System Development Bureau).
[40] *E.g.*, for Australia Payment Systems Board, *Annual Report,* Sydney: Reserve Bank of Australia, 1999.

community. Again, we know from anecdotal evidence that this is not always the case.

Conclusion: The Need for Continued Cooperation

Finally, on an international level, it is important that payment system experts work together. The Core Principles are after all a good example for such cooperation. It is important that payment system experts in the central banks know all the arguments, concerns, and solutions to concerns that the colleagues have found. After all, payment system overseers need to convince: they have hardly any regulatory or executory powers, as opposed to bank supervisors, and any good argument can help in their task. Some central banks that have identified a common goal or where there are common regional interests have created more or less formal groups of experts, like the CPSS, or the Group of Payment System Experts of the EMEAP (Executives' Meeting of East Asia and Pacific Central Banks) countries, or the group of payment system experts from the central banks/monetary authorities of the Gulf Cooperating Council (GCC).[41]

Where no formal arrangement exists, experts may meet in special events, such as workshops or roundtables organized, for instance by the CPSS in cooperation with local or regional institutions, or by the IMF and the World Bank (and the current event is a very good example of an expert meeting—for lawyers—organized by the IMF). Also the contribution of private or commercial initiatives,[42] and of more nationally oriented assistance and training programs,[43] to the discussion and dissemination of payment system expertise should not be neglected.

---

[41] Similar central bank initiatives are under way for some Eastern European ountries that have applied for accession to the European Union, and for countries of the Black Sea Group. In addition, regional political cooperation may include cooperation in the payment systems area, e.g., the PSSC (Payment and Settlement Systems Committee) within the ESCB, between the ECB and the candidates for accession to the EU, among central banks of the South African Development Community (SADC), or among the member countries of the Western African Monetary Union and the BCEAO as their central bank.

[42] *E.g.*, commercial seminars and workshops, S.W.I.F.T.'s annual SIBOS event, etc.

[43] *E.g.*, the U.S. "Financial Services Volunteer Corps," or programs organized by individual central banks.

I personally hope that the good cooperation between CPSS, IMF, and the World Bank, as shown in the elaboration of the CPSS Core Principles, will continue also when the principles are finalized and have become part of a living body of internationally accepted standards.

Annex 1: The Core Principles and Central Bank Responsibilities

Public Policy Objectives: Safety and Efficiency in Systemically Important Payment Systems

Core Principles for systemically important payment systems

The system should have a well-founded legal basis under all relevant jurisdictions.[44]

The system's rules and procedures should enable participants to have a clear understanding of the system's impact on each of the financial risks they incur through participation in it.

The system should have clearly defined procedures for the management of credit risks and liquidity risks, which specify the respective responsibilities of the system operator and the participants and which provide appropriate incentives to manage and contain those risks.

*The system should provide prompt final settlement on the day of value, preferably during the day and at a minimum at the end of the day.

*A system in which multilateral netting takes place should, at a minimum, be capable of ensuring the timely completion of daily settlements in the event of an inability to settle by the participant with the largest single settlement obligation.

Assets used for settlement should preferably be a claim on the central

---

[44] Committee on Payment and Settlement Systems, Bank for International Settlements, *Core Principles for Systemically Important Payment Systems*, Report of the Task Force on Payment System Principles and Practices.

bank; where other assets are used, they should carry little or no credit risk.

The system should ensure a high degree of security and operational reliability and should have contingency arrangements for timely completion of daily processing.

The system should provide a means of making payments that is practical for its users and efficient for the economy.

The system should have objective and publicly disclosed criteria for participation, which permit fair and open access.

The system's governance arrangements should be effective, accountable and transparent.

* Systems should seek to exceed the minima included in these two principles.

Responsibilities of the central bank in applying the Core Principles

The central bank should define clearly its payment system objectives and should disclose publicly its role and major policies with respect to systemically important payment systems.

The central bank should ensure that the systems it operates comply with the Core Principles.

The central bank should oversee compliance with the Core Principles by systems it does not operate and it should have the ability to carry out this oversight.

The central bank, in promoting payment system safety and efficiency through the Core Principles, should cooperate with other central banks and with any other relevant domestic or foreign authorities.

Annex 2: The "Lamfalussy Standards"

The Lamfalussy standards relating to netting schemes[45] are:

Netting schemes should have a well-founded legal basis under all relevant jurisdictions.

Netting scheme participants should have a clear understanding of the impact of the particular scheme on each of the financial risks affected by the netting process.

Multilateral netting systems should have clearly defined procedures for the management of credit risks and liquidity risks which specify the respective responsibilities of the netting provider and the participants. These procedures should also ensure that all parties have both the incentives and the capabilities to manage and contain each of the risks they bear and that limits are placed on the maximum level of credit exposure that can be produced by each participant.

Multilateral netting systems should, at a minimum, be capable of ensuring the timely completion of daily settlements in the event of an inability to settle by the participant with the largest net-debit position.

Multilateral netting systems should have objective and publicly disclosed criteria for admission which permit fair and open access.

All netting systems should ensure the operational reliability of technical systems and the availability of backup facilities capable of completing daily processing requirements.

---

[45] *Supra* footnote 3.

Annex 3: Members of the Task Force on Payment System Principles and Practices

Chairman: John Trundle (Bank of England)
Reserve Bank of Australia
National Bank of Belgium
Banco Central do Brasil
Bank of Canada
European Central Bank
Banque de France
Deutsche Bundesbank
Hong Kong Monetary Authority
National Bank of Hungary
Banca d'Italia
Bank of Japan
Bank Negara Malaysia
Banco de Mexico
Nederlandsche Bank
Central Bank of Russian Federation
Saudi Arabian Monetary Authority
Monetary Authority of Singapore
Federal Reserve Bank of New York
South African Reserve Bank
Sveriges Riksbank
Bank of England
Board of Governors of the Federal Reserve System
Central Bank of West Africa (BCEAO)
International Monetary Fund
World Bank
Bank for International Settlements (Secretariat)

Chapter 36

Institutional Framework and Implementation of the Core Principles for Systemically Important Payment Systems

OMOTUNDE E.G. JOHNSON

A payment system can be viewed as a set of instruments and means generally acceptable in making payments; the institutional and organizational framework governing such payments; and the operating procedures and communications network used to initiate and transmit payment information from payer to payee and to settle payments. Payment systems facilitate the exchange of goods and services between economic agents using some accepted medium of exchange (money). A modern domestic payment system typically has a range of specialized subsystems developed to serve particular sets of customers; some of these clear and settle small (retail) payments, some large (and time-critical) payments, while some cover both large and retail payments.

The manner in which the payment system works affects the financial sector as a whole: it influences the speed, financial risk, efficiency, and reliability of domestic and international transactions. Indeed, the payment system, among other things, can act as a conduit through which financial and nonfinancial firms and other agents affect overall financial system stability. The payment system also influences the effectiveness of monetary policy, inter alia via its impact on the transmission process in monetary management, the pace of financial deepening, and the efficiency of financial intermediation. Thus, monetary and financial sector authorities have typically been active in promoting sound and efficient payment systems and in seeking means to reduce related systemic risks.

It is against this background that the core principles for systemically important payment systems (CPSIPS) have been

---

Note: The author would like to thank May Khamis for comments on an earlier draft of the paper.

formulated.[1] These principles reflect consensus in payment system policy that has emerged over the last two or so decades. The public policy objectives specifically mentioned in stating the core principles are *safety* and *efficiency* in systemically important payment systems. From this perspective, the underlying message is that if every systemically important payment system satisfies the core principles, and if all payment systems (whether systemically important or not) are efficient, have good governance arrangements, and do not engender liquidity shocks that make difficult the achievement of the main monetary policy objective of long-run price stability, then the payment system as a whole will contribute to the soundness and stability of the financial system.

Six of the ten core principles are essentially the six so-called *Lamfalussy standards*.[2] The new principles are those relating to prompt settlement, the settlement asset, efficiency, and governance arrangements (namely, Principles IV, VI, VIII, and X). In addition, there are four principles dealing with the responsibilities of the central bank in applying the core principles.

Once the core principles are agreed, the next step would be for countries and systems to implement them. First and foremost, a country (and its systemically important system(s)) must be *willing and able* to implement the principles, however interpreted. As it attempts to do so in a resolute manner, a country (or system) must understand *what* to implement, which depends on its interpretation of the principles, and *how* to implement, which depends on a whole host of circumstances in which the country (or system) finds itself. Implementation will be via policies, practices, and procedures involving rules, and organizational, human, and physical resources.

This paper addresses selected issues in the institutional economics of implementing the core principles. The discussion is organized around three basic pillars: (1) risk control, (2) efficiency, and (3) governance. Of particular interest and focus are issues related to the willingness to implement, what to implement, and optimal rule making. In the first section, it is argued that as apparent norms with

---

[1] *See* Annex 1 in preceding chapter and BIS (1999).
[2] *See* Annex 2 in preceding chapter and BIS (1990), p. 26.

international legitimacy, countries will voluntarily try to implement the CPSIPS. Nevertheless, there could be significant differences among countries in the understanding of *what* to implement, which should be of much greater concern than differences in their understanding of *how* to implement, since a consensus on the latter is not really necessary and may not be possible for aspects of all the principles. It is, nevertheless, argued that certain basic economic principles could serve well the process of rule making (or legislation) for implementing the core principles whatever the particular circumstances of a country.

The next two sections bring out the tensions that could arise in trying to determine what to implement, due to the fact that, strictly speaking, the CPSIPS focus on particular systems, whereas the public policy perspective calls for a focus on the payment system as a whole and its place in monetary and financial sector policies as well as on the welfare of the society as a whole. The second section argues that although members of a systemically important payment system are required in the core principles to understand and manage legal, financial, and other risks, *given* the legal, economic, and financial environment in which the system operates, from a public policy perspective, the environment is not a given. Hence, in implementing the core principles, not only must systemically important payment systems (SIPS) be continuously evaluated, so also must the environment in which they operate. The third section discusses the efficiency concept, namely economic efficiency, that should really guide implementation of Principle VIII, from a public policy perspective. The next section discusses the meaning of Principle X on governance arrangements and argues that it implicitly assumes that those qualities of governance arrangements listed in the principle will be sufficient, other things being equal, to ensure that the objectives of the system are met. Finally, the last section contains concluding remarks.

The Institutional Economics of Implementing the Core Principles

As stated before, the core principles for systemically important payment systems (CPSIPS) reflect consensus that has emerged in major areas of payment system policy. Yet it is not realistic to expect the same kind of consensus on specific and detailed guidelines for implementation of the principles. This reflects the variety of country circumstances: for instance, countries' existing systems and the path taken in getting to them; the sophistication of financial markets; the state of technology and telecommunication systems; budgetary constraints; the likely evolution of demand for different payment services over some reasonable time horizon; and the legitimate political, economic, and legal institutions consistent with the fundamental values of their respective citizens.

The Core Principles as Legitimated Norms

The core principles for systemically important payment systems could be seen as broad norms that have been legitimated by the international community of market economies.[3] In other words, they have evolved from experience and widely accepted theory; have been arrived at by agreement (via discussion among free agents); are intended to regulate and coordinate interactions of individual agents (within payment systems); and are expected to be implemented by national authorities, without a central world authority, because such implementation of the principles is in the self-interest of the countries. At the same time, violation of the norms by a country is expected to invite costly punishment by other members of the community of nations—in this case, especially in the form of restrictions on the participation of other nations' financial organizations in the payment systems of the violating country.

An important hypothesis of the *theory and experience* which have motivated the core principles is that safe and efficient payment systems are critical to the effective functioning of the financial system. Another important hypothesis was mentioned above, namely, that the payment system can act as a conduit through which financial and nonfinancial firms and other agents affect overall financial system stability. The principles for the most part are minimum requirements (and hence necessary conditions) for SIPS to promote financial system stability. The consenting parties (to the principles)

---

[3] Like other institutions, norms coordinate expectations and constrain behavior in interactions of individuals, affect the transactions cost (the cost of doing business with each other) of such interactions, and determine the distribution of the costs and benefits that ensue from the interactions. Hence they are also at the core of the incentive structure that motivate behavior of the kind that creates wealth.

are silent on the issue of whether satisfying the core principles is sufficient for a systemically important payment system to promote financial system stability.

As regards the *experience*, financial market disruptions have been caused by payment system failures. Among such episodes, two are frequently cited: the failure of the Herstatt Bank in 1974[4] and the technical difficulties experienced by the Bank of New York in 1985.[5]

Experience in implementing risk management rules and procedures both before and since the Lamfalussy standards has also been relevant in focusing ideas, especially about the central role of settlement finality; various cost-effective arrangements that could be put in place to avoid unwinding, in particular, or settlement failures, in general, in netting systems, in the event of an inability to settle by some major participant; and about the value of shortening time lags in settlement. Moreover, with the growing worldwide concern with governance and transparency, it is no surprise that the core principles have something to say in this area as well.

The evolutionary *process* of getting to the CPSIPS has, therefore, involved a combination of experience and theoretical and technological developments. But reaching consensus on the exact principles and their wording has involved long and arduous debate and discussion among representatives of central banks, the International Monetary Fund, and the World Bank: to ensure wide

---

[4] In 1974, Bankhaus Herstatt, a German Bank, which was very active in the foreign exchange market, was closed by the German banking supervisory authority. At the time of the closure, several of Herstatt's counterparts had made irrevocable payments in deutsche mark in its favor, while the United States' dollar payments had not yet been received by the United States clearing system—Clearing House Interbank Payments System (CHIPS). Since Herstatt's corresponding banks suspended outgoing U.S. dollar payments from Herstatt's account at the same time as the closure in Frankfurt, several banks incurred losses. This risk of loss from nonsynchronous settlement of funds in two cross-border systems is now often called *Herstatt risk*.

[5] The Bank of New York, a major clearing bank in the United States's payment system, experienced a computer breakdown on November 21, 1985, so that it could settle only bought securities but not sold securities. To ensure settlement, the Federal Reserve Bank had to make an overnight loan of $22.6 billion from the discount window, collateralized by $36 billion in securities.

acceptability of the principles and to benefit from the rich and diverse experiences of the Task Force members.

The *self-interest of countries in observing the core principles* emanates from two basic sources: the quest for domestic financial stability and the desire to participate in the increasingly global and integrated system of markets involving trade and payment transactions; the latter is precisely why the punishment just referred to can be effective in providing the incentive for countries not to "defect" in the application of the core principles. If all countries are obeying the same norms then cooperation will be easier, the implementation will be less costly for all, and the benefits greater, as compared with a situation where some countries or systemically important payment systems are not complying with the CPSIPS.

Interpretation of What to Implement

For several reasons, despite the consensus in stating them, the interpretation of the principles may not be the same across countries, and the evolutionary process is bound to continue in that regard. Indeed, despite very serious attempts to minimize this problem through a reasonably thorough consultation process the attempt at implementation will bring out many difficulties in interpretation of the core principles. Differences in interpretation will result in major differences in *what* to implement. A few examples can be given.

First, and perhaps foremost, the *scope of the efficiency objective* being promoted by the CPSIPS is not transparent. It is easy to appreciate that a payment system should be efficient in using the resources put at its disposal (*intra-payment system efficiency*); ideally, in addition, all the resources put at the disposal of a payment system should be at their most valued uses in the society (*social efficiency*). It is not obvious that both these conditions are demanded by the core principles (in particular Principle VIII). In the attempt to reach consensus there has not obviously been complete clarity in this area. Indeed the problem is compounded by the fact that even the criterion of efficiency is not one that has universal meaning to persons who work in and on payment systems. Hence the word "efficiency" is variously invoked to connote "operational efficiency," "technical efficiency," and "economic efficiency." A new consensus will have to emerge on these issues. For this author, efficiency should relate to *economic efficiency* and it should be implicit that the institutional framework governing the payment system should foster *economic efficiency* from a social perspective (in other words, *social efficiency*).

Second, as regards *definitions*, it is essential for proper implementation of the core principles that major terms used in those principles have universal meanings. This may be simple to achieve for "ordinary" terms like credit risk, liquidity risk, and systemic risk, which have become core terms in specialized fields of study in economics and finance. For other terms, like "payment systems" and "systemically important payment systems," which have not benefited from the same systematic attempt at rigorous use, the problem may be harder. Of course, within any given country the problem may not be acute. But in order to realize one of the important objectives of the core principles (even if not explicitly stated)—namely, fostering global trade and payments in integrated markets—the application of important terms *across countries* would have to be fundamentally similar between counterparties, market participants, and country authorities. For example, whether a *particular arrangement* is a payment system and, if so, a systemically important one, *in any given country*, must be capable of the same answer by different persons across different countries. To the extent that this is the case, cooperation (trade and payment transactions, reliance on judgments of other oversight authorities) will be fostered.

Third, the same goes for *standards*. For several of the principles, judgments inevitably have to be made as to whether standards are high enough to pass the test. An example would be the criterion of "little or no credit risk," or "little or no liquidity risk," when the settlement asset is not a claim on the central bank (Principle VI). Another example where judgments can be tricky is the assessment of whether security and operational reliability are high enough and contingency arrangements adequate for timely completion of daily settlements (Principle VII). Clearly cooperation across countries would be promoted if such judgments in a particular context, when made by knowledgeable people, tend to be identical. Once again, the evolutionary process will have to continue toward consensus on interpretation. In general, I would posit that in the evolution of both definitions and standards, *peer reviews* would be very useful. So also may be *technical assistance* in some cases.

The Coverage of the Principles

As with every major institutional process (such as drafting a constitution), the *factors determining the content of the core principles* (and the principles for central bank responsibilities as well) have been many. As regards the core principles themselves, some of the factors could be deduced from what was stated above, namely: (1) a need for consensus and hence the necessity to confine the principles to policy areas where such a consensus had emerged; (2) the Lamfalussy standards which existed already and had served the global community well; and (3) a desire to broaden the scope of the existing (Lamfalussy) standards to cover systems other than netting systems (in particular, gross settlement systems and so-called hybrid systems). Still, deciding on the content of the principles has not been easy and there is always the risk in these kinds of exercises that the coverage is not comprehensive enough, say perhaps because the negotiating parties could not reach consensus on how to address an important policy issue.

We would conjecture that, because the core principles have been stated in very broad language, and the consultation process has been carefully managed, there is little or no risk that some major policy on which there is broad consensus and which would merit a separate principle has been left uncovered by the principles. Nevertheless, the absence of a principle that touches directly the link between *payment systems and monetary policy* appears, on face value, to be a significant omission. There is, after all, a separate core principle requiring that the legal basis of a system be well-founded. Hence why not something about the payment system and monetary policy?

There are, no doubt, a number of possible responses to this question of which two are important. One is that monetary policy is outside the control of the payment system itself and that as part of its responsibilities in applying the core principles, which is also an integral part of the institutional framework that has been developed, the central bank could consider issues of payment systems and monetary policy. The second response is that the range of topics that would need to be considered for a discussion of the payment system and monetary policy could be quite extensive, and deciding on what a core principle should address would invoke endless discussion at this point in time. In addition, as a minimum, those responsible for monetary policy would need to be drawn into such a debate on the development of any core principle in this area.

We believe that the more fundamental problem is that the core principles, strictly speaking, do not focus on the payment system as a whole but at particular payment systems. Once one begins to focus on the payment system as a whole, it becomes difficult not to mention more explicitly the importance of the payment system for monetary policy and to begin to ask if certain core principles can be agreed in that area as well. But even leaving aside such a broad-scale attack on the interrelationship between monetary policy and the payment system, we suspect that there would be great benefit in addressing more concretely at a broad international level (as done for the core principles under discussion) issues of liquidity and credit (quantity, price, collateral, role of markets, and the central bank) in the context of "responsibilities of the central bank in applying the core principles." Unfortunately, experience would indicate that a consensus would be hard to reach at this point in time. We also accept that such an exercise would need to include monetary policy personnel in addition to those dealing with payment system policy.

An implication that we draw would be that a more complete set of core principles needs to be developed in the future for the responsibilities of the central bank, which would address, more pointedly, issues such as the nature and content of oversight, the role of the central bank in provision of credit and payment services, and the determination of adequacy of liquidity for the payment system. The current treatment (at the level of general principles) of responsibilities of the central bank in the core principles document, of necessity, is rather thin. There is work for some future task force or task forces to develop core principles in some or all of these areas.

The Economics of Rule Making and Implementation of the Principles

In designing, assessing, and enforcing rules governing their systemically important payment systems each country will have to clarify the role of at least four parties, namely: (1) the individual participants of a payment system, (2) the governing body of the payment system, (3) outside regulatory/oversight body or bodies, and (4) the legal system(s)—laws and courts—within whose jurisdiction(s) the payment system operates. Whether substantive or procedural, specific rules are intended to serve certain functions and achieve certain objectives in any institutional framework. Thus, despite the absence of consensus at the international level about specific rules, certain fundamental principles can be used in conjunction with experience to guide the approach to rule making, whether in particular payment systems or for the payment system as a whole.

The most general principle in what may be called the economics of rule making is that rules should be designed and enforced to promote economic efficiency and wealth creation. Such rules in the payment system will address assignment of rights and obligations with regard to property, risks, and contractual relations. Having these rights and obligations clearly identified and understood is essential. In addition, the pure economics of rule making would lend great support to the view that the rules promote: complete internalization of costs and benefits of actions (taking into account the negotiation, enforcement, and other elements of the cost of internalization); freedom of contract within appropriate limits; and assignment of the obligation to manage risks according to comparative advantage in managing the risks (no matter how the management costs are then distributed).

In all of this, the history, traditions, and other underlying institutions of a country will play a role. Some countries resort to formal laws and regulatory and supervisory bodies only as a last resort; some others resort to self-regulation and rules by agreement among interacting parties only as a last resort, preferring formal laws covering most areas and having regulatory, supervisory, and oversight bodies responsible for ensuring observance of the rules. In today's world, at least for payment systems most countries probably lie somewhere on the spectrum between these two extremes.

Internalization of costs and benefits is a particularly useful principle in property rights formulation;[6] but it is also important in determining liability rules and assigning risk management

---

[6] Property rights are rights over assets: rights to use an asset (user rights); rights to reap income from the asset and to contract over the nature and amount of this income; and rights to transfer to another party the ownership or user rights to the asset.

obligations. Complete internalization is fostered by a cost-reward structure in which the values created by any particular activity are made to accrue to those who bore the cost of undertaking the activity. Each individual's wealth is made to depend solely upon the net value created by the resources under that individual's control. Improving the institutional framework by more clearly defining property rights, opening markets and allowing greater competition, and having full-cost pricing of payment services provided by the public sector including the central bank are some of the ways of fostering internalization. Complete internalization prevents divergence between private and social marginal costs and benefits and hence promotes social efficiency in the allocation and use of resources.

But it is not always possible or efficient to attain complete internalization, due to high cost of internalization or unquantifiable elements of private benefits (such as the value placed on "convenience"). A practical approach to facilitating social optimality could then be simply to ensure that institutional and organizational arrangements (rules and governance arrangements) are put in place that tend to promote social optimality and then to conclude that any residual divergences observed between private and social (marginal) costs and benefits, at the equilibrium point of private choice, reflect the impact of unquantifiable factors and of internalization costs.[7]

Freedom of contract with "appropriate" limits[8] is expected, in general, to foster economic efficiency and wealth creation. This would seem particularly pertinent for payment systems in today's world, as it would give flexibility in rule making in a rapidly changing financial and technological environment. In other words, given the basic legal framework, participants in a payment system, individually and as a group via their governing bodies, should be given broad freedom to formulate mutually advantageous rules that are enforceable in all relevant jurisdictions. This would enable members to design rules that take into account their special circumstances. Members will also be able to modify the system rules on a timely basis, to take account of changing circumstances or new opportunities consistent with the objectives of the organization.

---

[7] *See* Johnson et al. (1998), pp. 67–68.
[8] The appropriate limits to freedom of contract is one of the many contentious areas in law and economics. For an introduction *see, e.g.*, Trebilcock (1993).

A fundamental problem, as tends to be the case for standards in general, is that the core principles are all about limiting freedom of contract; hence the question of where or how to draw the line and set limits to freedom of contract becomes important in trying to implement the CPSIPS. Ultimately, a balance must be struck between the positive effect on incentives to participants of freedom and flexibility to alter policies, practices, and procedures, and the negative effects on third parties of not constraining the payment system participants from exercising this freedom in ways that have adverse effects on third parties without appropriate compensation.

In creating the institutional environment for implementing the core principles, we would accept that at least three considerations would be relevant in deciding the limits to freedom of contract. First, the participants of a payment system should not be allowed to contract freely to act in an unfair manner in restraining participation in the system. This is the essence of Principle IX. Second, the payment system participants should not be allowed to contract freely to impose costs on the guarantor of financial system stability, typically the central bank, by having settlement failures that induce injection of liquidity into the system to bail it out, which make difficult the achievement of monetary policy objectives. Compliance with Principles IV, V, and VI would ensure that this condition is met. Third, the payment system participants should not be allowed to contract freely to impose economic costs on third parities without prior agreement or appropriate compensation. The general method of handling this is to have policies and organizational arrangements in place to foster internalization of externalities. We believe that all the ten core principles are relevant to this consideration and that each helps to foster internalization of externalities.

We would argue that when the case for freedom of contract is placed next to the case for limiting this freedom, the conclusion as to how to draw the line appears straightforward. The participants in a payment system should be allowed to determine the rules, and hence the policies, practices, and procedures governing the system, and some public oversight agency should assess the rules to ensure that they conform to the core principles. In other words, when it comes to the policies, practices, and procedures being implemented by a payment system, there should be neither a regime of only self-regulation nor one of strict regulatory requirements (interpreted as rules and regulations imposed as minimum requirements by some public sector agency that also supervises and inspects the systems to ensure strict compliance).

Another element in the efficiency-enhancing approach to rule making is *assigning the responsibility for risk management* according to comparative advantage in managing such risks, as this should greatly reduce the social cost of risk management. It is sometimes argued that many legal systems which have emerged via a long evolutionary process, based on norms and customs of society, have tended to obey this principle. From this perspective, laws are frequently formalizations of actual and desired norms, with the advantage that having laws also helps to resolve the problem of who will bear the cost of enforcement.

Since Coase (1960), many economists have tended to argue that, in the absence of transaction costs, and with freedom of contract, it really does not matter how rights (and, ipso facto, risks) are initially assigned. Secondary reallocations will take care of apparent inefficiencies in the initial allocation. The initial assignments could, of course, engender important wealth effects. Also, with sufficiently high transaction costs, secondary reallocations could be frustrated. Nevertheless, it would appear that, for a payment system, freedom of the system participants as a group to set the rules and freedom of individual participants to negotiate the assignment of responsibilities for managing the risks that arise in their relations with each other should be sufficient to facilitate social efficiency.

The implications for the implementation of Principle III of the CPSIPS are immediate. General guidelines on risk management would be agreed by the participants. Some of these guidelines would involve centralized management and others decentralized management. Where decentralized management is involved participants should be allowed to work out their own solutions and the governing body of the payment system should assess the solutions to ensure that they conform to the guidelines and standards that have been set by the organization. Thus, for example, participants would be allowed to determine their bilateral exposure limits via bilateral negotiations.

Risk Management

Risk management is always central when one discusses payment systems: legal, financial, operational, and security risks. Indeed the core principles are mainly about risk measurement and management. Principle I is about legal risk, Principles II-VI about financial risks, and Principle VII about operational risk. Principle IX straddles both risk and efficiency.

Financial risks are usually classified as liquidity, credit, or systemic risks. In the area of risk controls, payment system policies and reforms proceed by focusing on the payment system directly and/or at the environment (including, especially the institutional context) in which the payment system operates. Indeed, the CPSIPS, strictly speaking, focus on particular systems and hence, on face value, would seem implicitly to take for granted the environment in which the payment systems operates. Members of a systemically important payment system are, from that perspective, being required to understand and manage legal, financial, and other risks, given the legal, economic, and financial environment in which they operate.

From a public policy perspective, the constraint—the environment—is not a given. The rules governing the financial system, the quality of the financial markets, the soundness of the financial organizations/institutions that operate in the payment system, and the macroeconomic policies being pursued by the authorities can all be changed in such a way as to reduce payment system risks, given the ability of the members of particular payment systems to manage the risks and given the governance of the systems by the operators. A change in the environment would, of course, typically induce a change in the rules of a particular payment system. In other words, there is a constant interaction between a payment system's rules and the legal, economic, and financial environment in which the system operates.

Systemic Risk

Given the environment, it is essential to have payment system policies, practices, and procedures in place that promote low systemic risk in the financial system. Systemic risk in this case would be the probability that liquidity or solvency problems of one or more individuals, institutions, or organizations in a payment system lead to liquidity or solvency problems on a large enough scale to threaten payment settlements in the economy at large. We believe that the CPSIPS adequately address the issue of systemic risk, and the scope for different emphasis in implementation is quite broad.

Easily the most effective way in which rules written for individual systems can also be made to address the problem of systemic risk is to have those rules foster internalization of externalities. We have argued above that the CPSIPS do foster internalization of externalities. In consequence, we will argue, they promote containment of systemic risk emanating from individual payment systems.

There is another perspective from which the adequacy of the CPSIPS for promoting containment of systemic risk could be analyzed. Discussion of systemic risks has highlighted the central role of *settlement finality*. One device used to facilitate settlement finality is ensuring that a system typically puts in place some mechanism(s) whereby settlement can occur even in the case of failure of a participant. Principle V addresses this issue for netting systems where a problem could arise.

Now, payment is final when it becomes irrevocable and unconditional. For this it is essential that the settlement asset be a claim on an institution that is highly creditworthy. Central banks typically stand ready to provide final settlement facilities for payment systems—both retail and large-value—subject to adequate safeguards to limit credit expansion. While banks can, as a matter of principle, settle using bilateral accounts with each other, or on the books of some private settlement agent (clearing bank), settlement by banks on the books of the central bank—whether gross or after deferred multilateral netting—can be seen as facilitating a reduction of systemic risk. Payments using central bank money result in claims on the central bank which cannot fail (become insolvent) or have liquidity problems. From the perspective of agents other than the central bank, such payments, therefore, do not have any credit or liquidity risk associated with them.

Despite the special qualification of the central bank for handling payment settlement, it does not necessarily follow, of course, that the legal framework should require private clearing systems to settle their final obligations across the books of the central bank. Nevertheless, there is growing consensus in favor of settlement in the books of the central bank as the normal approach, even if not the only legal approach, at least for systemically important systems. Hence Principle VI states that assets used for settlement should preferably be a claim on the central bank.

Finally, reducing the time lag in settlement is another way countries have found effective in containing systemic risk. For example, there has been an increasing tendency of central banks to build real-time gross settlement (RTGS) systems (when the demand justifies it). Also countries have pressed ahead to achieve same-day settlement for clearing and settlement systems, since net obligations do not get carried from one day to the next, avoiding the risk that a participant with a large debit position could fail overnight or over holidays and weekends. Principle IV is about same-day settlement.

The Legal Environment

In many countries, to reduce payment system risks the legal environment is often changed in major ways. These environmental changes often would go hand in hand with introduction of major payment systems. But the legal changes can also occur after a new payment system is in place and risk management problems have arisen that are best handled by changing the legal environment. For instance, in order to address issues that arise, related to finality of transfers, multilateral netting, the zero-hour rule, electronic signatures, and use of collateral, changes in the legal environment have been found useful. Among others, such changes typically involve modifications and amendments to the central bank, banking, insolvency, negotiable instruments, and funds transfer laws, all in the interest of strengthening the legal basis of certain payment system rules, practices, procedures, and instruments, and reducing legal risks faced by the payment system participants. We suspect that many countries, in trying to implement the CPSIPS, will find that substantial legal reforms are rational.

As regards finality of payment transfers, often there is lack of clarity within the current legal environment as to when in a payment system a payment is final and irrevocable. The legal framework may thus benefit from some revision to clarify the issue; for even where the rules of a payment system may be clear, those rules may not have a well-founded legal basis.

There is also sometimes a need to confirm that in all the relevant jurisdictions of a payment system, the laws contain or permit provisions that validate the use of electronic signatures (e.g., PINs or other authentication devices) associated with the message flows of a payment system.

Changes in insolvency laws have often been made during periods of financial sector reform, among other reasons to ensure that the laws accept the validity of multilateral netting. That way, a failed bank's liability to one survivor could be set off against its claim on another survivor. This usually means ensuring the validity, against a liquidator, of the multilateral net settlement of a payment system. Otherwise, there could, in the event of a liquidation, be a conflict between the insolvency law of the country and the rules governing a particular payment system.

The so-called "zero-hour rule" provides that when a bank (or other company) is placed in liquidation all the transactions that it had carried out from midnight of the previous day are automatically annulled. This rule can be disruptive depending on the time of the bank being put in liquidation, since it would automatically revoke all payments made by the bank, and all other drawings from its settlement account, if it was placed in liquidation after the clearing in some deferred net settlement payment system had taken place and settlement obligations calculated. There is sometimes a need to ensure, through modification of the legal environment, that in the relevant jurisdictions a judge cannot order the reversal of any payment made under any form of (valid) contract.

Collateral is sometimes used in connection with loss sharing in netting or deferred net settlement systems in case a member bank fails and is unable to meet its settlement obligations. The rules of the system will specify the nature of the pledged collateral and who is to hold it. In addition, a central bank or a commercial bank that extends intraday or overnight credit to a member of a payment system to facilitate settlement may want to demand collateral backing, with an appropriate haircut for the risk that the market value of the security will change and the holder may need to trade the security to recover its loan. A point that sometimes needs to be clarified, and legal changes made if necessary, is that if a bank fails the collateral pledgee will be able to take hold of pledged collateral for settlement and/or loss sharing, and a creditor bank or central bank can use pledged collateral of a borrowing bank for repayment of a loan. In other words, if the borrowing or pledging bank is placed in liquidation, there could be a risk (which must be eliminated) that the pledgee may be obliged by the relevant insolvency law to release the pledged securities to the liquidator without having any opportunity to realize them. The pledgee would then be left with an unsecured claim. In the case of a loan the creditor would have to try to recover from the liquidator of the failed bank.

The Soundness of the Financial System and the Legal Framework

Financial market development helps to reduce risk and increase efficiency in the payment system. Now payment system development fosters development of money markets—inter alia by increasing the speed, safety, and reliability of transfers, and by shortening settlement lags. The point now is that steps taken to improve the efficiency and liquidity of financial markets often help to reduce the costs to payment system participants of managing financial risks in the payment. An obvious example is the increased supply (relative to base money) of liquid assets that can be used as collateral in payment settlement. Financial market development typically also involves improvement in the treasuries of payment system participants—typically in connection with the provision of cash management services. Such progress benefits the payment system as the treasury improvements tend to enhance capacity for managing liquidity and queues in the payment system. In addition, a stable macroeconomic environment, including low and stable inflation, provides a favorable environment for financial market and payment system development.

A sound financial, and especially banking, system helps reduce the level of risk in the payment system. Such a system will contain predominantly banks with adequate capital to withstand most typical adverse shocks, with staff skilled in assessing conditions and coming up with solutions to manage liquidity, credit, market and other risks, whether related to the payment system or not. Hence, compliance with the CPSIPS will be easier if measures are taken to strengthen the banking system. In general, these measures would involve strengthening licensing and reporting requirements as well as the regulatory and the official banking supervision framework; and developing and maintaining strict exit policy in order to weed out weak banks on a timely basis. Particular attention may, in the process, need to be paid (within individual banks) to improving internal management; reducing the stock of nonperforming loans; improving risk management methods and procedures; improving internal controls, auditing, and accounting; and improving operational efficiency.

Creating a sound financial system and promoting financial market development often involves changes in the legal system, especially banking and central banking legislation, insolvency law, and contract law, with a view to increasing price and interest rate liberalization; strengthening banking and financial sector supervision and oversight authority of central banks and other agencies; and granting central bank instrument independence. The implications for the implementation of the CPSIPS are obvious.

Efficiency

Principle VIII of the CPSIPS is *the* efficiency principle. But, as stated before, Principle IX straddles both risk and efficiency, since fair and open access can encourage competition among banks and others in the provision of payment services, which tends to promote efficiency. Also, Principle X, the governance principle, has efficiency aspects to it, since governance arrangements that are effective, accountable, and transparent will tend to promote the efficiency with which resources are used in a payment system.

Earlier it was argued that efficiency should relate to *economic efficiency* in particular and that it should be implicit in the CPSIPS that any particular payment system should foster *social efficiency* in general. We explore briefly the meaning and implications of this position and the role that the legal framework can play in fostering efficiency.

A payment system produces economic goods (payment clearing and settlement services and payment instruments) using inputs that have alternative uses in the economy. The concern with efficiency is therefore a concern for avoiding waste of resources. A general approach to efficiency, hence, must take into account both demand and supply factors and both the present and the future.

The Meaning of Efficiency

From a public policy perspective, efficiency is attained when it is not possible to reallocate a society's resources between production activities and end up with an output mix, now and in the (foreseeable) future, that makes the society as a whole better off than before. At the point of efficiency, a number of things hold at the same time. First, the society is willing and able to pay for the quantity and quality of the various goods produced in the economy. Second, the production of every unit of every good (with its own quality) takes place at the lowest possible resource cost of producing that particular unit of that good. Third, starting with the actual mix of the various goods produced, society cannot change the mix without worsening the welfare of at least one person in the society. Fourth, society is saving and investing at a rate (flow per year) that maximizes the present value of consumption over time.

The general meaning of efficiency has immediate and important implications for the meaning of efficiency when applied directly to a payment system. When a payment system is efficient the resources used in it cannot be used to produce a more highly valued mix of means of making the same payments. The payment system, in addition, promotes social efficiency when no unit of the resources used in the system could be used in the production of other goods that are more highly valued in the society, taking into account both the present and the future. This implies the following.

First, the society is willing and able to pay for the mix of means of making payments and the payment services (quantities, attributes, and qualities) being provided. Second, the resources used in the payment services industry are allocated in such a way that they cannot (by a reallocation) produce a different mix of payment services more highly valued by the society. Third, the amount of resources used in the payment system cannot be reduced without eliminating or cutting back on some payment system service. Fourth, society cannot be made better off by taking some of the resources currently allocated to the payment system and using them instead to produce other goods in the society (both currently and in the future).

Inefficiency in Payment Systems

When one diagnoses a country's payment systems and one looks closely at, say, the most important—one that by any reasonable standard would be considered systemically important—one is sometimes struck by elements, practices, and procedures that on face value appear inefficient. These would include aspects of the design or the rules of the system that can lead to poor risk or liquidity management; poor operational performance (errors, long processing delays, and general unreliability) of the system; the rather limited way the system meets the needs of the users (perhaps because the financial system has been progressing while the payment system lags in its development); or the limited use of the system and hence the persistence of excess capacity. Or the central bank may be making losses due, among other things, to heavy spending on the payment system, including heavy subsidies to a large value payment system, or delivering cash to branches of commercial banks at heavily subsidized rates.

Addressing Inefficiency

Sometimes the solution to a diagnosed problem is easy and inexpensive, requiring perhaps only simple organizational and policy changes. For instance, in a paper-based clearing and settlement system, large and small values may be all lumped together. Separation of the two would facilitate, among other things, dedicated delivery services for the large values. Or the country might have just built a sophisticated RTGS system which banks ignore because of liquidity problems in using the RTGS system or because the banks benefit from float in using a rival netting (especially check) system. Or the pricing of the payment system services may not facilitate full-cost recovery and can be changed easily. Or simple steps could be taken to ultimately privatize certain payment services being provided by the central bank or the public sector; or competition could be increased in the provision of payment services by opening markets and addressing monopoly problems.

At other times the solutions are expensive and hence the search for efficiency becomes challenging, especially when it is public (including central bank) resources that are being spent. At such times, the organizational and policy changes require major investments in physical and human capital and in equipment. Even legal changes are often very difficult and expensive to decide and implement. To add to the problem, as argued above, in looking at what is efficient one must look at not merely the business requirements in the narrow sense but indeed in the broad social sense.

There are a few guiding principles useful in implementation to ensure that "reforms" are efficient. One is to create an environment that encourages the private sector to make investments in the payment system that are socially efficient so that the public sector is not forced to make these investments merely because of public policy that discourages private investment. A second guiding principle is to foster competition in the provision of payment services. A third guiding principle is that when the public sector—via the central bank especially—spends resources in current supply, or investing in future supply, of payment services it must always bear in mind that those resources have alternative uses in the economy. Central bank profits, for instance, could be transferred to the budget, where they *could* be used more efficiently in the society (directly through government spending or transfers or indirectly by making possible tax reductions). Hence there is great value to the public sector in taking the patience to do some reasonably good cost-benefit analysis to ensure that it is not wasting resources but rather is getting maximum value for society for the money it spends on the payment system. These guiding principles have implications for implementation of payment system projects or initiatives, including attempts to comply with the CPSIPS.

Most importantly, when a payment system is owned and managed by the public sector, especially the central bank, efficiency can be attained by adopting policies, practices, and procedures that involve essentially continuous application of cost-benefit analysis and use of open competitive bidding among suppliers of inputs. Cost-benefit analysis involves projecting the flow of benefits and costs associated with an investment (a particular reform, say) over some period of time (the time horizon), discounting such streams of benefits and costs to their present values by utilizing some discount rate (interest rate, social rate of discount), and calculating the ratios of present values of the benefits and costs of the investment (reform).[9] The benefits under consideration in the payment system include reduced operational and transaction costs, reduced risk, increased reliability, and new types of payment instruments. On the cost side, the inputs have to be identified and priced at what they are worth in alternative uses (their opportunity costs).

Another general principle of major importance is that when a payment system is owned and managed by the private sector, efficiency can be attained by policies, practices, and procedures that allow competition and market forces to operate while distortions arising mainly from externalities are addressed by public policy. When a payment system is owned and managed by the private sector, advantage should be taken of the fact that, most of the time, where there is competition there is a positive correlation between efficiency and profits, and the private sector supplier is interested in more profits than less. The main element in ensuring efficiency is, thus, maintaining open competition. That way the operation of the profit motive should normally enable the most efficient suppliers of services to weed out the less efficient—through pricing and services.

Thus public policy should develop a coherent and explicit *competition policy* that is continuously reviewed in light of changing real world economic forces. The formulation of such a policy will be greatly assisted by a clear institutional framework. For instance, freedom of entry in many areas of payments activity is often subject to licensing and specific entry requirements. Similarly, privately organized payment systems typically have rules for access that deny membership to certain potential entrants and this is usually permitted in most countries for objective reasons mainly related to risk. Nevertheless, such restrictions are often contained to the extent that risk control measures could be implemented that allow some of the less creditworthy to become members under specified conditions that are nondiscriminatory in an objective (that is risk-adjusted) sense.

As an element of competition policy, *the public authorities often regulate and oversee the private sector* to maintain the integrity of the market process, and sometimes intervene to influence market

---

[9] *See also* the discussion in Johnson, et al. (1998), pp. 61–63.

structure (antitrust rules and all that). Such authority for public action in the payment system area may be defined by the general laws of the country (including laws on industrial organization), as well as by banking and central banking legislation and payment system legislation.

A major problem for public policy when open competition is promoted, and particularly in the context of defining the appropriate oversight role of the public authorities, is how to identify and address situations in which there are *externalities*—which can happen when costs and benefits are not completely internalized (as discussed already). Sometimes, fostering greater competition or modifying official intervention in the form of pricing, taxation, and subsidization can promote internalization, basically by changing relative prices. At other times, it may be necessary to change the institutional framework, including liability rules, entry requirements, and the minimum standards for payment system operators.

The Legal Framework and Economic Efficiency

In general, there are at least three ways in which the legal framework can help promote the sort of economic efficiency in the payment system being discussed in this section. The first we have basically discussed: namely, by having in place an underlying legal framework with clearly defined property rights, freedom of contract, rules that internalize costs and benefits, and rules that assign responsibility for risk management in accordance with comparative advantage. Such laws must, of course, also be enforceable at relatively low costs to economic decision makers. In addition, we have indicated some specific areas in which the legal framework has often been reformed to reduce legal risks; then the positive effect of the reduction in risks on transaction costs would tend to have a positive impact on the allocation of resources and on saving and investment decisions.

A second way in which the legal framework will foster efficiency in the payment system is via establishing a well-founded legal basis for a competition policy that facilitates efficiency; in particular, such a legal framework will enshrine in the law statutes that support open markets in the provision of payment services and fair access to participate in payment systems. Typically industrial organization law (antitrust legislation, laws on branching, acquisitions, and mergers) as well as laws on price discrimination, collusion, and disclosure of information may all be relevant.

Third, the legal framework could promote efficiency in payment systems by specifying certain minimum requirements on the public sector when it operates in the payment system. A requirement to keep open the markets in which the central bank operates to entry by private sector providers of competing payment services as well as a requirement that there be full-cost recovery for payment services provided by the public sector are two important elements of such a legal framework.

For instance, a law requiring full-cost recovery would aim to cover not only variable costs but also the fixed costs, with a view to earning a rate of return on central bank investment in the payment services at least equivalent to competitive rates in private markets, after adjusting for risk. A basic reason is to promote efficiency by (1) discouraging excessive use of the services provided by the central bank; (2) ensuring that the central bank does not, by implicit subsidization, create competitive advantage for itself even though it may not be the least-cost provider of a service; and (3) forcing the central bank to make socially efficient decisions about what to produce and how it will invest its own resources.

Cost recovery has indeed become enshrined in practice in some countries (for example, the United States and Germany). In the United States the *Monetary Control Act of 1980* requires the Federal Reserve to charge prices for its payment services to recover the full fixed, variable, and imputed costs of providing the services (especially services such as check processing, automated check clearing, and large-value funds transfer). Imputed costs—the so-called Private Sector Adjustment Factor—are based on an estimate of the taxes and cost of capital that the Federal Reserve would incur were it a private firm.

Governance Arrangements and Good Governance

Principle X of the CPSIPS is about *governance arrangements.* Now *governance* in general refers to the arrangements (institutions and organizational structures), and how they are carried out in practice, for running the system by those responsible for doing so. Good governance will help ensure that the system achieves its objectives (ends and means). Principle X says that the system's governance arrangements should be effective, accountable, and transparent. There is an implicit expectation in the principle that if the governance arrangements are effective, accountable, and transparent, the governance of the system would be such that the objectives of the system are met.

The governance arrangements will include rules, contained in constitutions, charters, bylaws, and agreements, about organizational structure and about standards of appropriate behavior, codes of conduct, and the autonomy, discretion, and incentive structure for those carrying out the governance arrangements. The governance arrangements also include the resources (money, staff, and authority) available to those responsible for carrying out the governance arrangements.

For the governance arrangements to be *effective*, they must be appropriate to the circumstances, acceptable by those affected by the arrangements (the governed), and practical (that is, being capable of being put into practice).

For the arrangements to be *accountable*, they must come out of a decision-making process that properly takes into account the divergent interests of the members; the importance of the issues to the stability of the organization (for instance, some rules should be easier to change than others); and they must facilitate cooperation among the members. The governance arrangements must also contain elements that promote accountability by those who must carry out the arrangements. Such elements include internal controls, clear assignment of responsibilities, autonomy to achieve targets, and performance-based reward systems.

If the governance arrangements are *transparent*, the details and the rationale for rules and decisions are clear and easily understood by the members. Indeed, it could be argued that transparency facilitates effectiveness and accountability of the governance arrangements.

Poor governance will tend to show up in many ways. One is frequent turnover of skilled personnel, which would tend to indicate inadequate incentives; this turnover is directly costly (due especially to loss of experience and the enhanced training cost for new staff). A second piece of evidence would be disputes among members that are rather frequent, time consuming to resolve, and sometimes cannot be resolved without resort to outside parties, especially the courts and outside arbitrators. A third piece of evidence would be declining efficiency (in an economic sense) of the payment system.

Concluding Remarks

The core principles for systemically important payment systems are a great achievement, both in terms of their substantive content and the degree of cooperation and consensus that they manifest. They cover the fundamentals of best practices in payment system policy, even though their focus is on individual payment systems rather than the payment system as a whole. But the fact that they do not directly focus on the payment system as a whole is not without some cost: it leads to effective silence on important aspects of monetary policy and the payment system; and the concept of efficiency that they promote is obscured. In time, we expect it to become obvious that there is a need for development of core principles for aspects of the role of the central bank, including the nature and content of oversight and aspects of monetary policy and the payment system.

It is in the interest of countries to implement the principles and we expect them to do so. But problems in implementation will arise due to differences in interpretation of the principles, in particular as regards definition of some major terms and the exact determination of the level of standards to be maintained. International cooperation, peer reviews, and technical assistance will, therefore, be useful in building consensus on the interpretation of the principles.

In rule making—which is relevant for law reform—for the institutional framework governing oversight (by the central bank and other public agencies), and for internal governance of a particular system, countries should promote internalization of externalities, freedom of contract with appropriate limits, and assignment of responsibility for risk management according to comparative advantage in managing such risks. We believe that in many countries this kind of approach is now the normal practice; but there is still a need to do the same in some other countries.

The legal framework can play a role in ensuring that payment systems foster economic and social efficiency in resource use. In particular, the law can be used to promote competition and open markets as well as to mandate full-cost recovery in the pricing policy of payment services provided by the public sector (notably the central bank). Similarly, in many countries, there will be a need to effect major changes in the legal framework to reduce payment system risks, rather than force the payment systems to adapt to a legal framework that could use some major reforms.

References

Bank for International Settlements (BIS), 1990, *Report of the Committee on Interbank Netting Schemes of the Central Banks of the Group of Ten Countries* (Basel, November).

———, 1999, *Core Principles for Systemically Important Payment Systems: Report of the Task Force on Payment System Principles and Practices* (Basel: BIS).

Coase, R.A., 1960, "The Problem of Social Cost," *Journal of Law and Economics*, Vol. 3 (April), pp. 1–44.

Johnson, Omotunde E.G., Richard Abrams, Jean-Marc Destresse, Tonny Lybek, Nicholas Roberts, and Mark Swinburne, 1998, *Payment Systems, Monetary Policy, and the Role of the Central Bank* (Washington: IMF).

Trebilcock, Michael J., 1993, *The Limits of Freedom of Contract* (Cambridge: Harvard University Press).

| Chapter 37 | TARGET: Trans-European Automated Real-Time Gross Settlement Express Transfer System of the European System of Central Banks |

ERWIN NIEROP

On January 1, 1999, a historic event took place: the introduction of a single currency—the euro—in 11 of the 15 Member States of the European Union (EU).[1] The introduction of the euro was preceded by the establishment, on June 1, 1998, of the European Central Bank (ECB), the European System of Central Banks (ESCB), and the Eurosystem.[2] These events followed from the Treaty of Maastricht, which was concluded on February 7, 1992 and amended the Treaty establishing the European Community dated March 25, 1957 (the Treaty).

The introduction of the euro took place through the irrevocable fixing of the exchange rates of the currencies of Member States which introduced the single currency. As from January 1, 1999, monetary policy operations and payment systems transactions in the interbank

---

[1] Belgium, Germany, Spain, France, Ireland, Italy, Luxembourg, the Netherlands, Austria, Portugal, and Finland. On January 1, 2001, the euro was also introduced in Greece. Denmark, Sweden, and the United Kingdom will, at least for the time being, not introduce the euro.

[2] The ECB distinguishes between the ESCB and the Eurosystem. The ESCB is composed of the ECB and the national central banks (NCBs) of all 15 Member States of the EU. The Eurosystem is composed of the ECB and the NCBs of the 12 Member States which have introduced the euro. The notion "Eurosystem" cannot be found in the Treaty or any other statutory acts, but is used for reasons of convenience in order to make a clear distinction between the group of NCBs of those Member States which have introduced the euro, on the one hand, and the group of NCBs of those Member States which have not, at least not yet, introduced the euro, on the other hand. Institutional and operational features of the ECB, ESCB, and Eurosystem are addressed in a different chapter of this publication and are therefore not further elaborated here, unless this is appropriate in the framework of the subject of this specific chapter on TARGET. Since TARGET is an ESCB-wide system, this chapter will generally refer to the ESCB, unless it is unambiguously clear that only the Eurosystem can be meant.

circuit are executed in euro. On January 1, 2002, banknotes denominated in euro will be introduced. Up until that moment, the currencies of the participating Member States which have introduced the euro will continue to exist and will be regarded as subunits of the euro.[3] During the transitional period, at a retail level, scriptural payments may, on the basis of the principle "no compulsion, no prohibition," be made either in euro or in national currencies.[4] For EU-wide payment transactions in euro, the ESCB has developed the TARGET system, an acronym for Trans-European Automated Real-Time Gross Settlement Express Transfer system. This chapter will focus on the following issues:

- the technical structure of TARGET;

- statutory provisions in European Community law that are relevant for TARGET;

- the legal structure of TARGET;

- the impact of the Settlement Finality Directive and the Cross-Border Credit Transfers Directive on TARGET;

- the collateral requirements for TARGET; and

- by way of an epilogue, the implications of future developments for TARGET's legal framework.

The Technical Structure of TARGET

TARGET is the real-time gross settlement system for the euro. It consists of 15 national real-time gross settlement (RTGS),

---

[3] This follows from Article 6.1 of Council Regulation (EC) no. 974/98 of May 3, 1998 on the introduction of the euro.
[4] This follows from Article 8.3 of the Regulation mentioned in footnote 3.

systems—one for each EU Member State[5]—and the ECB payment mechanism (EPM). These systems and the EPM are interlinked and provide, thus, for a uniform platform for the processing of cross-border payments. The EPM has been established for the purpose of performing the following functions:

- processing the ECB's own payments;

- processing the payments of EPM customers such as central banks and European and international organizations; and

- supplying settlement services to cross-border clearing and settlement organizations.

TARGET is a real-time system, which means that payments can be executed in a very short period of time; it is also a gross settlement system in which each payment is handled individually. TARGET provides for intraday finality; settlement is final once the funds have been credited. This does not prevent the existence of netting mechanisms at a national level, as long as the top structure in each Member State is an RTGS system.

TARGET has been developed to achieve three main objectives:

- to serve the needs of the Eurosystem's monetary policy;

- to provide a safe and reliable mechanism for the settlement of cross-border payments on an RTGS basis; and

- to increase the efficiency of intra-EU cross-border payments.

---

[5]

Belgium	:ELLIPS	Luxembourg	:LIPS-GROSS
Denmark	:DEBES	The Netherlands	:TOP
Germany	:ELS	Austria	:ARTIS
Greece	:HERMES euro	Portugal	:SPGT
Spain	:SLBE	Finland	:BoF-RTGS
France	:TBF	Sweden	:euro-RIX
Ireland	:IRIS	United Kingdom	:CHAPS euro
Italy	:BIREL	ECB	:EPM

TARGET is available for all credit transfers in euro between EU Member States, including those Member States who have not introduced the euro yet (Denmark, Sweden, and the United Kingdom). It processes both interbank and customer payments without an upper or lower value limit.

Payments directly related to monetary policy operations involving the Eurosystem—as the recipient or the sender—have to pass via TARGET or the national RTGS environment. Cross-border large-value net settlement systems operating in euro also have to settle their end-of-day balances via TARGET.

NCBs grant intraday credit to TARGET participants up to an amount which participants determine themselves by providing adequate collateral. A list of eligible collateral has been established and such collateral may be provided on a cross-border basis.

There are at present approximately 5,000 RTGS participants in TARGET and almost all EU credit institutions are accessible via TARGET. Access to their respective domestic euro RTGS systems is sufficient to enable participants to make cross-border TARGET payments.

The system is available from 7 a.m. to 6 p.m. Frankfurt time, with a cutoff time for customer payments at 5 p.m. The system is closed on Saturdays and Sundays as well as on certain predefined public holidays. The fees charged for cross-border TARGET transactions are based on the number of transactions made.[6]

Finally, in order to give an impression of the numbers involved, on average TARGET processes at present 170,000 domestic and cross-border payments on a daily basis with a total value of

---

[6] The fees are at present calculated according to the following decreasing scale:
EUR 1.75 for each of the first 100 transactions per month;
EUR 1.00 for each of the next 900 transactions per month;
EUR 0.80 for each subsequent transaction in excess of 1,000 per month.
TARGET's fee structure is determined on the basic assumption of full-cost recovery. The fee is charged by the sending NCB only and is identical, irrespective of the destination or size of the payment.

approximately 1,000 billion EUR (by way of comparison, the Fedwire system processes a daily average of 400,000 payments).

Statutory Provisions in Community Law Relevant for TARGET

TARGET is a trademark and the name does not, therefore, appear itself in any provisions of Community law. There are, however, various statutory provisions establishing the legal framework in which TARGET is embedded. They can in particular be found in the Treaty and the Statute of the ESCB/ECB (the Statute) which is annexed to the Treaty and forms a part thereof. It would go beyond the scope of this chapter to provide an extensive elaboration of the legal features of those statutory provisions that may be relevant for TARGET, but the following table gives at least some indication of the features and allows one to put the legal acts and Articles that are mentioned below in their institutional context (see Table 1).

It would also go beyond the scope of this chapter to cite all Treaty and Statute Articles that may in one way or another be relevant for TARGET, but the main statutory provisions are summarized below.

Article 105.2, fourth indent, of the Treaty as repeated in Article 3.1, fourth indent, of the Statute state that one of the basic tasks to be carried out through the ESCB shall be to promote the smooth operation of payment systems.

Furthermore, in accordance with Article 17 of the Statute, the ECB and the NCBs may, in order to conduct their operations, open accounts for credit institutions, public entities, and other market participants and accept assets, including book securities, as collateral.

Table 1. Target Legal Provisions

Adopting Authority	Types of Legal Acts	Legal Basis	Legal Nature
Member States	Treaty establishing the European Community (Part II, Title VII), inclusive of the Protocol on the Statute of the ESCB/ECB		International Agreement between Member States
EC Council of Ministers	Regulations	Articles of the Treaty, dependent on the subject matter dealt with The formalities are laid down in Articles 250–254 of the Treaty	Generally applicable; binding in their entirety and directly applicable in all Member States
	Directives		Binding, as to the result to be achieved, upon each Member State to which they are addressed, but leave to the national authorities the choice of forms and methods
	Decisions		Binding in their entirety upon addressees
	Recommendations		No binding force
	Opinions		No binding force

Table 1 (continued)

Adopting Authority	Types of Legal Acts	Legal Basis	Legal Nature
ECB Governing Council	Regulations	Articles of the Treaty and the ESCB/ECB Statute, dependent on the subject matter dealt with See in particular Article 34.1, first indent, of the ESCB/ECB Statute The formalities are identical with those for EU Council legal acts	Directly applicable in all Member States, even though they are binding only in the euro area Member States
	Decisions	Article 34 of the ESCB/ECB Statute The formalities are laid down in the ECB's Rules of Procedure	Binding in their entirety upon addressees
	Recommendations		No binding force
	Opinions		No binding force
	Guidelines	Article 14.3 of the ESCB/ECB Statute The formalities for Guidelines are laid down in the ECB's Rules of Procedure	Binding on NCBs Require usually implementation in national legal acts
	Instructions		Binding on NCBs to which they are addressed

Also, in accordance with Article 22 of the Statute, the ECB and the NCBs may provide facilities and the ECB may adopt regulations (in the Community law sense of the word) to ensure efficient and sound clearing and payment systems within the Community and with other countries. Since such regulations are generally applicable in all EU Member States and binding in their entirety, this is a powerful instrument to ensure the efficiency and soundness of payment systems. However, up until now this instrument has not been applied for several reasons. The main reasons are (i) questions on the scope of regulations (should they only deal with technicalities or could they also address, for example, insolvency issues where other (Community) legislative authorities may have a competence) and (ii) the decentralized character of the TARGET system, which will be addressed below.

In addition, in accordance with Article 14.3 of the Statute, the ECB may adopt guidelines that are addressed to the NCBs and that usually require implementation in national legal acts.[7] In view of the ESCB's decentralized nature, guidelines are the cornerstones of the system's regulatory framework. They ensure that those matters are harmonized across the NCBs where harmonization is necessary to ensure a level playing field in the execution of ESCB-related tasks. Where appropriate, they may be topped-up by instructions to NCBs. At the same time, guidelines allow NCBs to tailor their implementation measures toward the requirements of their respective jurisdictions.

Finally, there are two other provisions that should be mentioned, namely Article 105 of the Treaty and Article 2 of the Statute. These Articles require the ESCB to act in accordance with the principle of an open market economy with free competition. On that basis, TARGET is not a monopolistic system, but coexists with other large value payment systems such as "Euro 1," a system operated by the Euro Banking Association Clearing Company. However, certain euro payments will have to go through TARGET and the ECB's central role in payment systems under the Treaty and the Statute implies that the ESCB also acts as overseer of other large value payment systems.

The Legal Structure of TARGET

TARGET is a decentralized system composed of the interlinking component and the EPM operated by the ECB as well as 15 national RTGS systems. This is in line with Article 12.1, third paragraph, of

---

[7] Article 14.3 of the Statute reads as follows: "The national central banks are an integral part of the ESCB and shall act in accordance with the guidelines and instructions of the ECB."

the Statute, which states that the ECB, to the extent deemed possible and appropriate, shall have recourse to the NCBs to carry out operations that form part of the tasks of the ESCB. Legally, this implies the existence of three layers of legal relations within TARGET.

Firstly, the relation between the ECB and the NCBs is governed by a guideline, the TARGET Guideline, adopted under Article 14.3 of the Statute. In addition, since guidelines are internal to the Eurosystem and cannot, thus, bind the three NCBs of the Member States which have not yet introduced the euro, there is also a multilateral agreement, the TARGET Agreement, which is signed by all 15 NCBs and the ECB. The TARGET Agreement mirrors the content of the TARGET Guideline in order to make these three NCBs subject to almost the same regime (almost, since there are certain differences, which mainly relate to monetary policy considerations which do not apply to these three NCBs).

The TARGET Guideline and the TARGET Agreement grant rights to, and impose obligations on, the NCBs which they, in their turn, where appropriate, have to reflect in their national RTGS documentation applicable to the legal relation between NCBs and their counterparties. This is the second layer of legal documentation. Such national legal RTGS documentation is tailored toward requirements of the legal systems in which it is intended to operate. Dependent on these legal systems and also on the practices of NCBs, national documentation may be of a regulatory or contractual nature or a mixture thereof. While the more northerly situated NCBs generally apply contractual "General Terms and Conditions," in the more southerly located NCBs there is a tradition to (also, in addition) apply regulatory means. In this context, it is interesting to note that the ECB's power to adopt regulations was introduced in Article 22 of the Statute at the initiative of the Italian delegation during the Treaty negotiations.

Since the Eurosystem has one single monetary policy and since TARGET is an instrument to implement such policy, it is important that access to euro liquidity is granted to counterparties in such a manner that there is a level playing field or, in other words, that there are economically no distortions across the Eurosystem in the terms and conditions under which such access is granted. The ECB has, therefore, reviewed the implementation of the TARGET Guideline (and the TARGET Agreement) by the NCBs in their national legal RTGS documentation and it monitors compliance therewith on a standing basis.

The third layer is the legal documentation between the national RTGS participants and their counterparties (for example, companies, private individuals) which may also bear the traces of the TARGET legal documentation. Again, this third layer is tailored towards the requirements of the legal system in which it is intended to operate.

The Impact of the Settlement Finality Directive and the Cross-Border Credit Transfers Directive on TARGET

One area of law that could not be conclusively addressed by the TARGET Guideline is the finality of payments through TARGET. The need to adjust national laws in order to ensure the nonretroactivity of insolvency procedures (including, in particular, the so-called "zero-hour rule") is instead addressed by an EU Directive on settlement finality in payment and securities settlement systems.[8]

The Settlement Finality Directive covers those payment and securities settlement systems, which have been notified by the competent authorities of the Member States to the European Commission, as well as collateral security provided in the framework of participation in such systems, with the objective to establish legal certainty by reducing systemic risk.

The Directive provides for the following five principles:

- Netting, bilateral or multilateral, shall be legally enforceable and binding on third parties (Article 3).

- System rules should define the point at which transfer orders become irrevocable and must be recognized (Recital 14, Article 3.3, Article 5).

---

[8] Directive 98/26/EC of the European Parliament and of the Council of May 19, 1998, on settlement finality in payment and securities settlement systems.

- Rules giving retroactive effect to the insolvency of a participant in a system, such as "zero-hour" rules, shall be abolished (Article 7).

- The insolvency of a participant in a system continues to be governed by the home country insolvency law. However, the rights and obligations in connection with participation in a system are to be governed by the insolvency law of the jurisdiction that the parties to the system have chosen to govern that system (Article 8).

- Collateral provided to a participant in a system (and in particular the ECB and NCBs), whether in the form of pledge, repo, or any other legal technique, shall not be affected by insolvency proceedings against the provider of such collateral (Article 9).

These provisions, as implemented at a national level by the EU Member State, will benefit also TARGET since all component national RTGS systems and the EPM have been notified to the European Commission as "systems" under the Directive.

Another new Community Directive in the field of payment systems is the Cross-Border Credit Transfers Directive.[9] This Directive is mainly of a consumer protection nature and aims at enhancing transparency of the conditions on which cross-border credit transfers are executed and the efficient and quick execution of such transfers. The main features of the Cross-Border Credit Transfers Directive are the following:

- The Directive is applicable to all EU cross-border credit transfers (excluding interprofessional transfers) for amounts not exceeding EUR 50,000 (Article 1).

- The Directive contains requirements for improved transparency of the conditions on which a credit transfer is executed, both prior and subsequent to the execution (Articles 3 and 4).

---

[9] Directive 97/5/EC of the European Parliament and of the Council of January 27, 1997 on cross-border credit transfers.

- The Directive contains requirements for an improved execution of credit transfers, in particular the suppression of unauthorized fee deductions, adherence to stipulated time schedules, recovery of misled or unexecuted credit transfers, and provisions of redress procedures with a money-back guarantee with a ceiling of EUR12,500 in case a credit transfer has gone astray (Articles 5 et seq.).

Since TARGET does not contain a lower limit under which payments cannot be made through the system, the provisions of the Cross-Border Credit Transfers Directive concerning information to customers, before and after the execution of transfers, and as regards the time and price of such transfers, are also relevant to TARGET. These provisions aim at enhancing transparency and to improve the level of service and efficiency for retail cross-border payments in Europe, an objective shared by the ECB.

The Collateral Requirements for TARGET

TARGET participants are granted intraday credit up to the amount of collateral that they have provided. This feature of collateralization stems from Article 18.1, second indent, of the Statute, which states that the ECB and the NCBs shall require "adequate collateral" in their credit operations with counterparties.[10]

This requirement of "adequate collateral" has led the ESCB to establish lists of eligible assets that are divided into tier one and tier two collateral. The tier one list consists of marketable assets that fulfill uniform euro area-wide eligibility criteria specified by the ECB. The tier two list consists of additional assets that the NCBs consider particularly important for their national financial markets

---

[10] Article 18.1, second indent, of the Statute reads as follows: "In order to achieve the objectives of the ESCB and to carry out its tasks, the ECB and the national central banks may . . . conduct credit operations with credit institutions and other market participants, with lending being based on adequate collateral."

and banking systems. The table below shows the main features of tier one and tier two as collateral.[11]

Table 2. TARGET Collateral Requirements

Criteria	Tier One	Tier Two
Type of asset	• ECB debt certificates; • Other marketable debt instruments (excluding "hybrid" instruments).	• Marketable debt instruments; • Nonmarketable debt instruments; • Equities traded on a regulated market.
Settlement procedures	• Instruments must be centrally deposited in book-entry form with national central banks or a CSD fulfilling the ECB's minimum standards.	• Assets must be easily accessible to the national central bank that has included them in its tier two list.
Type of issuer	• ESCB; • Public sector; • Private sector; • International and supranational institutions.	• Public sector; • Private sector.
Credit standard	• The issuer (guarantor) must be deemed financially sound by the ECB.	• The issuer/debtor (guarantor) must be deemed financially sound by the national central bank that has included the asset in its tier two list.

[11] Details may be found in "The single monetary policy in Stage Three: General documentation on ESCB monetary policy instruments and procedures," ECB, September 1998, p. 43.

Criteria	Tier One	Tier Two
Place of establishment of the issuer (or guarantor)	• European Economic Area (EEA).	• Euro area.
Location of asset	• Euro area.	• Euro area.
Currency	• Euro.	• Euro.
Memo item: Cross-border use	• Yes.	• Yes.

The decentralized nature of TARGET implies that collateral may be provided through those legal means that are tailored toward the jurisdiction in which the collateral is provided. The most common means are repurchase agreements and pledge and similar techniques. In an attempt to harmonize the terms and conditions of repurchase agreements, the ECB has developed a master repurchase agreement, which NCBs may use at their discretion, if necessary, in a form adapted to their respective legal systems. Similar projects such as the development of the European Master Agreement (EMA) by the European Banking Federation (EBF) are followed with great interest by the ESCB and may also result in templates of agreements for use by NCBs.

Collateral delivered in the framework of TARGET may also be provided on a cross-border basis. A counterparty of an NCB may activate collateral deposited in another Member State and deliver such collateral to the NCB of such other Member State. To this end, the ESCB has developed the Correspondent Central Bank Model (CCBM), where the correspondent NCB establishes, administers, and, where necessary, realizes the collateral on behalf of the NCB that provides the credit.

Summarized in a scheme (see Figure 1), the CCBM works as follows:

Figure 1.

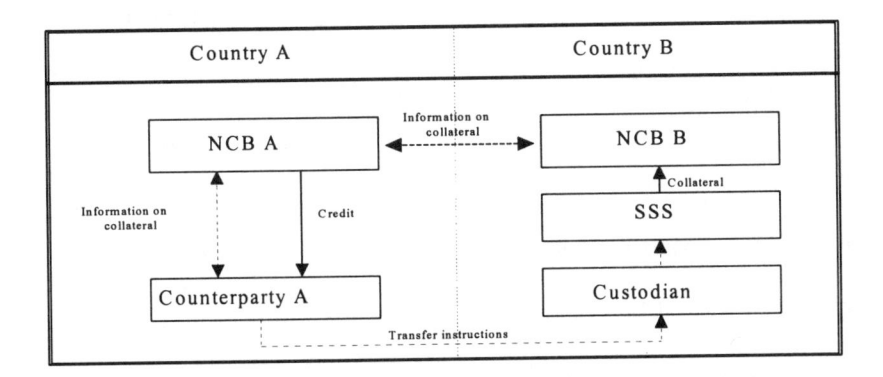

```
┌─────────────────────────────────┬─────────────────────────────────┐
│          Country A              │          Country B              │
├─────────────────────────────────┴─────────────────────────────────┤
│                        Information on                             │
│      ┌─────────┐       collateral        ┌─────────┐              │
│      │  NCB A  │ ◄---------------------► │  NCB B  │              │
│      └─────────┘                         └─────────┘              │
│        ▲   │                                  ▲ Collateral        │
│        │   │                             ┌─────────┐              │
│ Information│  Credit                     │   SSS   │              │
│ on         │                             └─────────┘              │
│ collateral │                                  ▲                   │
│        │   ▼                             ┌─────────┐              │
│      ┌───────────────┐                   │ Custodian│             │
│      │Counterparty A │                   └─────────┘              │
│      └───────────────┘                        ▲                   │
│              └----------Transfer instructions-┘                   │
└───────────────────────────────────────────────────────────────────┘
```

At present, there is a trend toward links between, and mergers of, Securities Settlement Systems (SSS) in the EU and this creates opportunities to deliver collateral directly on a cross-border basis to the NCB that provides credit. Meanwhile, there are more than 60 such links across the Community. In addition, recently the (German) Deutsche Börse Clearing (DBC) and the (Luxembourg) Cedel decided to merge into Clearstream and the Belgium-based Euroclear and French Sicovam have also announced merger plans. This implies that the CCBM will lose importance over time. As an important and large user of the services of SSS, the ECB has imposed certain requirements on SSS as a precondition to become eligible as vehicles for the ESCB's collateral operations. Along the lines of the Lamfalussy Report on netting,[12] these requirements are put in the form of minimum common standards[13] and the ECB regularly monitors compliance therewith. The ECB also reviewed links between SSS against, basically, the same standards. From a legal point of view, the main standard is standard 1 on the legal soundness of SSS and links between them. This standard reads as follows: "All

---

[12] Report of the Committee on Interbank Netting Schemes of the Central Banks of the Group of Ten Countries, Bank for International Settlements (BIS), November 1990.

[13] Report on "Standards for the Use of EU Securities Settlement Systems in ESCB Credit Operations," ECB, January 1998.

securities settlement systems (SSS) and the links between such systems must have a sound legal basis, ensuring that the settlement of payment and securities transfers is final, and must provide for adequate protection for the rights of the NCBs and the ECB in respect of securities held in their accounts in such systems." The ESCB has further elaborated this standard in substandards on matters such as

- the nature of the entitlement to securities held in the system for the holder;

- the liability for losses/error;

- the legal basis for settlement finality;

- the enforceability of netting; and

- the enforceability of risk management measures.

In addition, the ESCB has supported the adoption of legislation to improve the possibilities to establish and realize collateral. For example, Article 9 of the Settlement Finality Directive is very much inspired by the ECB's predecessor, the European Monetary Institute (EMI).

Yet, law and practices across the Community still show a wide diversity as far as collateral issues are concerned and there is a widely felt need for further harmonization. The EU Commission and the ECB, therefore, started projects to achieve such further harmonization and these projects are eventually expected to result in a new Directive especially dedicated to collateral issues. Collateral issues are within the ESCB, inter alia, discussed in a European Financial Market Lawyers Group (EFMLG), which has been established along the same lines as a similar group at the Fed New York (the Financial Markets Lawyers Group).

Epilogue: The Implications of Future Developments for TARGET's Legal Framework

It is expected that TARGET will evolve over time and so will its legal framework. Various developments may lead to adaptations of TARGET's legal framework as it currently stands.

The ESCB may once in a while be confronted with situations that require such adaptation. For example, at the end of January 1999, one of TARGET's national RTGS components broke down due to a computer failure that prevented the execution of payments from and into the national RTGS component concerned. This has led to a proposal to provide, through the TARGET Guideline and the TARGET Agreement, for a reimbursement scheme to compensate those participants that, in the unlikely situation that such an event would occur again, are forced to have recourse to the Eurosystem's standing facilities (the deposit facility and the marginal lending facility).

Technically, it would be possible to further consolidate the TARGET components. Any such consolidation is likely to affect the legal framework of TARGET.

Links between, and mergers of, SSS may have an impact on TARGET's legal framework as far as the establishment, administration, and realization of collateral are concerned.

The ECB has decided to disclose large parts of the TARGET Guideline to market participants and the general public. This is done in the framework of a project to enhance the ESCB's transparency through, inter alia, publication of the legal acts of which its regulatory framework is composed. Publication of the TARGET Guideline may lead to a general discussion on these documents, for example in academic circles. Although these documents have been carefully prepared and reviewed by a variety of groups (for example, legal experts, payment systems experts, inclusive of NCB representatives), it may, of course, not be excluded that such discussions, if any, will lead to useful suggestions for future amendments to TARGET's legal framework.

The accession of new Member States to the EU will have implications for TARGET and, thus, for its legal framework. Thirteen countries have applied for membership in the EU: Bulgaria, Cyprus, the Czech Republic, Estonia, Hungary, Latvia, Lithuania, Malta, Poland, Romania, Slovakia, Slovenia, and Turkey. Accession to the EU implies that the NCBs of these countries will become members of the ESCB and this will raise the question of participation in TARGET. Such participation will require adaptation of TARGET's legal framework, but it is too early to predict what kind of adaptation since TARGET, at the time of accession and at the time of the introduction of the euro by these countries, may be different from its present structure.

In addition, there is a variety of other developments that may, eventually, affect TARGET's legal framework, but it is not always possible to precisely predict how. For example, the increased importance of e-money and e-commerce, consolidation in the banking industry, and the creation of delivery-versus-payment systems in SSS (for collateral) may have an impact. Also, there is a project under way, the Continuous Linked Settlement (CLS), which will, once established, provide for a multicurrency system for the settlement of foreign exchange transactions on a payment-versus-payment basis. It is envisaged that the operator of the system would be a special purpose bank (Continuous Linked Settlement Bank International) located in New York with around 60 (indirect) shareholders, all of which are financial institutions located in 14 different countries. The ECB, through the EPM, is envisaged to settle payments in euro and oversee the euro part of CLS. Last but not least, the EU Commission has developed a Financial Services Action Plan (FSAP) to further enhance the internal market. The FSAP envisages further action in areas such as the implementation of the Settlement Finality Directive, the creation of a single market for payments, and the prevention of fraud in payment systems, e-commerce, and e-money.

Finally, it is noted that the ECB has to be consulted by the Community legislator and the legislative authorities of the EU Member States on draft legislation in the ECB's field of competence, which includes payment and settlement systems. This obligation is laid down in Article 105.4 of the Treaty as repeated in Article 4 of the Statute and in Article 2.1, fourth indent, of an EU Council Decision in this field.[14] In the past, the EMI (for which a similar obligation

---

[14] Article 105.4 of the Treaty, as repeated in Article 4 of the Treaty, reads as follows: "The ECB shall be consulted on any proposed Community act in its field of competence by national authorities regarding any draft legislative provision in its field of competence, but within the limits and under the conditions set out by the Council."

Article 2.1, fourth indent, of the Council decision of June 29, 1998 on the consultation of the European Central Bank by national authorities regarding draft

(continued)

existed) and the ECB have delivered approximately 30 opinions on draft legislation relating to payment and settlement systems. These consultation procedures, albeit resulting in nonbinding opinions, give the ECB an important instrument to influence the content of Community and national legislation on payment and settlement systems and to foster its consistency across the Community, which is particularly relevant when such legislation affects TARGET. This is the reason why the ECB has encouraged EU Member States to consult the ECB on the implementation of the Settlement Finality Directive, although they are formally not obliged to consult the ECB on legislation implementing directives. And this is also the reason, why the ECB stands ready to review draft legislation in accession countries in this field, although accession countries are not obliged to consult the ECB as long as they have not become members of the EU.

---

legislative provisions (98/415/EC) reads as follows: "The authorities of the Member States shall consult the ECB on any draft legislative provision within its field of competence pursuant to the Treaty and in particular on . . . payment and settlement systems."

IX. Dormant Accounts

Chapter 38

Swiss Law on the Treatment of Dormant Accounts: A Comparison with European and U.S. Law

MICHAEL BRADFIELD AND PAMELA SAK

Every year governments around the world take "temporary custody" of billions of dollars worth of abandoned or unclaimed assets, including dormant accounts, through a legal process known as "escheat." Through such a process, the rights of the original owners of the property may be protected and a mechanism is established for reuniting the owner with their property, and the government—rather than banks and other institutions—benefits from holding the property until such time as it is claimed. Recent technological developments—mainly, the development of the Internet and proliferation of its use—have drastically increased the ability of people to search for and locate such dormant accounts, and governments have taken notice and are facilitating the return of such assets to their owners. Enhancements in technology have also made it easier for banks to identify earlier when an account has evidence of inactivity and to locate the account holders.

While the focus here is the law on dormant accounts, a general description of the investigation of Swiss banks to identify dormant accounts of victims of Nazi persecution is useful, as this is the context in which the authors' research on the law on the treatment of dormant accounts arose. Then this chapter reviews the dormant account law in Switzerland and compares it to those in Germany, the United Kingdom, France, Australia, Canada, and finally, the United States.

The ICEP Investigation for Dormant Accounts in Swiss Banks

In May 1996, as a result of increasing public pressure, the Swiss banking community agreed to the establishment of the Independent Committee of Eminent Persons, or ICEP, as it is commonly known. The Committee was made up of five representatives of Jewish organizations and five members representing Swiss banks.

Paul Volcker, former Chairman of the Federal Reserve, was asked to serve as Chairman of the Committee, and Michael Bradfield was asked to serve as its Counsel. In September 1996, the Committee began its investigations of 59 Swiss banks, which in the end would span over three years and involve five of the then Big Six international accounting firms. The ensuing investigation was one of the largest accounting investigations in history.

Why was this investigation necessary? A partial answer to that question is the topic of this presentation today—if Switzerland had had a different law on the treatment of dormant accounts, then the ICEP investigation may never have happened. Consequently, not only can other countries that are trying to return assets to victims of Nazi persecution learn from the Swiss experience, but in fact many other countries can draw a valuable lesson from it. The lesson emphasizes the need for a law by which dormant accounts and other assets escheat (or are transferred to) the government after a statutorily defined period so that the owners are protected by locating them and restoring to them their property, as well as to give the state, rather than the holders of the unclaimed property, the benefit of its use. An escheat law also encourages discipline within banks to identify dormant accounts early so that they may maintain their relationships with their customers.

As part of the ICEP investigation, research was performed on the Swiss law on the treatment of dormant accounts, as well as such law in other European countries and the United States. In its final report—*The Treatment of Dormant Accounts of Victims of Nazi Persecution by Swiss Banks* (the ICEP Report)—released in December 1999, ICEP prepared a survey of the legal obligations of banks with respect to dormant accounts, in Switzerland, as well as in Germany, France, Belgium, the United Kingdom, and five individual states in the United States during the World War II era and presently.[1] This chapter draws largely from that survey.

---

[1] Independent Committee of Eminent Persons, *Swiss Law on the Treatment of Dormant Accounts*, Annex 9 on Report on Dormant Accounts of Victims of Nazi Persecution by Swiss Banks, 123–35 (December 1999) (hereinafter, "ICEP Report").

When analyzing the legal framework for the treatment of dormant accounts in the various countries, there are four basic issues to consider:

- first, whether dormant accounts eventually escheat, or are paid to, the sovereign government;

- second, whether the banks and/or the sovereign have a duty to notify the account holders or their heirs of the existence of a dormant account;

- third, whether the banks and/or the sovereign are obligated to repay dormant accounts to the rightful owners, and if so, the period of time for which the obligation stands; and,

- fourth, whether there are any particular procedures for claimants to recover their dormant accounts.

Comparison of Swiss Law on Dormant Accounts to Laws in Other European Countries and the United States

Switzerland, unlike other countries such as Canada, France, and the United States, does not have a statute that requires banks to hand over dormant accounts to the state for safekeeping. The Swiss system of law and banking practice with respect to dormant accounts had the effect of having dormant accounts remaining with the banks until such time as they are claimed by the account holders or their heirs. Under the Swiss system, the banks have had no or very little incentive to identify dormant accounts and return them to their owners. As a consequence, Swiss banks today hold very large amounts of open, dormant accounts. As a result of the ICEP investigation, we understand that the Swiss legislature is now focusing on this problem and is considering the adoption of an escheat law applicable to dormant accounts.[2] Moreover, the Swiss Bankers Association has

---

[2] *See* Statement by Ambassador Thomas Borer, Head of the Task Force: Switzerland-WWII to the Committee on Banking and Financial Services of the House of Representatives (June 25, 1997), stating that federal escheat legislation is under consideration and "would bring a lasting solution to the legal difficulties arising from dormant assets."

already adopted revised guidelines on the treatment of dormant accounts.[3]

Switzerland

In Switzerland, the relationship between banks and their customers is governed by the contract between them—the general terms of the documentation signed by the customer at the time the account was opened. Other relevant law applies in the absence of contractual provisions.[4]

During the 1930s and 1940s, most of the contractual relationships between the banks and their customers were governed primarily by what are known as the "General Conditions," which were signed by customers at the time they opened their account. Customer contracts were generally highly standardized, although the terms of the contract may have varied depending on the requirements of the parties.

Provisions of the Swiss Civil Code and Code of Obligations would apply only to the extent that the General Conditions were silent on the point at issue; however, the principle of good faith applied in all cases. Under Articles 2 and 3 of the Civil Code, every person is bound to exercise their rights and fulfill their obligations according to the principle of good faith. Swiss banks, therefore, were expected to exercise the principle of good faith, embracing the concept of mutual trust, in their dealings with their customers.

---

[3] Swiss Bankers Association, Guidelines of the Swiss Bankers Association on the Treatment of Dormant Accounts, Custody Accounts and Safe-Deposit Boxes Held in Swiss Banks (2000), replacing the guidelines dated September 8, 1995; Information for Customers of Swiss Banks Concerning the Avoidance of Dormant Assets (February 2000).

[4] Significant areas of civil legislation as it relates to agreements between parties are codified in the Swiss Civil Code and the Swiss Code of Obligations. These statutory laws became effective on January 1, 1912. The Code of Obligations pertains to certain aspects of civil legislation as they relate to the responsibilities of the parties to an agreement. The contractual relationship between a bank and its customer may be governed by various general provisions contained in the Code of Obligations but there is no specific provision regarding the relationship between a bank and its customer. The Code of Obligations was substantially revised in 1936, and this later version remained in force until 1992, when it underwent further revisions.

During the 1930s and 1940s, as well as today, theoretically, a Swiss bank holding a dormant account could voluntarily initiate a process whereby dormant assets could be transferred to the state.[5] Such process provides for the publication of the account, and if no heir is identified, then, in the case of assets of Swiss citizens, the estate will be managed by an appointed curator.[6] However, it is unknown whether any Swiss bank has ever utilized such procedure or whether this procedure could also be initiated for and applied to assets of a foreigner whose last domicile was outside of Switzerland.[7] Certainly, the banks had no incentive to initiate such a procedure. The newly adopted Swiss Bankers Association guidelines do not provide that such procedure would be used, but rather they provide that dormant accounts remain with the banks.

With respect to accounts of Holocaust victims, there was much debate in Switzerland on the fate of heirless assets during the period from the end of World War II up to the Federal Decree of 1962.[8] In 1947, a federal decree providing for the registration of assets dormant since May 9, 1945 was drafted, but the decree was never enacted. Again in 1952, the government tried to revive legislation pertaining to

---

[5] A person can be declared absent by the court if the person disappeared under circumstances of mortal danger or has not been heard of for a long time (Code Civil art. 35 (Switz.)). The declaration of absence can be requested one year after the mortal danger or five years after the last communication. The court will then order that a notice be published and if no information about the person is received within the time prescribed by the judge in the publication of the notice, which is at least one year, the court can declare the person dead (Code Civil art. 36 (Switz.)). It has been admitted by the courts that this procedure could also be applied to foreigners whose last domicile was outside of Switzerland when the sole purpose of the procedure is to deal with assets left by them in Switzerland (ATF 46 II 496 (Switz. 1920)).

[6] Code Civil art. 548 (Switz.); Code Civil art. 393 (Switz.).

[7] In the case of assets left at a bank, the appointment of a curator is necessary because it is not acceptable for the bank, as debtor, to manage the assets of its creditor (ATF 51 II 264 (Switz. 1926)). If the official management of the estate by a curator has lasted for more than ten years or the account holder would have reached the age of 100 years, then the judge may declare the heir absent. If no one claims to have an interest in the funds within a period set by the judge, then the funds revert to the canton or the municipality that would inherit if the absent person had no heir (Code Civil art. 550, Section 2 (Switz.)). The canton or the municipality remains responsible, however, to the beneficiaries to the dormant accounts (Code Civil art. 550, Section 3 (Switz.)).

[8] *See* ICEP Report, *supra* note 1, Annex 5: Treatment of Dormant Accounts of Victims of Nazi Persecution.

the issue of heirless assets. For a decade thereafter, discussions as to the merits of the proposed legislation continued. The Swiss Bankers Association and its members generally resisted such legislation. They argued that the existing legal framework was sufficient to manage the issue. They also sought to demonstrate that the value of such assets was not sufficiently great to justify the introduction of new legislation.[9] The ICEP Report is critical of the results of the prior surveys for dormant accounts and, in particular, the apparent reluctance of Swiss banks to cooperate with such surveys.[10]

As a result of the ICEP investigation, some 4.1 million accounts of an estimated 6.8 million accounts open in Swiss banks in the 1933 to 1945 period were identified. Of these accounts, some 46,000 accounts were determined to be probably or possibly related to victims of Nazi persecution and had not previously been published, and there was no evidence that they had been paid to victims of Nazi persecution or their heirs. ICEP recommended the publication of approximately 26,000 of these accounts with the highest probability of being accounts of victims of Nazi persecution. It also recommended that, using the claims filed by victims of Nazi persecution in the class action lawsuit pending in New York against the two largest Swiss banks, and other claims similarly filed, further database research be conducted to identify any additional accounts of victims of Nazi persecution that may not have been identified during the course of the investigation. The Swiss Federal Banking Commission recently authorized the publication of the 26,000 accounts recommended by ICEP for publication, and details with respect to further database research issues are still being resolved.

The finding after 50 years of such large numbers of accounts that are probably or possibly those of victims of Nazi persecution speaks for itself. In this context, the Committee was critical of the conduct of Swiss banks. Its final report stated:

> There is . . . confirmed evidence of questionable and deceitful actions by some individual banks in the handling of accounts of victims, including withholding of information from Holocaust victims or their heirs about their accounts, inappropriate closing of

---

[9] *See id.* at 89–92.
[10] *Id.* at 87 et seq.

accounts, failure to keep adequate records, many cases of insensitivity to the efforts of victims or heirs of victims to claim dormant or closed accounts, and a general lack of diligence—even active resistance—in response to earlier private and official inquiries about dormant accounts.[11]

The Committee "question[ed] whether their duty of due care in their dealings with customers was observed by a number of the banks and their officers in the special situation following World War II."[12] At the same time, it should be noted that the Committee also concluded that:

> The auditors have reported no evidence of systematic destruction of records of victim accounts, organized discrimination against the accounts of victims of Nazi persecution, or concerted efforts to divert the funds of victims of Nazi persecution to improper purposes.[13]

Comparison to Other Countries

Laws on the treatment of dormant accounts similar to that in Switzerland apply to dormant accounts in Germany and the United Kingdom. On the other hand, France, Australia, Canada, and the United States have laws providing that abandoned, dormant accounts are transferred to government authorities in periods ranging from 3 to 30 years, and that continuing efforts are made by the state to identify and return such dormant assets to their owners.

Germany

The German law and practice with respect to dormant accounts substantially mirrors that of Switzerland. Neither the Federal Republic of Germany, or its predecessor the German Reich, had or has enacted a law specifically on dormant bank accounts. As in Switzerland, the relationship between the bank and its customer is governed by the terms of the contract between them. Like the Swiss "General Conditions," in Germany, there are "General Business Conditions" that set forth basic rules governing the relationship

---

[11] *Id.* at 13.
[12] *Id.* at 14.
[13] *Id.* at 13.

between the customer and the bank. Under German law, a bank account is deemed a claim of the account holder against the bank, and after 30 years, the claim of an account holder or his or her heirs to an unclaimed bank account may be barred.[14]

Today, the Federal Association of German Banks states that it is an internal policy of its members to initiate research to locate the holder of an account that has been dormant for an unusual period of time. For example, the internal guidelines of Deutsche Bank provide that where the place of residence of the holder of a safe deposit box is unknown, the bank must investigate whether the holder has moved to a new residence without providing notice to the bank or is deceased. The Deutsche Bank Guidelines also provide that bank accounts exceeding $458 (DM 1,000) cannot be closed and never become dormant. Bank accounts with a balance of less than $458 (DM 1,000) are transferred to the bank's collection account when they have been dormant for two years and the bank is unable to locate the holder with reasonable efforts.

With respect to the treatment of accounts of Holocaust victims, during World War II the legal system of the German Reich was designed to transfer all Jewish assets to the Reich, and many laws were suspended until 1945.[15] In light of the reunification of Germany

---

[14] German law provides that the applicable statute of limitations period is 30 years (194, 195 BGB). The German courts, however, have not decided whether the limitation period begins from the last contact of the bank with the account holder or if other circumstances must be taken into consideration as well. In the context of savings accounts, the Court of Appeal Schleswig decided that only a notice of termination by the holder of the account would trigger the statute of limitations. Dormant savings accounts can therefore only exist if the account holder dies after sending a notice of termination to the bank and has not withdrawn the money from the account. This decision has not yet been applied to other forms of bank accounts or bank deposits.

[15] After World War II, a system of restitution and compensation was established for West Germany by the U.S. military government. One major goal of this system was to transfer all bank accounts, stocks, and other assets that were confiscated during the Nazi regime to victims of Nazi persecution, their heirs, and Jewish successor organizations. In furtherance of this goal, the U.S. military government enacted Law no. 59 on the Restitution of Identifiable Property ("USREG"). Gesetz Nr. 59—Rückerstattung feststellbarer Vermögensgegenstände. Banks were required to submit records to registration centers and failure to comply with this reporting requirement was punishable by up to five years of imprisonment (Id., arts. 73, 75). Assets for which there were no surviving heirs were to vest with "Jewish successor
(continued)

in 1990, the Federal Republic of Germany has passed laws providing restitution or compensation for all claims, including those to bank accounts, of victims of Nazi persecution in former East Germany.[16] A substantial humanitarian fund has also been established for persons with slave-labor and other claims against German industry.[17]

United Kingdom

The law and practice relating to dormant accounts in the United Kingdom is also parallel to that in Switzerland and Germany. It is worth noting at the outset that, according to one report, the value of unclaimed assets, including dormant accounts, unclaimed pensions, and unclaimed lottery winnings in the United Kingdom in 1999 was conservatively estimated at $116 billion (£77 billion).[18]

In the United Kingdom, the relationship between a bank and its customers is governed by the terms of their contract. Although there is a voluntary Code of Banking Practice, the treatment of dormant accounts varies among banks. For example, at NatWest Bank, accounts automatically become dormant after five years of inactivity, and the funds are then placed into a suspense account, where the

---

organizations" (*Id.* art. 10). The Federal Republic of Germany was to compensate all persons with claims relating to identifiable property, including stocks and bank accounts located in West Germany and West Berlin, under the Allied restitution program and the German restitution program. All property that had been confiscated in Germany and which had been brought later to the Federal Republic of Germany from occupied territories, including concentration camps, was retransferred to the rightful owner or compensated for.

[16] The Law on the Settlement of Open Property Issues, Gesetz zur Regelung Offener Vermögensfragen vom 23.9.1990 in der Fassung vom 24.7. 1997, Bundesgesetzblatt I. 1997, S. 1823. The Jewish Claims Conference is named as the successor organization authorized to file claims with regard to Jewish property that has been confiscated or that fell to the treasury as statutory heir in former East Germany (*Id.* Section 2). The Nazi Victim Compensation Law of September 27, 1994, NS-Verfolgten-Entschädigungsgesetz vom 27.9.1994, Bundesgesetzblatt I, S. 2632.

[17] *See* Agreement Reached on Allocating Nazi Labor Compensation Fund, Fox Marketwire (March 23, 2000) (http://www.foxmarketwire.com/wires/0323/f_ap_0323_15.sml) (visited May 3, 2000).

[18] Jonathan Guthrie, *Sniff Out Your Missing Cash: Dormant Accounts*, Financial Times (London), September 13, 1997 at 3; *See* http://www.unclaimedassets.com/uk.htm (citing London's *Financial Times*) (visited April 28, 2000).

dormant accounts no longer accrue any interest.[19] In order to claim a dormant account, the account holder must write to the specific bank to reclaim the funds. Another bank—Abbey National Bank—places a dormant account indicator on an account 18 months after a bank letter to the account holder has been returned by the post office. The funds remain in the customer's account until the holder or his or her heirs return to the bank to claim the account. Coutts & Co., a bank with a relatively small client base (about 50,000 clients), classes an account as dormant if there has been no entry in an account for at least two years, and all reasonable attempts to contact the client have failed. Again, in order to claim a dormant account, the account holder must contact the bank directly.

Because the procedures by which banks handled dormant accounts have varied, in July 1996, the British Bankers Association attempted to standardize the treatment of dormant bank accounts. Toward this end, they produced a standard "Dormant Bank Account" claim form, which may be submitted by claimants at the specific banks that they believe hold their dormant accounts.[20]

---

[19] *See id.* (noting that banks are within their rights to reduce or stop paying interest on dormant accounts).

[20] With respect to a dormant account, a demand for payment must be made and only then does the six-year time period for claiming such an amount start. Under Section 5 of the Limitation Act of 1980 and similar predecessor legislation, an action may not be brought after the expiration of six years from the date on which the cause of action accrued. In relation to debt recovery, time does not begin to run until there is a debt presently due and payable. In *Joachimson v. Swiss Bank Corporation*, 1921 3 KB 110, the Court held that a bank is not liable to pay the customer the full amount of his balance until demand is made. The Court further held that "the practical bearing of this decision [as to the necessity for a demand] is on the question of the statute of limitations...the result of this decision will be that for the future bankers may have to face claims for balances on accounts that have remained dormant for more than six years" (*Id.* at 130–131). Thus, under *Joachimson*, time does not begin to run against the customer until demand for payment has been made, irrespective of the amount of time that has elapsed since the last transaction relating to the account. See, however, the Court of Appeal decision *Mahomed v. Bank of Borada* (November 16, 1998), which held that if, following a demand for payment, the dormant account holder did not renew the claim within six years and the bank closed the account or transferred the account to a suspense account, the dormant account holder would be time-barred from making a fresh demand.

France

France is an example of a country with an escheat law, or a law pursuant to which the state takes custody and assumes title of dormant accounts and other abandoned property. In France, in the 1933–1945 period, dormant bank accounts, as well as unclaimed estates and other unclaimed assets, reverted to the state when no justified claim from any heir or assign was received over a period of 30 years.[21] In the 6 months before the expiration of the 30-year period, the Deposit and Consignment Office was required to notify the interested parties of which it had knowledge. A registered letter was to be sent to the last known residence of the depositor or, if no residence was known, to the state prosecutor. The date and place of the deposit and the names of interested parties were also published in the bulletin issued by the French government.

Present day laws in France authorize institutions holding deposits of cash or securities to close accounts on which there has been no movement recorded for a period of ten years,[22] and the Deposit and Consignment Office is empowered to receive such accounts.[23] Six months prior to transferring a dormant account to the Deposit and Consignment Office, the bank must notify the rightful claimants of which they have knowledge of the existence of the dormant assets by registered letter sent to their last known domicile. After an account has been dormant for 30 years, a bank must disgorge it to the tax bureau, provided it has not already been deposited with the Deposit and Consignment Office.[24]

The Deposit and Consignment Office is obligated to transfer to the state the balance, plus interest, of any account for which there has been no payment or repayment order, and for which no payment requisition has been received by the office over a continuous period

---

[21] State Property Code, Code du domaine de l'Etat, Art. L. 27 (Fr.).

[22] Law no. 77-4 of January 3, 1977, art. 2, Amending Article 189 bis of the French Commercial Code, concernant la prescription en matière commerciale (prescription concerning commercial matters) (J.O. 4 janv. 1977).

[23] Decree no. 79-894 of October 15, 1979, portant application de la loi n. 77-4 du 3 janvier 1977 modifiant l'article 189 bis du Code de commerce concernant la prescription en matière commerciale, J.O. Oct. 19, 1979.

[24] Decree no. 79-894 art. 2 set forth at Article R. 47 of the State Property Code (Code du domaine de l'Etat).

of 30 years. The statutory public notification procedure (that is, informing those concerned by registered letter of the forthcoming forfeiture along with publication in the government bulletin of the names and addresses of the owners of the relevant sums) is applied in all cases where the amounts involved exceed $136 (FRF 1,000).[25]

With respect to accounts of Holocaust victims, during World War II, the Germans occupied France and the Vichy Government undertook the "aryanization" of Jewish assets. Deposits of Jewish account holders with banks, notary publics, or other persons or entities in the occupied part of the country were frozen.[26] Approximately 67,000 deposit accounts, securities accounts, and savings accounts were declared frozen to the General Commission for Jewish Affairs in 1941. After the liberation of France, a number of measures were undertaken by the French authorities to restore the assets of those individuals who had suffered from the criminal activity of the military occupation forces and their accomplices.[27] New efforts to return assets to Holocaust victims or their heirs are under way in France today.[28]

---

[25] Law no. 67-1172 of December 22, 1967, art. 25.
[26] German Order of May 28, 1941 and an Act of July 22, 1941.
[27] *See* Government Order of November 14, 1944 (as extended on March 25, 1945) (Fr.); Government Order of April 15, 1945 (Fr.).
[28] As of June 1999, the Deposit and Consignment Office had been able to find evidence of repayment of 166 deposits to victims or heirs and assigns, out of a total of over 7,000 repayments made since the end of 1944. Generally, the amounts plus interest were refunded by bank transfer or postal order to the rightful owners on production of proof of identity. The deposited funds could be transferred to the owner's bank or postal checking account at the request of an interested party irrespective of his capacity or authority. In exceptional cases, the Deposit and Consignment Office reimbursed balances of less than FRF 5,000 to spouses on presentation of a certificate, issued by the government, vouching for the fact that the owner of the escrowed sum had been deported and had not yet returned. In 1997, the Study Mission into the Looting of Jewish Assets in France was established to examine the conditions under which assets belonging to individuals considered to be Jewish by the military occupier and the Vichy authorities were confiscated or, in general terms, acquired by fraud, violence, or other culpable means. The Study Mission into the Looting of Jewish Assets in France is an attempt to evaluate the extent of this theft and to indicate the identity of the private individuals and legal entities it benefited. The Study Mission has also been asked to determine what happened to the assets involved during the period between the end of the war and the present day and to endeavor to locate their whereabouts and legal status. The Study
(continued)

Australia and Canada

A brief description of the laws on dormant accounts applicable in Australia and Canada is also illustrative.

Australia has a law providing for the transfer of dormant accounts to the government.[29] After seven years of dormancy, banks must by March 31 of each year deliver to the Treasurer a list of all unclaimed accounts worth $59 (A$100) or more, which is then published in the *Government Gazette*. For 1998 alone, the total transferred was approximately $18 million (A$30.9 million). In order to claim an account, the account owners make a claim to the bank where the account was opened, and the Treasury refunds the money to the bank, which passes it along to the claimant. The Australian Treasury maintains an online searchable database on the Internet—www.treasury.gov.au—so that persons may easily identify any dormant accounts in their name or that of a relative.

Similarly, Canada also has a law providing for the transfer of dormant accounts to the government. Canadian banks must attempt to notify owners of dormant accounts in the second and fifth year of dormancy. In the ninth year of inactivity, the Office of the Superintendent of Financial Institutions publishes the names of owners of all unclaimed balances worth $7 (CAN$10) or more in the *Canada Gazette*. In the tenth year of inactivity, dormant accounts must be transferred to the Bank of Canada, Canada's central bank, which acts as custodian for the accounts. Accounts worth $335

Mission has set up two separate supervisory committees to investigate the issue of heirless property. In March 1998, the Banking Supervisory Committee was established to investigate whether the French banking and financial system still holds funds, securities, or safe deposit box contents that belonged to victims of Nazi persecution who perished during World War II. For this purpose, the Supervisory Committee oversees the work done in credit institutions and investment firms, proposes investigative methods, and compiles the findings. An inventory is to be made of dormant or heirless safe deposit boxes in institutions after the war that may have belonged to such victims. The investigation is also addressing the current accounts held with the post office, passbook savings accounts frozen in 1941, and heirless estates that have reverted to the state. The Deposit and Consignment Office is also undertaking an analysis on asset looting and asset restitution.

[29] Banking Act of 1954.

(CAN$500) or more are held indefinitely and interest is paid at the rate of 1.5 percent for 10 years. Balances under $335 (CAN$500) must be claimed within 20 years after the last transaction on the account. At the end of 1998, there were 770,000 unclaimed accounts worth $88.5 million (CAN$132 million), 88 percent of which were under $500. Like the Australian Treasury, the Bank of Canada maintains a searchable database on the Internet—ucbswww.bank-banque-canada.ca.

United States

In the United States, there is no federal law on dormant accounts; rather each state has its own law on the treatment of dormant accounts. California was the first state to adopt a law providing for the escheat of money deposited in a bank; New York adopted its law on abandoned property in 1835.[30] By the 1930s and 1940s, Texas, Massachusetts, and Florida were among the states that also had such laws. Today, over 30 states have, in whole or in part, enacted the Uniform Disposition of Unclaimed Property Act, which was recommended for enactment in 1955 by the National Conference of Commissioners on Uniform State Laws. The Act provides that holders of unclaimed property are to report and transfer the property to the individual state, that the owner is to receive notice by publication, and that the state is to maintain custody of the property until such time as the rightful owner comes forward with adequate proof of ownership.

California, Texas, Massachusetts, New York, California, and Florida are among the states that have adopted escheat laws. But only Florida has adopted the Uniform Disposition of Unclaimed Property Act in total.

California

During the 1930s and 1940s in California, bank funds could be declared abandoned and escheat to the state after 20 years of inactivity.[31] When the attorney general learned of abandoned deposits,

---

[30] *See* http://www.missingmoney.com/compliance/is_your_company.cfm (visited April 28, 2000).
[31] Cal. Civ. Proc. Code §1273 (A.V. Lake 1935) (repealed 1945).

he was to commence an action against the bank and the account owners on behalf of the state in order to recover the property.[32] If the court determined that the account was unclaimed, then judgment was rendered in favor of the state, and the court declared that the money had "escheated."[33] Even after the judgment was rendered, any person not a party to the escheat judgment could sue the state to recover the money for a period of five years.[34]

After 1955, California enacted a modified version of the Uniform Disposition of Unclaimed Property Act.[35] Deposits held by banks are presumed abandoned if the owners have not, within three years, caused activity in the accounts or with respect to them.[36] For accounts with $50 or more,[37] banks must make reasonable efforts to notify customers by mail that the account is to escheat to the state.[38] Notice must be given either between 2 and 22 years after the date of last activity or between 6 and 12 months before the account becomes reportable to the State Controller.[39] The holder of the abandoned property is required to report the existence of the property to the Controller before November 1 of each year.[40]

Within one year after the delivery of the escheated property to the Controller, the Controller must publish a notice in a newspaper of general circulation detailing the available information about the property.[41] Any person claiming an interest in the property may file a

---

[32] *See Matthews v. Savings Union Bank and Trust Co.*,184 P. 418, 419 (Cal. Ct. App. 1919).
[33] *Id.*
[34] *Id.*
[35] Cal. Civ. Proc. §1500–1580 (West 1982 and Supp. 1999).
[36] *Id.* §1513. In 1988, the statute was amended to lower the time of allowed inactivity from seven years to five years. In 1990, the statute was amended to decrease the time of allowed inactivity from five years to three years. *Id.* §15133, Historical and Statutory Notes (West Supp. 1999).
[37] *Id.* §1513.5 and Historical Statutory Notes (West Supp. 1999). Notice is not required for accounts of less than $50. In 1996, the threshold amount was changed from $25 to $50.
[38] *Id.* §1513.5(a).
[39] *Id.* In 1990, the notice provision was amended from between three and three and one-half years to between two and two and one-half years. *Id.* Historical and Statutory Notes.
[40] *Id.* §1530 (West Supp. 1999).
[41] *Id.* §1531 (West Supp. 1999).

claim with the Controller at any time.[42] Today, California, as well as most other states, now has a searchable database of unclaimed assets available on the Internet.[43]

Texas

During the 1930s and 1940s in Texas, the right of the state to bring an action of escheat depended upon whether there had been "reasonable diligence" used to discover claimants of the estate.[44] An account was deemed abandoned if no lawful claim had been asserted for more than seven years, and all beneficiaries had been absent for more than seven years.[45]

All accounts deemed abandoned were to be paid to the State Treasury.[46] Someone claiming title to an account that escheated to the state was required to institute a suit against the state within two years after the account had escheated.[47] Essentially, the purpose of Texas' escheat laws was to treat the State Treasurer as trustee for abandoned accounts, subject to certain regulations regarding time restrictions.[48]

Texas did not adopt in total the Uniform Disposition of Unclaimed Property Act. In Texas today, an account is deemed inactive if there has been no activity in the account for more than one year.[49] Inactive accounts are presumed abandoned if (1) the

---

[42] *Id.* §1540 (West Supp. 1999).
[43] *See* http://www.unclaimed.org (visited May 9, 2000).
[44] Tex. Civ. Stat. Ann. §3272-3289 (repealed 1984); *Manion v. Lockhart*, 114 S.W.2d 216, 218, (Tex. 1938); *Robinson v. Texas*, 87 S.W.2d 297, 298 (Tex. Civ. App. 1935).
[45] *Texas v. Reconstruction Finance Corp.*, 258 S.W.2d 869, 872 (Tex. Civ. App. 1953).
[46] *Manion*, supra, 114 S.W.2d at 218.
[47] *Id.* at 217.
[48] *Id.* at 218.
[49] Texas Prop. Code Ann. §73.003 (West Supp. 1999). In 1961, the Texas Legislature enacted Article 3272(a) covering property subject to escheat. *See Southern Pacific Transport Co. v. State of Texas*, 380 S.W.2d 123, 124 (Tex. Civ. App. 1964). Article 3272(a) was replaced in 1984 by Title 6 of the Texas Property Code. Chapter 73 of Title 6 pertains to inactive accounts held by banking organizations.

account . . . has been inactive for at least five years;[50] (2) the location of the depositor of the account . . . is unknown to the depository; and (3) the amount of the account . . . ha[s] not been delivered to the [State] comptroller.[51]

A holder of an abandoned account must file a detailed report with the State Comptroller.[52] The purpose of the report is to remove abandoned accounts from the possession of the current holder, relieve the holder of any further liability regarding the accounts, put the accounts in the hands of the state, and provide a means for reclaiming the accounts.[53] Each holder of an abandoned account must deliver the account to the Comptroller along with the report.[54]

Upon receipt of an account over $100, the Comptroller must notify each reported owner within the calendar year.[55] The state

---

[50] Prior to 1985, the dormancy period for abandoned accounts was seven years (Texas Prop. Code Ann. §73.101, Historical and Statutory Notes (West 1995)).

[51] Tex. Prop. Code Ann. §73.101 (West Supp. 1999).

[52] *Id.* §74.101 (West 1995 and Supp. 1999).

(c) The property report must include:

(1) the name and social security number, if known, and the last known address, if any, of each person who, from the records of the holder of the property, appears to be the owner of the property, or the name and address, if known, of any person who is entitled to the property;

(2) a description of the property, the identification number, if any, and if appropriate, a balance of each account, except as provided in Subsection (d);

(3) the date the property became payable, demandable, or returnable;

(4) the date of the last transaction with the owner concerning the property; and

(5) other information that the comptroller by rule requires to be disclosed as necessary for the administration of this chapter.

(d) Amounts due that individually are less than $50 may be reported in the aggregate without furnishing any of the information required by Subsection (c) (Tex. Prop. Code Ann. §74.101 (West 1995 and Supp. 1999)).

[53] *See Texas v. Melton*, 970 S.W.2d 146, 148 (Tex. App. 1998), *aff'd.*, 993 S.W.2d 95 (Tex. 1999). The holder must also keep a record of the account information for ten years (Tex. Prop. Code Ann. §74.103 (West Supp. 1999)).

[54] *See* Tex. Prop. Code Ann. §74.301 (West Supp. 1999).

[55] Such notice must be provided:

(a) Except as provided by Section 74.202, the comptroller may use one or more methods as necessary to provide the most efficient and effective notice to each reported owner in the calendar year immediately following the year in which the report required by Section 74.101 is filed. The notice must be provided:

(1) in the county of the property owner's last known address; or

(continued)

assumes custody and responsibility for the safe keeping of the account.[56] Any accounts received must be deposited in the General Revenue Fund with which the Comptroller has the authority to invest in various state-approved funds.[57] A holder who delivers an account in good faith is relieved of all liability to the extent of the value of the account for any claim that may arise. Additionally, the Attorney General will defend the holder against such claims.[58]

There is no time limit with respect to filing a claim for an abandoned account. Any claim filed after receipt of an account is handled by the Comptroller.[59] The Comptroller maintains a sophisticated website[60] and a toll-free number where individuals may search to determine whether they are the rightful owners of abandoned accounts that have escheated to the state. The state charges a handling fee for most claims.[61]

---

(2) in the county in which the holder has its principal place of business or its registered office for service in this state, if the property owner's last address is unknown.
(b) The notice must state that the reported property is presumed abandoned and subject to this chapter and must contain:
(1) the name and city of last known address of the reported owner;
(2) a statement that, by inquiry, any person possessing a legal or beneficial interest in the reported property may obtain information concerning the amount and description of the property; and
(3) a statement that the person may present proof of the claim and establish the person's right to receive the property (Tex. Prop. Code Ann. §74.201 (West Supp. 1999)).
Notice is not required for items worth less than $100, unless the Comptroller determines that notice is in the public interest (Tex. Prop. Code Ann. §74.202 (West Supp. 1999)). Between 1985 and 1997, this figure was $50 (*Id.* at Historical and Statutory Notes).

[56] *Id.* §74.304 (West Supp. 1999).
[57] *Id.* §74.601 (West Supp. 1999).
[58] *Id.* §75.405 (West Supp. 1999).
[59] Tex. Prop. Code Ann. §74.501 (West Supp. 1999).
[60] *See* Texas Comptroller of Public Accounts at http://www.window.state.tx.us/comptrol/unclprop/unclprop.html> (visited August 25, 1999).
[61] Claims over $500 are charged a 1.5 percent fee; claims between $100 and $5000 are charged a 1 percent fee and claims under $100 are without fee.

Massachusetts

During the 1930s and 1940s in Massachusetts, inactive accounts became property of the state on the application of the attorney general and after public notice.[62] As in France, inactivity was determined by an absence of transactions for more than 30 years.[63] So long as no claimant was known, and a depositor could not be found, an account was to escheat to the state.[64]

Essentially, the state served as a trustee for the owner of the account.[65] Anyone having and establishing a lawful right to an account that had escheated to the state was entitled to the account. In order to retrieve an account that had escheated to the state, it was necessary to file a petition with the court.[66] The court then determined if the claimant was the rightful owner of the account and ordered payment to the claimant accordingly.[67]

In Massachusetts, since 1950[68] and still today, a deposit of property is presumed abandoned if there has been no transaction or communication with respect to that property within three years.[69] Within one year thereafter, the holder is obligated to report abandoned property to the State Treasurer.[70]

Every person holding an account presumed abandoned is to report the account to the State Treasurer.[71] Additionally, if the account contains at least $100, the holder must send the owner notice that the

---

[62] *Malone v. Provident Institution for Savings*, 896 N.E. 912, 912 (Mass. 1909), aff'd., 221 U.S. 660 (1911).

[63] *Id.* According to the Commonwealth, such a long duration of inactivity furnished a strong presumption than an account has been abandoned.(*Id.* at 913–14).

[64] *Id.*

[65] *Id.* at 914.

[66] *Id.* at 912.

[67] *Id.*

[68] In 1950, the State Legislature enacted the Massachusetts Abandoned Property Act (Mass. Gen. Laws Ann. ch. 200A (West 1990 and Supp. 1999)).

[69] The length of the dormancy period has been reduced from 15 to 3 years. The dormancy period was 14 years from 1950–1975; 10 years from 1975-1980; 7 years from 1980-1981, and 5 years from 1981–1992 (*Id.* §3, Historical and Statutory Notes (West 1990 and Supp. 1999)).

[70] Mass. Gen. Laws Ann. ch. 200A, §3, 7 (West Supp. 1999).

[71] Mass. Gen. Laws Ann. ch. 200A, §7 (West Supp. 1999).

account is to be surrendered to the custody of the state within 60 days of the filing of the report.[72] Furthermore, no holder may impose any charges with respect to dormancy or inactivity on a bank account, or cease payment of interest, unless such charges were specifically agreed to by both parties, the customer is notified prior to the imposition of such charges, and it is not the policy of the holder to waive these types of charges.[73]

If an account remains unclaimed, the holder must pay or deliver the account to the Treasurer of the State by May 1 of each year.[74] The Treasurer in turn must publish a notice, no later than March 1 of the same year following the report, at least once a week for two consecutive weeks in an English-language newspaper of general circulation in each county in which an apparent owner had a last known address.[75] Notice is required for accounts worth at least $100.[76] Any account surrendered to the Treasurer vests in the Commonwealth.[77] Any money received is then placed in a special fund known as the Abandoned Property Fund. Whenever the amount of this fund exceeds $500,000, the excess is credited to the General Fund.[78] Anyone claiming an interest in accounts surrendered to the Treasurer may establish their claim at any time. The Treasurer possesses full and complete authority to determine all such claims. Massachusetts currently has an Internet site that contains lists of individuals and organizations who may be entitled to unclaimed assets.[79]

---

[72] This value was $25 from 1950 to 1984 and $50 from 1984 to 1992 (Mass. Gen. Laws Ann. ch. 200A, §7, Historical and Statutory Notes (West 1990 and Supp. 1999)).

[73] Mass. Gen. Laws Ann. ch. 200A, §15C (West 1990).

[74] Id. §8A (West Supp. 1999).

[75] Id. §8 (West Supp. 1999).

[76] This value was $25 from 1950 to 1984 and $50 from 1984 to 1992 (Mass. Gen. Laws Ann. ch. 200A, §7, Historical and Statutory Notes (West 1990 and Supp. 1999)).

[77] Id. §9 (West 1990).

[78] Id. §9 (e).

[79] This site is located at http://www.state.ma.us/scripts/treasury/abp.asp (visited on August 25, 1999).

New York

In New York, since 1835, holders of unclaimed property are to report and transfer the property to the state after a specified period of time, and the state is to maintain custody of the property until such time as the rightful owner comes forward with adequate proof of ownership.[80] During most of the 1930s and 1940s, all banks organized under the laws of the state of New York were required to report to the superintendent of banks any amount of 10 dollars or more that remained unclaimed for 15 years[81] as of July 1 of the year in question.[82] Banks were to publish a list of names and addresses of "persons appearing as the owners of unclaimed amounts" in a newspaper published wherever the bank was located "annually for not less than five years."[83] Banks were to transfer the reported accounts to the state no later than November 10 of each year.[84] Importantly, banks were not responsible for erroneously transferring to the state accounts as unclaimed or abandoned property.[85]

The state of New York today holds billions of dollars in unclaimed funds, including bank accounts. Today, unclaimed bank accounts are deemed abandoned property when the funds have remained unclaimed by the owner for five years, rather than 15 years.[86] There is no threshold reporting requirement: all unclaimed funds, regardless of amount, must be reported to the state.[87] The

---

[80] New York's unclaimed property statutes, now commonly known as the "Abandoned Property Law" trace their roots to 1835 (N.Y. Aband. Prop. Law (McKinney 1991)).

[81] Prior to the statutes' amendment in 1937, unclaimed funds were not deemed abandoned until 22 years had passed without contact with the account holder.

[82] N.Y. Banking Law §126 (Gould 1942) (applicable to banks and trust companies), N.Y. Banking Law §169 (Gould 1942) (applicable to private bankers) and N.Y. Banking Law 256 (Gould 1942) (repealed 1943) (applicable to savings banks).

[83] See, e.g., N.Y. Banking Law §126(2)(Gould 1942).

[84] See, e.g., N.Y. Banking Law §127 (Gould 1942).

[85] See id. (No action shall be maintained against any bank or trust company for the recovery of moneys paid over to the state comptroller pursuant to the provisions of this section or for damages alleged to have resulted from any such payment.)

[86] In 1943, the New York legislature consolidated its banking statutes and enacted Section 300 of the Abandoned Property Law, which is still in force today (N.Y. Aband. Prop. Law §300 (McKinney 1991 and Supp. 1999)).

[87] Id.

requirement to report such accounts to the state now applies to all banking organizations "organized under or subject to the provisions of the laws of [New York], or of the United States, [except for] federal reserve banks, not just those banks incorporated in the state of New York."[88] In addition, the state now pays interest on interest-bearing items (such as savings accounts) for a period of five years after it obtains custody of them.[89]

While the changes to the Abandoned Property Law since the 1930s and 1940s have been motivated by the state's desire to increase the interest income generated by its custody of abandoned property, changes in communication technology have facilitated the process of identifying and locating the rightful owners of unclaimed funds. The New York Office of the State Comptroller, which is responsible for the administration of claims to abandoned property, has a toll-free telephone number and an Internet website—www.osc.state.ny.us/ouf—that potential claimants may use to check the list of unclaimed property holders.[90]

Florida

In Florida, during the 1930s and 1940s, the holder of unclaimed funds was to file a bill of complaint in the circuit court when the lawful owner of those funds could not be found.[91] The action was to be brought against all persons or entities known or unknown, after a reasonable investigation and proper service, who may have had a

---

[88] N.Y. Aband. Prop. Law §103(c) (McKinney 1991). The difference has significant implications since many large national banks have headquarters in New York, irrespective of their state of incorporation. Since the Abandoned Property Law was enacted in 1943, there have been numerous high-profile cases regarding the respective rights of the different states to claim custody of dormant accounts. *See, e.g., Delaware v. New York*, 507 U.S. 490, 113 S. Ct. 1550 (1993), finding that states as sovereigns may take custody of abandoned personal property located or held in the state, regardless of the beneficial owner's last known address or the banking organization's state of incorporation.

[89] *See* N.Y. Aband. Prop. Law §1405 (McKinney 1991).

[90] *See* http://www.osc.state.ny.us/ouf (visited August 25, 1999).

[91] Florida's unclaimed property law was first enacted in 1927 by Laws of Florida, 1927, Chapter 12035, Section 1. This law was later codified in the first official version of the Florida Statutes in 1941 as Section 69.04–69.08 (Fla. Stat. Ann. §69.04-69.08 (1941) (repealed 1965)).

right to such funds.[92] If the circuit judge could not determine the lawful owner of the funds, the holder of the funds was obligated to deliver them to the State Treasurer.[93] The State Treasurer was obligated to keep the funds in a separate account for five years during which time an interested party could file a claim in the circuit court.[94] If no claims were brought during the five-year period, the State Treasurer could credit the unclaimed property to the state school fund.

As previously noted, Florida has adopted the Uniform Disposition of Unclaimed Property Act in total.[95] Bank accounts are presumed abandoned after five years of inactivity.[96] Holders of property presumed abandoned must file a report to the Department of Banking and Finance before May 1 of each year detailing the property held.[97] Not more than 120 days prior to filing the report, the holder of the property must send written notice to the apparent owner at the last known address informing the owner of the existence of the property.[98] The state is then required to make a single attempt to notify owners of the existence of abandoned property held by the department using any cost-effective means.[99] Such notice is required to be made within 13 months following the receipt of the report from the holders of the property.[100] The state retains up to $3 million of the abandoned properties in an account,[101] and any funds in excess of the $3 million are deposited in the state school fund.[102] Anyone claiming an interest in the property may file a claim with the department at any time.[103]

---

[92] *Id.* §69.05.
[93] *Id* §69.06.
[94] *Id.* §69.07.
[95] Florida's current Disposition of Unclaimed Property Law was enacted by Laws of Florida (LOF), 1987, ch. 87-105. This law essentially repealed the former unclaimed property provisions and replaced it with the Uniform Disposition of Unclaimed Property Act.
[96] Fla. Stat. Ann. §717.106 (West Supp. 1999).
[97] The report must detail accounts of $50 or more. Accounts of less value may be reported in the aggregate (*Id.* §717.117 (West Supp. 1999)).
[98] *Id.*
[99] *Id.* §717.118 (West Supp. 1999).
[100] *Id.*
[101] *Id.* §717.123 (West Supp. 1999).
[102] *Id.*
[103] *Id.* §717.124 (West Supp. 1999).

Conclusion

In conclusion, the Swiss experience has generated a worldwide interest in the treatment of dormant bank accounts. For example, until recently, in Ireland, there was no standard definition of a "dormant account" and such accounts remained with the banks until such time as account holders or their heirs file a claim.[104] In 1997, the Irish Department of Finance required financial institutions to estimate the value of dormant accounts held over the previous 25 years. Although the total estimate was initially $2.3 million (IR£2 million), in 1999, the Minister of Finance estimated that the true amount was closer to $23 million (IR£20 million) and may be as high as $46 million (IR£40 million).[105] In response to the survey of dormant accounts, new legislation, which would take effect later in 2000, was proposed. It provides for a five-year dormancy period after which the funds would be used to benefit social and community causes. However, owners or heirs would not lose the right to have their money refunded on submission of a valid claim. Until such legislation enters into force, banks retain dormant accounts, and claimants must file a dormant account claim form (which is available on the Internet from the Irish Banks' Information Service—www.ibis.ie/consumer/dormant/form.htm), with the branch of the bank that they believe holds the dormant account.

The purpose behind escheat laws in general is to protect the rights of beneficial owners to dormant assets as well as to allow the sovereign to use of the property during its dormancy. Enhancements in technology have made it easier for banks to identify earlier when an account has evidence of inactivity and to locate the account holders. In countries without the transparency and oversight implied by publication or state surveillance, the course of least resistance is for banks to neglect careful accounting for funds held in a fiduciary capacity over the years. However, in logic, an unlimited time obligation to repay deposits should create a concomitant obligation to carefully and fairly account for such deposits. The existence of an

---

[104] Siobhan Creaton, "State Plans to Seize Millions Sitting in Dormant Accounts," *Irish Times*, at 50 (Feb. 11, 2000).

[105] *See* http://www.unclaimedassets.com/ireland.htm (visited April 28, 2000).

escheat law encourages discipline by banks in accounting for the funds of its depositors.

Today, the development of the Internet has made it easier for governments to publish lists of dormant accounts and for beneficial owners to locate them. In addition to the various examples of such web pages mentioned above, one web page—www.unclaimedassets.com—[106] provides a brief overview of 16 countries' laws on unclaimed assets, including bank accounts. Another web page—www.missingmoney.com—is an on-line database that automatically searches by name for missing funds, whether at a bank or not, that are being held by approximately one-quarter of the 50 U.S. states.[107]

While ICEP's Report contained no recommendation that Switzerland adopt an escheat law applicable to dormant accounts, an annex to the ICEP Report on the treatment of dormant accounts under escheat laws certainly shows that such legislation not only has a precedent but is also beneficial to both government and account holders.[108]

---

[106] *See, supra,* note 18.
[107] *See, supra,* note 30.
[108] ICEP Report, *supra* note 1, at 123.

Chapter 39

Summary Review of the Claims Resolution Tribunal for Dormant Accounts in Switzerland

ROBERTS B. OWEN

My assignment is to explain—in a necessarily cursory way—the history and functions of an organization called the Claims Resolution Tribunal for Dormant Accounts in Switzerland. The CRT, as it is known, can probably best be described as a quasi-arbitral claims settlement tribunal. It was established just about two years ago to handle a mass of claims that were expected to be presented by Holocaust victims and their families against various Swiss banks. In a sense, the CRT was organized as a result of a suspicion, shared by many around the world, that some of the millions of people who were persecuted during the Nazi regime in Germany in the period 1933 through 1945 may have deposited large amounts of their life savings in Swiss banks, that the banks may have improperly retained the funds for 50 years, and that some sort of remedial mechanism should be established in order to insure that, at long last—some 50 years after the fact—justice would finally be done for the account holders or their heirs. The basic objective, obviously, was to return the funds to their rightful owners and to do so fairly and expeditiously. It was not an easy task to tackle under the best of circumstances.

History

Let me start with a somewhat oversimplified historical summary. In the relevant period, 1933–45, Switzerland became completely hemmed in by the Axis powers and found itself an isolated island of neutrality. It was therefore quite natural that it would become a financial haven for persons being persecuted in the Axis countries, particularly because it was widely known or believed that Swiss law required all Swiss banks to maintain complete confidentiality as to the identity of account holders and amounts on deposit. Although no one really knew how many Nazi persecution victims had actually taken advantage of the Swiss protection, or how much was on deposit, there was a widespread impression, particularly within the world Jewish community, that the Swiss banks had been "sitting on" a pile of ill-gotten wealth since 1945. Incidentally, in some other countries, including most of the United States, such an accumulation would not have been possible because dormant accounts legally escheat to the state after a period of years, but Swiss law contains no such requirement. Under Swiss law, it is open to a bank simply to retain the funds in a dormant account and eventually to absorb the funds as profits.

To me, one of the surprising aspects of this history is the time lag—that is, how long it took for non-Swiss groups to mobilize themselves to press for a remedy. In the immediate post-war period there was considerable debate within Switzerland as to whether Swiss law should be changed to provide new access to accounts that had become dormant during the war, but with the Swiss Bankers Association (SBA) opposing change, no effective internal steps were taken—and no effective outside pressure was brought to bear until 1995. By then, with the distractions of the Cold War effectively over, the world press, particularly in Israel, Western Europe, and the United States, began seriously to publicize the Swiss dormant account situation and, as a result, to create for the Swiss banks what some critics have characterized as a public relations disaster.

In the same year (1995), the SBA launched an initial damage control effort; they undertook a survey of Swiss bank accounts that had become dormant during the relevant period, 1933–45. In 1996, they initially announced that they had uncovered approximately 800 dormant accounts containing approximately 40 million Swiss francs, but that initial announcement was greeted with great skepticism, and another look was taken, and the numbers then went up. On the one hand, they reported 75,000 dormant accounts of *Swiss* residents, who were assumed not to be Holocaust victims, and then they identified 5,600 dormant accounts that apparently belonged to non-Swiss account holders with a book value of 72 million Swiss francs—some of which, it was assumed, belonged to Holocaust victims or their heirs. Although these larger figures were also suspected as being too low, at least the bankers had shed light on some part of the problem—and interested groups then began to think in terms of, first, a real audit of the Swiss banks to try to get at the true dimensions of the problem, and, second, the establishment of an impartial claims resolution mechanism.

In May 1996, bowing to worldwide pressure, the Swiss Bankers Association agreed to the establishment of the organization known as the Independent Committee of Eminent Persons, or ICEP, under the Chairmanship of Paul Volcker, the former Chairman of the U.S. Federal Reserve.

Immediately after its establishment in 1996, ICEP undertook the two-step remedial approach I just mentioned: first, it set out to organize a massive audit—to be conducted by five international accounting firms—to come up with a definitive assessment of the dimensions of the Swiss dormant account situation—and, second, it worked with the Swiss Bankers Association to establish a foundation (the Independent Claims Resolution Foundation), which would be funded by the SBA and which would organize and finance a new claims tribunal—the CRT. The initial workload of the CRT was to be the processing of all claims that might be asserted against the 5,600 foreign-owned dormant accounts that the banks had recently identified.

Before describing the structure and procedures of the CRT, let me say a word about the apparent motivations of the two sides of the controversy that led to the creation of the Claims Resolution Tribunal. On the bankers' side, there was obviously a desire for a quick and inexpensive procedure that could be concluded with minimum damage to the industry and its practices, including the secrecy principle. After all, the secrecy feature had attracted much business to the Swiss banks—including, ironically, an unknown number of victims of Nazi persecution. On the other hand, the banks recognized the need for the appearance and reality of complete fairness. One recognized factor was that many of the claimants would be without significant resources and usually without legal assistance. On the face of it, at least, the claimant group could be seriously out-gunned by the banks and their counsel—and that appearance of imbalance had to be dealt with. In addition, the banks had an incentive to keep potential claimants away from the Swiss judicial system and hence to design an impartial arbitral tribunal that would be more attractive to claimants than the Swiss courts. On the claimants' side, they wanted experienced impartial arbitrators and relaxed rules of evidence that would make due allowance for the fact that conventional proofs had long since disappeared through the destruction of World War II and through the mere passage of time. For those responsible for actually designing the CRT, the challenge would be to design a mechanism that would do justice to several thousand claimants without having the wheels of justice grind too slow.

Size and Structure

During 1997, in order to get the claims process started, the SBA published the names of the 5,600 account holders, together with cities and countries of residence, and gave notice, through broad publicity in 19 languages in 29 countries that claims against the listed accounts would be entertained. It was recognized that no claims at all would be asserted against some of the listed accounts; it was also expected, quite accurately, that multiple claims would be filed against many others. Accordingly, the new tribunal had to be equipped to entertain and dispose of many thousands of claims (the exact number, obviously, being unknown at the time), and adequate manpower had to be available. Ultimately, 17 experienced international arbitrators from seven countries were selected to become members of the Claims Resolution Tribunal, and from the outset they have been assisted by a Secretariat consisting of some senior lawyers from a distinguished Swiss law firm, approximately 20 so-called legal secretaries, all of them very bright young lawyers recruited from top law firms all around the world, and a fine administrative staff.

Burden of Proof

All interested parties recognized that 50 years after the disruptions of World War II, claimants simply could not be expected to come forward with conventional proofs of their claims. In the interests of fairness, the rules of the new Tribunal expressly provided that if any claimant made a showing that it was "plausible" that he or she was entitled to the funds in a specific dormant account, that would be enough for an award. On the other hand, in practice the CRT has found that a large proportion of the claims are unsupported by any sort of plausible showing. In many cases, a claimant has had nothing to say except that his surname is the same as the surname on the account—and the Tribunal, understandably, has not considered that sufficient. Although documentation is not required, no claimant can succeed without some sort of plausible explanation of why he or she may be entitled to the account, providing a family tree as necessary and other background information. To oversimplify, if a claimant comes forward with information which is consistent with unpublished information in the records of the bank involved—and if the claimant also provides some plausible explanation of a relationship to someone who fits the description of the account holder—and if the CRT has no information that refutes his or her story—the claimant will be held entitled to recover.

Fees and Interest

Measurement of the amount of the recovery has raised some very difficult issues. In many cases the contract between the bank and the holder of a demand account authorized the bank to charge service fees, and in literally thousands of such situations—despite dormancy, with no actual services being rendered after 1945—the bank continued to exercise its fee-charging privilege year after year—to the point, in many cases, where the account's balance was reduced virtually to nothing. A major question was how to value such accounts—and also what to do with managed accounts where little or no interest was paid and little or no appreciation took place.

To think through these problems, a special committee of economists was established and instructed to develop some "guidelines"—fee and interest guidelines—to help the arbitrators decide what, if anything, to add to the account's unadjusted book value (meaning the latest amount shown as the balance in the account). The authors of the guidelines had to work through a thicket of problems, but the essence of their approach has been that, where there has been a plausible showing that the claimant is entitled to an account originally belonging to a victim of Nazi persecution, any unadjusted book value shown in the account will be adjusted upward in three stages. The first step is to add back the estimated amount of any service charges imposed since 1945; the next is to deduct any interest credited to the account; and the final step is to multiply the resulting number by 10 in order to adjust the 1945 value to an estimated present value. The multiplier, I am told, is based on long-term Swiss rates of return.

I might note, incidentally, that the formulation of the guidelines was a difficult task and that, for some time, the CRT had to operate without knowing what adjustments were ultimately going to be made to the apparent book value of the account. During the interval before the guidelines were finally adopted, the simple solution was for the CRT in a given case to make a partial award in the amount of the apparent book value and to advise the claimant, in its decision, that the amount of the award might be increased following the publication of the guidelines. The process of making the appropriate guideline adjustments upward is now under way, and final awards are being made on that basis.

Now let me turn briefly to the decision-making procedures followed by the CRT in its daily work.

CRT Procedures, 1998–2000

Starting in 1998, the CRT developed three different procedural routes or "tracks" for dealing with the upcoming claims. The first track, known as the "fast track," commences with the submission of a particular claim to the bank involved to give it a chance to decide whether it wants to settle the case forthwith. In about 20 percent of all the cases, the bank has decided to settle, thus shortening but not entirely eliminating its involvement with the CRT. In each such case, the bank's records and the claimant's story are presented to a single CRT arbitrator who makes a quick review of available information to see whether the settlement appears to be fair to the claimant. If the arbitrator approves, as is normally the case, an unopposed partial award is made in favor of the claimant. Some of these awards will have to be adjusted upward under the guidelines, but it is clear that because of the need to show a connection to Nazi persecution, only a relatively small number will ever have to be adjusted in that way.

The second procedural "track," which comes into play for all unsettled cases, is called "initial screening"—performed, once again, by a single CRT arbitrator. Again, the arbitrator reviews the bank records and the claimant's submission, but this time for a different and very limited purpose: he or she is simply looking to see whether there is any possibility that the claimant might plausibly be entitled to the account. In some 60 percent of all the cases brought to the CRT, the single arbitrator has concluded either that the claim is based on pure speculation or that there are irrefutable facts that clearly show that the claimant cannot possibly be entitled to the account. In those instances, the claim, however well intentioned, must be dismissed simply because it has no possibility of succeeding.

In order to give you some "feel" for why it is that so many claims are dismissed during initial screening, I would simply note the not very surprising fact that a great many claims have been presented, not on the basis of any known relationship, but simply on the off chance that the claimant may have had a family relationship to the account holder. When the SBA list of 5,600 accounts was published in 1997, only the account holder's name and last residence were made known to potential claimants, thus leaving the door wide open for many purely speculative claims. Moreover, although in many cases the bank records relating to a specific account contain very little information about the account holder, in many other cases the existing bank documents reveal not only the account holder's name and last-known address, but also a variety of other biographical facts, including his or her profession, the name of the spouse, the identity of any holder of a power of attorney, and often sample signatures for one or more of these individuals. In many cases, therefore, the initial-screening arbitrator merely has to compare the allegations of the claim and the remaining bank records to reach a decision.

I should also note another major source of information for the CRT. As to many accounts, two or more claimants have come forward with relevant information, and it very frequently happens that facts submitted by one claimant will demonstrate the implausibility of another claim or claims against the same account. As a result, one of the functions of the single arbitrator with initial screening responsibility has been to review all of the multiple claims to a single account and to dismiss those that lack any plausible basis, leaving for later arbitration only those claims that have a chance of surviving that process.

I hardly need add, for those of you who are interested in the general subject of arbitration, that neither the fast-track settlement procedure nor the initial screening process involves arbitration in the true sense: in none of these cases is there any substantial dispute of fact or law. Accordingly, although most of us talk of the CRT as an arbitration tribunal, the vast bulk of its work product has been done prior to and without any true arbitration.

Before moving on to the third and only truly arbitral track, I should add that if a claimant suffers an adverse initial screening decision by a single CRT arbitrator, he or she has the right to appeal to a three-arbitrator CRT panel. In fact, such appeals are rarely taken, and it is even more rare for such a process to result in a reversal—a fact that some critics have regarded as demonstrating that this particular appellate arrangement has been a waste of time and money. As I will mention a little later, some thought is now being given to the revision of procedural steps of that kind.

This brings me to the third and final CRT track—a step that occurs only in those very few situations where a settlement has not occurred and the claim has survived the initial screening process. These rare cases, since they involve either factual or legal issues or both, are subjected to real arbitration under what is called the CRT's "ordinary procedure"—although that is a distinct misnomer because such cases are in fact quite extraordinary. If a particular case involves 3,000 Swiss francs or less, the arbitration is conducted by a single CRT arbitrator, subject to appeal to a three-person panel, while the larger cases involving more than 3,000 francs go to a three-person panel in the first instance. Obviously, a considerable number of these ordinary procedure cases result in affirmative awards.

CRT's Progress and Prospects

Let me say a word about the CRT's productivity in its first two years. Rounding the numbers for simplicity, approximately 10,000 claims have been presented as against approximately 2,500 of the 5,600 dormant accounts that were listed by the SBA in 1997. In two years' time, the Tribunal has made well over 9,000 decisions and has entered more than 2,500 affirmative awards aggregating 31 million Swiss francs—a number that will increase as the Tribunal finishes up its work on the original 5,600 accounts. There will be additional partial awards, and of course some final awards reflecting the effect of the guidelines. The hope is that this first stage of the Tribunal's work will be completed in the next few months.

On the other hand, there is in prospect a whole new wave of CRT work that is likely to start up as the Tribunal closes the first phase. The extensive ICEP audit that was initiated in 1997 was completed toward the end of 1999, and in December 1999 ICEP issued its final "Report on Dormant Accounts of Victims of Nazi Persecution In Swiss Banks." Although the blue volume is large because of elaborate appendices, the report itself consists of only 23 pages—albeit tightly written pages—and is essential reading for anyone interested in this general subject. Rather than attempt to summarize it here, I would simply note that this enormously painstaking three-year audit encompassed no less than 254 Swiss banks that existed in the 1933–1945 period, and it examined more than 4 million Swiss bank accounts that were open during that period. With those accounts entered into a database, an enormous forensic investigative effort was made to "match" those accounts with five and a half million names of Holocaust victims—and that difficult process has led ICEP to list approximately 26,000 dormant accounts which, in its judgment, are "probably or possibly" related to Holocaust victims. The Report is careful to explain that the inclusion of a specific account among the 26,000 does not mean that in fact such a relationship existed: it simply means that the account deserves to be subjected to an impartial claims resolution process by the existing CRT. It has not yet been firmly decided that the CRT will be given this awesome new responsibility, but that is the foreseeable outcome. Fortunately, this new responsibility, if assigned, will take hold just as the initial phase of the CRT's work is being completed.

CRT and Pending Class Actions

At this point, I should note that future proceedings of the Tribunal are likely to be intertwined with, and to some extent controlled by, a judicial proceeding that is now going forward in New York. As most of you know, in 1995 suits were filed in the U.S. District Court in New York on behalf, not of individually identified persons, but on behalf of a class of Holocaust victims with claims arising out of various different kinds of alleged misconduct, including the dormant account problem that we have been discussing. In January 1999, the three largest Swiss banks (which are now two as a result of a merger) entered into a settlement agreement under which they are to pay $1.25 billion into a settlement fund to be distributed to members of the class—an agreement which immediately raised the question whether, if the CRT were to make awards to class members, the settling banks would be given credit against the $1.25 billion. The answer is that such credit will be given under a formal Distribution Plan that is now being prepared and will be presented to the class action court in due course. Since I am not involved with the class action settlement, I cannot tell you what role, if any, the Distribution Plan will give the CRT to play in the settlement program, but I am told that a number of possible arrangements have been under discussion.

One possibility—that is foreshadowed by the ICEP Report—is that the CRT would be given the responsibility of resolving any dormant Swiss account claim in which it is alleged that the claimant was a victim of Nazi persecution (or is the heir of such a person) and as to which it is shown that the account "matches" with an account identified in the ICEP database. Under this suggestion the CRT would have to establish the "match" in the first instance and then adjudicate the claim, probably under the plausibility standard that is currently in use by the CRT.

Now, assuming that some such new responsibilities are placed upon the shoulders of the CRT, how heavy will the workload be and how will it be handled? Obviously it is too early to make anything like a real forecast, but simply judging by past experience, it would not be unreasonable to expect as many as 50,000 or even 100,000 claims to be presented against the large number of accounts identified by the ICEP as probably or possibly belonging to Holocaust victims. Of course, that sounds like an enormous task, but some very farsighted planning has been going forward, looking toward a new set of streamlined procedural rules intended to bring this substantial new burden within manageable proportions. Not surprisingly, the CRT has been able, in hindsight, to identify various arguable inefficiencies in its past practices, and the expectation is that with improved procedural rules and all of the latest modern high-tech mechanisms to assist in the process, sound and fair results can be achieved relatively efficiently.

Such new procedural devices are still being developed, and I therefore cannot tell you how the CRT of the future will be run in any exact terms, but I can give you one example of the kind of improvement that has been suggested by prior experience. Some of the cases that have been brought to the Tribunal have involved some quite complex issues as to inheritance rights under various national laws. In a given case, for example, the Tribunal might have to decide whether to apply the law of Switzerland or Germany or California—or some other relevant jurisdiction—and then determine the claimant's rights under the applicable law. The CRT's past experience in wrestling with such issues is probably going to make it possible to develop some formulaic principles that can be quickly applied to these inheritance problems and which should significantly increase the efficiency of the process.

Conclusion

In conclusion, let me touch briefly on the question of the lessons to be drawn from the CRT experience. Being an arbitrator, I am probably the least qualified person to tell you what lessons you should be drawing, but I probably will not be on too dangerous ground if I make two fairly obvious points.

First, there is a clear difference of view among the various banking nations of the world as to whether it is necessary or appropriate to require the escheat of dormant accounts to the state. I take no position as to that policy issue, but it seems clear that, if Switzerland had had an escheat regime in place in the period after World War II, its present public relations difficulties would have been enormously reduced. Whether particular Swiss banks engaged in any kind of misconduct, I do not know, but, as illustrated by the conclusions reached in the ICEP Report, the continuous possession of dormant funds has been seriously criticized—and those criticisms would have been much less forceful if the Swiss banks had supported an escheat regime many years ago. In addition, although it can be vigorously argued that Swiss bank secrecy is a perfectly proper and marketable banking attribute—indeed, an attribute sought by some Holocaust victims themselves—the secrecy practice has undoubtedly raised additional suspicions of concealed conduct and thus added to the Swiss banks' post-war difficulties. In the past, obviously, these arrangements—non-escheat and secrecy—have been regarded as being perfectly respectable, but in hindsight (which is always easy) it would seem that the Swiss banks might have been well advised to make greater efforts than they did to satisfy the public that the rights of heirs to Swiss accounts were and are fully protected.

Finally, although all of us here hope and expect that no part of the world banking industry will ever again have to face the kind of mass-claim situation that arose for the Swiss banks in 1995, many other industries have been facing similar mass-claim problems in recent years, and I think you are going to have to expect future mass-claim problems in your industry as well. If so, you will probably search for an appropriate private nonjudicial claims resolution process, and by that time there will be much to be learned from the CRT experience. Those of us who are involved in the CRT process are learning as we go, and by the time the CRT closes its doors, I am sure that a number of arbitration experts, not including myself, will be in a position to tell you—based on the CRT experience—exactly how your mass claims should be handled in the future.

X. Governance

Chapter 40
Managing the Global Economy: The Role of Governance

RAINER GEIGER

Governance in both the public and private sectors is a key aspect of managing globalization. It is essential for the stability of the financial systems and the functioning of domestic and international markets. In its broadest sense governance includes the legal and institutional framework conditions for governments and enterprises: i.e., the rule of law, efficiency and integrity of public administration, an appropriate regulatory system for economic activities, corporate governance, fight against corruption, and business integrity.

The different aspects of governance are closely interrelated: good governance is as needed in the public as in the corporate sectors and deficiencies in one area have pernicious effects on the other. Both are interacting within society and political systems. In a global economy governance has a strong international dimension. Good governance in one country has strong demonstration effects in others and bad governance, as the 1998 financial crises demonstrated, can send shock waves through the international financial system. A global economy does not suffer islands of dishonesty.

The present article is focused on three key components of governance: corporate governance, business ethics, and the fight against corruption. It draws on the experience with the instruments developed by the Organization of Economic Cooperation and Development (OECD) as well as other international players. It aims at demonstrating the contribution of these instruments to stability and integrity in global institutions and markets.

Democratic government and market economy rely on the same set of fundamental principles for governance: transparency, competition, integrity, and accountability. A disfunctioning in any of these areas leads to significant system risks.

If confidence in political systems is undermined, economic instability is the result. Criminal elements can take advantage of gaps and further damage the credibility of the systems in place. If anticompetitive practices in the corporate sector are tolerated, markets cannot function properly, resources are misallocated, and economic power may be accumulated by a few dominant enterprises. Corruption can turn into a terminal disease for political and economic systems.

Global markets need global rules and standards. In this respect, the OECD has proven well placed to provide constructive approaches. The OECD now includes 30 countries, which account for a large share in international trade and investment. It has long-standing experience with policy analysis, formulation of rules and best practices, and monitoring of implementation. In the area of governance, the following instruments are of particular importance: the 1999 Principles for Corporate Governance, the 2000 Guidelines for Multinational Enterprises, and the 1997 Convention and Recommendation on Combating Bribery of Foreign Public Officials in International Business Transactions.

Corporate Governance

What Is It About?

Corporate governance is a term of Anglo-Saxon origin that is difficult to translate into other languages. Yet it has become very popular and is widely used all over the world. The concept itself is not new: it emerged in the nineteenth century and was frequently referred to in the United States during the Great Depression, but during the last two decades it became the subject of much research and discussion. The 1998 financial turmoil in Asia and Russia dramatically underscored the importance of governance in economic and financial systems and after pioneering work in the private sector, a Business Advisory Group to the OECD led by Ira Millstein produced a comprehensive set of recommendations from a private-sector perspective.

If we cannot translate, let us describe the concept of corporate governance:

- It is about the organization of management and control of companies.

- It reflects the interaction among those persons and groups that provide resources to the company and contribute to its performance (i.e., shareholders, employees, creditors, long-term suppliers, and subcontractors).

- It helps define the relation between the company and its general environment, and the social and political systems in which it operates.

Corporate governance is linked to economic performance. The way management and control are organized affects the company's performance and its long-run competitiveness. It determines the conditions for access to capital markets and the degree of investors' confidence.

In today's economy, the private corporation has a fundamental role. Whereas over the last two decades, the role of the state in economic management has declined, private sector development has achieved a quantum leap through privatization and enterprise development. Privatization worldwide totals almost $850 billion since 1990 (and more than $1 trillion since 1980). International capital flows also showed unprecedented expansion since the 1980s and direct, as well as portfolio, investment accounts for a significant share. Companies, as well as countries, have to compete for funding in international capital markets, which reward good governance and sanction bad practices.

In the process of investment, corporate governance is important at all stages for

- mobilizing capital,

- allocating capital, and

- monitoring the use of capital.

To maintain confidence of investors and markets, property and shareholder rights need to be protected, there has to be timely and high-quality disclosure of information on the performance and financial situation of the company, and management needs to be accountable to shareholders and the company.

Who Are the Actors?

Obviously companies operate within legal frameworks but much of corporate governance is market driven. Regulators and the investors' community set high standards for access to financial markets, in particular in the areas of disclosure and accounting, and these standards are likely to be applied worldwide through the global operations of multinational enterprises. It is the responsibility of the board to ensure transparency and accountability of management and integrity in business transactions. Corporate culture depends on leadership and a motivated workforce. Internal programs for training, teambuilding, and control are essential.

Self-regulatory bodies, nongovernmental groups, and civil society at large exercise an increasing influence on the development of corporate governance patterns. A number of high-quality codes have been developed exclusively through private sector initiatives, with strong involvement by institutional shareholders. Pension funds, among others, tend to take an activist role in favor of socially responsible behavior and good environment management of investee companies.

Governments have not been inactive and in a number of countries corporate law reforms have been introduced in recent years, e.g., Canada, France, Germany, Ireland, Japan, Korea, Sweden, and the United Kingdom. The main thrust of these reforms is to improve corporate disclosure in accordance with international standards, to strengthen shareholder rights, and to provide the framework for accountability of corporate boards and management.

Finally, intergovernmental organizations like the OECD and the World Bank are playing an important role in encouraging good corporate governance worldwide. This is part of an attempt to develop internationally accepted standards to manage globalization and to provide a sound basis for international cooperation. Corporate governance has become an essential ingredient for the stability of the international financial system.

Increasing Convergence in Corporate Governance

Globalization has proved to be a powerful force in encouraging a strong move toward upgrading and convergence of corporate governance, at least as far as listed companies are concerned. Reaching beyond traditional differences, corporate laws and cultures have developed that made the elaboration of global standards possible.

In his book *Capitalism Against Capitalism*, Michel Albert distinguished two forms of corporate cultures: the so-called Anglo-Saxon one and the so-called rhenanian one of continental Europe and Japan, which is driven by insiders, cross-shareholders, and banks. The former is considered to promote flexibility and shareholder value, whereas the latter would privilege stability and long-term perspectives. These categories, if they ever reflected reality, are certainly no longer valid today.

Companies in whatever countries they operate are increasingly relying on equity finance through capital markets. Their disclosure practices tend to conform with international accounting standards. As a response to shareholder activism and pressure by civil society groups, corporate accountability has significantly increased and there is a new awareness of the importance of business ethics. The value of human capital and the quality of stakeholder relations are recognized.

The OECD Corporate Governance Principles of 1999 provide a strong basis for encouraging further convergence of corporate governance practices worldwide. Endorsed by the OECD Council of Ministers, the principles are the result of intensive discussions within a task force composed of governmental and private sector representatives. They are nonbinding and evolutionary. The provisions they contain are compatible with different legal systems, e.g., unitary boards or two-tier management and supervisory systems. The aim is not legal harmonization but a common framework in which good practices can develop consistently with national regulations and traditions.

The OECD principles are composed of five key elements:

1. Strengthening the right of shareholders through better communications and facilities to participate in decision making at general shareholders meetings. Markets for corporate control should remain open and not restricted through anti-takeover devices primarily designed to entrench incumbent management.

2. Protection of minority shareholders, which includes disclosure of complex corporate structures like shareholder agreements and shares with differentiated voting rights (e.g., nonvoting shares and shares with multiple voting rights). Insider trading and abusive self-dealing should be prohibited, and members of the board and managers should disclose material interests in transactions affecting the corporation.

3. Recognition of the role stakeholders play in wealth creation and the long-term sustainability of financially sound enterprises. Stakeholders include all persons and groups providing resources to the enterprise, i.e., investors, employees, creditors, and long-term suppliers. The principles encourage performance enhancing mechanisms of stakeholder participation in the corporation.

4. Transparency is crucial for investor confidence. Corporate disclosure should include financial information needed to assess the performance, the financial situation, and the risk management of the enterprise. The disclosure of nonfinancial information, including the governance patterns of the corporation, is also recommended.

5. Boards, whether they are unitary or have a two-tier structure (executive board/supervisory board), have the key functions of providing strategic guidance to the company as well as effective monitoring of management. Their composition and responsibilities should follow the following principles: competence, a sufficient degree of independence, and accountability to the company and its shareholders.

The OECD principles are primarily conceived for listed companies. For others, such as privately held and state-owned companies, they would need further elaboration. To be effective they need to be fully reflected in national practices, which may require adjustment to different legal frameworks. However, as they are based on broad consensus, they do provide a common reference for all systems and corporate cultures.

In order to promote good corporate governance worldwide, the OECD and the World Bank have entered into a cooperation agreement. The central element of this initiative is the conduct of reginal corporate governance roundtables. These roundtables bring together officials from emerging markets, transition economies, developing countries, and the private sector to elaborate on the principles and to set reform priorities in a national or regional context. So far, the following roundtables are operational: Russia, Eurasia, Asia, and Latin America. A roundtable for the countries of the countries of the Southeast European Stability Pact will be launched in September 2001.

Challenges Ahead

One of the key issues is regional disparity, and this is the main reason why the regional roundtables mentioned above have been established. Each region has its own specificity that needs to be addressed. For Russia and other countries of the former Soviet Union, the main problem is the lack of authority and credibility of state institutions, which has left a wide margin for dishonest behavior (e.g., asset stripping, self-dealing, and violation of the rights of shareholders). For Asia, the key problem is improvement of transparency of corporate structures and operations, while in Latin America concerns arise with respect to the presence in many companies of dominant shareholders or groups of shareholders. The approach used to improve the situation is the drafting, within each region, of a White Paper through which the development of local/regional best practices is encouraged. This is a participatory approach where governments, business associations, trade unions, and other civil society groups are closely associated with the drafting process.

The OECD Corporate Governance Principles are relevant to closely held corporations and enterprises that are wholly or majority owned by governments, but further elaboration is needed on the specific aspects of management and control of these entities.

Another area where more work is needed is the market for corporate control. In order to develop best practices, it would be useful to undertake a comparative study on individual country approaches and corporate practices with respect to voting rights linked to different categories of shares. A comparative assessment of anti-takeover devices would also be necessary in light of evolving experience with international mergers and acquisitions.

To prevent further corporate scandals, a major international effort is needed to improve disclosure of information by companies and to strengthen rules and standards to safeguard the integrity of corporate service providers, in particular, the accounting profession.

Measuring human capital as a major factor for the performance and prospects of the company is another challenge. Unfortunately, accounting practices for intangibles do not reflect the situation of an increasing number of enterprises for which the quality of human resources is crucial in terms of economic performance. Work in this area has started in the OECD, but more efforts are needed to develop best practices.

Modern information technology offers unprecedented opportunities for interaction among companies, shareholders, other stakeholders, potential investors, and the general public. It opens new avenues for communication. Absentee shareholder voting through electronic means is another possibility, which is already used by many companies.

Finally, no company that cares about its future can ignore the increasing expectations of civil society in the field of business ethics and corporate social responsibility. If investment is to contribute as it should to sustainable development, social and environmental considerations need to be integrated in corporate strategies.

Many companies have already responded by developing internal company codes setting forth standards of business ethics. There are also collective efforts undertaken by private sector groups, and the OECD Guidelines for Multinational Enterprises provide the first multilaterally agreed set of standards for responsible business behavior.

Standards for Business Ethics

In June 2001, the OECD Council of Ministers adopted a revised set of Guidelines for Multinational Enterprises together with strengthened implementation procedures. The original Guidelines had been in place since 1976 as part of the Declaration on International Investment and Multinational Enterprises. Also included in this Declaration is the Principle on National Treatment for Foreign Controlled Enterprises as well as provisions for international cooperation in the field of investment incentives and disincentives and conflicting requirements resulting from the extraterritorial application of national jurisdiction.

The Guidelines are designed as a contribution to a favorable climate for international investment. They express values shared by governments, businesses, trade unions, and the civil society with respect to corporate behavior. They are not legally binding and not intended as substitutes for national law. They do reflect expectations that enterprises cannot easily ignore and these expectations can reach beyond national law.

The Guidelines cover all aspects of corporate behavior and apply in all sectors of the economy and all types of multinational enterprises, whether large or small, whether private, state-owned, or under mixed ownership. They extend to corporate operations worldwide. The Guidelines are relevant for national enterprises as well, and enterprises are expected to encourage compliance by business partners, including suppliers and subcontractors.

The 2000 Revision of the Guidelines includes the following new elements:

- the chapter on employment and industrial relations includes a reference to the four core labor standards of the 1998 ILO Declaration (freedom of association and right to collective bargaining; elimination of all forms of forced and compulsory labour; effective abolition of child labor; elimination of discrimination in respect of employment and occupation);

- the chapter on environment sets forth recommendations for environmental management and contingency planning;

- the chapter on disclosure of information reflects the transparency provisions of the OECD Corporate Governance Principle and encourages social and environmental accountability;

- new chapters have been added on bribery concerning both public officials and private agents, as well as consumer protection including safety, labelling, and consumer complaints; and

- companies are expected to contribute to the respect of human rights.

The most important feature of the 2000 revision is the strengthening of the implementation procedures at national and international levels. All participating countries have to set up national contact points for handling inquiries and complaints. Governments remain free to determine the institutional setting of their contact points as long as they respect criteria of functional equivalence; i.e., the contact points need to be visible, easily accessible, transparent, and accountable.

The OECD Committee on International Investment and Multinational Enterprises (CIME) monitors national contact points. If national contact points do not fulfil their responsibilities, the matter can be raised directly with CIME. CIME can also act on a substantiated claim that an interpretation of the Guidelines issued by a national contact point was erroneous. National contact points are accessible for business, labor, NGOs, and other interested parties. For CIME, governments and the social partners, represented through their advisory bodies to the OECD (the Business and Industry Advisory Committee and the Trade Union Advisory Committee), have standing to raise specific cases and request clarification of the Guidelines in light of these cases. The clarification will refer to the issues raised by the case at hand but the Committee will not engage in fact finding, nor can it reach conclusions on the conduct of individual enterprises.

The effectiveness of the new procedures remains to be tested. In June 2001, national contact points of all adhering countries (all 30 OECD Member countries plus Argentina, Brazil, and Chile) will hold their first annual meeting to exchange experience. In the longer run, the success of the Guidelines will depend on leadership by governments, dialogue with social partners, and the continuing interest of civil society. The Guidelines are open for participation to those OECD nonmember countries that, after an initial examination of their investment policies, are invited by the OECD Council to adhere to the Declaration on International Investment and Multinational Enterprises.

Fighting Corruption in International Business Transactions

Globalization of markets, business transactions, and corporate structures has created opportunities for enhanced efficiency and growth in the world economy. Whether individual countries benefit will depend on comparative advantages and a mix of economic and regulatory policies that are perceived as favorable to trade and investment.

In the absence of proper rules, globalized markets driven by deregulation and technological progress can be breeding grounds for internationally organized crime, e.g., large-scale fraud, corruption, and money laundering. Criminal activities of this nature undermine political institutions, create financial instability, distort market competition, and hurt economic development. Individual countries acting in isolation are not able to stem the tide of international financial crime and vigorous action by the international community is urgently required. There is a need for international instruments and effective monitoring of application.

The OECD has taken a pioneering approach in fighting international corruption through its 1997 Convention and related Recommendations, which, taken together, constitute a comprehensive action program. Why has the OECD been involved? What is the value added of its instruments? How is effective implementation ensured? What are the implications for corporate responsibilities?

One can only measure the progress achieved by looking back to where the process started. Corruption of domestic public officials is an offense in all legal systems, but until recently, the U.S. Foreign Corrupt Practices Act was the only statute explicitly criminalizing bribery of foreign public officials. Some countries claimed that their law was applicable to international corruption as well but could not demonstrate cases of application. Corruption in international business was a universally condemned but widely tolerated phenomenon. It was against this background that work at the OECD started at the beginning of the 1990s with a feasibility study on alternative approaches to fight corruption in international transactions.

A first concrete result was achieved in 1994 with the adoption by the OECD Council of a recommendation committing member countries to take meaningful and effective steps against bribery in international transactions. A catalog of possible actions was provided but, in the absence of any specific obligations, was purely optional. A further step was taken by the OECD Fiscal Affairs Committee in 1996 when it agreed on a recommendation to eliminate tax deductibility of bribes.

At the same time, a dramatic change in public opinion occurred. Powerful business groups called for coordinated international action against bribery and anticorruption coalitions emerged in civil society under the leadership of Transparency International, a Berlin-based NGO with constituencies in many developed and developing countries. In many countries, the media mobilized against corruption, and a number of big corruption scandals created uproar in public opinion. In the OECD, a breakthrough occurred in May 1997 with the adoption of an expanded antibribery recommendation, which was followed six months later by the signature of a criminal law convention.

Key Elements

The OECD Convention on Combating Bribery of Foreign Public Officials in International Business Transactions is addressed to the supply side of corruption. It criminalizes "active" bribery, whereas passive corruption is left to the jurisdiction of the countries that are at the receiving end. In this manner, OECD countries, which are the main suppliers of capital, goods, and services, affirm their determination to dry up the sources of corruption.

The Convention takes a broad and comprehensive approach to fighting international bribery:

- a broad concept of a public official, which covers not only civil servants, elected officials, and judges but all persons performing a public interest activity (this may include executives of state-owned companies or even private companies if the latter exercise a monopoly or other function entrusted to them by the government);

- an autonomous definition of the offence of bribery, which does not allow any exceptions nor reservations by signatory countries;

- effective sanctions to include imprisonment of offenders, fines, corporate liability, and confiscation of illegal gains;

- an effective jurisdictional basis for action against bribery, i.e., a broad definition of territoriality or nationality (most countries apply a combination of both); and

- mutual legal assistance where bank secrecy cannot be invoked to refuse exchange of information.

The Convention provided a very brief period for ratification and transposition into national criminal law and, by February 15, 1999, the critical mass of ratification/implementation was achieved to allow the Convention to enter into force. By spring 2001, the quasi-totality of the 34 signatory countries (30 OECD Member and 4 non-OECD Member countries) had ratified, even if a few of these countries still lack national implementing legislation.

The Convention is part of a broader action program that includes measures to effectively deny tax deductibility (a handbook for tax inspectors is under preparation); improvement of accounting and auditing practices; integrity in public administration; and inclusion of anticorruption clauses into contracts financed by official development assistance.

Implementation

The Convention is not aimed at harmonizing national legal systems, which would have been a time consuming, if not impossible, task. The key notion is functional equivalence of implementation. National laws need to be in conformity with the standards of the Convention and have to be effectively enforced.

Monitoring of national legislation and enforcement is one of the most powerful features of the OECD approach. A two-phase process has been established. In the first phase, the Secretariat, together with two examining countries, assesses the implementing legislation of each signatory country to determine whether it complies with the Convention. The reports are discussed with the examined countries and reviewed by the OECD Working Group on Bribery in International Transactions. If deficiencies are found, the Group makes recommendations. The report and the recommendations are published. By spring 2001, 26 countries had been examined.

The result of monitoring in phase 1 is generally encouraging. The examinations were thorough and frank, and the examined countries cooperative. The overall picture is a large degree of conformity in many signatory countries. In one country, the United Kingdom, the Working Group was not convinced that there was any proper implementing legislation but remedial action was taken in December 2001. Deficiencies recorded in other countries include legal defenses not provided for in the Convention, the absence of corporate liability, inadequacies of sanctions, and short statutes of limitation. One country, Japan, introduced a restrictive definition of international business transactions, the so-called main office clause, which would exclude criminal action in cases where the foreign official is bribed by an employee of a subsidiary established in the country of that official. This exception is not in conformity with the Convention and, following the Working Group's recommendation, was subsequently removed through a change in legislation.

Phase 2—monitoring application—started in autumn 2001. It provides for on-site inspections conducted in each country by a team of examiners composed of the OECD Secretariat and experts from two examining countries. The team has the opportunity to discuss with competent ministries, judges and law enforcement agencies, tax authorities, and the business community; it can also collect the views of civil society organizations.

At a worldwide scale, the OECD, in cooperation with other international agencies and donor countries, has set up regional anticorruption networks bringing together governments with business and civil socitey representatives. Network meetings have been held in Manila and Seoul for Asian and Pacific countries, and in Istanbul for transition economies of Central and Eastern Europe and the former Soviet Union. An Anticorruption Initiative has been launched in the context of the Stability Pact for Southeast Europe and an Anticorruption Compact for Asia is being developed jointly with the countries of that region.

Business associations and individual companies have expressed their support for the exercise. The International Chamber of Commerce has developed guidelines that cover both corruption of officials and private agents. Trade unions and international trade union federations have also joined international anticorruption efforts and, together with businesses, participate in consultative meetings at the OECD and in regional network activities. Transparency International and its national constituencies provide major input to the OECD work and anticorruption activities worldwide.

Criminal law is important to deter and punish offenders, but compliance programs are as important for the purpose of prevention. Many companies have already developed codes of ethics and request commitment from their staff to abstain from corrupt activities. Training programs are being put in place and companies are seeking legal advice in order to distinguish permissible from illegal activities. Senior management and boards should be accountable for the implementation of these programs.

Conclusions

Public and corporate governance go hand in hand. Transparency, integrity, and social responsibility are fundamental to both the public and private sector. They build confidence, create stability, and contribute to economic performance.

Corporate social responsibility and business ethics, which include a strong commitment to fight corruption, should be firmly integrated into the governance structure of each corporation. These elements should be reflected in internal management and control, training programs for managers and staff, board responsibilities, disclosure practices, and stakeholder relations.

Internationally accepted standards in these areas are essential as part of a framework of rules for a globalized economy. In their absence, markets cannot function properly and will produce socially unacceptable results.

The OECD instruments discussed in this article are landmarks for international cooperation. Their relevance is not confined to industrialized countries nor big multinational enterprises; they reflect good practice for all. Where specific rules and standards are needed to meet local or regional conditions and legal systems, they can build on these principles.

As it already does in its partnership with the World Bank, the OECD is ready to deepen its dialogue with nonmember economies, strengthen cooperation with other international organizations, and contribute to global initiatives to construct a sound international financial architecture and to mobilize financial resources for development.

References

Albert, Michel, 1993, *Capitalism Against Capitalism* (London: Whurr Publishers).

Davies, Adrian, 1999, *A Strategic Approach to Corporate Governance* (Brookfield, Vermont: Gower).

Global Corporate Governance: Codes, Reports, and Legislation, 1999 (Washington: Investor Responsibility Research Center).

Gray, Cheryl W., and Rebecca Hanson, 1993, *Corporate Governance in Central and Eastern Europe,* Policy Research Working Paper No. 1182 (Washington: World Bank).

International Chamber of Commerce, 1999, *Fighting Bribery: A Corporate Practices Manual* (Paris: ICC Publishing SA).

Leading Corporate Governance Indicators 1999: An International Comparison, 1999 (Newton, Massachusetts: Davis Global Advisors, Inc.).

Nestor, Stilpon, 2001, *International Efforts to Improve Corporate Governance: Why and How?* (Paris: OECD).

OECD, 2000, *Corporate Governance in OECD Member Countries: Recent Development and Trends* (Paris: OECD). http://www.oecd.org/daf/corporate-affairs/

———, 1998, *Corporate Governance, State-Owned Enterprises and Privatisation* (Paris: OECD).

———, 2000, *Country Reports on the Implementation of the Convention on Combating Bribery of Foreign Public Officials in International Business Transactions and the 1997 Revised Recommendation*, June 27, http://www.oecd.org/daf/nocorruption/report.htm

———, 2000, *No Longer Business as Usual: Fighting Bribery and Corruption* (Paris: OECD).

Pieth, Mark, and Peter Eigen, eds., 1999, *Korruption im internationalen Geschäftsverkehr: Bestandesaufnahme, Bekämpfung, Prävention* (Neuwied: Luchterhand).

Sacerdoti, Giorgio, 1999, *The 1997 OECD Convention on Combating Bribery of Foreign Public Officials in International Business Transactions*, Italian Yearbook of International Law, Vol. IX (Milan: Dott. A. Giuffrè).

Transparency International (USA), 1996, *Corporate Anti-Corruption Programs: A Survey of Best Practices* (Washington).

OECD Instruments

OECD Convention on Combating Bribery of Foreign Public Officials in International Business Transactions (November 21, 1997): http://www.oecd.org/daf/nocorruption/

OECD Guidelines for Multinational Enterprises (Revised version of June 27, 2000): http://www.oecd.org/daf/investment/

OECD Principles of Corporate Governance (May 26–27, 1999): http://www.oecd.org/daf/corporate-affairs/

Revised Recommendation of the Council on Combating Bribery in International Business Transactions (May 23, 1997): http://www.oecd.org/daf/nocorruption/

Appendix

Appendix | Code of Good Practices on Transparency in Monetary and Financial Policies: Declaration of Principles

Introduction

In the context of strengthening the architecture of the international monetary and financial system, the Interim Committee in its April and October 1998 Communiqués called on the Fund to develop a code of transparency practices for monetary and financial policies, in cooperation with appropriate institutions. The Fund, working together with the Bank for International Settlements, and in consultation with a representative group of central banks, financial agencies, other relevant international and regional organizations,[1] and selected academic experts, has developed a *Code of Good Practices on Transparency in Monetary and Financial Policies*. The Code parallels the *Code of Good Practices on Fiscal Transparency* developed by the Fund and endorsed by the Interim Committee in April 1998.

The *Code of Good Practices on Transparency in Monetary and Financial Policies* identifies desirable transparency practices for central banks in their conduct of monetary policy and for central banks and other financial agencies in their conduct of financial policies. The definitions of "central bank," "financial agencies," "financial policies," and "government" as used in this Code are given in the attached Annex.

For purposes of the Code, transparency refers to an environment in which the objectives of policy, its legal, institutional, and economic framework, policy decisions and their rationale, data and information

---

[1] In addition to the Bank for International Settlements, the following international and regional organizations and international financial sector groupings were consulted: Basel Committee on Bank Supervision (BCBS), Center for Latin American Monetary Studies (CEMLA), Committee on Payment and Settlement Systems (CPSS), European Central Bank (ECB), International Association of Insurance Supervisors (IAIS), International Finance Corporation (IFC), International Organization of Securities Commissions (IOSCO), Organization for Economic Cooperation and Development (OECD), and the World Bank.

related to monetary and financial policies, and the terms of agencies' accountability, are provided to the public on an understandable, accessible, and timely basis. Thus, the transparency practices listed in the Code focus on (1) clarity of roles, responsibilities, and objectives of central banks and financial agencies; (2) the processes for formulating and reporting of monetary policy decisions by the central bank and of financial policies by financial agencies; (3) public availability of information on monetary and financial policies; and (4) accountability and assurances of integrity by the central bank and financial agencies.

The case for transparency of monetary and financial policies is based on two main premises. First, the effectiveness of monetary and financial policies can be strengthened if the goals and instruments of policy are known to the public and if the authorities can make a credible commitment to meeting them. In making available more information about monetary and financial policies, good transparency practices promote the potential efficiency of markets. Second, good governance calls for central banks and financial agencies to be accountable, particularly where the monetary and financial authorities are granted a high degree of autonomy. In cases when conflicts might arise between or within government units (e.g., if the central bank or a financial agency acts as both owner and financial supervisor of a financial institution or if the responsibilities for monetary and foreign exchange policy are shared), transparency in the mandate and clear rules and procedures in the operations of the agencies can help in their resolution, strengthen governance, and facilitate policy consistency.

In making the objectives of monetary policy public, the central bank enhances the public's understanding of what it is seeking to achieve, and provides a context for articulating its own policy choices, thereby contributing to the effectiveness of monetary policy. Further, by providing the private sector with a clear description of the considerations guiding monetary policy decisions, transparency about the policy process makes the monetary policy transmission mechanism generally more effective, in part by ensuring that market expectations can be formed more efficiently. By providing the public with adequate information about its activities, the central bank can establish a mechanism for strengthening its credibility by matching its actions to its public statements.

Transparency by financial agencies, particularly in clarifying their objectives, should also contribute to policy effectiveness by enabling financial market participants to better assess the context of financial policies, thereby reducing uncertainty in the decision making of market participants. Moreover, by enabling market participants and the general public to understand and evaluate financial policies, transparency is likely to be conducive to good policymaking. This can help to promote financial as well as systemic stability. Transparent descriptions of the policy formulation process provide the public with an understanding of the rules of the game. The release of adequate information to the public on the activities of financial agencies provides an additional mechanism for enhancing the credibility of their actions. There may also be circumstances when public accountability of decisions by financial agencies can reduce the potential for moral hazard.

The benefits for countries adopting good transparency practices in monetary and financial policies have to be weighed against the potential costs. In situations where increased transparency in monetary and financial policies could endanger the effectiveness of policies, or be potentially harmful to market stability or the legitimate interests of supervised and other entities, it may be appropriate to limit the extent of such transparency. Limiting transparency in selected areas needs to be seen, however, in the context of a generally transparent environment.

In the case of monetary policy, the rationale for limiting some types of disclosure arises because it could adversely affect the decision-making process and the effectiveness of policies. Similarly, exchange rate policy considerations, notably, but not exclusively, in countries with fixed exchange rate regimes, may provide justification for limiting certain disclosure practices. For example, extensive disclosure requirements about internal policy discussion on money and exchange market operations might disrupt markets, constrain the free flow of discussion by policymakers, or prevent the adoption of contingency plans. Thus, it might be inappropriate for central banks to disclose internal deliberations and documentation, and there are circumstances in which it would not be appropriate for central banks to disclose their near-term monetary and exchange rate policy implementation tactics and provide detailed information on foreign exchange operations. Similarly, there may be good reasons for the central bank (and financial agencies) not to make public their contingency plans, including possible emergency lending.

Additional concerns could be posed by some aspects of the transparency of financial policies. Moral hazard, market discipline, and financial market stability considerations may justify limiting both the content and timing of the disclosure of some corrective actions and emergency lending decisions, and information pertaining to market and firm-specific conditions. In order to maintain access to sensitive information from market participants, there is also a need to safeguard the confidentiality and privacy of information on individual firms (commonly referred to as "commercial confidentiality"). Similarly, it may be inappropriate for financial authorities to make public their supervisory deliberations and enforcement actions related to individual financial institutions, markets, and individuals.

Transparency practices differ not only in substance, but also in form. With regard to informing the public about monetary and financial institutions and their policies, an important issue concerns the modalities that these public disclosures should take. In particular with regard to monetary policy, should transparency practices have a legislative basis in a central bank law, or be based in other legislation or regulation, or be adopted through other means? The Code takes a pragmatic approach to this issue and recognizes that a variety of arrangements can lead to good transparency practices. On matters pertaining to the roles, responsibilities, and objectives of central banks (and for principal financial regulatory agencies), it recommends that key features be specified in the authorizing legislation (e.g., a central bank law). Specifying some of these practices in legislation gives them particular prominence and avoids ad hoc and frequent changes to these important aspects of the operations of central banks and relevant financial agencies. Information about other transparency aspects, such as how policy is formulated and implemented and the provision of information, can be presented in a more flexible manner. However, it is important that such information be readily accessible, so that the public can with reasonable effort obtain and assimilate the information.

In the context of good governance and accountability, as well as the promotion of efficient markets, reference to the public in this code should ideally encompass all interested individuals and institutions. In some cases, particularly for financial policies, it may be expedient for the purposes of administering or implementing certain regulations and policies to define the concept of the public more narrowly to refer only to those individuals and institutions that are most directly affected by the regulations and policies in question.

The focus of the Code is on transparency. While good transparency practices for the formulation and reporting of monetary and financial policies help to contribute to the adoption of sound policies, the Code is not designed to offer judgments on the appropriateness or desirability of specific monetary or financial policies or frameworks that countries should adopt. Transparency is not an end in itself, nor is transparency a substitute for pursuing sound policies; rather, transparency and sound policies are better seen as complements. In the realm of financial policies, there are complements to this code that go beyond transparency to promote good policies, notably the *Core Principles for Effective Banking Supervision* formulated by the Basel Committee for Banking Supervision, the *Objectives and Principles of Securities Regulation* formulated by the International Organization of Securities Commissions (IOSCO), and standards being developed by the Committee on Payment and Settlement Systems (CPSS), the International Association of Insurance Supervisors (IAIS), and the International Accounting Standards Committee (IASC). As these and other financial sector groupings develop and make significant adjustments in their principles and standards as they relate to transparency practices for financial agencies (e.g., in data dissemination requirements for financial agencies), this Code may have to be adjusted accordingly.

The Code is directed at the transparency requirements of central banks and financial agencies, not at the transparency procedures relating to firms and individual institutions. However, the benefits of transparency for monetary and financial policies may be fostered by appropriate policies to promote transparency for markets in general, for the institutions that are being supervised, and for self-regulatory organizations.

Monetary and financial policies are interrelated and often mutually reinforcing, with the health of the financial system affecting the conduct of monetary policy and vice versa. However, the institutional arrangements for these two types of policies differ considerably, particularly with regard to their roles, responsibilities, and objectives and their policy formulation and implementation processes. To take account of this, the Code is separated into two parts: good transparency practices for monetary policy by central banks and good transparency practices for financial policies by financial agencies. The basic elements of transparency for both policies are, however, similar. It should be recognized that not all transparency practices are equally applicable to all financial agencies, and the transparency objectives among different financial sectors vary. For some, the emphasis is on market efficiency considerations, for others the focus is on market and systemic stability, while for others the principal consideration is client-asset protection.

The operation of a country's payment system affects the conduct of monetary policies and the functioning of the financial system, and the design of payment systems has implications for systemic stability. The institutional structures of the payment system, however, are often significantly more complex than for monetary and other financial policies, and differ considerably across countries. In many instances, the operation of a country's payment system is split between the public and private sectors, including self-regulatory bodies. Nevertheless, most of the transparency practices listed in the Code for financial agencies are applicable for the roles and functions of central banks or other relevant public agencies exercising responsibility for overseeing the nation's payment systems. The coverage of transparency practices for financial policies in the Code includes those for the operation of systemically important components of the nation's payment system, and, where appropriate, makes allowance for the special nature of the payment system's operations (see section 5.3 of the Code).

The Code is of sufficient breadth to span and be applied to a wide range of monetary and financial frameworks, and thus to the full range of the Fund membership. Elements of the Code are drawn from a review of good transparency practices used in a number of countries and discussed in the professional literature. The Code thus represents a distillation of concepts and practices that are already in use and for which there is a record of experience. The manner in which transparency is applied and achieved, however, may differ, reflecting different institutional arrangements with respect to monetary and financial policies and legal traditions. The good transparency practices contained in the Code will, therefore, have to be implemented flexibly and over time to take account of a country's particular circumstances. A number of Fund members currently lack sufficient resources and the institutional capacity to implement all of the good transparency practices listed in the Code. These practices are included in the Code in the anticipation that countries would aspire over time to introduce such good practices.

Good Transparency Practices for Monetary Policy by Central Banks

I. **Clarity of Roles, Responsibilities, and Objectives of Central Banks for Monetary Policy**

1.1 **The ultimate objective(s) and institutional framework of monetary policy should be clearly defined in relevant legislation or regulation, including, where appropriate, a central bank law.**

1.1.1 The ultimate objective(s) of monetary policy should be specified in legislation and publicly disclosed and explained.

1.1.2 The responsibilities of the central bank should be specified in legislation.

1.1.3 The legislation establishing the central bank should specify that the central bank has the authority to utilize monetary policy instruments to attain the policy objective(s).

1.1.4 Institutional responsibility for foreign exchange policy should be publicly disclosed.

1.1.5 The broad modalities of accountability for the conduct of monetary policy and for any other responsibilities assigned to the central bank should be specified in legislation.

1.1.6 If, in exceptional circumstances, the government has the authority to override central bank policy decisions, the conditions under which this authority may be invoked and the manner in which it is publicly disclosed should be specified in legislation.

1.1.7 The procedures for appointment, terms of office, and any general criteria for removal of the heads and members of the governing body of the central bank should be specified in legislation.

1.2 The institutional relationship between monetary and fiscal operations should be clearly defined.[2]

1.2.1 If credits, advances, or overdrafts to the government by the central bank are permitted, the conditions when they are permitted, and any limits thereof, should be publicly disclosed.

1.2.2 The amounts and terms of credits, advances, or overdrafts to the government by the central bank and those of deposits of the government with the central bank should be publicly disclosed.

1.2.3 The procedures for direct central bank participation in the primary markets for government securities, where permitted, and in the secondary markets should be publicly disclosed.

1.2.4 Central bank involvement in the rest of the economy (e.g., through equity ownership, membership on governing boards,

---

[2] The practices in this area should be consistent with the principles of the International Monetary Fund's *Code of Good Practices on Fiscal Transparency*.

procurement, or provision of services for fee) should be conducted in an open and public manner on the basis of clear principles and procedures.

1.2.5 The manner in which central bank profits are allocated and how capital is maintained should be publicly disclosed.

1.3 Agency roles performed by the central bank on behalf of the government should be clearly defined.

1.3.1 Responsibilities, if any, of the central bank in (i) the management of domestic and external public debt and foreign exchange reserves, (ii) as banker to the government, (iii) as fiscal agent of the government, and (iv) as advisor on economic and financial policies and in the field of international cooperation should be publicly disclosed.

1.3.2 The allocation of responsibilities among the central bank, the ministry of finance, or a separate public agency,[3] for the primary debt issues, secondary market arrangements, depository facilities, and clearing and settlement arrangements for trade in government securities should be publicly disclosed.

II. Open Process for Formulating and Reporting Monetary Policy Decisions

2.1 The framework, instruments, and any targets that are used to pursue the objectives of monetary policy should be publicly disclosed and explained.

---

[3] The principles for transparency procedures listed in this Code, where applicable and adjusted as necessary, apply where a separate public agency has been designated to manage the country's public debt.

2.1.1 The procedures and practices governing monetary policy instruments and operations should be publicly disclosed and explained.

2.1.2 The rules and procedures for the central bank's relationships and transactions with counter parties in its monetary operations and in the markets where it operates should be publicly disclosed.

2.2 Where a permanent monetary policymaking body meets to assess underlying economic developments, monitor progress toward achieving its monetary policy objective(s), and formulate policy for the period ahead, information on the composition, structure, and functions of that body should be publicly disclosed.

2.2.1 If the policymaking body has regularly scheduled meetings to assess underlying economic developments, monitor progress toward achieving its monetary policy objective(s), and formulate policy for the period ahead, the advance meeting schedule should be publicly disclosed.

2.3 Changes in the setting of monetary policy instruments (other than fine-tuning measures) should be publicly announced and explained in a timely manner.

2.3.1 The central bank should publicly disclose, with a preannounced maximum delay, the main considerations underlying its monetary policy decisions.

2.4 The central bank should issue periodic public statements on progress toward achieving its monetary policy objective(s) as well as prospects for achieving them. The arrangements could differ depending on the monetary policy framework, including the exchange rate regime.

2.4.1 The central bank should periodically present its monetary policy objectives to the public, specifying, inter alia, their rationale, quantitative targets and instruments where applicable, and the key underlying assumptions.

2.4.2 The central bank should present to the public on a specified schedule a report on the evolving macroeconomic situation, and their implications for its monetary policy objective(s).

2.5 **For proposed substantive technical changes to the structure of monetary regulations, there should be a presumption in favor of public consultations, within an appropriate period.**

2.6 **The regulations on data reporting by financial institutions to the central bank for monetary policy purposes should be publicly disclosed.**

III. Public Availability of Information on Monetary Policy

3.1 **Presentations and releases of central bank data should meet the standards related to coverage, periodicity, timeliness of data, and access by the public that are consistent with the International Monetary Fund's data dissemination standards.**

3.2 **The central bank should publicly disclose its balance sheet on a preannounced schedule and, after a predetermined interval, publicly disclose selected information on its aggregate market transactions.**

3.2.1 Summary central bank balance sheets should be publicly disclosed on a frequent and preannounced schedule. Detailed central bank balance sheets prepared according to appropriate and publicly documented accounting standards should be publicly disclosed at least annually by the central bank.

3.2.2 Information on the central bank's monetary operations, including aggregate amounts and terms of refinance or other facilities (subject to the maintenance of commercial confidentiality) should be publicly disclosed on a preannounced schedule.

3.2.3 Consistent with confidentiality and privacy of information on individual firms, aggregate information on emergency financial support by the central bank should be publicly disclosed through an appropriate central bank statement when such disclosure will not be disruptive to financial stability.

3.2.4 Information about the country's foreign exchange reserve assets, liabilities, and commitments by the monetary authorities should be publicly disclosed on a preannounced schedule, consistent with the International Monetary Fund's Data Dissemination Standards.

3.3 The central bank should establish and maintain public information services.

3.3.1 The central bank should have a publications program, including an Annual Report.

3.3.2 Senior central bank officials should be ready to explain their institution's objective(s) and performance to the public, and have a presumption in favor of releasing the text of their statements to the public.

3.4 Texts of regulations issued by the central bank should be readily available to the public.

IV. Accountability and Assurances of Integrity by the Central Bank

4.1 Officials of the central bank should be available to appear before a designated public authority to report on the conduct of monetary policy, explain the policy objective(s) of their institution, describe their performance in achieving their objective(s), and, as appropriate, exchange views on the state of the economy and the financial system.

4.2 The central bank should publicly disclose audited financial statements of its operations on a preannounced schedule.

4.2.1 The financial statements should be audited by an independent auditor. Information on accounting policies and any qualification to the statements should be an integral part of the publicly disclosed financial statements.

4.2.2 Internal governance procedures necessary to ensure the integrity of operations, including internal audit arrangements, should be publicly disclosed.

4.3 Information on the expenses and revenues in operating the central bank should be publicly disclosed annually.

4.4 Standards for the conduct of personal financial affairs of officials and staff of the central bank and rules to prevent exploitation of conflicts of interest, including any general fiduciary obligation, should be publicly disclosed.

4.4.1   Information about legal protections for officials and staff of the central bank in the conduct of their official duties should be publicly disclosed.

Good Transparency Practices for Financial Policies by Financial Agencies

V.   **Clarity of Roles, Responsibilities, and Objectives of Financial Agencies Responsible for Financial Policies**[4]

5.1   The broad objective(s) and institutional framework of financial agencies should be clearly defined, preferably in relevant legislation or regulation.

5.1.1   The broad objective(s) of financial agencies should be publicly disclosed and explained.

5.1.2   The responsibilities of the financial agencies and the authority to conduct financial policies should be publicly disclosed.

5.1.3   Where applicable, the broad modalities of accountability for financial agencies should be publicly disclosed.

5.1.4   Where applicable, the procedures for appointment, terms of office, and any general criteria for removal of the heads and members of the governing bodies of financial agencies should be publicly disclosed.

---

[4] Refer to the Annex for definitions of financial agencies and financial policies.

5.2 The relationship between financial agencies should be publicly disclosed.

5.3 The role of oversight agencies with regard to payment systems should be publicly disclosed.

5.3.1 The agencies overseeing the payment system should promote the timely public disclosure of general policy principles (including risk management policies) that affect the robustness of systemically important payment systems.

5.4 Where financial agencies have oversight responsibilities for self-regulatory organizations (e.g., payment systems), the relationship between them should be publicly disclosed.

5.5 Where self-regulatory organizations are authorized to perform part of the regulatory and supervisory process, they should be guided by the same good transparency practices specified for financial agencies.

VI. Open Process for Formulating and Reporting of Financial Policies

6.1 The conduct of policies by financial agencies should be transparent, compatible with confidentiality considerations and the need to preserve the effectiveness of actions by regulatory and oversight agencies.

6.1.1 The regulatory framework and operating procedures governing the conduct of financial policies should be publicly disclosed and explained.

6.1.2 The regulations for financial reporting by financial institutions to financial agencies should be publicly disclosed.

6.1.3 The regulations for the operation of organized financial markets (including those for issuers of traded financial instruments) should be publicly disclosed.

6.1.4 Where financial agencies charge fees to financial institutions, the structure of such fees should be publicly disclosed.

6.1.5 Where applicable, formal procedures for information sharing and consultation between financial agencies (including central banks), domestic and international, should be publicly disclosed.

6.2 Significant changes in financial policies should be publicly announced and explained in a timely manner.

6.3 Financial agencies should issue periodic public reports on how their overall policy objectives are being pursued.

6.4 For proposed substantive technical changes to the structure of financial regulations, there should be a presumption in favor of public consultations, within an appropriate period.

VII. Public Availability of Information on Financial Policies

7.1 Financial agencies should issue a periodic public report on the major developments of the sector(s) of the financial system for which they carry designated responsibility.

7.2 Financial agencies should seek to ensure that, consistent with confidentiality requirements, there is public reporting of aggregate data related to their jurisdictional

responsibilities on a timely and regular basis.

7.3 Where applicable, financial agencies should publicly disclose their balance sheets on a preannounced schedule and, after a predetermined interval, publicly disclose information on aggregate market transactions.

7.3.1 Consistent with confidentiality and privacy of information on individual firms, aggregate information on emergency financial support by financial agencies should be publicly disclosed through an appropriate statement when such disclosure will not be disruptive to financial stability.

7.4 Financial agencies should establish and maintain public information services.

7.4.1 Financial agencies should have a publications program, including a periodic public report on their principal activities issued at least annually.

7.4.2 Senior financial agency officials should be ready to explain their institution's objective(s) and performance to the public, and have a presumption in favor of releasing the text of their statements to the public.

7.5 Texts of regulations and any other generally applicable directives and guidelines issued by financial agencies should be readily available to the public.

7.6 Where there are deposit insurance guarantees, policyholder guarantees, and any other client asset protection schemes, information on the nature and form of such protections, on the operating procedures, on how the guarantee is financed, and on the performance of the arrangement, should be publicly disclosed.

7.7 Where financial agencies oversee consumer protection arrangements (such as dispute settlement processes), information on such arrangements should be publicly disclosed.

VIII. Accountability and Assurances of Integrity by Financial Agencies

8.1 Officials of financial agencies should be available to appear before a designated public authority to report on the conduct of financial policies, explain the policy objective(s) of their institution, describe their performance in pursuing their objective(s), and, as appropriate, exchange views on the state of the financial system.

8.2 Where applicable, financial agencies should publicly disclose audited financial statements of their operations on a preannounced schedule.

8.2.1 Financial statements, if any, should be audited by an independent auditor. Information on accounting policies and any qualification to the statements should be an integral part of the publicly disclosed financial statements.

8.2.2 Internal governance procedures necessary to ensure the integrity of operations, including internal audit arrangements, should be publicly disclosed.

8.3 Where applicable, information on the operating expenses and revenues of financial agencies should be publicly disclosed annually.

8.4   Standards for the conduct of personal financial affairs of officials and staff of financial agencies and rules to prevent exploitation of conflicts of interest, including any general fiduciary obligation, should be publicly disclosed.

8.4.1   Information about legal protections for officials and staff of financial agencies in the conduct of their official duties should be publicly disclosed.

Annex: Definitions of Certain Terms

To facilitate presentation, certain general terms are used to capture different institutional arrangements in a summary fashion. The following descriptive definitions are used in the Code.

Central Bank

The institutional arrangements for assigning responsibility for the conduct of a country's monetary policy differ among the Fund's membership. For most Fund members, this responsibility is assigned to the central bank or to a system of constituent national central banks in a multinational central bank arrangement. There are a number of countries, however, where this role is designated to a "monetary authority" or to a "currency board." To facilitate presentation, the term "central bank" in the Code refers to the institution responsible for conducting monetary policy, which may or may not be a central bank.

Financial Agencies

A wide range of institutional arrangements prevail among Fund members with regard to which unit of government carries exclusive or primary responsibility for the regulation, supervision, and oversight of the financial and payment systems. In a few countries, an agency has been established with responsibility for regulating and supervising an array of financial institutions (banking, insurance, and securities firms) and markets (securities, derivatives, and commodity futures). For most countries, the oversight responsibility for the financial sector is shared among several agencies. Thus, responsibility for the conduct of bank regulation and supervision or for bank deposit insurance policies in some countries is assigned to the central bank, or to an independent bank supervisory or deposit insurance agency, or split among several units of government. Similarly, responsibility for the conduct of policies related to the oversight of certain categories of financial institutions is assigned to the central bank or to a specialized agency. In some cases (e.g., payment systems) a public agency oversees the activities of private sector self-regulatory bodies. To facilitate presentation, the phrase "financial agencies" is used to refer to the institutional arrangements for the regulation, supervision, and oversight of the financial and payment systems, including markets and institutions, with the view to promoting financial stability, market efficiency, and client-asset and consumer protection. (Where the central bank carries responsibility for financial policies, some of the good transparency practices listed for financial agencies in Sections V–VIII of the Code are already specified in the transparency practices listed for central banks in Sections I–IV of the Code.)

Financial Policies

The term "financial policies" in the Code refers to policies related to the regulation, supervision, and oversight of the financial and payment systems, including markets and institutions, with the view to promoting financial stability, market efficiency, and client-asset and consumer protection.

Government

Unless a particular unit of government is specifically identified in the Code, reference to "government" in the Code refers either to the executive branch of government or to a particular ministry or public agency, depending on the issue at hand or the established tradition of government in particular countries.

Biographical Sketches

Richard K. Abrams is an Advisor in the Monetary and Financial Systems Department (MFD), formerly Monetary and Exchange Affairs, of the International Monetary Fund. Before moving to MFD, he held various positions in the European and Policy Development Departments of the IMF. Prior to joining the IMF, Mr. Abrams worked at the Federal Reserve Bank of Kansas City. He is the author of numerous articles on finance as well as banking and banking supervision. Mr. Abrams obtained his Ph.D. in economics from the University of North Carolina at Chapel Hill.

Mark Allen received his Bachelor of Arts in mathematics and economics from Cambridge University in 1970. Thereafter, he completed two years of graduate studies in economics at Yale University, followed by one year at the Karl Marx Higher Economic Institute of Sofia, Bulgaria. He began his career with the International Monetary Fund as an economist in the Trade and Payments Division in 1974. He also served as an economist in the IMF's Geneva Office and as Senior Resident Representative in Poland. In 1994, he was named Deputy Director, Immediate Office, Policy Development and Review Department.

Tobias M.C. Asser received his law degree from Leyden University, the Netherlands, and his Ph.D. in private international law from Cambridge University. Before he joined the Legal Department of the International Bank for Reconstruction and Development (World Bank) in 1968, he was a practicing attorney in Amsterdam. Among other positions, he served at the World Bank as Assistant General Counsel, Operations, and Assistant General Counsel, Finance. In 1987, Mr. Asser transferred from the World Bank to the International Monetary Fund, where he served as Assistant General Counsel until his retirement in 1999. Since 1985, Mr. Asser has been Adjunct Professor of Law at the Georgetown University Law Center in Washington, D.C., where he teaches international finance and private international law.

Roy C.N. Baban, formerly Senior Counsel in the Legal Department of the International Monetary Fund, received the degrees of J.D. and LL.M.(Taxation) from Georgetown University Law Center, M.P.A. from Harvard University, and Ph.D. in economics from the University of Manchester (U.K.). He has served as an adjunct faculty member for international banking at the George Washington Law School and on the law of international financial institutions at the Summer Law Institute of the Colleges of Law of Case Western, Cleveland State, and St. Petersburg State Universities. He has conducted workshops on monetary and financial law for the Southeast Asian Central Banks (SEACEN) Research and Training Centre. Mr. Baban is a consultant, focusing on IMF legal matters, banking, and exchange control.

Tomás J.T. Baliño is Senior Advisor in the Monetary and Financial Systems Department of the International Monetary Fund. Since obtaining his Ph.D. in economics from the University of Chicago, Mr. Baliño has served at the Central Bank of Argentina as well as the IMF for numerous years. He has extensive experience in financial restructuring, corporate transparency, and examining monetary systems.

Thomas C. Baxter, Jr., received his B.A. from the University of Rochester in 1976 and his J.D. from the Georgetown University Law Center in 1979. He joined the Federal Reserve Bank of New York as an attorney in 1980 after serving as a law assistant to the Appellate Division of the New York Supreme Court. Currently, he is General Counsel and Executive Vice President of the Bank. He also serves as deputy general counsel of the Federal Open Market Committee. In addition, he has served as a legal advisor to the Current Payment Methods project of the National Conference of Commissioners on Uniform State Laws. Mr. Baxter has published articles on legal aspects of bank supervision, check collection, securities transfers, and electronic transfers of funds. He is a joint author of two textbooks, *Wire Transfers: A Guide to U.S. and International Laws Governing Funds Transfers* (Probus, 1993) and *The ABC's of the UCC: Article 4A Funds Transfers* (ABA, 1997).

William Blair graduated from Balliol College, Oxford, and was called to the English Bar in 1972. His practice focuses on banking and financial law. He has appeared in many leading cases and has an extensive international advisory practice. His publications include the *Encyclopedia of Banking Law*, which is now published online as part of Butterworths banking law direct service. He became the Queen's Counsel in 1994. Mr. Blair sits as a Recorder of the Crown Court and is a Visiting Professor at the London School of Economics and the Centre for Commercial Law Studies.

Michael Bradfield has extensive experience in legal aspects of U.S. and non-U.S. banking and monetary matters. His areas of expertise also include balance of payments and trade and development assistance, including U.S. participation in the international development banks. Prior to becoming general counsel of the Federal Reserve Board, he was in private law practice in Washington, D.C. from 1975 to 1981 with the law firm of Cole, Corette & Bradfield. In that capacity, he practiced in the areas of international finance and trade law as well as in resolving international claims.

Marco Cangiano has been with the International Monetary Fund since 1991, and currently serves as Assistant to the Director of the Fiscal Affairs Department (FAD). In addition to FAD, he has worked in the Asia and Pacific Department for five years. Prior to joining the IMF, Mr. Cangiano was an economist with the research department of ENI (Italian state oil company), and a consultant for cost benefit and financial feasibility studies for private companies and for the Italian government. He graduated from La Sapienza University in Rome and has a Master of Science in public finance from the University of York.

Mark Cymrot is an attorney with the law firm Baker & Hostetler LLP in Washington, D.C. concentrating his practice on international and commercial litigation and arbitration. He has represented both private clients and governments. Prior to joining Baker & Hostetler LLP, Mr. Cymrot served as Special Litigation Counsel in the U.S. Justice Department. In addition to his work with the American Bar Association Working Group's assessment of the *Foreign Sovereign Immunities Act*, Mr. Cymrot has published numerous articles on litigation and sovereign debt issues. He received his B.A. from George Washington University in 1969 and his J.D. from Columbia University in 1972.

Gregory C. Dahl received his graduate degree in economics from Harvard University. He joined the IMF in 1976 and has worked on a variety of countries including Pakistan, Nigeria, and Algeria. He has been posted overseas three times as the IMF's resident representative: in Haiti, Sierra Leone, and, most recently, Bulgaria. He is currently Advisor in the IMF Institute, where he provides training to country officials and IMF economists.

Ross S. Delston is a legal practitioner in Washington, D.C. specializing in banking law. He is also a legal consultant to the IMF and the World Bank on bank regulatory, insolvency, and deposit insurance issues. From 1991 to 1994, Mr. Delston was Of Counsel to the law firm of Jones, Day, Reavis & Pogue where he specialized in bank mergers and acquisitions. From 1986 to 1991, Mr. Delston was an attorney with the FDIC. From 1976 to 1986, Mr. Delston was an attorney specializing in trade finance with the U.S. Export-Import Bank. He is the author of *Statutory Protections for Banking Supervisors*, a 1999 survey of the laws of 20 countries. Mr. Delston received his B.A. (with special honors) in 1973 and his J.D. (with honors) in 1976 from The George Washington University.

Rainer Geiger is Deputy Director of the Directorate for Financial, Fiscal and Enterprise Affairs of the Organization for Economic Cooperation and Development. Mr. Geiger has also served as Professeur Adjoint at the Université Paris I (Panthéon—Sorbonne).

François Gianviti studied at the Sorbonne, the Paris School of Law, and New York University. He obtained a *licence ès lettres* from the Sorbonne in 1959, a *licence en droit* from the Paris School of Law in 1960, a *diplôme d'études supérieures de droit pénal et science criminelle* in 1961, a *diplôme d'études supérieures de droit privé* in 1962, and a *doctorat d'Etat en droit* in 1967. From 1967 to 1969, he was a Lecturer in Law, first at the Nancy School of Law and subsequently at the Caen School of Law. In 1969, Mr. Gianviti obtained the *agrégation de droit privé et science criminelle* of French universities and was appointed Professor of Law at the University of Besançon. From 1970 through 1974, he was seconded to the Legal Department of the International Monetary Fund, where he served as Counsellor and, subsequently, as Senior Counsellor. In 1974, he became Professor of Law at the University of Paris XII, where he taught civil and commercial law, banking and monetary law, and private international law. He served as Dean of its School of Law from 1979 through 1985. In 1986, Mr. Gianviti became Director of the Legal Department and, in 1987, General Counsel of the International Monetary Fund. He is a member of the Committee on

International Monetary Law of the International Law Association and has published books on property and many articles on aspects of French and international law.

Michael Gruson has been a partner of Shearman & Sterling since 1973 and is now Of Counsel. He has been primarily engaged in the representation of foreign banks and in international securities transactions. He received his legal education in Germany and in the United States (LL.B., 1962, University of Mainz; M.C.L., 1963, Columbia University; LL.B., 1965, cum laude, Columbia University; Dr. jur., 1966, Freie Universität Berlin). Mr. Gruson is a past Vice-Chairman of the Committee on Banking Law and the past Chairman (1984–1995) of the Subcommittee on Legal Opinions of the Committee on Banking Law of the International Bar Association. He has also served as a lecturer at various law schools including the University of Illinois at Urbana-Champaign, Columbia University School of Law, and the University of Osnabrück, Germany, and he is a visiting Professorial Fellow at the Centre for Commercial Law Studies, Queen Mary and Westfield College, University of London. Mr. Gruson is the author of a number of publications on banking and securities law and has frequently lectured on these topics.

Gregor Heinrich is presently Head of the Secretariat to the Committee on Payment and Settlement Systems (CPSS) at the Bank for International Settlements (BIS) in Basle, Switzerland. He studied law and romance languages in Bonn, Lausanne, and Hamburg and holds a German law degree from the University of Hamburg as well as a Second State Degree in Law from the State of Hamburg with admission to the bar ("Assessor") in Germany. After completing his law studies, he worked as assistant to the Faculty of Law at Hamburg University. From 1982 to 1984, when he joined the BIS, he held a research position at the Max Planck Institute for Foreign and Private International Law in Hamburg and worked as an attorney for the law offices of Franke & Jacob in Hamburg. Mr. Heinrich has published several articles on various aspects of comparative law. He is a member of the Editorial Council of the journal, "Payment Systems Worldwide," of the International Advisory Council for the World Bank's "Western Hemisphere Payments Initiative," and a member of the Consultative Group on the Supporting Document to the IMF Code of Good Practices in Monetary and Financial Policies.

Ricki Tigert Helfer is a law professor at the Washington College of Law of American University, where she teaches domestic and international banking and finance. She previously served as Chairman and Chief Executive Officer of the Federal Deposit Insurance Corporation (FDIC) in Washington, D.C. While Chairman of the FDIC, Ms. Helfer was a member of the Basle Committee on Banking Supervision. Ms. Helfer has previously served as a Nonresident Senior Fellow at The Brookings Institution in Washington. She has also served for seven years as the senior international lawyer for the Board of Governors of the Federal Reserve System in Washington and was a Governor of the Philadelphia Stock Exchange. Ms. Helfer has contributed to a wide range of publications, including articles and chapters in books, on banking and financial issues. Ms. Helfer graduated with honors from the University of Chicago Law School and has an M.A. in political development from the University of North Carolina at Chapel Hill. She received her B.A., magna cum laude, from Vanderbilt University and served as a law clerk at the U.S. Court of Appeals for the Fifth Circuit.

John Hicklin received his B.A. and M.A. in modern history and economics from University College, Oxford, and his M.Sc. in economics from the London School of Economics. He is currently Senior Advisor in the Policy Development and Review Department of the International Monetary Fund. He has also held positions in other departments, including the Middle Eastern and Asia and Pacific Departments, and the Office of the Deputy Managing Director, since joining the IMF in 1982 from H.M. Treasury.

Luis Jácome Hidalgo is a senior economist in the Monetary and Financial Systems Department of the International Monetary Fund, having served previously as a Technical Assistance Advisor in the same department. Mr. Hidalgo has held positions with the Central Bank of Ecuador, the Ministry of Finance, and the Corporación de Estudios para el Desarrollo. Mr. Hidalgo obtained his undergraduate degree in macroeconomics from the Universidad Computeres, an M.Sc. in macroeconomics from Queen Mary College, and a Ph.D. in international economics from Boston University.

William E. Holder received his LL.B. and B.A. from the University of Melbourne. He subsequently earned an LL.M. from Yale University and a Diploma from the Hague Academy of

International Law. He has served as a Tutor in Law at the University of Melbourne, a Professor of Law at the University of Mississippi, a Reader in Law at the Australian National University, and an advisor on international law for the Australian Department of Foreign Affairs. Mr. Holder joined the International Monetary Fund in 1976 and has served as Deputy General Counsel since 1986. He is coeditor of *The International Legal System: Cases and Materials with Emphasis on the Australian Perspective* (Butterworths, 1972) and is the author of many articles on international law.

George Iden is a senior economist in the Monetary Operations Division in the Monetary and Financial Systems Department (MFD), formerly the Monetary and Exchange Affairs Department. He served on a departmental task force that was assigned to work on the *Code of Good Practices on Transparency in Monetary and Financial Policies* and an associated *Supporting Document to the Code*. In this connection, he coordinated a Regional Consultative Meeting on the Code held in Abu Dhabi and participated in another such meeting in Singapore. He has also participated in several missions that have focused on issues associated with transparency in monetary policy, including Hong Kong SAR, Russia, and Ghana. Mr. Iden, who has his Ph.D. in economics from Harvard, joined the International Monetary Fund in 1992. Before joining the IMF, he worked for the U.S. Congressional Budget Office (CBO) where he served as Chief of the Special Studies Unit. Prior to CBO, he taught economics at American University and the University of North Carolina, Chapel Hill, and served as an economist for the Joint Economic Committee of the U.S. Congress.

Alain Ize received an engineering degree from L'Ecole Centrale de Paris, an M.B.A. from Columbia University, and a Ph.D. in engineering economic systems from Stanford University. Before joining the Monetary and Financial Systems Department of the International Monetary Fund, in which he currently serves as Advisor, he held various positions in the Fiscal Affairs Department. He joined the IMF in 1985 after holding teaching, research, and consulting positions at the Colegio de Mexico and Banco de Mexico.

Karen H. Johnson is Director of the Division of International Finance at the Board of Governors of the Federal Reserve System, a position she has held since October 1998. Ms. Johnson earned a

Ph.D. in economics from the Massachusetts Institute of Technology in 1973 and later joined the faculty of the economics department of Stanford University, where she taught for six years. In 1979, she moved to Washington, D.C., as an economist in the Division of International Finance at the Federal Reserve Board. She became Chief of the World Payments and Economic Activity Section in 1984, Assistant Director of the Division of International Finance in 1985, and Associate Director in 1997.

Omotunde E.G. Johnson studied economics at the University of California, Los Angeles (UCLA), where he received his B.A. in 1965 and Ph.D. in 1970. He was Lecturer at the University of Sierra Leone (1969–73) and Visiting Assistant Professor and Research Associate at the University of Michigan (1973–74), before joining the International Monetary Fund in 1974. In the IMF he has worked in the Exchange and Trade Relations Department (now the Policy Development and Review Department), the African Department, the Research Department, and, since 1990, the Monetary and Financial Systems Department, formerly Monetary and Exchange Affairs, where he was formerly Assistant Director. He was also IMF Resident Representative in Ghana during 1987–90. Mr. Johnson has written on various topics in the field of economics and coauthored a book, *Payment Systems, Monetary Policy, and the Role of the Central Bank*, published by the IMF in 1998.

Jennifer Johnson-Calari is a Principal Investment Officer, Investment Management Department (IMD), World Bank. She joined the IMD ten years ago and has been responsible for client investment strategy. Since joining the IMD, she has been a fixed income portfolio manager in all of the major currency blocs and has had responsibility for the fixed income sector of the pension plan. Before joining the World Bank, she was with the Comptroller of the Currency where she specialized in multinational bank management of market risks. From 1981 to 1988, she was with the Board of Governors of the Federal Reserve System in international bank supervision. She holds a master's degree in international economics from the Johns Hopkins University and is a Chartered Financial Analyst.

Ross Leckow is Senior Counsel in the Legal Department of the International Monetary Fund. Mr. Leckow holds a B.A. (Honors) from the University of Winnipeg, an LL.B. from the University of Manitoba, and an LL.M. from York University (Canada). Previously, he served as Legal Counsel in the Legal Services Division and Treasury Officer in the Corporate Finance Department of the Export Development Corporation of Canada.

John Jin Lee is Vice President and Managing Senior Counsel at Wells Fargo Bank, N.A.. In this capacity, he has extensive experience with legal issues in retail banking, ranging from depositary matters to consumer credit transactions and cyberspace banking. Prior to joining the bank in 1977, Mr. Lee was an associate in the law firm of Manatt, Phelps & Rothenberg. He graduated magna cum laude with a B.A. from Rice University in 1971 and received his J.D. and M.B.A. from Stanford University in 1975. Mr. Lee has served on various committees of the American Bar Association in the area of financial services. He is also a member of the Lawyers Committee of the Consumer Bankers Association and has been elected to the American College of Consumer Financial Services Attorneys. Mr. Lee has written numerous articles for *The Business Lawyer* and other publications. He is a member of the California State Bar.

Jerome I. Levinson is a graduate of the Harvard College, 1953, and the Harvard Law School, 1956. He was a Fulbright scholar in India, 1956–57. He is presently the Distinguished Lawyer in Residence at the Washington College of Law, where he has been for the last five years. Professor Levinson previously served as Assistant Director of the Agency for International Development Office in Brazil (1964–66); Deputy Director of the AID Latin American Capital Assistance program (1966–68); Chief Counsel to the Senate Foreign Relations Committee, Sub-Committee on Multinational Corporations and U.S. Foreign Policy (1972–77); General Counsel to the Inter-American Development Bank (1977–89); and Of Counsel to the Washington law firm of Arnold & Porter (1990–92). Professor Levinson is also currently a research associate of the Economic Policy Institute.

Cynthia Lichenstein is a visiting professor at George Washington University School of Law after retiring from active teaching at Boston College Law School in the spring of 2001. Ms. Lichtenstein graduated magna cum laude from Radcliffe College in 1955, and earned her J.D. magna cum laude from Yale University in

1959. She also holds a master's degree in Comparative Law from the University of Chicago. Ms. Lichtenstein began her career by association with a major New York law firm where she specialized in international banking, returning to the same firm in the 1980s. In 1971, she joined the faculty of Boston College Law School, where she was one of the first female professors. She was elected President of the American Branch of the International Law Association in 1986, has served as chair of the ILA's International Securities Regulation Committee, and has been a member of the Board of Editors of the *American Journal of International Law*. Ms. Lichtenstein also served as a guest scholar in the Legal Department of the International Monetary Fund in early 2000.

Jéan-Victor Louis is professor at the European University Institute, Florence, and at the Université Libre de Bruxelles. He has also been a visiting professor at the Université de Paris 1 (Panthéon–Sorbonne) and the Université Robert Schuman at Strasbourg. He is the president of the "Study Group on European Politics" (the Belgian branch of the TransEuropean Political Studies Association (TEPSA)). From 1980 to 1992, he was the president of the Institute of European Studies of the ULB and, up to 1998, Head of the Legal Department of the National Bank of Belgium. He is now honorary General Counsel of the NBB. He has published extensively on institutional and other aspects of European Community Law, especially in the field of EMU, and on external relations law of the EU.

Carol Mates is Principal Counsel with the International Finance Corporation, the private-sector affiliate of the World Bank. At the IFC, she specializes in project finance and particularly the financing of private infrastructure projects. Her work has entailed syndication of loans with banks in Asia, Europe, and the United States, as well as cofinancing arrangements with bilateral and other multilateral development agencies and local development banks. She obtained her A.B. from Barnard College and J.D. from Columbia Law School.

John W. Moscow is Deputy Chief of the Investigations Division of the New York County District Attorney's Office, where he started prosecuting street crime in 1972. He has spent more than 20 years prosecuting thefts, tax fraud, money laundering, securities fraud, and bank fraud. A graduate of the University of Chicago and Harvard, his best known case is the prosecution of the Bank of Credit and Commerce International (BCCI).

Erwin Nierop studied law at the State University of Leiden, the Netherlands. He then joined the legal department of the Dutch Central Bank in Amsterdam. Subsequently, he served as member of a team that set up the European Bank for Reconstruction and Development in London; member of the Secretariat of the Committee of Governors of the Central Banks of the Member States of the European Economic Community at the Bank for International Settlements in Basle, Switzerland, which created the basis for the European Monetary Institute; and Deputy General Counsel of the European Monetary Institute in Frankfurt am Main, Germany. Mr. Nierop is presently Deputy General Counsel and Head of the Financial Law Division of the European Central Bank, based in Frankfurt am Main.

Joseph Norton holds an A.B. from Providence College; an LL.B. from the University of Edinburgh; an LL.M from the University of Texas; a Diplôme (droit privé) from the Hague Academy of International Law; an S.J.D. from the University of Michigan; and a D.Phil. (Law) degree from Oxford University. He has held appointments at the Centre for Commercial Law Studies-University of London; the Southern Methodist University (SMU) Law School; and the University of Hong Kong. He has served as editor-in-chief of *The International Lawyer* and the *Yearbook of International Financial and Economic Law* as well as other international legal publications. He has been a visiting professor at Soochow University, Taipei; the University of Tokyo Law Faculty; and the University of Münster, Germany. He is Executive Director of the London Institute of International Banking, Finance and Development Law, and of the SMU Institute of International Banking and Finance. Before joining the SMU law faculty full time in 1981, Professor Norton was a director of a major Dallas law firm, practicing in the banking/capital markets/corporate areas. He has written more than 120 articles, chapters, and research monographs on domestic and international business and banking matters.

Roberts B. Owen, a graduate of the Harvard Law School and Cambridge University, practiced law as a litigator for Covington & Burling of Washington, D.C., for many years and has now retired from the litigation practice. He served as the Legal Adviser to the U.S. Department of State in 1979–81 and as Senior Adviser to the Secretary of State in 1995–99. He participated in drafting the 1981 Algerian Accords (establishing the U.S.-Iran Claims Tribunal) and the 1995 Dayton Accords. He continues to practice as an international arbitrator. He is a member of the arbitration panels of the International Center for Settlement of Investment Disputes and the Claims Resolution Tribunal for Dormant Accounts in Switzerland.

Vincent Raymond Reinhart is Director of the Division of Monetary Affairs at the Board of Governors of the Federal Reserve System and Secretary of the Federal Open Market Committee since July 2001. Previously, he was Deputy Director of the Division of International Finance for two years and held a variety of positions in the Division of Monetary Affairs. Before joining the Board in 1988, he was Senior Economist in the International Research Department of the Federal Reserve Bank of New York. His academic publications primarily concern the conduct of policy and issues related to the monetary transmission mechanism as well as an analysis of alternative Treasury auction techniques and Treasury debt management. After his undergraduate training at Fordham University, he received graduate degrees in economics at Columbia University.

Antonio Sáinz de Vicuña is a graduate in economic sciences and law, Universidad Complutense de Madrid, and received a Diploma in International Law, Cambridge University (U.K.). He is a member of the Corps of Government Attorneys (*Abogado del Estado*). He served as Legal Adviser to the Ministry of Finance (1974–77), the Deputy Prime Minister and Minister of Economy (1977–78), the Ministry of Foreign Affairs (1979–85), the Secretariat of State for the European Communities (1980–83), and as Chief Legal Adviser to the Ministry of Foreign Affairs (1985–87). He was Chief International Legal Counsel of the Banco Español de Crédito (1987–94), General Counsel of the European Monetary Institute (Frankfurt) (1994–98), and General Counsel of the European Central Bank (since 1998). He serves as Chairman of the Legal Committee of the European System of Central Banks (ESCB) and a Member of the International Monetary Law Committee. He is the author of *International State Contracts* (*La contratación exterior del Estado*), and of some 20 professional articles on Community, International, and Banking Law.

Pamela Sak is a member of the Financial Transactions Practice of Jones Day, specializing in the areas of banking and corporate matters. Prior to joining Jones Day, she worked in the Legal Department of the International Monetary Fund, where she gained broad experience in banking, commercial, monetary, and international law. Ms. Sak is a member of Women in Housing and Finance and cochair of its International Task Force. She is a coauthor of *Swiss Law on the Treatment of Dormant Accounts* and *Bankruptcy Law Reform in Eastern Europe* and is author of *Environmental Law in Ukraine*.

Garry J. Schinasi received his Ph.D. in economics from Columbia University in 1979. He worked on the staff of the Board of Governors of the U.S. Federal Reserve System from 1979 to December 1989, when he joined the staff of the International Monetary Fund. Mr. Schinasi is currently the Chief of the International Capital Markets and Financial Studies Division in the International Monetary Fund's Research Department, which is responsible for writing the IMF's annual *International Capital Markets Report*. He has published articles in *The Review of Economic Studies, Journal of Economic Theory, Journal of International Money and Finance*, and other academic and policy journals. His recent research has focused on international capital markets, the interplay of monetary and financial stability, and the relevance of asset prices in the formulation of monetary and financial policies.

Brian W. Smith is a partner in the Washington, D.C., office of Mayer, Brown & Platt where he heads the Financial Regulatory and e-commerce practices of the firm. Mr. Smith was formerly chief counsel to the Office of the Comptroller of the Currency and a member of the Comptroller's Policy Group. Formerly, he was senior vice president, general counsel, and corporate secretary to MasterCard International, Inc. Mr. Smith received his undergraduate and law degrees from St. John's University in New York and a master's degree from Columbia University's Graduate School of Business.

Kazuaki Sono is currently Dean and Professor of Law, Faculty of Law and Policy, Tezukayama University, Nara; Professor Emeritus, Hokkaido University, Sapporo; and served as Secretary of the United Nations Commission on International Trade Law

(UNCITRAL) and Chief of the International Trade Law Branch, Office of Legal Affairs, United Nations, 1980–85. Formerly, he served as Assistant General Counsel in the Legal Department of the International Monetary Fund, 1990–93. He has also been a member of the International Monetary Law Committee of the International Law Association (ILA) since 1979. Mr. Sono holds an LL.M. from Kansai University and a J.D. from the University of Washington.

Bernhard Steinki is Counsel in the Legal Department of the International Monetary Fund. He obtained his law degree (1. Juristisches Staatsexamen) from the University of Freiburg in 1992 and has a Master of Laws degree from the University of London (King's College). After completing his professional training (Rechtsreferendariat), Mr. Steinki joined the Legal Department of the Deutsche Bundesbank in 1996 where he worked on a broad range of issues of preparatory work for European Monetary Union. He joined the Legal Department of the IMF in April 1999.

Michael W. Taylor is currently the Monetary and Financial Systems Department's Financial Sector Issues Representative in Indonesia, where he is engaged in financial sector reform issues. He holds his D.Phil. and B.A. from Oxford University and before joining the IMF, he was Reader in Financial Regulation at Reading University (U.K.) and worked for six years with the Bank of England.

Victor Thuronyi received his undergraduate degree in economics from Cambridge University and his law degree from Harvard Law School. He joined the International Monetary Fund's Legal Department in 1991. He has practiced tax law, served in the U.S. Treasury Department, and taught tax law at several law schools. Mr. Thuronyi, who currently serves as Senior Counsel (Taxation) of the IMF, has supervised and participated in legislative drafting projects for roughly 40 countries. He is the author of several articles on taxation and editor of a book, *Tax Law Design and Drafting*.

Robert B. Toomey has been Counsel at the Federal Reserve Bank of New York since December 1997. Prior to joining FRBNY in 1995, Mr. Toomey spent three years with the Securities and Exchange Commission in the Division of Corporation Finance. From 1987 to 1992 he was an associate with Reid & Priest in New York. Mr. Toomey currently serves as Secretary to the Financial Markets

Lawyers Group and acts as Counsel to the Foreign Exchange Committee. He received his B.A. from Haverford College and his J.D. from Fordham University Law School.

Jan-Willem van der Vossen is Deputy Division Chief in the Banking Supervision and Regulation Division of the Monetary and Financial Systems Department (MFD), formerly Monetary and Exchange Affairs of the International Monetary Fund. Prior to taking up the position of Deputy Division Chief, Mr. van der Vossen served as Technical Assistance Advisor from 1993 to 1997 and as Senior Economist from 1997 to 1999. Before joining the IMF in 1993, he held positions in the private sector as well as with the Netherlands Ministry of Foreign Affairs. Mr. van der Vossen obtained his M.A. in Law from Leyden University in 1970.